Texas Criminal Law

Texas Criminal Law

Principles and Practices

Jerry L. Dowling, J.D.

College of Criminal Justice
Sam Houston State University

Prentice Hall
Upper Saddle River, New Jersey
Columbus, Ohio

Library of Congress Cataloging-in-Publication Data

Dowling, Jerry L.
    Texas criminal law : principles and practices / Jerry L. Dowling.—1st. ed.
      p. cm.
    Includes bibliographical references and index.
    ISBN-13: 978-0-13-172139-5 (alk. paper)
    ISBN-10: 0-13-172139-9 (alk. paper)
    1. Criminal law—Texas.   I. Title.
    KFT1761.D69 2009
    345.764—dc22

                                   2008017596

Vice President and Executive Publisher: Vernon Anthony
Senior Acquisitions Editor: Tim Peyton
Editorial Assistant: Alicia Kelly
Media Project Manager: Karen Bretz
Director of Marketing: David Gesell
Marketing Manager: Adam Kloza
Marketing Coordinator: Alicia Dysert
Production Manager: Kathy Sleys
Creative Director: Jayne Conte
Cover Design: Jayne Conte
Cover Illustration/Photo: Getty Images/National Geographic
Full-Service Project Management/Composition: Sadagoban Balaji/Integra Software Services, Inc.
Printer/Binder: Hamilton Printing Company
Cover Printer: Phoenix Color Corp.

Credits and acknowledgments borrowed from other sources and reproduced, with permission, in this text-book appear on appropriate page within text.

Pearson Education Ltd., London
Pearson Education Singapore, Pte. Ltd
Pearson Education Canada, Inc.
Pearson Education–Japan
Pearson Education Australia PTY, Limited

Pearson Education North Asia, Ltd., Hong Kong
Pearson Educación de Mexico, S.A. de C.V.
Pearson Education Malaysia, Pte. Ltd.
Pearson Education Upper Saddle River, New Jersey

Prentice Hall
is an imprint of

www.pearsonhighered.com

10 9 8 7 6 5 4 3 2 1
ISBN-13: 978-0-13-172139-5
ISBN-10:   0-13-172139-9

To Katherine,
Jared, Colin,
Natalie, Allison,
Margaret, and Davis,
each of whom enrich my life daily
in their own special way

Contents

Preface

Texas Criminal Law—Principles and Practices is much different than existing undergraduate criminal law textbooks. First, while Texas-related supplements exist for most of the generic substantive criminal law texts, *Texas Criminal Law* is believed to be unique among undergraduate college texts in its exclusive emphasis on the criminal laws of the Lone Star State. This state-specific focus exists because contemporary penal law is almost totally a product of legislative enactments. While many similarities exist across each of the 50 states' criminal codes, each state is also unique in how it defines and imposes the various criminal sanctions. These differences range from variations in terminology (e.g., larceny versus theft) to whether or not certain conduct (e.g., public intoxication) is even a crime at all. Accordingly, for students of the criminal law who reside in Texas or plan a post-graduation career with a Texas justice agency, a text that centers on the laws of this state serves their needs best.

Second, historical antecedents such as the English Common Law are important to understanding the origins of modern criminal statutes. Each chapter of this text introduces the offenses with discussion of their English Common Law roots. Likewise, early Texas laws are mentioned as relevant. However, modern criminal statutes, particularly those in Texas, have so modified the traditional definitions of crimes that in many instances the only thing recognizable between the Common Law and the modern statute is the name of the offense. Additionally, as appropriate, the general state of a particular criminal offense throughout the nation is presented. For example, Chapter 5, "Criminal Homicide," contains a discussion of the primary methods by which other states classify criminal homicides. Similarly, in Chapter 15 the rules used in other jurisdictions to determine whether a criminal defendant was entrapped are explored. This discussion serves to broaden the reader's perspective on the topic of entrapment because Texas has its own unique approach to this defense, an approach out of the mainstream of American criminal law. However, the thematic focus remains on the elements of the major criminal offenses and defenses in Texas as described in the Texas Penal Code.

Third, frequently statute books say one thing but the actual implementation of the law occurs in practice in a different manner. *Texas Criminal Law*, where relevant, overviews the actual practices throughout the state based on the author's three decades of experience with the state's criminal justice system. For example, the manner in which theft by check and issuance of worthless check offenses are handled in actuality is not easily determined from only reading the relevant Penal Code sections. Likewise, the Texas court system and the variations in the manner in which prosecutors file formal charges are overviewed in Chapter 3. While the text is not intended to substitute for an introduction to the Texas criminal justice system book, the day-to-day procedures used by Texas law enforcement, prosecutorial, and correctional agencies are highlighted where their understanding will assist the student of the criminal law.

The reader is strongly encouraged to have at hand a current copy of the Texas Penal Code when reading this text. While the pages of *Texas Criminal Law* do contain many excerpts from Texas criminal statutes, many other important sections are not included because of space considerations. Only by reading and analyzing the referenced statutes can one fully understand the content and scope of application of the particular law being examined in this text. The appendix contains directions on understanding the organizational structure of the Texas Penal Code and suggestions regarding how best to read and comprehend its contents. This material should be reviewed prior to embarking on Chapter 1.

The style of the text is a bit more informal than traditional criminal law textbooks. A large number of scenarios are used and much of the text is conversational in tone. In my years of teaching the topic, I have found that many students learn best by exploring examples as opposed to discussing abstract concepts. In much of the book, criminal law principles are presented by playing off of a particular fact situation. Many of these factual scenarios are relevant to college-age individuals, such as date rape or the question of when does a loud party rises to the level of disorderly conduct. Similarly, the use of questions in the text requires the student to apply his or her understanding of the material presented to a new situation or factual variation of the topic discussed. In this manner, the student must digest the material presented in order to arrive at a reasonable answer.

The informal style found in *Texas Criminal Law* does not mean, however, that the content is less than scholarly. Rather, each chapter contains a large number of references to the source of the content. These footnotes serve several purposes. First, the footnotes establish the origin of the principles of law and their interpretation found in the text narrative. In most instances, this is a reference to either a particular section of the Texas Penal Code or to a Texas court decision interpreting a portion of the Penal Code. When constitutional issues are implicated, references to U.S. Supreme Court cases are given. The footnotes also serve to provide parenthetical material that may be tangential to the main content under discussion. This use of the footnote avoids a digression from the topic at hand. However, the reader should exam this explanatory material to expand his or her understanding of the narrative. Third, much material in the footnotes provides the reader the opportunity for further research on the particular topic. Scholarly books, law review articles, collected annotations, and the like are referenced for the reader who wishes to explore a particular matter in greater depth.

Needs of an undergraduate criminal justice student studying the criminal law, or just the laymen wanting to know about their state's criminal statutes, are different in both degree and kind from the needs of a law school student preparing to become a practicing attorney. While the traditional casebook method may serve the latter well, a more direct, narrative approach seems most effective for the first group. The goal of *Texas Criminal Law—Principles and Practices* is to meet this need in an interesting and intellectually stimulating manner without the reader's quest becoming obstructed by legal jargon and the tedium that can arise in examining statutes. I trust that *Texas Criminal Law* will assist the college instructor in educating his or her criminal justice students in the important topic of substantive criminal law.

PROFESSOR JERRY L. DOWLING, J.D.

Acknowledgments

The author would like to acknowledge the many that assisted personally or through emotional support in the creation of this text. First are the reviewers who provided critiques and suggestions that helped in making the book a better, more useful classroom text. Thanks to Ivan Bliss, Prince George's Community College; Diana Clayton, Rogers State University; Alexis Kennedy, University of Nevada, Las Vegas; Mike Penrod, Kirkwood Community College; Karen Youngblood, Cameron University; and Jason Waller, Tyler Junior College.

Second, I would be remiss in not acknowledging the support provided by Sam Houston State University. Access to the university library's legal holdings and electronic databases was crucial to the successful completion of the text. Of special note is the opportunity to write a substantial portion of the text while on faculty development leave from the College of Criminal Justice. This leave was made possible to a large degree through the support of SHSU Provost and Vice President for Academic Affairs David E. Payne and the former Dean of the College of Criminal Justice Richard H. Ward. To both I owe thanks.

Senior Acquisitions Editor Tim Peyton and the staff at Pearson Prentice Hall deserve special recognition for their patience and direction in the development and production of this textbook.

A major thanks goes out to the hundreds of Texas peace officers and SHSU undergraduates who I have had the pleasure of training and teaching about the criminal laws in my three decades residing in the state. Not a class meeting or training session occurred where the students did not educate me as well. The teacher becomes better because of the insights provided by the students.

Finally, a special thanks goes to my family and friends, and especially my wife Katherine, for their encouragement, tolerance, support, and most importantly patience during the writing of this text.

About the Author

Jerry L. Dowling is Professor of Criminal Justice at Sam Houston State University, Huntsville, Texas. He has taught courses on criminal law and criminal procedure at both the undergraduate and graduate levels at SHSU for over 35 years. During the same period, he has conducted numerous legal training sessions for Texas peace officers, police chiefs, and sheriffs. He holds the Doctor of Jurisprudence degree from the College of Law at the University of Tennessee. Prior to becoming a university teacher, Professor Dowling served as a Special Agent of the Federal Bureau of Investigation.

CHAPTER

Foundations of Criminal Law

1

The reader should be on the lookout (BOLO) for the meaning of the following terms. Knowledge of the meaning of these terms will greatly assist the reader in understanding the primary elements of the chapter.

- Breach of the peace
- Codification movement
- Common Law
- Crime
- Crimes involving moral turpitude
- *Ex post facto* law
- Felony
- General deterrence theory
- Incapacitation
- *Malum in se*
- *Malum prohibitum*

- Misdemeanor
- Penal Code
- Preemption doctrine
- Principle of legality
- Rehabilitation
- Retribution
- Specific deterrence
- *Stare decisis*
- Substantive criminal law
- Territorial jurisdiction
- Treason

INTRODUCTION

This text examines the substantive criminal law in Texas. **Substantive criminal law** concerns the definitions of crimes and their penalties, in contrast to procedural criminal law, which focuses on the implementation of the criminal sanction through the laws of arrest, search, seizure, and confessions, and the courtroom rules of evidence. While some overlap exists between the two categories of criminal law (e.g., Is the defense of entrapment a substantive issue or a procedural one?), an understanding of each is necessary to fully appreciate the legal complexities of the state's modern justice system. Knowledge of the kinds of behavior that are condemned by society as highly undesirable and thereby criminal forms one of the cornerstones of the study of criminology and criminal justice.

Virtually everyone has a basic notion of what is legal and what is illegal. This knowledge comes from being reared in a particular society, with its culture, customs, religions, and value systems being imprinted from birth. Additionally, mass media—particularly television and motion pictures—imprint citizens with ideas about society's rules concerning crime and punishment.

For the average citizen, such indoctrination likely provides enough guidance to be a productive member of society. One can function reasonably well knowing that stealing is unlawful, driving while intoxicated is dangerous and illegal, and engaging in sexual relations without the consent of the other person is subject to criminal prosecution. For the student of the American criminal justice system, such a cursory understanding is far from sufficient. Individuals who seek to work in the justice system must possess a clear understanding of the criminal law in both theory and application. Indeed, many veteran justice professionals are more knowledgeable about the criminal law than most attorneys, the bulk of whom rarely engage in this specialized area of legal practice. The need for an in-depth understanding of the criminal law is particularly acute for police officers, individuals who frequently must make the initial determination of whether or not cause exists to believe a crime has been committed. Likewise, individuals employed in community supervision, probation, parole, and institutional correctional agencies should possess an understanding of the criminal sanction. Their daily work exists because of the criminal law. Appreciating the rules and foundations of the criminal law places their job in the larger context of the justice system.

Study of American criminal law is complicated by a single fact: While there exists a great commonality in the coverage of the criminal law from state to state, subtle and sometimes very important variations also exist. These variations may range from labeling, such as whether taking someone's property without consent is called "larceny" or "theft," up to whether the conduct itself is even declared unlawful—public intoxication, for example. While the broad principles of criminal law operate in every state, the "devil lies in the details."

Under our federal system of government, every state has enacted its own set of criminal laws, usually called the **Penal Code**, Criminal Code, or something similar.[1] Further, a separate criminal code exists for the District of Columbia and the armed forces, as well the federal government. Thus, more than 50 possible definitions of murder, robbery, rape, and disorderly conduct exist.[2] As a consequence, creation of a single text that is useful and accurate for every jurisdiction is virtually impossible.

This text focuses on the substantive criminal law of the State of Texas. While it is anticipated that the reader will be either a student in a Texas college, a cadet in a Texas police training facility, or simply a citizen interested in the topic, Texas law actually serves as an excellent guide for understanding the criminal law not only of the state but of the nation as well. The Texas Penal Code is a modern compilation of criminal laws. It is reflective of the contemporary thinking of criminal law scholars and policy makers. The code does not contain arcane and oddball statutes that have long outlived their usefulness. Both the definitions of offenses and the punishment ranges are reflective of current criminological thought. Indeed one group of legal scholars has ranked it as the top compilation of criminal law in the United States.[3] Credit for this can largely be laid at the feet of the drafters of the Model Penal Code, which greatly influenced the content and structure of the Texas Penal Code, and the nearly 100 individuals and organizations who worked for eight years to update Texas' criminal laws.

In 1931, the American Law Institute (ALI), an organization of judges, lawyers, and legal scholars, proposed the development of a comprehensive penal code that state legislatures could use for a guide in the revision of their criminal laws. It was not until 1962, however, after 13 tentative drafts, that the prototype code was published. ALI's Model Penal Code has served as a basis for the revision of the criminal codes of many states, including Texas.[4]

Using the Model Penal Code as a basis, a committee of the State Bar of Texas in 1965 began the work of revising the then existing Penal Code. The State Bar undertook

TABLE 1-1   Historical Development of Criminal Law in Texas

Date	Government	Penal Laws
1824–1829	Austin's Colony	Rules of conduct drafted by Austin and approved by Mexican authorities
1824–1836	Mexican States of Coahuila and Texas	Mexican civil law system
1836–1845	Republic of Texas	English Common Law and a few legislative enactments
1845–1856	State of Texas	English Common Law and a few legislative enactments
1856	State of Texas	First written Penal Code enacted
1879	State of Texas	Limited revision of 1856 Penal Code
1895	State of Texas	Limited revision of existing Penal Code
1911	State of Texas	Limited revision of existing Penal Code
1925	State of Texas	Limited revision of existing Penal Code
1973	State of Texas	Enactment of completely new Penal Code (effective Jan. 1, 1974)
1994	State of Texas	Major revision of penalty structure within Penal Code

the revision effort because, as the chair of the revision committee noted, "The existing Texas Penal Code is a bulky, confusing, and conflicting compilation of the original Texas Penal Code of 1856 plus additions and amendments. The accumulation of 110 years of legislation today [1967] rests uneasily upon a foundation laid twenty-one years after the Texas Revolution."[5] A draft of a proposed new Penal Code was presented to the Legislature in 1970, but lawmakers waited until 1973 to take action.[6] This 1973 Penal Code, with some modifications over the intervening years, contains the primary criminal offenses for the state.

PRIMARY ATTRIBUTES OF A CRIME

Definition

To study and understand criminal law, the reader must first comprehend the legal concept of a "crime." From a definitional perspective, the term "crime" can be characterized in a variety of ways. Cynics might say that a crime is anything the legislature says is a crime. They are correct, of course, in a general sense. In Texas, and every other state, conduct can become a crime through legislative enactment. Likewise, behavior is normally not considered to be a crime unless a legislative body actually enacts a law so declaring.[7]

Others might opt for a more formal definition of "crime." Sir William Blackstone (1723–1780), a famous scholar of the English Common Law, defined the term as, "A crime, or misdemeanor, is an act committed, or omitted, in violation of a public law, either forbidding or commanding it."[8] Blackstone's definition includes three important aspects that will be discussed subsequently: the notion that crime involves an act, a public law declares the conduct criminal, and the illegal behavior can involve either actual conduct or a failure to act.

More modern legal scholars have defined the term as, "Crime is any social harm defined and made punishable by law."[9] This definition adds two other important concepts: First, crime involves social harm and, second, conduct that is deemed to be a crime is subject to punishment. Harm and punishment will be explored subsequently.

Interestingly, most states, including Texas, do not specifically define "crime" in their respective penal codes but rather only present the elements of behavior that constitute a specific offense, such as murder, robbery, burglary, and the like.

Whichever definition—or nondefinition—one prefers, scholars generally agree that "crime" contains several important attributes that distinguish it from other aspects of the law. These elements are:

- Government defines the illegal conduct.
- Government is the victim.
- Government prosecutes case.
- Judgment is payable to the government.

Attributes of a Crime

Government Defines the Illegal Conduct

Crimes are created by a governmental body. This means that Congress, in the case of federal criminal law, and state and local legislative bodies, such as the Texas Legislature or a city council, formally pass a bill barring (or in rare instances, requiring) certain behavior by the citizenry and providing a penalty for noncompliance. This **principle of legality** is expressed by the Latin phrase *nullum crimen sine lege* (no crime without law). This requirement, while somewhat obvious, is nonetheless quite important. Suppose, one July 4th evening about 9 p.m. a police officer is called to the scene of a party at your apartment complex. You and other revelers are frolicking about the swimming pool, dancing to recorded music, drinking beer, and otherwise enjoying yourselves. A few of the revelers are shooting fireworks. Which of these behaviors is a crime? Maybe all; maybe none. If the music is so loud it disturbs the peace, then disorderly conduct is being committed. If the partiers are underage, a violation of the alcoholic beverage laws may be occurring. However, the officer determines that the audio player's sound level is not excessive and everyone at the pool appears to be an adult. But, what if the apartment manager has posted a rule at the pool that prohibits electrical devices (the CD player), hazardous objects (the fireworks), and alcoholic beverages (the beer) at the poolside? No criminal law violation has occurred! The apartment manager as part of the lease, or in establishing "house rules," can certainly bar alcohol and fireworks at the poolside or limit the hours for the use of the pool. However, the rules violations by the party participants are not contrary to the state or local *criminal* law because the rules, even though they may well help maintain social order within the apartment complex, were not enacted by a governmental body. The rules violations could result in termination of the participants' apartment leases or a ban on the use of the pool or some other sanction by the apartment manager, but the conduct is not criminal as no statute is violated.

This concept that only a governmental entity with lawmaking authority can create criminal law has become increasingly relevant in suburban Texas. Recent decades have seen the rise of planned residential communities, often outside the incorporated limits of a city. In order to make the lands attractive to potential residents, land use is often limited through so-called deed restrictions. These land restrictions are enforced through a community association in which each resident is a member. While these restrictions often concern home design criteria, lot size, and the like, they may also place limits on certain other aspects of life; for example, no hunting, no fireworks, and no powerboats on community lakes. Violation of these restrictions is not a crime but a civil matter. Accordingly, peace officers will not normally enforce these rules. Rather, habitual violators will be subject to civil suit by the owners' association.

Government Is the Victim of Crime

As odd as it may initially seem, when Joe punches Roger in the nose, Roger's nose may bleed but it is the State of Texas that is offended. A governmental body enacts the criminal law for the benefit of society as a whole, not for the benefit of individuals. While the government may hold broad responsibility for the safety and well-being of the citizenry, it does not normally have legal responsibility for the misfortunes that befall an individual. Consequently, when a criminal law is violated, the interests of society as a whole are impacted. This principle is manifested in the justice system in several ways. First, all criminal prosecutions are filed in the name of the state. A criminal charge based on the previous example will be styled "*State v. Joe.*" This stylistic form emphasizes that the action is being brought in the name of the State of Texas.

Second, Texas statutes specify that legal documents ranging from charge complaints to indictments conclude with the specific phrase "against the peace and dignity of the state."[10] The Texas Constitution requires this phrase to appear in all indictments.[11] The phrase, which has been ruled to be absolutely mandatory, reinforces the principle that it is the public, through its government, that is offended by the criminal behavior.[12]

Finally, the notion that the sovereign is the victim permits the government to proceed with a prosecution even with a missing or reluctant complainant. Obviously, no living complainant is needed in order for the state to initiate a murder prosecution. The rule is generally no different for other offenses. Likewise, even if a human victim does not wish to pursue the matter, the state may still prefer charges. A district attorney may accede to a victim's wishes to drop charges, particularly if the case is minor and the testimony of the victim is the primary evidence, but this decision is based more on practicality than on law. For example, increasingly prosecutors are filing charges in domestic assault cases even when the victim of the abuse wants the charges dropped. The notion being that prosecution of all domestic assaults will have a deterring effect on future acts of household violence.

Government Prosecutes Case

In the American adversarial system, the prosecutor is a government employee, paid with tax dollars, whose compensation is normally not dependent on which or how many cases he or she prosecutes. In Texas, district attorneys and county attorneys are popularly elected and are thereby accountable to the electorate.

The office of public prosecutor is largely an American invention. In colonial times, private lawyers were hired or appointed to prosecute criminal cases.[13] For example, during the trial of the British soldiers involved in the Boston Massacre of 1770, the trial judge appointed a pro-British prosecutor, while the people of Boston raised money to pay for a second prosecutor who was pro-colonists. Today, society recognizes the desirability of a governmental officer performing the prosecutorial function. The public prosecutor holds broad discretion as to which cases to pursue and which to drop. While a prosecutor may confer with the victim prior to accepting a plea bargain offer or a court may order a victim impact study be conducted before considering sentencing, the human victim has little direct control over the sanction a defendant receives.

Many persons believe that the human victim of a crime should have a stronger voice in the prosecutorial process. As a result, Texas, along with many other states, has enacted victim rights laws. Additionally, a victim rights constitutional amendment is gaining political support. The Texas victims' rights statute requires notice of case status, court dates, parole hearings, and the like be given to the victims of certain violent crimes. The statute permits the victim to provide input to the pre-sentencing investigation. Despite the expanded rights of crime victims, the district attorney retains the power to control the overall prosecutorial process.[14]

The government also absorbs the expense of investigating and prosecuting criminal offenses, although court costs are often assessed against a guilty defendant. Collection of these costs occurs most often in misdemeanor cases but rarely after a felony conviction, as most felons either lack the resources to pay or have little fear of the consequences of not paying.

Judgment Is Payable to the Government

The government also extracts the penalty from the guilty on behalf of society. A convicted defendant may be incarcerated or fined for his offense, and in a few instances sentenced to death. Often the human victim of the crime—the homeowner whose residence was burglarized or the driver whose car was stolen—receives nothing as part of the sentencing of the defendant. All fines and other costs are payable to the government and society as a whole through its governmental entities funds the cost of incapacitating the offender or overseeing his or her probation.

RELATIONSHIP OF CRIMINAL AND NONCRIMINAL LAW

The popular notion that law can be divided into criminal and noncriminal (i.e., civil) law is a relatively modern idea. Historically, however, such a sharp division has not long existed. Early English law was unconcerned with maintaining a distinction between legal matters of public interest and those of private concern. This mixture is likely the result of a society governed by an absolute monarch; every legal matter was the king or queen's concern so categorizing the law served little purpose. Even today, legal circumstances exist that are unclear regarding whether or not the conduct in question is a crime or a civil matter: Is a parking violation on a state university campus a criminal violation? It is certainly a violation of a preexisting rule established by a branch of government and is often subject to a monetary fine. Or how about the recent practice in many large Texas communities of using cameras to record motorists who ignore red traffic signals? The motorist is sent a notice of the violation and a demand for payment of a "civil" penalty. Yet, the entire process seems very similar to the procedure used if one were cited for disorderly conduct or some other petty violation of the Penal Code. The point is simply that the technical legal definition of a crime and the popular view of a crime may be somewhat different.

Virtually any criminal offense that involves injury to a person or damage or destruction of private property can also serve as the basis for a civil suit. Such suits are relatively rare, however, because many criminal offenders simply lack the financial resources to pay a monetary judgment. Hence, it would be a waste of time and money to sue the individual who burglarized your home and stole your television set. The burglar, who likely is sitting in jail, has neither the resources nor the motivation to satisfy a civil suit judgment.

Civil suits do occur, however, but normally at each arise only in the extremes of either relatively minor offenses or very serious crimes. First, the minor traffic offender who runs the stop sign and collides with another vehicle may be sued for monetary damages as well as face a criminal citation. At the other end of the spectrum, wealthy or high profile individuals who commit offenses, often crimes against the person, may find themselves subject not only to criminal prosecution but also to civil suit. A famous example in recent years is the 1995 prosecution of former football star and actor O.J. Simpson for the murder of his ex-wife and her acquaintance. Simpson was found not guilty of the criminal offense but was sued a year later on behalf of the ex-wife's estate and by the parents of the dead acquaintance for the tort of wrongful death. A multimillion dollar monetary judgment was rendered against him. Since the standard of proof in a civil suit is less than that required in a criminal case, the two verdicts are not legally inconsistent. Professional basketball star Kobe Bryant suffered a similar fate following allegations of sexual assault in 2003. Rape charges were dropped when the victim became reluctant to pursue the matter but Bryant reportedly made a financial settlement of a civil suit filed by his accuser.

SOURCES OF CRIMINAL LAW

Common Law of England

When America was colonized, the settlers soon recognized the need for a system of law. Since most of the newly settled territory was claimed by the British Crown and most early settlers emigrated from the British Isles, the English system of law was adopted. This system was based on the so-called **Common Law** of England.

The Common Law of England is a body of legal rules that developed largely from custom and case law as supplemented by monarchial decrees and Parliamentary enactments. Beginning with the Norman Conquest of England in 1066, a new system of government and, consequently, law was established in the British Isles, replacing the crude Anglo-Saxon system. While the early English kings and queens were absolute monarchs, the implementation of their decrees, as well as the resolution of disputes not covered by direct pronouncements, came to be resolved by the various judicial tribunals throughout the land. Many of these decisions were based on the customs of the country as interpreted by judges, not enacted legislation. Over time, as reports of these decisions became collected, a body of consistent law began developing. Utilizing the concept of legal precedent (*stare decisis*), where stability of the law was viewed as more important than the correctness of the decision, judges generally rendered their rulings in accord with prior, similar decisions. This technique created a consistency of legal rules and a system of building blocks upon which controversies could be resolved with some degree of predictability. Given the nature of this approach, case law, instead of statutory law, became the primary vehicle for capturing legal principles. This evolving set of laws became known as the Common Law largely because it developed from cases defining the rights and responsibilities of the common people as a whole.

With the establishment of the first form of a Parliament in the late thirteenth century, a British legislative body began supplementing the Common Law. Interestingly, the evolution of the unwritten Common Law continues today in England though these changes have scant direct influence on contemporary American law.

One often hears the statement that the early colonists brought the Common Law of England to America, as if a set of books were placed in a trunk and transported across the sea. This is a misnomer because no single set of books contains a precise compendium of all of the Common Law.[15] Rather, the traditions and influence of the rules of law developed under the Common Law provided a template for the American legal system. In this country's formative years, whenever a dispute arose over whether certain behavior constituted a crime, for example, American officials would refer to the crimes known to the Common Law. In fact, many states after 1776 adopted the Common Law crimes as their "penal code," initially leaving the definitions of crimes in their unwritten form.

For some states, such as Florida,[16] the unwritten Common Law crimes are considered still to be in force today when they do not conflict with an offense enacted by the legislature. In these jurisdictions, a violation of one of the unwritten Common Law offenses is normally a misdemeanor. A few states (e.g., North Carolina) rely exclusively on statutory crimes but utilize the Common Law to provide definitions for the elements of the statutory offenses. Most other states, including Texas, have by statute explicitly abolished the Common Law crimes altogether, declaring that only offenses enacted by their respective legislatures are punishable. The federal government, because of its organic structure, does not enforce the unwritten Common Law crimes.[17] But, even in the overwhelming majority of jurisdictions where the Common Law crimes are not enforceable, the underlying principles of the old English law served as the primary influence on both the substantive and procedural criminal law.

Laws of Other Countries

While British law has served as the predominant influence on Texas criminal law, other countries' legal systems have had minor influence. Because, during its early settlement, Texas was a part of Spain (1716–1821), and later Mexico (1821–1836), the Spanish and Mexican legal systems have been somewhat influential. For example, Texas' **territorial jurisdiction** extends into adjacent waters based on the Spanish law of three leagues, not the Common Law three-mile limit used by most coastal states.[18] The Texas tradition of small-town mayors and rural county judges serving as both municipal administrator and judicial officer likely evolved from the Texas colonial period, when each town had an alcalde, a multifunction government official established by Spanish and later Mexican law.[19]

Codification Movement

Despite the early adoption of the Common Law crimes, all states subsequently became active in passing legislation that clearly spelled out in written form the elements of criminal offenses so confusion and ambiguity would be minimized. Additionally, by the mid-nineteenth century a movement developed to codify all laws, meaning collecting statutes of like topics and placing them together in organized topical volumes called codes.[20] Texas was an early participant in the **codification movement**. The state Legislature abolished the Common Law crimes and adopted its first comprehensive written Penal Code in 1856.[21]

State Statutory Enactments

Enactments of the state legislatures constitute the primary source of criminal laws in every state, including Texas. The Texas Legislature convenes starting from the second Tuesday in January every two years in odd-numbered years for a period of 140 days. Special called sessions are also possible but they rarely involve consideration of penal laws.

The Texas Constitution grants to the Legislature the power to enact any law on any subject or in any field that is not explicitly denied to it.[22] This rather broad grant of power vests the Legislature with the authority to define crimes and fix penalties.[23]

It is within the power of the State to define as criminal conduct whatever acts it sees fit, so long as such acts bear some reasonable relation to the needs of society and the safety and general welfare of the public. This power of the State extends not only to overt acts which are naturally immoral or wrong in themselves, but also to lawful acts negligently or maliciously done, as well as mere inaction in certain circumstances.[24]

Criminal laws enacted by the Legislature traditionally go into effect on September 1 of the same year. In some instances, a criminal statute does not become effective until January 1 of the following year. Other statutes become effective immediately upon the governor's signature if the Legislature finds an "emergency" exists.[25] The time lag between a law's passage and its effective date gives both citizens and justice system personnel time to learn of and adapt to the changes.

While the bulk of the serious criminal statutes are codified into the Texas Penal Code, many other statutes with criminal penalties are scattered throughout other of the state's codes. For instance, motor vehicle laws are contained in the Texas Transportation Code, drug laws are found in the Texas Health and Safety Code, and hunting and fishing statutes are placed in the Texas Parks and Wildlife Code. One source estimates about 1,900 crimes ranging from selling infant formula at a flea market[26] to body piercing an intoxicated person[27] are to be found in Texas statute books other than the Penal Code![28]

Municipal Ordinances

All states permit cities to enact their own criminal laws in the form of city ordinances. Additionally, some states, such as Florida and New York, also grant counties relatively broad ordinance-making authority. Texas counties have very limited authority to enact laws, whether criminal or otherwise. Consequently, county-enacted criminal laws are rare in Texas; state statutes are nearly the exclusive laws in effect outside the city limits. Counties do have authority to enact animal control laws and laws controlling sexually oriented businesses, and to set speed limits in certain situations.

Texas cities, however, often enact a broad array of ordinances containing a criminal penalty. While the state has chartered about 900 cities, only about 300 are "home rule" cities, which are authorized broad ordinance-making authority. These 300 cities enact city ordinances that supplement state statutes; for example, traffic laws, laws on disorderly conduct, and ordinances that speak to areas not covered by state law, such as animal control laws and anti-fireworks laws. The penalty for violation of these ordinances is a fine up to $500, although state law permits a fine up to $2,000 for cases involving fire safety, zoning, or public health and sanitation laws.[29] Texas city ordinances may not impose jail terms. Although some city ordinances may duplicate state misdemeanors, the constitutional prohibition against double jeopardy would bar prosecution for the same conduct under both the state law and a city ordinance.[30]

Uniform Laws

Certain offenses have become highly standardized across the states. Traffic laws and anti-narcotics laws are nearly identical in every jurisdiction. This circumstance exists because of the leadership of the federal government in the creation of the Uniform Vehicle Code and the Uniform Controlled Substances Act, which most states have adopted. Once again, the penalty for violating one of the uniform statutes may vary slightly from state to state, but the rules of conduct are very similar. For example, a red traffic signal means stop in every state and almost every state classifies controlled substances in five categories according to the drugs' potential for abuse.

Federal Criminal Law

Despite frequent political posturing in Congress to declare certain violent or predatory conduct a violation of federal law, the national government is, in fact, quite limited in its power to impose criminal sanctions. At the time of the creation of the Constitution, the states chose to retain the primary responsibility for criminal laws and granted the newly formed federal government the explicit authority to punish counterfeiters but otherwise limited federal authority in the criminal law field. Under the U.S. Constitution, Congressional power to create crime is largely limited to areas of inherently federal interest, such as espionage, use of the mail to commit fraud, or crimes committed on federal property, and to criminal conduct that involves interstate or foreign activity.[31] Indeed, relatively few federal criminal statutes existed prior to the gangster era of the 1920s and 1930s, when Congress sought to stem the country's first nationwide crime problem.

Many federal criminal laws rely upon the power of Congress to regulate interstate commerce. Thus, the 1992 federal anti-carjacking law[32] applies only to vehicles that have been transported or received in interstate or foreign commerce. Similarly, the famous Lindbergh Law,[33] which declares kidnapping for ransom a federal offense, is applicable only when the victim is transported from one state to another.

Under the American justice system, the responsibility for dealing with everyday crime remains with the states, a fact about which the Supreme Court must occasionally remind Congress. For example, in the 1995 case of *United States v. Lopez*,[34] the high court justices ruled that Congress exceeded its constitutional authority when it passed legislation creating "gun-free zones" around public school grounds. The court reasoned that mere possession of a firearm near a school had no substantial effect on interstate commerce and Congress' claim that such conduct significantly impacted interstate commerce was not proven.

CLASSIFICATION OF CRIME

English Common Law Classification

Anglo-American law has long recognized that some offenses are more serious than others and worthy of differing punishments. Accordingly, our forbearers found it convenient to classify crimes in a variety of ways. These classification labels are useful in understanding the structure of the criminal law in modern society.

The early English legal system created an arrangement whereby criminal conduct was deemed to be a treason, a felony, or a trespass. The differences across the classifications lay in the severity of the offense and the punishments attached thereto. If the Duke of Essex plotted against the king, he would have committed a treason. Punishment for the treason, besides the death of the duke, included forfeiture of his land to the monarch. In contrast, the broad range of serious crimes, such as robbery and murder, were deemed to be felonies. Again, the punishment was often death, transportation, or branding as no system of prisons existed, but any lands held were forfeited to the overlord, not the monarch, during this feudal period. Finally, more minor offenses were called trespasses. While the term today is generally thought of as involving nonpermissioned entry onto another's land, in early England the term covered a wide range of lesser offenses, offenses similar to today's misdemeanors. For many years, the sanction for a trespass was a monetary penalty paid to the victim or whipping or being placed in the stocks.

Traditional American Classification

American law has developed a classification of offenses based on the English model. Since forfeiture of estates was abandoned early on as part of American criminal law, the distinction between treasons and felonies is not well preserved. **Treason** is no longer considered a class of crimes but rather treated as a specifically defined offense. With the exception of New Jersey,[35] all American jurisdictions divide their criminal offenses into felonies and misdemeanors, depending primarily upon the severity of the offense. A few states also classify very minor offenses, such as traffic violations, as infractions or petty offenses, subject to a small fine.

While the felony–misdemeanor terminology is widely used, far less agreement exists as to the definitions of the terms. For example, in Texas, a felony is determined by the location the punishment is served.[36] Thus a **felony** is any offense for which death or incarceration in the state prison is the punishment. A **misdemeanor** is one which calls for a monetary fine or serving time in the local jail.

Many jurisdictions, including the federal system, consider the length of time of the incarceration, holding that death or incarceration for a period in excess of one year is a felony. Correspondingly, a misdemeanor would be an offense with only a fine or jail time less than one year. Texas law rejects the length of sentence approach. In fact, an individual convicted of a Class A misdemeanor could theoretically receive a longer sentence to be served in the county jail than a person convicted of a more serious state jail felony: The maximum sentence for a Class A misdemeanor is one year, while the minimum sentence for a state jail felony is 180 days' confinement.[37]

The felony–misdemeanor distinction has consequences outside of the criminal law. Individuals convicted of a felony may be barred from certain professions such as law or medicine, or from serving as a peace officer, or be prohibited from holding public office, and temporarily lose the right to vote.

Other Ways to Classify Crimes

In early Anglo-American law, it proved useful to classify crime in other ways. Perhaps the best known was to distinguish between *malum in se* and *malum prohibitum* offenses.[38] Since many early crimes were judge-made, not the acts of legislative bodies, discriminating between the two forms of criminal offenses assisted courts in applying legal rules and consequences. A case excerpt from the last century explains the difference in the terms:

> An offense *malum in se* is one which is naturally evil, as murder, theft, and the like. Offenses at common law are generally *malum in se*. An offense *malum prohibitum*, on the contrary, is not naturally an evil, but becomes so in consequence of being forbidden.[39]

Because most states, including Texas, now rely exclusively on legislatively enacted penal codes, the distinction between *malum in se* and *malum prohibitum* has lost much of its previous usefulness. However, new statutory enactments—all *malum prohibitum*—do serve as a reminder of the value system of the society.

A traditional classification retaining some modern utility is the definition of **crimes involving moral turpitude**. As one court noted,

The term "moral turpitude" has been used in the law for centuries. It has been the subject of many decisions by the courts but has never been clearly defined because of the nature of the term. Perhaps the best general definition of the term "moral turpitude" is that it imports an act of baseness, vileness or depravity in the duties which one person owes to another or to society in general, which is contrary to the usual, accepted and customary rule of right and duty which a person should follow.[40]

While theft-related crimes, perjury, vice offenses, murder, and sexual assaults are generally considered to be crimes involving moral turpitude, most states do not have a written list of such crimes but must define the phrase on a case-by-case basis. A conviction of a crime involving moral turpitude often produces collateral consequences, such as loss of an occupational license, deportation if a resident alien, and ineligibility to hold public office. In Texas, the fact of conviction of a crime of moral turpitude can also be presented in the cross-examination of a witness to discredit his or her testimony.[41]

A final classification of offenses used by Texas and most other states is those crimes labeled breaches of the peace. While the term **breach of the peace** originally referred to upsetting the peaceful, violence-free state that the king's realm should endure at all times, the modern use of the term is different. A Texas court ruled,

The term "breach of the peace" is generic, and includes all violations of the public peace or order, or decorum; in other words, it signifies the offense of disturbing the public peace or tranquility enjoyed by the citizens of a community; a disturbance of the public tranquility by any act or conduct inciting to violence or tending to provoke or excite others to break the peace; a disturbance of the public order by an act of violence, or by any act likely to produce violence, or which, by causing consternation and alarm disturbs the peace and quiet of the community.[42]

Misdemeanors such as disorderly conduct and public intoxication are commonly held to be breaches of the peace. Texas law limits a peace officer's authority in making an arrest for misdemeanors the officer did not personally observe. However, the law permits a warrantless arrest for a nonviewed offense if the offense was a breach of the peace.[43]

PURPOSES OF CRIMINAL LAW

The criminal sanction does not exist in a vacuum apart from the society at large. Rather, like all social institutions, criminal laws are enacted to accomplish certain societal goals. Throughout history, however, society's view of which of those goals should be primary has changed. In preparation for study of the criminal law, the reader should conduct a self-assessment about which goals of the criminal law he or she believes is most important.

Criminologists traditionally view the criminal law as addressing five broad objectives. When legislatures enact new laws and when judges or juries mete out consequences, they are, at least theoretically, attempting to accomplish one or more of the following objectives.

- General deterrence
- Specific deterrence
- Rehabilitation
- Retribution (just deserts)
- Incapacitation (public protection)

General Deterrence

An overarching objective of the criminal law is to prevent the occurrence of the very behavior that is prohibited. The Penal Code is largely a composition of "thou shall nots"; the government's goal being to apprise citizens of prohibited behaviors and encourage conformance by threatening punishment. This is the **general deterrence theory**. The theory is based upon the proposition that if individuals will suffer punishment for engaging in certain behavior, they will not engage in that behavior.

Criminologists have long debated the effectiveness of the general deterrence theory. Millions of crimes occur each year, including many serious ones. Clearly some proportion of the population is not being deterred. On the other hand, it is impossible to measure the number of crimes *not* committed because an individual who might think about engaging in the socially undesirable behavior fears being caught and punished. If the individual chooses not to commit the offense out of fear of punishment, he has been deterred.

Legislative bodies operate with high faith in the general deterrence theory. Frequently, when a societal problem arises, the legislature passes a law criminalizing the conduct. If the conduct continues unabated, the legislature often increases the punishment, reasoning that the "pain did not exceed the gain" from the perspective of the potential offender. A prime example of this logic is nationwide legislative efforts to curb intoxicated driving. Presumptive levels of blood alcohol have been reduced from 0.10 to 0.08 in all states, bringing more drinking drivers within the scope of the law. Penalties have been increased, including mandatory confinement periods and loss of operator licenses. Each of these efforts is a message to drivers that if they drink and drive, they will be punished. Whether these approaches have indeed reduced drunk driving is in dispute.

On occasion, so-called white-collar criminals will be prosecuted and sentenced as an example to other corporate executives that they are not above the law. The prosecution of various corporate figures in the early 2000s was as much about deterring others as handing out individual punishments. Similarly, the occasional criminal prosecution of an individual for income tax evasion serves as a reminder to the public that cheating on their income tax could have serious consequences.

Because the general deterrence theory is grounded in the idea of free will, only offenses involving conscious, intentional choice-making are likely deterred. Deterring reckless and negligent conduct is more difficult. The well-known prohibition against arson may deter certain "firebugs" but likely has little effect on preventing an individual from destroying his neighbor's house through carelessness in burning leaves on a windy day. The individual simply does not consider possible criminal liability when beginning the otherwise innocent act of setting his leaves ablaze. Additionally, general deterrence theory assumes the potential offender knows the contours of the law and the punishment for its violation. While everyone in society knows that murder is unlawful and that the punishment is severe, the same cannot be said for more obscure offenses. Is it unlawful to drive a motor vehicle that has a cracked windshield? Is robbery with a toy pistol punished more severely than robbery with no pistol? Is burning brush on one's own property without first obtaining a permit a crime? Unless the prospective offender considers the possibility that his conduct may be criminal, he or she is unlikely to be deterred.

To avoid the ignorance problem, the state may actually provide notice that certain behavior is unlawful. Consider signs reading "Fine for littering" or "School Zone, 20 mph." The state is seeking to deter undesirable behavior under a circumstance where it might not be apparent that the behavior is inappropriate. On the other hand, no signage exists at the local convenience store reading, "It is a serious crime to rob this store," as everyone is presumed to know that fact.

Specific Deterrence

Unlike general deterrence, which focuses on the population as a whole, **specific deterrence** (also called special deterrence) seeks to deter identified individuals from future criminality. This concept is best exemplified by the existence of enhanced punishments for repeat offenders. Assume Albert is tried and convicted of burglary. He is sentenced to two years. After his release from prison, Albert commits another burglary and is again arrested and convicted. Obviously the first prison term was insufficient to specifically deter Albert from future criminal behavior. His sentence for the second burglary conviction will likely be much greater than the first. Given relatively high recidivism rates, the validity of specific deterrence theory also is open to question.

Rehabilitation

Rehabilitation means altering someone's behavior so he or she will function appropriately in society. While rehabilitation is generally viewed as one goal of correctional institutions, most persons do not view the criminal law as having a rehabilitation element. While criminologists disagree on the viability of a rehabilitative correctional system generally, some percentage of offenders is sentenced with rehabilitation as the judge or jury's primary concern.

All American correctional institutions operate rehabilitation programs for felons, ranging from education to job training activities. Some misdemeanor facilities may also offer programs geared toward improving socialization of the offender. Most such programs require voluntary participation on the part of the offender. For lower-level offenders, however, mandatory attendance at a drug and alcohol treatment program or participation in a "boot camp" program is directed toward modifying the offender's behavior through rehabilitation.

Many post-incarceration programs such as parole and mandatory supervision involve monitoring the rehabilitative process of the offender.

Retribution (Just Deserts)

Many Americans strongly believe that some persons need to be punished because they deserve it. This is the concept of **retribution**, sometimes called "just deserts." This principle is best typified by capital punishment. Polls reveal that a majority of society still demands retribution for at least the most serious of offenses. Texas provides as an alternative to the death penalty: life without parole. Such a sentence is rooted in the mentality of "lock'em up and throw away the key." The offender is deprived of his liberty for life because that is what society believes the offender deserves for killing another human being.

This principle is further seen when the Legislature requires certain sentences be served day-for-day without accumulation of "good time" credit toward parole or discharge. A prime goal of such laws is sheer punishment of offenders.

Incapacitation (Public Protection)

The final goal of the criminal law concerns protection of the public from future harm by the offender. This goal is attained through **incapacitation**. The goal is not often overtly stated in the sentencing process but hangs over the trials of particularly heinous offenders. Consequently, the long sentences handed out to serial murderers, child molesters, serial rapists, violent robbers, and the like manifest this concern for the future safety of the public. While the particular offender's sentence is for the criminal conduct of the past, the judge or jury certainly has an eye on the future. Likewise, life without parole or a similar sentence is intended to keep the violent offender away from society permanently. Death, of course, is the ultimate form of incapacitation.

Incapacitation is also manifest in the politically popular habitual offender laws. These laws hold that upon conviction of a third felony, an offender will receive a life sentence, irrespective of the punishment prescribed for the most recent felonious act. The theory here is that the offender has had three chances to show he can function appropriately within society and has failed each chance. So society essentially banishes the offender from normal everyday life.

PURPOSES OF TEXAS CRIMINAL LAW

The Texas Legislature has adopted a formal statement of public policy regarding criminal law within the state. This policy, as reflected in Sec. 1.02 of the Texas Penal Code, emphasizes which goals lawmakers consider the most important. Additionally, the statute lays out other specific objectives that the Penal Code is supposed to accomplish.

The first goal of the Penal Code is to insure public safety through general deterrence, rehabilitation, and specific deterrence. Interestingly, despite leading the nation in the number of executions[44] and having the second highest incarceration rate, the Texas statute lists neither retribution nor incapacitation as formal goals of the penal law. Various statutory changes in recent decades would suggest that the stated legislative goals found in Sec. 1.02 and the state's actual goals are inconsistent. For example, in 1989,

§ 1.02. Objectives of Code

The general purposes of this code are to establish a system of prohibitions, penalties, and correctional measures to deal with conduct that unjustifiably and inexcusably causes or threatens harm to those individual or public interests for which state protection is appropriate. To this end, the provisions of this code are intended, and shall be construed, to achieve the following objectives:

1. To insure the public safety through:
   a. the deterrent influence of the penalties hereinafter provided;
   b. the rehabilitation of those convicted of violations of this code; and
   c. such punishment as may be necessary to prevent likely recurrence of criminal behavior;

2. by definition and grading of offenses to give fair warning of what is prohibited and of the consequences of violation;

3. to prescribe penalties that are proportionate to the seriousness of offenses and that permit recognition of differences in rehabilitation possibilities among individual offenders;

4. to safeguard conduct that is without guilt from condemnation as criminal;

5. to guide and limit the exercise of official discretion in law enforcement to prevent arbitrary or oppressive treatment of persons suspected, accused, or convicted of offenses; and

6. to define the scope of state interest in law enforcement against specific offenses and to systematize the exercise of state criminal jurisdiction.

the name of the prison system was altered from the Texas Department of Corrections (a rehabilitation focus?) to the Institutional Division of the Texas Department of Criminal Justice (an incapacitation focus?).[45] Likewise, legislative changes restricting violent offenders' eligibility for probation and increasing the amount of prison time they must serve prior to becoming eligible for parole certainly suggest a retribution and incapacitation orientation.[46]

Texas law also formally recognizes the idea that the public should receive fair warning of what conduct is unlawful and that penalties should be proportionate to the seriousness of the offenses. As will be seen in the next chapter, the range of sanction for offenses is quite wide. The Legislature did this purposely because of the "differences in rehabilitation possibilities" among offenders. Further, by defining what conduct is criminal, the law also defines that which is not criminal. The written Penal Code protects innocent conduct from being deemed to be criminal conduct.

Finally, one purpose of the code is to guide the exercise of discretion by police, court, and corrections officials. Importantly, the Legislature recognizes that discretion is necessary in the implementation of the criminal law and that it should be controlled, not eliminated.

These greater public policy purposes of the criminal law often become lost in the day-to-day implementation of the justice system.

LIMITATIONS ON POWER TO CREATE CRIMINAL LAW

Practical Limits

Any effort by a legislative body to enact a criminal statute is doomed to failure unless the proposal is supported by the bulk of the population. Lawmaking is, after all, a political process. No legislator who expects reelection is going to propose a criminal statute that is not reasonable on its face and that is not likely to be supported by the overwhelming majority of the electorate.

In recent years, Texas, like many states, has enacted new criminal laws covering identity theft.[47] Despite the fact that existing law likely covers most concerns of the public, these proposals have enjoyed wide support because the public perceives a serious problem exists, a broad segment of the population are potential victims of the fraudulent behavior, and most individuals know someone who has had her credit rating or other personal identity information used by a thief without the victim's knowledge. The personal aggravation the theft has caused the victim makes for an interesting story over dinner. Accordingly, broad public support, and correspondingly only minor opposition, exists for creation of identity theft laws.

In contrast, the American experience with mandated seatbelt rules, motorcycle helmet laws, and laws against speeding has been mixed at best. Why? Because a significant portion of the population views these laws as either unnecessary or unreasonable. Many drivers contend seatbelts are uncomfortable, while motorcyclists argue that not only do helmets obscure their vision but mandated wearing of a helmet violates their freedom to control their own lives.

The classic example of a law effectively becoming a nullity due to nonsupport by the population was the 55 miles per hour national speed limit mandated in 1974 as a means to save fuel during a period of shortage of gasoline. In jurisdictions where the legal speed limit had previously been much higher—as high as 75 miles per hour in some states—the "double nickel" was widely ignored because citizens either did not believe it saved fuel, doubted that a fuel shortage actually existed, or found the law to be a personal annoyance and generally unreasonable. Police soon began granting wide tolerance to speeders. Many local authorities, recognizing the political unpopularity of the law, ordered that only minor fines be assessed against violators. Congress finally acknowledged the extent of the noncompliance as well as the political liability of the lower speed limit, and the law was repealed in 1995, over 20 years after the population had effectively repealed it by noncompliance.

In a similar vein, laws prohibiting the possession of marijuana exist in every state. Yet, the aggressiveness with which the laws are enforced varies from community to community, largely depending upon the social composition of the community and residents' views regarding the reasonableness of a law barring private use of marijuana.

Legal Limits

Constitutional Conflict

Important legal limits also exist on the power of a legislative body to criminalize behavior. Foremost among these limits are provisions of the U.S. Constitution. *Ex post facto* laws are prohibited, for example.[48] An ***ex post facto* law** is a law passed after the occurrence of an event or action that retrospectively changes the legal consequences of the event or action. Thus, a legislative body may not criminalize conduct that occurred in the past or enhance the punishment for the conduct between the time the event occurred and the time of conviction at trial. Legislatures today attempt to avoid *ex post facto* problems by establishing a prospective effective date of most new legislation. Thus, a bill changing the punishment for theft, though signed by the governor on July 15, might not go into effect until September 1.

Most importantly, a criminal statute cannot be contrary to the personal liberties guaranteed by the Bill of Rights and the Fourteenth Amendment of the U.S. Constitution. Thus, a legislature in crafting anti-riot laws and public disturbance statutes has to be cautious not to violate the First Amendment protections of free speech and peaceful assembly. In 2003, the Supreme Court ruled the Texas homosexual conduct statute unconstitutional on the grounds that it violated the Fourteenth Amendment right to liberty.[49]

The Texas Constitution also contains a Bill of Rights that guarantees certain personal liberties.[50] As with the U.S. Bill of Rights, legislative enactments may not conflict with the Texas Bill of Rights. While the language between the federal Bill of Rights and the state Bill of Rights is similar in many sections, it is not exactly the same. For example, on the question of private ownership of firearms, the Texas Bill of Rights states,

> Every citizen shall have the right to keep and bear arms in the lawful defense of himself or the State; but the Legislature shall have power, by law, to regulate the wearing of arms, with a view to prevent crime.[51]

This constitutional provision prohibits the Legislature from criminalizing mere possession of a firearm but not the carrying thereof. Thus, Sec. 46.02 of the Texas Penal Code prohibits unlawful *carrying* of a weapon, not unlawful possession.

Statute Must Relate to Conduct

Criminal offenses must relate to conduct or behavior of the individual. No crime may punish an individual for what she thinks, her evil intent, or for her status. Criminal liability must be based on an act, or in limited circumstances, a failure to act. This principle, tied to the concept of *actus reus*, which will be discussed in the next chapter, is based on the idea that no societal harm flows from mere thoughts of an individual.[52] The principle is best exemplified in the law of conspiracy where two or more persons may actually agree to commit a crime but no violation occurs until at least one of them engages in an overt act—some conduct—in furtherance of the agreement.

Conduct need not be limited to actual physical movement. Uttering of a verbal threat in an assault case fits the requirement.[53] Similarly, a legislature may criminalize failing to act, as in the common offense of failure to stop and render aid following a traffic accident.[54]

Statute Cannot Lend Itself to Arbitrary Enforcement

Another requirement of a modern criminal statute is that it cannot lend itself to arbitrary enforcement. As the Supreme Court has noted, this principle, known as the void-for-vagueness doctrine, involves two circumstances:

> First, it may fail to provide the kind of notice that will enable ordinary people to understand what conduct it prohibits; second, it may authorize and even encourage arbitrary and discriminatory enforcement.[55]

The first rule requires that terminology in a statute contain clearly defined or commonly understood meanings.[56] Thus, the Supreme Court ruled unconstitutional a Chicago city ordinance that prohibited criminal street gang members from loitering in any one place with no apparent purpose.[57] While the term "loiter" might have a common, everyday meaning, "[i]t is difficult to imagine how any citizen of the city of Chicago standing in a public place with a group of people would know if he or she had an 'apparent purpose,' " Justice John Paul Stevens wrote.

Secondly, the language of a law must be sufficiently distinct to limit arbitrary enforcement. The Supreme Court, while recognizing the need for discretionary decision making by police officers, has ruled that vesting a police officer with virtually total discretion to determine whether or not an individual is in compliance with a law is unconstitutional.[58]

It should be noted that the necessity of a police officer to exercise discretion does not automatically doom a statute for being vague. For example, many minor offenses, such as disorderly conduct, require the officer to determine if a person is making "an unreasonable noise." Likewise, a public intoxication law may charge the police officer with determining whether a citizen is "a danger to himself or others" in order to arrest him. The key point in these types of offenses is that while fairly broad discretion is granted the police officer, the penalty for the violation is relatively low. Imprecision in defining the illegal conduct is balanced against attachment of a minor penalty, often only a monetary fine. Such an approach apparently complies with the constitutional requirements of due process.

Proportionality of Punishment

The U.S. Supreme Court has ruled that the Eighth Amendment's cruel and unusual punishment ban "prohibits not only barbaric punishments, but also sentences that are disproportionate to the crime committed."[59] The concept of proportionality is deeply rooted in Common Law jurisprudence, being embodied in the British Magna Carta.

Courts have generally deferred to legislative bodies on the question of the appropriate penalty range for a particular offense. Barbaric punishments, such as torture or burning at the stake, no longer occur in our society. Consequently, modern Eighth Amendment challenges tend to focus on the issue of proportionality of sentence to harm. With the exception of death cases, the disproportionality argument has rarely been successful.

Recent disproportionality challenges before the Supreme Court have concerned the application of habitual criminal laws. These laws, which are discussed more fully below, provide for life imprisonment for individuals who continually commit a series of criminal offenses, even if the offenses are nonviolent. For example, the Supreme Court did find that a sentence of life without parole for a seventh nonviolent felony was contrary to the Eighth Amendment.[60] The felony was passing a $100 no-account check. In this 1983 case, the justices said that reviewing courts should look at the gravity of the offense and the harshness of the penalty, as well as the punishment imposed for other crimes in the same jurisdiction. Additionally, appeals courts should examine the penalty imposed for the same crime in other jurisdictions. By 1991, however, the Supreme Court appeared to backtrack on its suggestion of appellate court review of sentences. In *Harmelin v. Michigan*, the court held that the fixing of prison terms for specific crimes involves a substantial penological judgment that, as a general matter, is properly within the province of the legislature, and reviewing courts should grant substantial deference to legislative determinations.[61] Further, the Eighth Amendment does not require a state to adopt any particular penological theory, whether retribution, deterrence, incapacitation, or rehabilitation. The court also recognized that divergences both in sentencing theories and the length of prescribed prison terms are the inevitable, often beneficial, result of our structure of government, and differing attitudes and perceptions of local conditions may yield different, yet rational, conclusions regarding the appropriate length of terms for particular crimes. Perhaps most importantly, the justices ruled that "the Eighth Amendment does not require strict proportionality between crime and sentence, but rather forbids only extreme sentences that are grossly disproportionate to the crime."[62] Accordingly, a claim of disproportionality of sentence will be a tough sell for a state criminal defendant so long as his punishment falls within the specified statutory range.

The primary exception to the general deference to legislative bodies has come with the sentence of death. In recent decades, the Supreme Court has rejected as disproportionate the sentence of death for rape[63] and burglary and has only upheld it for certain forms of murder. While the high court has not passed on the issue, death would likely be upheld as a penalty for the traditional capital crimes of treason, espionage, and sabotage during wartime.

The Supreme Court has largely eliminated death as a penalty for any offense other than intentional murder.[64] However, the justices have sent mixed signals on the level of scrutiny appellate courts should give to claims of sentence disproportionality in noncapital cases. Generally, the courts will defer to the legislature's judgment regarding the appropriate range of sentence for a particular criminal violation and to a judge or jury's judgment in imposing a particular term of years in an individual case.

Preemption Doctrine

The pyramidal structure of government that exists in America provides the opportunity for criminal laws to be enacted at the local, state, or federal level. Indeed, criminal offenses frequently overlapped in terms of the behavior prohibited. State law bars robbery, while federal law criminalizes robberies in certain circumstances, such as those involving a federally insured bank. Likewise, state statutes often proscribe the offense of disorderly conduct, while local ordinances add to the list of behaviors that constitute the crime of disorderly conduct. In some limited instances, the higher governmental entity prohibits a lower governmental entity from enacting a statute covering a particular topic. This is the **preemption doctrine**, whereby the higher-level sovereign assumes total authority for the lawmaking responsibility for a particular topic. The federal preemption doctrine proceeds from the Supremacy Clause of the U.S. Constitution, which provides that the law of the United States "shall be the supreme Law of the Land. . . ."[65] For example, the federal government has likely preempted the topic of criminalizing acts of treason, espionage, and sabotage as these are areas of concern to the nation as a whole regardless of where the act occurs.

A state statute criminalizing espionage probably would not pass court scrutiny. In a more contemporary example, Congress has preempted the field on the sale of intoxicating liquors on interstate airlines. An air carrier does not need to terminate sale of beer, wine, and liquor depending on whether the county over which it is flying at any given point in time is "wet" or "dry."

A similar rule applies in most states. State constitutions often limit the criminal law making authority of counties and cities to offenses not covered by state law or not in conflict with state law. Thus, a city cannot enact criminal ordinances on a particular topic unless the legislature has granted such authority. A city can establish no-parking zones within its corporate limits under authority granted by state law. But, a city could not raise the speed limit to 70 miles per hour when state law sets it at 65.

Federal–state preemption issues in criminal law rarely come up because of the dual sovereign doctrine, discussed in a later chapter. Preemption is occasionally raised as a defense to a municipal ordinance violation.

JURISDICTION

Common Law Territorial Jurisdiction

Criminal laws are limited in their application in many ways. One important limitation is whether or not the undesirable conduct occurred within the jurisdiction of the sovereign. Put another way, under what circumstances do the penal laws of Texas apply to individuals.

Under the Common Law, criminal offenses were enforceable against individuals who committed the forbidden act within the territory of the sovereign. Conduct outside the territory controlled by the monarch was not normally deemed to violate that government's laws. Thus, in the eighteenth century an English citizen who stole property in Paris might be subject to the criminal law of France but had done nothing to offend his own sovereign, the King of England. Hence, the English criminal law would not be applicable.

In contrast, European countries adhered to the Roman basis of jurisdiction, which held their citizens accountable for their conduct no matter where they committed the unlawful behavior. Thus, a French citizen who committed a crime in Spain was subject to French criminal law.

During the age of exploration, the territorial principle was extended to cover ships on the high seas that flew the flag of the homeland. A British flagship was viewed as a floating piece of England and a crime committed aboard the boat was subject to English law, even if it occurred in the Pacific Ocean.

State Criminal Jurisdiction

Given their strong Common Law heritage, it is not surprising that American states initially adhered to English notions of criminal jurisdiction. Eventually problems arose because the Common Law held that a crime had only one situs; that is, could occur in only one place. This notion worked well enough in a country separated from other countries by water and one which had a single lawmaking body. America was another story because each state passed its own laws. And, every state abutted at least one other state, thereby permitting easy movement from one jurisdiction to another. Occasionally, odd problems manifested themselves. In one case an individual standing in North Carolina fired a gun across the state line and killed another person in Tennessee. The court ruled that the crime occurred in Tennessee and reversed the North Carolina murder conviction.[66]

Over time states began expanding the application of their criminal statutes. For example, a century ago, a Californian who mailed a box of poison candy to a resident of Delaware was properly tried for murder in California after the Delaware recipient died.[67]

Today, states continue to adhere primarily to the principles of territorial jurisdiction. However, partially influenced by the reform efforts of the Model Penal Code, many states, including Texas, have expanded the coverage of their penal laws to where any element of an offense, or the result of an offense, occurring within the state is sufficient to give that state jurisdiction. Likewise, most states will not allow their territory to serve as a staging ground for committing crimes in another state. The criminal conspiracy law of the host state would be invoked against conspirators who plot in one state to commit an offense in another.

Little constitutional impediment seems to exist to the expansion of a state's criminal jurisdiction beyond that state's boundaries, providing some harm occurs within the state. As Supreme Court Justice Oliver Wendell Holmes noted long ago, "Acts done outside a jurisdiction, but intended to produce or producing detrimental effects within it, justify a State in punishing the cause of the harm as if he had been present at the effect. . . ."[68] The key factor is that the legislature must enact a statute that clearly expands the state's territorial jurisdiction. Failure to do so means the laws will not apply beyond the state's boundaries, even if the particular state arguably has an interest in the criminal act. For example, the Iowa Supreme Court ruled that no violation of that state's criminal code had occurred when an inmate from the Iowa State Penitentiary escaped in Texas as he was being transported from Iowa to New Mexico. The court found that no Iowa statute existed that applied to escapes by its inmates that occur outside the state's boundaries.[69]

State territorial jurisdiction extends to the sky above the state and, for states with water boundaries, to the territorial waters of that state. For coastal states, except Texas and Florida, this is three nautical miles from the mean high tide line. Thus, a murder committed on a boat within the adjacent territorial waters of a state is subject to the criminal laws of that state. In a bit of an unusual jurisdictional claim, Minnesota and Wisconsin assert criminal jurisdiction over the entire portion of the Mississippi River adjacent to the states even though the states' boundaries with each other and with Iowa is the middle of the river.[70] Similarly, by congressional legislation, Oregon and Washington assert concurrent territorial jurisdiction on the waters of the Columbia River.[71] Exercising criminal jurisdiction over the entire river is largely a matter of practicality.

In recent years, because of acts of terrorism against American citizens abroad, the federal government, by statute, has claimed jurisdiction over many criminal acts that occur against American persons or property in foreign lands.[72] Traditionally, a legal presumption has existed against applying extraterritorial jurisdiction of federal law to American citizens.[73] Under the territorial principle, the host country also holds jurisdiction over the criminal act.

Texas Criminal Jurisdiction

Sec. 1.04 of the Penal Code sets forth Texas' jurisdictional claims.

Subsection (d) of the statute notes that the territorial jurisdiction of Texas includes not only its land but also its waters and air space above the land. The physical territory of Texas is a bit odd. On the east, as previously noted, the territorial waters extend into the Gulf of Mexico for three leagues (10.35 miles). On the north to the Oklahoma line, due to a language quirk in the annexation treaty of 1845, Texas extends only to the

§ 1.04. Territorial Jurisdiction

a. This state has jurisdiction over an offense that a person commits by his own conduct or the conduct of another for which he is criminally responsible if:

1. either the conduct or a result that is an element of the offense occurs inside this state;

2. the conduct outside this state constitutes an attempt to commit an offense inside this state;

3. he conduct outside this state constitutes a conspiracy to commit an offense inside this state, and an act in furtherance of the conspiracy occurs inside this state; or

4. the conduct inside this state constitutes an attempt, solicitation, or conspiracy to commit, or establishes criminal responsibility for the commission of, an offense in another jurisdiction that is also an offense under the laws of this state.

b. If the offense is criminal homicide, a "result" is either the physical impact causing death or the death itself. If the body of a criminal homicide victim is found in this state, it is presumed that the death occurred in this state. If death alone is the basis for jurisdiction, it is a defense to the exercise of jurisdiction by this state that the conduct that constitutes the offense is not made criminal in the jurisdiction where the conduct occurred.

c. An offense based on an omission to perform a duty imposed on an actor by a statute of this state is committed inside this state regardless of the location of the actor at the time of the offense.

d. This state includes the land and water and the air space above the land and water over which this state has power to define offenses.

south bank of the Red River, not to the center as is traditional. The center of the Sabine River is the boundary with Louisiana.[74] The 100th meridian forms the boundary with New Mexico, while the center of the Rio Grande River is the boundary with Mexico.

Sec. 1.07 broadens the Common Law rule that a crime can have only one location by asserting jurisdiction over both conduct which occurs in the state and results that occur in the state. Only a single element of the offense need occur in the state. For example, a capital murder conviction was upheld where the victim was kidnapped in Texas but actually killed in Mexico.[75]

Suppose Mutt and Jeff become involved in a barroom fight in Oklahoma. Mutt stabs Jeff with a knife. Subsequently, Jeff is transported to the nearest available hospital emergency room, which happens to be across the state line in Texas. Jeff dies in the emergency room. Texas could claim jurisdiction over the incident since Jeff died in the state. This principle is further expanded by subsection (b) in raising a presumption that a dead body found in the state was killed in the state. In one murder case, the appeals court found that Texas had jurisdiction over skeletal remains found in the Rio Grande River, the center of the river being the boundary with Mexico. The court ruled that the defendant failed to rebut the presumption that the body was in Texas.[76]

Extraterritorial jurisdiction is also asserted over individuals who, though out of state, attempt or conspire to commit an offense in Texas. Similarly, Texas will not be a safe haven for criminals as the state will exercise jurisdiction over individuals who use the state as a place to attempt or conspire to commit crimes elsewhere. With the advent of the Internet and the various criminal offenses that can be committed with its technology, the extraterritorial reach of the state's penal laws may prove useful in establishing a place of prosecution. Thus, an individual running an Internet fraud from outside Texas would be subject to Texas law if any victims reside in the state. Similarly, an individual running the same fraud from Texas, but without any Texas victims, would still be subject to the state's laws.

Finally, subsection (c) speaks to the problem of failing to perform a legally required duty within the state though being located outside the state. One Texas court found that the statute granted criminal jurisdiction over a Colorado resident who did not pay child support for an offspring who resided in Texas.[77]

Notes

1. Asian, African, and most European countries operate with a single, nationwide set of penal laws.
2. State criminal codes are often supplemented by local ordinances, further expanding the variations in terminology and definition.
3. *See* Paul H. Robinson et al., *The Five Worst (and Five Best) American Criminal Codes*, 95 Nw. U. L. Rev. 1 (2000).
4. *See* Richard Singer, *The 25th Anniversary of the Model Penal Code: Forward*, 19 Rutgers L.J. 519 (1988), for an overview of the influence of the Model Penal Code on American criminal law.
5. W. Page Keeton and William G. Reid, *Proposed Revision of the Texas Penal Code*, 45 Tex. L. Rev. 399 (1967).
6. Act of Jun. 14, 1973, 63rd Leg., R.S., ch. 399, 1973 Tex. Gen. Laws 883.
7. Some jurisdictions, but not Texas, still recognize and enforce unwritten Common Law crimes.
8. 4 William Blackstone, Commentaries *5.
9. Rollin M. Perkins & Ronald N. Boyce, Criminal Law 12 (3rd ed. 1982).
10. Tex. Code Crim. P. art. 21.02 and 21.21.
11. Tex. Const. art. V, § 12.
12. *Ex parte* Warnell, 606 S.W.2d 923 (Tex. Crim. App. 1980).
13. Texas permits, but does not require, a crime victim to hire a "special prosecutor" to assist the elected district attorney. *See* Lopez v. State, 437 S.W.2d 268 (Tex. Crim. App. 1968).
14. *See* Tex. Code Crim. P. art. 56.01–56.64.
15. The most commonly used reference for determining the nature of the Common Law is William Blackstone, Commentaries on the Laws of England, originally published in 1765.
16. Fla. Stat. § 775.01.
17. U.S. v. Hudson & Goodwin, 11 U.S. 32 (1812).
18. A league is roughly 3.45 miles. Thus, Texas claims territorial jurisdiction reaching 10.35 statute miles into the Gulf of Mexico, while Florida exercises a similar jurisdiction into both the Gulf of Mexico and the Atlantic Ocean. The Supreme Court upheld the validity of the Florida claim in Skiriotes v. Florida, 313 U.S. 69 (1941).
19. See Tex. Code Crim. P. art. 2.09 including mayors and county judges in the list of who are magistrates.
20. Many consider the first penal code on the North American continent to have been The Massachusetts Body of Liberties adopted in colonial New England in 1641. It contained written definitions of degrees of criminal homicide, theft, sodomy, adultery, and public rebellion.
21. Act approved Aug. 28, 1856, effective Feb. 1, 1857, 6th Leg., Adj. S.
22. Brown v. City of Galveston, 75 S.W. 488 (Tex. 1903).
23. McNew v. State, 608 S.W.2d 166, 176 (Tex. Crim. App. 1980).
24. Crawley v. State, 513 S.W.2d 62, 66 (Tex. Crim. App. 1974).
25. The Texas Constitution, art. III § 39, provides that no law shall go into effect until 90 days after adjournment unless an emergency is declared by two-thirds vote of each house.
26. Tex. Bus. & Com. Code § 35.55.
27. Tex. Health & Safety Code § 146.0124.
28. *See* Diane Burch Beckham, *Thrashing Pecans and Other Non-PC Crimes*, 69 Tex. B.J. 262 (2006).
29. Tex. Loc. Gov't. Code § 54.001.
30. Waller v. Florida, 397 U.S. 387 (1970).
31. U.S. Const. art. I, § 8.
32. Anti-Car Theft Act of 1992, Pub. L. No. 102–519, 106 Stat. 3384 (codified as amended at 18 U.S.C. § 2119).
33. 18 U.S.C. § 1201.
34. 514 U.S. 549 (1995).
35. New Jersey uses the term "high misdemeanor" instead of "felony." N.J. Stat. Ann. § 2C:1–4.
36. *See generally* Chapter 12 of Tex. Penal Code.
37. *Compare* Tex. Penal Code §§ 12.21 and 12.35.
38. *Malum in se* and *malum prohibitum* are the plural forms of these Latin terms. *Mala in se* and *mala prohibita* are the singular forms.
39. State v. Horton, 51 S.E. 945, 946 (N.C. 1905).
40. The Committee on Legal Ethics of the West Virginia State Bar v. Scherr, 143 S.E.2d 141 (W.Va. 1965).
41. Tex. R. Evid. 609.

42. Woods v. State, 213 S.W.2d 685 (Tex. Crim. App. 1948).
43. *See* Tex. Code Crim. P. art. 14.03.
44. Texas has executed over 400 individuals since 1976. Virginia is second with about 100 executions over the same time frame.
45. Act of Jun. 15, 1989, 71st Leg., R.S., ch. 785 § 1.01, 1989 Tex. Gen. Laws 3471.
46. *See* Tex. Code Crim. P. art. 42.12(3g) and Tex. Gov't. Code § 508.145(d).
47. *See* Tex. Penal Code § 32.51.
48. U.S. Const. art. I, § 9.
49. Lawrence v. Texas, 539 U.S. 558 (2003).
50. Tex. Const. art. I §§ 1–30.1.
51. Tex. Const. art. I § 23.
52. A second reason for limiting the criminal sanction to actual conduct is a reaction to some British monarchs' penchant for punishing political enemies for plotting against the sovereign when no actual action had been taken and the king only suspected the individual might be disloyal.
53. Tex. Penal Code § 22.01(a)(2).
54. Tex. Transp. Code § 550.023.
55. City of Chicago v. Morales, 527 U.S. 41, 56 (1999), *citing* Kolender v. Lawson, 461 U.S. 352 (1983).
56. But see Rose v. Locke, 423 U.S. 48 (1975), upholding a conviction for violating the Tennessee statute prohibiting "crimes against nature" on the ground that Tennessee courts had sufficiently interpreted the phrase to provide notice of the conduct prohibited.
57. City of Chicago v. Morales.
58. Kolender v. Lawson.
59. Solem v. Helm, 463 U.S. 277, 284 (1983).
60. *Id.*
61. 501 U.S. 957 (1991).
62. *Id.* at 1001.
63. Coker v. Georgia, 433 U.S. 584 (1977).
64. Whether the death penalty is still a constitutionally acceptable punishment for treason, espionage in time of war, and military desertion has not been considered in recent years. These offenses have historically been sanctioned with death. Likewise, Texas and several other states have enacted statutes establishing death as a penalty for serial child sexual assault. Whether these statutes will pass constitutional scrutiny has yet to be determined.
65. U.S. Const. art. VI, § 8, cl. 2.
66. State v. Hall, 19 S.E. 273 (N.C. 1894).
67. People v. Boykin, 64 P. 286 (Cal. 1901).
68. Strasheim v. Daily, 221 U.S. 280, 285 (1911).
69. State v. Wagner, 596 N.W.2d 83 (Iowa 1999).
70. Minn. Const. art. II and Wis. Const. art. IX, § 1.
71. Acts of Mar. 2, 1853, c. 90, 10 Stat. 172, and of Feb. 14, 1859, c. 33, 11 Stat. 383.
72. See, for example, 18 U.S.C. § 1203, criminalizing hostage-taking whether inside or outside the territory of the United States.
73. U.S. v. Kim, 246 F.3d 186 (2nd Cir. 2001).
74. Amazingly, the dispute with Louisiana over the eastern boundary was not formally settled until 1973! *See* Texas v. Louisiana, 410 U.S. 702 (1973).
75. Rodriguez v. State, 146 S.W.3d 674 (Tex. Crim. App. 2004).
76. Torres v. State, 141 S.W.3d 645 (Tex. App.—El Paso 2004).
77. State v. Paiz, 817 S.W.2d 84 (Tex. Crim. App. 1991).

CHAPTER 2
Elements of a Crime

BOLO

The reader should be on the lookout (BOLO) for the meaning of the following terms. Knowledge of the meaning of these terms will greatly assist the reader in understanding the primary elements of the chapter.

- But for test
- Act
- *Actus reus*
- Attendant circumstances
- Causation
- Concurrence
- Constructive possession
- Criminal negligence
- Doctrine of transferred intent
- Elements of an offense
- Intentionally
- Knowingly
- *Mens rea*
- Nature of conduct
- Omission to act
- Possession
- Recklessly
- Result of conduct
- Status offenses
- Strict liability
- Victimless crimes

INTRODUCTION

Remember your high school chemistry classroom? Hanging on the wall was a copy of the periodic table. The periodic table displays the 118 scientifically accepted elements in the universe, ranging from hydrogen to ununoctium. Every bit of matter is composed of one or more combinations of these elements in varying amounts. The breakfast cereal you ate this morning or the bus you rode to class or this textbook all are made up of some combination of these 118 basic units of matter. Each element is describable and behaves in a particular, predictable manner, at least to the degree that scientists understand them.

For the less scientifically inclined, consider English grammar instruction. A traditional tool for teaching grammar and writing is the sentence diagram. Using a standardized format, the student of English is required to deconstruct sentences by identifying the subject, predicate, adjectives, adverbs, participles, objects, and other parts of speech. These elements of the sentence are placed in the appropriate spots on a diagram, thereby giving a visual picture of the sentence.

Criminal offenses have much in common with chemistry and English grammar. Each offense is composed of a combination of basic building blocks—elements—which are describable and reasonably consistent across different crimes. When you examine a particular crime, for example a robbery, you will notice that it has some, but not all, of the same components (i.e., elements) as burglary. Similarly, assault consists of many of the elements of murder, while sexual assault contains a few, but not all, of the same factors that appear in an entirely different offense, such as public lewdness. Thus, while both your morning cornflakes and your television set seem completely different in appearance, each contains certain chemical elements, such as carbon and oxygen, but each is constructed of additional chemical elements not shared by the other. Hence, cornflakes and television sets are at the same time similar and different. This sentence is different in content than the prior sentence but shares a similar structure as each is composed of a subject, predicate, adjectives, prepositions, and the like—so it is with criminal offenses. Each crime has a similar construction but varying elements.

Understanding the elements of a particular offense is the key to differentiating criminal behavior from innocent, or noncriminal, behavior. If John purposely inflicts a serious injury upon Jack, but thanks to rapid medical care Jack survives the attack, John cannot be prosecuted for Jack's murder because the death of a human victim is a necessary element of the crime of murder. Similarly, if Jennifer mistakenly takes Patricia's umbrella believing it to be her own, Jennifer has not committed an offense because she lacks the element of intent, which is necessary for the crime of theft. Often a single component (element) of an offense is all that separates criminal from noncriminal behavior. For example, sexual intercourse between consenting adults is not a crime. But, if the same conduct occurs in public view, a public lewdness offense has occurred. The addition of the sole element of the location of the behavior determines whether criminal or innocent behavior has occurred, just as a chocolate cake will not be a chocolate cake without, of course, chocolate!

Not only must each element of a criminal offense be proven beyond a reasonable doubt to obtain a criminal conviction, but the negation of a single element is sufficient to defeat the prosecutor's case. To convict an individual of theft through the possession of stolen property, the prosecutor must establish that the property was indeed stolen and the defendant possessed it and knew the property was stolen. If the defense attorney can raise a question in the jurors' minds about whether the defendant *knew* the stolen nature of the property, failure to convince the jury as to that single element will be sufficient to refute the charge. A not guilty verdict will result.

To understand any particular offense, you should be able to identify and understand its component elements. Indeed, the subsequent chapters, which focus on specific crimes and their definitions, will highlight the requisite elements of major crimes in order to facilitate your study of the offenses. Crimegraphs are provided to assist in understanding the elements of the offenses and how each differs from the other.

BASIC ELEMENTS OF A CRIME

To better grasp the concept of **elements of an offense**, Figure 2-1 may prove helpful. The diagram displays the skeletal structure of a crime. It can depict almost any crime as all serious crimes, at least in theory, contain the same generic components. The Common Law legal tradition holds that all crimes contain the following basic structural components:[1]

- Conduct (*actus reus*)
- Culpable mental state (*mens rea*)
- Concurrence
- Causation
- Harm
- Penalty

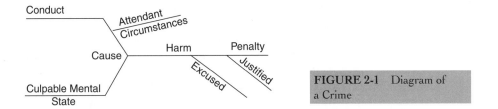

FIGURE 2-1   Diagram of a Crime

Simply put, the diagram shows that conduct (often with special or attendant circumstances) and a culpable mental state combine to cause some harmful result, to which, unless the result is excused or justified, society attaches a penalty. This is the fundamental structure of every crime.

CONDUCT (*actus reus*)

The most obvious element of a penal offense is the unlawful conduct: the killing of another in a murder, the entering of the home in a residential burglary, or the verbal threat to do bodily injury to another in an assault. Traditionally, this conduct element has been called the ***actus reus***, a Latin phrase meaning "guilty act."

The concept of a guilty act, however, is somewhat more complex than it may first appear. To start, modern American law sanctions only what people *do*, not what they may be or what they may think. The punishment of one's status did not receive close judicial scrutiny until 1962, when the U.S. Supreme Court struck down a California statute criminalizing being addicted to narcotics.[2] The justices ruled that sanctioning personal status violates the Eighth Amendment prohibition against cruel and unusual punishment. Such a statute is the equivalent of penalizing an individual for contracting a disease. As Justice Potter Stewart observed, "Even one day in prison would be a cruel and unusual punishment for the 'crime' of having a common cold."[3] The court was clear, however, that possession of narcotics or appearing in public under the influence of narcotics does constitute "conduct" that can be subject to a criminal penalty.

The prohibition against **status offenses**[4] casts doubt upon the constitutionality of vagrancy-type crimes that seek to sanction the status or condition of a person as opposed to some conduct in which he engages. In 1972, the Supreme Court struck down a Florida city's vagrancy ordinance. While the court did not rely on the status crime argument in its decision, the justices did find that the language of the ordinance "fails to give a person of ordinary intelligence fair notice that his contemplated conduct is forbidden by the statute."[5]

Recent efforts to use criminal sanctions to control homeless persons and other "street people" in urban communities have met with mixed success in the courts. Likewise, offenses condemning "being a fortune teller" or "being a common prostitute" are likely unconstitutional for punishing status, not behavior. Most recently, in 1999, the Supreme Court voided a Chicago city ordinance that granted police officers the authority to order "gang members" to disperse when observed together on a city street. If the individual refused the officer's command, he was subject to arrest for loitering. The high court essentially found a constitutional right to loiter and struck down the ordinance as vague because it failed to distinguish between gang members who "might loiter near Wrigley Field . . . to rob an unsuspecting fan" and those who are there "just to get a glimpse of Sammy Sosa leaving the ballpark."[6]

A second aspect of the conduct requirement is that of voluntariness. American law punishes only voluntary conduct. An underlying assumption of American criminal law is that individuals are rational beings who make freewill choices. The law may punish the individual when his freewill choice is deemed harmful to society.

Penal Code Sec. 6.01(a) puts forth the Texas version of the concept of voluntariness by stating that "A person commits an offense only if he *voluntarily* engages in conduct. . . ." To the contrary, if conduct is not voluntary, the individual is normally excused from sanction.

The Court of Criminal Appeals has wrestled with the meaning of the word "voluntary" and its relationship to accidental harm. The issue comes up primarily when a defendant raises the defense of accident. Case law suggests that the voluntary act requirement of Sec. 6.01(a) relates to the perpetrator's conduct, not the result of his conduct. The result of the conduct may be accidental. This question will be dealt with below in the discussion of culpable mental state. While the high court has refused to impose an explicit freewill component into the definition of "voluntary,"[7] it has defined the term as follows:

> "Voluntariness," within the meaning of Section 6.01(a), refers only to one's own physical body movements. If those physical movements are the nonvolitional result of someone else's act, are set in motion by some independent non-human force, are caused by a physical reflex or convulsion, or are the product of unconsciousness, hypnosis or other nonvolitional impetus, that movement is not voluntary.[8]

The Texas refusal to explicitly embody free will into the criminal statutes has little practical effect. The only way one can commit the elements of the various criminal offenses is by making freewill choices to engage in some conduct. This voluntary conduct must be proven even though unintended and unforeseen harm may result. Suppose Warren is an individual with epilepsy. While in class he suffers a grand mal seizure. During the incident his foot strikes and breaks the classroom's glass door. Warren will not be held criminally responsible for the damage to the door as his destructive behavior was not voluntary.[9]

To reiterate, the student of criminal law should not confuse the idea of voluntariness with blameworthiness. Just because an individual's conduct produces an unintended result does not mean the individual did not act voluntarily. Drunk drivers who strike and kill pedestrians do not intend that harm but their conduct that produced the death was nonetheless voluntary.

Under Texas law, voluntary conduct subject to criminal liability takes one of three forms:

- Acts
- Omissions to act
- Possession

Acts

The most common form of conduct subject to criminal liability is an affirmative act by the offender. State law defines an **act** as "a bodily movement, whether voluntary or involuntary, and includes speech."[10] The subject engages in some body movement—swinging his fist, firing a pistol, entering a building, starting a fire—as required by the statute. Evil thoughts by themselves are insufficient to constitute an "act" for the purposes of criminal liability. The notion is that mere thoughts produce no harm to others. Obviously a practical problem of proof would exist if mere thoughts were subject to criminal prosecution.

A somewhat more difficult issue arises when the required act involves written or oral communication. If Julie, angry at her ex-boyfriend, says, "I hope you die, die, die," no offense has been committed. If she adds to her statement, "And I am going to cut your guts out right now," an assault by threat has occurred. The second statement becomes a crime because the words now are a required element of the offense of assault. Julie's words constitute a threat to do bodily injury to the ex-boyfriend. Her first statement did not express any threatening words, only a wish.

The same can be true of written communication where the content of a note or letter can constitute a threat. Suppose Betty writes Veronica a letter saying, "You'd better stay away from Archie or else!" Is this statement an act sufficient to constitute a threat? Obviously, a judge or jury would need to consider the context in which the letter was written, as well as Betty's purpose in sending it to Veronica.

Consider the following Dallas city ordinance:

SEC. 31-13. SLEEPING IN A PUBLIC PLACE.

(a) A person commits an offense if he:

    (1) sleeps or dozes in a street, alley, park, or other public place; or

    (2) sleeps or dozes in a vacant lot adjoining a public street or highway.[11]

Is sleeping a voluntary act? One might argue that sleeping involves doing nothing as opposed to doing something. Dallas, along with many other Texas cities, criminalizes sleeping under certain factual situations. In this instance, the law views sleeping as a conscious act of the defendant.[12] Would a criminal act occur if the same defendant suffered from narcolepsy, a neurological disorder caused by the brain's inability to regulate sleep–wake cycles? Would his or her sleeping be a voluntary act?

Omissions to Act

American legislative bodies have been reluctant to criminalize failures to act. From a public policy perspective, criminalizing **omissions to act** would require determining the extent to which an individual is "his brother's keeper," a concept that runs counter to the criminal law's general focus on freewill choice and personal responsibility.[13] Additionally, a basic philosophical purpose of criminal law is the deterrence of undesirable social behavior, not the encouragement of desirable conduct. Accordingly, most offenses that declare it a crime to fail to act involve circumstances where either (1) the defendant's conduct instigates the harmful condition in question; (2) the defendant possesses an explicit legal responsibility to act under the circumstances; or, in rare incidents, (3) the social harm in failing to act far outweighs any potential risk to the individual. It is important to note that the first two types of statutes limit their application to a defined category of specific individuals, not the public at large. Only the third form applies to the general public.

As to the first circumstance, suppose Paul, while driving to work, comes upon an accident involving a school bus and a train. The bus is partially on fire and young children are trapped inside. Should it be a crime if Paul, a healthy 30-year-old male, decides not to assist in the rescue of the children? Should Paul be required to risk his life or else face criminal prosecution? Will other factors (e.g., personal morals, peer pressure, culture) accomplish the desired social result without using the threat of the government's criminal sanction? No state's criminal code mandates that Paul assist in the rescue of the children. Indeed, no state's criminal code requires Paul to attempt a rescue even if he could do so with little risk of injury to himself.[14] However, suppose instead that Paul's automobile, not the train, strikes the school bus and causes it to catch afire. Under the motor vehicle laws of every state, Paul has a legal obligation to stop and render reasonable aid to the driver and children on the bus. If he flees the scene, he will be subject to prosecution as a hit-and-run driver.[15]

The second circumstance regarding omissions to act is exemplified by child and elder neglect laws. The laws of every state define the responsibilities parents have toward their minor children. Normally, a parent must provide food, shelter, clothing, and medical care for their offspring under age 18. The parent is also responsible for seeing that the child attends school. Consequently all jurisdictions criminalize the failure of a parent or guardian to care for a minor child. Thus, if an infant is starving because the parent neglects to feed the baby, the parent may face criminal charges of child neglect or injury to a child. Similar charges would be forthcoming if the child suffered physical injury through other neglectful behavior, such as failure to provide medical treatment. In Texas, similar laws apply to individuals who have assumed the care of elderly individuals or individuals with disabilities and then fail to provide an appropriate level of care. For example, nursing homes and their personnel are occasionally prosecuted for elder neglect.

A recent trend fitting this category is the requirement that convicted sex offenders register their residence addresses with local law enforcement authorities. Failure to perform such registration is itself a criminal offense. In each of foregoing examples, the failure to act is grounded in the fact that the law imposes a statutory duty to perform the act; failure to perform the mandated act is criminalized.

In the third area of concern, legislatures on occasion impose a legal duty on the citizenry as a whole to engage in certain conduct. Refusal to perform the prescribed act is a crime. These limited situations normally involve topics of great concern to society. Further, the duty imposed on the citizen rarely subjects the citizen to personal risk. Examples include the mandate that all persons must report to authorities suspected acts of child abuse or the occurrence of a felony or the location of a dead body.[16] Prosecutions for violating these types of statutes are rare. Rather, it is primarily the threat of criminal sanction that is used to encourage the desired behavior on the part of the general public.

Sec. 6.01(c) limits the failure to act to those to whom a law requires a duty to act. While normally this means a statutory duty mandating an act, such as the previously mentioned mandate for all persons to report child abuse, case law holds that Common Law duties also fall within the scope of the statute.[17] However, the appellate courts have yet to delineate nonstatutory examples wherein an individual can be successfully prosecuted for failure to act.

The principle that a legal duty must exist before an omission to act is criminal holds true even in circumstances where the citizen could act easily and in circumstances where the average person probably would act. Assume Jose is walking along the beach. He observes Linda in the ocean obviously having difficulty swimming. She cries for help. Jose ignores her pleas even though he could easily rescue her or summon others to assist. Jose has committed no criminal offense. While Jose may have had a moral duty to save Linda, he had no *legal* mandate to do so. He did not cause her peril nor is he related to her by blood or marriage.

Possession

The third form of conduct covered by the criminal sanction is possession. The criminalization of mere possession of objects was largely unknown among our Common Law ancestors. Given the overarching principle that evil conduct fell under the criminal law, English law, and by extension early American law, rarely concerned itself with persons who merely *had* something as opposed to *did* something. The singular exception to this rule appears to be the colonial ban on possession of obscene and blasphemous publications.[18]

Beginning in the mid-1800s the federal government began to declare many items to be contraband—originally defined as objects unlawful for the average citizen to possess unless taxes had been paid on the items. The contraband items were subject to forfeiture to the government and the possessor of the item subject to criminal prosecution.

Subsequently, the prohibition on contraband was expanded to cover socially harmful items, although the tax laws continued to be used as the legal justification for regulation. Initially, contraband items consisted mainly of objects on which excise taxes had not been paid, such as opium[19] and marijuana.[20] Later Congress began using the taxing power of the federal government to attack narcotics abuse and organized crime activity. The government did not actually expect traffickers in narcotics and illegal liquor to pay the tax because the taxes were set at exorbitant rates.[21]

Meanwhile, the states, with their inherent power to enact criminal law for the public safety and welfare, began passing legislation that simply banned possession of narcotics. With the rise of the gangster era of the 1920s, many jurisdictions also banned the weapons of choice of gangsters—submachine guns and sawed-off shotguns. By the 1970s, anti-narcotics tax laws had morphed into comprehensive drug control legislation that banned many substances with no recognized medical use.

The 1970s also saw the rise of the use of the contraband concept to enforce legislation as diverse as the endangered species laws and import/export regulations. Today, under state statutes, most items of contraband fall in the categories of illegal gaming devices, obscene matter, prohibited weapons, and illicit drugs. The federal law also criminalizes private possession of many of these items but also declares as contraband an array of objects ranging from bald eagle feathers to Cuban cigars![22]

The term **possession** may be defined as "actual care, custody, control, or management" of an item.[23] The concept of possession under the criminal law, however, is slightly more restrictive than the ordinary use of the term. The criminal law requires that the possession be *knowing* possession; that is, the possessor must be aware of the nature of the object possessed. If Frank buys a bag of cocaine from his drug dealer, he certainly is in knowing possession of the contraband drug. But, if Frank takes the same cocaine and ships it by FedEx to his brother in Texas as a birthday gift, the FedEx delivery person is not in *unlawful* possession of the cocaine as she is unaware of the contents of the package.

Possession takes one of two forms: actual possession or constructive possession. In actual possession, the individual has direct care, custody, control, or management over the item. If Maria has marijuana in her purse, she has actual possession of the contraband. But, if she takes the purse and locks it in the trunk of her automobile while she is attending class, her possession becomes constructive in nature. **Constructive possession** occurs when the individual has dominion over the object without the item being in their actual presence.

Note that possession is not necessarily the same thing as ownership. If Ken steals an automobile, he does not acquire ownership of the vehicle because a thief obtains no title. But, Ken certainly is in possession of the stolen vehicle.

ATTENDANT CIRCUMSTANCES

Some conduct becomes criminal only if it occurs under particular circumstances, also known as **attendant circumstances**. The behavior is not unlawful unless the special situation arises. For example, the driving while intoxicated (DWI) statute applies only in public places.[24] If Joe is drinking and driving his ATV around his private hunting lease, he likely does not violate the DWI law, no matter how intoxicated he is. But, should he venture on to the nearby public roadway, he becomes an intoxicated driver within the meaning of the law. This attendant circumstance shifts lawful behavior to criminal behavior because of the location of the conduct. In other instances, the existence of attendant circumstances may change the potential punishment for the criminal conduct. While a wide range of attendant circumstances may alter the nature of a penal offense, commonly these factors focus on who, when, where, why, and how.

Who

Texas and many other states declare certain behavior to be criminal if it is committed by designated individuals or if particular persons are the victim. If Julie, a teenager, gives her little brother Ray a dollar not to tell their mother that Julie smokes cigarettes, Julie has bribed Ray. Yet, no criminal offense occurs because the crime of bribery normally can only be committed if one of the parties is a government official.[25] Similarly, sexual assault of a child can be committed only if the victim is under the statutorily designated age, 17 in Texas.[26]

When

Time of day can determine whether an offense has occurred. As will be seen in Chapter 11, the Common Law definition of the crime of burglary required the act occur in the nighttime. This requirement carries over in a few states today. If the would-be burglar commits all of the elements of the offense but does so at high noon, the traditional definition of burglary is not met. Texas, like the majority of jurisdictions, has dropped the nighttime requirement from the elements of burglary although many states still punish night burglaries more severely than those occurring in the daytime.

Today, the time element appears primarily in regulatory-type offenses. For instance, if you operate a motor vehicle, the headlamps must be turned on while driving at night.[27] Similarly, the sale and consumption of alcoholic beverages are restricted to certain times of day.[28]

Where

The most common attendant circumstance which determines whether behavior is an offense, or determines the level of severity of the offense, is location. Most disorderly conduct is dependent on the proscribed conduct occurring either in a public place or within public view. The same behavior outside of public observation is normally not a crime. If Suzy drinks alcohol to excess in the privacy of her apartment, her punishment will only be a next-day hangover. If she appears in a public place in an intoxicated condition, she could awake in a jail cell with her hangover.[29] Likewise, being nude is not an offense but might bring charges if the individual is nude in a public place.[30]

In recent years many cities have limited the smoking of tobacco in particular public locations. Smoking in a nonapproved place may result in a citation.

Many statutes use location as a circumstance which defines a particular form of a crime or determines the severity of the crime. Texas, for example, has enacted separate statutes covering burglary of buildings, burglary of motor vehicles, and burglary of vending machines. The location of the unlawful act determines the specific offense. Other states modify the penalty for an offense depending on its location. In recent years, some legislatures have increased the punishment for arson if the location of the incident is a place of worship. Possession of firearm laws traditionally have varying punishment depending on whether the unlawful act occurs on the grounds of a school, public building, licensed premises, polling place, or other designated locale.

Why

While motive—the "why" a crime occurs—is normally not an element of an offense, in a few instances the reason for the conduct must be proven. If Roger shoots and kills his professor because the professor gave Roger an "F" in his criminal law course, Roger will be prosecuted for murder. But, if Roger shoots and kills the professor because Wendy, who received the "F," hired him to do so, Roger will face capital murder charges.[31] His reason for the murder—he was paid to commit the criminal homicide—changes the level of offense. Similarly, if Jack strikes Bill with his fist, an assault has occurred. If, however, Jack commits the assault because Bill served as a witness for Jill in the trial of her divorce from Jack, many states, including Texas, will enhance Jack's punishment.[32]

How

In a few instances, the manner in which a crime is committed may affect the nature of the charge or the level of punishment. In California, for example, if a murder is committed using poison, the death penalty becomes an option for punishment.[33] In Texas, if the offender used a firearm or other deadly weapon, he is ineligible for a probated sentence.[34]

CULPABLE MENTAL STATE (*mens rea*)

This afternoon following class you enter your automobile and drive toward your residence. You are driving within the speed limit and operating your car in the normal manner. As you approach an intersection, the glare from the bright afternoon sun prevents you from seeing clearly. Being overly cautious you slow your car as you enter the intersection. Suddenly a motorcycle approaches from your right and proceeds into the intersection. You strike the motorcycle, knocking the rider off the bike. As a result, the rider breaks several bones and his motorcycle is damaged beyond repair. Should you be criminally charged for causing the injuries to the rider? Should you be criminally charged for destroying the motorcycle? Your conduct certainly produced harm to both a person and his property, but did your behavior rise to the level of a penal offense?

The scenario presented is commonly called an accident. Did you ever consider what the word "accident" means? The common definition of the word "accident" refers to producing unintended harm. You accidentally break your friend's nose when your elbow strikes him during a pickup basketball game. You accidentally damage your roommate's DVD player when you insert the disk improperly. While individuals cause harm to each other's persons and property every day, not all of these acts rise to the level of a penal offense. Only those instances where the law says one is criminally blamable constitute crimes. So, when does harmful conduct elevate to a criminal offense?—when the individual possesses a degree of criminal culpability. "Culpability" simply means deserving of blame.

In the Common Law tradition, every crime contained a requirement of a culpable mental state. Traditionally this has been known as the ***mens rea*** of the crime. The phrase derives from a quotation from the eminent English jurist Sir Edward Coke (1552–1634), who wrote *actus non facit reum nisi mens sit rea*, which roughly translated means, "an act does not make someone a criminal unless (their) mind is guilty."[35]

The idea that harmful conduct alone is insufficient to impose criminal liability is rooted in part in the theory of general deterrence. The general deterrence goal of the criminal sanction would not be served if criminal liability were based solely on harmful result. Rather, general deterrence theory assumes that the potential criminal will make a conscious choice whether to engage in the harmful behavior. If the individual chooses to commit the offense, then morally he can be held accountable for his freewill decision. If the individual chooses not to commit the offense, then the risk of punishment has deterred him. But, reconsider the earlier motorcycle crash scenario. The issue of deterrence did not come into play when you chose to drive into the intersection. You had no intent to harm the motorcyclist or his property. Indeed, you were exercising as much caution as possible yet bad things still occurred. You were not deterred from injuring the rider simply because you did not make a conscious choice to strike his motorcycle. No moral or practical reasons exist to hold you criminally responsible in this case.

Many individuals equate *mens rea* with the word "intent." Under modern concepts of criminal law, this view is far from accurate. As will be seen, intent is only one form of culpable (blameworthy) mental state in modern criminal law. The *mens rea* concept developed during the Common Law period, and during that timeframe, intentional conduct was largely the only form of conduct subject to criminal sanction. Common Law crimes, such as murder, larceny, robbery, and rape, required as an element that the offender purposefully (intentionally) commit the offense. Thus, a death that was unintended did not constitute murder. Under the early Common Law, had matters gone awry in the legendary story of William Tell shooting the apple off his son's head with an arrow, Tell would not have committed a murder because he did not purposefully kill the child.[36]

Over the course of time, however, public policy makers recognized that other levels of blameworthiness might be appropriate. Thus, conduct or results that were not entirely purposeful became subject to criminal sanction. Today, every state extends its criminal laws beyond purely intentional behavior.

Whatever approach a jurisdiction takes in establishing levels of culpability, a hierarchy of blame normally exists. As the U.S. Supreme Court has noted, "Deeply ingrained in our legal tradition is the idea that the more purposeful is the criminal conduct, the more serious is the offense, and, therefore, the more severely it ought to be punished."[37] The degree of blame assigned for a particular harm varies depending on the level of culpable mental state. Hence, harm produced through an intentional act will normally be subject to greater sanction than the same harm produced through reckless or negligent behavior, lower levels of culpable mental state. For example, if Sam intentionally runs over Dick with his automobile, breaking Dick's leg, Sam will face a more severe prison sentence than if Sam had caused the same injury to Dick through reckless behavior, such as striking Dick while driving under the influence.

Texas Penal Code Sec. 6.03 establishes four levels of *mens rea*, or criminal culpability. These categories of culpability are

- Intentional
- Knowing
- Reckless
- Criminal negligence

§ 6.03. Definitions of Culpable Mental States

a. A person acts intentionally, or with intent, with respect to the nature of his conduct or to a result of his conduct when it is his conscious objective or desire to engage in the conduct or cause the result.

b. A person acts knowingly, or with knowledge, with respect to the nature of his conduct or to circumstances surrounding his conduct when he is aware of the nature of his conduct or that the circumstances exist. A person acts knowingly, or with knowledge, with respect to a result of his conduct when he is aware that his conduct is reasonably certain to cause the result.

c. A person acts recklessly, or is reckless, with respect to circumstances surrounding his conduct or the result of his conduct when he is aware of but consciously disregards a substantial and unjustifiable risk that the circumstances exist or the result will occur. The risk must be of such a nature and degree that its disregard constitutes a gross deviation from the standard of care that an ordinary person would exercise under all the circumstances as viewed from the actor's standpoint.

d. A person acts with criminal negligence, or is criminally negligent, with respect to circumstances surrounding his conduct or the result of his conduct when he ought to be aware of a substantial and unjustifiable risk that the circumstances exist or the result will occur. The risk must be of such a nature and degree that the failure to perceive it constitutes a gross deviation from the standard of care that an ordinary person would exercise under all the circumstances as viewed from the actor's standpoint.

In addition, a close reading of the definitions of these culpable mental states reveals that the issue of blameworthiness may relate to the nature of the suspect's conduct, the result of his conduct, or the circumstances surrounding his conduct as the elements of the particular offense require. That is, in some cases the actor's behavior is harmful because of what he or she does (conduct), because of the consequences of their behavior (result), or because the behavior occurs under certain specific conditions (circumstances). In an effort to explain this approach to *mens rea*, the Court of Criminal Appeals has noted,

> To begin with, we have consistently recognized that Penal Code, Sec. 6.03 delineates three "conduct elements" which may be involved in an offense: (1) the nature of the conduct; (2) the result of the conduct; and (3) the circumstances surrounding the conduct. An offense may contain any one or more of these "conduct elements" which alone or in combination form the overall behavior which the Legislature has intended to criminalize, and it is those essential "conduct elements" to which a culpable mental state must apply. For example, where specific acts are criminalized because of their very nature, a culpable mental state must apply to committing the act itself. On the other hand, unspecified conduct that is criminalized because of its result requires culpability as to that result. Likewise, where otherwise innocent behavior becomes criminal because of the circumstances under which it is done, a culpable mental state is required as to those surrounding circumstances.[38]

In applying this concept, one finds that assault by threat is an offense where the nature of the conduct is criminalized and it is to that nature that the culpable mental state applies. The crime occurs when the suspect threatens bodily injury to another.

The reaction of the victim is irrelevant to the commission offense; whether the victim is frightened does not matter. The crime is complete when the offender makes the threat. In contrast, murder is a result of conduct offense. Sec. 19.02 states that "a person commits an offense if he intentionally or knowingly causes the death of an individual." Thus, the culpable mental states of intent or knowledge must be connected to the resultant death, not necessarily to the conduct in which the offender initially engaged. Finally, issuance of a bad check is a circumstance surrounding the conduct offense. Passing a bank check, an otherwise lawful act, becomes unlawful when the individual knows he does not have sufficient money in the bank to cover the check. To prove the offense, the culpable mental state of knowledge must be related to the factual circumstances surrounding the act (i.e., knowledge of lack of sufficient funds), not the act itself.

In some instances a criminal statute may contain several *mens rea* and may mix result of conduct and nature of conduct. Consider the following excerpt from the definition of robbery in Sec. 29.02:

(a) A person commits an offense if, in the course of committing theft as defined in Chapter 31 and with intent to obtain or maintain control of the property, he:
   (1) intentionally, knowingly, or recklessly causes bodily injury to another;

To prove robbery, the state must establish the *actus reus* of the crime but also must establish two different *mens rea*. The district attorney must prove that the offender possessed the "*intent* to obtain or maintain control of the property" (nature of conduct) and also that he "*intentionally, knowingly, or recklessly* causes bodily injury to another" (result of conduct). By the way, the crime can be elevated to the more serious offense of aggravated robbery under Sec. 29.03 if the prosecutor can establish that the defendant exhibited a deadly weapon. However, no culpable mental state relates to the deadly weapon element. Thus the state need not prove whether the robber intentionally or knowingly or recklessly or with criminal negligence exhibited the deadly weapon, only that a deadly weapon was exhibited. In theory, a robber could see his offense elevate to aggravated robbery if during the commission of the crime a pistol inadvertently falls out of his coat pocket. The pistol, a deadly weapon, is "exhibited" and it matters not that its exhibition was purely inadvertent; the statute attaches no culpability requirement to the exhibition of the deadly weapon.

While the concept of the three conduct elements and their relationship with the *mens rea* appears complex at first blush, one simply needs to bear in mind that the requirement of a specific culpable mental state can relate to some or all of the elements of a particular offense. Examples are provided below to demonstrate how this triad of conduct elements works in practice with each form of culpability.

Intentional

At the top of the scale is intent. Offenses committed **intentionally** are viewed as the most serious because they represent a conscious choice by the offender—a freewill decision. Historically, the criminal law concerned itself with two forms of intent: general intent and specific intent. General intent meant that the actor purposefully engaged in the conduct in question. Specific intent meant that the actor possessed an identified purpose or goal in committing the act. Thus, in a burglary, the offender had the general intent to break and enter the home while possessing the specific intent to commit a felony once inside. Given the language in Sec. 6.03, Texas no longer concerns itself with the notions of general and specific intent.

Assume that Mary threatens to kill John. A few days later, Mary stabs John six times with a knife and causes his death. It is reasonable to assume that she acted intentionally in bringing about his death.

Read closely the definition of "intent" reproduced above. Under the language of Sec. 6.03, the culpable mental state of intent is limited in application to either of two possibilities:

1. Nature of the actor's conduct
2. Result of the actor's conduct

Nature of Conduct

Recall the conflict between Mary and John in the above scenario. When she threatens John, she has committed assault under Sec. 22.01(a)(1). She engaged in the conduct—made the threat—in an intentional manner. But suppose instead that John simply becomes fearful of Mary because of her recent bizarre and erratic behavior. John is afraid of what Mary might do. Has Mary committed assault? No. The assault statute requires that she *intentionally* threaten him. She has not done so even though he may be fearful of her.

Result of Conduct

In contrast, when Mary stabs John to death, the state need not establish that the stabbing was intentional but rather only that she intended to cause his death. If this fact is established, she has committed murder under Sec. 19.02(a)(1). But suppose Mary claims she intentionally stabbed John but it was not her intent to cause his death; she only wanted to hurt him real badly. Is Mary absolved of a murder charge because she did not intend to cause his death? Look at Sec. 19.02(a)(2) for the answer.

Knowing

During the early Common Law period, judges were faced with the issue of conduct that was not directly intended to produce harm but nonetheless harm was obviously likely to result. If from the top of the castle wall, Richard dumped a box of stones on to the crowd below, he may not have intended to injure any particular individual but it would come as no surprise that one or more persons would be injured. Common Law jurists initially expanded the concept of intent to cover such situations where the result of the conduct was certain to follow.

Modern statutes tend to deal with this problem through use of the culpable mental state of knowledge. To act **knowingly** means the offender is *aware* of his conduct or that his conduct is reasonably certain to cause the result. Late one evening, Fred accidentally strikes Ricky with his automobile. Fred stops immediately and determines that Ricky is still alive but needs medical attention. Fred, fearing he will be arrested for the incident, flees the scene. Ricky subsequently dies lying by the side of the highway. Fred did not intend to kill Ricky but was aware that Ricky will die without medical attention. In Texas and most other jurisdictions, Fred would be guilty of murder, not because he initially struck Ricky but because he *knew* Ricky would die without medical care.

Under the Texas statute, the culpable mental state of knowledge can relate to any of the three conduct elements:

1. Nature of the actor's conduct
2. Result of the actor's conduct
3. Circumstances surrounding the actor's conduct

Nature of Conduct

An infrequently used statute, Sec. 37.101 declares it a crime to "knowingly present for filing . . ." a false financial statement. The legislative history of the statute suggests that it applies to erroneous reports of financial status relative to judicial and other governmental proceedings.[39] The crime is complete upon the filing of the statement regardless of whether anyone is defrauded or deceived. Suppose Ronda is charged with a criminal offense and is seeking a court-appointed attorney on the grounds that she is indigent. The court requests that she complete a statement of her financial worth. She files the statement but it contains errors regarding her assets and earnings. Does she violate Sec. 37.101? Her conduct is criminal only if at the time of the filing of the statement she is "*aware* of the nature of her conduct." Thus, if Rhonda is aware that the statement contains false information, she commits the offense. If the errors are simply mistakes, such as typos or transposed numbers, she commits no offense. The difference between a crime and no crime is whether Rhonda *knowingly* files the false statement.

Result of Conduct

Suppose Raul, a terrorist, places a bomb in a bus station. The bomb explodes, killing six people. Raul is apprehended and charged with murder. He testifies at trial that it was not his intent to kill anyone; he just wanted to make a political statement. Even assuming Raul's testimony is accurate, he knew that his conduct was reasonably certain to cause the result. Thus he acted knowingly in producing the deaths.

Circumstances Surrounding the Actor's Conduct

The culpable mental state of knowledge often applies to situations which require actual awareness of a fact or circumstance. Recall the earlier scenario concerning the FedEx delivery person who transported the box of cocaine. She lacked awareness of the contents of the package and thereby an element of the offense was missing: *knowing* possession. Her lack of awareness of the package's content saves her from criminal liability.

Another common application of the culpable mental state of knowledge occurs with possession of stolen property. Warren buys a new plasma television at a flea market. He pays $700 for an object that normally sells retail for several thousand dollars. Subsequently, Warren is contacted by the police and informed that the television is stolen property. Is Warren guilty of theft through possession of stolen property? Probably not.[40] The Texas theft by receiving stolen property law requires that the individual actually be aware of the stolen nature of the property. While Warren may have had some suspicion that the television was stolen given the price he paid, that suspicion likely does not rise to the level of actual awareness or knowledge. The requirement that the state prove that a possessor of stolen property actually *know* the property is stolen makes prosecution of fences and other traffickers in stolen goods difficult.[41]

Suppose Karl has sexual intercourse with an underage female. Karl can be convicted of sexual assault of the child even if he believes she is an adult. As will be seen in the section on sexual assault, knowledge of the child's age is not an element of the crime. In other words, the sexual assault statute (Sec. 22.011) contains no requirement that the offender be aware (know) of the age of the consenting youthful victim.

Reckless

Suppose you are late to your criminal law exam. You drive to the campus at a faster than normal speed. You approach an intersection protected by a stop sign in your direction of traffic. In the interest of saving time you decide to slow down slightly and proceed through the intersection without coming to a complete stop. As you move into the intersection, a vehicle approaches from your right. You are unable to stop before striking the vehicle. The driver of the vehicle is killed. Are you criminally blamable? Yes. While you did not intend to kill the driver, nor were you aware that entering the intersection without stopping might cause a death, you were reckless. **Recklessness** occurs when the individual is aware of a risk and consciously disregards it. A reckless person is essentially saying, "I know my conduct is risky but I am willing to take my chances." The law takes the view that one who engages in dangerous conduct is going to be criminally responsible if another person or property is injured. Normally, harm produced through reckless behavior is punished at a penalty level less than the same conduct committed intentionally or knowingly.

Not every type of risky behavior rises to the level of recklessness. Texas law, following the influence of the Model Penal Code, requires that the risk be substantial and unjustified. The conduct must be a gross deviation from the standard of care the ordinary person would exercise under the same circumstances. Consider a child who darts out from between two parked cars to retrieve a baseball. He is struck and killed by a passing automobile. The vehicle was moving in excess of the posted speed limit—by five miles per hour. Is that excessive speed a *gross* deviation from the standard of care the ordinary citizen would exercise? Probably not. But what if a vehicle strikes and kills the child while moving at 75 miles per hour through a school zone? Most would agree that the driver was engaged in a gross deviation from the ordinary standard of care and should be considered to be reckless.

A violation of another criminal statute during the course of committing the offense charged is often used as proof of recklessness. The logic is that the underlying statute establishes the standard of care the ordinary person would use under the circumstances. Thus, suppose Tyrone owns and operates a chicken processing facility. In order to speed up the processing of the poultry, Tyrone purposefully disregards various worker health and safety regulations applicable to the plant. One day, Juanita, an employee at the plant, is seriously injured because the safety device on a saw has been removed to make slicing quicker. Tyrone may well face charges of reckless injury to Juanita because the injury was a result of Tyrone failing to adhere to the worker safety laws.

As to the conduct triad, recklessness applies only to

1. Result of the actor's conduct
2. Circumstances surrounding the actor's conduct

Result of Conduct

The above example of Tyrone's failure to adhere to worker safety rules is an example of a result of conduct event. His knowing lack of compliance with the regulations is not a violation of the Penal Code but serves as the basis of prosecution when a harmful result, Juanita's injury, occurs. Tyrone is aware of the risk of failing to adhere to the safety rules and makes a conscious decision to ignore them. He is responsible for the harmful consequences of his decision.

Circumstances Surrounding the Actor's Conduct

Since recklessness concerns risk awareness and subsequent disregard of that awareness, the culpable mental state is often the basis of a criminal act in situations where only the potential for harm exists. Consider the offense of deadly conduct (Sec. 22.05). It is a crime if the actor recklessly places another in imminent danger of serious bodily injury. Note that no actual bodily injury need occur, only the potential for such injury. The same statute notes that danger and recklessness are presumed if a firearm is pointed at another. Texas law considers inappropriate use of firearms as an inherently dangerous action. Such a dangerous act constitutes reckless behavior.

Criminally Negligent

Criminal negligence as a form of culpability is a modern-day concept with no basis in the Common Law of crimes. The idea of negligence focuses on what an individual *ought* to have done, not what he or she consciously chose to do. In intentional, knowing, and reckless behavior, the defendant has made a conscious decision to engage in some conduct that is either harmful in itself or produces harmful results or the potential of harmful results. Criminal negligence lacks this conscious decision-making process and focuses on a societal standard of care.

Ordinary negligence serves as the basis for many civil lawsuits. A negligence lawsuit asserts that the defendant had a duty to the injured plaintiff not to cause him harm and that the defendant breached that duty. In the typical car collision suit, one party asserts that the other was negligent in not keeping his vehicle under control, or having inadequate brakes, or not being attentive to his driving, or some other requirement that society recognizes is important in safely operating a car.

Criminal negligence is a higher form of negligence than the negligence standard used in civil suits. While the concepts are difficult to distinguish in the abstract, criminal negligence involves what is known as gross negligence. That is, it is a *substantial* deviation from the ordinary standard of care in the particular situation. Because of difficulties in drawing the line between reckless behavior and criminally negligent behavior and drawing the line between gross negligence and ordinary negligence, the Texas Legislature has enacted very few criminal statutes predicated on criminal negligence.

Under Sec. 6.03(d) criminal negligence applies only to result of conduct and circumstances surrounding conduct offenses.

Result of Conduct

Criminally negligent homicide is a good example of a result of conduct statute involving the culpable mental state of criminal negligence. Under Sec. 19.05, the defendant is responsible if she causes the death of another by criminal negligence. Thus, it is the result of the negligence (the death), not negligent behavior that is criminalized. Marla is driving down the street in her automobile on her way to work. She is also putting on her makeup. The latter task distracts her attention from the road. She inadvertently strikes a pedestrian who is attempting to cross the street. He is killed. Was Marla criminally negligent? Should she have been aware of the risk of harm her multitasking activity could cause? Did she grossly deviate from the standard of care the ordinary motorist would have used under the same circumstances?

Circumstances Surrounding the Actor's Conduct

Offenses that criminalize being negligent about the surrounding circumstances are very rare under the Texas Penal Code. Only harboring a runaway child (Sec. 25.06) appears to be concerned about someone being criminally negligent relative to the surrounding circumstances of the event. In this offense, the actor harbors a child and is criminally negligent about whether the child is under 18 and an escapee from a detention facility or absent from home without parental consent.[42] The statute does not require actual knowledge of those facts but effectively places a duty of reasonable care upon the actor to determine age and detention/runaway status. Experience suggests that in most harboring of a child cases, the defendant actually knows that the child is underage and a runaway. "Proof of a higher degree of culpability than that charged constitutes proof of the culpability charged."[43] Thus, the low culpable mental state of criminal negligence simply makes the charge easier to prove.

Strict Liability

The time-honored principle of a culpable mental state for each crime began to erode in the middle of the nineteenth century as legislators started to use the criminal sanction as a means to enforce matters that were primarily regulatory in nature. No longer was criminal law limited to *malum in se* behavior or conduct where an identifiable person or property was injured. Rather, the criminal sanction became an easy way to encourage the citizenry to comply with a series of rules that benefited the public welfare generally. The invention of the automobile and subsequent enactment of rules of the road in the twentieth century saw a proliferation of violations for which no culpable mental state was specified. The absence of a culpability requirement has been expanded to a wide variety of public welfare offenses ranging from air and water pollution standards to food processing rules to sale of alcoholic beverages. Violation of the rules carries a sanction, usually a fine, irrespective of the culpable mental state of the violator.

Sheila is stopped by a state trooper for driving 80 miles per hour in a 55 miles per hour zone. The trooper asks Sheila if any reason exists as to why she is driving so fast. Sheila replies, "I didn't realize I was driving that fast," essentially claiming she was not intentionally speeding. Is this a defense to the speeding charge? Or, Sheila might respond, "My speedometer is malfunctioning. I was on my way to the garage to have it repaired." Is this a defense?

All jurisdictions provide that a driver will not exceed the posted speed limit. This mandate comes without a culpable mental state requirement; the mandate is essentially one of strict liability.[44] Indeed automobiles had not long been operating on Texas roadways when the Court of Criminal Appeals in 1911 determined that a motorist could be convicted of exceeding the state's 18 miles per hour speed limit without establishing that he did so willfully: "Very few people in driving a car have an evil intent, but the Legislature, in protection of the public, has decreed it wise to limit the speed at which these cars may run, and each one is required to keep within that limit."[45]

The Supreme Court in 1952 recognized the popularity of regulatory offenses lacking a *mens rea* but ruled that the offense of theft of government property required proof of intent even though the written statute in dispute contained no culpable mental state. The court reasoned that the Common Law tradition of the law of larceny required proof of an evil mind and Congress did not intend to dispense with that requirement. The court did note, however, that criminal statutes that do not require a culpable mental state are permissible if

1. the violation involves neglect or omission rather than an assertive act;
2. there is no direct injury to a person or property but rather the danger that such injury will occur;
3. the penalty is small; and
4. conviction has no significant effect on the individual's reputation.[46]

Violation of traffic control laws, health and safety rules, and environmental standards normally meet these four standards. Hence, the Legislature may dispense with the requirement of a culpable mental state.

While prior law suggests the possibility of offenses without a *mens rea*, the current Texas Penal Code casts a bit of doubt on the possibility of that circumstance. The Penal

Code explicitly speaks to the question of whether *every* offense, even minor traffic infractions, requires proof of at least one culpable mental state. Sec. 6.02(b) states,

> If the definition of an offense does not prescribe a culpable mental state, a culpable mental state is nevertheless required unless the definition plainly dispenses with any mental element.

As the statutory section reveals, a *mens rea* must be proven unless the statute in question "plainly dispenses" with the mental elements. This statute would indicate that **strict liability** offenses exist in the state only if the Legislature has explicitly authorized them. However, Texas courts have had some difficulty in determining the offenses from which the Legislature has eliminated the culpable mental state primarily because the Legislature has failed to be precise on the matter.[47] Most potential offenses, such as the speeding statute, are simply silent on the question of *mens rea*. Does such total absence of a *mens rea* indicate the Legislature intended to plainly dispense with the requirement?

In the leading case on the question of the necessity of proving a *mens rea*, the Court of Criminal Appeals ruled that the statute means what it says. Unless the statute plainly dispenses with a *mens rea*, the state must prove one.[48] Sec. 6.02(c) teaches that

> If the definition of an offense does not prescribe a culpable mental state, but one is nevertheless required under Subsection (b), intent, knowledge, or recklessness suffices to establish criminal responsibility.

Note that criminal negligence is not one of the *mens rea* options that can be used to prosecute statutory violations which lack a culpability requirement. Thus, in theory, the state must allege and prove that the defendant engaged in the conduct charged with a *mens rea* of at least recklessness. Recall that the definition of recklessness under Sec. 6.03(c) requires an awareness and conscious disregard of the surrounding circumstances. Does this rule provide a possible defense to Sheila in the speeding scenario above?

The question of *mens rea* and regulatory offenses, such as traffic violations, is one area where theory and practice often diverge. Because the sanction is small for violations and the average person does not wish to spend the time and money to contest the charge, few of these regulatory-type offenses receive close court scrutiny. However, based on existing court decisions one can certainly make a credible argument that many traffic violations, for example speeding, running a stop sign, or making an illegal turn, entail more than just proof of the act; proof of a culpable mental state of at least recklessness may also be required.

Effect of Accident or Mistake on Culpability

Recall the concept of "accident"—unintended harm. If while shooting bottle rockets on the Fourth of July, Randy "accidentally" sets fire to a neighbor's house, should Randy be held criminally responsible? Probably not, but also recall that modern levels of culpability extend beyond mere intentional behavior. Modern statutes now sanction reckless and criminally negligent conduct. Consequently, an "accident" within the day-to-day meaning of the term could still generate criminal responsibility if the behavior were criminally negligent. Such is the condition found in many motor vehicle "accidents" or hunting "accidents." Marge does not see the red stop signal, enters the intersection, and strikes and kills a pedestrian. While the next morning's newspaper headline may read "Car accident kills pedestrian," Marge may face criminal homicide charges because of her negligence in running the traffic light. While the term "accident" may mean the opposite of "intentional" in everyday language, the two terms are no longer antonyms within the criminal law.

Assume Wayland goes to dinner at a chic restaurant. He leaves his red sports car with the valet to be parked. Upon concluding his meal, Wayland hands the valet his claim ticket and in a few moments the valet produces the red sports car. Halfway home Wayland realizes that the red sports car he is driving is not his but another of the same make and model. Has Wayland committed theft of the sports car? The answer clearly is no. Wayland lacks the requisite *mens rea* to commit the offense of auto theft; Wayland did not intend to deprive the owner of the sports car. This mistake of fact by Wayland negates the required culpable mental state, that is, he had no intent to commit the offense.[49] A mistake of fact which negates the kind of culpability required for the crime is a defense to the charge. This principle is embodied in Sec. 8.02 as the mistake of fact defense.

CONCURRENCE

Phillip, angry that he did not receive a pay raise, decides to murder his boss Jake. Phillip decides to buy a pistol and shoot Jake later that evening. While driving to the gun shop, Phillip's car accidentally strikes Jake when Jake steps off the curb before the "Walk/Don't Walk" sign changes in his favor. Jake dies instantly. Has Phillip committed murder? Phillip presumably gained the result he sought: Jake's death. Phillip certainly intended to kill Jake. Phillip also engaged in conduct that produced Jake's death. But, at the moment Phillip's car struck Jake, Phillip lacked the required culpable mental state. The conduct (*actus reus*) and the culpable mental state (*mens rea*) did not concur. They were not in place at the same moment when the harm was produced. Not only must an offender possess a culpable mental state and commit some prohibited act, but a temporal connection must exist between the two elements. Under normal circumstances, **concurrence** between the mind and the act or result is obvious.

CAUSATION

Just as the culpable mental state and the proscribed conduct must occur at the same time, the resultant harm must have been caused by the offender. **Causation** implicates two distinct concepts: cause-in-fact and legal cause. Cause-in-fact means that the behavior produced the result. Tom sets fire to a building. The building burns to the ground. Tom's conduct caused the result. Mary stabs her abusive husband ten times. The husband bleeds to death. Mary's conduct caused her husband's death. These examples highlight the cause-in-fact requirement.

Cause-in-fact is normally established using the "but for" test. The **but for test** holds that the result would not have occurred *but for* the conduct of the offender.[50] This is the rule followed in Texas as evidenced in Sec. 6.04(a). The linkage between the conduct and the harmful result is usually fairly obvious.

A more complex aspect of causation is legal cause, sometimes called proximate cause. Legal cause relates to a sociolegal policy issue regarding when one will be held accountable for his conduct. Suppose Don intends to kill Linda. He places a bomb under her car. When the bomb explodes, the metal floor of the vehicle protects Linda from harm but flying debris strikes and kills Jacob, who is standing across the street selling newspapers. Did Don commit murder in relation to Jacob's death? His conduct was the cause-in-fact of the death but should society hold him criminally responsible for the death of an unintended victim? Or, assume Carlos stabs Reynaldo during a gang fight. The stab wound is minor and Reynaldo is treated at the hospital emergency room and released. Reynaldo subsequently exits the emergency room and is struck by lightening while walking across the parking lot. Should Carlos be charged with Reynaldo's death since Reynaldo would not have been in a position to be hit by the lightening bolt but for Carlos stabbing him?

The preceding examples raise issues about the extent to which an offender will be held responsible under the criminal law for harm produced through a series of unintended and unforeseen events. This is where legal cause comes to the forefront.

The Don–Linda–Jacob example illustrates the Common Law **doctrine of transferred intent**. This principle holds that if an offender seeks to harm one person or property but through a change in factual circumstances another unintended person or property is harmed, the offender is nonetheless liable. The law says that the offender's *mens rea* toward the intended victim is transferred to the actual victim. Thus, in the example, Don would be blamable for the murder of Jacob even though he was trying to kill Linda. The doctrine of transferred intent is, of course, a legal fiction, something untrue but treated as true to make a rule of law work efficiently. The rule can also apply to harm to property. Joe sets fire to Bill's house. The wind shifts and the fire spreads to Becky's house. Becky's house is destroyed. Joe is guilty of arson of Becky's house.

The Texas version of the law of causation and the doctrine of transferred intent is found in Sec. 6.04.

Sec. 6.04(a) adopts the approach that an offender is not responsible for his or her conduct if a concurrent cause is "clearly sufficient" and the conduct of the actor "clearly insufficient" to cause the result. In the Carlos and Reynaldo scenario above, Carlos' conduct in stabbing Reynaldo is clearly insufficient to kill him and the lightening strike is clearly sufficient. Carlos is thereby not criminally responsible for Reynaldo's death. But suppose Carlos had stabbed Reynaldo in the heart and on the way to the hospital the ambulance is involved in a traffic collision. Reynaldo is ejected from the vehicle and his neck breaks upon striking the pavement. He dies immediately. Would the intervening traffic collision save Carlos from responsibility? Probably not, as Carlos' initial stabbing was not *clearly* insufficient to bring about Reynaldo's death. If the medical examiner is willing to testify that Reynaldo's wound would have killed him anyway, Carlos will be responsible for the criminal homicide, the intervening traffic collision notwithstanding.

Similarly, Sec. 6.04(b) incorporates a version of the doctrine of transferred intent. Once an offender puts a set of circumstances into motion, he or she becomes criminally responsible for the results even if they are unintended or unanticipated. The Court of Criminal Appeals has held that the subsequent different offense committed need not

---

§ 6.04. Causation: Conduct and Results

a. A person is criminally responsible if the result would not have occurred but for his conduct, operating either alone or concurrently with another cause, unless the concurrent cause was clearly sufficient to produce the result and the conduct of the actor clearly insufficient.

b. A person is nevertheless criminally responsible for causing a result if the only difference between what actually occurred and what he desired, contemplated, or risked is that:

1. a different offense was committed; or
2. a different person or property was injured, harmed, or otherwise affected.

even be foreseeable.[51] For example, during a domestic dispute, Suzy fires a pistol at her husband Roy. The shot misses Roy and ricochets off the wall. The bullet flies into the house next door, striking baby Waldo. The baby bleeds to death because until the next morning no one realizes that he has been shot. Suzy later tells the police she was only trying to scare Roy. Suzy may well be looking at a manslaughter charge even though her victim was different than she desired (Waldo instead of Roy) and a different crime was committed than intended (manslaughter instead of aggravated assault). Although Waldo's death may not have been foreseeable under the circumstances, Suzy is still responsible for the results of her conduct.

HARM

A prime purpose of criminal law is to protect society. Thus, only behavior detrimental to society should be deemed to be criminal. Recall that while all crimes are created by the sovereign and subsequently viewed as offenses against the sovereign, harm, in the normal sense of the term, is often thought of in the context of direct injury to a human victim or the human victim's property. The broken nose Ralph receives when punched by Mike or the loss Marilyn suffers when Jay steals her sports car are simple examples of harm done in the course of the commission of a crime. With traditional crimes against person and property, such as assault and theft, the direct harm is fairly obvious. For some offenses the party directly harmed actually may be the government, such as in the crimes of escape, perjury, or resisting arrest. For other crimes, the broader society as a whole may be viewed as the direct victim. Disorderly conduct offenses, public intoxication, and traffic offenses are but a few of the crimes that potentially affect a large segment of the community.

The fact that the punch in the nose and the wrongful taking of the automobile are harmful is rarely explicitly recognized in the language of a criminal statute. Thus, while it may be accurate to state that all crimes are rooted in some harm to an individual, the government, or society at large, the actual existence of the harm is normally not an element of the offense that must be proven. It is unnecessary for the prosecutor to establish that Marilyn, who has a net worth of $50 million, suffered significant economic loss when Jay stole her sports car. It is simply sufficient to establish that he did the act; the economic loss is assumed. A few exceptions exist to the idea that the conduct alone is sufficient to establish harm. If Mike punches Ralph in the nose but Ralph suffers no injury, is there still harm? Is there still a crime?

A similar issue arises with property damage offenses. In most states, including Texas, a person cannot be convicted of criminal mischief unless some damage actually occurs to the property. Likewise, tampering with another's property is an offense only if economic loss or substantial inconvenience results (Sec. 28.03). Assume your roommate without your permission uses your iPod, shifting songs every few seconds. Unless it can be shown that his nonpermissioned behavior produces economic loss or inconvenience to you, his tampering with the iPod is not a crime.

The requirement of harm lies at the heart of the debate over so-called victimless crimes. **Victimless crimes** are offenses where the parties involved are consenting to the behavior (e.g., prostitution), or a single offender engages in conduct that does not appear to directly hurt any other person or property (e.g., smoking marijuana or failing to wear a seatbelt). A close examination of victimless crimes reveals that virtually all involve enforcement of the cultural and moral code of society or are simply protective in nature.

As to the question of harm, supporters of the morality-based offenses, such as prostitution, fornication, public intoxication, and use of narcotics, assert that cultural norms are an appropriate area of coverage by the criminal law. Indeed, as cultural norms change, so too do the victimless crimes. In the last 50 years, the majority of society's view of alcohol use has changed; correspondingly, the laws on possession and consumption of alcohol have also lessened. On the other hand, while sex out of wedlock has become much more accepted, virtually no change has occurred regarding society's opinion of prostitution. Consequently, anti-fornication laws have largely vanished, but prostitution statutes remain in the Penal Code and are enforced.[52]

The protective offenses exist due to two factors: the propensity of government to operate in a paternalistic manner and the corresponding use of the criminal sanction as an efficient enforcement mechanism of that paternalism. Mandated seatbelt use,[53] mandatory helmet use by motorcyclists,[54] and laws prohibiting underage smoking[55] are three examples of victimless crimes aimed at protecting the individual from oneself. Supporters of such legislation argue that the government has a responsibility to guide individuals in what is best for them. They further argue that society broadly will have to bear the medical costs of the injured motorist or motorcyclist or the youth who develops health problems from smoking. Hence, it is appropriate that the government require the individual to take steps to reduce the potential for such costs by mandating seatbelts and helmets and limiting tobacco use to those with the maturity to make the smoking decision. Victimless crimes are almost always misdemeanors and rarely expose a perpetrator to significant penalty.

While state legislatures are granted wide discretion in enacting criminal statutes, the U.S. Supreme Court has occasionally struck down laws on the grounds that any harm to societal interests are outweighed by the constitutional rights of the individual. Examples are laws prohibiting use of contraceptives by married persons,[56] prenatal abortions,[57] private possession of obscene matter,[58] and private consensual homosexual conduct.[59]

Until 1993, the Texas Penal Code contained the following statute:

Sec. 32.49. Issuance of Checks Printed on Red Paper.

(a) A person commits an offense if he issues a check or similar sight order for payment of money printed on dark red or other colored paper that prevents reproduction of an image of the order by microfilming or other similar reproduction equipment, knowing that the colored paper prevents reproduction.

Occasionally, a statute such as Sec. 32.49 will be enacted where the harm is not obvious to the reader. In these cases, the harm the Legislature is seeking to prevent may be discovered by researching the law's legislative history. Proceedings of state legislatures and the Congress are published in written form. The debate over a particular law will reveal the harm the legislature is seeking to deter through the law's enactment. As to the example, at the time of the statute's enactment, banks and other financial institutions photographed the checks they processed, rather than digitizing them. Apparently, some of the film stock used was not sensitive to red light waves. Thus, any check written in red would appear blank on the film. To deter frauds against banks, the Texas Legislature declared checks printed on red paper to be unlawful. Since a change in technology eliminated the potential for harm, the law was repealed.

Another example is an offense which has taken on near mythical proportions: spitting on the sidewalk. Jurisdictions with reputations for vigorous enforcement of the criminal law are often said to be so intolerant of deviant behavior that they will arrest a person for spitting on the sidewalk.[60] At first impression, spitting on the sidewalk, while culturally uncouth and potentially unsightly, hardly seems like behavior worthy of arrest and prosecution. Yet, in the early 1900s many communities outlawed the practice in a misguided effort to control the spread of tuberculosis. Some medical experts at the time believed the disease was spread by human saliva. In recent years, a few cities have used the old law in an attempt to control the public congregating of urban gang members by aggressively enforcing no spitting and other public disorder statutes.

EXCUSE AND JUSTIFICATION

You turn on the television just in time to see a live broadcast of a police chase. An individual has stolen a car and several police cars have given chase. During the pursuit the driver sideswipes several vehicles, nearly strikes a pedestrian, and violates numerous traffic laws. After an hour the vehicle runs out of gasoline and police officers apprehend the driver. Subsequent investigation reveals that the car thief is Anthony, an 11-year-old child. Anthony will be excused from prosecution in the adult justice system.

Rhonda intentionally shoots and kills Peter. Detectives determine that Rhonda killed Peter because he had broken into her apartment and was attempting to rape her. Rhonda will escape criminal sanction because her action was justified.

In both examples, all of the elements of one or more criminal offenses are present yet the two individuals are not held accountable under the law. Anthony is *excused* from prosecution because society has decided that children will not be held under the criminal law to the same standard as adults. Similarly, Rhonda's conduct of killing Peter would normally be considered murder except for the factual circumstances under which the behavior was committed. Thus, her act of self-defense was *justified* under the circumstances.

The specific requirements of the various Texas excuses and justifications are found in Chapter 15.

PENALTY

Introduction

Legislative bodies may enact hundreds of laws each session. These laws describe what various members of society may and may not do. However, a law may properly be labeled as a criminal offense only when some penalty is attached for noncompliance. A state's criminal code is only one volume in a multivolume set of statutes. Texas law is organized in 30 different codes, covering subjects from agriculture to water. Only a relatively few of these laws contain a direct penalty for noncompliance. Most statutes make clear whether an act is a crime by using language such as, "A person commits an offense if . . . " or "It is a felony to . . . "

With the elimination of corporal punishment, such as flogging and shaming, the American justice system has settled into a criminal penalty model limited to death, incarceration, and monetary fine. Except for the death penalty, generally applicable only in certain cases of criminal homicide, all criminal offenses are punished with some combination of incarceration or monetary fine. For a particular offense, the time range of incarceration or the range of fine is largely left to the wisdom of the Legislature, subject only to the constitutional requirement prohibiting cruel and unusual punishments. The actual penalty within the range imposed on an offender is, of course, determined by the judge or jury, depending on the defendant's choice. Over the years, a wide variety of correctional alternatives such as probation, deferred adjudication, suspended sentences, mandatory educational programs, and the like have been developed in an effort to better tailor to the individual offender the attainment of the goals of the criminal sanction. However, at the core remains the possibility of deprivation of life (death penalty), liberty (jail or prison time), or property (fine).

Penalty Classification

All jurisdictions recognize that some criminal offenses are more harmful to society than others. Minor offenses are sanctioned by a fine or a relatively small amount of time in jail. Felonies, however, impose incarceration for extended time frames in state penitentiaries. Over the history of the American justice system, jurisdictions have struggled with the appropriate approach to use in determining the sentence of offenders. This divergence in approach to some degree is a product of the varied, and sometimes conflicting, societal goals of the criminal sanction.

As a point of departure it should be noted that the Legislature, not the courts, are responsible for establishing the penalties for violations of criminal statutes. The Legislature has determined the break point between misdemeanors and felonies and decided the level of severity for each offense. The Legislature has also determined the possible range of punishment for each crime.

Texas classifies most criminal offenses into one of eight penalty categories. Misdemeanors are classified as Class A, B, or C while the felony categories consist of capital felony, followed by felonies of the first, second, or third degree and the state jail felony. In this manner the Legislature creates a public policy regarding relative offense severity. Each penalty group contains a range of sanctions, since each case is likely to have varying facts. For example, assume speeding in a motor vehicle is a Class C misdemeanor. While the severity of the offense of speeding is minor compared to other crimes, varying severities of speeding also exist. Should the motorist who is driving 15 miles per hour over the speed limit receive the same penalty as one going 40 miles over? Likewise, should the convenience store robber who has no prior arrests and was intoxicated at the time of the crime receive the same sentence as a robber with an extensive record of violent criminal conduct who physically batters the store clerk?

Table 2-1 displays the punishment ranges for each of the penalty classifications.

If Harry is convicted of robbery, a second degree felony, he could receive a sentence of any term of years between 2 and 20 as well as a fine of up to $10,000. Similarly, if Sally is convicted of possession of marijuana, a Class B misdemeanor, she could receive jail time or a monetary fine, or some combination of both. Note that, except for corporate defendants, all felonies involve deprivations of liberty. A fine may be added. However, for misdemeanors, a fine or incarceration, or both can be used.

Both felony and misdemeanor offenses are subject to a variety of enhancements depending on whether the defendant is a repeat or habitual offender or if the offense was a hate crime. Sentences may also be enhanced if the offender used a deadly weapon.[61] With the exception of capital murder, murder, aggravated sexual assault, aggravated robbery, and a few other crimes, all sentences are subject to being suspended, deferred, or probated as provided by law.[62]

TABLE 2-1 Texas Penalty Classifications

Classification	Penalty Range
Capital felony	death or life without parole
First degree felony	5 to 99 years in state prison and fine up to $10,000
Second degree felony	2 to 20 years in state prison and fine up to $10,000
Third degree felony	2 to 10 years in state prison and fine up to $10,000
State jail felony	180 days to 2 years in state jail and fine up to $10,000
Class A misdemeanor	up to one year in county jail and/or fine up to $4,000
Class B misdemeanor	up to 180 days in county jail and/or fine up to $2,000
Class C misdemeanor	fine up to $500

Notes

1. TEX. PENAL CODE § 1.07(22) states that "Element of offense" means (A) the forbidden conduct; (B) the required culpability; (C) any required result; and (D) the negation of any exception to the offense.
2. Robinson v. California, 370 U.S. 660 (1962).
3. *Id.* at 667.
4. In juvenile law, many children are often labeled as "status offenders." They may be children in need of supervision or delinquent children. This form of status is constitutionally permissible because it is based on the child's conduct.
5. Papachristou v. City of Jacksonville, Florida, 405 U.S. 156, 162 (1972).
6. City of Chicago v. Morales, 527 U.S. 41, 60 (1999).
7. Alford v. State, 866 S.W.2d 619 (Tex. Crim. App. 1993).
8. Rogers v. State, 105 S.W.3d 630, 638 (Tex. Crim. App. 2003).
9. See People v. Grant, 360 N.E.2d 809 (Ill. App. Ct. 1977), finding that jury should have considered whether defendant was suffering psychomotor seizure at the time he committed an assault.
10. TEX. PENAL CODE § 1.07(a)(1).
11. DALLAS CITY CODE § 31–13.
12. But see Pollard v. State, 687 S.W.2d 373 (Tex. App.—Dallas 1985), requiring proof of a culpable mental state to successfully prosecute a violation of the Dallas city ordinance.
13. This concept is sometimes called the "American bystander rule."
14. Even if Paul were a trained firefighter or police officer, he probably commits no *criminal* offense by failing to act in this circumstance.
15. *See* TEX. TRANSP. CODE § 550.021.
16. *See* TEX. FAM. CODE § 261.101 *and* TEX. PENAL CODE § 37.09(d)(2).
17. State v. Zascavage, 216 S.W.3d 495 (Tex. App.—Fort Worth 2007).
18. Today, the First Amendment prevents criminalization of possession of obscene and blasphemous materials. *See* Stanley v. Georgia, 394 U.S. 557 (1969).
19. Harrison Act, ch. 1, 38 Stat. 785.
20. Marijuana Tax Act of 1937, ch. 533, 50 Stat. 551.
21. For example, the Marijuana Tax Act imposed a $100 per ounce transfer tax on certain transactions.
22. 16 U.S.C. § 668; 31 CFR 515.204.
23. TEX. PENAL CODE § 1.07(a)(39).
24. TEX. PENAL CODE § 49.04.
25. *See* TEX. PENAL CODE § 36.02.
26. TEX. PENAL CODE § 22.011(c)(1).
27. TEX. TRANSP. CODE § 547.302.
28. *See generally* TEX. ALCO. BEV. CODE §§ 105.01–105.08.
29. TEX. PENAL CODE § 49.02.
30. TEX. PENAL CODE § 42.01(a)(10).
31. TEX. PENAL CODE § 19.03(a)(3).
32. TEX. PENAL CODE § 22.01(b)(1).
33. CAL. PENAL CODE § 190.2.
34. TEX. CODE CRIM. P. § 42.01(3g).
35. III EDWARD COKE, INSTITUTES OF THE LAWES OF ENGLAND (1633), reprinted in II THE SELECTED WRITINGS AND SPEECHES OF SIR EDWARD COKE 961 (Steve Sheppard, Liberty Fund 2003).
36. In the interest of accuracy, the fifteenth-century William Tell legend comes from Switzerland, not England.

37. Tison v. Arizona, 481 U.S. 137, 156 (1987).

38. McQueen v. State, 781 S.W.2d 600, 603 (Tex. Crim. App. 1989).

39. *See* HOUSE COMM. ON CRIMINAL JURISPRUDENCE, BILL ANALYSIS, Tex. H.B. 1185, 75th Leg. R.S. (1997).

40. Although Warren cannot be successfully prosecuted for possession of the stolen television, he does not get to keep it! A thief acquires no title to property and cannot thereby pass to another what he does not have.

41. The problem of proving knowledge in possession of stolen property cases will be explored further in Chapter 9.

42. A curious aspect of the statute is that it essentially defines "child" as a person under 18 years old, while the sexual assault of a child statute (§ 22.011) applies to a child under 17. Thus, if an individual picks up a 17-year-old runaway and they have consensual sexual intercourse, the harboring statute might apply, but not the more serious sexual assault law. From another perspective, the 17-year-old victim can lawfully consent to sex without parental consent as long as she doesn't runaway from home.

43. TEX. PENAL CODE § 6.02(e).

44. *See* TEX. TRANSP. CODE § 545.351.

45. Goodwin v. State, 138 S.W. 399 (Tex. Crim. App. 1911).

46. Morissette v. U.S., 342 U.S. 246 (1952).

47. See Lomax v. State, 233 S.W.3d 302 (Tex. Crim. App. 2007), holding that the Legislature had clearly dispensed with the need to prove a culpable mental state in the felony murder statute, § 19.02(b)(3).

48. Honeycutt v. State, 627 S.W.2d 417 (Tex. Crim. App. 1982). *See also* Aguirre v. State, 22 S.W.3d 463 (Tex. Crim. App. 1999).

49. Should Wayland not return the automobile promptly, he could well face theft-related charges.

50. TEX. PENAL CODE § 6.04(a).

51. *See* Thompson v. State, 2007 Tex. Crim. App. LEXIS 871.

52. Until 1974, fornication by cohabiting with another and engaging in sexual intercourse was subject to a fine of $50 to $500. *See* 1925 TEX. PENAL CODE art. 503.

53. TEX. TRANSP. CODE § 545.413.

54. TEX. TRANSP. CODE § 661.003.

55. TEX. HEALTH & SAFETY CODE § 161.252.

56. Griswold v. Connecticut, 381 U.S. 479 (1965).

57. Roe v. Wade, 410 U.S. 113 (1973).

58. Stanley v. Georgia, 394 U.S. 557 (1969).

59. Lawrence v. Texas, 539 U.S. 558 (2003).

60. *See* "Police use of spit law blasted," Cincinnati Enquirer Online, *at* http://www.enquirer.com/editions/2003/05/09/loc_spitting09.html.

61. *See, e.g.,* TEX. PENAL CODE §§ 12.41–12.43; and 12.47.

62. *See* TEX. CODE CRIM. P. art. 42.12(3g).

The Criminal Law in Daily Practice

3

BOLO

The reader should be on the lookout (BOLO) for the meaning of the following terms. Knowledge of the meaning of these terms will greatly assist the reader in understanding the primary elements of the chapter.

- Bias crime
- Bifurcated trial
- Complaint
- *Corpus delicti*
- Direct filing
- Discretion
- Double jeopardy
- Dual sovereign doctrine

- Hate crime
- Indictment
- Information
- Lesser included offense
- Magistrate
- Proof beyond reasonable doubt
- Statute of limitations

INTRODUCTION

While this text examines the substantive criminal law of Texas, the procedural aspect of the law cannot be completely ignored. Additionally, many practical issues concerning the process of implementing the criminal sanction directly affect the manner in which the penal laws are used in reality. A study of criminal law would not be complete without the examination of some of these matters. Initially, it is noteworthy that despite the Penal Code's stated objective to "systematize the exercise of state criminal jurisdiction,"[1] wide variation exists across the state in implementing the criminal law. As one set of experts on Texas criminal law have noted,

> In any realistic sense, there is not one Texas criminal process, but many of them. At the day-to-day operational level, the criminal process differs markedly between urban areas of the state and rural ones, between the panhandle and the valley and even between adjacent counties. Local customs, attitudes of the relevant officials and the like determine the nature of the criminal process to a significant extent and, of course, those are subject to change, and do change, over time.[2]

While this text cannot cover every variation in the application of the criminal law in each of the state's 254 counties, the more common variations in practice are noted as appropriate.

THE POLICE AND THE CRIMINAL LAW

Have you ever attended a party where police officers showed up in response to a complaint of loud noise? This is a common police activity, particularly in college towns where fraternities, sororities, and other student congregations can become quite loud in their celebration of the weekend. In virtually every instance of police response to a loud party call, the officers simply request the organizer or host of the party to do something to reduce the noise.

The police reluctance to arrest anyone in this circumstance stems not from the fact that no law is being broken; indeed a disturbance of the peace is likely what prompted the initial complaint. Rather, the police officers recognize that the threat of enforcement of the criminal law, not its actual use, often is sufficient to resolve situations such as this.

However, each year the nation's law enforcement officers make about 14 million nontraffic full custody arrests. Texas officers make about 8 percent of those arrests.[3] Additionally, officers issue tens of thousands more citations for minor criminal offenses. In each of these incidents, the arresting or citing officer possesses the required level of facts to support the belief the suspect committed one or more violations of the state's penal laws.

Depending on the circumstances, the arresting officer may know exactly which offense the suspect has committed or may have only a broad notion of the criminal violation. Consider the case of Bob who is apprehended after shoplifting merchandise at a discount store. Officer Terry certainly knows that Bob has violated the theft statute but may not know whether the incident is a felony or misdemeanor until the value of the stolen property has been determined. At the other extreme, assume Officer Terry responds to a domestic disturbance call and finds John and Marsha screaming at each other. Each individual exhibits signs of physical injury and many items in their apartment are scattered and damaged. Initially, Officer Terry may not even be able to determine which individual is the victim and which is the offender, even though clearly one or more crimes likely occurred and John, or Marsha, or both have committed them!

Fortunately, for Officer Terry, the U.S. Supreme Court has held that the Constitution does not mandate that an arresting officer know precisely what crime has occurred at the moment of making an arrest, only that she has probable cause to believe a crime has been or is being committed.[4] Determination of the precise charges is reserved for the time of filing a formal **complaint** in court.

Law enforcement officers serve as the primary gatekeepers to the criminal justice system. They initially determine whether a possible violation of the criminal law has occurred and what form of formal action if any to take. Through the use of **discretion** they may opt to cite or arrest an offender and thereby put the justice system in play. However, at the low end of Penal Code violations, many offenders are simply ignored or warned to cease their behavior, even though the elements of an offense are present. In any case, it is important to recognize that not every incident that fits the elements of a criminal offense results in an arrest or the filing of charges. Many petty offenses go unprosecuted because a peace officer makes a judgment that the public interest is better served without invoking the criminal sanction.

THE PROCESS OF FILING CHARGES

Simply because an individual has been arrested does not mean that he or she will be prosecuted. Following the taking into custody of an offender, a decision has to be made regarding the filing of formal charges. Some offenders may be released from jail without being charged, such as in public intoxication cases. Charges might also be dropped due to insufficient evidence, an illegal search, or some other reason that makes further pursuit of the matter legally difficult. More commonly, however, the arrested offender will be brought before a judge within 48 hours and notice of formal charges read to him.

Prosecution of Penal Code and other serious criminal violations lies in the hands of either the district attorney or the county attorney.[5] Both positions are filled by popular vote. In many smaller counties, the positions are part-time or several counties may share the same district attorney. While the process of filing charges varies from community to community within the state, the presumptive legal structure calls for the district attorney to handle felony-level matters and the county attorney to prosecute misdemeanors. However, over the years special laws and local practice have modified this split of responsibilities. In the largest counties, and many of the smaller ones as well, the district attorney's office processes all felony and state-level misdemeanors; the county attorney handles only civil matters. Violations of municipal ordinances are prosecuted by the city attorney. The Texas Attorney General possesses no general prosecutorial authority although the position is authorized to assist local prosecutors in handling certain specific offenses such as hate crimes, computer crimes, telecommunications crimes, money laundering, and insurance fraud.[6]

Formal charges are normally initiated by a peace officer filing a sworn compliant.[7] It is at this point that a decision must be made regarding the actual charge to file. For example, in the case of Bob the shoplifter, the level of misdemeanor or felony theft must be decided since this decision affects subsequent steps in the process, most notably which court will hear the case.

Whether charges must be cleared with the prosecutor prior to being filed varies from county to county. In some counties, the police officer will directly file the case. This means that the arresting officer is responsible for deciding which crime or crimes to list on the formal sworn complaint to be filed with the court. **Direct filing** is common with petty offenses, such as traffic violations, and minor misdemeanors, such as disorderly conduct and shoplifting. It is a less common practice with felony and serious misdemeanor cases. Prosecutors who will be handling the matter in court prefer to have control over the kind and level of offense charged since they are responsible for proving the elements at trial. Since police officers need only to possess probable cause to file charges, this level of evidence may never increase sufficiently to prove guilt. Likewise, police officers, while knowledgeable in the criminal law, may be less acquainted with formal rules of evidence and the subtleties of establishing guilt in the courtroom.

The alternative process, and the one often used in more serious cases, involves prosecutorial review of the case prior to the filing of formal charges. Under this model, if Officer Brown arrests Herby after finding him inside a closed building on a cold snowy night, the officer will book Herby into jail and contact the in-take unit of the district attorney's office. The officer will present the facts of the case to an assistant district attorney (ADA) along with the nature of the evidence available. The ADA will decide whether to authorize the filing of charges and the specific charges to be filed.

The American Bar Association Standards for Criminal Justice hold that "The duty of the prosecutor is to seek justice, not merely to convict."[8] Similarly, the Texas Code of Criminal Procedure commands that "It shall be the primary duty of all prosecuting attorneys, including special prosecutors, not to convict, but to see that justice is done."[9] Like many legal concepts, the word "justice" is difficult to define with precision. In a general sense, "justice" is seen as the effort to do right. Of course, reasonable people may disagree on what is right in a particular circumstance. As a consequence, obtaining justice often requires the making of tough choices in a given case through the exercise of discretion.

Prosecutors control the flow of a criminal case through the court system. The prosecutor determines whether or not to charge an individual, what type and level of charge to file, whether to agree to a plea bargain with the defendant, when to set the case for trial, and the subsequent strategy to follow at trial. Additionally, the prosecutor often has a strong say in the sentence that a convicted offender will receive, particularly if a plea agreement has been negotiated. Thus, the exercise of prosecutorial discretion has a major effect on the implementation of the criminal sanction.

In Herby's case, the ADA may decide to authorize burglary charges against Herby. Or the ADA may authorize only criminal trespass charges, reasoning that she will be unable to prove Herby's motivation for being in the building. Or, the ADA may simply decline to authorize any charges on the grounds that Herby likely entered the building to get out of the snowstorm and it is simply not worth expending resources on prosecuting him for conduct that may not even be a crime under the circumstances in which it occurred.

If charges are approved, a sworn complaint will be filed in the proper court and the judicial process will be underway. The suspect will be taken before a **magistrate**, told of the charges that have been filed, advised of his rights, and have bail set, if eligible.[10]

Texas and about half the other states use the grand jury system for felony cases. Unless the defendant waives his or her right, a true bill **indictment** must be issued from the grand jury before any felony case can proceed to trial.[11] Texas law does not explicitly state the amount of evidence a grand jury must receive to issue an indictment. Thus, if the indictment is valid on its face, the courts will not review the sufficiency of the evidence presented to the grand jury; the grand jury's determination is conclusive.[12] Often, the grand jury will come forth with an indictment for an offense other than the one for which the defendant was originally arrested. For example, assume the police arrest Alf for snatching Rhonda's purse and file a complaint charging him with robbery. When the case is presented to the grand jury, the victim testifies that although Alf grabbed her purse without permission and fled, he did not injure her nor did he threaten her or otherwise display a weapon. The district attorney will likely opt for an indictment for felony theft because the elements of robbery cannot be conclusively established. If the grand jury "no bills" the accused, the matter is dropped.

Misdemeanor cases are prosecuted based on filing with the court an **information**, a written statement charging an offense and signed by the district, county, or city attorney as appropriate.[13] Only rarely an individual is indicted by the grand jury for a misdemeanor. Most such cases involve acts of misconduct by public officials.

TEXAS COURT SYSTEM

While some states operate a unified court system, the Texas system is a bit of a structural hodgepodge. Felony cases are tried in the District Court or Criminal District Court,[14] while Class A and B misdemeanors are handled at the county level in the constitutional County Court, County Court at Law, or County Criminal Court at Law.[15] Class C misdemeanors are prosecuted in Justice Court or Municipal Court depending on whether the incident occurred within or outside the city limits.[16] The Municipal Court also processes city ordinance violations.[17]

Appeals of convictions of felonies and Class A and B misdemeanor convictions go to one of 14 regional Court of Appeals by right.[18] This means that the convicted defendant has the absolute right to have his case reviewed by an appellate court. These appellate courts review whether legal errors occurred in the conduct of the defendant's trial. They do not reconsider the facts of the case or consider items of evidence not introduced at the original trial. Because the various Court of Appeals are assigned to hear cases from a limited geographical area of the state, it is possible for conflicting rulings of law to exist. For example, in very similar factual cases, the Court of Appeals in San Antonio ruled that peace officers are not exempt from the application of the criminal trespass statute, while the appeals courts in Dallas and Houston held that the officers are exempt.[19] This potential for conflicting interpretation of the provisions of the Penal Code makes the study of Texas criminal law particularly challenging.

The highest appellate court in the state is the Court of Criminal Appeals, with the Texas Supreme Court having only civil jurisdiction. With one exception, the Court of Criminal Appeals grants review solely on a discretionary basis. The judges may choose or not choose to review a decision of one of the Court of Appeals. However, a mandatory appeal in capital cases goes directly to the Court of Criminal Appeals, bypassing the intermediate Court of Appeals. Thus, if Alf is convicted of felony theft, he has the right to have his conviction reviewed by the Court of Appeals. If his appeal is unsuccessful, he may petition the Court of Criminal Appeals to review the matter but has no absolute right to such a review. On the other hand, if Alf were convicted of capital murder and given the death penalty, his case will bypass the intermediate appeals courts and be reviewed initially by the Court of Criminal Appeals. Figure 3-1 shows the relationship among the various Texas courts.

FIGURE 3-1   Texas Courts With Criminal Jurisdiction

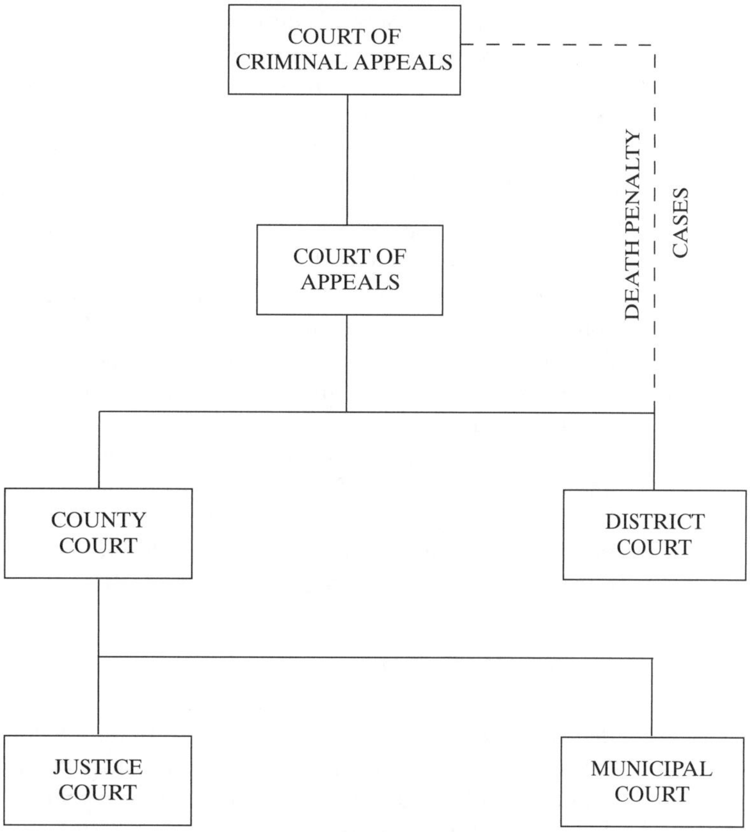

PROBLEMS OF PROOF

Proof beyond a Reasonable Doubt

To successfully prosecute a criminal defendant for a violation of the penal laws, several fundamental criteria of the American justice system must be met. Perhaps the best known of these criteria is the requirement of **proof beyond a reasonable doubt**. While police officers need possess only the relatively low standard of probable cause to make an arrest, at trial, each element of an offense, whether felony or misdemeanor, must be established at a level of proof beyond a reasonable doubt. The government's prosecutor bears the burden of coming forth at trial with evidence that is sufficient to convince the trier of fact, be it jury or judge, that the defendant committed the offense charged. The proof presented must reach the level of proof beyond a reasonable doubt. As one federal court has noted,

> It is not required that the government prove guilt beyond all possible doubt. The test is one of reasonable doubt. A reasonable doubt is a doubt based upon reason and common sense—the kind of doubt that would make a reasonable person hesitate to act. Proof beyond a reasonable doubt must, therefore, be proof of such a convincing character that you would be willing to rely and act upon it unhesitatingly. Putting it in another way, a reasonable doubt means a doubt based on reason and not the mere possibility of innocence.[20]

To explain this level of proof, one federal circuit issues the following standardized instruction to jurors:

> A reasonable doubt is a doubt based upon reason and common sense, and not the mere possibility of innocence. A reasonable doubt is the kind of doubt that would make a reasonable person hesitate to act. Proof beyond a reasonable doubt, therefore, must be proof of such a convincing character that a reasonable person would not hesitate to rely and act upon it. However, proof beyond a reasonable doubt does not mean proof beyond all possible doubt.[21]

Texas no longer mandates that juries be instructed with a particular definition of "beyond a reasonable doubt."[22] Rather, the Court of Criminal Appeals has taken the position that the phrase has a commonly accepted meaning and the jury is just as competent to define the phrase as is the court. This approach is consistent with a U.S. Supreme Court ruling that the Constitution does not require that any particular form of words be used in advising the jury of the government's burden of proving its case beyond a reasonable doubt.[23]

The prosecutor may introduce direct or circumstantial evidence; witness testimony and the results of scientific examination of evidence; photographs and documents. Any form of lawfully admissible evidence may be used. However, if the quantity of proof falls short of the beyond a reasonable doubt standard, the defendant is entitled to either an acquittal or conviction of a lesser offense, as the evidence establishes.

Corpus Delicti Rule

A second criterion that must be met in many cases is the establishment of the *corpus delicti* of the crime. ***Corpus delicti***, from Latin meaning "body of crime," refers to the principle that evidence independent of a suspect's confession must establish that a crime has occurred before a person can be convicted of committing that crime. For example, a person cannot be convicted of theft unless it can be shown that property has been stolen. Likewise, in order for a person to be tried for arson, it must be proven that a criminal act resulted in the burning of property. In criminal homicide cases, the corpse of the victim is used as evidence of the *corpus delicti*, although, as will be seen in Chapter 5, a criminal homicide violation can be legally established without the actual body of the deceased being recovered.

In the Anglo-American legal system, the concept of *corpus delicti* has its outgrowth in the important legal principle that an accused cannot be convicted solely on his or her uncorroborated confession. Other evidence of the existence of a crime must be shown—the *corpus delicti*. The rule originated in England over 300 years ago to prevent conviction of individuals who confessed to nonexistent crimes due to torture or mental illness. Indeed, English courts, and to a lesser extent American courts, have traditionally maintained a strong suspicion of the truthfulness of extra-judicial (i.e., out of court) confessions.

> *Corpus delicti* generally involves only two elements: (1) an injury or loss (e.g., death or missing property), and (2) someone's criminal act as the cause thereof . . . . Generally, proof of identity of a person who committed a crime is not part of *corpus delicti*, which only requires proof that a crime was committed by someone.[24]

Every American jurisdiction adhered to the *corpus delicti* rule by the end of the nineteenth century, but in the last 50 years, nearly a dozen states and the federal government have altered or repealed the rule. States that have dropped the requirement of proof of the *corpus delicti* have generally done so on the grounds that modern legal protections (e.g., the *Miranda* warning and prompt appearance before a magistrate) are sufficient to protect against coerced and false confessions.[25] Texas, however, retains the *corpus delicti* rule and holds that "an extrajudicial confession of wrongdoing, standing alone, is not enough to support a conviction; there must exist other evidence showing that a crime has in fact been committed. This other evidence need not be sufficient by itself to prove the offense. All that is required is that there be some evidence which renders the commission of the offense more probable than it would be without the evidence."[26]

Statute of Limitations

Suppose you leave class one day and discover that your prized sports car, your high school graduation gift, has been stolen from the campus parking garage. You notify the police, who dutifully take a report and enter the vehicle's descriptive information into the national database of stolen cars. You also call your insurance agent and report the theft. Days pass and it becomes apparent that your automobile is unlikely to be recovered. Your insurance company ultimately pays you the fair market value of the sports car. You purchase a new car and go on about your life. A decade later you learn that your sports car was recently discovered when an individual, Henry, sought to drive it into this country from Canada. Upon questioning by authorities, Henry, a former classmate, admitted that he stole the vehicle years earlier and took it with him when he returned to his home country Canada. Should Henry be subject to prosecution for stealing your car? Does the fact that ten years have passed since the theft affect your answer? Does it matter that Henry and the sports car have been out of the country all of those years? Does it matter that you technically no longer own the vehicle due to the insurance payment? Would any social purpose be served by prosecuting Henry at this late date?

The solution to the problem of you, Henry, and the sports car revolves around issues concerning **statutes of limitations**. These laws, which exist in one form or another in all states except Wyoming,[27] hold that a prosecution must be commenced within a specific time period following the commission or discovery of the offense. Curiously, the historical evidence is unclear as to why American jurisdictions even have statutes of limitations. The concept was not part of the Common Law, nor is the idea part of current British law. Indeed the time restrictions imposed on certain criminal prosecutions "are not a matter of right but legislative grace."[28] The length of a particular time limitation is purely a decision of the Legislature, as is the question of extending or reducing the time frame.

Equally unclear is the public policy purpose the time limitations on prosecution are attempting to accomplish. One might argue that all offenders should be subject to sanction for violating society's most important rules. On the other hand, is justice served by prosecuting old, forgotten criminal incidents? The U.S. Supreme Court has noted that

> The purpose of a statute of limitations is to limit exposure to criminal prosecution to a certain fixed period of time following the occurrence of those acts the legislature has decided to punish by criminal sanctions. Such a limitation is designed to protect individuals from having to defend themselves against charges when the basic facts may have become obscured by the passage of time and to minimize the danger of official punishment because of acts in the far-distant past. Such a time limit may also have the salutary effect of encouraging law enforcement officials promptly to investigate suspected criminal activity.[29]

Other legal scholars have suggested that additional societal and legal objectives are served by the existence of statutes of limitation. These scholars argue that:

- prosecutions should proceed only with fresh evidence;
- as time passes, the likelihood that the offender has reformed increases;
- after an extended period of time, society's retributive impulse may be replaced with sympathy for a defendant being prosecuted for a long forgotten crime; and
- the possibility of blackmail by one who is aware of the offense is cut off.[30]

Little uniformity exists from state to state on the time frames for statutes of limitation. However, the limitation on misdemeanors is usually about two to three years, while felonies must be prosecuted within five to ten years, depending on the type of felony—crimes against persons often having longer limitation periods than property crimes. As to murder, no American jurisdiction has a statute of limitation on this offense, hence the trend toward the creation of "cold case" squads in police departments. Some states expand this absence of a time restriction to lower levels of criminal homicide.

A recent trend has been to expand the time frame on the statute of limitations in cases of child sexual abuse and incest. The reasoning is that the offense might occur at an age when the child is too young to effectively report the incident to authorities. Thus, the offender should not be able to escape sanction because of his victim's lack of maturity. In addition, several states have expanded the statute of limitations for prosecutions of the most serious forms of sexual assault, regardless of the age of the victim. The extension of the time limit may be based on a set number of years from the date of the crime, the date the child reaches adulthood (usually at age 18), the date the crime is first reported to law enforcement, the date the victim discovers the crime, or whether DNA evidence exists.

The Texas Code of Criminal Procedure establishes limitations of actions. This means that a felony indictment or misdemeanor information must be presented within a specified period of time, depending on the offense, or no prosecution may proceed.

For misdemeanors, two years from the date of the commission of the offense is the limitation.[31] Thus, if Barbara embezzles $350 from her employer, any effort at prosecuting Barbara must be formally initiated within two years from the date she took the money. What if the theft goes undiscovered for more than two years, can Barbara be charged once the loss is discovered? No. The statute is clear that the time runs from the date of the commission of the crime.

Statutes of limitations for felonies are much more complicated. Once again the time begins to run from the date of commission of the offense, but the time limits vary widely.[32] For specific circumstances, Chapter 12 of the Texas Code of Criminal Procedure should be consulted. But, in general, the rules for the more common felony offenses are shown in Table 3-1.

The Legislature has chosen different time levels for different offenses. The relative time differences are based on the seriousness of the offenses (e.g., murder compared to burglary), the likelihood that the matter will be readily discovered (e.g., theft by public servant), and the ability to prove the case at a remote time (e.g., forgery, sexual assault with DNA). The idea that the statute does not begin to run until the child victim's

---

TABLE 3-1   Texas Statute of Limitations for Felonies

- No limitation
    - Murder and manslaughter
    - Sexual assault of child
    - Indecency with child
    - Sexual assault with existing DNA evidence
    - Failure to stop and render aid where death results
- Ten years
    - Theft by a fiduciary
    - Theft by public servant
    - Sexual assault
    - Forgery
    - Injury to child, elderly individual, or disabled individual (serious bodily injury)
    - Arson
- Ten years from 18th birthday of victim
    - Indecency with a child
    - Sexual assault of child
- Seven years
    - Credit card or debit card abuse
    - Identity theft
- Five years
    - Theft
    - Burglary
    - Robbery
    - Kidnapping
- Three years
    - Most other felonies (e.g., aggravated assault, criminally negligent homicide, escape, possession of prohibited weapon)

18th birthday is a recent change in the law. Under this rule, a child molester who assaults a six-year-old could be charged up to 22 years after the incident (18 – 6 = 12 plus 10).

The Texas rule is that the statute of limitation clock begins to run when the crime occurs and stops when formal charges are received by the court.[33] Texas and most other states hold that the statutory time clock pauses, called "tolling," while the defendant is continuously out of the state. Thus, in the example of the stolen sports car, the five-year statute of limitation for theft would begin to run the moment the vehicle was stolen. However, the time period would be suspended while Henry was in Canada. Texas authorities could lawfully prosecute Henry despite the fact that more than five calendar years had passed since the theft. Whether a prosecution for auto theft at this late date is good public policy is a decision left to the district attorney's discretion.

Double Jeopardy

A final issue that affects the implementation of the criminal sanction is the Fifth Amendment prohibition against **double jeopardy**.[34] "[N]or shall any person be subject for the same offence to be twice put in jeopardy of life or limb . . . " On the surface, the prohibition against "twice being put in jeopardy" seems straightforward enough. However, its application in practice is a far different matter. Indeed, when the double jeopardy clause is violated is a complicated topic that is beyond the scope of this text. In general, however, the U.S. Supreme Court has ruled that the prohibition covers three possible circumstances:

1. A second prosecution for the same offense after acquittal;
2. A second prosecution for the same offense after conviction; or,
3. Multiple punishments for the same offense.[35]

In its simplest application, the rule prevents an individual from being tried and convicted for an offense for which he or she has already been acquitted. Thus, the State of California is barred from reprosecuting former football star O. J. Simpson for the murder of his ex-wife and a friend because Simpson was found not guilty of that charge following a trial in 1995. Such reprosecution is prohibited even if new evidence of Simpson's guilt were found or Simpson himself were to now confess to the murders.

The problem of a second prosecution for the same offense after conviction arises occasionally. Certainly no rational district attorney would attempt to prosecute a convicted rapist a second time for the same rape. However, consider the case of Phillip, an intoxicated driver who is involved in a fatal traffic collision. Phillip is charged with misdemeanor driving while intoxicated (DWI) and intoxication manslaughter. He pleads guilty in County Court to the misdemeanor DWI charge. The state later attempts to prosecute him for the criminal homicide. Would such a prosecution constitute double jeopardy? In a similar fact situation, the U.S. Supreme Court ruled that the motorist's Fifth Amendment right was violated because the homicide case relied upon an offense for which he had already been convicted, the DWI.[36]

Similarly, assume that Lex, a previously convicted felon, is in need of quick cash. Armed with a pistol, Lex enters the First National Bank of Smallville and demands money. The frightened bank teller gives him $5,000. Lex flees, only to be apprehended by police a short time later. Lex is charged with aggravated robbery, felony theft, and unlawful possession of a firearm. Lex is convicted of all three offenses. On appeal,

Lex's attorney argues that the convictions violate the double jeopardy clause of the Fifth Amendment. Is he correct? Which, if any, of the three offenses are in conflict?

In 1932, the U.S. Supreme Court created the "*Blockburger* Test" (from a case of the same name)[37] to determine whether conviction of several crimes arising from the same factual incident violates the double jeopardy clause. Under the *Blockburger* Test, punishment for two offenses arising out of the same criminal transaction does not violate the double jeopardy prohibition if each crime requires proof of an additional element which the other does not. As a rule of thumb, if one offense is a lesser included offense of another, the double jeopardy prohibition bars a conviction for both crimes. Thus, in the example, Lex may not be lawfully convicted of both aggravated robbery and theft because the theft is a necessary element, and lesser included offense, of robbery. However, conviction for unlawful possession of a firearm by a felon can be had as it does not involve the same elements as the aggravated robbery charge.

In recent years, a popular motion picture portrayed Libby, a wife who is erroneously convicted of murdering her husband, Nick.[38] According to the storyline, Nick fakes his death, moves to another city, and starts a new life, while Libby is imprisoned for causing his supposed death. Upon being paroled, Libby searches for Nick with possible intentions of actually killing him. While the movie plot takes a different turn, what if Libby did indeed kill Nick? Could she be prosecuted for his death or would the double jeopardy clause of the Constitution prevent a second trial for the same "murder"?

Bart is charged with murder. A jury convicts him of manslaughter and sentences him to ten years in prison. While in prison, his case is appealed. The appellate court subsequently finds error occurred at his trial, reverses his conviction, and orders a new trial. At the new trial, the double jeopardy clause comes into play in two ways. First, Bart may not be convicted for any form of criminal homicide higher than manslaughter because the jury's verdict in the original trial, while convicting him of manslaughter, also found him not guilty of murder, the more serious offense. Second, if Bart is convicted in the second trial, he may lawfully receive a sentence greater than ten years but must be credited with the time he has already served. Failing to credit him with time served would constitute multiple punishments for the same crime.[39]

Consider again the above scenario of Lex and the bank robbery. Robbing a bank is not only a violation of the Texas robbery statute[40] but also a violation of federal law.[41] Would it violate the constitutional prohibition against double jeopardy to convict Lex in both state and federal court for his single act of bank robbery? What if Lex is tried in state court and found not guilty, followed by a trial in federal court where he is convicted? The Supreme Court has ruled that the double jeopardy prohibition normally is not violated with this form of multiple trials.[42] Because each prosecuting entity is a separate sovereign, under the American system of government, each entity, state and federal, has an interest in prosecuting the robber. Lex's conduct has violated the criminal law of each sovereign and he is subject to being held accountable by each. While such multiple prosecutions are constitutional, they are relatively rare. Often, when conduct violates both a federal and a state law, the federal government will defer to the state to conduct the initial prosecution. According to U.S. Department of Justice policy, the Assistant Attorney General must personally approve any subsequent federal prosecution of individuals who are acquitted in state court for the same incident.[43]

Traditionally, federal prosecution following a state prosecution has been used largely in cases of governmental misconduct, such as incidents of police brutality.[44] In an infamous example from 1992, several white Los Angeles police officers were acquitted in state court of assaulting a black motorist named Rodney King. Many individuals were surprised at the verdict since the beating had been recorded on videotape. Massive rioting erupted in south central Los Angeles following the announcement of the acquittal. The next year the federal government prosecuted the officers for violating King's civil rights. Two of the officers were convicted. A federal appeals court, citing the **dual sovereign doctrine**, rejected the former officers' claims of double jeopardy.[45]

The dual sovereign doctrine also applies in the very rare instances where two states seek to prosecute an individual for the same offense.[46] Indeed it is theoretically possible for multiple states and the federal government each to have a jurisdictional claim over an offender for a single criminal incident. If Paul steals Peter's car in Texas and drives it into Georgia, he has violated Texas law (theft),[47] Georgia law (theft by bringing stolen property into state),[48] and federal law (interstate transportation of stolen motor vehicle)[49] and is subject to prosecution by each jurisdiction. As a practical matter, the likelihood of prosecution by more than one of the entities is slim. Normally, the jurisdiction where the underlying offense occurred will handle the initial prosecution. In this example, Paul would be extradited back to Texas for trial.

LESSER INCLUDED OFFENSES

If the state is unable to establish each element of a particular offense, the defendant is not guilty of that crime. Roscoe is killed by a bullet from Fred's pistol. Fred is indicted for murder in the death of Roscoe. At the murder trial, Fred claims Roscoe was killed when the bullet ricocheted after Fred shot over Roscoe's head to scare him. If the state proves that Fred intentionally shot Roscoe, Fred is culpable for murder. But, if the jury believes Roscoe's version of the facts, that he acted only recklessly, Roscoe would be found guilty of manslaughter, not murder. In this instance, manslaughter is a lesser included offense of murder.

Lesser included offenses are crimes that have some, but not all, of the elements of a more serious offense. Theft is a lesser included offense of robbery. Criminal trespass is a lesser included offense of burglary. Assault is a lesser included offense of aggravated assault and attempted murder is a lesser included offense of murder, to name a few. Under the merger doctrine, lesser crimes are merged into the more serious crime. If Sam pushes Jennifer to the ground and snatches her purse, Sam cannot be convicted of both theft and robbery. The lesser crime of theft is merged into the greater offense of robbery.

The Texas Code of Criminal Procedure (Art. 37.09) states that a crime is considered to be a lesser included offense if:

1. It is established by proof of the same or less than all the facts required to establish the commission of the offense charged;
2. It differs from the offense charged only in the respect that a less serious injury or risk of injury to the same person, property, or public interest suffices to establish its commission;
3. It differs from the offense charged only in the respect that a less culpable mental state suffices to establish its commission; or
4. It consists of an attempt to commit the offense charged or an otherwise included offense.

Lesser included offenses help ensure a just system by avoiding an "all or nothing" approach at trial. Justice would not be served if because of selection of the wrong charge or a strategic decision to pursue a particular charge resulted in a defendant being found not guilty. If the judge or jury only had two choices—convict the defendant of the stated charge or acquit him—many factually guilty persons could go free due to the failure of the government to prove a single element of an offense. Existence of lesser included offenses also benefits the defendant. Prosecutors are often accused of "overcharging," filing a more serious charge than the evidence warrants. The lesser included offense rule allows the defendant to be convicted of the offense established by the courtroom evidence, not just the offense charged.

Lesser included offenses also guide prosecutors in the plea negotiation process. A prosecutor may be willing to take a plea to a lesser charge to save the cost and uncertainty of a trial or to spare the victim the emotional stress of having to testify. If Bob is charged with aggravated assault, the parties may agree for Bob to plead guilty to simple assault, thereby resolving the matter through compromise. An estimated 95 percent of criminal cases in America are resolved through the plea bargaining process, often with a plea to a lesser offense than originally charged.

Under Texas law, however, a defendant is entitled to a jury instruction on a lesser included offense only if there is some evidence in the record that if the defendant is guilty, he is guilty only of the lesser offense.[50] Thus, in the criminal homicide hypothetical of Roscoe and Fred discussed above, Fred would likely be entitled to have his jury instructed on the crime of manslaughter in addition to the crime of murder as charged. Fred, through his testimony, presented evidence that he might be guilty of manslaughter instead of murder. "Anything more than a scintilla of evidence is sufficient to entitle a defendant to a lesser charge."[51]

ISSUES IN SENTENCING

Judge Sentencing versus Jury Sentencing

Assume you are convicted of a serious crime. Would you rather have a judge impose your sentence or place your fate in the hands of the jury? Would your decision vary depending on the nature of the offense? Or, on whether you were tried in a major city or a small town? Do other factors exist that would affect your choice?

The Sixth Amendment to the Constitution grants a criminal defendant "the right to a speedy and public trial, by an impartial jury." The Supreme Court has interpreted this provision to mean that a defendant has a right to have his or her guilt determined by a jury but not the right to have the sentence assessed by a jury.[52] While jury sentencing was common in the nineteenth century, the trend in the last century has been to restore sentencing authority to judges. However, a few state constitutions or state statutes continue to grant the defendant a right to jury sentencing if he or she so chooses. Texas, along with Missouri, Oklahoma, and Virginia, has retained for the convicted defendant the option of jury sentencing, while the federal system, the District of Columbia, and the remaining states use a judge-based sentencing process.[53]

In Texas and the three other states that currently utilize the option of jury-based sentencing, the legal range of punishment is limited by statute. Legislatures in these states have revised their respective penal codes or corresponding punishment schedules fairly recently and have classified offenses by relative severity.[54] Each criminal offense has been assigned to one of the penalty categories.

Because evidence relevant to sentencing may be legally inadmissible or irrelevant to the issue of guilt, Texas courts utilize a **bifurcated trial**. This means that a criminal trial consists of two parts: a guilt or innocence phase and a punishment phase.[55] In the first phase, the prosecution and defense try the issue of the defendant's guilt. If the judge or jury, as the case may be, renders a guilty verdict, a second trial follows. This is the punishment phase. In this segment the prosecution may place into evidence the defendant's prior criminal history and other evidence to support the level of punishment sought. The defense is likewise permitted to put on proof seeking to mitigate the level of punishment. Upon completion of this phase, the sentencing authority, judge or jury, announces the sentence. For example, assume Alex is charged with robbery. He opts to have a jury trial. The jury returns a verdict of guilty. Alex further decides to let the jury set his punishment. Following the trial on punishment, the jury returns a sentence of

12 years, appropriately within the statutory range of 2 to 20 years as provided for in the Penal Code.[56] Capital cases follow a similar bifurcated trial system except during the punishment phase, when, depending on the circumstances of the case, the jury answers two or three special issue questions. The answers to these questions determine whether the judge imposes a death sentence or life without parole. This process is discussed more fully in Chapter 5.

Hate and Bias Crimes

With few exceptions the criminal law has traditionally been unconcerned with why an individual commits an offense. Although determining the motive for a crime may prove useful in identifying the offender or establishing that the offender engaged in the conduct purposely, statutes rarely include the "why" of a crime in the elements of the offenses. If a thief steals your red convertible, the Penal Code does not distinguish between the thief who steals because he plans to resell the vehicle and the thief who takes the vehicle to impress his new girlfriend. Similarly, the drug addict burglar and the skilled burglar are similarly culpable for taking your giant-screen plasma television set. But should all similar offenses be handled the same?

Suppose Rob strikes Bob in the face, causing Bob's nose to bleed. Should it matter if Rob commits the assault because he disapproves of Bob dating his ex-wife? What if the reason Rob strikes Bob is because Rob thinks Bob is a homosexual? Should the law treat the two bloody noses differently? What if high school students paint graffiti on the exterior walls of a rival school? On the school they write, "Go Eagles!" This form of mischief is certainly punishable under the criminal law, although most would agree it is not a major breach of society's rules of conduct. But suppose, instead, the students write, "Death to all Jews!" Is the societal concern different due to the motives of the students as evidenced by the content of their message? Should their punishment be based on their motives and beliefs in addition to the underlying physical damage done to the property?

Concern over **hate crimes**, also known as **bias crimes**, has caused many state legislatures to enact special statutes or enhanced penalties for offenses that are motivated by hatred of certain groups. Over 40 states and the District of Columbia have enacted hate crime laws since the mid-1980s. These laws impose higher penalties for crimes that are motivated by bias and prejudice. However, the scope of such laws is not uniform. For example, over 20 states include persons with mental and physical disabilities to the list of bias crime victims. About two dozen states include sexual orientation to the list, while others omit that particular factor. The Texas Code of Criminal Procedure defines a "bias crime" as occurring when the person or property affected was intentionally selected "because of the defendant's bias or prejudice against a group identified by race, color, disability, religion, national origin or ancestry, age, gender, or sexual preference."[57] Application of the Texas statute is limited to offenses against the person and arson, criminal mischief, and graffiti.[58] If during the guilt or innocence phase of the trial, a factual finding is made that the defendant's conduct fits the definition of a bias crime, the defendant is subject to the sentencing range from the next higher penalty category. Thus, if Roger is convicted of setting fire to Elton's store because Elton is a homosexual, the arson, normally a felony of the second degree, will be treated as a felony of the first degree for purposes of setting the punishment. The sentencing judge in a bias crime case may also require as a condition of punishment attendance in an educational program that teaches tolerance and acceptance of others.

Critics have raised several objections to hate crime legislation. First, they argue that the Anglo-American tradition punishes criminal offenders for their crimes, not for their motives or beliefs. They assert that enhancing a penalty because of the defendant's beliefs, no matter how repugnant, violates the First Amendment. The Supreme Court in 1993 rejected this claim. In a factually unusual case, an African American was convicted under Wisconsin law for aggravated assault of a white boy. Evidence in the case showed that the white victim was selected because of his race. Under the state's hate crime statute, an enhanced punishment was imposed. On appeal, a unanimous Supreme Court ruled the statute valid because it was aimed at conduct unprotected by the First Amendment. Additionally, the state's desire to redress individual and societal harm thought to be inflicted by bias-motivated crimes provided an adequate explanation for the penalty enhancement and went beyond mere disagreement with the offender's beliefs or biases.[59]

It is unclear whether the same result would be forthcoming if actual speech were involved as in the graffiti example earlier. However, the Supreme Court has ruled that a Virginia law that criminalizes cross-burning with intent to intimidate another does not violate the First Amendment protection of freedom of speech. In *Virginia v. Black*,[60] the court held,

> The First Amendment permits Virginia to outlaw cross burnings done with the intent to intimidate because burning a cross is a particularly virulent form of intimidation. Instead of prohibiting all intimidating messages, Virginia may choose to regulate this subset of intimidating messages in light of cross burning's long and pernicious history as a signal of impending violence.[61]

To avoid possible conflict with the First Amendment, many states, including Texas, have made a portion of their hate crime laws' content neutral. This means that the actual content of any speech in the case is irrelevant. Thus, "Death to all Jews!" painted on a synagogue wall would be treated the same as "Bobcat football is the greatest!" painted on the same synagogue. But, penalty enhancement is based on the location of the message. The statutes list specific locations where "hate speech" is most likely to manifest itself. For example, the Texas criminal mischief statute declares it a felony to place inscriptions, slogans, drawings, and paintings on "a place of worship or human burial, a public monument, or a community center that provides medical, social, or educational programs."[62]

Since the underlying purpose of a hate crime is to sanction the offender for his motive in committing the offense, what if the offender is mistaken about the nature of his victim? Jake and Bubba are members of a neo-fascist group that believes that heterosexual whites of European descent are the superior race. While driving around one evening they observe Louis exiting a local bar that is known to cater to homosexuals. Assuming Louis to be a homosexual, the pair follows him and assaults him in a parking lot. Police officers happen upon the scene and arrest Jake and Bubba. It is subsequently determined that Louis is not a homosexual but rather had gone into the bar in an attempt to sell the owner a new sound system. Have Jake and Bubba committed a hate crime?

In Texas, the assault of Louis would be considered a bias crime. Recall that the statutory definition of a bias crime touches upon selection of the victim due to the defendant's bias or prejudice against the particular group. Whether the offender's perception is or is not correct is not important for the purposes of the legislation. Since a major goal of hate crime laws is to deter criminal acts based on protected classifications, the purpose is violated when the unlawful act is motivated by the suspect's perception, regardless of the reality of the matter.

In 2006, the Texas Department of Public Safety collected reports of 245 hate crime incidents. Over three-quarters of these events were assaults or acts of vandalism.[63]

The degree to which Texas prosecutors seek to enhance a defendant's punishment on the basis that the conduct was a hate crime is unknown. However, one Texas legislator asserts that the enhancement statute has been used only seven times since its original enactment in 2001.[64]

Nontraditional Sentences

What if your family physician were limited to treating any disease or condition with either aspirin, radiation therapy, or vascular surgery? Certainly some of your medical conditions would improve by one of these treatments but other conditions would be unaided. Indeed, in many instances your condition might actually worsen if you received one of these treatments. Yet modern society finds itself in a similar situation when it comes to dealing with criminal offenders. For most offenses, the sentencing authority, be it judge or jury, is quite limited in what sanctions it can impose. Legislatures have generally restricted judges and juries to using monetary fines or incarceration to accomplish the diverse goals of general deterrence, specific deterrence, rehabilitation, incapacitation, and retribution. While death also is an occasional option, in the vast majority of prosecutions only some combination of incapacitation or monetary fine is imposed. Certainly, probation or other forms of deferred adjudication may be a possibility, but these options have traditionally been more of a generic "second chance" for the offender than a directed effort at rehabilitation or specific deterrence.

Recognizing the inherent limitations in using fines and incarceration as the "treatment" for any and all criminal acts, legislatures recently have begun to broaden sentencing options. While no state has reinstituted corporal punishment (whipping) or shaming (placing the offender in the pillory or stocks), other possibilities have become available in recent years. One of the more common is the use of community service, whereby a misdemeanor offender is required to pick up litter or work at a recycling center for a stated number of hours. A controversial form of sanction has been the use of boot camps for youthful offenders. The idea, a rehabilitation one, is that placing young offenders in a militaristic environment would teach them self-discipline and coping skills. While initially popular in the 1980s, the number of boot camps has diminished after research questioned their effectiveness in reducing recidivism and prison crowding.[65]

While legislatures have expanded sentencing options somewhat, some state judges have also adopted innovative approaches to sentencing while remaining within appropriate statutory boundaries. Many of the innovative sanctions have come in dealing with intoxicated drivers. The intoxicated driver is a particularly good candidate for adaptive sentences because the crime is one of the few that cuts across all social and economic classes. The sanction can be modified to the particular offender with an objective of preventing a reoccurrence. Among creative sanctions imposed on drunk drivers have been:

- Attendance at hospital emergency rooms to view traffic collision victims
- Attaching a "I'm a drunk driver" bumper sticker on a defendant's vehicle
- Requiring the defendant to periodically place flowers on the grave of an individual killed as a result of his drunken driving
- Requiring a defendant to place an advertisement in the local newspaper notifying the public that he is a drunk driver

Other offenders have also received their share of innovative sentences. One Massachusetts judge required offenders to read classic literature as part of their sentence, while a Texas jurist has required a shoplifter to stand in front of a discount store wearing a signboard reading "I was caught shoplifting." The same Texas judge mandated that the perpetrator of an act of family violence conduct a public meeting on the steps of the city hall and apologize for battering his wife. A Michigan teen convicted of violating a loud noise ordinance was required to listen to Wayne Newton songs. In one of the more creative sentences on record, two youthful offenders were convicted of desecrating a nativity scene on Christmas Eve. The judge ordered them to walk through the town's snow-spattered streets leading a donkey bearing a sign that read, "Sorry for the offense." Most of these unusual sanctions are officially a term of a probated sentence to which the offender must agree.[66]

Notes

1. TEX. PENAL CODE § 1.02(6).
2. ROBERT O. DAWSON AND GEORGE E. DIX, TEXAS CRIMINAL PROCEDURE 1–2 (1984).
3. FEDERAL BUREAU OF INVESTIGATION, CRIME IN AMERICA-UNIFORM CRIME REPORTS 2005 (2006).
4. *See* Devenpeck v. Alford, 543 U.S. 146 (2004).
5. TEX. CODE CRIM. P. art. 2.01–2.02.
6. TEX. PENAL CODE §§ 12.47(b); 33.04; 33A.06; 34.03; 35.04.
7. TEX. CODE CRIM. P. art. 15.05.
8. STANDARD 3–1.2, ABA STANDARDS FOR CRIMINAL JUSTICE: PROSECUTION FUNCTION AND DEFENSE FUNCTION.
9. TEX. CODE CRIM. P. art. 2.01.
10. TEX. CODE CRIM. P. art. 14.06; 15.17.
11. TEX. CODE CRIM. P. art. 1.05; 1.41. If the right to an indictment is waived, an information is used as the charging instrument. *See* TEX. CODE CRIM. P. art. 21.20–21.23.
12. Tarpley v. State, 565 S.W.2d 525 (Tex. Crim. App. 1978).
13. TEX. CODE CRIM. P. art. 21.20.
14. TEX. CODE CRIM. P. art. 4.05. District Courts also handle misdemeanors involving acts of official misconduct.
15. TEX. CODE CRIM. P. art. 4.07.
16. TEX. CODE CRIM. P. art. 4.11; 4.14.
17. TEX. CODE CRIM. P. art. 4.14.
18. Appeals of Class C misdemeanor convictions are given a completely new trial by the County Court. For these petty offenses, appeal beyond County Court is limited. *See* TEX. CODE CRIM. P. art. 4.08.
19. *Compare* State v. Howell, 824 S.W.2d 317 (Tex. App.—San Antonio 1992); Rosalez v. State, 875 S.W.2d 705 (Tex. App.—Dallas 1993); and Rue v. State, 958 S.W.2d 915 (Tex. App.—Houston [14th Dist.] 1997). See Chapter 11 for further discussion of this issue.
20. U.S. v. Conley, 523 F.2d 650, 655 (8th Cir. 1975).
21. INSTRUCTION 3.11, MANUAL OF MODEL JURY CRIMINAL INSTRUCTIONS FOR THE DISTRICT COURTS OF THE EIGHTH CIRCUIT (2002).
22. *See* Paulson v. State, 28 S.W.3d 570 (Tex. Crim. App. 2000), *overruling* Geesa v. State, 820 S.W.2d 154 (Tex. Crim. App. 1991).
23. Victor v. Nebraska, 511 U.S. 1 (1994).
24. State v. C.M.C., 40 P.3d 690, 692 (Wash. Ct. App. 2002).
25. See David A. Moran, *In Defense of the Corpus Delicti Rule*, 64 OHIO ST. L.J. 81 (2003), for a list of jurisdictions that have dropped or altered the rule's requirements.
26. Rocha v. State, 16 S.W.3d 1, 4 (Tex. Crim. App. 2000).
27. Vernier v. State, 909 P.2d 1344 (Wyo. 1996).
28. 1 CHARLES E. TORCIA, WHARTON'S CRIMINAL LAW 628–629 (15th ed. 1993).
29. Toussie v. United States, 397 U.S. 112, 114–115 (1970).
30. MODEL PENAL CODE § 1.06 cmt. 1 (1985).
31. TEX. CODE CRIM. P. art. 12.02.
32. TEX. CODE CRIM. P. art. 12.01.
33. TEX. CODE CRIM. P. art. 12.06.
34. Originally, the federal constitutional prohibition against double jeopardy applied only in federal cases. In 1969, in the case of *Benton v. Maryland*, 395 U.S. 784 (1969), the Supreme Court ruled that the ban is an essential part of due process of law and is binding on state prosecutions as well.
35. U.S. v. Halper, 490 U.S. 435 (1989).
36. Grady v. Corbin, 495 U.S. 508 (1990).
37. Blockburger v. U.S., 284 U.S. 299 (1932).
38. *Double Jeopardy*, Paramount Pictures (1999).
39. Pearce v. North Carolina, 395 U.S. 711 (1969).
40. TEX. PENAL CODE § 29.02.
41. 18 U.S.C. § 2113.
42. Bartkus v. Illinois, 359 U.S. 121 (1959).
43. U.S. DEPARTMENT OF JUSTICE, UNITED STATES ATTORNEYS' MANUAL § 9-2.031.
44. In recent years, an increasing number of federal domestic violence prosecutions have been initiated. The bulk of these involved cases where the abuser used a firearm. Under a 1994 law, possession of a firearm by anyone with a prior misdemeanor conviction for domestic violence, or who is

currently subject to a protective order, is a federal felony. *See* MATTHEW R. DUROSE ET AL., FAMILY VIOLENCE STATISTICS (NCJ 207846) (U.S. Department of Justice, Bureau of Justice Statistics 2005) and 18 U.S.C. § 922.

45. Koon v. United States, 34 F.3d 1416 (9th Cir. 1994).
46. Heath v. Alabama, 474 U.S. 82 (1985).
47. TEX. PENAL CODE § 31.03.
48. GA. CODE § 16-8-9.
49. 18 U.S.C. § 2312.
50. Rosseau v. State, 855 S.W.2d 666 (Tex. Crim. App. 1993).
51. Bignall v. State, 887 S.W.2d 21, 23 (Tex. Crim. App. 1994).
52. Spaziano v. Florida, 468 U.S. 447 (1984).
53. Jury discretion to select sentences in felony cases was first adopted in the United States as part of the 1796 penal code of the Commonwealth of Virginia. The idea of jury sentencing apparently originated with a proposed penal code drafted by Thomas Jefferson. *See* Nancy J. King, *The Origins of Felony Jury Sentencing in the United States*, 78 CHI.-KENT L. REV. 937 (2003).
54. Missouri 1977, Oklahoma 1999, Texas 1994, and Virginia 1975.
55. A bifurcated trial is not used in trials of Class C misdemeanors in Justice Courts or Municipal Courts. TEX. CODE CRIM. P. art. 37.07(2)(a).
56. TEX. PENAL CODE § 29.02.
57. TEX. CODE CRIM. P. art. 42.014.
58. *Id.*
59. Wisconsin v. Mitchell, 508 U.S. 476 (1993).
60. 538 U.S. 343 (2003).
61. *Id.* at 363.
62. TEX. PENAL CODE § 28.03(f).
63. TEX. DEP'T OF PUB. SAFETY, THE TEXAS CRIME REPORT FOR 2006 (2007).
64. Letter from Senator Rodney Ellis to Lieutenant Governor David Dewhurst (May 26, 2006), *at* www.rodneyellis.com/news/pressreleases?id = 0006.
65. *See* CORRECTIONAL BOOT CAMPS: LESSONS FROM A DECADE OF RESEARCH (NIJ 197018) (U.S. Department of Justice, National Institute of Justice 2003).
66. *See* Dale Lezon, *Judge tries a serial killer's message to warn prostitutes; Defendants cry, but the jury's out on whether it makes a difference*, HOUSTON CHRONICLE, Jan. 20, 2006, at B2, *and* Ron Wood, *More unusual sentences given—but do they work?*, HOUSTON CHRONICLE, Nov. 4, 2007, at A33.

Parties to Offenses

BOLO

The reader should be on the lookout (BOLO) for the meaning of the following terms. Knowledge of the meaning of these terms will greatly assist the reader in understanding the primary elements of the chapter.

- Accessory after the fact
- Accessory before the fact
- Accomplice testimony rule
- Corporation
- High managerial agent
- Law of complicity

- Misprision of a felony
- Party to an offense
- Principal in first degree
- Principal in second degree
- *Respondeat superior*
- Vicarious responsibility

INTRODUCTION

Assume that Joey, Ross, and Chandler hatch a scheme to rob the local bank. Ross is assigned to drive the getaway car. Since he does not own an automobile, he borrows Rachel's car. The three men go to the bank. Joey enters the bank while Ross remains outside in the car. Chandler stands as a lookout just inside the bank while Joey points a pistol at a bank employee and collects several thousand dollars. Joey and Chandler exit the bank and flee in the car. The three decide they need a place to hideout and go to their friend Monica's apartment. Monica agrees to allow the trio to stay at her place for a few days. Who among the five is criminally culpable for the robbery? Do they all share equal blame? Are any of the individuals not criminally responsible at all?

The question of when one is responsible for the criminal acts of someone else is called the **law of complicity**. Anglo-American law has long recognized that when a criminal event involves more than one perpetrator, each individual may play a distinct role before, during, or after the event. Should these individuals, referred to as **parties to an offense**, also have differing levels of blameworthiness for their respective roles in the criminal act?

COMMON LAW APPROACH TO LAW OF PARTIES

For many years, prosecutors struggled with rigid Common Law distinctions between principals in the first degree, principals in the second degree, accessories before the fact, and accessories after the fact.[1] These distinctions originally developed when most felonies were capital offenses. By the twentieth century, most felonies were not capital but the culpability distinctions among parties remained in the criminal law. Various

TABLE 4-1	Law of Parties Under the Common Law
Principal in first degree	Individual who performs the actual criminal act. Every crime needs at least one principal in the first degree. More than one person can be a principal in the first degree, such as when two individuals or more perform the *actus reus* of the crime, as in a gang rape. No legal limit exists on the number of principals in the first degree. The famous Agatha Christie novel *Murder on the Orient Express* (1934) involves a dozen principals in the first degree.
Principal in second degree	An individual who is present at the crime and aids the principal in the first degree but does not perform the *actus reus*. A lookout or getaway car driver in a robbery is a principal in the second degree.
Accessory before the fact	An aider and abettor of the commission of the crime but who is not present at the scene. This individual can range from the mastermind of the event to simply someone who provided a weapon or vehicle to assist in the commission of the criminal act.
Accessory after the fact	An individual who provides post-crime assistance with knowledge that the crime has occurred but did not participate in the planning or implementation of the criminal event.

arcane procedural rules also made it difficult to prosecute persons other than the direct participants in the criminal event.

Table 4-1 displays the traditional Common Law distinctions between principals and accessories.

TEXAS LAW OF PARTIES

Introduction

The terms "principals," "accessories," "accomplices," and "aiders and abettors" have pretty much lost their traditional legalistic meanings. However, many courts continue to use the terminology to label those who are direct perpetrators of harm (principals) and those who have derivative liability for their own acts or the criminal conduct of someone else (accomplices and accessories). Today, the legal focus is generally on establishing a criminal relationship between the parties to an offense. If that relationship is shown, all parties who participate in the planning and execution of the offense are treated as equally guilty regardless of their actual factual role in the crime. As one court observed, "When an accomplice chooses to become a part of the criminal activity of another, she says in essence, 'your acts are my acts,' and forfeits her personal identity."[2]

§ 7.01. Parties to Offenses

a. A person is criminally responsible as a party to an offense if the offense is committed by his own conduct, by the conduct of another for which he is criminally responsible, or by both.

b. Each party to an offense may be charged with commission of the offense.

c. All traditional distinctions between accomplices and principals are abolished by this section, and each party to an offense may be charged and convicted without alleging that he acted as a principal or accomplice.

Adopting the modern view of the topic, Texas Penal Code Sec. 7.01(c) abolishes the Common Law distinctions among participants in a criminal event. Specifically, the statute asserts that "each party may be charged and convicted without alleging that he acted as a principal or accomplice." This statute accomplishes two purposes. First, it recognizes that culpability is not dependent on the extent to which one participated in the commission of the crime in question. Rather, the concern is simply did the defendant participate at some level? If so, the individual bears criminal responsibility for the entire offense; the degree of blameworthiness becomes a consideration for the jury or judge at time of sentencing. Second, the district attorney is saved from adherence to the complicated charging and proof rules that existed under the Common Law. A procedural misstep with these old rules could result in a legal acquittal of a clearly factually guilty individual. Such an unjust result is much less likely to happen today.

Note that under the Texas statute the underlying criminal conduct may be felony or misdemeanor in degree. The law of parties could be applied to individuals who disturb the peace as a participant in a loud party and to acts of criminal mischief by a group of youthful offenders. How much noise each reveler made or which acts of damage were done by which youth probably need not be precisely proven.

Personal and Vicarious Responsibility

Under current Texas law, a person is responsible for his or her own criminal conduct, and he or she *may* be responsible for another's criminal conduct. The first line of responsibility is so obvious that it is a bit surprising that the matter is even mentioned in the Penal Code. If Barry intentionally strikes Jose in the head with a baseball bat, Barry is criminally responsible for his conduct (assault) and for any harmful result, such as Jose's death (murder). The overwhelming bulk of criminal offenses are committed by individual conduct wherein one person causes some harm through his intentional, knowing, reckless, or criminally negligent conduct.

More complicated are circumstances when one person is held criminally responsible for the illicit conduct of some other person. This form of legal responsibility is sometimes called **vicarious responsibility**. Sec. 7.02 sets forth the three circumstances where this complicity liability can arise:

Aiding Innocent/Nonresponsible Person
Acting with the appropriate culpable mental state, the defendant causes or aids an innocent or nonresponsible person in committing a crime. In his classic tale *Oliver Twist*, Charles Dickens recounts the story of a ten-year-old boy in Victorian England who falls under the control of a career criminal named Fagin. Fagin houses runaways and orphans and trains them to be pickpockets. The young men bring their loot back to Fagin in exchange for food and shelter. Now, as then, Fagin would be responsible for the thefts committed by the young men. Modern criminal law punishes individuals who cause legally or factually innocent individuals to commit crimes at their behest. A modern day Oliver Twist would not be accountable in the adult justice system due to his young age, but Fagin would be accountable for Oliver's criminal deeds. Today, adults occasionally use juveniles to commit burglaries and thefts on their behalf. If Jack, an adult, sends Ted, his 12-year-old brother, into the store to shoplift a six-pack of beer, Jack is responsible for Ted's behavior. The crime of theft requires intent to steal, which Jack certainly has. Jack "causes" his brother to commit the crime. Ted, however, is "nonresponsible" because he is too young to be processed in the adult court system. While the juvenile may avoid the sanction of the criminal law, the adult will not.

§ 7.02. Criminal Responsibility for Conduct of Another

a. A person is criminally responsible for an offense committed by the conduct of another if

  1. acting with the kind of culpability required for the offense, he causes or aids an innocent or nonresponsible person to engage in conduct prohibited by the definition of the offense;

  2. acting with intent to promote or assist the commission of the offense, he solicits, encourages, directs, aids, or attempts to aid the other person to commit the offense; or

  3. having a legal duty to prevent commission of the offense and acting with intent to promote or assist its commission, he fails to make a reasonable effort to prevent commission of the offense.

b. If, in the attempt to carry out a conspiracy to commit one felony, another felony is committed by one of the conspirators, all conspirators are guilty of the felony actually committed, though having no intent to commit it, if the offense was committed in furtherance of the unlawful purpose and was one that should have been anticipated as a result of the carrying out of the conspiracy.

In an actual case, the father of two juveniles was found guilty of a felony violation of the Parks and Wildlife Code for assisting his children in illegal hunting. The sons shot several deer on private land. The father, who was not present at the time of the shooting, assisted the sons in dragging the deer to his truck. The court applied the law of parties to sustain the father's guilt.[3]

On rare occasions, a factually innocent person is duped into committing a crime. Roger observes a well-dressed man drop his parking lot claim check. Roger picks up the ticket and places it in his pocket. An hour later, Roger asks his friend Andy to do him a favor and pick up his new car at the parking garage. He gives Andy the claim ticket. Andy presents the ticket at the garage, pays the parking fee, and drives off in an automobile which he erroneously believes belongs to Roger. He delivers the vehicle to Roger. Roger later sells the vehicle. Roger is guilty of theft through Andy's actions but Andy is not guilty of theft because he lacked the intent to steal.

Intentional Assistance/Encouragement/Direction

Acting with intent to promote or assist the commission of the offense, the defendant "solicits, encourages, directs, aids, or attempts to aid" the other person. This theory is the most common application of the law of parties. Suppose Ethel hires Vincent to kill her ex-husband Fred. Vincent agrees to perform the deed for $5,000. Vincent hails a taxicab being driven by Max. Vincent tells Max to drive him to an apartment house at 231 Elm Street, Fred's residence. Upon arrival, Vincent tells Max to wait for him. While inside the apartment, Vincent murders Fred. He exits and directs Max to drive to the airport. At the airport, Vincent pays the cab fare and never sees Max again. Can Ethel be successfully prosecuted as a co-principal to murder? Can Max?

Ethel's conduct meets the requirements of this section. She purposefully solicits Vincent to commit murder, which he does.[4] But, Max will escape punishment. While he certainly aids Vincent in committing the murder, he lacks the required culpable mental state for his conduct to create criminal liability. Texas law is explicit that mere presence at a scene without more is not sufficient to be considered an aider and abettor.[5] This rule is consistent with the broader notion that American law punishes conduct and not guilt by association. However, presence can result in criminal liability if the goal were to assist the commission of the offense, as with Chandler serving as a lookout in the opening scenario.

Perhaps the minimum conduct necessary for collateral criminal liability is speech. Recall that the statute contains the term "encourages." Verbal statements are certainly a form of encouragement. Assume Homer learns that his wife Marge is having an affair with Ned. Homer tells his friend Barney about the affair. Barney says, "If that were my wife, I would beat her and Ned within an inch of their lives. That's what you ought to do Homer. Give them a good whipping." If Homer assaults the lovers, is Barney an accomplice because of his verbal encouragement? Must his encouragement be more forceful in order for liability to attach? The Court of Criminal Appeals has held that a suspect's presence at the crime scene along with encouragement by words or other agreement is sufficient to support a conviction.[6] Would the same rule apply if the defendant were not present?

Breach of Legal Duty

Having a legal duty to prevent the commission of the offense and acting with intent to promote the commission of the offense, the offender fails to make a reasonable effort to prevent its commission. Instead of some affirmative act by the defendant, this section focuses on the failure of the defendant to act. As with other areas of the law, sanctions for failure to act arise in very limited circumstances. All too common a mother of an abused child is prosecuted for failing to shield her child from an abusive boyfriend. In Texas and most other states, the mother has a legal duty to protect the child and purposeful failure to act results in injury to a child charges against her based on the acts of the boyfriend.[7]

Assume Rafael observes Barry chasing Jose with a raised baseball bat. Rafael stands by and does nothing as Barry strikes Jose several times. Does Rafael have collateral criminal responsibility for Barry's assault on Jose? Probably not. Liability in this situation attaches only if Rafael both intends to assist the commission of the assault and has a legal duty to prevent it. In this incident, Rafael likely has neither. But, suppose Rafael is a correctional officer and Barry and Jose are inmates. Does that change Rafael's blameworthiness? Only if Rafael intends for the assault to occur. If he is just unable to stop it before it occurs, Rafael has no criminal liability because he lacks the intent to assist the crime's commission.

While the existence of intent certainly must be proven, the tougher issue may be the element of a legal duty. The statute does not define when one has a legal duty to prevent the commission of a crime. Few appellate court decisions have interpreted this provision. In one case, an off-duty deputy sheriff's conviction for assault was upheld on the basis that he had a legal duty to prevent an acquaintance from cutting an individual with a knife during a tavern dispute.[8] The application of the criminal law in this factual situation is curious given that the police rarely have civil liability for failure to prevent a crime from occurring. A stronger case could be made against a correctional officer who allows an inmate to escape by purposefully leaving the cell door unlocked. In this example, the intent and the breach of the legal duty are clear.[9]

An unanswered question turns on the meaning of "legal duty." Does that mean a statutorily created responsibility only or could it extend to mere contractual duties? It seems logical that the private security guard who leaves the building alarm inactive to facilitate the commission of a burglary should be held accountable as a co-principal to the criminal incident.

ISSUES IN LAW OF PARTIES

Unanticipated Crimes

May an individual be convicted under the law of parties if a co-principal commits offenses which the individual did not intend? Suppose Zelda hires Scott to go to Maynard's apartment and steal his priceless Van Gogh painting. Scott slips into the apartment but encounters Maynard before he can take the painting. A struggle ensues and Scott kills Maynard. Is Zelda culpable for Maynard's murder? Apparently yes. Sec. 7.02(b) holds co-conspirators responsible for acts "in furtherance of the unlawful purpose." The act must be one that "should have been anticipated." Should Zelda have anticipated that a burglary of Maynard's apartment might result in a confrontation between Scott and Maynard and that Maynard might be killed?

Suppose Bob and Ray decide to give whiskey to Shirley, a 16-year-old, in order to lower her inhibitions so she will agree to have sex with them. The plan succeeds. Shirley agrees to engage in sexual intercourse with the two men. While Ray and Shirley are engaged in the sex act, Ray becomes angry and chokes her to death. Is Bob culpable for the murder? One can make a persuasive argument that Shirley's murder should not have been anticipated under the circumstances. Likewise, while a felonious sexual assault is occurring (Shirley is underage),[10] the murder is not "in furtherance of the commission" of the underlying felony as required by the felony murder statute.[11] Arguably, Ray's act was an independent impulse and not attributable to Bob.[12]

While case law is scant on the matter, the "should have been anticipated" limitation in Sec.7.02(b) would appear to be a restriction on the application of the statutory rule that "a person is nonetheless criminally responsible for causing a result if the only difference in what he intended and what occurred is a different offense was committed."[13] However, in the case of Maynard's death, the potential for murder seems more compelling. Burglaries which involve offender–homeowner confrontations are known to often result in violence. The language of the felony murder rule reinforces the appropriateness of also charging Zelda with Maynard's murder.[14] The message society sends is, "Don't put a criminal act in motion unless you are willing to accept the *likely* consequences."

Capital cases present a slight modification to this general rule of vicarious responsibility. While an accomplice may still have liability, he may escape the death penalty. The U.S. Supreme Court has held that death as a penalty cannot be imposed by mere operation of law unless the accomplice either intended to kill or was recklessly indifferent to human life. In Enmund v. Florida, an individual was assessed the death penalty after being determined to be a principal in the second degree in a robbery–murder case.[15] The vehicle in which the defendant was riding overheated. While two associates went to a house to ask for some water for the car's radiator, Enmund remained in the vehicle. Unknown to Enmund, his two associates decided to rob and kill the elderly residents of the house. Under the Florida law of parties, Enmund was punishable as a co-principal and eligible for the death penalty. The Supreme Court voided the death penalty for Enmund saying,

> For purposes of imposing the death penalty, Enmund's criminal culpability must be limited to his participation in the robbery, and his punishment must be tailored to his personal responsibility and moral guilt. Putting Enmund to death to avenge two killings that he did not commit and had no intention of committing or causing does not measurably contribute to the retributive end of ensuring that the criminal gets his just deserts.[16]

In another case, however, the death penalty was upheld on two brothers who supplied weapons to help their father escape from prison. They were present when their father and another escapee murdered a family of four they had kidnapped during the escape.[17] The high court found that the brothers had a reckless disregard for human life.

Acquittal of Co-defendant

Suppose Bonnie and Clyde are charged with robbery. Clyde committed the act and Bonnie served as the lookout. At trial, Clyde is found not guilty. Since Bonnie's culpability is drawn from Clyde's conduct, can she be convicted if Clyde is acquitted? Under the Common Law, Bonnie would have avoided responsibility. The Common Law held to the notion that no one could be an accomplice unless the principal was convicted.

Sec. 7.03(2) provides a fairly clear answer to this matter in this state. Texas legislators, like those in many other states, understand that a variety of reasons exist as to why the prime offender might be acquitted. The perpetrator might hold a legal defense such as insanity; he might die before being tried; or, he might escape sanction due to a constitutional violation such as an unlawful search. Since in order to convict the accomplice, the underlying offense must be established anyway, whether other partners in the crime are convicted is not relevant to the accomplice's culpability. In fact, under this legal theory, it is legally possible for the co-principal to be convicted of a more serious offense than the individual who assisted him.[18] In the example, Bonnie could be convicted of the robbery regardless of Clyde's acquittal.

Pre-crime Assistance

Because of the statutory language, one who assists the commission of an offense can be prosecuted as a co-principal. In the chapter's opening scenario Rachel becomes criminally liable for the bank robbery only if she intends to assist in the robbery when she loans her automobile to Ross. Thus, not only must the individual in fact help in the commission of the crime but she must be aware that a crime will be occurring. More facts would be necessary before determining Rachel's culpability.

A hardware store clerk who sells a hammer to an individual who later uses the tool to bludgeon to death his spouse is unlikely to be held culpable as an accomplice. Likewise, "[a] clerk in a clothing store who sells a dress to a prostitute knowing that she will be using it in plying her trade is not guilty of aiding and abetting. The sale makes no difference to her illegal activity. If the clerk didn't make the sale, she would buy, at some trivial added expense in time or money, an equivalent outfit from someone ignorant of her trade. That is where the requirement of proving the defendant's desire to make the illegal activity succeed cuts off liability. The boost to prostitution brought about by selling a prostitute a dress is too trivial to support an inference that the clerk actually wants to help the prostitute succeed in her illegal activity. If on the other hand he knowingly provides essential assistance, we can infer that he does want her to succeed, for that is the natural consequence of his deliberate act."[19] However, another federal judge has observed, "One who sells a gun to another knowing that he is buying it to commit a murder would hardly escape conviction as an accessory to the murder by showing that he received full price for the gun."[20]

The language of the statute speaks of "acting with intent" but that does not mean that liability arises only if the co-principal's *mens rea* fits the definition of "intent" under Sec. 6.03(a). The Court of Criminal Appeals has upheld an involuntary manslaughter[21] conviction where one party intentionally assisted another in committing a reckless act.[22]

Recall that when one acts recklessly, he or she intends the conduct but not the result. In another case, the mother of a 15-year-old girl was found guilty of manslaughter when she purchased heroin and allowed another individual to inject the substance into her and her daughter. The daughter died of an overdose. The court viewed the mother's conduct as passively reckless.[23] But in another case, a manslaughter conviction of an individual who had supplied alcohol to minors at a high school graduation party was overturned.[24] One underage reveler left the party and subsequently crashed his pickup truck, killing two passengers. The appeals court ruled that the facts established that the party host was not acquainted with the youthful drunk driver, did not serve alcohol to him, and was unaware he was intoxicated when he left her premises. "However misguided or wrong [defendant's] judgment was in allowing the party and participating in it, we will not punish her for what she did not have the intention of doing and did not do."[25]

Post-crime Assistance

What about Monica in the opening scenario? What is her level of criminal responsibility? Or, how about Carmine who assists Guido, a professional hit man, in disposing of one of his victim's corpse? To use the traditional terminology, both are accessories after the fact. Monica provided assistance to the bank robbers after the event. She had no prior knowledge that the crime was going to be committed. Similarly, assuming Carmine knew nothing of the initial killing of the deceased, he is a mere post-crime accessory.

While early American law treated such individuals as accomplices, today Texas follows the modern view that post-crime assistance is generally a distinct offense. Neither Monica nor Carmine are assisting or aiding the commission of the underlying offenses because the offenses have already been committed. Their respective conduct, providing a hideout and assisting in disposal of a body, are not elements of the crimes of robbery and murder. Thus, any criminal violation by Monica or Carmine will have to be found elsewhere in the Penal Code. Typical offenses that might relate to individuals who serve as after-the-crime accessories are tampering with or fabricating evidence (Sec. 37.09), hindering apprehension or prosecution (Sec. 38.05), interference with public duties (Sec. 38.15), resisting arrest, search, or transportation (Sec. 38.03), and abuse of a corpse (Sec. 42.08).

For many years it was considered an offense to fail to report a felony. This crime was known as **misprision of a felony**. The concept fell into disuse but has been revived in recent years, at least in limited form. Statutes criminalizing failure to report crimes against children are commonplace across the country, including in Texas. Texas is also among the states that declare it a misdemeanor to fail to report to authorities the occurrence of a violent felony[26] or to fail to report existence of a dead body.[27] These statutes have been applied to individuals who knowingly provide post-crime assistance to other offenders.

Accomplice Testimony Rule

As a safeguard against unjustified prosecution, Texas follows the **accomplice testimony rule**. The rule, located in Art. 38.14 Code of Criminal Procedure, provides that "a conviction cannot be based on the testimony of an accomplice unless corroborated by other evidence tending to connect the defendant with the offense committed." This rule comes into play in the law of parties. To convict an individual as a party to an offense based on the conduct of another person, the state must present evidence other than the testimony of the primary offender or the co-conspirator.

CRIMINAL LIABILITY OF CORPORATIONS

Introduction

From the 1930s until the 1950s, the New York-centered organized crime syndicate operated an entity which the media dubbed "Murder, Inc." Murder, Inc., was the enforcement arm of the syndicate. Syndicate objectives were carried out by killing any associate that proved a hindrance. Contract killers were used to perform the "hits." Contracts had to be approved unanimously by the syndicate's controlling members. Murder-for-hire contracts were issued from various cities throughout the nation. If a killing needed to be completed in Philadelphia, Murder, Inc., would hire someone from Pittsburgh or Chicago and bring them to Philadelphia for a week to study the victim's routine. The hired killers used various means to eliminate their targets—automobile collisions, strangulation, or simply gun them down in the street. Generally, the hoodlums only killed other members of the underworld, such as informants or individuals who had embezzled mob money.[28]

Murder, Inc., of course, was not a true corporation, although superficially it had many of the attributes of a corporation, such as an identified group of "shareholders," a stated business purpose, a board of directors, and a self-sustaining existence. What it lacked was a charter from a state to engage in *lawful* business.

While Murder, Inc., was entirely a criminal syndicate, many real corporations have over the years been held responsible for misconduct, not only through civil suits and regulatory enforcement action but also through the application of the criminal sanction. Criminal liability by corporate officials and corporations has received a high degree of public attention in recent years. Frauds committed in the name of former high-flying corporations such as Enron, WorldCom, Tyco, and HealthSouth have dominated the pages of financial newspapers for a decade. Likewise, high-profile entrepreneurs such as Kenneth Lay, Jeffrey Skilling, and Martha Stewart caught the public's attention for their alleged "white collar" criminal activity. Often lost in the sensationalism, at least for the student of criminal law, is any discussion of the criminal liability of the business entities themselves, separate and apart from the crimes of corporate officers. As to the latter, an individual, whether Wall Street financier or street thug, is responsible for his or her own violations of the penal statutes of the state. If a corporate executive steals company assets or defrauds others through unlawful business practices, the executive is as criminally culpable as the thief who might burglarize that executive's suburban mansion.

However, this section of the text will explore the liability of business enterprises themselves. Is Stardoe Coffee Company, Inc., criminally responsible if a customer becomes ill after drinking a cup of its coffee? What if the customer dies? Can the coffee company be prosecuted for criminal homicide? Is Stardoe Coffee Company, Inc., criminally liable if its delivery truck strikes and kills a pedestrian crossing the street? Is Stardoe Coffee Company, Inc., subject to criminal prosecution if its regional manager advertises a 50 percent off-sale, then sells cups of coffee for their normal price? When does the conduct of a Stardoe employee create criminal liability for the company?

The Nature of Corporations

To understand the issues surrounding the criminal liability of corporations, it is helpful to understand the nature of a corporation and how it differs legally from a natural person. A **corporation** is an organization formed with state governmental approval to act as an artificial person to carry on business, which can sue or be sued, and (unless it is not-for-profit) can issue shares of stock to raise funds with which to start a business or increase its capital.[29] Issuance of stock of less than $300,000, with no public solicitation and relatively few shareholders, is generally exempt from extensive state or federal regulation. Larger stock offerings or those offered to the general public require approval by the federal Securities and Exchange Commission (SEC) after close scrutiny and approval of a public prospectus which details the entire operation of the corporation. Corporations can range from very small ones such as Pat's Corner Liquor Store, Inc., to the world's largest company, Wal-Mart, Inc.[30]

Note that a corporation is an "artificial person." It is this characterization that both places the entity under the coverage of the penal law and at the same time creates difficulties in holding it accountable. As a "person," the corporation is subject to legal rules, but being artificial means it is incapable of acting on its own, incapable of forming a culpable mental state in the normal manner, and incapable of being executed or incarcerated as punishment.

Historical Liability of Corporations

In England, corporations were created by royal charter. The British law developed early on that a corporation was not subject to the criminal law in its corporate capacity but that individual employees could be criminally prosecuted.[31] This rule was not adhered to in America, however. While prosecutions of corporations were rare in the nineteenth century, the few states that had considered the issue reasoned that if corporations were civilly responsible for misconduct, no reason existed to excuse them from prosecution for criminal misconduct as well. When the U.S. Supreme Court first considered the question in 1909, the justices had no difficulty in concluding that Congress had the power to subject corporations to the federal criminal law for acts of their agents which benefited the company.[32] In the same year, a New York court ruled that a corporation could be held criminally accountable for manslaughter.[33] As time passed, most states extended the application of their criminal codes to corporations. Texas became the sole holdout, refusing to hold corporations criminally accountable until 1974 when the newly enacted Penal Code added provisions creating corporate criminal liability.[34]

While this text is primarily concerned with traditional forms of criminal law, one needs to recall that in modern times the criminal sanction has been expanded well beyond *malum in se* behavior. This is of particular importance where corporate criminality is concerned. While much corporate criminal liability arises when a corporation runs afoul of regulatory-type statutes, in rare circumstances corporations and other business associations can be held culpable for many of the same Penal Code offenses that individuals commit.

Traditional Criminal Offenses

Perhaps the most difficult area of the criminal law to apply to artificial persons is traditional *malum in se* offenses such as murder, theft, robbery, and arson. It is difficult to conceive of a reasonable set of facts whereby a corporation would be held criminally culpable for purposeful crimes against person such as assault and murder. Likewise, by the very nature of the offense it is impossible for a corporation to commit perjury or sexual assault.[35]

The drafters of the Texas Penal Code may have desired to separate those offenses which could be committed only by human offenders from those which could be attributed to corporations and associations. The effort was rooted in distinguishing between the terms "person" and "individual." Sec. 1.07 defines "person" as "an individual, corporation, or association." On the other hand, the statute defines "individual" to mean "a human being who is alive . . . ." However, the Legislature has not been consistent in maintaining this distinction. For example, the relevant Texas Penal Code sections provide that only "individuals" can be victims of assaults, criminal homicides, and kidnappings but all of these offenses, as well as sexual assaults, theoretically can be committed by "persons."

The two prime issues in establishing criminal culpability for a corporation are determining which actions of employees (*actus reus*) are attributable to the corporation and how is the required *mens rea* established. Since an artificial person, such as a corporation, can only act through its agents and employees, any criminal liability of the corporation is going to flow from employee conduct. On the question of attributing criminal responsibility to the corporation, courts use one of two theories. The first approach, which has its origins in tort law, is the concept of *respondeat superior*. This term translates from Latin as "let the master answer." A key doctrine in the law of agency, **respondeat superior** means that a principal (employer) is responsible for the actions of its agent (employee) in the course of their employment. When applied to the idea of criminal responsibility for a corporation, Texas law holds that if an employee, whether menial or executive, acts within the scope of his authority on behalf of the corporation and for the benefit of the corporation, criminal responsibility can be attributed to the corporation (Sec. 7.22). One could argue that a criminal act is never in the scope of an employee's authority unless specifically authorized by senior management. However, that is not the meaning of the concept of scope of employment. Rather, scope of authority simply means the conduct is related to the job. Thus, if Fred the bookkeeper makes false entries into the financial records of the corporation, he is acting within the scope of his authority even though such conduct is obviously not in his job description nor was it explicitly authorized by the board of directors. However, that is not sufficient for the *actus reus*. The conduct also must be for the benefit of the corporation. If Fred makes the fraudulent entries to cover his own embezzlements, the corporation is the victim not the beneficiary of his behavior. But if Fred makes the phony financial entries so the company can avoid paying taxes, then the act is for the benefit of the corporation and becomes an act of the corporation with corresponding corporate criminal liability.

An alternative way of establishing the conduct element of an offense is showing that the criminal behavior is the official policy of the corporation. If the misconduct were performed, authorized, ratified, adopted, or tolerated by a majority of the governing board or a high managerial agent of the corporation, the acts are attributable to the corporation. **High managerial agent** generally means corporate officers or others who are empowered to make corporate policy.[36]

Texas law combines both of the above approaches, holding corporations criminally responsible under the *respondeat superior* theory only as to misdemeanors. For a corporation to be responsible for a felony, a high managerial official or a majority of the board of directors must have "authorized, requested, commanded, performed, or recklessly tolerated" the conduct.[37]

Somewhat more problematic is the *mens rea* requirement. For strict liability offenses this is not a barrier to prosecution. Likewise, if a statute specifies criminal negligence as the culpable mental state, no affirmative authorization by senior corporate personnel is needed since criminal negligence focuses not on what the entity consciously choose to do but rather what it *ought* to have done. But, as one moves up the culpability hierarchy, new difficulties present themselves. Unlike Murder, Inc., the members of which actually voted on the question of whether to kill someone, a corporate board of directors is unlikely to take such a vote, even regarding its strongest competitor! On the other hand, corporate directors and high corporate officers have been known to make conscious decisions to violate certain laws to benefit the corporation. In addition to their own personal culpability, are their actions criminally imputable to the company? The answer is usually "yes". Thus, if the president of the Rustbelt Chemical Company, Inc., decides to cheat vendors on behalf of the corporation, his intentional theft and fraud are attributable to the corporation.

Appellate court challenges to criminal convictions of corporations are few. This suggests that Texas has held corporations criminally responsible in relatively few instances. In one case, a corporation was fined for violating the harassment statute in its bill collection efforts. This case is noteworthy because the culpable mental state, intent, was supplied by low level workers.[38] Intent was also an issue in a case upholding conviction of a corporate owner of an adult bookstore for exhibiting obscene material. In this misdemeanor, pursuant to the statute, the required culpable mental state was supplied by the clerk at the store.[39]

A trucking company was found guilty of criminally negligent homicide as a result of the conduct of one of its drivers.[40] At the time of the conviction, criminally negligent homicide was a misdemeanor. Today, with criminally negligent homicide being designated as a felony, traffic deaths caused by low level employees are unlikely to impose vicarious criminal liability on the corporate employer. In 1985, Texas instituted the nation's first murder trial against a corporately owned nursing home. The corporation and four employees were charged in the death of an 87-year-old resident. After a six-month long trial, the case ended in a mistrial due to a hung jury. The local prosecutor chose not to refile the charges.[41]

In a most unusual case, the Court of Appeals allowed prosecution to proceed against a public school district for tampering with records. The appellate court reasoned that since the word "person" includes an "association" and the term "association" is statutorily defined to include a governmental subdivision, the Penal Code was applicable to governmental entities including school districts.[42]

Assessing Criminal Penalties on Corporations

Suppose that a corporation is found criminally responsible. What is the appropriate penalty to levy? Whereas serious human offenders tend to be incarcerated for their wrongdoings, a corporation, being an artificial person, cannot be placed in prison. Consequently, monetary fines, which are used against human beings in minor cases, are levied against corporations in virtually all instances of criminal guilt. Under Texas statute (Sec. 12.51), the fine levied against a corporation upon a criminal conviction may range up to $50,000 depending on the level of the offense. Under limited circumstances the fine can be doubled.

Serious questions can be raised as to whether a monetary fine can serve the goals of the criminal sanction in every situation. The problem lies in the nature of a corporation. For example, Ford Motor Company has nearly two billion shares outstanding in the hands of hundreds of thousands of shareholders. Each of these shareholders is a proportionate owner of Ford, some owning more than others. Were the company to be fined, the value of each shareholder's proportionate level of ownership would be diminished. If the fine were $100,000, the absolute maximum under Texas law, it would not be noticed by individual shareholders as the amount could be absorbed through the general corporate assets. Does such a fine serve the traditional purposes of the criminal law: deterrence and punishment? How great would a fine need to be to deter the company and others in the industry from misconducting themselves in the future? How high a fine would impose on the company what it deserves as punishment?

Assume a fine of $100 million were imposed. (No jurisdiction currently allows such a high level of fine.) Could the company, which sells about three million motor vehicles a year, recover the fine simply by adding $3.34 to the price of each car? Hardly a deal breaker.

Even if the $100 million were taken from profits without being passed on to consumers, the $100 million would amount to dividends not payable to stockholders. Employee pension plans holding the stock and innocent stock owners around the world would suffer for conduct of the corporation's executives, conduct essentially outside the control of the bulk of stockholders.

But suppose the offending corporation were LMC Auto Parts, Inc. For business ease, Larry, Moe, and Curly operate their auto parts store as a corporation. Last year, the store had total sales of less than $500,000 and each owner drew a salary of about $40,000. A $50,000 criminal fine against the auto parts store would have a strong effect on its operations. The small number of owners who control the company would be hit directly in their respective pocketbooks. Their business practices would certainly be reformed, or the fine might actually force them to close. In the case of a small, closely held corporation, the monetary fine might well serve the purposes of the criminal law.

The foregoing examples are meant to highlight some issues that arise when attempting to apply to artificial persons a system of criminal law designed for natural persons. The difficulty of determining an appropriate punishment level is one reason why Texas prosecutors continue to be reluctant to press criminal charges against corporate entities except in the most egregious of cases. So long as human defendants are available to be prosecuted, the goals of the criminal law can be served easier if maybe not as well.

Criminal Liability of Noncorporate Entities

While the use of the criminal law to artificial persons largely focuses on corporations, the state's penal laws are more broad in application. The same laws that create possible criminal liability for corporations may also apply to partnerships and other business organizations.

Assume the brothers at Delta House are having their annual toga party. The music is loud and goes on into the early morning hours. Neighbors residing near the fraternity house call the campus police. Campus police officers arrive at Delta House and decide to issue a citation for disorderly conduct. Who should be named as the defendant in the citation? Should it be chapter president Hoover? Is he legally responsible for the behavior of his fraternity brothers? Or, should the fraternity as an association be cited? Under the theory that artificial persons are subject to the Penal Code, a persuasive case can be made the Delta House as an organization should be charged with disorderly conduct, not the chapter president. This result would appear to be the most just for all involved. Citing the president might deter members from agreeing to serve as president but will likely do little to deter future loud parties. Citing the fraternity, thereby hitting all members in their wallets, might be a more effective approach.

Notes

1. *See generally* WAYNE R. LAFAVE, CRIMINAL LAW (4th ed. 2003) *and* ROLLIN M. PERKINS & RONALD N. BOYCE, CRIMINAL LAW.

2. Joshua Dressler, *Reassessing the Theoretical Underpinnings of Accomplice Liability: New Solutions to an Old Problem*, 37 HASTINGS L.J. 91, 111 (1985).

3. Mitchell v. State, 2003 Tex. App. LEXIS 5269.

4. Ethel actually commits solicitation of capital murder [§ 15.03], conspiracy to commit capital murder [§ 15.02], and capital murder [§ 19.03(a)(3)].

5. Beardsley v. State, 738 S.W.2d 681 (Tex. Crim. App. 1987).

6. *See, e.g.*, Ransom v. State, 920 S.W.2d 288 (Tex. Crim. App. 1994), *and* Salinas v. State, 163 S.W.3d 734 (Tex. Crim. App. 2005).

7. *See generally* TEX. PENAL CODE § 22.04.

8. Rasberry v. State, 757 S.W.2d 885 (Tex. App.—Beaumont 1988).

9. See TEX. PENAL CODE § 38.07 declaring it an offense for an employee of a correctional institution to knowingly permit or facilitate the escape of a prisoner.

10. TEX. PENAL CODE § 22.011(a)(2)(A).

11. TEX. PENAL CODE § 19.02(b)(3).

12. *See* Mayfield v. State, 716 S.W.2d 509 (Tex. Crim. App. 1986), *overruled in part*, Solomon v. State, 49 S.W.3d 356, 368 (Tex. Crim. App. 2001).

13. TEX. PENAL CODE § 6.04(b)(1). But see Gutierrez v. State, 681 S.W.2d 698 (Tex. App.—Houston [14th Dist.] 1984), adhering to an "ordinary and probable" test.

14. See discussion of felony murder rule in Chapter 5.

15. 458 U.S. 782 (1982).

16. *Id.* at 800.

17. Tison v. Arizona, 481 U.S. 137 (1987).

18. Reece v. State, 521 S.W.2d 633 (Tex. Crim. App. 1975).

19. U.S. v. Zafiro, 945 F.2d 881, 887 (7th Cir. 1991).

20. Backun v. United States, 112 F.2d 635, 637 (4th Cir. 1940).

21. Conduct previously considered involuntary manslaughter is now prosecuted under either the manslaughter (§ 19.04) or intoxicated manslaughter (§ 49.08) statutes.

22. Mendez v. State, 575 S.W.2d 36 (Tex. Crim. App. 1979).

23. Clair v. State, 2006 Tex. App. LEXIS 1661.

24. Henkel v. State, 2001 WL 258624 (Tex. App.—El Paso).

25. *Id.* at *2.

26. TEX. PENAL CODE § 38.171.

27. TEX. PENAL CODE § 37.09(d)(2).

28. *See* www.murderinc.com.

29. A few not-for-profit corporate charters have been issued by the federal government. For example, the American Red Cross, the Boy Scouts of America, and AMTRAK hold federal corporate charters.

30. Adapted from definition of "corporation" found *at* www.law.com.

31. 1 WILLIAM BLACKSTONE, COMMENTARIES *464.

32. New York Central and Hudson River Railroad Co. v. United States, 212 U.S. 481 (1909).

33. People v. Rochester Railway & Light Co., 88 N.E. 22 (N.Y. 1909).

34. See Vaughan & Sons, Inc. v. State, 737 S.W.2d 805 (Tex. Crim. App. 1987), discussing the history of corporate criminality in the state.

35. Civil lawsuits against corporations that are an outgrowth of someone else's criminal acts are fairly common. Lawsuits are often brought against corporate owners of apartment complexes or shopping malls by crime victims, usually robbery or sexual assault victims, claiming the corporate owners provided inadequate security.

36. TEX. PENAL CODE § 7.21(2).

37. TEX. PENAL CODE § 7.22(b).

38. Collection Consultants, Inc. v. State, 556 S.W.2d 787 (Tex. Crim. App. 1977).

39. N.W. Enterprises, Inc. v. State, 1986 Tex. App. LEXIS 11866.

40. *See* Vaughan & Sons, Inc. v. State.

41. *See Mistrial declared after 6 months in murder trial of nursing home*, NEW YORK TIMES, Mar. 26, 1986, at B24.

42. *Ex parte* Austin Independent School District, 23 S.W.3d 596 (Tex. App.—Austin 2000).

CHAPTER 5

Criminal Homicide

BOLO

The reader should be on the lookout (BOLO) for the meaning of the following terms. Knowledge of the meaning of these terms will greatly assist the reader in understanding the primary elements of the chapter.

- Adequate Cause
- American System of classification
- Capital murder
- Criminal homicide
- Criminally negligent homicide
- Depraved heart murder
- Felony murder rule
- Fetal homicide
- First degree murder
- Homicide
- Individual
- Intent-to-cause serious bodily injury murder

- Intent-to-kill murder
- Intoxication manslaughter
- Involuntary manslaughter
- Malice aforethought
- Manslaughter
- Motive
- Murder
- Second degree murder
- Sudden passion
- Suicide
- Voluntary manslaughter
- Year-and-a-day rule

INTRODUCTION

If you were to walk into police headquarters in any large city in Texas, you might well observe a door labeled "Homicide Division." One function that virtually every municipal or county law enforcement agency performs is the investigation of not only known murders but also unattended and suspicious deaths. The law specifies when governmental authorities—the police, the justice of the peace, or the medical examiner—must be notified of a death, and when an inquest into the cause and manner of death must be conducted.[1] While various reasons exist for the government to investigate the death of one of its citizens, a primary goal is to distinguish criminal from noncriminal incidents. If the death is initially believed to have occurred because of the unlawful conduct of another, a full investigation potentially resulting in criminal prosecution will be initiated.

Each year just under one percent of the population of the country dies.[2] According to data collected by the Federal Bureau of Investigation, about 16,000 of those deaths are willful killings amounting to **criminal homicides**.[3] Slightly over that same number are killed annually by intoxicated drivers under circumstances where criminal responsibility may also arise. Further, several more thousand persons are estimated killed in traffic incidents due to driver negligence. An unknown number are killed in other acts of negligence, such as work-related events, hunting incidents, and the like. And, several hundred die under justifiable circumstances, such as self-defense or police use of deadly force. Each of these incidents requires an inquiry to confirm or reject that a criminal act has taken place.

In Texas, about 1,400 murders and nonnegligent manslaughters occur each year.[4] Drinking drivers are involved in traffic collisions that cause the death of over 1,600 individuals, while other traffic crashes produce nearly 2,000 fatalities.[5]

Police agencies are thus tasked with sorting which of these deaths violate the criminal laws of the state, hence, the label "Homicide Division." A **homicide** is defined as one human being causing the death of another human being. The police role is to investigate all homicides and determine which are *criminal* homicides. Just because someone dies as a result of the conduct of another person does not mean a criminal homicide has occurred. Recall that criminal liability arises when the proscribed conduct is paired with a culpable mental state. Accordingly, many homicides are deemed not criminal because the necessary culpable mental state is missing.

Consider two automobile–pedestrian encounters. In the first, an eight-year-old child chasing a baseball darts out in front of an automobile. The driver has no time to stop. The child is struck and killed. In the second, an eight-year-old child walking along the shoulder of a country lane is struck and killed by an intoxicated driver. Neither of these deaths was purposely brought about, yet each was a homicide. The police will investigate each. But, criminal charges will only be filed in the second example because the Penal Code holds intoxicated drivers responsible for deaths they cause regardless of the driver's culpable mental state. This death is a *criminal* homicide while the first is not. The first is simply considered an unfortunate and sad accident.

It should be noted that the legal definition of homicide excludes some conduct that the law may handle in another manner. If an individual intentionally poisons his neighbor's dog, a death is purposely caused by a human but the act fails to meet the definition of a homicide because the victim was not a human being. Similarly, if the neighbor's dog attacks the individual and kills him, no homicide has technically occurred because while the victim is a human, the killer is not.[6] Finally, a **suicide** is not considered a homicide because it lacks the requirement of death caused by another, since the perpetrator and victim are the same individual.

COMMON LAW CRIMINAL HOMICIDE

As with most criminal offenses in the United States, the British Common Law shaped the elements of criminal homicide. Over time, the Common Law came to recognize two forms of criminal homicide: murder and manslaughter.

Common Law Murder

Murder under the Common Law was defined as the unlawful killing of another human being with malice aforethought. Initially, the offense of murder was applied only to premeditated killings. But over the course of years, the law came to recognize that the death of a human can occur under a variety of circumstances, which, while factually different, should be treated similarly under the law. As a result, an unlawful killing could occur under a range of situations from a purposeful act to an inadvertent death during the commission of another felony.

The elements of Common Law murder included **malice aforethought**. The words "malice" and "aforethought" have historically been defined in law somewhat differently than their ordinary, everyday meanings. A dictionary definition of "malice" connotes hatred, ill will, spite, or disrespect toward another. As one Texas court put it some years ago, malice is "that condition of the mind which shows a heart regardless of social duty and fatally bent on mischief."[7] If Cain intentionally kills Abel because Cain believes Abel cheated him, the murder is certainly motivated by malice within the common meaning of the word. But if Cain purposely kills Abel to collect as beneficiary of a life insurance policy, does malice exist? Certainly not in the everyday meaning of the term. Cain may hold no ill will toward his victim but is simply using his death for economic gain. But Cain's conduct would be considered malicious under the traditional law of murder because he engaged in the conduct with intent to harm Abel.

A similar definitional issue arises with the notion of "aforethought." This term is often equated to the idea of premeditation. Certainly long-term planning or lying in wait before killing someone would constitute premeditation. However, the legal view of the concept is much broader. Assume Jack is committing a robbery of a fast food restaurant. Ronald, the cashier, attempts to telephone the police. Jack fires his pistol directly at Ronald and kills him. Was Jack's decision one of malice aforethought? Did Jack act in a premeditated manner? Or, was the decision to kill Ronald made on the spur of the moment? While hundreds of years ago the assumption may have been that murder must be planned well ahead of the event, such a rigid view no longer survives in modern times.

Common Law Manslaughter

The absence of malice is the factor that traditionally distinguished **manslaughter** from murder. In a practical sense, however, manslaughter came to cover any unlawful killing that did not meet the definition of murder.[8] A killing was "unlawful" if it was not justified or excused. Thus, through a process of elimination, if Jack killed Jill, the initial question would be whether the conduct met the elements of murder. If the answer were in the negative, the next question would be whether the killing was justified or excused under existing principles of law. If the answer here is also no, then Jack has committed manslaughter. Jill's death was not murder but it was unlawful, hence manslaughter.[9]

Note that all Common Law criminal homicides involved some form of purposeful conduct on the part of the offender. The Common Law did not punish deaths caused by negligence.

AMERICAN SYSTEM OF CLASSIFICATION

Murder and Manslaughter

Were you to examine the penal codes of the 50 states and the federal government regarding criminal homicide, you would find that most criminal homicide statutes are structured along the so-called **American System of classification**. The American System, while greatly influenced by the English Common Law structure, developed in reaction to the British "all or nothing" approach wherein a death either fit the rigid definitions of murder and manslaughter or did not. But, American courts and legislatures recognized that some intentional killings were more blameworthy than others. Accordingly, the idea of degrees of criminal homicide began to take hold. The notion of degrees of murder originated in Pennsylvania in 1794.[10] The concept quickly gained popularity and became widespread during the codification movement of the nineteenth century. Over the years, the model has been expanded in many states to degrees of manslaughter as well. The American System of classifying criminal homicides is well known to the public because California and New York, where most movies and television shows are produced, follow this approach. Talk of "first degree murder" and "murder two" permeate the cinema and television crime dramas.

Under the modern version of the American System, first degree murder covers intent-to-kill murders described above. Many jurisdictions have dropped the malice aforethought element, doing by statute what the courts already have been doing slowly through their generous definition of the concept. Influenced by the approach taken in the Model Penal Code, these states simply rely on the culpable mental state of purposefulness. If the killing were purposeful (intentional), the offense is murder in the first degree. The simplicity of this approach is the recognition that what society seeks to prevent, or punish as the case may be, is deliberate killing of its members. Regardless of whether those killings are based on prior planning or the existence of evilness in one's heart, the result is the same: a human being's life has been taken purposely.

Not surprisingly, the dividing line between first degree murder and second degree murder (and in a few states, third degree murder) is not drawn at precisely the same place in every jurisdiction. Under most modern statutes, **first degree murder** encompasses only intent-to-kill type murders and so-called felony murders involving inherently violent felonies. Some jurisdictions use the first/second division to distinguish between purposeful murders that are truly premeditated and those that are not. An intentional killing where the offender actually plans out the crime would be a first degree murder, whereas the spontaneous decision to kill would fall in the second degree category. Others use the categorization to distinguish capital from noncapital criminal homicides.

Second degree murders tend to encompass all other purposeful killings. Some statutes simply define murder, state what conduct constitutes first degree murder, and then assert that "all other murders" are second degree. Other statutes explicitly place no-intent-to-kill behavior and depraved heart behavior in the second degree category. Illinois, in a somewhat unique fashion, uses second degree murder to cover what most states include in voluntary manslaughter.[11]

The effective difference in first and second degree murder is the range of possible punishment. First degree murder is commonly life, life without parole, up to 99 years imprisonment, or death, while second degree murder penalties usually top out with a maximum of 30 years imprisonment.

American jurisdictions generally have divided manslaughter into two forms, voluntary and involuntary, with differing punishments.[12] **Voluntary manslaughter** is defined as a purposeful killing under the influence of a sudden rage of passion arising from adequate provocation. With voluntary manslaughter, the law is recognizing that human nature sometimes causes individuals to do things they might not have done had they thought the matter out. Indeed, emotions can override clear, rational decision making. While a killing under such an emotional circumstance will not be excused, the level of blameworthiness is less than that of a premeditated murder.

Romeo comes home and finds his wife Juliet engaged in sexual intercourse with Paris. Enraged at the betrayal of his wife and Paris, Romeo beats Paris to death with the bedroom lamp. Has Romeo committed murder? Or, does Romeo's conduct only constitute voluntary manslaughter?

For Romeo's intentional killing to be considered voluntary manslaughter instead of murder, it must meet several criteria:

1. Did adequate provocation exist for Romeo's conduct?
2. Did Romeo kill the individual who provoked him?
3. Did the killing arise from the heat of passion?
4. Did a causal connection exist between the provocation and the killing?

Other Forms of Voluntary Manslaughter

Some, but not all, jurisdictions have used the crime of voluntary manslaughter to cover incidents of so-called imperfect self-defense. Normally, an individual is not blameworthy for murder if he or she acts in self-defense (see Chapter 15—General Defenses and Justification). But, what if in an act of self-defense the individual overreacts or otherwise engages in unreasonable behavior. Bart attacks Terry in an attempt to commit a strong-arm robbery. Unknown to Bart, Terry is a professional wrestler and easily thwarts Bart's effort. But instead of simply subduing Bart until the police arrive, Terry continues to beat him. Bart dies from the beating. Assuming Terry's response was excessive and unreasonable under the circumstances thereby forfeiting his justification defense, Terry would be held for some level of manslaughter in many states. Similarly, without legal justification, Dick, a police officer, is beating a prisoner in his custody. In the struggle the prisoner manages to gain control of Dick's nightstick. In an attempt to protect himself, the prisoner begins striking Dick. Dick, now fearing for his life, draws his pistol and shoots and kills the prisoner. Dick's conduct is not justified because he was the initial unlawful aggressor in the incident. Both Terry and Dick have committed voluntary manslaughter. They have intentionally killed another individual but lack the element of malice in their acts.

Involuntary Manslaughter

Involuntary manslaughter is the catch-all term for other unlawful killings. Whether lethal conduct is involuntary manslaughter is determined largely through the process of elimination—that is, if a death does not fit the elements of murder or voluntary manslaughter but is also not justified (e.g., self-defense) nor excused, an involuntary manslaughter has occurred. Looked at another way, involuntary manslaughter is an unintended death resulting either from the commission of an unlawful act or from criminally negligent behavior in performing a lawful act.

Some states further divide unlawful act involuntary manslaughter by whether the fact situation involves *malum in se* behavior or merely *malum prohibitum* behavior. Recall that *malum in se* is conduct that is viewed as evil in itself. The best example of unlawful act involuntary manslaughter with the *malum in se* component is the intoxicated driver who inadvertently kills another person. The law would excuse the accidental death except for the fact that the driver was committing an unlawful act at the time, driving under the influence.[13] But consider Dana who is driving well within the speed limit when her vehicle strikes and kills a pedestrian who steps off the curb without looking. Investigation reveals that Dana was not in possession of her operator's license at the time of the incident. She was committing an unlawful act at the time of the event (driving without a license), but the act was *malum prohibitum*. Should her lack of a driver's license elevate an accident to involuntary manslaughter? In most jurisdictions the answer would be no because no causal connection exists between the death and the absence of the piece of paper in her purse.

The other form of involuntary manslaughter involves negligent behavior while engaged in otherwise lawful conduct. Negligence is frequently the basis for tort suits. A person has breached a duty of care owed to another and injury has resulted. Thus, a civil suit arises when a driver strikes another motor vehicle and damages the automobile or injures the fellow motorist. What if the victim motorist is killed? Should criminal charges be forthcoming or should the matter simply be considered an accident? This issue bedeviled the Common Law and continues to be a difficult issue for modern jurisdictions that seek to expand the law of criminal homicide beyond intentional acts. The Common Law, and accordingly American jurisdictions adhering to its traditional principles, punish as involuntary manslaughter certain, but not all, negligent deaths.

Modern law recognizes that more than ordinary negligence—the standard for civil liability—is needed for criminal responsibility. Where the states disagree is whether the offender must be aware of the risky nature of his act (recklessness) or merely engage in a substantial deviation from the level of care the ordinary person would exercise under the circumstances. In many jurisdictions the risk must also be one related to the possibility of serious bodily injury or death.

One practical outgrowth of the ambiguity in defining criminal negligence has been the reluctance of prosecutors to pursue cases of involuntary manslaughter through negligence. Only the most egregious cases get filed. Some would argue that many deaths in industrial settings where safety regulations are violated should be prosecuted as involuntary manslaughter. Others assert that nursing home deaths where the staff fails to care for the deceased appropriately should be considered as involuntary manslaughters. While a few such cases are filed each year, many more possible prosecutions arise but are handled as civil suits. Is society's interest sufficiently served using the civil justice system?

Today, Texas is one of only six states that do not use some variation of the American System to classify the levels of criminal homicide.[14] Instead, the Texas criminal homicide statutory forms are influenced by the structure within the Model Penal Code. For example, Texas does not utilize the idea of degrees of murder. Prior to 1974, the Penal Code did distinguish between murders with malice and murders without malice but did not refer to them as degrees of murder. Also, over the course of years, Texas has used the terms "voluntary manslaughter" and "involuntary manslaughter" in its criminal homicide laws. Currently, neither term is an accurate label within the Texas Penal Code.

ISSUES IN CRIMINAL HOMICIDE

Introduction

Before discussing the elements of criminal homicide in Texas, it will prove useful to consider several issues and terms. In many instances these issues arise regardless of the level of homicide or the particular definition of the offense.

Motive

Alan is found shot to death. Homicide detectives respond to the scene and launch an investigation. Since the facts indicate a criminal homicide, not a suicide, the detectives will attempt to identify possible suspects. The standard protocol for this task is to determine who had a reason, a motive, to kill Alan. Logically, humans kill other humans only when they perceive they have a good reason. Determine who has the reason to kill another and a suspect can be identified. Use of motive as an investigative tool is not always productive. If Alan is found dead in his home under circumstances indicating he knew his killer, establishing motive will likely be quite helpful. If, on the other hand, Jack, a clerk in a liquor store, is killed in a robbery, the motive is obvious but of scant use in identifying the offender. The reason for the killing was to cover the robbery but without knowing the identity of the robber, determination of the motive is of little use.

In addition to its use as an investigative guide in cases of criminal homicide, motive can be important for several reasons when a case goes to court. A prosecution of murder rarely gets very far without the question of the killer's motive arising. Indeed, the issue of motive so permeates the law of murder that it is easy to believe it is an important element of the offense. In fact, evidence of motive is nearly always presented during a murder trial, yet motive is an actual element of the offense that must be proven in only a few forms of criminal homicide. More commonly, the prosecutor presents evidence of motive to establish that the killing was intentional, not accidental. Additionally, evidence of motive is put forward as a trial strategy to satisfy the innate curiosity of the jury.

Assume investigators charge Barry with Alan's death. Without additional facts we do not know whether Barry's conduct is a murder, a noncriminal accident, or some level of criminal homicide between these two poles. How might the district attorney show the killing was intentional and, therefore, murder? Surrounding facts of the killing might raise inferences of purposeful behavior. An eyewitness or multiple shots fired would be helpful in establishing an intentional act as might the existence of forensic evidence. But, lacking such evidence the prosecutor can fall back on motive.

Barry admits the shooting but claims the shooting was accidental. Evidence shows that the day before his death Alan had terminated Barry's employment as an executive at Alan's company. Would that give Barry a motive to kill Alan? Or maybe Alan was having a sexual fling with Barry's girlfriend. Does that raise an inference that the shooting was intentional? Such motives would be used by the district attorney in an effort to convince a jury that Barry acted intentionally and was culpable for murder.

Suppose the investigation reveals that Barry was not acquainted with Alan but shot him because Paul paid Barry $10,000 to kill Alan. Now the motive (the monetary payment) not only establishes that Barry acted intentionally but also elevates the crime to a capital offense in Texas and many other states. The monetary gain Barry received becomes an element of the offense that must be established beyond a reasonable doubt if Barry is to be convicted of the capital crime. In this scenario, proving motive serves a dual purpose: establishment of the culpable mental state and establishment of an element of the offense of capital murder.

Finally, suppose you were a member of Barry's jury. The prosecutor demonstrates that Barry purposefully killed Alan but never introduces a single bit of evidence about the reason Barry committed the act. Wouldn't you find that odd? Certainly you would. Human curiosity wants to know "what happened and why." Prosecutors realize that winning jury support includes satisfying this curiosity, even if no legal requirement exists to tell the complete story of the case. In some instances, the motive in the case may be bizarre and irrational. For example, notorious convicted killer Charles Manson claimed that his motive for orchestrating several murders in Southern California in 1969 was to start a race war. He was motivated to this effort by listening to record albums of The Beatles. Similarly bizarre was a claim, later refuted by an FBI profiler, that David Berkowitz, New York City's "Son of Sam" killer in the mid-1970s, was motivated to kill several young women because his neighbor's dog told him to do so.

Corpus Delicti Revisited

Recall from Chapter 3 that when the prosecution seeks to use a confession as the basis of guilt, it is required to establish the *corpus delicti* of the crime. Factual establishment of the *corpus delicti* of a criminal homicide is often accomplished by proving the existence of the dead body under circumstances indicating a criminal act.

Suppose the killer disposes of the victim's body so that it is never recovered. Is a criminal homicide prosecution still possible? Both logic and law tells us that the answer is yes in the overwhelming number of American jurisdictions that have considered the matter.[15] If the rule were otherwise, killers would be encouraged to dismember or otherwise dispose of their victims' corpses in order to escape sanction. Clearly, society would not want to encourage such behavior. This public policy is reflected in the law as well where numerous successful prosecutions have been had without physical discovery of the deceased's corpse.[16] However, Texas appears to follow the rather curious rule that discovery of the body is necessary to establish the *corpus delicti* when a confession is offered in evidence but is not necessary if no confession is presented in the case.[17]

Who Is a Human Being?

Suppose that Bart, in a fit of rage, stabs his pregnant girlfriend Julie. The knife thrust instantly kills the fetus although Julie is only injured. Does the law of homicide apply to the death of the fetus? Would it matter if the injured fetus were born alive and then died?

The Common Law rule and the view initially adopted in the United States required the fetus to be born alive to fall within the scope of the law of criminal homicide. Case law generally required that the baby be viable, capable of existence independent of the mother. This required proof that the child was born alive and breathed on its own.

The "born alive" rule became complicated by the famous 1973 Supreme Court decision in *Roe v. Wade*.[18] The *Roe* case challenged the constitutionality of the Texas criminal abortion statute. The Supreme Court struck down the statute and said a right to privacy limits the authority of a state to criminalize a woman's qualified right to terminate her pregnancy. To date, efforts of various religious organizations and political interest groups to encourage the high court to overturn the *Roe* decision as well as efforts to amend the Constitution to ban abortions have been unsuccessful.

What have been successful in the last decade are state efforts to expand criminal homicide and assault laws to cover unborn fetus. Many jurisdictions have concluded that it is possible to extend coverage of criminal homicide statutes to the unborn so long as consensual medical abortions are not criminalized. The federal government and about two dozen states, including Texas, extend their penal code coverage to unborn fetus. The Texas statute [Sec. 1.07(26)] defines **individual** as "a human being who is alive, including an unborn child at every stage of gestation from fertilization until birth." Texas lawmakers have been careful to craft the statutes to avoid conflicting with the *Roe* decision. For example, Sec. 19.06 specifically excludes deaths caused by lawful medical procedures from the scope of coverage of the criminal homicide offenses.

In 2004, Scott Peterson was convicted in California of killing his wife Laci and their unborn son Conner. Peterson received the death penalty because he killed more than one individual—his wife and the unborn child—during the same transaction. The Peterson case, which received nationwide attention, prompted Congress to enact legislation clarifying that the mother and the fetus are separate persons for the purposes of federal criminal law.[19] In jurisdictions, such as Texas, which extend the coverage of the law to fetus, the death of mother and fetus would be two homicides. By default, intentional killing of a pregnant female potentially becomes capital in Texas, assigning the death penalty for more than one murder during the same course of conduct. In the first case to present the question, the Court of Criminal Appeals upheld a capital murder conviction of an individual who intentionally killed a female who was four to six weeks pregnant. The fetus was reportedly only one-half a centimeter long.[20]

Application of the criminal law to unborn fetus creates some challenging evidentiary problems. Suppose Jamal is driving while intoxicated (DWI). He crashes into a car driven by Rita, a pregnant female. Rita is seriously injured. At the hospital, Rita delivers a stillborn baby. Is Jamal criminally responsible for the child's death? In this example, the district attorney would have to establish that the wreck caused the baby's death. To do so, the prosecutor would first have to establish that the fetus was alive at the time of the collision.[21,22] If the child were already dead at the time, there is no criminal homicide. Assuming the state can clear this hurdle, the prosecutor would then have to establish beyond a reasonable doubt that Jamal's conduct—the collision—not some independent event caused the fetus to expire. While forensic medicine has made great strides in recent years, making a post-mortem determination of the viability of a fetus at a given time can prove difficult.

While engaged in a residential burglary, Roger encounters the homeowner Martha. In an effort to make good his escape he stabs Martha with a pair of scissors. Unknown to Roger, Martha is pregnant. The stab wound causes the death of the fetus. Is Roger culpable for the death of the fetus even though he did not know that Martha was pregnant?

One curious result of crafting **fetal homicide** statutes that do not conflict with the *Roe* case involves exempting the mother from the law's coverage. Texas and several other jurisdictions explicitly state that their respective homicide statutes do not apply to a pregnant woman who purposely terminates her pregnancy by killing her fetus.[23] While the intent of the Legislature appears to be to prevent criminal prosecution of a female who obtains an otherwise lawful abortion, the statute is not limited to that factual situation but provides blanket immunity to the mother. Thus, if Pamela, a pregnant female, self-induces an abortion, no matter at what stage of gestation, she is not subject to prosecution. On the other hand, if Pamela gives birth to her child and then immediately suffocates the baby, she has committed a capital offense.[24] Likewise, while mother gets a free pass under the law, father does not! If the father induces an involuntary abortion on the mother, he is subject to criminal homicide charges. Do you think this is fair?[25]

It is difficult for a legislative body to anticipate every factual situation that might arise in this new effort to apply the criminal homicide laws to unborn children. Despite the Legislature's best intentions, difficult fact cases may arise. It can be expected that fetal homicide laws may be modified in coming years to prevent their unjust application.

When Is One Dead?

A criminal homicide is not complete until the victim dies. But what is death? Consider the individual who suffers a blow to the head and ceases breathing. Is he dead? What if CPR is administered and the individual begins to breathe again. Was he dead during the period before the CPR?

While individual human cells, for example skin, are dying all of the time, the law is concerned with irreversible death of the entire human organism. Medical science was far from developed when the Common Law was first faced with determining when an individual was legally dead. Accordingly, our English ancestors relied on what they could observe. A person was considered legally dead with the cessation of the natural beating of the heart. This became known as clinical death. Such a rule did not anticipate use of mechanical life support systems, implanting of artificial hearts, and other miracles of modern medical science. If a crime victim is placed on life support, how could death ever be determined?

Fortunately, statutory enactments have largely resolved this problem. Forty states and the District of Columbia have adopted either the Uniform Determination of Death Act (UDDA) or a substantially similar law.[26] The Texas statute for death determination, found in Sec. 671.001 of the Health & Safety Code, is similar to the UDDA.

This approach codifies the Common Law standard of clinical death and adds to that definition so-called biological death, the cessation of brain function. Note that either definition is legally sufficient. As to the second definition, the requirement of cessation of the functioning of the entire brain including the stem means that a person in a coma or persistent vegetative state is not dead for the purposes of the law.

Medical personnel who make death determinations in adherence to this law are not criminally or civilly liable for their actions. However, the death determination must be made in compliance with accepted medical standards. Thus, if Dr. John makes a death determination while intoxicated, he could face manslaughter charges if it were later determined that the now deceased individual did not meet the statutory definition of death at the time the pronouncement was made.

Texas Health & Safety Code

§ 671.001. STANDARD USED IN DETERMINING DEATH

a. A person is dead when, according to ordinary standards of medical practice, there is irreversible cessation of the person's spontaneous respiratory and circulatory functions.

b. If artificial means of support preclude a determination that a person's spontaneous respiratory and circulatory functions have ceased, the person is dead when, in the announced opinion of a physician, according to ordinary standards of medical practice, there is irreversible cessation of all spontaneous brain function. Death occurs when the relevant functions cease.

c. Death must be pronounced before artificial means of supporting a person's respiratory and circulatory functions are terminated.

* * *

§ 671.002. LIMITATION OF LIABILITY

a. A physician who determines death in accordance with Section 671.001(b) or a registered nurse or physician assistant who determines death in accordance with Section 671.001(d) is not liable for civil damages or subject to criminal prosecution for the physician's, registered nurse's, or physician assistant's actions or the actions of others based on the determination of death.

b. A person who acts in good faith in reliance on a physician's, registered nurse's, or physician assistant's determination of death is not liable for civil damages or subject to criminal prosecution for the person's actions.

Causation in Criminal Homicide

As with any offense, the resultant harm must be caused by the offender's conduct. As noted in Chapter 2, while the relationship between the *actus reus* and the harm is usually obvious, such is not always the case. Consider a real instance. Clyde and Fred engage in an argument. Ultimately Clyde shoots Fred. Fred receives medical treatment but is forced to spend the next 20 years in a wheelchair as a paraplegic. Fred dies and the justice of the peace rules that his death is a direct result of the gunshot wound suffered two decades earlier.[27] Did Clyde cause the death of Fred? Should Clyde face criminal homicide charges?

Because of the crudity of medical science at the time, in the thirteenth century the English adopted a rule that the victim of a homicide must die within one year and one day of the infliction of the fatal wound in order for criminal liability to attach.[28] This **year-and-a-day rule** subsequently became part of the early American legal culture. Texas had a curious application of the rule. Until 1974, a statute applied the year-and-a-day rule specifically to deaths from poisoning but was silent as to its application to homicides caused by other means.[29]

In recent years, the rule has fallen into disfavor and has been legislatively or judicially abrogated by the majority of jurisdictions that have considered the issue. As the U.S. Supreme Court has noted,

> The year and a day rule is widely viewed as an outdated relic of the common law . . . . as practically every court recently to have considered the rule has noted, advances in medical and related science have so undermined the usefulness of the rule as to render it without question obsolete.[30]

The modern view is to treat the matter as a pure issue of causation: If the prosecution can prove that the defendant's conduct caused the victim's death, that is sufficient regardless of the amount of time that lapses between the infliction of the wound and the actual death. This is the approach followed in Texas.[31] It should be noted that no statute of limitation exists for the crimes of murder or manslaughter.[32]

TEXAS LAW OF CRIMINAL HOMICIDE

Introduction

Despite the verbiage of Sec. 19.01, the Texas Penal Code criminalizes five, not four, types of homicide.[33] These offenses are the following:

Murder—Sec. 19.02

Capital Murder—Sec. 19.03

Manslaughter—Sec. 19.04

Intoxication Manslaughter—Sec. 49.08

Criminally Negligent Homicide—Sec. 19.05

To a large degree, the prime difference across the various forms of homicide is the culpable mental state of the killer. Sec. 19.01 emphasizes this point. Murder and capital murder focus on intentional or knowing conduct while manslaughter concerns recklessness. In intoxication manslaughter the act of being intoxicated is deemed the equivalent of being reckless. Finally, as its name indicates, criminally negligent homicide involves deaths through criminal negligence. Thus the district attorney is faced with proving a specific *mens rea*, while a defense strategy would be to establish a lower culpable mental state or the entire absence of *mens rea*.

§ 19.01. Types of Criminal Homicide

a. A person commits criminal homicide if he intentionally, knowingly, recklessly, or with criminal negligence causes the death of an individual.

b. Criminal homicide is murder, capital murder, manslaughter, or criminally negligent homicide.

None of the Texas forms of criminal homicide requires proof of premeditation or malice. Nor are there, strictly speaking, any degrees of murder, although the penalty structure uses the term "degree" to refer to the level of felony punishment.

Elements of Murder

Introduction

While capital murder is the most serious offense, its underlying offense is murder. So any discussion of criminal homicide logically starts with examining the law of murder. Murder in Texas exists in three forms: intent-to-kill murder, intent-to-cause-serious-bodily-injury murder, and felony murder.

Intent-to-kill Murder [Sec. 19.02(b)(1)]

Intentionally or knowingly causing the death of an individual is murder. This is the conduct one immediately thinks of in the ordinary course of the use of the term

§ 19.02. Murder

a. In this section:
   1. "Adequate cause" means cause that would commonly produce a degree of anger, rage, resentment, or terror in a person of ordinary temper, sufficient to render the mind incapable of cool reflection.
   2. "Sudden passion" means passion directly caused by and arising out of provocation by the individual killed or another acting with the person killed which passion arises at the time of the offense and is not solely the result of former provocation.

b. A person commits an offense if he:
   1. intentionally or knowingly causes the death of an individual;
   2. intends to cause serious bodily injury and commits an act clearly dangerous to human life that causes the death of an individual; or
   3. commits or attempts to commit a felony, other than manslaughter, and in the course of and in furtherance of the commission or attempt, or in immediate flight from the commission or attempt, he commits or attempts to commit an act clearly dangerous to human life that causes the death of an individual.

c. Except as provided by Subsection (d), an offense under this section is a felony of the first degree.

d. At the punishment stage of a trial, the defendant may raise the issue as to whether he caused the death under the immediate influence of sudden passion arising from an adequate cause. If the defendant proves the issue in the affirmative by a preponderance of the evidence, the offense is a felony of the second degree.

"murder" and is probably the most common variant of the crime. Intentional murder is a result of conduct offense, meaning the actor's conscious objective is to cause the death of another individual.[34] If Juanita stabs Pablo 16 times and he dies, Juanita's conduct will be judged as intending to cause Pablo's death. Note that the issues of malice, premeditation, and motive are not elements of the offense. The prosecution is not required to establish whether the act was pre-planned or the result of a sudden decision. Also, the prosecutor does not need to prove the reason for the killing or whether the actor had an evil intention. All that is necessary is to show that the actor made a conscious decision to produce the death.

Texas law adds the culpable mental state of "knowing" to this traditional category of murder. For knowing murders, the distinction between result of conduct and nature of conduct blurs because awareness of the result of the conduct necessarily entails awareness of the nature of the conduct as well. Murder is committed knowingly when the actor engages in conduct while aware that death is reasonably certain to result from his conduct. To be aware that his conduct is reasonably certain to result in death, the actor must also be aware of the lethal nature of his behavior.[35] This covers several potential situations that might otherwise be missed by a rigid requirement of intent, for example, where the offender does not select a particular victim but his or her conduct brings about the death of an individual. If Paul aims his pistol at Peter and shoots him dead, Paul has certainly intentionally killed Peter. But, if Paul fires his pistol randomly into a crowded room and a bullet strikes and kills Peter, Paul did not intentionally kill Peter but did so knowingly. Paul was aware that his conduct (firing the pistol) was reasonably certain to produce the result (someone's death).

The addition of the culpable mental state of knowing also can cover much, but not all, of what other jurisdictions refer to as **depraved heart murders**.[36] Roy fires several shots from his rifle at a passing passenger train. One bullet strikes and kills a passenger. Although Roy does not necessarily intend to cause a death, his conduct evidences a total disregard for the safety of others and is such that the reasonable person would be aware that the conduct is likely to cause the resultant death. In contrast, if Roy shot at a freight train and the bullet strikes and kills a hobo who is riding in a boxcar, Roy's conduct likely does not rise to the level of knowledge that his conduct would produce the result. In this latter case, Roy would probably be guilty only of criminally negligent homicide.

Intent-to-cause-serious-bodily-injury Murder [Sec. 19.02(b)(2)]

This form tracks the traditional approach that specific intent to kill is not necessary in every murder situation. Rather, the actions of the actor are to cause serious bodily injury. The actor tries to produce one result and a result other than he intended occurs. Assume Joanne is angry at Paul because he comes home drunk. An argument ensues. In a rage, she stabs him with a kitchen knife. The wound proves fatal. Joanne claims that she had no intention of killing Paul. She did intend to cause him serious bodily injury. But, her dangerous act certainly could result in death. Thus, she is responsible for the probable consequences of her conduct through her purposeful act, in this case Paul's death.

The Texas statute restricts this form of murder to acts that are clearly dangerous to human life. The use of the term "clearly dangerous" means that not all intent-to-do-serious-bodily-injury cases that result in a death constitute murder.[37] The definition of serious bodily injury includes permanent disfigurement and protracted loss of body members, neither of which is life-threatening. Thus, for the fatal act to result in a murder conviction, the act must be objectively clearly dangerous.[38] Suppose during a fistfight Mike bites off Evander's ear. Loss of the ear meets the definition of serious bodily injury. But assume further that Evander bleeds to death. Has Mike committed an act "clearly dangerous to human life"? As a practical matter, few factual situations will likely arise where one engages in conduct desiring to cause serious bodily injury and death results, yet his or her conduct was not *clearly* dangerous.[39]

Felony Murder [Sec. 19.02(b)(3)]

Suppose late one night, Juanita, hoping to collect the insurance on her restaurant, sets the restaurant building afire. Unknown to her, Hector, the cook, is working late. He dies in the blaze. Under the Common Law, Hector's unintended death during the commission of any felony could be prosecuted as murder. The logic was that the underlying felony provided the necessary *mens rea*. This so-called **felony murder rule** originally elevated to murder any unintended homicide that occurred during the course of the commission of another felony. The rule developed during the Common Law period to deter the commission of felonies. However, over the years, the volume and types of criminal behavior that have been elevated to felony level has expanded greatly. As a result, several states, including Texas, have placed limits on the application of the felony murder rule.[40]

One should initially separate intended and unintended deaths during felonious acts. Under Texas law, the former, such as the killing of a convenience store clerk during a robbery, would most often be punished as capital murder [Sec. 19.03(a)(2)]. Only the latter, the unintended deaths, fall under the felony murder rule.

The Texas version of the felony murder rule is found in Sec. 19.02(b)(3) displayed above. For an unintended death to raise to the level of murder under the felony murder rule it must meet certain factual criteria. First, the underlying offense must be a felony, any felony except manslaughter and its lesser included offenses.[41,42] Unlike some jurisdictions, Texas does not have a misdemeanor murder rule. A death in the course of commission of a misdemeanor could, depending on the circumstances, be treated as manslaughter. Second, the death must be related to the commission of the felony either by being "in furtherance" of the offense or "in the immediate flight" from the crime. This requirement would appear to take incidental deaths from under the rule. Roger is passing a forged check at the bank. During the transaction the bank teller has a heart attack and dies. Roger likely is not culpable for the teller's death even though the death occurred during commission of the felony of forgery. The death was not in furtherance of the commission of the crime. Additionally, the statute requires an act "clearly dangerous to human life." Suppose that Justin is committing a bank robbery. He hands the bank teller a note saying, "Your money or your life." He has no gun or other weapon, only the threatening note. The bank teller keels over and dies of a heart attack. Robbery is a violent and dangerous felony in the abstract, but not in this instance. Here, Justin did not commit an act that was "clearly dangerous to human life," even though his act of presenting a threatening note may well have caused the teller's heart attack and death.[43] Similarly, if Carl is printing counterfeit money in his basement and his two-year-old daughter Brenda stumbles and fatally strikes her head on the printing press, is this murder under the felony murder rule? Probably not as no clearly dangerous act was involved.

On the other hand, an individual's conviction under the felony murder rule was upheld where a burglar and his two partners set fire to a fast food restaurant to cover up their deed. Two firefighters became trapped in the building and died while fighting the blaze.[44] Similarly, an individual with two prior DWI convictions was held to have committed murder when he killed a five-year-old girl while committing a third DWI.[45] A car thief who collided with and killed an innocent motorist while fleeing the police was found to have committed murder under the rule.[46] Each of these individuals engaged in an act clearly dangerous to human life that facilitated the commission of their underlying felony.

Penalty

A conviction for any of the three forms of murder under Sec. 19.02 constitutes a felony of the first degree. Accordingly, the defendant can receive a sentence of between five and 99 years or life in prison and a $10,000 fine.

However, under certain circumstances at the punishment phase of the bifurcated trial the sentencing authority, be it judge or jury, can treat the conviction as a felony of the second degree. In 1993, the Texas Legislature abolished the offense of voluntary manslaughter and made the issue of sudden passion killings a matter of punishment level.[47] Any of the three forms of murder can be reduced from a felony of the first degree to a felony of the second degree for purposes of punishment if the defendant demonstrates the traditional elements of voluntary manslaughter: committing the murder while being under the immediate influence of **sudden passion** arising from **adequate cause**. The jury's decision to reduce the level of the offense must be unanimous.[48] The effect of successfully arguing this point would be to cap possible imprisonment at 20 years, the maximum for a felony of the second degree.

In an effort to guide juries in their decision making, Sec. 19.02(a) defines the operative terms "adequate cause" and "sudden passion." Mere words alone are not sufficient to reduce the murder to a second degree felony. "You're a rotten bastard" is legally insufficient to provoke a person of ordinary temperament. Likewise, a killing in reaction to a racial slur has been held to be murder. However, if words convey a message, such as "I want a divorce because I'm having an affair with your brother," the words might serve as sufficient provocation.

The standard is based on what the ordinary person would do under the same circumstances. Accordingly, if the defendant has a reputation as a "hot head" or of otherwise acting impetuously, the adequacy of the provocation will be judged not by whether he was in fact provoked but whether the reasonable man under the same circumstances would have been provoked.

Should a killing precipitated by uncontrollable road rage be reduced? Does impatience with the driving of others qualify as adequate provocation? Probably not because the reasonable person does not respond to another's poor driving by killing someone![49]

What form of provocation is adequate to cause an individual to kill another? Which behavior constitutes adequate provocation is a jury question. No laundry list of situations exists in the Penal Code. Sudden passion killings have been found in cases where an individual died during mutual combat, a death resulting from a fistfight between two males and the killing of a spouse's lover.

To qualify for the penalty mitigation, the victim of the act must be the provocateur. This is important as the law will not allow the killer to take out his or her rage on innocent parties. Incidents of workplace violence where job stress or other traumatic influences lead an individual to engage in random acts of bloodshed do not qualify for reduction of the severity of the offense. These and other incidents of being angry at the world in general receive little sympathy under the law.

Finally, note that the provocation may not be solely the result of former provocation. This raises questions as to whether the penalty mitigation is available in battered spouse cases. Assume Fred frequently beats his wife Joanne. If Joanne kills Fred during one of the abusive episodes, she has available the punishment mitigation. But suppose after years of abuse Joanne decides she has had enough of Fred. She purchases a pistol and when Fred comes home she shoots him dead. Is this a murder with a first degree felony penalty or a murder with a reduced penalty? Is Joanne's conduct *solely* the result of former provocation? Because of current statutory constraints, evidence of the prior years of abuse would be admissible only if Joanne can establish its relevancy. However, Fred's prior bad acts can be raised if she offered self-defense as her defense.[50]

Elements of Capital Murder

A Person Commits Murder under Sec. 19.02(b)(1)

A widely held belief is that murder that occurs under certain attendant circumstances is a capital offense. Thus, many believe that the killing of a police officer or firefighter, for

§ 19.03. Capital Murder

a. A person commits an offense if the person commits murder as defined under Section 19.02(b)(1) and:
   1. the person murders a peace officer or fireman who is acting in the lawful discharge of an official duty and who the person knows is a peace officer or fireman;
   2. the person intentionally commits the murder in the course of committing or attempting to commit kidnapping, burglary, robbery, aggravated sexual assault, arson, obstruction or retaliation, or terroristic threat under Section 22.07(a)(1), (3), (4), (5), or (6);
   3. the person commits the murder for remuneration or the promise of remuneration or employs another to commit the murder for remuneration or the promise of remuneration;
   4. the person commits the murder while escaping or attempting to escape from a penal institution;
   5. the person, while incarcerated in a penal institution, murders another:
      A. who is employed in the operation of the penal institution; or
      B. with the intent to establish, maintain, or participate in a combination or in the profits of a combination;
   6. the person:
      A. while incarcerated for an offense under this section or Section 19.02, murders another; or
      B. while serving a sentence of life imprisonment or a term of 99 years for an offense under Section 20.04, 22.021, or 29.03, murders another;
   7. the person murders more than one person:
      A. during the same criminal transaction; or
      B. during different criminal transactions but the murders are committed pursuant to the same scheme or course of conduct;
   8. the person murders an individual under six years of age; or
   9. the person murders another person in retaliation for or on account of the service or status of the other person as a judge or justice of the supreme court, the court of criminal appeals, a court of appeals, a district court, a criminal district court, a constitutional county court, a statutory county court, a justice court, or a municipal court.

b. An offense under this section is a capital felony.

c. If the jury or, when authorized by law, the judge does not find beyond a reasonable doubt that the defendant is guilty of an offense under this section, he may be convicted of murder or of any other lesser included offense.

example, is a capital crime. That belief is only partially correct. While Texas criminalizes three forms of murder under Sec. 19.02, only the first form [Sec. 19.02(b)(1)], the intent-to-kill form of murder, can elevate to a capital crime.[51] The **capital murder** statute begins with the phrase "[a] person commits an offense if the person commits murder as defined under Section 19.02(b)(1)." For example, this limitation explains why the death of the firefighters at the fast food restaurant fire mentioned earlier was only murder, not capital murder. The deaths of the firefighters were unintended.

As the Texas Criminal Homicide Crimegraph reflects, an intent-to-kill type murder perpetrated under any one of numerous attendant aggravating factors elevates the offense to a capital crime. A review of each aggravating factor is presented below. It should be noted, however, that the factors that elevate a murder to a capital offense in Texas may well be different than the factors used in other states.

Murders a Peace Officer or Fireman [Sec. 19.03(a)(1)]

The definition of who is a peace officer is covered in Art. 2.12 of the Code of Criminal Procedure. Currently, about three dozen different law enforcement-related positions and assignments are named. The statute lists occupations ranging from Texas Rangers to municipal police officers and deputy sheriffs. But the law also covers a number of individuals one might not normally consider to be peace officers, such as game wardens, investigators for the state fire marshal, and officers commissioned by the state Board of Dental Examiners. While their respective day-to-day responsibilities may vary widely, each of the individuals named in the statute as a "peace officer" is employed by a governmental entity.

Curiously, the capital murder statute neither defines nor cross-references to any other definition of "fireman." Presumably the Legislature intends for the law to cover firefighters who work for fire departments. However, unlike law enforcement agencies, many firefighters are not employed by governmental units. These individuals may serve as industrial firefighters at oil refineries or as members of a community volunteer fire department. Indeed, there may be more volunteer firefighters in the state than professional paid firefighters. Texas courts apparently have not been faced with having to define who is a fireman for the purposes of the capital murder statute.

Two other elements of the statute should be noted. First, the peace officer or firefighter must be in the lawful discharge of an official duty. Thus, it is not only the victim's occupation that is important but also that he or she is performing an official function. If Andy becomes involved in a barroom argument with Barney, a deputy sheriff, and Andy purposefully kills Barney, no capital murder occurs. While Barney's occupation may be that of a peace officer, he is not engaged in that function at the time of his death. The second element is the awareness of the fact that the victim is a peace officer or firefighter. Thus, if Rex, a drug dealer, intentionally kills an undercover police officer, the state would have to establish beyond a reasonable doubt that Rex knew his victim was a peace officer. If that element cannot be shown, Rex would be guilty only of murder.

Intentionally Commits Murder during Dangerous Felony [Sec. 19.03(a)(2)]

The most common form of capital murder is an intentional killing during the commission or attempt to commit certain dangerous felonies. A murder during the commission of a robbery or a sexual assault provides the basis for a substantial number of capital murder convictions. Less frequent are killings during arsons and commission of terroristic threats.

The dangerous felony form of the crime is limited to seven felonies which by their very nature present factual circumstances particularly hazardous to human life. Thus, the district attorney must establish that not only did the defendant intentionally or knowingly killed the victim but that the death occurred while the defendant was committing one of the specified felonies.

At first glance, this section would appear to overlap the felony murder rule. Bear in mind, however, that capital murder is limited to intentional or knowing deaths, a restriction not placed on murder under the felony murder rule discussed earlier. Thus if Ted kidnaps and sexually assaults Rita and then purposefully kills her, he has committed capital murder. But suppose he kidnaps and sexually assaults her and than abandons her in the desert at night. Rita dies of hypothermia before she can walk to safety. Has Ted committed murder or capital murder? Did he intentionally kill Rita as Sec. 19.03(a)(2) requires?

Murders for Remuneration [Sec. 19.03(a)(3)]

This subsection, often referred to as the murder-for-hire provision, is actually much broader. Not only does the statute apply to those who purposefully kill because they have been hired to do so, but it also applies to any murder where the perpetrator's motive is financial gain. The term "remuneration" has been defined by the courts to mean economic gain.[52] The state must establish that the reason for the crime was to obtain a benefit or financial settlement such as proceeds from an insurance policy or retirement plan or to inherit money or property.[53] Thus, if Cain kills his brother Abel in order to inherit the family farm, a capital murder has occurred. Likewise, if Martha poisons her aged grandmother because she is the beneficiary under the grandmother's life insurance policy, Martha has committed capital murder. On the other hand, if John kills his wife Marsha in order to be able to marry his secretary Bambi, the motive may be love but that is not a form of remuneration within the meaning of the statute. As for the economic aspect of the statute, note that the offender need not actually receive the compensation but only need to be operating under the promise of such compensation.

As to the murder-for-hire application of the law, the statute applies both to the killer and to the individual who employed the killer. If Sadie pays Barry $500 to kill her romantic rival Trixie, both Sadie and Barry have committed capital murder. The state is not required to rely on the law of parties to establish Sadie's culpability because the statute is explicit on the matter.

Murders while Escaping from Penal Institution [Sec. 19.03(a)(4)]

The capital murder statute applies to those who commit a murder during the escape from a jail or prison unit. By definition, the only person culpable under this subsection would be a prisoner as only a prisoner can escape. The prisoner must be incarcerated in the penal institution. Presumably a murder committed by a prisoner who was being transported outside the institution would fall under another section of the law, such as the prohibition on the murder of a peace officer.

Note that the application of the statute is not limited to victims who are employees of the institution. Bruno, a county inmate, is secretly crawling under the fence at the jail. A pedestrian who is walking by sees Bruno and attempts to alert the guards. Bruno kills the pedestrian to stop his outcry. Bruno commits capital murder.

One bedeviling part of this statute concerns the phrase "while escaping." On the surface, it would appear the Legislature was concerned about killings close in time to an inmate's efforts to breach the prison walls. But, suppose Bobby, an inmate, is successful in exiting the prison. Two weeks later Bobby murders Roger over a matter totally unrelated to his status as a prisoner. Has this murder occurred "while escaping"? Should Roger's death be considered a capital murder? Probably not. Current case law holds that the crime of escape is not a continuing offense.[54] The Court of Criminal Appeals has ruled that once an inmate is outside the confines of the penitentiary, the escape is complete.[55]

Murders Prison Employees or Gang Member [Sec. 19.03(a)(5)]

This section also applies only to individuals who are inmates in city jails, county jails, or state penal facilities. Additionally, under subsection (A), the victim must be an individual who is employed in the operation of the penal institution. While the most likely victim would be a jailer or correctional officer, the phrase is broad enough to cover wardens, the warden's secretary, the librarian, a teacher in the prison, and just about anyone else who is regularly employed in the penal institution.

Under subsection (B), the victim is almost always going to be another inmate. Here motive—the intent to participate in a combination—is a key factor in raising the killing from an ordinary murder. The term "combination," while not otherwise defined in the chapter, apparently refers to organized criminal activity within the correctional institution.[56] Prison gang initiation as well as maintenance of authority over members of a prison gang often involves acts of violence. One inmate killing another inmate to facilitate the operation of the gang becomes a capital offense. The Legislature added this provision after the Court of Criminal Appeals in 1991 refused to expand the meaning of the murder for remuneration section to apply to killings related to the economic interests of prison gangs.[57]

Inmate Murders another Inmate [Sec. 19.03(a)(6)]

Many jurisdictions declare it a capital offense for one prison or jail inmate to murder another inmate. The reasoning for these statutes lies primarily in the notion that by being incarcerated one is limited in his ability to protect himself. Therefore, the government will seek to protect the inmate through the deterrence theory by seriously punishing certain criminal acts perpetrated against the inmate.

Texas law does not go so far as to cover the intentional killing of any inmate by any other inmate. Rather Sec. 19.03(a)(6) creates a capital offense for any murder of an inmate by another who is serving any amount of time for capital murder or murder, or who is serving life or 99 years for aggravated kidnapping, aggravated sexual assault, or aggravated robbery. If Jon is serving a 30-year sentence for murder and purposefully kills his cellmate Bruno, Jon has committed a capital offense under this section. But if Jon is serving 30 years for aggravated robbery and murders his cellmate, Jon has committed only murder because he is not serving life or 99 years for this aggravated robbery conviction. Likewise, if Jon is serving eight years for burglary and murders Bruno, the act is not a capital offense. Does the limitation of this subsection only to certain inmates serving certain specified sentences seem logical or desirable?

Commits Mass Murder or Serial Murder [Sec. 19.03(a)(7)]

Under the 1974 Penal Code, if an offender murdered more than one person in an incident the matter was treated as simply multiple violations of Sec. 19.02. Similarly, a serial murderer, one who killed more than one person over the course of time, was simply facing multiple murder charges. Prompted by a 1984 shooting in a Dallas nightclub in which seven people were murdered, the Texas Legislature the next year amended the capital murder statute to provide the possibility of the death penalty for those who murder more than one person during the same criminal transaction.[58] During the same time frame, several serial murderers, for example, Ted Bundy and Henry Lee Lucas, were receiving nationwide media attention. The Legislature added to the new statute the possibility of death as a penalty for serial murder.

Relatively few prosecutions have occurred under the serial murder provision of the capital murder statute. This is due primarily to the fact that serial murderers often kidnap and sexually assault their victims. Depending on the facts of a particular case and the availability of evidence, it is often easier to prosecute such killers under Sec. 19.03(a)(2) rather than under this subsection. Double jeopardy concerns also arise in the case of a serial murderer. Suppose an individual is charged with killing three individuals during the same scheme or course of conduct, serial murder. The individual is subsequently acquitted by the jury. Does that mean that the constitutional protection against double jeopardy would bar further prosecution for any of the individual murders? Probably so. In contrast, had he been prosecuted for only one of the murders with a capital enhancement based, for example, on kidnapping or sexual assault, his acquittal would leave open the very real possibility of prosecution for the other two killings.

While the phrase "same criminal transaction" would seem to connote deaths close in time and space, the expression "same scheme or course of conduct" is more difficult to define. The concept seems to intertwine motive with some time frame. For example, assume Phillip decides to imitate the Zodiac killer of California from the 1970s. Over the course of four years Phillip kills three persons. After each killing, he sends the local newspaper a poem in which he claims credit. Phillip's murderous conduct would seem to most people to fit within the concept of the "same scheme or course of conduct." But assume over the course of 20 years, Phillip murders three individuals and sends no notes to the media. Does Phillip violate Sec. 19.03(a)(7)(B) under these facts? Or, are these simply three single acts of murder subject to prosecution under Sec. 19.02? The Court of Criminal Appeals has interpreted the term "same criminal transaction" to encompass a continuous and uninterrupted chain of conduct occurring over a very short period of time. The murders must occur in a rapid sequence of unbroken events. Thus the distinction between mass murder and serial murder is the continuity of the killing.[59] Using this distinction, an appeals court in another case ruled that an individual who murdered a woman and then killed her son and his friend over four hours later had committed serial murder, not mass murder.[60]

Murders a Child [Sec. 19.03(a)(8)]

Several Texas penal statutes recognize the special vulnerability that young children have as potential victims of crime.[61] The capital murder law is no exception. Under Sec. 19.03(a)(8), an intentional killing of a child under six years of age is a capital offense. Why did the Legislature draw the line at six? The lawmakers' logic appears to be that children who are six years old have sufficient maturity to appreciate dangerous circumstances, take action to protect themselves, and recognize the importance of reporting to an authority figure if someone seeks to harm them. Accordingly, those under six are in most need of the protection of the capital murder statute.

Under Sec. 1.06, "[a] person attains a specified age on the day of the anniversary of his birthdate." The capital murder statute is applied based on chronological age, not mental age or some other comparative standard. The state bears the burden of proof to establish that the child victim was less than six years old at the time of the murder. The state need not prove that the defendant knew the age of the child at the time of the death.

Suppose the child was five years old at the time of the infliction of the fatal wound but does not die until turning six. Is this murder a capital offense? Texas courts have not had the opportunity to answer that question. But, given that murder, and presumably capital murder, is a result of conduct offense, logic would suggest that the incident would not be capital because the crime is not complete until the victim dies.

Murders a Judge [Sec. 19.03(a)(9)]

The most recent expansion of the capital murder statute is to coverage of judges as victims. The statute appears to cover anyone who acts as a state judge, even a small town mayor who occasionally serves as a municipal court judge. Note that as with the murder of a peace officer or firefighter, the killing must be related to the judge's performance of his or her official duties. Because of this factual requirement, the statute appears to be redundant to Sec. 19.03(a)(2) which declares it a capital offense to murder another in the course of committing retaliation or obstruction. Retaliation or obstruction (Sec. 36.06) prohibits, among other things, harming another due to his or her service as a public servant. The definition of "public servant" under Sec. 1.07 does not explicitly mention judges but rather refers to officers, employees, and agents of government. (Jurors are specifically mentioned in the statute.) Perhaps the Legislature feared that this broad definition was insufficient to cover judicial officers.

What Does Not Constitute Capital Murder

Dallas, Texas, Nov. 22, 1963, President John F. Kennedy dies as a result of an assassin's rifle shot. Lee Harvey Oswald is subsequently arrested and charged with the offense of murder with malice, the highest form of criminal homicide then in force in the state.[62] Oswald never lived long enough for a jury to determine his guilt and whether to sentence him to death. Were the same set of tragic events to occur again today in Texas, the presidential assassin would only be facing a murder charge, not a capital murder charge. While Sec. 19.03(a)(2) elevates to capital the purposeful retaliatory killing of a public servant, the definition of who is a public servant is limited to officials of state and local government.[63] Federal officials are nowhere listed. Under the same logic, the murder of a federal judge does not violate the Texas capital murder statute. Whether the purposeful killing of a federal law enforcement agent is a state capital offense is an open question. A generous interpretation of the term "peace officer" could include FBI, DEA, and other federal law enforcement officers. However, in granting limited arrest authority to certain federal agents, one Texas statute explicitly states that the federal agents "shall not be deemed peace officers."[64] Thus, capital prosecutions of the murder of federal officials within the state appears limited to violations of the U.S. Code.[65]

However, assuming a killing would be in retaliation for their governmental service, the murder of the Governor, a member of the Legislature, or any other public employee ranging from a probation officer to a public school teacher would qualify as a capital offense.

One justice-related occupation not included within the capital murder statute is that of a private security officer. A purposeful killing of a private security officer could become a capital offense, however, if the act occurred during the commission of a robbery or burglary or fell within one of the other qualifying categories under Sec. 19.03.

Unlike other states, the Texas capital murder law is largely unconcerned with the means by which the offense occurs. For example, California declares murders committed through poisoning to be a capital crime as are killings that are particularly heinous in nature and those wherein the victim was tortured.[66] Under Texas law a poisoning would be capital murder only if done under one of the qualifying circumstances such as to gain remuneration.

Penalty

The current penalty upon conviction for capital murder is death or life without parole. Which sentence is meted out depends on several procedural and factual factors. First, the district attorney might choose not to seek death even if the facts of the case fit one of the definitions of capital murder. Perhaps the defendant has no prior criminal record or is mentally deficient. Perhaps the cost of a capital trial would significantly impact the budget of a small county. Or perhaps the available evidence is weak and the prosecutor fears that a jury would acquit rather than risk the possibility of an innocent person being executed.

In most capital cases, either the defendant pleads guilty or opts for a jury trial and, if convicted, jury sentencing.[67] In cases where the death penalty is not sought and the defendant is convicted, the judge automatically imposes a sentence of life without parole.[68] Despite the state's reputation regarding use of capital punishment, in recent years only about 7 to 10 percent of capital murder cases brought to trial resulted in the imposition of the death penalty.[69]

A jury faced with determining the convicted defendant's sentence for capital murder will hear testimony and review evidence in the penalty phase of the bifurcated trial. Whether the defendant receives the death penalty turns on a jury determination of three issues:

1. Is there a probability the defendant will be a continuing threat to society?
2. If the defendant were merely an accomplice to the offense, did the defendant cause or anticipate the victim's death?
3. Do mitigating factors exist that warrant life without parole instead of death?[70]

For a death sentence to be imposed, the jury must be unanimous in answering "yes" to question one and question two, if applicable. To answer "no" to either question, at least ten jurors must so indicate. As to question three regarding mitigating evidence, the jury may not return a "no" answer unless it is unanimous and may not respond "yes" unless at least ten agree. Thus, for the death penalty to be imposed, the jury's decision on questions one and three, and two if applicable, must be unanimous. If the jury is not unanimous in any of its decisions, the trial judge automatically imposes a sentence of life without parole.

Any death sentence must receive a statutorily mandated review by the Court of Criminal Appeals.[71] If the death penalty is upheld, most defendants pursue a series of appeals first to the U.S. Supreme Court and then through the lower federal courts. Since 1976, the period of time between conviction and execution of a defendant has ranged from as little as 248 days to as long as 24 years! The average time spent on death row is slightly more than ten years.[72] When all appeals has been exhausted, the original trial judge sets an execution date.[73]

Texas follows the majority of states and uses lethal injection as its method of execution. Since reinstatement of the death penalty in 1976, Texas has executed over 400 individuals. At any one time, another 400 men and women are on death row processing appeals or awaiting the setting of an execution date. The men's death row is maintained at the Polunsky Unit of the Texas Department of Criminal Justice in Livingston. Women's death row is housed at the Mountain View Unit in Gatesville. Currently, executions are carried out at the Huntsville Unit in downtown Huntsville. Condemned prisoners are transferred to the death house at the Huntsville Unit the day before the scheduled execution.

Manslaughter

Deaths caused through reckless behavior are considered manslaughter and punished as a felony of the second degree (Sec. 19.04). Covered here are circumstances where the defendant intends to engage in the risky behavior but does not intend to produce the death. Although manslaughter is believed not to be a frequently filed charge in

§ 19.04. Manslaughter

a. A person commits an offense if he recklessly causes the death of an individual.

b. An offense under this section is a felony of the second degree.

Texas, murder defendants often seek a jury instruction on manslaughter in an effort to provide the jury an option to convict them of a lesser offense. The cases that are filed often involve traffic-related deaths where the defendant engaged in extremely reckless conduct such as driving 87 mph in a 45 mph zone on a two lane, hilly roadway.[74] In a recent case, a peace officer who was operating his patrol vehicle at night at a high rate of speed and without headlamps or emergency lights illuminated was found guilty of manslaughter after the police car collided with another motorist and killed a passenger in the other vehicle.[75]

Another class of manslaughters involves deaths through careless handling of firearms.[76] Various Texas laws view firearms as dangerous instruments and misuse of a firearm is deemed to be inherently reckless conduct.[77] Thus, assume Mary points a loaded shotgun at Ralph and pulls the trigger, killing Ralph. Mary claims that she did not know anything about guns and had forgotten that the shotgun was loaded. A jury could properly convict her of manslaughter on the basis that her forgetfulness was a conscious disregard of a mortal danger.[78]

Recall that the law of manslaughter occasionally arises in cases where the actor may be justified in using force to defend himself or his property but exerts more force than is permitted under the law and an unintended death occurs. Or where the defendant's use of deadly force is an unreasonable response to the circumstances presented. Thus, manslaughter is the appropriate charge for an individual who shoots and kills an unarmed man who had earlier damaged his property.[79]

Intoxication Manslaughter

Unfortunately, a very common charge within the state is **intoxication manslaughter** (Sec. 49.08). Also a second degree felony, this offense essentially substitutes the defendant's intoxication for the culpable mental state of recklessness required for Sec. 19.04 manslaughter.[80] Note that the offense can be committed only if the defendant is operating a motor vehicle or watercraft, or assembles or operates an amusement park ride.[81] An intoxicated individual who stabs, shoots, chokes, or otherwise causes the death of another would be prosecuted under the murder or general manslaughter statute as the facts dictate.

The standard for intoxication is the same used for driving while intoxicated (Sec. 49.04), either a 0.08 blood alcohol concentration (called the *per se* law) or loss of

§ 49.08. Intoxication Manslaughter

a. A person commits an offense if the person:
   1. operates a motor vehicle in a public place, operates an aircraft, a watercraft, or an amusement ride, or assembles a mobile amusement ride; and
   2. is intoxicated and by reason of that intoxication causes the death of another by accident or mistake.

b. An offense under this section is a felony of the second degree.

normal physical and mental faculties due to ingestion of any substance. This latter standard could apply to persons intoxicated by alcohol with less than a 0.08 alcohol concentration as well as individuals using marijuana, cocaine, hallucinogens, or any other mind-altering substance. Neither statutory law nor case law provides a defense to the intoxicated driver whose condition is the result of use of lawful substances. Specifically, the fact that the vehicle operator is entitled to use alcohol, controlled substances, or other drugs does not create a legal defense.[82]

The defendant's conduct is criminal only because of his intoxication. The statute recites that the conduct is otherwise "by accident or mistake." Recall that events that occur by accident and mistake are not criminal because they lack a culpable mental state.

A key element of intoxication manslaughter that is often overlooked is the requirement of a causal relationship between the death and the intoxication. Assume that late one rainy night, Rodney is driving his pickup truck in an intoxicated condition. Larry, who is wearing dark clothing, attempts to cross the roadway. Because of poor visibility due to the weather, Rodney does not see Larry and the truck strikes and kills him. Rodney has not committed intoxication manslaughter if Larry's death would have occurred even if Rodney were sober. In other words, Rodney's intoxicated state was not the cause of Larry's death. On the other hand, if Wilma, with a blood alcohol level of 0.21, is driving at 100 miles per hour and strikes a disabled vehicle and kills the occupant, Wilma will be culpable for intoxication manslaughter. The sober driver operating her car within the speed limit could have avoided striking the disabled vehicle.[83] A causal link between the intoxicated state of the driver and the death must be established in court.

Intoxication manslaughter is a result of conduct offense. This means the defendant is criminally responsible for the result of his behavior, not the behavior alone. Thus, if Bud, while intoxicated, crashes his automobile into another vehicle carrying several persons and three passengers are killed, Bud has committed three, not one, counts of intoxication manslaughter. He may be prosecuted for each death.

Finally, suppose Jack, while operating his motorboat at dusk, runs over and kills Jose who is scuba diving. Tests reveal that Jack's blood alcohol level was 0.05. Can Jack be properly convicted of some form of criminal homicide? Since Jack's blood alcohol level is below 0.08, the state cannot take advantage of the conclusive presumption that he was intoxicated. Accordingly, the prosecutor would have to establish that the lower alcohol level still caused Jack to lose normal use of his mental or physical faculties. In the alternative, the district attorney could charge Jack with Sec. 19.04 manslaughter and use his blood alcohol level as part of the evidence that his conduct in the incident was reckless.

Criminally Negligent Homicide

Prosecution for death through criminal negligence focuses not on what the defendant consciously chose to do but what he ought to have done under the circumstances (Sec. 19.05). Because proving what the reasonable person would do under the same circumstances can be difficult, relatively few **criminally negligent homicide** cases are

§ 19.05. Criminally Negligent Homicide

a. A person commits an offense if he causes the death of an individual by criminal negligence.

b. An offense under this section is a state jail felony.

initiated. Most that are prosecuted involve clear violations of traffic laws, health and safety regulations, or other statutes. These laws, which are primarily regulatory in nature, establish the level of conduct society expects, so one knows what one ought to do. The same cannot be said for many other aspects of social interaction.

Distinguishing between manslaughter and criminally negligent homicide appears difficult at first glance. However, manslaughter requires actual awareness of a risk while criminally negligent homicide mandates that the defendant failed to perceive risk but should have. Assume Dale runs a stop sign in his delivery truck and strikes and kills Jeff who is riding a bicycle. Dale says, "I didn't see the sign." Dale is criminally negligent because he is required by the Transportation Code to be aware of traffic signals and obey them. Dale did not do what he ought to have done. Had Dale made the intentional choice to run the stop sign but unintentionally hits and kills Jeff, a manslaughter charge would be more appropriate.

Texas prosecutors have also successfully used criminally negligent homicide to hold corporations accountable in a few cases. Since the required culpable mental state does not necessitate a conscious, purposeful decision, artificial entities can be prosecuted for what they ought to have done. Thus, when two deaths resulted from a trench cave-in after a construction company failed to follow appropriate safety standards, the construction company could be found guilty of criminally negligent homicide.[84]

Criminally negligent homicide is a state jail felony.

CRIMEGRAPH
Criminal Homicide Offenses

Offense	Underlying offense/behavior	Culpable mental state	Conduct	Who?	Why?	When?	Specific knowledge	Penalty
Murder 19.02(b)(1)		1. Intentionally or 2. Knowingly	Causes death	Individual				F2 to F1
Murder 19.02(b)(2)	Intending to cause serious bodily injury	1. Intentionally, or 2. Knowingly, or 3. Recklessly*	Commits act clearly dangerous to human life that causes death	Individual				F2 to F1
Murder 19.02(b)(3)	1. Commits or attempts to commit felony and in furtherance of felony or 2. During immediate flight from felony	1. Intentionally, or 2. Knowingly, or 3. Recklessly*	Commits act clearly dangerous to human life that causes death	Individual				F2 to F1
Capital Murder 19.03(a)(1)	Murder 19.02(b)(1)		Murders	1. Peace officer or 2. Fireman		In lawful discharge of duties	Knowing person is peace officer or fireman	CF

Offense	Underlying offense/behavior	Culpable mental state	Conduct	Who?	Why?	When?	Specific knowledge	Penalty
Capital Murder 19.03(a)(2)	Murder 19.02(b)(1)	Intentionally	Murders	Individual		In the course of: 1. Kidnapping, or 2. Burglary, or 3. Robbery, or 4. Aggravated Sexual Assault, or 5. Arson, or 6. Obstruction or Retaliation		CF
Capital Murder 19.03(a)(3)	Murder 19.02(b)(1)		Murders	Individual	1. For remuneration, or 2. For promise of remuneration, or 3. Employs another to commit for remuneration			CF
Capital Murder 19.03(a)(4)	Murder 19.02(b)(1)		Murders	Individual		While escaping from a penal institution		CF
Capital Murder 19.03(a)(5)(A)	Murder 19.02(b)(1)		Murders	Employee of penal institution		While incarcerated in a penal institution		CF
Capital Murder 19.03(a)(5)(B)	Murder 19.02(b)(1)		Murders	Individual	To participate in combination	While incarcerated in a penal institution		CF
Capital Murder 19.03(a)(6)(A)	Murder 19.02(b)(1)		Murders	Individual		While incarcerated in a penal institution		CF

Offense	Underlying offense/ behavior	Culpable mental state	Conduct	Who?	Why?	When?	Specific knowledge	Penalty
Capital Murder 19.03(a)(6)(B)	Murder 19.02(b)(1)		Murders	Individual		While serving life or 99 years for: 1. Aggravated Kidnapping, <u>or</u> 2. Aggravated Sexual Assault, <u>or</u> 3. Aggravated Robbery		CF
Capital Murder 19.03(a)(7)(A)	Murder 19.02(b)(1)		Murders	More than one person		During same criminal transaction		CF
Capital Murder 19.03(a)(7)(B)	Murder 19.02(b)(1)		Murders	More than one person		During different criminal transactions pursuant to same scheme of conduct		CF
Capital Murder 19.03(a)(8)	Murder 19.02(b)(1)		Murders	Individual under 6				CF
Capital Murder 19.03(a)(9)	Murder 19.02(b)(1)		Murders	State judge	1. In retaliation for, <u>or</u> 2. On account of service, <u>or</u> 3. On account of status			CF
Manslaughter 19.04(a)		Recklessly	Causes death	Individual				F2

Offense	Underlying offense/behavior	Culpable mental state	Conduct	Who?	Why?	When?	Specific knowledge	Penalty
Intoxication Manslaughter 49.08(a)		1. Accident or 2. Mistake	Causes death by reason of intoxication	Individual	While intoxicated	1. Operating motor vehicle in public place, or 2. Operating aircraft, or 3. Operating watercraft, or 4. Operating amusement ride, or 5. Assembles mobile amusement ride		F2 to F1
Criminally Negligent Homicide 19.05(a)		Criminal negligently	Causes death	Individual				SJF

*Required by Texas Penal Code § 6.02

Notes

1. See Tex. Code Crim. P. art. 49.04 regarding circumstances under which an inquest on dead bodies must be conducted.

2. In 2004, the Centers for Disease Control estimated that 2,398,000 Americans died from all causes. The U.S. population for the same year was placed at 293,656,000.

3. Federal Bureau of Investigation, Crime in America-Uniform Crime Reports 2005 (2006).

4. Tex. Dep't of Pub. Safety, The Texas Crime Report for 2006 (2007).

5. Nat'l Highway Traffic Safety Admin., Traffic Safety Facts—State Alcohol Estimates (2005).

6. The offending animal in such a situation is most often euthanized, even if the animal's conduct was arguably justified. In medieval Europe, animals that caused property damage or death were placed on trial. In one reported case in France, a pig that entered a house and disfigured a child's face was convicted and hanged. Historical records are unclear as to the societal goal in putting animals on trial. At least one motion picture about animal trials has been produced (*The Advocate*, BBC Films, 1994).

   In 1916, in a bizarre incident in American history, a five-ton elephant that killed its handler was executed by being hanged by a railroad crane in Erwin, Tennessee. Some historians believe that "Murderous Mary" was unjustifiably lynched.

7. Gonzales v. State, 397 S.W.2d 440, 441 (Tex. Crim. App. 1965).

8. The idea of manslaughter originated in the Common Law to avoid the fixed penalty of death for all murders. Jurists recognized that even in criminal homicides, mitigating factors often arise.

9. Texas followed this elimination approach for many years to distinguish murder from other forms of criminal homicide. *See* 1925 Tex. Penal Code art. 1256.

10. Penna. Laws 1794, ch. 257, §§ 1–2.

11. 720 Ill. Comp. Stat. 5/9–2.

12. English Common Law recognized the two divisions of manslaughter but affixed the same punishment to each.

13. While courts that have considered the matter view drunk driving as *malum in se*, the conclusion appears to be illogical given that the crime was unknown during the Common Law era and is completely the product of legislative enactment.

14. Connecticut, Georgia, Maine, Mississippi, South Carolina, and Texas do not divide murder into degrees although they may utilize separate statutes for capital murder, murder, and felony murder.

15. For a list, see Government of the Virgin Islands v. Harris, 938 F.2d 401 (3rd Cir. 1991).

16. *See, e.g.*, Williams v. State, 629 S.W.2d 791 (Tex. App.—Dallas 1981); Fisher v. State, 851 S.W.2d 298 (Tex. Crim. App. 1993); McDuff v. State, 939 S.W.2d 607 (Tex. Crim. App. 1997); Stanford v. State, 2005 Tex. App. LEXIS 570; and Trejos v. State, 243 S.W.3d 30 (Tex. App.—Houston [1st Dist.] 2007).

17. Penry v. State, 691 S.W.2d 636 (Tex. Crim. App. 1985).

18. 410 U.S. 113 (1973).

19. Unborn Victim's of Violence Act or Laci and Conner's Law, Pub. L. No. 108–212, 118 Stat. 568 (codified at 18 U.S.C. § 1841).

20. Lawrence v. State, 240 S.W.3d 912 (Tex. Crim. App. 2007).

21. See Tex. Code Crim. P. art. 38.40. "EVIDENCE OF PREGNANCY. (a) In a prosecution for the death of or injury to an individual who is an unborn child, the prosecution shall provide medical or other evidence that the mother of the individual was pregnant at the time of the alleged offense."

22. However, the prosecutor is not required to establish that the fetus was viable, that is, capable of living outside the womb. *See* Lawrence v. State.

23. *See* Tex. Penal Code § 19.06(1).

24. *See In re* C.M.G., 180 S.W.3d 836 (Tex. App.—Texarkana 2005). *See also, South Texas teen accused of murder in newborn's death*, Associated Press State & Local Wire, Jun. 7, 2007.

25. See Flores v. State, 215 S.W.3d 520 (Tex. App.—Beaumont 2007), rejecting the argument that limiting the law's exemption only to the mother violates the equal protection clause of the U.S. Constitution.

26. The UDDA was developed in 1980 by the Uniform Law Commissioners in cooperation with the American Bar Association, the American Medical Association, and the President's Commission on Medical Ethics.

27. *See Death of man 20 yrs. after being shot poses problem over charges*, Houston Post, Jan. 17, 1981, at A24. See also Ben Finley, *Making a Case*, The Intelligencer *at* http://www.phillyburbs.com/pb-dyn/news/113–08232007–1396716.html (Aug. 23, 2007), concerning a case wherein the death of a Philadelphia police officer was alleged to have been caused by a gunshot fired 41 years earlier.

28. Statutes made at Gloucester on the Fourth of October, 1278, 6 Ed. I, ch. 9.

29. *See* 1925 Tex. Penal Code art. 1199.

30. Rogers v. Tennessee, 532 U.S. 451, 462–463 (2001).

31. *See* Martin v. State, 732 S.W.2d 743 (Tex. App.—Ft. Worth 1987).

32. Tex. Code Crim. P. art. 12.01(1)(a).

33. When the Legislature created the offense of intoxication manslaughter (§ 49.08) in 1993, it neglected to

amend § 19.01(b) to include the offense. The omission of § 49.08 has no effect upon its enforceability.

34. Cook v. State, 884 S.W.2d 485 (Tex. Crim. App. 1994).

35. Medina v. State, 7 S.W.3d 633 (Tex. Crim. App. 1999).

36. The idea of depraved heart murder is based on wanton disregard of an unreasonable human risk.

37. Lugo-Lugo v. State, 650 S.W.2d 72 (Tex. Crim. App. 1983).

38. *Id.* at 81.

39. Indeed death is listed as a type of "serious bodily injury" in the term's statutory definition. TEX. PENAL CODE § 1.07(46).

40. For a discussion of the history of the felony murder rule, see Lawson v. State, 64 S.W.3d 396 (Tex. Crim. App. 2001).

41. Jurors do not have to be unanimous as to which underlying felony the defendant committed. They simply must agree that the defendant committed some felony. White v. State, 208 S.W.3d 467 (Tex. Crim. App. 2006).

42. Texas courts have chosen to exclude from the coverage of the felony murder rule only manslaughter and its lesser included offenses. As a result, a felony murder conviction can be had in cases wherein the felony and the act causing the death are one and the same. Thus, a felony murder conviction will lie where an unintended death results during the commission of injury to a child. *See* Johnson v. State, 4 S.W.3d 254 (Tex. Crim. App. 1999). Similarly, a felony murder conviction will stand when the underlying felony is an intentional aggravated assault because the crime is not a lesser included offense of manslaughter. *See* Lawson v. State, 64 S.W.3d 396 (Tex. Crim. App. 2001). Would an aggravated assault by recklessness be viewed as a lesser included offense of manslaughter?

43. Bank robbery example adapted from Lawson v. State (Cochran, J., concurring).

44. Loredo v. State, 130 S.W.3d 275 (Tex. App.—Houston [14th Dist.] 2004).

45. Lomax v. State, 233 S.W.3d 302 (Tex. Crim. App. 2007).

46. White v. State.

47. Act of May 29, 1993, 73rd Leg., R.S., ch. 900, § 1.01, 1993 Tex. Gen Laws 3586.

48. Sanchez v. State, 23 S.W.3d 30 (Tex. Crim. App. 2000).

49. A study funded by the National Institute of Mental Health suggests that up to 16 million Americans may suffer from intermittent explosive disorder (IED). IED may help explain some incidents of road rage. *See* Ronald C. Kessler et al., *The Prevalence and Correlates of DSM-IV Intermittent Explosive Disorder in the National Comorbidity Survey Replication*, 63 ARCHIVES OF GEN. PSYCHIATRY 669 (2006).

50. See TEX. CODE CRIM. P. art. 38.36 and discussion of battered spouse defense in Chapter 15—General Defenses and Justification.

51. Threadgill v. State, 146 S.W.3d 654 (Tex. Crim. App. 2004).

52. Beets v. State, 767 S.W.2d 711 (Tex. Crim. App. 1988).

53. *Id.*

54. See Lawhorn v. State, 898 S.W.2d 886 (Tex. Crim. App. 1995). But see also Hobbs v. State, 175 S.W.3d 777 (Tex. Crim. App. 2005), holding that evading arrest is a continuing offense.

55. *See* Fitzgerald v. State, 782 S.W.2d 876 (Tex. Crim. App. 1990).

56. See TEX. PENAL CODE § 71.01(a) defining "combination" as "three or more persons who collaborate in carrying on criminal activities, although: (1) participants may not know each other's identity; (2) membership in the combination may change from time to time; and (3) participants may stand in a wholesaler-retailer or other arm's-length relationship in illicit distribution operations."

57. Rice v. State, 805 S.W.2d 432 (Tex. Crim. App. 1991).

58. Act of Apr. 16, 1985, 69th Leg., R.S., ch. 44, § 1, 1985 Tex. Gen. Laws 434. *See also* GARY M. LAVERGNE, WORSE THAN DEATH: THE DALLAS NIGHTCLUB MURDERS AND THE TEXAS MULTIPLE MURDER LAW (2003).

59. Vuong v. State, 830 S.W.2d 929 (Tex. Crim. App. 1992).

60. Burkett v. State, 173 S.W.3d 250 (Tex. App.—Beaumont 2005).

61. *See e.g.*, TEX. PENAL CODE § 21.11 (indecency with a child); § 22.021 (aggravated sexual assault of a child); § 22.04 (injury to a child); § 22.041 (abandoning or endangering a child); and § 22.10 (leaving a child in a vehicle).

62. *See* 1925 TEX. PENAL CODE art. 1256–1257.

63. *See* TEX. PENAL CODE §§ 1.07(41)(A) and 1.07(24).

64. See TEX. PENAL CODE § 1.07(36) defining who is a "peace officer." See also, Art. 2.122 of the TEX. CODE CRIM. P. designating certain federal law enforcement personnel as "special investigators" but stating they "shall not be deemed peace officers."

65. *See generally*, 18 U.S.C. §§ 351; 1111; 1114; & 1751.

66. *See* CAL. PENAL CODE § 190.2.

67. *See District Courts Activity Summary by Case Type from September 1, 2005 to August 31, 2006*, Texas Courts Online, *at* http://www.courts.state.tx.us/pubs/AR2006/dc/4-dc-summary-of-activity-by-case-type-fy06.pdf.

68. TEX. CODE CRIM. P. art. 37.01.

69. *District Courts Activity Summary*, *supra*.

70. *Id.*

71. TEX. CODE CRIM. P. art. 37.071(h).

72. *See Death Row Facts*, Texas Department of Criminal Justice, *at* http://www.tdcj.state.tx.us/stat/drowfacts.htm.

73. TEX. CODE CRIM. P. art. 43.141.

74. Newman v. State, 49 S.W.3d 577 (Tex. App.—Beaumont 2001).

75. Martinez v. State, 2006 Tex. App. LEXIS 9809.

76. *See e.g.*, Davis v. State, 757 S.W.2d 386 (Tex. App.—Dallas 1988), *and* Zarate v. State, 2006 Tex. App. LEXIS 23.

77. *See* TEX. PENAL CODE § 22.05(c).

78. *In re* E.U.M., 108 S.W.3d 368 (Tex. App.—Beaumont 2003).

79. Lewis v. State, 2006 Tex. App. LEXIS 8141.

80. Rathmell v. State, 653 S.W.2d 498 (Tex. App.—Corpus Christi 1983).

81. The rather unusual addition of amusement park ride operators to the intoxication manslaughter statute was motivated by a 1998 incident in Austin, in which a teenage girl was thrown to her death from a ride that had a defective safety bar. Murder indictments against the owner of the ride and nine employees were ultimately dropped. Curiously, no formal allegations surfaced that any of the parties charged were intoxicated when assembling the ride. Two individuals were ultimately convicted, one of manslaughter and the other of deadly conduct.

82. TEX. PENAL CODE § 49.10. See also Parr v. State, 575 S.W.2d 522 (Tex. Crim. App. 1978), interpreting prior version of statute.

83. Glauser v. State, 66 S.W.3d 307 (Tex. App.—Houston [1st Dist.] 2000).

84. Sabine Consolidated, Inc. v. State, 816 S.W.2d 784 (Tex. App.—Austin 1991).

CHAPTER 6

Assault and Sexual Assault

BOLO

The reader should be on the lookout (BOLO) for the meaning of the following terms. Knowledge of the meaning of these terms will greatly assist the reader in understanding the primary elements of the chapter.

- Bodily injury
- Child
- Common Law assault
- Common Law battery
- Common Law mayhem
- Consent
- Corroboration requirement
- Danger
- Deadly weapon
- Disabled individual
- Elderly individual
- Exhibit deadly weapon
- Lord Hale instruction
- Penetration
- Physical contact
- Serious bodily injury
- Sexual contact
- Stalking
- Threat
- Use deadly weapon

INTRODUCTION

Suppose Rob, angry because he has been fired from his job as a waiter, punishes the restaurant manager in the nose. Or what if Nick comes home drunk and strikes his wife Yolanda with his fist because dinner is not ready. Or maybe Jack points a pistol at Geoff and says, "If you don't stay away from my wife, I'm going to kill you." Perhaps Carl as a protest against the war hits a local politician in the face with a pie. Or Freddy, a drunk driver, crashes his vehicle into another car seriously injuring Katie. All of these examples implicate the modern law of assault.

With the possible exception of theft, perhaps no other offense can be committed in more factually different ways than the crime of assault. And also like theft, the law of assault has been adapted from its traditional forms to fit new behaviors that result in fear or the mere potential for fear, such as stalking and terroristic threats. Special laws also now exist for battering children, the disabled, and the elderly.

Additionally, the traditional law of rape has been reconfigured in Texas and many other jurisdictions into a particularized form of assault—sexual assault. Combine this modern expansion of assaultive-type crimes with significant statutory modifications to the traditional definitions of assault and battery and one is left with a group of offenses that can be a bit confusing unless the actual statutory elements of the offenses are examined closely.

COMMON LAW ASSAULTIVE CONDUCT

Like many crimes, assaultive offenses have their origin in the Common Law. Also, like all Common Law crimes, assaultive crimes had very specific definitions. Understanding the nuances of the Common Law definitions will assist in understanding why the modern elements of the offense are structured in the manner in which they are now written.

Under the Common Law, three assaultive offenses evolved: battery, assault, and mayhem. (Rape as a form of sexual assault will be discussed later in this chapter.)

Battery

A **battery** resulted when the assailant purposefully caused bodily injury to another or touched another in an offensive manner. Suppose Jerry is angry at Tom. Jerry walks up behind Tom and without warning strikes him with a club. Tom is knocked unconscious. Under the Common Law, Jerry has committed a battery because Tom suffered bodily injury. But a battery could also be committed where Forrest is riding on an elevator with Julianne, an attractive coed. Forrest extends his hand and pats Julianne on the buttocks. Julianne moves away, offended and outraged. Even though Julianne suffers no bodily injury, Forrest has committed a battery because his touching of her was nonconsensual and offensive.

Assault

Under the Common Law, **assault** was originally viewed as an attempt to commit a battery. If Ron takes a swing at Mike and misses, he commits assault under the Common Law view because he was trying to batter Mike. The Common Law also recognized a second form of assault, but only as a civil matter not as a criminal act. This second form of assault concerned intentionally frightening another by placing him in fear of bodily injury. Suppose that Ron swings at Mike from behind. Mike moves at the last moment and the fist misses its target. An assault of the first form has occurred but not of the second form; Ron is attempting a battery but Mike is not placed in fear of injury because he is unaware of Ron's conduct. On the other hand, if Ron, in a rage, shakes his fist in Mike's face but does not swing, under the Common Law he is committing a civil assault through his threatening conduct. American law ultimately incorporated the civil concept of assault by threat into the statutory criminal law and thereby added intent-to-frighten as a form of the crime.

When Ron takes his swing at Mike and Mike sees the fist coming toward him, Mike is placed in fear of bodily injury and an assault occurs at that moment. If the fist strikes Mike, Ron has committed both assault and battery under the ordinary view of those crimes. Other traditional issues that arise in the law of assault are considered below.

Mayhem

The Common Law did not recognize aggravated forms of assault and battery. Accordingly, a special offense was created for circumstances where serious injury occurred and felony-level punishment was deemed appropriate. This offense was called mayhem. **Mayhem**, also called "mahemium," was defined as "the violently depriving another of the use of such of his members, as may render him the less able in fighting, either to defend himself, or to annoy his adversary." Thus, intentionally maiming the victim or permanently disabling him was viewed as more serious than a mere battery. Cutting off hands or fingers and gouging out eyes were considered mayhem. The focus on the crime of mayhem seems more on the loss of the victim as a potential soldier for the king than to punish the particular harm done to the individual. With a few exceptions, the crime of mayhem today is incorporated within the offenses of aggravated assault or aggravated battery, depending on the particular state's penal law structure.

Note that each of the three assaultive offenses, like most Common Law crimes, required a general *mens rea* of intent. Later in this chapter, criminal liability for assaultive conduct committed with lesser culpable mental states will be explored.

MODERN TERMINOLOGY

Under modern criminal codes whether threatening and injurious conduct is called an "assault" or a "battery" is simply dependent on the statutory labeling. While all states have laws that cover the traditional notions of assault and battery, the modern trend is to merge both forms of conduct into a single offense, usually called "assault." This style of labeling, which is followed in Texas, flows from the approach initiated by the Model Penal Code where the classic behaviors of assault and battery are grouped together as assaults and any such behavior that produces serious injury or involves use of firearms or other deadly weapons is elevated to aggravated assault. The word "battery" is nowhere used. If Mark threatens to punch Jared, the matter is an assault. Likewise, if Mark purposefully strikes Jared, the incident is also considered to be an assault, not a battery as that labeling is eliminated. If Mark's unlawful conduct causes serious bodily injury or if he uses a deadly weapon, his criminal behavior rises to aggravated assault. Simple assaults, as they are sometimes called, are misdemeanors while aggravated assault is a felony-level crime.

Unless otherwise noted, the terms "assault" and "aggravated assault" will be used throughout the chapter to refer to the conduct previously encompassed within the Common Law terms of assault, battery, and mayhem.

TEXAS LAW OF ASSAULT

Introduction

With one exception, Chapter 22 of the Penal Code contains the assault-type offenses applicable in Texas. These statutory offenses greatly expand the coverage of the old Common Law crimes in terms of both the *mens rea* and the *actus reus*. The culpable mental states necessary for a crime to occur have been broadened and the forms of conduct constituting an offense have been enlarged. Additionally, specialized offenses and punishments have been enacted to cover certain types of victims, such as children, elderly individuals, and persons with disabilities.

The primary assault-type offenses recognized under Texas law are the following:

- Assault—Sec. 22.01
- Aggravated Assault—Sec. 22.02
- Intoxication Assault—Sec. 49.07
- Deadly Conduct—Sec. 22.05
- Terrorist Threat—Sec. 22.07
- Injury to a Child, Elderly Individual, or Disabled Individual—Sec. 22.04

Each of these offenses will be discussed in order along with several miscellaneous assault-related crimes.

§ 22.01. Assault

(a) A person commits an offense if the person:

1. intentionally, knowingly, or recklessly causes bodily injury to another, including the person's spouse;
2. intentionally or knowingly threatens another with imminent bodily injury, including the person's spouse; or
3. intentionally or knowingly causes physical contact with another when the person knows or should reasonably believe that the other will regard the contact as offensive or provocative.

Forms of Assault

A close reading of Sec. 22.01 reveals that it criminalizes three forms of behavior:

- Assault with bodily injury—Sec. 22.01(a)(1)
- Assault by threat—Sec. 22.01(a)(2)
- Assault by contact—Sec. 22.01(a)(3)

Each of the three forms largely mirrors the Common Law crimes of assault and battery. Assault with bodily injury is the equivalent of one type of Common Law battery, assault by threat is the equivalent of one form of Common Law assault, and assault by contact is similar to a version of battery. An assault as an attempted battery is not explicitly mentioned. Whether taking a swing and missing at a victim who is unaware of the act violates the Texas assault statute will be discussed later in the chapter.

Elements of Assault with Bodily Injury

A Person Intentionally, Knowingly, or Recklessly   While assault with bodily injury is traditionally thought of as an intentionally perpetrated crime, Texas extends the concept to two lower levels of culpable mental state—knowledge and recklessness. If Blair purposefully strikes Gene with his fist, bloodying Gene's nose, an assault with bodily injury has certainly occurred. But what if Blair's elbow strikes Gene's nose during a pickup basketball game? Is this a violation of Sec. 22.01(a)(1)? Certainly not, as the incident was an accident, that is, no culpable mental state.

But what if as a prank, Tim drops a concrete block off the overpass of a highway. The block hits the roadway in front of Rhonda's automobile. Rhonda swerves to avoid striking the object but runs off the road and hits a pole. Rhonda suffers a bloody nose and bruises as a result of the collision. Tim has committed assault with bodily injury because he acted in a reckless manner. He was aware of the risk that his conduct could cause injury but disregarded the risk.

Anecdotal evidence suggests that few cases of assault with bodily injury through recklessness are initiated because many Texas prosecutors continue to adhere to the notion that assault is an intentional or knowing act, regardless of the broadened language of the state statute.

One particular area where recklessly caused bodily injury often arises is in traffic collisions. Traffic collisions frequently involve one motorist violating some provision of the Transportation Code, such as speeding, following too closely, or running a stop sign. These violations of the law arguably constitute recklessness. When the motorist collides with another vehicle, occupants in either or both vehicles are often injured. These bodily injuries could provide the basis for an assault charge. In many parts of the state, police and prosecutors do not appear to consider applying Penal Code sections to incidents involving motor vehicles. An exception to this perspective is the offenses related to drunk drivers contained in Chapter 49. As will be discussed below, if an intoxicated driver causes serious bodily injury to another person, he has committed intoxication assault (Sec. 49.07).

Bodily injury caused through criminal negligence does not generally constitute assault. (One exception to this rule is injury to children and the elderly discussed below.) Many incidents of negligent injury occur, particularly in motor vehicle collisions. The civil suit, not the criminal law, is the primary remedy available to victims who suffer injury through another's negligence.

Causes   Assault with bodily injury is a result of conduct offense. In the typical assault with bodily injury case, the offender purposely strikes the victim with the conscious goal of causing bodily injury. But suppose Melvin is arguing with Vince, his supervisor. The argument heats up and Melvin shoves Vince in the chest. Has an assault with bodily injury occurred? Probably not, assuming Vince suffered no pain from the shove.[1] But what if Vince falls backward as a result of the shove and strikes his head? He goes unconscious. Melvin has certainly "caused" the injury. Melvin is responsible for the harm done to Vince even if Melvin did not intend to knock him unconscious.[2]

Bodily Injury   At a minimum, some physical harm must result for conduct to be considered an assault with bodily injury. (If no "bodily injury" occurs, the act may still be an assault by contact.) Sec. 1.07(a)(8) provides the statutory definition of "bodily injury".

The statutory definition includes three possibilities: physical pain, illness, or any impairment of physical condition. The first is physical pain. Note that mental distress, fear, or other psychological reactions do not fall within the definition of "bodily injury." Any pain must be physical in nature. However, unlike some jurisdictions, Texas does not require that the physical pain be substantial.[3] If the victim testifies that the defendant's contact hurt, physical pain has occurred, no matter how minor. As one Texas court noted, "This definition [of bodily injury] appears to be purposefully broad and seems to encompass even relatively minor physical contacts so long as they constitute more than mere offensive touching."[4]

As to illness, Texas courts have had limited opportunity to discuss situations where the transference of an illness constituted an assault. Presumably the knowing transfer of any disease or illness could constitute an assault. The most likely scenario here would be sexually transmitted diseases, such as herpes and HIV. The relationship between sexually transmitted diseases and the law of assault is discussed later in the chapter.

Recall Vince who was knocked unconscious after being shoved to the ground. Vince's loss of consciousness is a form of bodily injury, an impairment of physical condition. Also included within the concept of an impairment of physical condition would be bruises, sprains, and muscle strains. If Trevor punches Mike and blacks his eye, bodily injury has occurred.

§ 1.07. Definitions

(a) In this code:

* * *

(8) "Bodily injury" means physical pain, illness, or any impairment of physical condition.

To Another, Including the Person's Spouse   As with other offenses, causing harm to oneself is not a criminal act. There must be injury to another person. Likewise, producing bodily harm to an animal does not constitute an assault but rather would more likely be considered criminal mischief (Sec. 28.03), reckless damage (Sec. 28.04), or cruelty to animals (Sec. 42.09) depending on the violator's culpable mental state.

The statutory reference to "the person's spouse" is redundant language. Certainly one's spouse is "another." The Texas Legislature added this phrase to the statute in 1979 as part of broader anti-domestic violence legislation.[5] The phrase simply emphasizes that one spouse has no legal right to physically abuse his or her mate. Such conduct is a crime in the same manner as if the victim were a stranger. The original absence of the phrases does not mean that spousal abuse was previously lawful.

Elements of Assault by Threat

A Person Intentionally or Knowingly   Unlike an assault with bodily injury which can be committed with the lesser culpable mental state of recklessness, an assault by threat can only be committed intentionally or knowingly. This is an important point as it demonstrates that the intent of the perpetrator, not the reaction of the supposed victim, is the focus of the statute. For example, suppose late one night Brittney is walking alone on the way from the library to her apartment. From behind her she hears a noise. She turns quickly and observes Chad, an individual she does not know. Chad is dressed in Goth-style attire. His sudden appearance and manner of dress frighten Brittney. She immediately becomes fearful that she may be robbed or assaulted or otherwise suffer some personal harm. Has Chad committed assault by threat? Not unless he intends for his actions and demeanor to be a threat to Brittney. The fact that his dress and surrounding circumstances makes someone fearful does not translate into an intentional or knowing threat.

Threatens Another with Imminent Bodily Injury, Including the Person's Spouse   Suppose an angry Craig approaches Mitch and says, "You may be sorry one of these days." Has Craig threatened Mitch with imminent bodily injury and thereby assaulted him? Probably not. Craig's expression of displeasure with Mitch would be a verbal assault only if the words were indeed a "threat," the supposed threat related to possibly bodily injury, and the prospects of the injury were "imminent." Texas law requires these three coordinated circumstances.

Curiously, while the key term in the statute is the word "threatens," the term is nowhere defined in the Penal Code. So what does it mean to threaten? Initially, a **threat** is essentially an intention to commit a battery. One Texas appeals court's definition of "threat" expands on this notion with "[a] threat is defined as, 'a declaration of intention or determination to inflict punishment, loss or pain on another, or to injure another by the commission of an unlawful act.' "[6]

It should be noted that a threat need not be verbal. Certainly gestures can be threatening. Shaking of one's fist in a provocative manner could be interpreted as being threatening for the purposes of the law of assault since fists are a common means by which to strike another. Brandishing a weapon in a provocative manner would be viewed as a threat by the average person. However, simply making a rude or obscene gesture at another, while certainly communicative, does not assert an intention to cause bodily injury. Threats to do bodily injury also can be transmitted by written note, letter, email, or telephone. For reasons discussed below, such communication, while arguably threatening in nature, would not normally be an assault, although they likely constitute terroristic threat.

Any threat must be to impose imminent bodily injury since this form of assault is essentially a precursor to being battered. In Craig's case, telling Mitch he will be sorry is ambiguous at best. Craig might be intending to file a lawsuit against Mitch; or, he might be intending to tell others of his low opinion of Mitch; or, he might intend to take steps to affect Mitch's economic circumstance, such as endeavoring to get Mitch fired from his job. If Craig is successful in any of these ventures, Mitch might well "be sorry one of these days." However, none of those outcomes involves possible physical injury to Mitch. Threats to ruin one's reputation, report them to their boss, or tell their mother do not reach the necessary level to be an assault.

A written, emailed, or telephoned threat is unlikely to be considered an assault. Recall that an assault in this context is defined as a threat to commit imminent bodily injury. One cannot suffer physical injury from an email or a conversation over the telephone. The menacing email or phone call is not an *imminent* threat. Although other criminal statutes, such as terroristic threat discussed below, may cover this conduct, these transmitted threats fall outside the scope of Sec. 22.01. Assault requires an imminent or immediate assertion to commit physical harm. In most instances that would necessitate a near face-to-face confrontation between the would-be assailant and his intended victim. This is another reason that Craig's statement does not constitute an assault. He makes no assertion that immediate physical injury is about to befall Mitch. Rather, Craig says some form of harm may occur "one of these days." Such a statement of future happening is unlikely to be viewed as a threat to commit bodily injury *now*.

Assume Phillip, a college student full of beer and testosterone, recognizes Larry, a professional football player, standing at the other end of the bar. Phillip, in what all would agree is a potentially foolish decision, walks up to Larry and says, "You are the fattest, most overpaid player in the league. You have ruined my fantasy league season. You could use your butt kicked and I'm the guy who's going to do it!" Larry looks at Phillip and sees a 5'8" drunk college student. He laughs. Despite Larry finding humor in the incident, has Phillip committed an assault by threat? Does it matter whether Larry is placed in fear of Phillip? The answer to these questions concern two important aspects of the law of assault. First, since assault by threat is rooted in the law of battery, must the assailant be able to actually carry out his proposed battery? And second, must the victim of the assault actually be placed in fear?

In many jurisdictions, the answer to the first question would turn on the legal distinction between the concepts of "present ability" and "apparent ability." Must the offender have the actual wherewithal to carry out his threat to injure or only the apparent ability to do so? Most jurisdictions today hold that an actual ability to commit a battery is not essential in simple criminal assault, an apparent ability to do so being sufficient. The Texas statutory language is silent on the matter but one Texas appeals court has held that an ability to commit a battery is no longer necessary to prove an assault.[7] The traditional present ability/apparent ability concept is a moot point under the modern Texas law of assault.[8] Texas courts view assault by threat as a "nature of conduct" offense.[9] This means that the focus of the crime is the behavior of the offender, not the actual result or harm he produces. Thus, whether Phillip has the actual ability to harm Larry is irrelevant. Once he makes the threat, the crime is complete without regard to his ability to deliver the threat.[10]

As to the need for the victim to be actually placed in fear of a battery, the national majority view holds that no assault occurs unless the victim is actually frightened. Texas, however, charts a different course. Whether the victim is actually placed in fear is not an element of assault by threat.[11] This is because of the above discussed view that it is the making of the threat that is the harm the statute seeks to prevent, not a particular result.

Must the victim even be aware of the defendant's conduct in order for an assault to occur? Suppose Raymond throws a rock at Kim. The rock sails by Kim's head. She is unaware that Raymond threw the object. Has an assault by threat occurred? Or is the conduct an attempted assault with bodily injury? In a 2006 case, the Court of Criminal Appeals upheld an assault by threat conviction of an individual who shot at the victim but the victim was unaware of the assault, only at a later time discovering the bullet holes in her vehicle. Citing the fact that the defendant's conduct in recent days had caused the victim to feel threatened, the court upheld the conviction and strongly suggested that the law does not require that the victim be aware of the offender's conduct at the moment of the act for that conduct to constitute a "threat."[12]

Would the previous case simply have been better resolved as an attempted assault with bodily injury?[13] Texas appellate courts have never explicitly held that the offense of attempted assault with bodily injury exists under the Penal Code.[14] There seems to be no reason why such an offense should not exist. However, a charge of attempted assault by threat would appear to violate the traditional and statutory rule that attempts to attempt an offense is no crime.[15]

Suppose Ethel says to Lucy, "If you don't stay away from my boyfriend Fred, I'm going to shoot you." Two days later Ethel sees Lucy with Fred and immediately fires a pistol at her. It is no defense for Ethel that Lucy could have avoided the risk of the assault by simply staying away from Fred. Ethel had no legal right to prevent Lucy from seeing Fred.[16] Therefore, her threat of future harm was still a threat and thereby unlawful. However, suppose Roger says to Andy, "If you were not so stupid, I would punch you in the nose." Is this an assault by threat? No. Roger's comment, although using the word "if" like the other example, is not really a conditional assault. Rather, if you examine Roger's comments closely, you realize he is saying he is *not* going to punch Andy in the nose. Whether or not Andy is actually stupid is irrelevant. Roger is simply being rude at worst.

Just as an individual's spouse can be the victim of an assault with bodily injury, the statute also criminalizes threatening one's mate with bodily injury. All individuals (e.g., wives, fathers, sons, mothers, and daughters), regardless of their relationship to the offender can be victims of an assault by threat.

Elements of Assault by Contact

A Person Intentionally or Knowingly As you exit the class today you may be subject to bumping and jostling by your fellow students. While you may find this behavior impolite, it is not criminal as one can reasonably expect such social contact in a crowded situation. Contact that is reckless or merely negligent, as with exiting the classroom, is no criminal offense.

But what if one student purposefully shoves another? Or puts their hand on another's buttocks? Those actions would constitute assault by contact even though no bodily injury results. This variation of assault sanctions the intentional or knowingly touching of another in offensive or provocative circumstances.

Causes Physical Contact with Another Individuals enjoy a broad social and legal right to control their personal security, and in particular, who may touch them. Accordingly, the law has long considered any intentional, nonconsensual offensive, insulting, or provocative contact by another person as constituting a crime. The harm comes not from any physical injury the victim suffers but rather from the violation of his or her right to control personal space.

The physical contact requirement excludes words from serving as the basis for an assault by contact charge. If John directs obscene, rude, and demeaning language toward Rudy, even though Rudy may find the words offensive, no assault occurs because there is no physical contact.[17]

Texas appellate courts have yet to decide the scope of the meaning of **physical contact**. Suppose Joan is deathly afraid of snakes. Jerry waives his pet boa constrictor in front of Joan. Joan screams in terror. There is no assault by contact.[18] But suppose Jerry places the boa on Joan's shoulder. A Texas court seems likely to find that such an act is "physical contact." The same logic would hold true in cases where thrown objects strike another. Consider the prankster who hits a politician in the face with a cream pie or the prisoner who tosses human feces at a correctional officer. These acts probably fit within the broad sense of "physical contact."

When the Person Knows Others will Regard the Contact as Offensive or Provocative   Unwanted contact alone is insufficient to constitute the offense. A *mens rea* element related to the surrounding circumstances is also required. The offender must know or reasonably believe that the victim will find the contact offensive or provocative. You are attending a Christmas holiday party at a private home. While leaning in the doorway enjoying a cup of eggnog, you are unaware that a sprig of mistletoe is hanging above your head. Suddenly a complete stranger walks up and gives you a kiss. Is the stranger's conduct an assault by contact? Would it matter if the kissing stranger were the same sex as you? Does the partier *know* that you will find the uninvited kiss offensive? Should the partier believe you will find the kiss offensive?

Reconsider the prankster who hits a politician in the face with a pie. One can certainly assume that the prankster should believe the politician will be offended. Or consider Pat and Mike who get into an argument. Pat, in an effort to make his point, continuously pokes his finger in Mike's chest. Mike tells him to stop but Pat continues the gesture. Pat is likely violating Sec. 21.01(a)(3). The range of offensive or provocative contact is virtually limitless. In one case involving a juvenile, a Florida court reluctantly conceded that hitting a fellow student in the lunchroom with a forkful of ravioli violated that state's assault statute![19]

Provocative touching of a child under 17 years of age for purposes of sexual arousal is covered by the indecency with a child statute (Sec. 21.11). In what some might consider as a legal loophole, the provocative touching of an adult for sexual gratification only violates Sec. 22.01(a)(3).

Penalty

The three forms of assault have different penalties. An assault by threat and an assault by contact are Class C misdemeanors. An assault with bodily injury is a Class A misdemeanor. However, each of the penalties can increase depending on the circumstances or the particular victim. Of particular note is that an assault with bodily injury against a public servant, such as a peace officer or school teacher, elevates the crime to a felony of the third degree. Table 6-1 displays the penalty schedule for the various forms of assault.

§ 22.02. Aggravated Assault

(a) A person commits an offense if the person commits assault as defined in § 22.01 and the person:

1. causes serious bodily injury to another, including the person's spouse; or
2. uses or exhibits a deadly weapon during the commission of the assault.

TABLE 6-1 Penalties for Assault-Type Offenses

Assault with Bodily Injury [§ 22.01(a)(1)]	Class A misdemeanor
Victim is public servant	Third-degree felony
Victim is family member and defendant has prior domestic violence conviction	Third-degree felony
Victim is security officer	Third-degree felony
Victim is private correctional officer	Third-degree felony
Assault by Threat [§ 22.01(a)(2)]	Class C misdemeanor
Victim is sports participant	Class B misdemeanor
Assault by Contact [§ 22.01(a)(3)]	Class C misdemeanor
Victim is elderly individual	Class A misdemeanor
Victim is disabled individual	Class A misdemeanor
Victim is sports participant and actor is not sports participant	Class B misdemeanor
Aggravated Assault [§ 22.02(a)]	Second-degree felony
Actor uses deadly weapon and causes serious bodily injury to family member	First-degree felony
Offender is public servant	First-degree felony
Victim is public servant	First-degree felony
Victim is witness, prospective witness, informant, or person who reported crime	First-degree felony
Victim is security officer	First-degree felony
Intoxication Assault [§ 49.07]	Third-degree felony
Injury to a Child, Elderly Individual or Disabled Individual [§ 22.04]	
Intentionally or knowingly by act or omission causes serious bodily injury; or serious mental deficiency, impairment or injury	First-degree felony
Recklessly by act or omission causes serious bodily injury or serious mental deficiency, impairment or injury;	Second-degree felony
Intentionally or knowingly by act or omission causes bodily injury or exploitation	Third-degree felony
Recklessly by act or omission causes bodily injury or exploitation	State jail felony
Causes serious bodily injury; serious mental deficiency, impairment or injury; bodily injury; or exploitation by an act of criminal negligence	State jail felony
Deadly Conduct [§ 22.05]	
Recklessly placing in danger of serious bodily injury	Class A misdemeanor
Discharging firearm at individual, habitation, building, or vehicle	Third-degree felony
Terroristic Threat [§ 22.07]	Third-degree felony
Causing reaction from emergency services agency	Class B misdemeanor
Placing individual in fear of serious bodily injury	Class B misdemeanor
Placing individual in fear of serious bodily injury and victim is family member	Class A misdemeanor
Placing individual in fear of serious bodily injury and victim is public servant	Class A misdemeanor
Interrupt occupation of public facility (loss less than $1,500)	Class A misdemeanor
Interrupt occupation of public facility (loss $1,500 or more)	State jail felony

Elements of Aggravated Assault

The Person Commits an Assault

Under certain conditions an assault can elevate to an aggravated assault, a felony. Note that the first element of aggravated assault is the commission of an assault as defined under Sec. 22.01. If there is no assault, there can be no aggravated assault. While aggravated assaults generally have their base as an assault by threat or an intentional assault with bodily injury, other forms of assault can also rise to the aggravated level. With the correct additional factors, an assault with bodily injury through recklessness can be an aggravated assault as could an assault by contact. In a real case, a college fraternity member was found guilty of aggravated assault by recklessly causing serious bodily injury during the hazing of a fraternity pledge. The pledge suffered his injuries after being forced to drink large quantities of water.[20]

And the Person Causes Serious Bodily Injury to Another

If the victim's injuries rise from bodily injury to serious bodily injury, the assault is considered to be aggravated. **Serious bodily injury** is bodily injury that is serious. While that statement sounds a bit silly, it is highly accurate. Simply stated, the law tries to segregate ordinary bodily injury from injuries that create a substantial risk of death or produce long-term or permanent injuries. "To be a serious bodily injury, the injury 'must be grave, not trivial,' that is, it must be 'such an injury as gives rise to apprehension of danger to life, health or limb,'" the Court of Criminal Appeals has said.[21] The concept of seriousness means either a prolonged injury or a permanent injury or disfigurement. Al, seeking revenge against Jack for a stock investment tip that went sour, attacks Jack and beats him continuously with his fists. When the attack ends, Jack transports himself to the emergency room where it is determined that he has two black eyes, assorted bruises and cuts, and a bloody nose. Jack is a sad sight. Is this a misdemeanor assault with bodily injury or do Jack's injuries constitute serious bodily injury? In Texas, despite Jack's unfortunate appearance, the offense would be simple assault with bodily injury. While his injuries are both ugly and painful, they are unlikely to be permanent. In a few weeks, Jack will appear the same as before the attack. But, suppose Al also knocked out one of Jack's front teeth during the fight. Case law holds that the loss of the tooth elevates the crime to an aggravated assault because a body member, the tooth, is permanently destroyed.[22]

Does the definition of serious bodily injury cover being knocked unconscious, a broken nose, a ruptured spleen, a severed artery, a broken leg, a sprained ankle, a detached retina, a one-inch permanent scar on the face, or permanent brain damage? Obviously a wide range of injuries could possibly fit the definition. Whether an injury is a serious bodily injury is determined on an ad hoc basis.[23] However, the key to whether personal injury is serious seems to turn on two factors: First, was the injury permanent, long-term, or possibly fatal? Under this standard the law is recognizing

§ 1.07. Definitions

(a) In this code:

* * *

(46) "Serious bodily injury" means bodily injury that creates a substantial risk of death or that causes death, serious permanent disfigurement, or protracted loss or impairment of the function of any bodily member or organ.

that medical problems that are resolved in a relatively short period of time fall outside the scope of an aggravated crime. Perhaps most problematic under this criteria is the broken bone. Part of the issue here is that bones "break" in a variety of ways ranging from cracks to complete, splintering separations. While most persons consider a break serious at the time it occurs, recovery with few to no permanent problems is quite common given competent medical care. However, it should be noted that the fact the victim received rapid medical care and never was actually in danger of death or permanent disability is not a factor in considering the severity of the injury.

The second, unwritten criterion is the social distinction between a misdemeanor offense and a felony. Is the injury of such a magnitude that it is worthy of sentencing the assailant to prison? Felonies connote the major offenses in our society. Is breaking someone's leg or knocking them temporarily unconscious worthy of possible incarceration with murderers, robbers, and rapists? This standard may be one of the subtle reasons that prosecutors invoke their discretion and plea-bargain many potential aggravated assault charges down to misdemeanors. The nature of the injury, while meeting the statutory standard, is simply not worthy of prison time.

Table 6-2 displays a range of injuries that have been deemed by Texas courts to constitute "serious bodily injury" for the purposes of the aggravated assault statute.

Or, the Person Uses or Exhibits a Deadly Weapon

The aggravated assault statute speaks of **using or exhibiting deadly weapon**. Clearly these are two different acts. As the Court of Criminal Appeals has explained,

> Thus, "used . . . a deadly weapon" during the commission of the offense means that the deadly weapon was employed or utilized in order to achieve its purpose. Whereas "exhibited a deadly weapon" means that the weapon was consciously shown or displayed during the commission of the offense . . . . [U]sed . . . during the commission of a felony offense refers certainly to the wielding of a firearm with effect, but it extends as well to any employment of a deadly weapon, even

---

TABLE 6-2   Injuries Deemed Bodily Injury or Serious Bodily Injury by Texas Courts

Appellate courts have ruled that under the facts of a particular case, the following conditions constituted "bodily injury" or "serious bodily injury" within the meaning of the Penal Code:

Bodily Injury	Serious Bodily Injury
Pain	Death
Bruises	Skull fracture
Muscle strain	Fractured nose
Skin cut	Loss of ear
Fractured jaw	Loss of tooth
Causing burning sensation in mouth	Loss of ability to walk
Passing out	Loss of eye
Striking with fists	Broken finger, hip, or pelvis
Sprained finger	Broken arm or leg
	Shattered cheek bone
	Dislocated toe
	Extreme dehydration
	Internal bleeding
	Stab wound

§ 1.07. Definitions

(a) In this code:

* * *

(17) "Deadly weapon" means:

A. a firearm or anything manifestly designed, made, or adapted for the purpose of inflicting death or serious bodily injury; or

B. anything that in the manner of its use or intended use is capable of causing death or serious bodily injury.

its simple possession, if such possession facilitates the associated felony. However, to "exhibit" a deadly weapon it need only be consciously displayed during the commission of the required felony offense. Thus, one can "use" a deadly weapon without exhibiting it, but it is doubtful one can exhibit a deadly weapon during the commission of a felony without using it.[24]

The assailant who fires a shotgun at his victim or stabs him in the back with a knife has used the deadly weapon even though the victim may never have seen the weapon. On the other hand, if Charles waives a gun in the air while threatening his victim, he has exhibited the deadly weapon even though the firearm is never directly pointed at the victim.[25] Meanwhile, the offender who threatens to shoot the victim while pointing a pistol at him has both exhibited and used the deadly weapon under the court's definitions. The use comes from the fact that display of the weapon facilitates the offense by placing the victim in fear. But suppose Tom and Jerry get into a fistfight while on a hunting trip. Tom is wearing a pistol but never draws it. Assuming that Tom is the assailant in this incident, does his offense rise to the level of an aggravated assault because he is wearing the pistol? Is he exhibiting the deadly weapon?

The Texas definition of "deadly weapon," while set within two statutory subsections, actually covers three possibilities. A **deadly weapon** can be:

* A firearm
* Anything designed, made, or adapted for causing death or serious bodily injury
* Anything that in its manner of use is capable of causing death or serious bodily injury

Firearm   The only object that is always a deadly weapon for purposes of the law of aggravated assault is a firearm. While the term "firearm" is not defined in the general Penal Code definitions found in Sec. 1.07, a definition does appear in Chapter 46. This definition has been applied in aggravated assault cases.

§ 46.01. Definitions

In this chapter:

* * *

(3) "Firearm" means any device designed, made, or adapted to expel a projectile through a barrel by using the energy generated by an explosion or burning substance or any device readily convertible to that use.

The definition encompasses traditional firearms such as pistols, rifles, and shotguns. It also includes machine guns and similar military-type weaponry. However, because the definition requires a projectile be expelled by an explosion or burning substance, weapons which look like a firearm may not fit the definition. For example, a pellet pistol, a B-B gun, and a water pistol do not meet each part of the definition.[26]

What if:

- The firearm is not loaded?
- The firearm is broken?
- The firearm is actually a toy?
- The firearm is actually a toy but the victim thinks it is real?
- The assailant feigns a pistol by placing his finger in a jacket pocket?

Texas and the vast majority of states follow an objective standard: a pistol, rifle, or shotgun is a firearm regardless of whether it is loaded or broken.[27] Similarly, a toy pistol is just that a toy, not a pistol, and thereby not a firearm.

If Jack feigns a pistol by placing his finger in a jacket pocket and tells Jill, "I'm going to kill you." Jill's reaction would likely be identical if Jack held a real concealed pistol. But Jack has only committed assault by threat, not aggravated assault. The assault sections of the Texas Penal Code are unconcerned with the victim's reaction, only the offender's actual conduct.

But suppose in reaction to Jack's nonexistent pistol, Jill draws her own pistol and shoots him. Can she make a valid claim of self-defense? Yes, while the state follows the objective standard for criminal offenses—a firearm must really be a firearm—it follows a subjective standard for defenses. Jill can avail herself of the theory of self-defense if she "reasonably believes the deadly force is immediately necessary . . . to protect himself against the other's use or attempted use of unlawful deadly force."[28] Thus, for purposes of a substantive offense, a firearm must actually be a firearm, but for purposes of the law of self-defense, the actor's perception that the device is a deadly weapon, not reality, controls.

Anything Designed, Made, or Adapted for Causing Death or Serious Bodily Injury On occasion, devices will be constructed that are capable of causing death or serious bodily injuries. Military ordinance, such as hand grenades and plastic explosives, fit within this category of deadly weapons. Improvised devices such as baseball bats adorned with nails, pipe bombs, and a bag full of rocks fall within the scope of this definition of the term.

Anything in the Manner of Its Use Capable of Causing Death or Serious Bodily Injury The fake or toy firearm is not an issue in aggravated assault cases as the object is incapable of discharging a bullet and thus is not a "firearm." But a gun, real or toy, could, of course, cause serious bodily injury if used as a bludgeon. In such cases, its inherent dangerousness is not important but rather its manner of use. In this regard, virtually *anything* could be a deadly weapon depending on how it is used. Table 6-3 lists various items that Texas courts have found to be deadly weapons based on their manner of use in the particular circumstances.

Knives, chains, rocks, and even an automobile have been used as a deadly weapon. In one bizarre case in Illinois, a woman was charged with assault after allegedly pummeling a dog breeder with a dead Chihuahua.[29] In many jurisdictions, including Texas, live dogs have been considered deadly weapons under the facts of the particular case.[30] Similarly, throwing acid on another could be a deadly weapon if the acid were capable

TABLE 6-3   Articles Deemed Deadly Weapons Under Specific Factual Circumstances

Appellate courts have ruled that under the facts of a particular case and based on their manner of construction or use, the following items were deadly weapons within the meaning of the Penal Code:

Firearm (specifically designated as deadly weapon in statute)
Automobile
Knife
Human bite
Iron bar
Hot coffee
Glass bottle
Broken plate
Hands
Feet
Plastic bag
Plastic cord
Video cassette recorder
Metal pipe
Ripped aluminum can
Golf club
Spear
Tree branch
Sharpened toothbrush handle
Walking cane

of producing permanent disfigurement. Likewise, hitting a victim's head on a nearby lamppost constitutes use of a deadly weapon as does striking the victim's head on a concrete roadway. As an Oregon judge once observed, "Whether the pitcher hits the stone or the stone hits the pitcher, it will be bad news for the pitcher."[31]

One bit of lore surrounding the concept of deadly weapon is the notion that the hands and feet of professional boxers and martial arts experts are inherently deadly weapons due to the individual's level of training and expertise in assaultive-type behavior. No American statute is known to exist that declares hands and feet of skilled individuals to be deadly weapons *per se* or that requires the appendages be registered with authorities as a deadly weapon in the same manner as a handgun might. Indeed, the prevailing rule is that bare hands and feet are not intrinsically dangerous weapons; were the rule to the contrary, every fistfight would elevate to an aggravated assault. However, in some jurisdictions, including Texas, fists and feet, given their particular manner of use, have been ruled to be deadly weapons where the beating was particularly savage.[32] Of course, a victim battered by a professional boxer is likely to suffer serious bodily injury and the charges can be based upon the harmful result rather than the type of weaponry.

During the 1990s, some prosecutors filed aggravated assault charges against certain individuals who were infected with acquired human immunodeficiency virus (HIV). In some cases, the individual had transmitted the virus to an uninformed sex partner or to a sexual assault victim. In other instances, the infected person spat at or threw bodily fluids at a police officer or correctional officer. While Texas courts have recognized that HIV-infected semen is a deadly weapon in a sexual assault case,[33] to establish aggravated assault the state would have to prove that the disease is capable of being transmitted in the manner in question. In one case, the court found that an HIV-infected inmate who bit a jail nurse had used a deadly weapon within the meaning of the statute.[34] But, transmittal of AIDS by spittle or by mere contact with another's bodily fluids is generally viewed as unlikely to near impossible.[35] From 1989 until 1994, the Texas Penal Code contained a statute specifically criminalizing the intentional passing of HIV to another person.[36] Today, the matter is simply absorbed within the aggravated assault statute, placing the burden on the state to establish that the manner in which the actor attempted to transfer bodily fluids to the victim fits within the definition of a deadly weapon. For persons who work in jails and other correctional facilities, a statute decrees it a third degree felony if an individual commits an assault by contact through use of human or animal bodily fluids or feces, regardless of whether they are HIV-infected.[37]

Alternative Theories in Charging Aggravated Assault

Many aggravated assaults occur wherein the offender threatens the victim with a deadly weapon or actually uses the deadly weapon in an effort to physically harm the victim. Since a deadly weapon by definition is capable of causing death or serious bodily injury, many such offenses do in fact produce serious personal injuries to the victim. Pam threatens to shoot Sam and actually discharges a pistol in his direction, missing him but shattering the television set. Pam has committed an aggravated assault because of the use of a firearm. Likewise, were she lacking the pistol, if Pam were to take a swing at Sam with a fireplace poker, an aggravated assault has also occurred as the poker could cause serious bodily injury. If Larry shoots Moe with a rifle and the bullet shatters Moe's ribs, Larry has committed two forms of aggravated assault and the prosecutor could file the charge based on either the use of the deadly weapon or the extent of Moe's injuries. A district attorney can charge Larry with aggravated assault by deadly weapon or aggravated assault with serious bodily injury, whichever is easier to prove. On the other hand, if the bullet merely grazes Moe's arm, aggravated assault with a deadly weapon has occurred but not aggravated assault with serious bodily injury. Constitutional prohibitions against double jeopardy may bar two convictions using both theories.[38]

Penalty

Aggravated assault is a felony of the second degree. If the offender knows the victim is a public servant lawfully discharging an official duty, the offense rises to a first degree felony. Thus, an aggravated assault on a peace officer is this level of crime. But suppose the officer is undercover when the assault occurs? It may be difficult to prove that the offender knew the victim was an officer. Aggravated assaults on security officers, witnesses, informants, and persons who report crime also become a felony of the first degree. Interestingly, the offense is also a felony of the first degree if committed by a public servant under color of authority. This means that a police officer or correctional officer who uses excessive force and causes serious bodily injury to a prisoner may be looking at felony of first degree charges.

Intoxication Assault

While public awareness about deaths caused by drunk drivers is high, less attention is paid to injuries that alcohol-impaired drivers cause. The National Highway Traffic Safety Administration estimates that while about 1,600 persons are killed each year

§ 49.07. Intoxication Assault

a. A person commits an offense if the person, by accident or mistake:
  1. while operating an aircraft, watercraft, or amusement ride while intoxicated, or while operating a motor vehicle in a public place while intoxicated, by reason of that intoxication causes serious bodily injury to another; or
  2. as a result of assembling a mobile amusement ride while intoxicated causes serious bodily injury to another.
b. In this section, "serious bodily injury" means injury that creates a substantial risk of death or that causes serious permanent disfigurement or protracted loss or impairment of the function of any bodily member or organ.
c. An offense under this section is a felony of the third degree.

in Texas in alcohol-related crashes, over 63,000 persons are injured due to intoxicated drivers. The intoxication assault statute is directed toward sanctioning the drivers for this harm. The statute is not contained in Chapter 22 with other assaultive offenses but is found in Chapter 49 among the alcohol-related crimes. Intoxication assault, Sec. 49.07, is geared toward sanctioning intoxicated drivers who cause significant bodily harm. Commission of intoxicated assault is the equivalent of committing aggravated assault with serious bodily injury, although intoxicated assault is a felony of the third degree.

Elements of Intoxicated Assault

By Accident or Mistake   The accident or mistake element of intoxicated assault underlines the intention of the Legislature to punish conduct which would otherwise not be a crime. If a sober driver causes serious bodily injury in a vehicle collision, no offense occurs because no *mens rea* exists; the event is deemed an accident. But under Sec. 49.07, the fact of intoxication substitutes for the culpable mental state. The Legislature has created a strict liability offense and the offender's mental state is irrelevant.[39]

While Operating Aircraft, Watercraft, Amusement Ride, or Motor Vehicle in Public Place   The overwhelming bulk of intoxicated driving and intoxication assault offenses are committed by individuals operating motor vehicles on public roadways. The statute, however, also covers intoxicated operators of aircraft, watercraft, and amusement rides. Drunken boaters, water-skiers, and jet ski riders occasionally are prosecuted for intoxication assault as a result of injuries they cause.

The statute is not applicable to intoxicated individuals on horseback or bicycles. Likewise, the law would appear not to apply to injuries resulting from persons who operate industrial machinery while drunk or high on drugs. Application of the intoxication assault statute is directed to individuals who place the general public at risk through their impaired driving.

While Intoxicated   Sec. 49.01 sets forth the two alternative definitions of "intoxication." These are the same definitions used for intoxication manslaughter discussed in Chapter 5 of this text. Recall that an individual is intoxicated if he or she lacks normal use of their mental and physical faculties through the introduction of alcohol and/or drugs into their body. This standard requires a finding of fact by the judge or jury. The alternate criteria—the *per se* law—holds that one is deemed intoxicated by law if his or her blood alcohol level is 0.08 or higher.

Causes Serious Bodily Injury to Another Intoxication assault is limited to incidents wherein serious bodily injury occurs, not ordinary bodily injury. Suppose Lindsey, an intoxicated driver, crashes her car into a lamppost. Her passenger Brittney is injured. If Brittney's injuries meet the definition of "serious bodily injury," Lindsey can be prosecuted for intoxication assault. If the injuries are merely bumps and bruises, any assault charge against Lindsey would have to be predicated upon Sec. 22.01(a)(1), assault with bodily injury by recklessness. Such charges are rarely filed.

Injury to a Child, Elderly Individual, or Disabled Individual

Texas, like most states, provides enhanced punishment for assaults that involve certain highly vulnerable victims. These increased penalties are an effort to deter the use of unlawful force against these individuals or to protect those who may be less able to protect themselves. Falling within the special victim classification are children, elderly individuals, and individuals with physical and mental disabilities. Child abuse is viewed as particularly abhorrent behavior in modern society. The federal government estimates that annually about 175,000 children are victims of physical abuse.[40] Similarly, elder abuse, long hidden from public view, has emerged as a significant social problem. Often the offender in such abuse cases is a relative, babysitter, or caregiver. The Texas statute contains a specific subsection applicable to group home and nursing home operators and employees.

For the purposes of the statute (Sec. 22.04), a **child** is someone 14 years old or younger while an **elderly individual** is a person 65 years of age or older. The definition of "child" also covers fetus, although not if the mother is the perpetrator of the injury.[41] A **disabled individual** is someone over 14 who due to age or mental or physical disease, defect, or injury is unable to protect or care for themselves.

The law imposes enhanced punishment beyond that for ordinary assault with bodily injury behavior under Sec. 22.01 and 22.02. All injuries to children, elderly individuals, or individuals with mental or physical impairments are felonious with the level of the felony primarily determined by the culpable mental state of the offender. The statute covers harm caused by acts of the defendant and by omissions to act when the defendant has a legal duty to act.

As a general rule, if the victim of bodily injury is a child, elderly individual, or individual with a disability, prosecution under Sec. 22.04 provides a potential higher level of punishment than would arise under the assault and aggravated assault statutes. However, Sec. 22.04 does not cover assaults by threat or assaults by contact. The standard statutes would be used in these cases even though the victim might be a child or elderly individual. Sec. 22.04 is complex and the exact language should be reviewed prior to applying it to a particular fact situation.

Deadly Conduct

Suppose Lindsey, who is intoxicated, finds herself driving down a street. Because of her impaired condition she is slow to observe a group of school children crossing the street. Lindsey's car is in the crosswalk before she slams on the brakes. The school children jump out of the way. No one is injured but several children are nearly struck by Lindsey's car. Or suppose Eddie is a member of an urban gang. One night he and a fellow gang member drive past the home of Calvin, a member of a rival gang. Eddie fires a shotgun through Calvin's front window. No one is injured because Calvin is not at home at the time.

Although no one is physically harmed in either of the previous hypothetical incidents, the actions constitute the crime of deadly conduct. The Texas deadly conduct

§ 22.05. Deadly Conduct

a. A person commits an offense if he recklessly engages in conduct that places another in imminent danger of serious bodily injury.

b. A person commits an offense if he knowingly discharges a firearm at or in the direction of:
   1. one or more individuals; or
   2. a habitation, building, or vehicle and is reckless as to whether the habitation, building, or vehicle is occupied.

c. Recklessness and danger are presumed if the actor knowingly pointed a firearm at or in the direction of another whether or not the actor believed the firearm to be loaded.

d. For purposes of this section, "building," "habitation," and "vehicle" have the meanings assigned those terms by Section 30.01.

e. An offense under Subsection (a) is a Class A misdemeanor. An offense under Subsection (b) is a felony of the third degree.

statute covers two entirely separate forms of antisocial behavior. The first is conduct that places others at great risk of serious injury and the second explicitly criminalizes so-called drive-by shootings.

Elements of Deadly Conduct by Placing in Imminent Danger

A Person Recklessly   The *mens rea* for the first form of deadly conduct is recklessness. This fills a gap in the law of assault by threat. If Martha intentionally, but unsuccessfully, tries to injure Robert, either an assault by threat or an attempted assault with bodily injury has occurred. But if she only recklessly places Robert in danger of injury, no assault occurs. That is where deadly conduct fits in the statutory scheme. If harm exists in knowingly threatening a person, there is also harm in placing that individual in danger unintentionally but through reckless conduct.

Engages in Conduct   The offender must engage in some act for liability to attach. If the victim places himself in peril, the offender normally commits no offense by failing to extract him from the potential harm.

That Places Another in Imminent Danger of Serious Bodily Injury   The actor's conduct must result only in the potential for *serious* bodily injury, not injury itself. Likewise, the statute is not violated if only bodily injury is the potential outcome of the deed. In short, Sec. 22.05(a) applies to acts that fall short of injuring another.[42] Of course, if the actor's conduct actually produces serious bodily injury, an aggravated assault has occurred.

While the term **danger** is not defined in the statute, one court has ruled that it means "exposure or liability to injury, pain or loss; jeopardy; peril."[43] Many, but not all, reckless conduct cases involve firearms. To assist in proving these cases, Sec. 22.05(a) provides that recklessness and danger are presumed if the actor points a firearm at another. For nonfirearms cases, the prosecution has to establish that the victim was in peril of serious bodily injury.

The exposure to serious bodily injury must be "imminent." Recall that the term "imminent" means "near, close at hand." Driving a vehicle at a high speed along the open spaces through West Texas may not be lawful but it does not place a youthful passenger in the car in "imminent" danger. But twice attempting to force a car off the road during an incident of road rage places its youthful passenger in imminent danger of serious bodily injury.[44]

Elements of Deadly Conduct by Discharging Firearm

Knowingly Discharges a Firearm at an Individual, Habitation, Building, or Vehicle   Discharging a firearm is a common category of deadly conduct. This may take the form of unjustifiably firing over the head of the victim in an effort to scare him or participating in a drive-by shooting of a home, building, or vehicle. Depending on the factual circumstances, this subsection could overlap aggravated assault by threatening with a deadly weapon. On the other hand, the law of assault is not implicated if the actor shoots at an unoccupied house, building, or vehicle. In the case of Eddie and Calvin above, Eddie commits deadly conduct. But, if Calvin or someone else had been struck by the bullets, Eddie would be guilty of aggravated assault, that is, Eddie recklessly caused bodily injury with a deadly weapon.

And Is Reckless as to Whether the Habitation, Building, or Vehicle Is Occupied   The final element of this form of deadly conduct requires an additional level of culpability—recklessness. The actor must be reckless about whether the structure or vehicle is occupied; the offender must be aware of the risk that the structure or vehicle may contain a person. Establishing this *mens rea* element will vary with the facts of the case, but should not prove difficult in most applications.

But what if Jeffery is using his 0.22 caliber rifle to take target practice at a vehicle that has been abandoned along a desert road? He certainly is knowingly discharging a firearm at a vehicle but is not being reckless about whether the vehicle is occupied. This missing final element prevents deadly conduct charges in this case. Any offense Jeffrey might be committing would appear to better fall under the criminal mischief law.

Penalty

Deadly conduct involving placing others in danger of serious bodily injury is a Class A misdemeanor. Discharging a firearm at a person, building, habitation, or vehicle is a third degree felony.

Consenting to Assault

Suppose early one morning a masked man gives Natalie a substance which renders her unconscious. Then a woman wearing a mask and gloves and using a sharp knife slices open her abdomen. Has the woman and her confederate committed an aggravated assault? Not if she is a licensed physician performing the delivery of a baby through a Caesarian section. Recall the earlier scenario regarding the injury of Gene's nose in the basketball game. Has an assault occurred? Or suppose this Halloween you pay five dollars to tour a "haunted house" established as a charitable fund-raiser. Over a dozen times during your tour, you are momentarily placed in fear of imminent bodily injury. Have the haunted house organizers committed assault by threat?

At one time or another, every human has consented to conduct that could under other circumstances be considered an assault. Medical treatment and contact sports are but two of several circumstances where knowing consent prevents any claim of a criminal incident. Every state recognizes the idea that one can consent to being assaulted. Boxers certainly do in a most direct sense as do surgery patients. But so do college students when engaged in intramural sports. Whether playing full contact sports, such as football, or supposedly noncontact sports, such as soccer and softball, participants implicitly recognize the possibility of some level of grabbing, twisting, bumping, and even outright pain. Inadvertent bodily injury, such as sprains, strains, and broken bones, may also result from aggressive play.

Sec. 22.06 of the Penal Code establishes **consent** as a defense to allegations of assault, aggravated assault, and deadly conduct. Consent forms a defense if the victim has consented in fact or the actor reasonably believes the victim has consented and the conduct does not threaten or inflict serious bodily injury. Or, the victim knows the conduct is a risk of his occupation, medical treatment, or scientific experimentation. The individual's consent may be either explicit or implicit. When you have surgery, for example, you are required to execute extensive informed consent forms prior to the procedure. But, a pickup basketball game is certainly not preceded by players signing consent forms. Players are rightly assumed to have consented to the contact involved in the game.

However, criminal prosecutions have been instituted in some jurisdictions when the level of contact exceeds that to which a reasonable person could assume to have agreed to. The best known incident is likely the 2000 conviction by a Canadian court of National Hockey League (NHL) player Marty McSorley. A 17-year professional hockey veteran with the Boston Bruins, McSorley was convicted of assault with a weapon after striking Vancouver Canucks forward Donald Brashear with his hockey stick during a game. The McSorley incident is not unique among assault charges in sporting contests. In 1988, another NHL player, Dino Ciccarelli, received a day in jail and a fine for striking an opponent with his stick. In 2005, a South Dakota college basketball player was charged with assault for throwing an elbow during a game. The elbow resulted in a concussion and 14 stitches in the opponent's face. A jury subsequently found him not guilty of simple assault. No assault charges are known to have ever been filed as a result of injuries incurred in sporting events in Texas.

So long as serious bodily injury is not intended, one can usually consent to forms of contact that would otherwise be an assault. Some jurisdictions have banned ultimate fighting, mixed martial arts,[45] combative fighting, and "tough-man" contests because of their emphasis on disabling the opponent through particularly brutal punching and kicking.[46] About three dozen states have statutes outlawing "no-holds-barred" fighting. In recent years, many promoters of such matches have altered their rules to reduce the possibility of serious bodily injury and thereby permit participants to be regulated under state sports commissions as well as avoid indictment under aggravated assault statutes. Currently in Texas, such events fall under the purview of the Texas Department of Licensing and Regulation (TDLR). Mixed martial arts contests are permitted providing they are licensed by TDLR and comply with the agency's rules.[47]

Terroristic Threat

Introduction

The offense of terroristic threat has no Common Law antecedent but certainly responds to contemporary needs. The terroristic threat law actually predates the 9/11 tragedy and societal concerns about terrorism, although the statute certainly is applicable to many acts of political terrorism. Sec. 22.07 seeks to sanction two broad categories of behavior. The first is conduct intended to place an individual in fear of bodily injury. The other is threats against broader elements of society where the public at large is affected by the threatening conduct.

§ 22.07. Terroristic Threat

(a) A person commits an offense if he threatens to commit any offense involving violence to any person or property with intent to:

1. cause a reaction of any type to his threat by an official or volunteer agency organized to deal with emergencies;
2. place any person in fear of imminent serious bodily injury;
3. prevent or interrupt the occupation or use of a building, room, place of assembly, place to which the public has access, place of employment or occupation, aircraft, automobile, or other form of conveyance, or other public place;
4. cause impairment or interruption of public communications, public transportation, public water, gas, or power supply or other public service;
5. place the public or a substantial group of the public in fear of serious bodily injury; or
6. influence the conduct or activities of a branch or agency of the federal government, the state, or a political subdivision of the state.

Elements of Terroristic Threat

A Person Threatens to Commit Any Offense Involving Violence to Any Person or Property Suppose Brad confronts Helen and threatens to shoot her. An assault by threat has occurred as Brad has threatened Helen with imminent bodily injury. But what if Brad, living in El Paso, telephones Helen at her home in McAllen? Helen is not at home. However, Brad leaves the following message on Helen's voice mail. "This is your worst nightmare. I am coming to your house and I'm going to kill you." Has Brad committed an assault? Probably not. Brad's conduct lacks the traditional view of an assault: a face-to-face confrontation and an apparent ability to immediately deliver upon the threat.

Brad has certainly made a threat. Recall from earlier in the chapter that "[a] threat is defined as, 'a declaration of intention or determination to inflict punishment, loss or pain on another, or to injure another by the commission of an unlawful act.' "[48] For the offense of terroristic threat, any offense involving violence to persons or property is covered. This section is intended to be very broad and cover all threats of violence where the intent is to cause fear, emergency action, or substantial inconvenience. However, Texas appellate courts have not to date identified which offenses in the Penal Code "involve violence to persons or property." Presumably, threats to do bodily injury, commit a robbery, perpetrate a sexual assault, or damage property through arson would be considered crimes of violence. However, a threat to steal one's property, paint graffiti on the side of one's house, or damage one's automobile would not seem to fall within the ordinary dictionary definition of "violence."

Note that an actor could also make a threat to one person to harm another person. The intended victim of the harm and the recipient of the threat need not be the same person. Suppose Junior writes a note, intended for a classmate, that reads, "I am going to kick your butt after school." The teacher intercepts the note before the intended recipient reads it. For the purposes of the statute, Junior has made a threat to commit a crime of violence.

With Intent to Terroristic threat requires a general *mens rea* of at least recklessness in making the threat but also a specific intent to accomplish one of six goals.[49] It must be proven that the actor's conscious objective was to accomplish one of the six alternative results. Like assault by threat, this is a nature of conduct offense. It is not necessary that the victim or anyone else be actually placed in fear or that the offender had the capacity to carry out his or her other threats. The statute requires only that the defendant sought the desired reaction, not that the victim actually reacted.[50]

The threat must occur under one of the following six conditions:

1. *Cause a reaction of any type to his threat by an emergency agency* The first subsection of the terrorist threat statute overlaps to some degree the false alarm statute found in Sec. 42.06. This statute sanctions a threat of a future offense with intent to cause a reaction by an emergency services agency, while Sec. 42.06 covers present, past, and future false incidents. The terrorist threat statute is unconcerned with the truth or falsity of the actor's threat. Indeed, unlike the false alarm statute, the individual who makes a terroristic threat may actually intend to place a bomb, start a fire, or commit some other violent offense.

2. *Place any person in fear of imminent serious bodily injury* Anecdotal evidence suggests that this is the most commonly committed form of terrorist threat: a threat made to place another in fear of serious bodily injury. Several elements are important to note. First, the law does not apply to threats to do ordinary bodily injury. If Harry sends Jim an email threatening to punch him in the nose, that threat concerns only ordinary bodily injury. Second, unlike the law of assault where making the threat is the *actus reus*, this offense requires a goal of placing the victim in fear, a slightly different circumstance. However, it is important to remember that the offense is complete whether or not the victim actually becomes fearful.

A curious portion of this subsection is the placement within the sentence of the word "imminent." As written, the word modifies the term "serious bodily injury," meaning that the threat must be of causing imminent serious bodily injury. This conduct would appear already to be covered by the assault statute, which requires "threatening another with imminent bodily injury." However, Texas courts seem inclined to interpret the statute as if the term modified "fear," so that the statutory phrase reads "place any person in imminent fear of serious bodily injury." For example, one Court of Appeals held that a terroristic threat occurred when a husband, who was several miles away, threatened his estranged wife over the telephone. The court rejected the argument that due to his locale the defendant could not place his wife in fear of *imminent* serious bodily injury. The court ruled that it was reasonable for the victim to believe he was close at hand.[51] In another case, the appeals court found that two messages left on the answering machine of an individual who was out of town constituted threats to place in fear of imminent serious bodily injury, even though the actor repeatedly called for the victim to "come find me" and never suggested he was coming to the victim's home.[52] However, another Texas court has recognized that the word "imminent" requires a present, not a future harm. This appeals court reversed the terroristic threat conviction of an individual who said to a county commissioner "I'll kick your g__ d __ ass if you aren't out grading my road tomorrow." The court found that the threat was not imminent as it was conditioned on the occurrence or nonoccurrence of the road grading the following day.[53]

3. *Prevent or interrupt the occupation or use of a building . . . or other public place* The classic case of a bomb threat that disrupts a meeting and causes evacuation of a building falls within this subsection. If Ferris, at home because of illness, telephones his high school and states that a bomb is in the cafeteria, he has committed terroristic threat. The fact that Ferris has not placed a bomb nor has any real intention of actually harming anyone is irrelevant to the commission of the offense.

In one real case, a 12-year-old was found to have violated the statute when he twice told school officials, "I'm going to blow up the school." The statements were made in an apparent effort to forestall disciplinary action about to be taken by the principal. The reviewing court admitted that the juvenile lacked the capacity to blow up the school and likely did not really intend to carry out his threat. Nonetheless, his behavior fit the elements of the offense.[54]

In what may be the oddest application of this subsection to date, a terroristic threat conviction was upheld against an individual who told the victim "I have put snakes in your house." The appeals court rejected the argument that no offense occurred because the accused did not say they were dangerous snakes.[55]

4. *Cause impairment/interruption of public communications . . . or other public service* This subsection, along with the next two, is directed particularly at terrorist acts which place the public as a whole in fear of mass harm. If Roger threatens to poison the public water supply or place the Ebola virus on city busses, he is violating this subsection of the statute. While it does not matter whether Roger has a political agenda in making the threat, one would expect the offense would be committed primarily by those with a motive to panic the public.

5. *Place the public or a substantial group of the public in fear of serious bodily injury* Any threat to do violence that places the public, as opposed to a particular individual, in fear of serious bodily injury falls within the coverage of the statute. A terrorist who posts an item on the Internet threatening to set off a "dirty nuclear bomb" somewhere in Texas violates this subsection. Once again, it is the intent of the actor, not whether he carries out the threat that constitutes the offense.

6. *Influence the conduct . . . a branch or agency of . . . government . . . of the state* Threats to commit violent acts to influence government conduct has been shown to be a common goal of political terrorists. To date, no terrorist is known to have been prosecuted for violating this section of Texas law.

Penalty

Commission of the first two subsections of Sec. 22.07 is a Class B misdemeanor. Other subsections, if violated, generally constitute a Class A misdemeanor, state jail felony, or felony of the third degree depending on the surrounding circumstances and the nature of the victim.

Stalking

Modern statutes have also expanded the criminal law to another circumstance where only a potential harm to persons exists. This is nowhere more evident than with the enactment of anti-stalking laws.[56] California enacted the first such law in 1990[57] and the other 49 states have since enacted their own anti-stalking statutes.[58] The issue of stalking was viewed as of sufficient national importance that in 1996 Congress declared it a federal offense to travel across a state line for the purposes of stalking someone.[59]

In a general sense, **stalking** places the victim in fear, but unlike assault where fear of personal injury arises, the fear in stalking is a more generic one; the victim is fearful of the unknown, the next move the stalker may make. One author has characterized stalking as a form of mental assault.[60]

The extent of stalking in Texas is unknown. The crime is believed to be highly underreported. One Texas survey of the general population found that over 18 percent of respondents had been the victim of a stalking incident within the previous two years. According to the survey, men and women were about equally likely to be the victim of a stalking incident. The most common reason given for the stalking was jealousy on the part of the offender.[61]

§ 42.072. Stalking

a. A person commits an offense if the person, on more than one occasion and pursuant to the same scheme or course of conduct that is directed specifically at another person, knowingly engages in conduct, including following the other person, that:
   1. the actor knows or reasonably believes the other person will regard as threatening:
      A. bodily injury or death for the other person;
      B. bodily injury or death for a member of the other person's family or household; or
      C. that an offense will be committed against the other person's property;
   2. causes the other person or a member of the other person's family or household to be placed in fear of bodily injury or death or fear that an offense will be committed against the other person's property; and
   3. would cause a reasonable person to fear:
      A. bodily injury or death for himself or herself;
      B. bodily injury or death for a member of the person's family or household; or
      C. that an offense will be committed against the person's property.

b. An offense under this section is a felony of the third degree, except that the offense is a felony of the second degree if the actor has previously been convicted under this section.

Texas has placed its stalking statute in Chapter 42 (Disorderly Conduct and Related Offenses). The content of the law, however, seems more applicable to assaultive and threatening behavior.

One unique aspect of the Texas statute and other states' anti-stalking laws is the element of repeated conduct. The statute requires either a repeated pattern of behavior or that the harassing incidents occur on more than one occasion. This unusual requirement can create difficulty in proving the offense unless some official record of at least two incidents of stalking was made. However, in one case the prosecution established the defendant's threatening conduct through use of telephone records showing 34 calls in a two-day period.[62] Unlike most criminal offenses, if the victim is subjected to the actor's antisocial behavior only once, the stalking law has not been violated.

Another interesting element of the offense is a factor that might normally be considered lawful conduct: following the other person. In cases wherein the victim claims to be unlawfully followed, the evidence must clearly establish that the actor's appearance in the vicinity of the victim was purposefully threatening, not a mere coincidence.

The conduct of the offender must place the victim in fear of injury to herself or himself, their property, or their family. Accusations of stalking often occur in the context of domestic disputes. The Texas statute requires that not only must the offender know his or her conduct is threatening but, unlike terrorist threat, the victim must actually be placed in fear. Finally, to prevent individuals from being accused unjustifiably, it must be proven that the offender's conduct would cause a reasonable person to be placed in fear. These three requirements attempt to prevent petty bickering among former friends and ex-spouses from being viewed as a crime.

Anti-stalking statutes, including Sec. 42.072, have generally passed constitutional scrutiny despite the fact that the terminology used in the laws is fairly broad and not given to precise definition.[63] Courts recognize the difficulty for the Legislature in trying to precisely describe each form of harassing conduct that it deems to be illegal. Accordingly, some judicial latitude is granted in the use of broad terms to describe the prohibited conduct.[64]

SEXUAL ASSAULT

Archie and Betty, both college students, have been out on several dates together. Late one Saturday night, after having consumed a large amount of liquor, Archie and Betty find themselves in Archie's apartment. They begin kissing. Soon they are semi-naked. Before long, Archie is on top of Betty and attempts to engage in sexual intercourse. Betty says nothing. Archie successfully enters Betty at which point she says, "Don't. We shouldn't be doing this." Betty says nothing further and Archie does not withdraw until a minute later after reaching orgasm. The two fall asleep. The next morning, Betty leaves Archie's apartment and contacts the campus police and says Archie raped her. Assume you are a prosecutor. Would you file criminal charges against Archie? How would you prove your case beyond a reasonable doubt? Are there more facts you need to know in order to make your decision?

COMMON LAW RAPE

Under the Common Law, rape was the carnal knowledge of a female by a male, not her husband, forcibly and against her will. The crime was limited to female victims and male offenders. A variant of this definition was followed in most American jurisdictions until the 1970s.

Under traditional law, a successful prosecution required proof of three elements: carnal knowledge, force, and lack of consent. Penile penetration was the sole method by which carnal knowledge could be established. Any other form of sexual contact was not rape but sodomy or some other offense.

Rape also had to be forcible. Accordingly, under the Common Law rule a female victim was obligated to "resist to her utmost," otherwise the possibility was raised that she had consented. This rule placed victims in grave danger of being seriously injured or killed. If Adam threatens to stab Eve with a knife unless she submits to sexual intercourse, is it reasonable to expect Eve to resist Adam? Our ancestors thought so!

Traditional law also excluded husbands from the class of persons who could commit the crime of rape, the logic being that by marrying, the woman agreed to be subservient to her husband.[65]

TEXAS LAW OF SEXUAL ASSAULT

Introduction

In the 1970s, a movement led by legal scholars and feminist activists resulted in major reforms to the law of rape. The Texas Legislature ultimately responded to this movement and in the 1980s significantly changed the state's approach to sexual assault. While some critics have suggested that the intended goals of the reforms have not been completely met, most would agree that the state of the law is more just than it was only a generation ago.

The reform movement focused on five major changes to the law of rape. Most of these changes are now reflected in one form or another in the Texas sexual assault statutes.

- Renaming the offense
- Redefining the scope of the offense
- Changing evidentiary rules
- Redefining statutory rape offenses
- Altering the penalty structure

§ 22.011. Sexual Assault

(a) A person commits an offense if the person:

1. intentionally or knowingly:
   A. causes the penetration of the anus or sexual organ of another person by any means, without that person's consent;
   B. causes the penetration of the mouth of another person by the sexual organ of the actor, without that person's consent; or
   C. causes the sexual organ of another person, without that person's consent, to contact or penetrate the mouth, anus, or sexual organ of another person, including the actor; or

2. intentionally or knowingly:
   A. causes the penetration of the anus or sexual organ of a child by any means;
   B. causes the penetration of the mouth of a child by the sexual organ of the actor;
   C. causes the sexual organ of a child to contact or penetrate the mouth, anus, or sexual organ of another person, including the actor;
   D. causes the anus of a child to contact the mouth, anus, or sexual organ of another person, including the actor; or
   E. causes the mouth of a child to contact the anus or sexual organ of another person, including the actor.

Elements of Sexual Assault

Causes Penetration or Contact

The sexual assault statute (Sec. 22.011) incorporates two harms. First, subsection (a)(1) speaks to intentional or knowing nonconsensual sexual penetration or sexual contact. Subsection (a)(2) covers sexual penetration and sexual contact with a child. In this case, consent is not an element since the law does not grant children the authority to consent.

Both subsections appear to cover most possible combinations of contact or penetration between sexual organs, the anus, and the mouth of the offender and the victim. Thus, oral, vaginal, or anal sex all fall within the scope of the statute. Mouth-to-mouth contact, that is, kissing, is not within the scope of the statute.[66]

Note should be made of the fact that the sexual assault statute is gender free except as anatomically required. This means that the perpetrator of a sexual assault can be a male or female and the victim can also be either a male or female. This approach is a significant departure from Common Law rape which was limited to male offenders and female victims.

In keeping with the Common Law tradition, however, Texas follows the rule that **penetration**, no matter how slight, is sufficient to establish the element of the offense.[67] The penetration may be made by sex organ, finger, tongue, or any other means.[68] If Abraham is forcibly assaulted by having a wooden rod inserted in his rectum, penetration has occurred. Likewise, the law does not require ejaculation as an element of the offense, only penetration.[69] The statute criminalizes alternative methods by which penetration can occur. Since sexual assault is a conduct-oriented offense, use of different types of penetration during the same incident constitutes multiple offenses.[70]

The statute utilizes the phrase "causes penetration." A defendant violates the statute if he or she brings about a penetration even if they do not personally penetrate the victim. In one case, a sexual assault of a child conviction was upheld where the defendant held his dog in a position to penetrate the victim.[71]

"Sexual contact" is not defined in this statute although it is defined in two other sections of the Penal Code, Sec. 21.01(2) and Sec. 21.11(a).[72] Appellate courts of the state have not had the opportunity to determine if either of these two definitions of the term or some other definition should be used in Sec. 22.011 prosecutions.

Of Another Person

Crime statistics suggest that the stereotypical stranger-to-stranger sexual assault occurs in only about one-third of reported cases.[73] Other studies put the figure at under 20 percent.[74] More common are allegations of acquaintance rape, such as in the Archie and Betty example at the beginning of this section.

The Texas statute applies to any person, including the husband or wife of the victim. While the Common Law exempted husbands from the class of individuals who could perpetrate the crime of rape, this state's law has dropped that exclusion. When this trend arose in the 1970s, many were concerned that spouses would unjustly accuse their mates of rape out of anger or to gain leverage in some collateral domestic dispute, such as a divorce. This concern has proven largely unfounded. As a practical matter, given the historical reluctance of women to report sexual assaults, it seems unrealistic that a false report would be made on a whim or in a small effort at revenge. While no national data is captured on the number of spousal rape charges filed annually, anecdotal evidence suggests they are few. Those charges that are filed often involve individuals who are legally married but no longer living together, in the process of divorce, or who have otherwise severed the emotional bonds of matrimony.

Since the statutory definition of "person" includes an "individual," a human being who is alive, sexual relations with a corpse would not constitute sexual assault.[75]

Without Consent

In neither subsection of Sec. 22.011 is the issue of force mentioned. This is because the cornerstone issue in sexual assault of an adult is the question of consent, not the issue of force. Sec. 1.07(a)(11) defines **consent** as "assent in fact, whether express or apparent." Recall the scenario of Archie and Betty. Betty has not given Archie express assent. Is, under the circumstances, Betty's failure to object to Archie's behavior apparent assent? In some states a defendant is allowed to raise the issue that he mistakenly believed the sexual encounter was consensual. The role of the jury becomes to determine if the defendant's belief that the alleged victim had given affirmative permission was reasonable.[76] Although Texas courts appear not to have considered this question, how would Archie fare with a defense of apparent assent?

In an effort to separate consensual sex from sexual assault, the Texas Legislature has codified not what constitutes consent but rather what is lack of consent. It is important to note that unlike the law of theft, which is concerned with *effective* consent, sexual assault speaks just of consent. This distinction would seem to evidence an intention on the part of the Legislature to limit the consent/nonconsent question to those situations listed in Sec. 22.011(b) rather than apply the more generic concepts of force, threat, or fraud contained in the definition of effective consent.[77] Of particular question is the issue of obtaining consent by fraud, which is examined below.

The 11 circumstances that do not constitute consent under Sec. 22.011(b) cover most situations that the ordinary individual would consider nonconsensual sex. The first two subsections along with subsection (b)(7) encompass the traditional notions of forcible sexual assault. Note that the force or threat of force can be used against the victim or some other person, such as threatening to harm the victim's child unless the victim submits. Note also that the victim is not required to resist to the utmost and the actor is not required to actually force the victim to submit; the threat

§ 22.011. Sexual Assault

* * *

(b) A sexual assault under Subsection (a)(1) is without the consent of the other person if:

1. the actor compels the other person to submit or participate by the use of physical force or violence;

2. the actor compels the other person to submit or participate by threatening to use force or violence against the other person, and the other person believes that the actor has the present ability to execute the threat;

3. the other person has not consented and the actor knows the other person is unconscious or physically unable to resist;

4. the actor knows that as a result of mental disease or defect the other person is at the time of the sexual assault incapable either of appraising the nature of the act or of resisting it;

5. the other person has not consented and the actor knows the other person is unaware that the sexual assault is occurring;

6. the actor has intentionally impaired the other person's power to appraise or control the other person's conduct by administering any substance without the other person's knowledge;

7. the actor compels the other person to submit or participate by threatening to use force or violence against any person, and the other person believes that the actor has the ability to execute the threat;

8. the actor is a public servant who coerces the other person to submit or participate;

9. the actor is a mental health services provider or a health care services provider who causes the other person, who is a patient or former patient of the actor, to submit or participate by exploiting the other person's emotional dependency on the actor;

10. the actor is a clergyman who causes the other person to submit or participate by exploiting the other person's emotional dependency on the clergyman in the clergyman's professional character as spiritual adviser; or

11. the actor is an employee of a facility where the other person is a resident, unless the employee and resident are formally or informally married to each other under Chapter 2, Family Code.

to use force and the victim's belief that the actor has the present ability to deliver the threat is sufficient to constitute no consent.

Subsection (b)(3) covers situations where the victim is unconscious or physically unable to resist. Thus, an individual who has passed out through self-induced intoxication is still protected under the law from being sexually assaulted. In one case, the court held that a female had been sexually assaulted by a midwife during a consensual medical exam. The midwife's conduct exceeded the scope of a proper medical exam and the victim was physically unable to resist because of the manner in which she was positioned on the examining table.[78]

The Court of Criminal Appeals has taken a very broad view of when one is unable to resist. "We hold that where assent in fact has not been given, and the actor knows that the victim's physical impairment is such that resistance is not reasonably to be expected, sexual intercourse is 'without consent' under the sexual assault statute."[79]

The sexual assault statute also protects those whose mental impairment prevents them from appraising the nature of the sexual act. The state will not permit sexual predators to prey upon the mentally impaired. Consent from a mentally retarded individual is the equivalent of no consent at all.[80]

On the surface, subsection (a)(5) appears to be the most curious. But a close reading of the statute reveals that the victim is not unaware that something is happening, just he or she is unaware they are being sexually assaulted. This provision could come into play with medical exams that exceed the scope of standard medical procedures.

Subsection (a)(6) speaks to impairing the victim's judgment by administering any substance without the victim's knowledge. (Use of "date rape" drugs is an enhancing factor that raises the crime to aggravated sexual assault.) Thus if Mark secretly adds vodka in Jennifer's lemonade and then obtains her consent for sexual activity solely because she is intoxicated, her consent is not valid. But reconsider the case of Betty and Archie. Suppose Betty consents to sex but does so only because of her self-induced intoxication. Has Archie committed sexual assault? The current state of Texas law on this question is unclear. On one hand, the consent statute speaks only to administering the substance without the victim's knowledge. Does that mean that if victims knowingly become intoxicated, the decisions they make about sexual conduct, even if foolish, still constitute consent? Certainly actual assent to sexual intercourse or other conduct has been given. Case law suggests that if consent is given and the victim's situation does not fit within one of the expressed provisions of Sec. 22.011(b), no sexual assault occurs.[81]

The remaining subsections of the statute relate to individuals who hold a superior position of power or authority over the victim. Accordingly, if a government official coerces the victim into the sexual conduct, no consent has occurred. Suppose Harry, a police officer, stops Suzy for speeding. Harry tells Suzy she is going to jail unless she performs oral sex on him. Suzy agrees and engages in the act. Harry has committed sexual assault under Sec. 22.011(b)(8).[82,83]

Similarly, purported consent obtained by counselors and clergy from emotionally dependent individuals is not recognized as valid consent and a sexual assault violation occurs. Falling under this provision are social workers, counselors, therapists, psychologists, and members of the clergy. In an unusual application of this provision, an individual who claimed to be a Hindu priest was convicted of sexual assault after bullying a woman into sexual intercourse. He persuaded the victim that she needed holy sperm to cleanse her womb.[84]

In an apparent strict liability approach to sexual assault, the Legislature has declared in Sec. 22.011(b)(11) that no employee of a nursing home or adult extended care facility can lawfully have sex with a resident unless they are married. The state is extending the same protection to these residents as it extends to children by refusing to allow them to consent to sexual conduct, at least with facility employees who are in a position to influence them.

Consent obtained by fraud is one area of the law not clearly covered in the statute. A traditional view holds that consent for intercourse obtained through fraud is normally not a sexual assault. For example, if Jennifer agrees to engage in sexual intercourse with Bruce because he promises to marry her in the morning and Bruce later recants on his agreement, no sexual assault has occurred because Jennifer agreed to the act. Likewise, if Brenda agrees to have sex with Norman because she wrongly mistakes him for a famous movie star, no crime occurs. Such would appear to be the rule under current Texas law because the fraud was in the inducement to the act, not in the act itself; the nominal victim agreed to the act, albeit for reasons different than reality. She voluntarily agreed to engage in sexual conduct. On the other hand, if Wanda visits her gynecologist for a checkup and he engages her in sexual intercourse while she thinks she is receiving a pelvic examination, the doctor has committed sexual assault because Wanda did not consent to the act of intercourse.[85] This latter situation is covered by Sec. 22.011(b)(5).

Assume Naomi is married to Raul. Late one night, Raul's cousin Pedro climbs into Naomi's bed. Naomi, believing her bedmate to be her husband, willingly engages in sexual intercourse. She subsequently discovers that her sex partner was Pedro. This is an offense under traditional rules regarding rape. Is this a nonconsensual sexual act under current Texas law?

The Betty and Archie scenario presents the problem of ambiguous consent. For many years the "lack of consent" element of the offense was established concurrent with the use of force. But since the sexual assault law has expanded to nonforcible acts, establishing lack of consent becomes more problematic. The modern trend is to presume lack of consent if the victim states that he or she did not consent to the act. However, lack of consent is an element of the offense that must be proven beyond a reasonable doubt. This evidentiary rule places the fact finder in a "who to believe" dilemma.

Contemporary social thinking holds that "no means no," "silence means no," "maybe means no," and in some situations "yes means no." Texas case law has yet to fully embrace this principle.

Assume Archie and Veronica engage in consensual sexual intercourse. During the act Veronica changes her mind and tells Archie to stop. Archie ignores her request and continues. Is Archie now committing a sexual assault? The few courts that have considered the matter have come to conflicting results with no clear trend on the question.[86] California holds that "a withdrawal of consent effectively nullifies any earlier consent and subjects the male to forcible rape charges if he persists in what has become nonconsensual intercourse."[87] Illinois has addressed the matter with a statute stating that consent withdrawn during sexual conduct terminates any existing consent.[88]

Neither Texas statutes nor court decisions provide much guidance on the answer to the withdrawal of consent question. Sexual assault is a conduct-oriented offense.[89] As such, one could argue that once penetration has occurred with consent, there is no sexual assault because the actor's conduct does not meet the elements of the offense. A counter argument would be that while sexual assault may be a conduct-oriented crime, penetration is a continuing event. Thus, when consent is withdrawn, a penetration without consent begins occurring and thereby a sexual assault.

Sexual Assault of a Child

The second form of sexual assault, Sec. 22.011(a)(2), is commonly referred to as sexual assault of a child. While children can certainly be victims of nonconsensual sexual assault under Sec. 22.011(a)(1), such as through a forcible rape, the second form of the offense dispenses with the issue of consent. The Legislature has declared that a child is incapable of giving legally recognized consent for sexual activity. While the so-called age of consent varies from state to state from 16 to 18, Texas considers a person under 17 to be a "child" and legally incapable of granting consent for sex.[90] (The age of consent bar does not apply to a person under 17 who is the spouse of the actor.) Remember that the age of consent applies to both males and females. Thus if Carla, a 23-year-old female, performs an act of oral sex on Jerome, a 15-year-old male, Carla has committed sexual assault no matter how willing a participant Jerome may be. But what if Jerome told Carla that he was 18? This matters not in Texas. Texas, like most states, views the sexual assault statute as a means to protect children. Accordingly, it is applied in a strict liability fashion. A mistake of age on the part of the actor, no matter how reasonable the mistake, does not absolve he or she of criminal responsibility.

But suppose Charles comes home early one evening and finds his 15-year-old daughter Brittney on the living room couch engaged in sexual intercourse with Kevin, her 16-year-old boyfriend. Which, if either, of the underage children are committing sexual assault of a child? Is each assaulting the other? While Charles is certainly likely to be unhappy with this turn of events, neither Kevin nor Brittney is culpable for sexual assault of a child. The Legislature recognizes that while it is socially undesirable for an underage child to engage in sex and that children must be protected from adult sexual predators, the hormones of teenagers may overpower good judgment. Accordingly, Sec. 22.011(e) establishes an affirmative defense to sexual assault of a child. The offender has a perfect defense to the charge if he or she is not a registered sex offender, the victim was at least 14 years old, and the offender was no more than three years older than the victim. In the prior example, Kevin and Brittney both fit this criterion, so no criminal charges will be forthcoming.

Even if Kevin is only one year older than Brittney he still could face a sexual assault charge if Brittney did not consent to the sex act. If Kevin forced Brittney to engage in sexual intercourse against her will, it matters not that he is close to her age. Such nonconsensual conduct constitutes sexual assault under Sec. 22.011(a)(1).

Penalty

Sexual assault is a felony of the second degree punishable by imprisonment for a term of two to 20 years and a fine up to $10,000.

Elements of Aggravated Sexual Assault

Structurally, aggravated sexual assault is similar to other aggravated offenses such as aggravated assault. Commission of the underlying offense, that is, sexual assault, must be established before the aggravated form can exist. In what at first glance appears odd and inconsistent with the approach taken in defining other aggravated offenses in the Penal Code, the aggravated sexual assault statute repeats the language of the underlying sexual

---

§ 22.021. Aggravated Sexual Assault

(a) A person commits an offense:

1. [*if he commits sexual assault under Sec. 22.011*] and
2. if:
   A. the person:
      i. causes serious bodily injury or attempts to cause the death of the victim or another person in the course of the same criminal episode;
      ii. by acts or words places the victim in fear that death, serious bodily injury, or kidnapping will be imminently inflicted on any person;
      iii. by acts or words occurring in the presence of the victim threatens to cause the death, serious bodily injury, or kidnapping of any person;
      iv. uses or exhibits a deadly weapon in the course of the same criminal episode;
      v. acts in concert with another who engages in conduct described by Subdivision (1) directed toward the same victim and occurring during the course of the same criminal episode; or
      vi. administers or provides flunitrazepam, otherwise known as rohypnol, gamma hydroxybutyrate, or ketamine to the victim of the offense with the intent of facilitating the commission of the offense;
   B. the victim is younger than 14 years of age; or
   C. the victim is an elderly individual or a disabled individual.

assault statute instead of simply incorporating it by reference. This approach to statutory draftsmanship exists to reinforce the above-mentioned principle that each form of contact or penetration is a separate offense even when it occurs during the same episode or time frame.[91] Often, an offender will violate the victim in more than one way. Each act can be raised to a separate aggravated sexual assault charge without running afoul of the constitutional prohibition against double jeopardy. In contrast, under the law of assault an actor who threatens his victim several times during the same incident or causes more than one form of serious bodily injury is charged with only one assault or aggravated assault.

Assuming sexual assault without consent or sexual assault of a child can be established, the behavior elevates to aggravated sexual assault if one of several factual circumstances exists at the time. While the reader should refer to the displayed statute for the exact language, these circumstances may be summarized as follows:

- Causing serious bodily injury or death to the victim
- Threatening to cause serious bodily injury, death, or kidnapping to the victim or any other person
- Using or exhibiting a deadly weapon
- Acting in concert with another (i.e., gang rape)
- Administering a "date rape" drug
- Victim is under 14 years old
- Victim is an elderly person (65 or older)
- Victim is a disabled individual

Penalty

Aggravated sexual assault is a felony of the first degree punishable by imprisonment for a term of five to 99 years or life and a fine up to $10,000.

SPECIAL EVIDENTIARY RULES IN LAW OF SEXUAL ASSAULT

Lord Hale Instruction

"Rape is an accusation easily to be made, hard to be proved, and harder yet to be defended by the party accused, tho' never so innocent." So spoke Sir Matthew Hale, Lord Chief Justice of England, in the seventeenth century.[92] **The Lord Hale instruction** was a caution that a claim of rape was both difficult to prove and difficult to defend. This perspective influenced the trial of rape cases for several hundred years. Juries were told to be particularly careful to avoid convicting an innocent man. Critics claimed that such an instruction unfairly cast doubt upon the victim's credibility and was not required in trials of robbers, burglars, thieves, or any other criminal offenders. Many claimed this added to the reluctance of rape victims to report the crime or to be willing to testify in court. The reform movement in recent years has seen the elimination of the Lord Hale instruction in most jurisdictions either by case decision or statutory enactment.[93] Researchers found no supporting data for the admonition that the charge was easy to make. In fact, data suggests exactly the opposite is true, given that sexual assault is widely regarded as underreported. Likewise, studies suggest that rape is one of the easiest violent crime charges to disprove.[94] Because the state's legal tradition has long barred trial judges from commenting on the weight of the evidence,[95] Texas has never required any version of the Lord Hale instruction to be given to a jury in a rape or sexual assault case.[96]

Victim's Reputation

Since consent negates an element of the offense, the defendant in a sexual assault trial has a right to attempt to establish that the sexual intercourse was consensual. As recently as 30 years ago, one method of establishing consent was to show that the victim had previously engaged in consensual sex with other individuals, the argument being that the victim must have consented to the incident in question. Additionally, the defendant was permitted to offer evidence of the victim's reputation for chastity. If the jury could be convinced that the victim was an individual of loose morals, then it was likely she consented to the sex act.

In 1974, Michigan responded to this arcane logic and enacted the nation's first rape shield law, which greatly limits the defendant's ability to attack the victim's reputation and character. In the last three decades, every jurisdiction has adopted some form of rape shield law.[97] Rule 412 of the Texas Rules of Evidence is similar to the rape shield law found in many other states. Essentially, the rule bars the admissibility of evidence of the victim's sexual reputation as well as prior sexual history. Incidents of specific prior sexual

---

Rule 412. Evidence of Previous Sexual Conduct in Criminal Cases

a. Reputation or Opinion Evidence. In a prosecution for sexual assault or aggravated sexual assault, or attempt to commit sexual assault or aggravated sexual assault, reputation or opinion evidence of the past sexual behavior of an alleged victim of such crime is not admissible.

b. Evidence of Specific Instances. In a prosecution for sexual assault or aggravated sexual assault, or attempt to commit sexual assault or aggravated sexual assault, evidence of specific instances of an alleged victim's past sexual behavior is also not admissible, unless:

  1. such evidence is admitted in accordance with paragraphs (c) and (d) of this rule;
  2. it is evidence:
      A. that is necessary to rebut or explain scientific or medical evidence offered by the State;
      B. of past sexual behavior with the accused and is offered by the accused upon the issue of whether the alleged victim consented to the sexual behavior which is the basis of the offense charged;
      C. that relates to the motive or bias of the alleged victim;
      D. is admissible under Rule 609; or
      E. that is constitutionally required to be admitted; and
  3. its probative value outweighs the danger of unfair prejudice.

c. Procedure for Offering Evidence. If the defendant proposes to introduce any documentary evidence or to ask any question, either by direct examination or cross-examination of any witness, concerning specific instances of the alleged victim's past sexual behavior, the defendant must inform the court out of the hearing of the jury prior to introducing any such evidence or asking any such question. After this notice, the court shall conduct an in camera hearing, recorded by the court reporter, to determine whether the proposed evidence is admissible under paragraph (b) of this rule. The court shall determine what evidence is admissible and shall accordingly limit the questioning. The defendant shall not go outside these limits or refer to any evidence ruled inadmissible in camera without prior approval of the court without the presence of the jury.

d. Record Sealed. The court shall seal the record of the in camera hearing required in paragraph (c) of this rule for delivery to the appellate court in the event of an appeal.

activity with the defendant in an effort to establish consent is admissible only after the judge, out of the jury's presence, conducts a hearing and finds that the value of the evidence substantially outweighs the danger of harm to the victim and of unfair prejudice to any party. For example, at Fred's trial for the sexual assault of Ginger, Fred's attorney may not introduce evidence of Ginger's reputation for "sleeping around" nor may he introduce evidence that Ginger has had ten prior sex partners. However, the judge would likely allow evidence that Fred and Ginger had engaged in consensual sexual intercourse with each other three times in the two weeks prior to the alleged assault. But, the judge is unlikely to allow the jury to hear evidence that Fred and Ginger had consensual sex 15 years earlier on the night of the high school prom.

Corroboration Requirement

Partly because of Lord Hale's belief that a great risk of false accusation existed, the law developed that the absence of consent had to be corroborated by other evidence. Initially, the existence of immediate outcry was used to corroborate the claim. If a woman had been raped, she would cry out and tell someone be it the police, a friend, or a family member. If she failed to tell anyone within a short time of the event, the victim's credibility was suspect.[98] Later, physical evidence, such as the results of a medical examination, was used as corroboration of the claim of lack of consent.

Today, in most states, making outcry or otherwise producing corroborating evidence of the absence of consent is not necessary.[99] Article 38.07 of the Texas Code of Criminal Procedure retains the **corroboration requirement** to some extent. Since the statute of limitations on sexual assault is 10 years, an allegation of the crime could be made many years after the incident occurred.[100] Article 38.07 requires independent evidentiary support of the assault unless the victim makes outcry to someone within one year. The corroboration requirement is eliminated entirely if the victim is less than 17 years old, over 65, or mentally or physically disabled. The elimination of the outcry requirement in sexual assault of children is contrary to the prevailing law in most states.

However, for practical reasons, timely reporting of the assault, prompt medical examination of the victim, and immediate processing of the crime scene greatly assist the prosecution in establishing that a sexual assault occurred. Additionally, the advent of popular television shows featuring the wonders of forensic science have led some to believe that juries now expect to see DNA and other corroborating physical evidence in sexual assault cases.[101]

Art. 38.07. Testimony in Corroboration of Victim of Sexual Offense

a. A conviction under Chapter 21, Section 22.011, or Section 22.021, Penal Code, is supportable on the uncorroborated testimony of the victim of the sexual offense if the victim informed any person, other than the defendant, of the alleged offense within one year after the date on which the offense is alleged to have occurred.

b. The requirement that the victim inform another person of an alleged offense does not apply if at the time of the alleged offense the victim was a person:
   1. 17 years of age or younger;
   2. 65 years of age or older; or
   3. 18 years of age or older who by reason of age or physical or mental disease, defect, or injury was substantially unable to satisfy the person's need for food, shelter, medical care, or protection from harm.

OTHER SEX CRIMES

Indecency with a Child

Somewhat overlapping the sexual assault of a child statute is the indecency with a child law, Sec. 21.11. It covers **sexual contact** and is often invoked in child molestation cases. In order to engage in sexual penetration, one obviously must first contact the sexual organ of the victim.[102] But, the definition of "sexual contact" adds the touching of the child's breast as well as anus and genitals. It also explicitly includes touching through clothing. Thus, in many cases with a child victim, the prosecutor has the option of filing sexual assault of a child or indecency with a child charges. Since indecency with a child by contact is a felony of the second degree, the same as sexual assault of a child, the prosecutor can choose the easier offense to prove.

The other form of indecency with a child is by exposure. An offense is committed if with the specific intent to arouse or sexually gratify, the actor exposes his or her genitals in the presence of a child or causes the child to expose his or her genitals or anus. Exposure of genitals in circumstances that are not sex-related are normally prosecuted as disorderly conduct [Sec. 42.01(a)(10)]. Individuals who expose themselves to children commit a felony of the third degree.

In a manner similar to the sexual assault of a child law, the three years of age defense is available [Sec. 21.11(b)]. However, in a curious limitation, the defense applies only if the actor and the victim are of the opposite sex. This results in the possibility, for example, of a 17-year-old male escaping prosecution for either indecency with a child or sexual assault of a child after having consensual sexual intercourse with a 16-year-old female. On the other hand, a 17-year-old male who has oral sex with a 16-year-old male, while having an affirmative defense to a charge of sexual assault of a child, is not immune from prosecution for indecency with a child. The Legislature has drawn a line between heterosexual conduct with a child and homosexual conduct with a child.

---

§ 21.11. Indecency with a Child

a. A person commits an offense if, with a child younger than 17 years and not the person's spouse, whether the child is of the same or opposite sex, the person:
   1. engages in sexual contact with the child or causes the child to engage in sexual contact; or
   2. with intent to arouse or gratify the sexual desire of any person:
      A. exposes the person's anus or any part of the person's genitals, knowing the child is present; or
      B. causes the child to expose the child's anus or any part of the child's genitals.

* * *

c. In this section, "sexual contact" means the following acts, if committed with the intent to arouse or gratify the sexual desire of any person:
   1. any touching by a person, including touching through clothing, of the anus, breast, or any part of the genitals of a child; or
   2. any touching of any part of the body of a child, including touching through clothing, with the anus, breast, or any part of the genitals of a person.

§ 21.08. Indecent Exposure

a. A person commits an offense if he exposes his anus or any part of his genitals with intent to arouse or gratify the sexual desire of any person, and he is reckless about whether another is present who will be offended or alarmed by his act.

b. An offense under this section is a Class B misdemeanor.

Indecent Exposure

Indecent exposure criminalizes exposure of the anus or genitals for purposes of sexual gratification under circumstances where someone could be offended or alarmed. In particular, the offender must be reckless about whether another is present. In one case, the court held the elements of the offense were met when an undercover vice officer testified he was alarmed and offended when the defendant exposed his penis in an enclosed booth in an adult video arcade.[103]

Additionally, the statute does not require that anyone actually see the actor's genitals or actually be offended or alarmed but only that the possibility such reaction could occur.[104] While incidents of indecent exposure often occur in public places, there is no such requirement in the statute.[105] If actual exposure occurs in the presence of someone under 17 years of age, the offense is indecency with a child as discussed above. Otherwise the offense is a Class B misdemeanor.

Public Lewdness

Otherwise lawful sexual behavior can be a crime depending on the circumstances. If an act of consensual sex occurs in a public place or under circumstances where the offender is reckless about whether another is present who will be offended or alarmed, the crime is public lewdness (Sec. 21.07). Thus engaging in sexual intercourse in the backseat of an automobile parked on a public street is likely a violation.

Curiously, public lewdness is the only statute that speaks to sexual contact with animals. Sexual contact with an animal or fowl under the same circumstances mentioned above violates the statute. Texas would not appear currently to have any criminal prohibition against bestiality so long as the conduct does not occur in a public place. Any form of public lewdness is a Class A misdemeanor.

Homosexual Conduct

In 1973, the Legislature repealed the state's sodomy statute and replaced it with Sec. 21.06—Homosexual Conduct, a Class C misdemeanor. Thirty years later, in a case involving what is believed to be the only prosecution ever initiated under the statute, the U.S. Supreme Court declared the law to be unconstitutional. In *Lawrence v. Texas*, the high court ruled the law unenforceable because it infringed upon an individual's vital interests in liberty and privacy protected by the due process clause of the Fourteenth Amendment.[106] Thus, while the statute continues to appear in the Penal Code, it is legally unenforceable.

CRIMEGRAPH
Assaultive Offenses—Part One

Offense	Underlying offense	Culpable mental state	Conduct	When?	What?	Who/where?	Specific knowledge	Penalty
Assault 22.01(a)(1)		1. Intentionally, or 2. Knowingly, or 3. Recklessly	Causes		Bodily injury	Another, including person's spouse		AM to F3
Assault 22.01(a)(2)		1. Intentionally or 2. Knowingly	Threatens	Imminent	Bodily injury	Another, including person's spouse		CM to AM
Assault 22.01(a)(3)		1. Intentionally or 2. Knowingly	Causes		Physical contact	Another	Knowing or should believe conduct will be regarded as offensive or provocative	CM to AM
Aggravated Assault 22.02(a)(1)	Assault 22.01		Causes		Serious bodily injury	Another, including person's spouse		F2 to F1
Aggravated Assault 22.02(a)(2)	Assault 22.01		1. Uses or 2. Exhibits		Deadly weapon			F2 to F1

152

Assaultive Offenses—Part Two

Offense	Underlying offense	Culpable mental state	Conduct	When?	What?	Who/where?	Specific knowledge	Penalty
Deadly Conduct 22.05(a)		Recklessly	Places in	Imminent	Danger of serious bodily injury	Another		AM
Deadly Conduct 22.05(b)(1)		Knowingly	Discharges		Firearm	At or in direction of an individual		F3
Deadly Conduct 22.05(b)(2)		Knowingly	Discharges		Firearm	At or in direction of: 1. Building, or 2. Habitation, or 3. Vehicle	Reckless about whether occupied	F3
Terroristic Threat 22.07(a)		Recklessly*	Threatens		Any offense involving violence to	1. Person or 2. Property	With intent to: 1. Cause reaction by official or volunteer agency, or 2. Place any person in fear of imminent serious bodily injury, or 3. Prevent occupation of public building, airplane, vehicle, etc., or 4. Cause interruption of utility services, or 5. Place public in fear of serious bodily injury, or 6. Influence conduct of governmental operations	BM to F3

*Required by Texas Penal Code § 6.02

Assaultive Offenses—Children, Elderly, or Disabled

Offense	Culpable mental state	Conduct	What/when?	Who/where?	Penalty
Injury to a Child, Elderly Person, or Disabled individual 22.04(a)	1. Intentionally, or 2. Knowingly, or 3. Recklessly, or 4. Criminal negligence	Act causes	1. Serious bodily injury, or 2. Serious mental deficiency, impairment or injury, or 3. Bodily injury	1. Child, or 2. Elderly individual, or 3. Disabled individual	SJF to F1
Injury to a Child, Elderly Person, or Disabled individual 22.04(a)	1. Intentionally, or 2. Knowingly, or 3. Recklessly	Omission causes	1. Serious bodily injury, or 2. Serious mental deficiency, impairment or injury, or 3. Bodily injury	1. Child, or 2. Elderly individual, or 3. Disabled individual	SJF to F1
Abandoning or Endangering a Child 22.041(b)	Intentionally	Abandons	Circumstances that exposes child to unreasonable risk of harm	Child younger than 15 who is under custody, care, or control	SJF to F2
Abandoning or Endangering a Child 22.041(c)	1. Intentionally, or 2. Knowingly, or 3. Recklessly, or 4. Criminal negligence	1. By act or 2. By omission	Places in imminent danger of: 1. Death, or 2. Bodily injury, or 3. Physical impairment, or 4. Mental impairment	Child younger than 15	SJF

Sexual Assaultive Offenses—Part One

Offense	Culpable mental state	Conduct	Of what?	How?	When?	Penalty
Sexual Assault 22.011(a)(1)(A)	1. Intentionally <u>or</u> 2. Knowingly	Penetrates	1. Anus <u>or</u> 2. Sexual organ	By any means	Without consent	F2 to F1
Sexual Assault 22.011(a)(1)(B)	1. Intentionally <u>or</u> 2. Knowingly	Penetrates	Mouth	By sexual organ of actor	Without consent	F2 to F1
Sexual Assault 22.011(a)(1)(C)	1. Intentionally <u>or</u> 2. Knowingly	1. Contacts <u>or</u> 2. Penetrates	1. Mouth, <u>or</u> 2. Anus, <u>or</u> 3. Sexual organ	By sexual organ of: 1. Actor <u>or</u> 2. Another person	Without consent	F2 to F1
Sexual Assault 22.011(a)(2)(A)	1. Intentionally <u>or</u> 2. Knowingly	Penetrates	1. Anus of child <u>or</u> 2. Sexual organ of child	By any means		F2 to F1
Sexual Assault 22.011(a)(2)(B)	1. Intentionally <u>or</u> 2. Knowingly	Penetrates	Mouth of child	By sexual organ of actor		F2 to F1
Sexual Assault 22.011(a)(2)(C)	1. Intentionally <u>or</u> 2. Knowingly	1. Contacts <u>or</u> 2. Penetrates	Sexual organ of child	1. Mouth of another, <u>or</u> 2. Anus of another, <u>or</u> 3. Sexual organ of another		F2 to F1
Sexual Assault 22.011(a)(2)(D)	1. Intentionally <u>or</u> 2. Knowingly	Contacts	1. Anus of child <u>or</u> 2. Sexual organ of child	Mouth of another		F2 to F1

Sexual Assaultive Offenses—Part Two

Offense	Underlying offense	Culpable mental state	Conduct	Who?	Specific intent	Specific knowledge	Penalty
Aggravated Sexual Assault 22.021(a)(1)(A)	Sexual Assault 22.011(a)(1)		1. Causes serious bodily injury, or 2. Places in fear of death, serious bodily injury, or kidnapping, or 3. Threatens death, serious bodily injury, or kidnapping to any person, or 4. Uses/exhibits deadly weapon, or 5. Acts in concert with another, or 6. Administers date rape drug.	Another			F1
Aggravated Sexual Assault 22.021(a)(1)(A)	Sexual Assault 22.011(a)(1)			1. Elderly victim or 2. Disabled victim			F1
Aggravated Sexual Assault 22.021(a)(1)(B)	Sexual Assault 22.011(a)(2)			Child younger than 14			F1
Indecency with a Child 21.11(a)(1)		1. Intentionally, or 2. Knowingly, or 3. Recklessly*	Sexual contact	With child younger than 17			F2
Indecency with a Child 21.11(a)(2)(A)		1. Intentionally, or 2. Knowingly, or 3. Recklessly*	1. Exposes anus or 2. Exposes genitals.	To child younger than 17	With intent to arouse or gratify sexual desire	Knowing child is present	F3
Indecency with a Child 21.11(a)(2)(B)		1. Intentionally, or 2. Knowingly, or 3. Recklessly*	Causes child to expose anus or genitals		With intent to arouse or gratify sexual desire		F3

*Required by Texas Penal Code § 6.02

156

Notes

1. The incident up to this point is an assault by contact, however.
2. TEX. PENAL CODE § 6.04(b).
3. *Compare* N.Y. PENAL LAW § 10.00(9).
4. Lane v. State, 763 S.W.2d 785, 786 (Tex. Crim. App. 1989).
5. Acts 1979, 66th Leg., R.S., ch. 164, 1979 Tex. Gen. Laws 366.
6. Cook v. State, 940 S.W.2d 344, 347 (Tex. App.— Amarillo 1997). *See also* Olivas v. State, 203 S.W.3d 341 (Tex. Crim. App. 2006). In this case the Court of Criminal Appeals considers various definitions of "threat" but never settles on any particular one.
7. *See* Miller v. State, 741 S.W.2d 501 (Tex. App.— Corpus Christi 1987). This rule is a departure from prior Texas law, which by statute required a threat to be "coupled with ability to commit" a battery. *See* 1925 TEX. PENAL CODE art. 1138; 1141.
8. The question of present ability to carry out a threat does arise in the law of sexual assault discussed later in the chapter.
9. See discussion of distinction between nature of conduct and result of conduct offenses contained in Chapter 2.
10. *See* Olivas v. State; Dolkart v. State, 197 S.W.3d 887 (Tex. App.—Dallas 2006), *and* McGowan v. State, 664 S.W.2d 355 (Tex. Crim. App. 1984).
11. Nelson v. State, 2002 Tex. App. LEXIS 2164.
12. Olivas v. State.
13. See discussion of the law of criminal attempt in Chapter 14.
14. See Olivas v. State, wherein the offense of attempted assault with bodily injury is mentioned in a hypothetical discussion.
15. *See* TEX. PENAL CODE § 15.05.
16. See Tanksley v. State, 656 S.W.2d 194 (Tex. App.— Austin 1983), upholding an assault conviction of an inmate who told jailer that the next time jailer came into locked holding cell inmate would stab him in the eye. Assault occurred even though inmate was separated from jailer by glass window and could not then carry out threat.
17. If the words constitute a threat to cause bodily injury, then an assault by threat has occurred.
18. Does an assault by threat occur?
19. D.C. v. State, 436 So.2d 203 (Fla. Dist. Ct. App. 1983). The court noted, "This case presents a perfect example of a disturbing societal proclivity toward settling all disputes through resort to a severely overburdened judicial system."
20. *See* Michael Grabell, *Probation for SMU hazing*, DALLAS MORNING NEWS, Jun. 27, 2006.
21. Hatfield v. State, 377 S.W.2d 647, 648 (Tex. Crim. App. 1964).
22. *See* Lenzy v. State, 689 S.W.2d 305 (Tex. App.— Amarillo 1985), *and* Campbell v. State, 1999 Tex. App. LEXIS 1055.
23. Moore v. State, 739 S.W.2d 347 (Tex. Crim. App. 1987).
24. Patterson v. State, 769 S.W.2d 938, 941 (Tex. Crim. App. 1989).
25. Montgomery v. State, 99 S.W.3d 257 (Tex. App.—Fort Worth 2003).
26. Mosley v. State, 545 S.W.2d 144 (Tex. Crim. App. 1976). But see Vaughn v. State, 600 S.W.2d 314, (Tex. Crim. App. 1980), suggesting that the definition of "firearm" in § 46.01 is not binding in defining the meaning of the term for purposes of offenses in other chapters of the Penal Code.
27. *See* Walker v. State, 543 S.W.2d 634 (Tex. Crim App. 1976).
28. TEX. PENAL CODE § 9.32(a).
29. *See Ill. woman charged in alleged dead puppy attack*, USA TODAY, *at* http://www.usatoday.com/news/nation/2006–06–18-puppy-charges_x.htm (Jun. 18, 2006).
30. See Garrett v. State, 619 S.W.2d 172 (Tex. Crim. App. 1981), holding that the defendant used his Doberman pincer to threaten the victim, and thus, an assault was committed. *See generally* Fern L. Kletter, Annotation, *Dog as Deadly or Dangerous Weapon for Purposes of Statutes Aggravating Offenses Such as Assault and Robbery*, 124 A.L.R.5TH 657 (2006).
31. State v. Reed, 790 P.2d 551 (Or. Ct. App. 1990).
32. *See* Vitauts M. Gulbis, Annotation, *Parts of Human Body, Other than Feet, as Deadly or Dangerous Weapons for Purposes of Statutes Aggravating Offenses Such as Assault and Robbery*, 8 A.L.R.4TH 1268 (1981). *See also*, Lane v. State, 151 S.W.3d 188 (Tex. Crim. App. 2004), *and* Jefferson v. State, 974 S.W.2d 887 (Tex. App.—Austin 1998).
33. Mathonican v. State, 194 S.W.3d 59 (Tex. App.— Texarkana 2006).
34. Degrate v. State, 2005 Tex. App. LEXIS 547.
35. *See* Rene Lynch, *Misdemeanor Filed in Alleged AIDS Spit Case*, LOS ANGELES TIMES (ORANGE COUNTY EDITION), Jun. 15, 1993, at Metro 1.
36. TEX. PENAL CODE § 22.012, repealed by Acts 1993, 73rd Leg, ch. 900, § 1.01, eff. Sept. 1, 1994.
37. TEX. PENAL CODE § 22.11.
38. Is such an incident one crime or two? Since the elements of aggravated assault with a deadly weapon can be committed without committing the elements of aggravated assault with serious bodily injury,

a credible argument can be made that although only one individual is victimized, two crimes have occurred. This argument is also supported by the notion that aggravated assault with a deadly weapon is a conduct-oriented offense while aggravated assault with serious bodily injury is a result-oriented offense.

39. Burke v. State, 28 S.W.3d 545 (Tex. Crim App. 2000).

40. *See Child Maltreatment: Fact Sheet*, National Center for Injury Prevention and Control, Centers for Disease Control, *at* http://www.cdc.gov/ncipc/factsheets/cmfacts.htm.

41. Tex. Penal Code § 22.12(1).

42. Gallegos v. State, 548 SW.2d 50 (Tex. Crim. App. 1977).

43. Bell v. State, 693 S.W.2d 434, 438 (Tex. Crim. App. 1985).

44. *See* Rich v. State, 823 S.W.2d 420 (Tex. App.—Fort Worth 1992).

45. Mixed martial arts (MMA) includes karate, jiu-jitsu, boxing, kickboxing, grappling, wrestling, sumo, and other combat sports.

46. Missouri and New York are two states that have explicitly outlawed such events although certain forms of the contests are now permitted and regulated by New York. *See* Mo. Rev. Stat. § 317.018 and N.Y. Unconsol. Law, ch. 7, § 5-a. Utah declares it no defense to a charge of criminal homicide or assault that the victim consented to participate in the ultimate fighting match. *See* Utah Code § 76–5–104. Legislation to ban the events in other states has largely been unsuccessful, although a few municipalities have banned the contests. In some jurisdictions, event promoters avoid the oversight of existing state boxing commissions by structuring the matches to fall outside the definition of "boxing." *See* Joseph T. Hallinan, *Fancy Footwork: How Impresario of Fight Events Evades Regulation, The Wall Street Journal* Online, *at* http://www.wsj.com (Aug. 25, 2003).

47. *See* www.license.state.tx.us/sports/sports.htm.

48. Cook v. State.

49. Tex. Penal Code § 6.02(c).

50. Dues v. State, 634 S.W.2d 304 (Tex. Crim. App. 1982), *and* Jarrell v. State, 537 S.W.2d 255 (Tex. Crim. App. 1976).

51. George v. State, 841 S.W.2d 544 (Tex. App.—Houston [1st Dist.] 1992).

52. Cook v. State.

53. Bryant v. State, 905 S.W.2d 457 (Tex. App.—Waco 1995).

54. *In re* C.S., 79 S.W.3d 619 (Tex. App.—Texarkana 2002).

55. Redfearn v. State, 738 S.W.2d 28 (Tex. App.—Texarkana 1987). In this case the court assumed that the subsection applies to a private residence. A close reading of the statute suggests that it was originally intended to apply only to disrupting occupation of public buildings and facilities. This case would probably have been better handled as a violation of § 22.07(a)(2), placing in fear of imminent serious bodily injury.

56. California, Florida, Illinois, New York, and a few other states, as well as the federal government, have also enacted cyberstalking laws that apply specifically to using the Internet or other electronic means to harass another person.

57. Cal. Penal Code § 646.9.

58. For a comprehensive list of state anti-stalking legislation, see The National Center for Victims of Crimes, *Stalking Laws*, Stalking Resource Center, *at* http://www.ncvc.org/src/main.aspx?dbID=DB_Register204.

59. 18 U.S.C. § 2261A.

60. Lambèr Royakkers, *The Dutch Approach to Stalking Laws*, 2 Cal. Crim. L. Rev. 1, 7 (2000).

61. See generally, Glen Kercher and Matthew Johnson, *Stalking in Texas* (2007), available at www.crimevictims institute.org.

62. Criswell v. State, 2004 Tex. App. LEXIS 1502.

63. See Lewis v. State, 88 S.W.3d 383 (Tex. App.—Fort Worth 2002), and Sisk v. State, 74 S.W.2d 893 (Tex. App.—Fort Worth 2002), upholding the statute's constitutionality.

64. *See generally* Majorie A. Caner, Annotation, *Validity, Construction, and Application of Stalking Statutes*, 29 A.L.R.5th 487 (1995).

65. Another rationale was the marital unity theory. When a man and woman are married they become one legal unit. Hence, one cannot commit a crime against himself. This view fell into disuse with the legal emancipation of women.

66. Depending on the circumstances, a nonconsensual kiss might constitute assault by contact.

67. Cowan v. State, 562 S.W.2d 236 (Tex. Crim. App. 1978).

68. For a definition of "penetration," see Vernon v. State, 841 S.W.2d 407 (Tex. Crim. App. 1992).

69. Vela v. State, 209 S.W.2d 128, 139 (Tex. Crim. App. 2006).

70. Vick v. State, 991 S.W.2d 830 (Tex. Crim. App. 1999).

71. Karnes v. State, 873 S.W.2d 92 (Tex. App.—Dallas 1994).

72. For a discussion concerning the difference between "contact" and "penetration," see Vernon v. State.

73. *See* Criminal Victimization in the United States (2004) *at* http://www.ojp.usdoj.gov/bjs/pubalp2.htm.

74. *See* Dana Berliner, *Rethinking the Reasonable Belief Defense to Rape*, 100 Yale L.J. 2687, n.1 (1991).

75. Attempted sexual assault would be the more appropriate charge.

76. *Id.*
77. See Elliot v. State, 858 S.W.2d 478, n.1 (Tex. Crim. App. 1993), suggesting the list is exclusive. See also Johnson v. State, 227 S.W.3d 180 (Tex. App.— Houston [1st Dist.] 2007), holding that the general definition of "consent" found in § 1.07 is inapplicable in a sexual assault prosecution. The rape statute in force until 1974 used the phrase "without her consent obtained by force, threats, or fraud." *See* 1925 TEX. PENAL CODE art. 1183.
78. Suarez v. State, 901 S.W.2d 712 (Tex. App.—Corpus Christi 1995).
79. Elliot v. State at 485.
80. Rider v. State 735 S.W.2d 291 (Tex. App.— Dallas 1987).
81. Elliot v. State.
82. Harry has also violated § 39.03 official oppression.
83. The conduct is nonconsensual only if the public servant coerces the other person into sexual activity. If there is actual consent and no coercion, the sexual assault statute is not violated.
84. *See* Steve Brewer, *Hindu priest gets two years in rape case*, HOUSTON CHRONICLE, May 31, 2000, at A17.
85. For an extended discussion of consent obtained by fraud and deception, see Patricia J. Falk, *Rape by Fraud and Rape by Coercion*, 64 BROOK. L. REV. 39 (1998).
86. See State v. Siering, 644 A.2d 958 (Conn. App. 1994); State v. Crims, 540 N.W.2d 860 (Minn. Ct. App. 1995); State v. Robinson, 496 A.2d 1067 (Me. 1985); and State v. Jones, 521 N.W.2d 662 (S.D. 1994), holding a forcible rape has occurred. But see Battle v. State, 414 A.2d 1266 (Md. 1980), and State v. Way, 254 S.E.2d 760 (N.C. 1979), which hold that if there was consent to sexual intercourse preceding penetration, the crime of rape is not committed if the consent is withdrawn following penetration.
87. People v. John Z., 60 P.3d 783, 784 (Cal. 2003).
88. *See* 720 ILL. COMP. STAT. 5/12–17(c).
89. *See* Mathonican v. State.
90. Under the state's first penal code the age of consent was 10! *See* 1856 TEX. PENAL CODE art. 523.
91. *See* Vick v. State.
92. 1 M. Hale, PLEAS OF THE CROWN 635 (1680).
93. *See* Kristine Cordier Karnezis, Annotation, *Propriety of, or Prejudicial Effect of Omitting or Giving, Instruction to Jury, in Prosecution for Rape or Other Sexual Offense, as to Ease of Making or Difficulty of Defending Such a Charge*, 92 A.L.R.3D 886 (1979).
94. *See* Turner v. State, 892 P.2d 579 (Nev. 1995).
95. *See* TEX. CODE CRIM. P. art. 36.14.
96. *See* Hamilton v. State, 58 S.W. 93 (Tex. Crim. App. 1900).
97. For an up-to-date summary of rape shield laws in each state, see *Rape Shield Statutes*, American Prosecutor's Research Institute, *at* http://www.ndaa-apri.org/apri/programs/vawa/statutes.html.
98. *See* Topolanck v. State, 40 Tex. 160 (1874).
99. *See* Vitauts M. Gulbis, Annotation, *Modern Status of Rule Regarding Necessity for Corroboration of Victim's Testimony in Prosecution for Sexual Offense*, 31 A.L.R.4TH 120 (1984).
100. TEX. CODE CRIM. P. art. 12.01(2)(E). If DNA evidence exists, there is no statute of limitations to the filing of sexual assault charges. *See* TEX. CODE CRIM. P. art. 12.01(1)(B).
101. *See* '*CSI effect' has juries wanting more evidence*, USA TODAY, *at* http://www.usatoday.com/news/nation/2004–08–05-csi-effect_x.htm (Aug. 8, 2004).
102. See Barnes v. State, 165 S.W.3d 75 (Tex. App.— Austin 2005), holding that genital-to-genital contact that occurs in the course of penile penetration is subsumed in the completed act. The constitutional prohibition against double jeopardy is violated if a person is convicted of both the completed act of penetration and the contact incident to the penetration.
103. Hankins v. State, 85 S.W.3d 433 (Tex. App.—Corpus Christi 2000).
104. Metts v. State, 22 S.W.3d 544 (Tex. App.—Fort Worth 2000).
105. Young v. State, 976 S.W.2d 771 (Tex. App.—Houston [1st Dist.] 1998).
106. 539 U.S. 558 (2003).

CHAPTER 7

Kidnapping and Related Offenses

BOLO

The reader should be on the lookout (BOLO) for the meaning of the following terms. Knowledge of the meaning of these terms will greatly assist the reader in understanding the primary elements of the chapter.

- Common Law kidnapping
- Restrain
- Abduct

- Asportation
- Safe place
- Parental abduction

KIDNAPPING

Introduction

A warm July day in Philadelphia. Charley, age four, and his brother Walter, age six, join two men for a promised trip to buy fireworks. The two unnamed men had given the boys candy on previous occasions. When Walter goes into the store to buy fireworks with money the men had given him, the two adults depart with Charley. A ransom demand is subsequently made to Charley's father. But to no avail as Charley was never seen again.

The abduction of Charley Ross from in front of his parent's mansion in 1874 caught the attention of the nation. Thousands daily followed the search for Charley through sensational newspaper accounts of every investigative step. The event raised in every parent a primal fear of their child being abducted, never to be seen again.[1] But as far as the nation's criminal codes were concerned, the disappearance of Charley Ross generated another problem. No specific statutes existed criminalizing kidnapping for ransom.[2] Young Charley's abduction was the first recorded instance in America of such a crime.[3]

Not surprisingly, the notoriety of the Ross case and the success of the kidnappers of Eddie Cudahy in Omaha in 1900 prompted many of the nation's legislatures to expand their kidnapping statutes to include abductions for ransom and other forms of involuntary restraint.[4] In hopes of deterring such behavior, many jurisdictions substantially increased the penalty for kidnapping. The reaction is noteworthy because high-profile kidnappings seem to have that effect on legislatures to this day. Consider the 1932 kidnapping of Charles Lindbergh, Jr. Once again, massive media coverage and a high level of public interest regarding the abduction of an American hero's toddler ultimately led to passage of the "Lindbergh Act," a statute authorizing the Federal Bureau of Investigation to investigate ransom kidnappings.[5] Many legal scholars view the

Lindbergh Act as the beginning of the trend toward federalization of many heretofore state criminal violations. In more recent years, the abduction and subsequent murder of Polly Klaas by a parolee with numerous prior convictions gave impetus to resurrection of habitual criminal ("three-strike") laws. The public interest in the abductions of Adam Walsh in 1981 and Amber Hagerman in 1996 focused attention on child abductions and the need to create better means for preventing and reporting such events. Code Adam[6] and AMBER alert[7] systems are widely used today to enlist the assistance of the general public in thwarting suspected child abductions. Most recently, the 2005 kidnapping, rape, and murder of nine-year-old Jessica Lunsford has given rise to additional state and federal legislation concerning sex offenders.[8]

In modern times, kidnapping is also used as a political tool. The abductions of journalists, relief workers, soldiers, and other foreign citizens during the recent conflicts in the Middle East are prime examples. Rather than demanding a monetary ransom, changes in political positions are sought. The abductors seek release of supporters being held in prisons, removal of foreign troops, or other acts related to their particular political agenda. Politically motivated kidnappings have been very rare events in America. The best known is likely the abduction of newspaper heiress Patricia Hearst in San Francisco in 1974. Her abductors, the self-styled George Jackson Brigade of the Symbionese Liberation Army (SLA), demanded, among other things, release from prison of other SLA members and distribution of food to California's poor. The demands were not met.

Over the years, some of the domestic airplane hijackings, which resulted in an incidental kidnapping of the crew and passengers, have also had political motivations. During the September 11, 2001, tragedy the terrorists committed kidnappings when they forcibly took control of the three airplanes.

Society's interest in kidnapping cases arises because such abductions are very rare. While each year sees a large number of missing children and adults, few are victims of abduction by strangers. Yearly, the number of domestic kidnappings for ransom, adult and children, probably totals less than two dozen,[9] while the total number of children abducted by strangers is about 115.[10] The number of abducted children who are murdered is estimated at less than 100 per year nationwide.[11]

Today, the bulk of incidents of kidnapping and related offenses occur in one of three circumstances: unlawful restraint, kidnapping incidental to the commission of some other felony, and parental abduction. Even within these three categories, the filing of criminal charges does not come about with great frequency.

COMMON LAW KIDNAPPING

During early Common Law times kidnapping meant the forcible abduction of a person and sending him to another country. The removal to another country was called **asportation**, the same term used in the law of larceny to describe the taking of property.[12] The act was an aggravated form of false imprisonment since it incorporated that crime with taking the victim out of his own country, thus removing the victim from the protection of his sovereign. During the Common Law period, kidnappings occurred for political reasons to force individuals into involuntary servitude, and to conscript soldiers. If a ransom were demanded, it was usually in a political context, such as the capture of King Richard I by the King of Austria in 1192 as the British monarch was returning from the Third Crusade.

Texas law early on held to a similarly limited view of the crime of kidnapping. The 1856 Texas Penal Code stated that kidnapping was a crime only if a person was falsely imprisoned for the purpose of being removed from the state, sold as a slave, or, if a minor, being taken from the custody of their parent.[13]

As a criminal act, kidnapping developed into a prohibition against both the abduction of an individual and the secreting of an individual. Thus a kidnap victim might be carried away (asportation) or simply concealed where they would not likely to be found. In either case, the offense apparently did not occur with much frequency over the years.

TEXAS LAW OF KIDNAPPING

Unlawful Restraint

At the lowest level of kidnapping-type offenses is unlawful restraint. The offense of unlawful restraint is a recognition that an individual has the right to move unimpeded by others, unless authorized by law as with a lawful arrest. While civil suits for the tort of false imprisonment are brought when illegal arrests or detentions are alleged, criminal charges of unlawful restraint are rarely filed against public officials.

Unlawful restraint requires a *mens rea* of intent or knowledge and an *actus reus* of restraint. If Paul locks up his restaurant for the evening forgetting that Roderick is still in the kitchen washing dishes, Paul does not commit unlawful restraint because he lacks the appropriate culpable mental state. He did not restrain Roderick's freedom of movement intentionally or knowingly. On the other hand, assume Pascal, the high school math teacher, purposefully locks Ronald, the class clown, in the classroom closet. He leaves him there for an hour "to teach him a lesson." No matter how deserving of the lesson Ronald may be, Pascal has committed unlawful restraint because he had no

§ 20.01. Definitions

In this chapter:

1. "Restrain" means to restrict a person's movements without consent, so as to interfere substantially with the person's liberty, by moving the person from one place to another or by confining the person. Restraint is "without consent" if it is accomplished by:
   A. force, intimidation, or deception; or
   B. any means, including acquiescence of the victim, if:
      i. the victim is a child who is less than 14 years of age or an incompetent person and the parent, guardian, or person or institution acting in *loco parentis* has not acquiesced in the movement or confinement; or
      ii. the victim is a child who is 14 years of age or older and younger than 17 years of age, the victim is taken outside of the state and outside a 120-mile radius from the victim's residence, and the parent, guardian, or person or institution acting in *loco parentis* has not acquiesced in the movement.
2. "Abduct" means to restrain a person with intent to prevent his liberation by:
   A. secreting or holding him in a place where he is not likely to be found; or
   B. using or threatening to use deadly force.
3. "Relative" means a parent or stepparent, ancestor, sibling, or uncle or aunt, including an adoptive relative of the same degree through marriage or adoption.
4. "Person" means an individual, corporation, or association.
5. Notwithstanding Section 1.07, "individual" means a human being who has been born and is alive.

§ 20.02. Unlawful Restraint

a. A person commits an offense if he intentionally or knowingly restrains another person.

b. It is an affirmative defense to prosecution under this section that:
　1. the person restrained was a child younger than 14 years of age;
　2. the actor was a relative of the child; and
　3. the actor's sole intent was to assume lawful control of the child.

c. An offense under this section is a Class A misdemeanor, except that the offense is:
　1. a state jail felony if the person restrained was a child younger than 17 years of age; or
　2. a felony of the third degree if:
　　A. the actor recklessly exposes the victim to a substantial risk of serious bodily injury;
　　B. the actor restrains an individual the actor knows is a public servant while the public servant is lawfully discharging an official duty or in retaliation or on account of an exercise of official power or performance of an official duty as a public servant; or
　　C. the actor while in custody restrains any other person.

d. It is no offense to detain or move another under this section when it is for the purpose of effecting a lawful arrest or detaining an individual lawfully arrested.

e. It is an affirmative defense to prosecution under this section that:
　1. the person restrained was a child who is 14 years of age or older and younger than 17 years of age;
　2. the actor does not restrain the child by force, intimidation, or deception; and
　3. the actor is not more than three years older than the child.

lawful right to deprive Ronald of his freedom of movement. Pascal has purposefully restrained Ronald.

Sec. 20.01(1) defines **restrain** as "to restrict a person's movements without consent, so as to interfere substantially with the person's liberty, by moving the person from one place to another or by confining the person." Several parts of the definition affect whether particular conduct is a crime. First, note that the restriction on a person's movement must be without consent. The same section defines "without consent" to include

- force, intimidation, or deception
- taking a child under age 14 or an incompetent without parental or guardian consent
- taking a child of age 14 to 17 outside the state and beyond 120 miles from home without parental or guardian consent.

The statute thereby criminalizes both forcible restraint and nonforcible taking of children without parental permission. With a goal of protecting children who might be lured into accompanying strangers, any child under 14 is legally incapable of consenting to restriction of their movement. If the child is between 14 and 17, being taken out of state and more than 120 miles from home is nonconsensual by legal definition.

Second, the restriction on the victim's movement must involve either confinement or a substantial interference with their liberty. The statute imposes no time limit on the period of confinement or the time during which the victim is deprived of his or her liberty.[14] Thus a "restraint" within the meaning of the statute occurred when the defendant climb into a high school student's car and threatened her with a knife. The student struggled with the defendant for about two minutes until a gathering crowd caused the defendant to abandon his intentions. The offender had thereby substantially interfered with the victim's liberty.[15] On the other hand, temporarily blocking a classmate's ability to walk down the hallway is likely not a *substantial* interference with his liberty.

Some cases of unlawful restraint happen under extreme factual circumstances. Unlawful restraint charges are filed where mentally disabled children or adults suffering from dementia are shackled to a bed or locked in their rooms. While the caregiver's intentions may be good though misguided, such conduct is normally not permissible under the criminal law.

Unlawful restraint is a Class A misdemeanor. It moves to a state jail felony if the victim is under 17 years old and to a felony of the third degree under certain other factual circumstances. Because the definition of "restraint" is similar to the definition of an "arrest," the statute declares that a lawful arrest is not an unlawful restraint.[16] Presumably, an unlawful arrest could meet the definition of a criminal act. Additionally, the statute does not criminalize the efforts of a parent, sibling, or other relative to regain lawful control of a child under 14 years old. Likewise, if the offender and victim are within three years of age of each other and no force or intimidation was involved, an affirmative defense is available. Thus, if Suzie, age 16, runs away from home with her boyfriend, Jeff, age 18, Jeff is not guilty of unlawful restraint.[17]

Kidnapping

The offense of kidnapping exists in the statute books of every state, including Texas, despite the relatively rare occurrence of the event.[18] The Texas kidnapping statute requires an "abduction" of the victim. "Abduction" is the modern equivalent of the asportation element needed under the Common Law and involves either restraining a person in a secret place or threatening or using deadly force. In Texas terminology, **abduct** is an aggravated form of "restraint."[19] Katie leaves a message on Tom's answering machine that she no longer wishes to be his girlfriend. Tom becomes enraged that Katie would terminate their relationship. He goes to Katie's apartment and forces her to get into his car. He drives around the neighborhood waiving a firearm and threatening to kill himself or her if she does not change her mind. Tom has committed kidnapping.

In the alternative, kidnapping can also occur when a person is confined against his or her will. For this conduct to elevate from the crime of unlawful restraint to kidnapping, an element of secrecy must often be proven. Thus, the traditional notion of the taking of a child to be held for ransom falls within this class since the child may be

§ 20.03. Kidnapping

a. A person commits an offense if he intentionally or knowingly abducts another person.

b. It is an affirmative defense to prosecution under this section that:
   1. the abduction was not coupled with intent to use or to threaten to use deadly force;
   2. the actor was a relative of the person abducted; and
   3. the actor's sole intent was to assume lawful control of the victim.

c. An offense under this section is a felony of the third degree.

deceived into accompanying the abductor but is then held in a secret location until the ransom is paid.

Suppose Jose decides to kidnap Rodney, a 15-year-old child, and make a ransom demand from Rodney's parents. Jose is successful in taking Rodney against his will. He ties up Rodney with ropes and hides him in the bedroom of an abandoned house. When Jose leaves to telephone Rodney's parents, Rodney slips from the ropes and escapes. Rodney has been abducted within the meaning of the statute.

One unusual aspect of the Texas kidnapping statute is treating the requirement of secreting the victim where he or she will likely not be found as part of the *mens rea* of the offense, not the *actus reus*. As a result, if the offender at any time during the restraint intended to secret the victim, the offense of kidnapping is complete.[20] For example, luring an underage boy into a motel room for the purposes of sex has been found to evidence an intent to secret the child.[21]

The same rule regarding the *mens rea* would appear to hold true in a case where deadly force is threatened. The logic for this view is twofold. First, the statute speaks in terms of "an intent to prevent his liberation." The offender need not be successful in attaining his goal; he or she need only have the intent. Second, abduction is a continuing event. It is not necessary that the intent to prevent liberation by secreting the victim or the threat or use of deadly force occur at the time of the initial restraint.[22] Suppose Mary, a stranger, enters the hospital and takes the infant Hugh from the nursery, intending to raise him as her own child. When Mary comes home with the child, her sister Louise decides to notify the police of Mary's actions. Mary threatens to kill Louise if she tries to contact authorities. Mary's conduct, due to the threat to use deadly force, elevates from unlawful restraint of Hugh to kidnapping.

The Texas kidnapping statute is limited to "persons" as offenders and victims. While Sec. 20.01(4) defines "person" as "individual, corporation, or association," it is difficult to imagine how anyone or anything other than an individual could be a victim of the offense. In a point of clarification, the Legislature has evidenced an intent that the law not be applied to abductions of nonhumans, such as animals. Thus, taking a prized race horse and holding him for ransom implicates the law of theft not kidnapping.

Unlike the criminal homicide and assault statutes which apply to unborn fetus, the Legislature has excluded fetus from the scope of the kidnapping statute. If Steve abducts Maria, a pregnant female, only one kidnapping offense, not two, has occurred.

Kidnapping is a felony of the third degree.

Aggravated Kidnapping

If a kidnapping includes one or more of six attendant circumstances, the offense elevates to aggravated kidnapping. Anecdotal evidence, as well as reported case opinions, suggests that aggravated kidnapping is a more common offense than ordinary kidnapping. A review of the additional elements that inflate the offense reveals most of the common motives for abducting another person. If the abduction is committed with intent to do one of the following, the offense becomes an aggravated kidnapping. As with plain kidnapping, the specific intent of the offender is the element of the offense, not the actual accomplishment of the result. Kidnapping becomes aggravated kidnapping if the victim is abducted with intent of:

- *Holding victim for ransom or reward*—An actual demand for ransom certainly establishes this element but is not required. Holding for ransom applies to adults as well as children.
- *Using victim as hostage*—See discussion below of hostage-taking as a form of aggravated kidnapping.

§ 20.04. Aggravated Kidnapping

a. A person commits an offense if he intentionally or knowingly abducts another person with the intent to:
1. hold him for ransom or reward;
2. use him as a shield or hostage;
3. facilitate the commission of a felony or the flight after the attempt or commission of a felony;
4. inflict bodily injury on him or violate or abuse him sexually;
5. terrorize him or a third person; or
6. interfere with the performance of any governmental or political function.

b. A person commits an offense if the person intentionally or knowingly abducts another person and uses or exhibits a deadly weapon during the commission of the offense.

c. Except as provided by Subsection (d), an offense under this section is a felony of the first degree.

d. At the punishment stage of a trial, the defendant may raise the issue as to whether he voluntarily released the victim in a safe place. If the defendant proves the issue in the affirmative by a preponderance of the evidence, the offense is a felony of the second degree.

- *Using victim to facilitate attempt, commission, or flight from another felony*—If Peter robs the bank and then carjacks Adam and forces him at gunpoint to assist his getaway, an aggravated kidnapping occurs under this provision. Likewise, holding the bank president's family at gunpoint at their home while an accomplice goes to the bank with the president to obtain cash violates this subsection.

- *Inflicting bodily injury or sexual abuse on victim*—One all too common form of kidnapping is the abduction of an adult or child victim in order to sexually assault them.

- *Terrorizing the victim or a third party*—While "terrorize" is not defined in the statute, case law says the term means to fill with anxiety, coerce by violence, or create an atmosphere of fear of imminent bodily injury or death.[23] Tom's abduction of Katie in the earlier example could fit within this provision.

- *Interfering with government or political functions*—Any kidnapping wherein the motive is to alter government policies or other political decisions elevates to an aggravated form of the offense.

- *Using or exhibiting deadly weapon during commission of offense*—As with most other crimes against person, the offense rises to the elevated form if a deadly weapon is used or exhibited during its commission.[24] Recall that the threat to use deadly force elevates an unlawful restraint to a kidnapping. The actual use of deadly force thereby raises the crime one more level.

ISSUES IN KIDNAPPING

Felix and Oscar decide to rob a jewelry store in Fort Worth. Wearing masks and armed with pistols they enter the store. Felix forces all store employees and customers into the employee break room while Oscar takes jewelry from the display cases. Just as the two bandits are about to flee the store, the police arrive. In a panic, Felix grabs the store manager. Using her as a hostage, he and Oscar exit the store. In addition to an aggravated robbery charge, will Felix and Oscar be facing kidnapping charges?

While more than one crime can arise out of a single event, American jurisdictions are split on the question of whether an abduction that is merely incidental to an underlying felony can be prosecuted as a kidnapping. The majority view is that kidnapping statutes do not apply to unlawful confinements or movements incidental to the commission of other felonies. In the jewelry store robbery case, one can certainly argue that herding the employees and customers into the next room was simply inherent in the act of the robbery. But, the taking of the hostage is a significant, stand-alone event that increased the danger to the store manager. The majority of jurisdictions would likely allow a kidnapping prosecution for the hostage-taking but not for the movement of the individuals into the break room. Texas follows a minority view on this question. Because of the language of the aggravated kidnapping statute, Texas will permit a prosecution for either or both the movement into the break room and the taking of the hostage. "There is also nothing in the statute indicating that the Legislature intended to bar the prosecution of a kidnapping that is part and parcel of another offense."[25]

A similar issue arises in many sexual assaults, particularly those involving children. The child is abducted and taken to a remote locale and sexually assaulted. Has the assailant also committed kidnapping as an incident to the assault? Most jurisdictions, including Texas, would view the abduction as a second offense because the elements of the offense are complete prior to any sexual act being perpetrated. The offender could be convicted of both aggravated sexual assault and aggravated kidnapping without violating the prohibition against double jeopardy.[26]

Penalty

A basic violation of the aggravated kidnapping statute is punished at the felony of the first degree level. One interesting aspect of the penalty for aggravated kidnapping is grounded in the general deterrence theory. If the existence of the criminal sanction deters individuals from committing offenses, can it also encourage the same individuals to mitigate the level of harm they might otherwise produce? Texans apparently believe so. Sec. 20.04(d) provides that upon conviction of aggravated kidnapping, the offense drops to a second degree felony if the defendant establishes that he voluntarily released the victim in a **safe place**.[27,28] The purpose of this provision is to encourage kidnappers to take measures to ensure that their victims survive. Like all laws based on the general deterrence theory, it presupposes that the offender knows which conduct aggravates his plight and which reduces his level of culpability.

Whether the location is a "safe place" is dependent on a variety of factors. Case law has held that the jury should consider the remoteness of the location; the proximity of authorities or persons who could aid or assist; the time of day; the climatic conditions; the victim's condition; and the character of, and the victim's familiarity with, the location or neighborhood.[29] Releasing the victim in their own home does not necessarily constitute a "safe place" if the victim is still at risk of harm from the kidnapper.[30]

ABDUCTION-RELATED OFFENSES

Parental Abduction

Roger and Dolores after 12 years of marriage have separated and are in the process of a divorce. Their son Eddie is eight years old and in the third grade. One day, instead of taking the school bus home, Eddie is met at the school door by his father Roger. Eddie and Roger depart in Roger's automobile. When Eddie does not come home on the bus,

Dolores becomes worried and calls the police. Inquiry at the school reveals that Eddie left with his father. Roger and Eddie are never seen again by Dolores. Has Roger committed a crime?

The scenario is one faced by the criminal justice system on a frequent basis. A federally funded study of the problem of **parental abductions** found that approximately 200,000 children are abducted annually by a noncustodial family member, usually the father.[31]

Traditional views of kidnapping do not fit parental abductions very well. First, under our Common Law tradition, each parent has an equal right to custody of their children. Second, in most such cases, the parent-abductor intends no harm to the child and is committing the act out of fear of losing their relationship with the child or out of dissatisfaction with a judicial determination regarding legal custody. On occasion, the abduction is an attempt to gain leverage during a divorce proceeding. Whatever the motive, the act is quite dissimilar to the harm the law of kidnapping has traditionally sought to prevent and punish.

For many years law enforcement and other elements of the criminal justice system considered parental abductions as a civil matter not a criminal offense. Any effort to regain lawful custody of the child had to be pursued through the slow civil court process. Adding to the reluctance of the police to become involved in such matters was the lack of legal clarity as to which parent actually was entitled to custody and the authority of the police to enforce that claim. This issue was further complicated if the parents had recently resided in another state. For example, the mother might have a judicially issued custody order from California while father possessed a similar order from a Texas court. Police officers were uncomfortable trying to make judgments about which of the two conflicting orders should be enforced. Accordingly, little assistance was afforded to the parent from whose physical custody the child had been taken.

Legislative bodies have responded to these problems in two ways. On the national level, Congress enacted the Parental Kidnapping Prevention Act of 1980.[32] This statute clarified the responsibilities of a state in enforcing out-of-state custody orders. The statute goes a long way in clearing up questions of which state's custody order is valid. Second, Texas and other states, recognizing that parental abductions, while not classic kidnappings, should be discouraged, have enacted specific interference with child custody laws. In effect, these laws give the police a legal basis to intervene in a parental abduction case until custody rights can be clearly established and enforced by the civil court system.

Sec. 25.03 establishes a state jail felony for several different forms of custody interference. First, it is an offense for any person to take or retain a child under age 18 in violation of the express terms of a court custody order. However, the offender must know of the existence of the court order. Assume Ken and Barbara are divorced. During the divorce proceedings, custody of their twins, Rob and Roberta, was awarded to Barbara. Ken was granted certain visitation rights every other weekend. One weekend Ken picks up the children but without telling Barbara decides to take the twins on a vacation to the beach. They stay at the beach for a week. Assuming such a period of custody is outside the limits the court order establishes for Ken, he has violated Sec. 25.03(a)(1).

The statute also criminalizes taking a child under age 18 from the jurisdiction of the court without court permission, knowing that custody proceedings are pending. Interestingly, the geographical jurisdiction of the court wherein the proceeding is pending may vary from case to case. For example, while statutory County Courts at Law only have jurisdiction within the geographical limits of the particular

§ 25.03. Interference with Child Custody

a. A person commits an offense if the person takes or retains a child younger than 18 years when the person:
1. knows that the person's taking or retention violates the express terms of a judgment or order of a court disposing of the child's custody; or
2. has not been awarded custody of the child by a court of competent jurisdiction, knows that a suit for divorce or a civil suit or application for habeas corpus to dispose of the child's custody has been filed, and takes the child out of the geographic area of the counties composing the judicial district if the court is a district court or the county if the court is a statutory county court, without the permission of the court and with the intent to deprive the court of authority over the child.

b. A noncustodial parent commits an offense if, with the intent to interfere with the lawful custody of a child younger than 18 years, the noncustodial parent knowingly entices or persuades the child to leave the custody of the custodial parent, guardian, or person standing in the stead of the custodial parent or guardian of the child.

c. It is a defense to prosecution under Subsection (a)(2) that the actor returned the child to the geographic area of the counties composing the judicial district if the court is a district court or the county if the court is a statutory county court, within three days after the date of the commission of the offense.

d. An offense under this section is a state jail felony.

county, some Texas District Courts cover single counties (such as in the largest counties of the state) while those in sparsely populated parts of the state serve three or more counties. Recognizing that the higher goal of the law is not to punish the individual but to protect the welfare of the child, the statute provides an absolute defense if the violator brings the child back within the jurisdiction of the court within three days.

While the first section of the statute could apply to virtually anyone with a custody interest in the child, such as grandparents, siblings, and former foster parents, the second section [Sec. 25.03(b)] is explicitly limited to noncustodial parents. This section declares it an offense for the noncustodial parent to knowingly persuade the child to leave the custody of the individual to whom the court has awarded custody. Assume Susan, the birth mother of Jenna a 14-year-old, has had troubles with drug and alcohol abuse. She has also served time in prison. While in prison, Susan's parents obtained legal custody of their grandchild. If Susan subsequently persuades Jenna to leave the grandparents and come live with her, Susan has violated the statute.[33]

Unlawful Transport

The unlawful transport statute was enacted in 1999 to place on the law books a state statute regarding the commercial transportation of undocumented migrant workers. While foreign immigration issues are generally viewed as falling with the purview of the federal government, the extensive boundary that Texas shares with Mexico has made the state a major location for the smuggling of Mexican and Central American migrants. Sec. 20.05 grants state and local officers a basis for interceding into commercial

§ 20.05. Unlawful Transport

a. A person commits an offense if the person for pecuniary benefit transports an individual in a manner that:
   1. is designed to conceal the individual from local, state, or federal law enforcement authorities; and
   2. creates a substantial likelihood that the individual will suffer serious bodily injury or death.
b. An offense under this section is a state jail felony.

smuggling operations. The offense requires, among other elements, that the manner of transportation place the immigrants at substantial risk of serious bodily injury or death.[34]

Trafficking of Persons

An entire chapter of the Penal Code, albeit a small one, Chapter 20A, covers trafficking in humans. Human trafficking has been receiving increased attention in the international legal and human rights communities. In many places in the world an extensive market for forced labor or forced prostitution exists.[35] America is not immune to this tragic circumstance. "Women and girls, largely from East Asia, Eastern Europe, Mexico and Central America are trafficked to the United States into prostitution. Some men and women, responding to fraudulent offers of employment in the United States, migrate willingly—legally and illegally—but are subsequently subjected to conditions of involuntary servitude at work sites or in the commercial sex trade. An unknown number of American citizens and legal residents are trafficked within the country primarily for sexual servitude and, to a lesser extent, forced labor."[36] While human trafficking numbers in Texas are unknown, nationwide an estimated 20,000 individuals annually are believed to be smuggled into the United States to be enslaved to work in small factories or forced to serve as prostitutes.[37]

The Texas law creates a high level felony for anyone who entices, recruits, transports, or harbors by force or deception another individual with intent to place him or her into forced labor or prostitution.

CRIMEGRAPH
Kidnapping and Related Offenses

Offense	Culpable mental state	Conduct	Who?	Specific Intent/Knowledge	How?	What/Where	Penalty
Unlawful Restraint 20.02(a)	1. Intentionally or 2. Knowingly	Restrains	Another person				AM to F3
Kidnapping 20.03(a)	1. Intentionally or 2. Knowingly	Abducts	Another person				F3
Aggravated Kidnapping 20.04(a)	1. Intentionally or 2. Knowingly	Abducts	Another person	With intent to: 1. Hold for ransom or reward, or 2. Use as shield or hostage, or 3. Facilitate commission of another felony, or 4. Inflict bodily injury or abuse sexually, or 5. Terrorize victim/third party, or 6. Interfere with performance of governmental or political function			F2 to F1
Aggravated Kidnapping 20.04(b)	1. Intentionally or 2. Knowingly	Abducts	Another person		1. Uses or 2. Exhibits	Deadly weapon	F2 to F1
Interference with Child Custody 25.03(a)(1)	Recklessly*	1. Takes or 2. Retains	Child under 18	Knowing the taking or retention violates court custody order			SJF
Interference with Child Custody 25.03(a)(2)	Recklessly*	Takes	Child under 18	Knowing court custody proceeding is pending	Without lawful custody	Out of court's geographical jurisdiction	SJF
Interference with Child Custody 25.03(b)	Recklessly*	Noncustodial parent: 1. Entices or 2. Persuades	Child under 18	With intent to interfere with lawful custody of another		To leave custodial parent, etc.	SJF

*Required by Texas Penal Code § 6.02

171

Notes

1. The kidnapping of Charley Ross may well be the origin of the parental admonition about taking candy from strangers.

2. One individual, who was shot during a residential burglary in New York, made a deathbed confession to the kidnapping. The individual believed to be his partner in the kidnapping was killed instantly in the same shoot-out. One additional individual, a relative of the kidnappers, was prosecuted for assisting with commission of the crime. *See* ERNEST KAHLAR ALIX, RANSOM KIDNAPPING IN AMERICA, 1874–1974: THE CREATION OF A CAPITAL CRIME (1978).

3. It should be noted that during the colonial period, several incidents occurred where Native Americans required a ransom for settlers who had been kidnapped. No historical record exists suggesting that anyone was ever prosecuted for such an act.

4. *See* ALIX, *supra*, at 18–20.

5. Lindbergh Act, ch. 271, 47 Stat. 326 (1932), now codified as 18 U.S.C. § 1201.

6. Many department and discount store chains participate in the Code Adam program. When a child is reported separated from his or her parents in the store, an announcement is made of the child's description. Store employees have previously assigned areas to search and monitor in an effort to locate the missing child. Shoppers are also urged to be vigilant for the child's location. If the child is not found in 10 minutes, law enforcement authorities are notified.

7. In known child abduction cases, the child's description and descriptive information about the abductor and his vehicle are broadcast over participating radio and television stations. Electronic signage on area freeways also post the information.

8. *See* Adam Walsh Child Protection and Safety Act of 2006, Pub. L. 109–248, 120 Stat. 587, and list *at* www.jmlfoundation.org/StatesJMLLaw.htm.

9. The offense is so infrequent that even the FBI, which has investigative responsibilities over the crime, does not collect and publish the number of incidents annually in its UNIFORM CRIME REPORTS. The logistical problems of perpetrating a kidnapping for ransom combined with the aggressive response by federal and state authorities make the crime a rare one.

10. DAVID J. FINKELHOR ET AL., NONFAMILY ABDUCTED CHILDREN: NATIONAL ESTIMATES AND CHARACTERISTICS 6 (2002).

11. CHRISTINE O. GREGOIRE, CASE MANAGEMENT FOR MISSING CHILDREN HOMICIDE INVESTIGATION 2 (1993).

12. *See* Chapter 9—Theft.

13. 1856 TEX. PENAL CODE art. 515.

14. Rodriguez v. State, 646 S.W.2d 524 (Tex. App.—Houston [1st Dist.] 1982).

15. *Id.*

16. Peace officers enjoy a level of immunity from criminal prosecution for making arrests, even those that turn out to be unlawful. *See* TEX. PENAL CODE § 9.51. This statutory immunity does not normally extend to private citizens. On occasion, well-meaning citizens and bail enforcement agents (bounty hunters) will be charged with unlawful restraint when they fail to follow state law regarding citizen's arrest or apprehension of bond jumpers.

17. Jeff might be facing enticing a child charges. *See* TEX. PENAL CODE § 25.04.

18. Jurisdictions are inconsistent in whether to spell the offense with one "p" or two. Perkins and Boyce argue that the one "p" version "is to be preferred" because the term is a word "ending in a single consonant preceded by a single vowel." *See* ROLLIN M. PERKINS & RONALD N. BOYCE, CRIMINAL LAW 229 n.1 (3rd ed. 1982). Their argument, though likely grammatically correct, appears to have failed to persuade the overwhelming majority of legislatures. Although Congress opted for the single "p" in constructing the U.S. Code, California, Florida, New York, and Texas lawmakers prefer the double letters. Illinois, wishing to straddle the issue, has officially created the offenses of kidnaping (one "p") and aggravated kidnapping (two "p")! [*Compare* 720 ILL. COMP. STAT. 5/10–1 *and* 720 ILL. COMP. STAT. 5/10–2.]

19. Carpenter v. State, 551 S.W.2d 724 (Tex. Crim. App. 1977).

20. Clark v. State, 24 S.W.3d 473 (Tex. App.—Texarkana 2000).

21. Price v. State, 35 S.W.3d 136 (Tex. App.—Waco 2000).

22. Kemple v. State, 725 S.W.2d 483 (Tex. App.—Corpus Christi 1987).

23. *See* Teer v. State, 895 S.W.2d 845 (Tex. App.—Waco 1995), *and* Padgett v. State, 683 S.W.2d 453 (Tex. App.—San Antonio 1984).

24. *See* TEX. PENAL CODE § 22.02(a)(2) (aggravated assault); TEX. PENAL CODE § 22.021(a)(2)(iv) (aggravated sexual assault); and TEX. PENAL CODE § 29.03(a)(2) (aggravated robbery).

25. Hines v. State, 75 S.W.3d 444, 448 (Tex. Crim. App. 2002).

26. Rodriguez v. State, 766 S.W.2d 358 (Tex. App.—Texarkana 1989).

27. The safe place requirement includes the victim being alive at the time of the release. *See* Teer v. State.

28. The defendant has the obligation of establishing the existence of the safety of the place of release by the preponderance of the evidence.

29. Ballard v. State, 193 S.W.3d 916 (Tex. Crim. App. 2006).

30. McLaren v. State, 104 S.W.3d 268 (Tex. App.—El Paso 2003).

31. *See* HEATHER HAMMER ET AL., CHILDREN ABDUCTED BY FAMILY MEMBERS: NATIONAL ESTIMATES AND CHARACTERISTICS 4 (2002).

32. 28 U.S.C. § 1738A. In 1993, Congress also enacted the International Parental Kidnapping Crime Act (18 U.S.C. § 1204) declaring it a federal felony to take a child under 16 years of age out of the country for the purposes of interfering with the lawful exercise of parental rights.

33. The statute uses the verbs "entice" and "persuade." No appellate court has to date decided whether the act of enticement must be successful or whether the simple act of encouraging the child to leave the individual with lawful custody violates the law.

34. During a 2003 smuggling attempt from South Texas to Houston, more than 70 illegal immigrants were packed inside an airtight trailer. Nineteen were discovered dead inside the abandoned trailer stopped along the highway near Victoria. The truck driver and several associates were subsequently prosecuted in federal court for the fatal smuggling attempt.

35. *See* U.S. DEPARTMENT OF STATE, TRAFFICKING IN PERSONS REPORT (Jun. 2007), *at* http://www.state.gov/g/tip/rls/tiprpt/2007/.

36. *Id.* at 49.

37. *See* Okereke, Godpower, *The International Trade in Human Beings: A Critical Look at the Casual Factors*, CRIME & JUST. INT'L 4, 6 (May/Jun. 2005), *at* http://www.cjcenter.org/cjcenter/publications/cji/archives.

CHAPTER 8

Property Destruction Offenses

BOLO

The reader should be on the lookout (BOLO) for the meaning of the following terms. Knowledge of the meaning of these terms will greatly assist the reader in understanding the primary elements of the chapter.

- Building
- Burning
- Common Law arson
- Content neutral
- Curtilage
- Damage
- Destroy
- Explosion
- Fire

- Habitation
- Open-space land
- Security agreement
- Tagging
- Tamper
- Tangible property
- Vandalism
- Vehicle

INTRODUCTION TO ARSON

A cold winter night. Firefighters are called to the scene of a raging blaze at a restaurant. Despite their efforts, the structure is a total loss. Subsequent investigation reveals the restaurant's owner had been experiencing financial troubles and the restaurant had been losing money for over a year. A case of arson?

A crisp autumn afternoon. Carl is raking leaves in his backyard. As the leaves accumulate into large piles, Carl sets them afire. Things go well until a quick shift in the wind direction causes sparks to fly onto the roof of a neighbor's house. The house catches fire. Has Carl committed arson?

Will robs a bank. He flees the scene in an automobile that he stole earlier in the day. He drives to a secluded area and sets the vehicle on fire to destroy any fingerprints or other evidence that could be used against him. In addition to auto theft and robbery charges, has Will also committed the crime of arson?

Each of the above incidents would attract the attention of arson investigators and raise a possibility of arson-related charges being filed against the perpetrator.

While historically considered one of the major crimes in society, acts of arson, in fact, occur relatively infrequently. About 30,000 intentionally set structural fires and another 17,000 purposeful vehicle fires are known to happen each year throughout the country.[1] In Texas, authorities become aware of about 6,800 arsons annually.[2] In the crimes against property category, the number of arsons pales by comparison with over 1,000,000 motor vehicle thefts and over 2,000,000 burglaries nationwide.

The early law of arson applied only to the intentional burning of the dwelling house and adjoining outbuilding of another. Burning of a business or of one's own property did not constitute arson, unless the fire spread and consumed someone else's home. The felony offense of arson developed in the Common Law out of concern for both the sanctity of one's home and the great possibility of injury or death due to fire. As the great legal scholar Sir William Blackstone observed,

> This is an offense of very great malignity, and much more pernicious to the public than simple theft: because, first, it is an offense against that right, of habitation, which is acquired by the law of nature as well as by the laws of society; next, because of the terror and confusion that necessarily attends it; and, lastly, because in simple theft the thing stolen only changes it's master, but still remains *in esse* [in being] for the benefit of the public, whereas by burning the very substance is absolutely destroyed. It is also frequently more destructive than murder itself, of which too it is often the cause: since murder, atrocious as it is, seldom extends beyond the felonious act designed; whereas fire too frequently involves in the common calamity persons unknown to the incendiary, and not intended to be hurt by him, and friends as well as enemies.[3]

Perhaps fittingly, during the thirteenth century England punished the crime of arson by death by burning.[4]

The English held an understandable concern not only for the homeowner but for their ability to control the spread of a fire. For example, the City of London was heavily damaged by fire in 1135 and again in 1212. In 1666, during what has become known as the Great Fire, over 13,000 houses and 100 churches and chapels, including old St. Paul's Cathedral, were destroyed. Over 100,000 persons, one-sixth of the population, were rendered homeless.[5] Even today, with modern fire-fighting apparatus, a major blaze is difficult to suppress. One can only imagine the level of concern of individuals in the Middle Ages.

COMMON LAW ARSON

As originally developed under the Common Law, arson was the willful and malicious burning of the dwelling or outbuildings of another. As background for understanding the modern law of arson, each of the Common Law elements is considered in order below.

Willful and Malicious

The *mens rea* for arson under the Common Law definition was being willful and malicious. Burnings thus had to be willful, meaning purposeful. Damage to property through negligent or careless burning did not qualify. Consider the earlier scenario of Carl burning leaves. His negligent conduct would not have been viewed as an act of arson under the Common Law. Likewise, the element of malice had to be established. While malice is normally thought of as possessing evilness in one's heart, in the context of arson the term also covered conduct that created a high risk of burning. While all intentional burnings were viewed as malicious, an act that evidenced an extreme disregard for the safety of others also would be considered malicious. For example, if John, angry at his boss, sets fire to his employer's shop in a densely populated city and the fire spreads to an adjacent dwelling, John has committed arson under the traditional definition. Even though John may not have intended to damage the adjacent home, his act was so irresponsible that an English court would view it as malicious. Certainly purposeful fires were considered to be malicious but so were those that today might be deemed to be merely reckless.

Burning

Much of the litigation in arson prosecutions under the Common Law definition concerned what constituted a **burning**. The law of arson focused on whether a "burning" had occurred because without a burning, no harm had resulted. The existence of a burning, no matter how slight, no matter whether the structural integrity of the dwelling was affected, and no matter if it extinguished itself, was a necessary element of arson. One American court described the traditional test as whether "there is actual ignition, and the fiber of the wood or other combustible material is charred, and thus destroyed, even in small part . . ."[6] Additionally, material that is merely blackened by smoke, smudged, or discolored by heat was customarily viewed as not having been burned within the meaning of the law of arson.[7]

Dwelling or Outbuildings of Another

As with the early law of burglary, the crime of arson was concerned with the sanctity of the habitation of persons other than the perpetrator. The historical law was limited to dwellings and outbuildings of a person other than the offender. The outbuilding inclusion reflected the Common Law concept of curtilage. The **curtilage** was the series of domestic buildings that surrounded and supported a residence and might include a detached kitchen and privy.[8] Additionally, the law of arson applied only to houses that were occupied. This does not mean that the resident had to be in the house at the time of the fire but rather that it actually functioned as a habitation as compared to some other use such as a storage building.

Additionally, one could not be guilty of arson for burning his own home. Nor could one commit the offense by burning a barn, carriage, shop, or other nonresidential property. Even the burning of mortgaged or insured property was originally viewed as falling outside the scope of the law of arson because the target was not the dwelling of another.

TEXAS LAW OF ARSON

Introduction

As with most other Common Law offenses, the modern Texas arson statute bears only a passing resemblance to the old law. The Texas Legislature has recognized that the malicious burning of dwelling houses is not the only harm caused by purposefully set fires. On the other hand, fire and explosions can have lawful and useful purposes. The Legislature has attempted to craft an arson statute that criminalizes that which is harmful to society without making innocent behavior an offense. This has been an ongoing endeavor as the statute has been modified and expanded several times since its original enactment in 1973.

With this goal of balancing harm and utility in mind, the Texas arson statute seeks to prevent and punish those persons who use fire and explosions to:

- Destroy someone else's property
- Create a risk of destruction of someone else's property
- Create a danger to the public safety
- Perpetrate insurance fraud

. . . while at the same time permitting fire and explosions to be used in a socially useful manner.

§ 28.01. Definitions

In this chapter:

1. "Habitation" means a structure or vehicle that is adapted for the overnight accommodation of persons and includes:
   A. each separately secured or occupied portion of the structure or vehicle; and
   B. each structure appurtenant to or connected with the structure or vehicle.

2. "Building" means any structure or enclosure intended for use or occupation as a habitation or for some purpose of trade, manufacture, ornament, or use.

3. "Property" means:
   A. real property;
   B. tangible or intangible personal property, including anything severed from land; or
   C. a document, including money, that represents or embodies anything of value.

4. "Vehicle" includes any device in, on, or by which any person or property is or may be propelled, moved, or drawn in the normal course of commerce or transportation.

5. "Open-space land" means real property that is undeveloped for the purpose of human habitation.

6. "Controlled burning" means the burning of unwanted vegetation with the consent of the owner of the property on which the vegetation is located and in such a manner that the fire is controlled and limited to a designated area.

§ 28.02. Arson

a. A person commits an offense if the person starts a fire, regardless of whether the fire continues after ignition, or causes an explosion with intent to destroy or damage:
   1. any vegetation, fence, or structure on open-space land; or
   2. any building, habitation, or vehicle:
      A. knowing that it is within the limits of an incorporated city or town;
      B. knowing that it is insured against damage or destruction;
      C. knowing that it is subject to a mortgage or other security interest;
      D. knowing that it is located on property belonging to another;
      E. knowing that it has located within it property belonging to another; or
      F. when the person is reckless about whether the burning or explosion will endanger the life of some individual or the safety of the property of another.

a-1. A person commits an offense if the person recklessly starts a fire or causes an explosion while manufacturing or attempting to manufacture a controlled substance and the fire or explosion damages any building, habitation, or vehicle.

b. It is an exception to the application of Subsection (a)(1) that the fire or explosion was a part of the controlled burning of open-space land.

c. It is a defense to prosecution under Subsection (a)(2)(A) that prior to starting the fire or causing the explosion, the actor obtained a permit or other written authorization granted in accordance with a city ordinance, if any, regulating fires and explosions.

d. An offense under Subsection (a) is a felony of the second degree, except that the offense is a felony of the first degree if it is shown on the trial of the offense that:
   1. bodily injury or death was suffered by any person by reason of the commission of the offense; or
   2. the property intended to be damaged or destroyed by the actor was a habitation or a place of assembly or worship.

e. An offense under Subsection (a-1) is a state jail felony, except that the offense is a felony of the third degree if it is shown on the trial of the offense that bodily injury or death was suffered by any person by reason of the commission of the offense.

f. It is a felony of the third degree if a person commits an offense under Subsection (a)(2) of this section and the person intentionally starts a fire in or on a building, habitation, or vehicle, with intent to damage or destroy property belonging to another, or with intent to injure any person, and in so doing, recklessly causes damage to the building, habitation, or vehicle.

g. If conduct that constitutes an offense under Subsection (a-1) or that constitutes an offense under Subsection (f) also constitutes an offense under another subsection of this section or another section of this code, the actor may be prosecuted under Subsection (a-1) or Subsection (f), under the other subsection of this section, or under the other section of this code.

To a large degree, the statute sorts lawful and unlawful behavior based on the perpetrator's *mens rea* and the surrounding factual circumstances of the fire. As to *mens rea*, arson may be unique when compared to other Texas criminal laws. It can require proof of three *mens rea* elements within a single offense. As will be further explored below, an act of arson generally requires an intentionally set fire with the specific intent of damaging property combined with the knowledge of the circumstances surrounding the fire. The *mens rea* requirement certainly separates criminal from noncriminal conduct but makes prosecution of some arson cases particularly difficult.

Regarding the surrounding factual circumstances of the incident, the statute declares an arson when the object of the fire or explosion falls within either of two broad possibilities. One level of arson occurs when the object is vegetation, fences, and structures on open-space land and the other level of crime occurs when buildings, habitations, or vehicles are attacked under any one of six factual circumstances. These are discussed in detail below.

An act of arson also can have collateral consequences. A purposeful killing during an arson can constitute capital murder.[9] Likewise, since arson is a felony, its commission with a resulting unintended death can support a charge of murder under the Felony Murder Rule.[10]

As will be seen later in the chapter, damage to property through use of fires and explosions can occasionally not violate the arson statute but rather be covered under the criminal mischief or reckless damage statutes.

Elements of Arson

Starts a Fire or Causes Explosion

Arson has been expanded in Texas to cover both fires and explosions. However, the Penal Code does not provide a definition of a "fire" or of an "explosion." One Texas court has said, "**Fire** is defined in terms of its tangible aspects and effects—'fire' is 'the phenomenon of combustion as manifested in light, flame, and heat and in heating, destroying, and altering effects.' "[11] From a scientific perspective, a fire may be defined as a rapid, persistent chemical change that releases heat and light and is accompanied by flame, especially the exothermic oxidation of a combustible substance. While fires commonly produce heat, light, and smoke and ultimately consume their hosts, such visible conditions are not always necessary. For example, a fire fueled by methyl alcohol burns with no visible smoke and no visible flame but is nonetheless a fire. Likewise, burning propane emits little smoke.

Unlike the Common Law definition of arson that required burning, the Texas statute focuses upon "starting a fire." Can one start a fire without a resultant burning? Suppose Walter constructs a Molotov cocktail, lights the wick, and tosses it at Katherine's house.[12] The burning device shatters and falls to the ground. A bush and some grass are burned and the garage door is scorched. Has Walter started a fire within the meaning of the arson statute? Yes. In a similar case the appellate court held that the offense of arson was complete when Walter lit the wick with the intent to damage Katherine's house. He started a fire by lighting the bottle of gasoline. The failure to cause the house to burn did not affect whether the elements of the offense were met. The fact that the house was not damaged by his actions did not make his conduct only an attempted arson. His conduct created a completed arson.[13] The crime of arson is complete whether or not any damage is done. This principle is reinforced by the statutory language "regardless of whether the fire continues after ignition." This phrase emphasizes that the focus of the statute is on the offender's efforts not his results. While no case law yet speaks to the issue, presumably the mere striking of a match as the prelude to burning a structure would meet the definition of "starting a fire."

Explosions may be created in a variety of ways. Any sudden increase in volume and release of energy in a violent manner, usually with the generation of high temperatures and the release of gases, constitutes an explosion and is potentially covered under Texas arson law. The most common forms of explosions encountered by justice system personnel are homemade devices, such as black powder-based pipe bombs, stolen commercial explosives, such as dynamite, and stolen military ordinance, such as hand grenades.

While the statute does not explicitly require a general *mens rea*, the Court of Criminal Appeals has ruled that for a standard arson conviction to stand, the fire must be of an incendiary nature.[14] This means that the fire (and presumably an explosion) was started intentionally or knowingly.[15,16] Thus, when an electrical short ignites a fire and destroys several adjacent buildings, no arson has occurred because the fire was not intentionally set. But, Will the bank robber in the opening scenario certainly intentionally and knowingly set fire to the stolen automobile.

With Intent to Damage or Destroy

The second *mens rea* to be proven is the specific intent requirement to damage or destroy. Reconsider the opening scenario of Carl burning leaves. He certainly purposefully set the leaves afire but he did not do so with the conscious objective to damage the neighbor's home. Any potential charge of arson against Carl collapses due to his lack of intent to destroy or damage the house. If Carl is viewed as being reckless in causing the residential fire, the offense is not arson. A charge of reckless damage or destruction (Sec. 28.04) might be appropriate. If his conduct in burning the leaves is merely criminally negligent, he has committed no violation of Chapter 28 as negligent destruction of property is not an offense.

The specific intent element is important because this factor creates the essential distinction between arson and noncriminal conduct. Many intentionally set fires spread and damage someone else's property. However, in many of those incidents the individual who set the fire had no intent to damage or destroy someone else's property. The perpetrator, like Carl, may have civil liability for negligence but will not face criminal charges.

The statute nowhere defines the phrase "damage or destroy." An ordinary dictionary definition suggests that the utility of an object is reduced when it is damaged but can be repaired. Property that is destroyed cannot be repaired. For the purpose of the arson statute, either will suffice. No distinction in penalty is drawn between items that are merely damaged and those that are fully destroyed. However, recall that the crime of arson is complete whether or not any damage actually occurs to the property. The operative factor is the specific intent of the offender, not what he or she succeeds in accomplishing.

Any Vegetation, Fence, or Structure on Open-space Land

Extending the law of arson to crops, grass, trees, fences, and the like is certainly not in the tradition of the Common Law notion of arson. However, in 1989 the Legislature extended the crime of arson to such purposeful burnings. Periodically, farmers will discover that someone has intentionally set fire to one of their fields or burned their fence posts or corn crib. Such conduct is now a form of arson. **Open-space land** is defined in Sec. 28.01(5).

Suppose Ronda is driving down the highway and tosses her lit cigarette butt out the window. The butt lands on the edge of the road and ignites the adjacent grass. The grass fire spreads to an alfalfa field owned by farmer McDonald and destroys two acres of plants. No arson has occurred because although Ronda lit the cigarette initially and caused a fire to erupt on open-space land, she lacked the intent to damage or destroy the property.

On occasion, farmers and ranchers will conduct controlled burns of land to prepare for planting or to kill undesirable vegetation. Such burns are an exception to the arson statute [Sec. 28.02(b)]

Any Building, Habitation, or Vehicle

The most frequent targets of arson are **buildings**, **habitations**, and **vehicles**. These forms of property are defined in Sec. 28.01, and are identical to the terminology used in the law of burglary. To eliminate redundancy in this text, a detailed discussion of these terms is found in Chapter 11, which covers burglary. The reader should review the relevant pages as needed. At this point, it is important to note that the Texas arson statute makes no distinction as to ownership of the building, habitation, or vehicle in question or whether effective consent of the owner has been obtained. The theft-related concepts of "effective consent" and "owner" are nowhere mentioned in the statute. The prohibited behaviors are just as illegal whether committed against another's property without consent or against property owned by the perpetrator. Although the bulk of arsons involve persons with no ownership interest in the property, acting out of revenge or vandalism causing harm to a third-party owner, the arson statute can ensnare individuals who use fire or explosives to destroy their own property for whatever reasons.

Causing a bomb to explode under a car or purposely setting a building or home afire becomes a crime if perpetrated under any one of the six statutory circumstances outlined in Sec. 28.02(a)(2)(A) through 28.02(a)(2)(F). These factual situations are the most common basis for an arson prosecution. Note, however, that each of these possibilities adds a third *mens rea* element that the prosecutor must prove. For the first five alternatives, the culpable mental state of knowledge must be shown. The sixth alternative uses recklessness.

Within the Limits of an Incorporated City   Consider that Hal has an old garage on his property. He wants to remove it in order to construct a new facility. He decides that the easiest way to destroy the structure is to burn it down. Does Hal commit arson if he sets the garage ablaze? He does if the property is inside the city limits. As a general rule, fires within the limits of a city potentially put other properties at risk far more than a similar fire out in the countryside. Accordingly, Hal could commit arson even when burning his own property! The public policy concern here is the risk to the public safety as a whole that is created by burning one's own property in close quarters. He can avoid the possibility of criminal charges by obtaining a fire permit from the city fire marshal prior to setting the fire [Sec. 28.02(c)].

A similar issue arises with commercial demolition companies. Companies that use high-order explosives to demolish large buildings are required to obtain permits to ensure that surrounding properties will not be adversely affected by their explosions. Using the dynamite without the appropriate permit could raise possible arson charges.

The rise of suburbs in unincorporated areas around a city with high residential and business densities creates the same potential for danger when a fire is set. Houston, Dallas, San Antonio, and other major Texas cities have suburban areas that are every bit as densely populated as the central city. However, counties are not required to establish the office of fire marshal and a county commissioner's court to establish fire regulations in unincorporated areas is very limited at this time.[17]

Insured against Damage or Destruction Recall the restaurant fire scenario at the beginning of the chapter. Assuming the fire was intentionally set, the incident would be an arson if the structure were covered by a fire insurance policy. This provision of the arson law sanctions those who attempt to perpetrate a fraud against insurers of property. While building and home insurance normally covers loss from fire, most automobile policies also protect against this risk.

A unique provision of the Texas statute is that, unlike many states, the crime is complete simply if an insurance policy exists on the property. There is no requirement that the owner of the policy actually file an insurance claim. Nor does the statute require a showing of an actual intent to defraud. The purposeful burning of buildings, homes, and vehicles that are insured constitutes arson under this subsection of the Penal Code.

Suppose Jack purchases a new sports car and finances the purchase through the brand's financial services arm. Over the next two years, the vehicle suffers a constant array of problems and breakdowns. It is essentially a lemon. Jack seeks to have the dealer swap the vehicle for a new one. The dealer refuses. Out of frustration, Jack drives the vehicle to the dealer's lot and sets it on fire. Has Jack committed arson of the vehicle because it is insured against damage? A literal reading of the statute suggests that he has. However, the insurance policy likely excludes damage purposefully inflicted by the owner. Since Jack cannot collect on the insurance, should his conduct be considered an arson? Texas courts have yet to rule on this factual situation.

Subject to a Mortgage or Other Security Interest An arson is committed when the building, habitation, or vehicle is subject to a mortgage or other security agreement. Mortgages and **security agreements** are legal contracts wherein money is loaned to the borrower and certain property is used as collateral for the loan. If the borrower does not pay back the loan and any interest, the holder of the security agreement often can seize the property and sell it to satisfy the outstanding loan balance. This is the common method by which houses and automobiles are financed.

Setting fire to property subject to a security agreement devalues the collateral of the loan. If the property were destroyed, the lender would have no recourse to recover the money he loaned. Accordingly, any arson of property subject to such a loan agreement affects the interests not only of the property owner but also of the lender.

Recall Jack and his "lemon" automobile above. Regardless of whether he has criminal liability for burning insured property, a more compelling case for harm can be argued based on the fact the automobile financing company no longer has viable collateral to force collection of its loan to Jack. Jack would certainly appear to commit arson under this provision of the statute.

Located on Property Belonging to Another   Whenever a building, habitation, or vehicle is burned while located on real estate belonging to another, that individual's property is placed at risk as well. The arson statute criminalizes such conduct in an effort to protect the property or third parties and the public safety as a whole. Once again, when Jack sets his convertible affair on the dealer's lot, he commits arson because the blaze presents a risk to the dealer's property.

Has Located within it Property Belonging to Another   In a similar vein, when someone burns his or her own property but that building, habitation, or vehicle contains property belonging to another, the other party's property is placed at risk of damage.

Recklessly Endangers Life or Property of Another   Regardless of where they occur, by their very nature structural and vehicle fires and explosions place the general public at risk of personal injury and property damage. Indeed when a substantial accidental fire erupts, firefighters often spend much of their efforts in preventing the fire from spreading to adjacent property and in rescuing persons who may be at risk of injury. Because of mankind's inability to quickly control or extinguish large fires, even with modern firefighting equipment and tactics, the arson law will sanction those who recklessly place the lives and property of others in danger.

Under this subsection a third culpable mental state that must be proven is recklessness. To show arson, it must be established that the arsonist started the fire in the building, vehicle, or habitation intending to damage or destroy the target and that he or she was reckless about placing another's life or property at risk. Evidence must show that the arsonist was aware of the risk and consciously disregarded it.

Any intentional burning of real estate or vehicles belonging to someone other than the arsonist indicates a reckless endangerment of that individual's property and completes the elements of the offense. This subsection serves as a catchall provision for any factual circumstance where the arsonist is burning property owned by someone else. The same rule also applies to arsonists who might burn their own property. Suppose Ben owns a small apartment house. He hires Derek to burn the building down. If Derek sets the facility ablaze while it is occupied, he is certainly aware of the risk the fire will pose to the tenants. His conduct constitutes arson.

Recklessly Causes Fire/Explosion While Manufacturing Controlled Substance

The methamphetamine epidemic of the early twenty-first century led several states, including Texas, to amend their arson statutes to further sanction the unlawful production of the drug. The chemicals used and the process by which methamphetamine is illicitly manufactured are considered hazardous materials because they are highly volatile and toxic to humans. As a consequence, fires at clandestine labs are common occurrences. To punish the drug dealers who put their families as well as their neighbors at risk, the Texas Legislature in 2005 expanded the definition of arson. An arson occurs if an individual recklessly causes a fire or explosion as a result of the manufacturing of illicit drugs and a building, habitation, or vehicle is damaged

[Sec. 28.01(1-a)]. If Bubba is cooking "meth" in his trailer house and the ether or acetone used in the process explodes, Bubba is facing an arson charge even if the only habitation damaged is his own.

Defenses to Arson

Assuming all other elements of the offense are in place, it is no defense to an arson charge that the property damaged or destroyed belonged to the offender or that the offender had the owner's permission to start the fire. Even a lawful fire started by a property owner can become arson if another person also has an interest in the property and no consent has been obtained. Assume Patricia is in a dispute with her business partner Molly. Patricia tries to set fire to the company office building. Firefighters arrive and extinguish the blaze before much harm has been done. Patricia has committed arson because Molly also has an ownership interest in the building. The fact that Patricia is a part owner of the building does not give her the right to destroy her partner's interest in the structure (Sec. 28.05).

Penalty

Arson is normally a felony of the second degree. The crime rises to a first degree felony if bodily injury or death occurs as a result of the crime. The offense also becomes a first degree felony if the intended target is a habitation or place of worship. Thus, arson of a private residence is a first degree felony. Also, out of legislative concern about hate crimes, arson of a church or similar religious meeting place is a felony of the first degree. FBI data suggests arsons constitute a substantial percentage of the hate crimes that occur annually.[18]

An arson under subsection (a-1) is a state jail felony, except it elevates to a third degree felony if injury or death occurs.

Distinguishing Arson from Criminal Mischief

Not surprisingly, the crimes of arson and criminal damage can often overlap. Indeed, criminal damage is often a lesser included offense of arson since arson involves destruction of property, albeit by fire or explosion. On the other hand, not all destructive acts involving fire constitute arson. Suppose Phil, angry that he lost a golf match to Eldrick, sets Eldrick's golf bag afire. That action destroyed property by fire but is not arson.

A three-part sequential test can be used to sort arsons from other forms of destructive behavior:

1. Did the destructive act involve use of fire or an explosion? If no, the event is criminal damage.

2. Was the intended target or damaged property on open-space land, a building, a habitation, or a vehicle? If the property in question does not fit within this list, the crime is not arson even though a fire or explosion was involved.

3. Are the required culpable mental states present? Was the fire/explosion intentionally caused? Did the offender know the surrounding circumstances that deem the act criminal? Other than fires and explosions erupting during illicit drug manufacturing, all arsons require intent to start the fire, an intent to damage or destroy designated property, and knowledge of the surrounding circumstances.

CRIMINAL MISCHIEF

Introduction

Cooter and two of his high school pals are driving around in his pickup truck late one Saturday evening. As they pass the crosstown rival high school, Cooter says, "Watch this!" He turns the steering wheel and guides the truck off the roadway into the flowerbed in front of the school. Cooter spins the wheels of the truck, throwing dirt and daffodils in all directions. After making a total mess of the plants, he returns to the roadway.

As he motors down the road, another group of youths spy the red pickup. As Cooter and his friends pass, the youths emerge from the shadows and hurl eggs at the truck. Several splatter on its shiny finish. The youths scatter in all directions, laughing at the accuracy of their aim. Cooter is not amused.

Meanwhile, across town Louise sees her boyfriend Rodney kissing Thelma. Enraged at her cheating beau, Louise picks up a large rock and begins bashing Rodney's sports car. She smashes the windshield and puts large dents in the hood and fenders.

The trenching of the flowerbed and the egging of the truck are but two examples of modern acts of vandalism. Louise's out-of-control behavior likewise is sadly a not uncommon occurrence. Such damage to property is, not surprisingly, illegal. Society calls this conduct vandalism. Some states label the conduct "criminal damage." Texas uses the term "criminal mischief." While the term "mischief" normally connotes playful pranks which produce no real harm, in extreme cases *criminal* mischief is punishable as a felony of the first degree.

TRADITIONAL VIEW OF CRIMINAL DAMAGE TO PROPERTY

The societal revulsion against the destruction of another's property has its origin in the term **vandalism**. The Vandals, an eastern Germanic tribe, stormed Rome in the fifth century. The tribe looted the city for two weeks in the year 455 A.D. Although scholars suggest that Vandals were no worse than the other barbarian tribes that sacked Rome during this period, their name became synonymous with acts of property damage and destruction. However, only in more recent years the term "vandalism" has become associated with senseless destructive acts, often perpetrated by youthful offenders.

While the record is scant, the English Common Law apparently considered malicious mischief to be a crime although it is unclear the circumstances which actually constituted the offense. Initially the Common Law viewed such damage to property as a petty trespass, which may explain the lack of written historical record regarding the crime. But over the years the English Parliament passed statutes increasing the penalty for certain forms of property damage.

Early American courts generally accepted property damage and destruction as a criminal act. For example, an 1808 Tennessee judge suggested that stabbing a horse might violate the Common Law rules regarding damaging property.[19] During the codification movement of the nineteenth century, many states clarified the issue by enacting statutes prohibiting certain forms of property damage. Initially, these offenses were characterized as "malicious mischief" and required proof of a malicious intent. The type or value of property damaged determined the level of offense.

No comprehensive count is made of the number of criminal damage incidents that occur nationwide or statewide. Data collected by the FBI shows about 780,000 persons arrested each year for "vandalism." The Texas Department of Public Safety reports over

8,000 adult arrests and about 4,700 juvenile arrests annually.[20] Human observation suggests that the actual number of incidents where property is damaged or destroyed vastly exceeds the number of arrests.

The opening scenarios demonstrate the range of conduct that falls under criminal mischief statute. Acts of vandalism by juveniles to purposeful damage to another's property all fall within the law's scope. Occasionally, acts of criminal mischief result in supplemental charges to other offenses, such as the intoxicated driver who is arrested and in his drunken and angry condition damages the police car in which he is placed. He will likely see criminal mischief charges filed in addition to the DWI charge.

TEXAS LAW OF CRIMINAL MISCHIEF

Introduction

1. The Texas Penal Code chapter on criminal damage to property takes several approaches to injuries done to another's property. The primary statute, criminal mischief, covers three different undesirable behaviors. First, the statute criminalizes purposeful damage to property. Second, intentional or knowing tampering with property becomes a crime when monetary loss or substantial inconvenience is the result. Finally, the inscription of graffiti is declared criminal. As to graffiti, a separate offense (Sec. 28.08) also exists. The two statutes overlap slightly in regard to the harm they seek to sanction. As to nonintentional damage to property, any reckless damage or destruction is declared to be a Class C misdemeanor under Sec. 28.04. Finally, a special statute, Sec. 28.07, covers various acts of vandalism that occur on railroad property.

Elements of Criminal Mischief

Without Effective Consent of Owner

As with robbery, burglary, theft, and other similar property-based offenses, the conduct in question is criminal only if it occurs without the effective consent of the owner of the property. Essentially, lack of effective consent means that the offender either is missing any assent whatsoever from the property owner—the normal circumstance in the vast majority of criminal mischief incidents—or has the permission of the owner but the permission was obtained through deception, coercion, or under some other circumstance where a rational person who not have consented. If Billy shoots his pellet pistol at the globes of streetlamps and breaks them, he certainly does not do so with the consent of the electric company. Likewise, in the opening hypotheticals, Cooter and Louise were totally lacking the consent of the individuals whose property they damaged.

§ 28.03. Criminal Mischief

a. A person commits an offense if, without the effective consent of the owner:
1. he intentionally or knowingly damages or destroys the tangible property of the owner;
2. he intentionally or knowingly tampers with the tangible property of the owner and causes pecuniary loss or substantial inconvenience to the owner or a third person; or
3. he intentionally or knowingly makes markings, including inscriptions, slogans, drawings, or paintings, on the tangible property of the owner.

Suppose Callie is attending a magic show. The main performer is part magician and part comedian. During the performance he asks Callie for her cellphone. He tells her, "Don't worry. Nothing will happen to it." Callie hands the phone to the performer. He crushes the phone with his foot and places the parts in his magic hat. The magician utters a few words and reveals to the audience the fact that the phone is still crushed. "Whoops! This trick worked last week," he says as the audience laughs uproariously. Would Callie have given the performer the cellphone had she known it would be damaged beyond repair? Certainly not. The performer obtained the phone from Callie with her consent, but did not have her *effective* consent because he deceived her. The entertainer has committed an act of criminal mischief.

The statute focuses on consent of the "owner" and damage to property of the "owner." "Owner" is defined in Sec. 1.07(35). A detailed discussion of the concept may be found in Chapter 9—Theft—but the term essentially means the property titleholder or the individual with a superior right of possession when compared to the offender. If one purposely damages his or her own property, no offense occurs. Likewise, if one destroys property with the permission of the owner, no offense has been committed. This latter event occurs frequently. Consider the building owner who hires another to demolish the structure in order to construct a new facility. Such a demolition is conducted with the owner's permission and obviously violates no criminal statute. But if the demolition occurred without the consent of the owner, a criminal offense has taken place.

Suppose Rita and Jerome are married. During a domestic dispute, Rita hits Jerome's expensive sports car with a hammer. The hood of the sports car is damaged. Rita is charged with criminal mischief but asserts at trial that since Texas is a community property state, she is actually the owner of the sports car as well. And, the statute does not apply to damaging your own property. Will the court agree with Rita's position? Probably not. As with the law of arson, it is no defense to the charge of criminal mischief that the offender held an interest in the property damaged if another person also had an interest in the property that she is not entitled to infringe upon.[21]

Intentionally or Knowingly

Suppose during class, a fellow student leans backward in his chair. The chair leg breaks, dumping the student onto the floor. Has the student committed the offense of criminal damage to property? The chair is certainly damaged but criminal charges are highly unlikely to be forthcoming. The student did not damage the chair intentionally or knowingly. Like other offenses, criminal damage statutes contain a *mens rea*. In Texas, liability attaches only for intentional or knowing behavior. Willful destruction of another's property is the harm the law is seeking to deter.

The Common Law offense of property destruction was labeled *malicious* mischief. When Cooter runs over the flowers in the opening example, was he motivated to do so out of ill will? Possibly as he may have held some form of dislike for the rival school and its students. Similarly, when Thelma trashes Rodney's sports car, she is acting out of rage and hatred for Rodney. But, when the teens egged Cooter's truck, was it due to ill will toward Cooter? No. He was merely the first vehicle to pass by. Is their conduct any less an offense than the other two incidents? While the eggers may not have caused the same level of damage as Cooter and Thelma, their conduct would still constitute criminal mischief because they acted in an intentional manner. The presence or absence of actual ill will or malice is not an element of the crime.

Property destruction is a prime example of a societal harm where social institutions other than the criminal law are better equipped to deal with the problem. With 200,000,000 registered motor vehicles in the United States, it is no surprise that about 6,000,000 collisions occur annually, ranging from minor "fender-benders" to multi-fatality incidents.[22] While charges for violating various provisions of the Transportation Code may be filed following a collision, rarely is a criminal damage to property charge filed. The reasons being threefold: First, most of these events are indeed true accidents, or at worst involve negligent behavior and, for the reasons discussed in Chapter 2, negligence is rarely criminalized. Second, many police officers psychologically separate traffic laws from penal laws, viewing the former as the sole legal basis for handling matters involving motor vehicles. Third, society has adopted insurance as a better means to deal with these property losses. The criminal law rarely makes the victim whole for his or her loss but in the case of vehicle collisions, insurance does a fairly good job of accomplishing that goal. Hence, little motivation exists to criminalize property destruction that is other than purposeful.

While only intentional or knowing behavior falls under Sec. 28.03, reckless damage to property can also be a criminal offense, albeit a Class C misdemeanor. The crime of reckless damage or destruction is discussed below.

Damage, Destroy, or Tamper

Each of the criminal damage statutes utilize the *actus reus* of damaging property, destroying property, or tampering with property. Curiously, none of the statutes define the words "damage" or "destroy" and only the interference with railroad property statute expressly defines "tamper." Accordingly, the statutes leave it to juries and judges to consider whether or not the conduct in a particular case fits within the ordinary meanings of the terms.

One court has suggested that the term **destroy** in its ordinary sense means "to reduce (an object) to useless fragments, a useless form, or remains, as by rending, burning, or dissolving; injure beyond repair or renewal" or "to ruin completely; spoil so that restoration is impossible."[23] The term **damage** refers to harm that reduces value or usefulness. Notice that both definitions speak in terms of the utility or value of the item. It is this diminution of usefulness or value, either partially or completely, that creates the harm in an act of criminal mischief and distinguishes these two terms from the term "tamper." If Anna is angry with Marta and "keys" the paint on her car, the vehicle has been damaged because of the reduction in value between a vehicle with a pristine paint job and one with an unsightly scratch.[24]

Damage or destruction can be perpetrated in any manner of ways. Physical force, for example, hands and feet, may be used. Tools, such as hammers and prybars, may be used. The damage may be committed through use of a firearm. Even found objects, such as rocks, bricks, and articles of furniture, may be employed to cause damage.

Suppose Johnny flushes a "cherry bomb" down the toilet in the school restroom. The firecracker explodes and cracks the toilet bowl. An act of criminal mischief has occurred. Similarly if Tom sets fire to the trash in a dumpster behind a store, he has committed criminal mischief. Even though Johnny and Tom caused an explosion or started a fire, their conduct does not rise to the level of an arson because the object of their destructive behavior was not a building, habitation, or vehicle. Thus, some acts of property destruction by fire may not qualify as an arson due to the target of the vandalism.

To meddle or misuse would be synonyms for **tamper**. But where is the harm in misusing an object? Suppose Jack and Jill are driving up a hill in Jack's car with the radio playing. Jill begins to push the radio buttons, causing the station to change every few seconds. Jack, finding her conduct distracting, says, "Stop changing stations. That's real annoying." Jill replies, "I am just trying to find something to listen to," and continues to push the buttons. Is Jill "tampering" with the radio? Does her conduct constitute a criminal offense?

Whatever minimal wear and tear Jill is inducing in the radio is of such a small amount that no significant harm is being done. Even though her conduct may be annoying to Jack, it is not a crime. For her tampering with the radio to become a criminal offense, the element of a "pecuniary loss or substantial inconvenience" must exist. In other words, the tampering has to produce some measurable harm before the criminal sanction is imposed.

A pecuniary loss is one measurable in money. Suppose, as a prank, Albert lets the air out of the tires on Professor Newton's automobile. Does the professor suffer a monetary loss due to this prank? He certainly is likely to have to pay someone to come and reinflate the tires.

Is Professor Newton substantially inconvenienced by Albert's actions? Many acts in life are inconvenient. Is the delay and annoyance of dealing with the flat tires a "substantial inconvenience"? When do such acts become substantial? Reconsider the egging of Cooter's truck. Assuming the eggs did not dent the sheet metal on the vehicle, what is the nature of the harm caused? Is there a pecuniary loss for Cooter? Is Cooter inconvenienced substantially because of the egging?

Assume Paul, an environmental advocate, is vehemently opposed to the clearing of a wooded area for a new shopping mall. Late one evening, he pours sugar into the fuel tanks of the logging equipment. Paul's conduct amounts to criminal mischief because the sugar will not only contaminate the fuel and damage the motors in the equipment but also cause substantial disruption of the project. This is certainly an inconvenience. The owner will have to expend a substantial sum to have the equipment cleaned and repaired. But suppose instead that Paul, in a symbolic act, merely places a daisy in the exhaust stack of each piece of logging equipment. Does his conduct rise to the level of criminal mischief? Has he tampered with the equipment? Has he caused substantial inconvenience? What forms of tampering with the logging equipment would create an inconvenience that you would consider to be substantial?

Tangible Property of the Owner

The criminal mischief statute is limited in application to acts against the **tangible property** of another person who fits within the broad concept of "owner." Property in this context includes both personal property and real property. So Cooter's trenching of the yard or the poisoning of a tree[25] or the knocking down of fencing or other damage to real estate is within the coverage of the statute. Likewise is damage to automobiles, wristwatches, works of art, and other types of personal property. Note, however, that the statute applies only to *tangible* property. Not covered are more ephemeral items of property like one's reputation, one's good name, or the idea for an invention. While these matters certainly have value, any damage done to them is a subject for civil courts not the criminal law.

The coverage of both personal and real property solves the dilemma occasionally encountered in the law of theft regarding crops and other vegetation and whether they constitute real or personal property.[26] So when Cooter drives over the daffodils, it matters not whether the flowers are viewed as real property or personal property as either form is covered.

The Texas criminal code is silent on the matter of whether purposeful harm to domestic animals falls under the criminal mischief statute.[27] For example, if Rob purposely poisons his neighbor's prized bird dog, is this an act of criminal mischief or an act of animal cruelty or both?[28] Case law suggests that answer is likely both. While privately owned domesticated animals can be considered "property" under Sec. 28.03,[29] animal cruelty charges alone are probably used more frequently in such cases.

One ingenuous application of the Texas criminal mischief statutes is to the problem of diversion of utilities. While stealing of electricity, water, gas, and telecommunication service arguably involves property (e.g., electric impulses or water), the concept of electrical charges as property is a bit difficult to comprehend. Thus, the criminal mischief statute is applied to bypassing an electric meter, water meter, or gas meter. This approach has the secondary benefit of relieving the prosecution of the burden of proving the quantity of electricity, water, gas, and so forth that was stolen by focusing on the act of tampering.

Penalty

Much like the law of theft, the penalty for criminal damage is normally established by a scale based on the fair market value/replacement value of the property damaged or destroyed.[30] Damage to highly valued items in excess of $1,500 raises the offense to a felony. If the amount of damage or destruction exceeds $200,000, a felony of the first degree has been committed.[31] For prosecution purposes, the Penal Code allows aggregation of multiple acts of criminal damage.[32] The multiple acts are handled as one case, felony or misdemeanor as the total value of the damage dictates.

The cost of replacing or repairing the damaged property is a crucial element of the offense because it forms the basis of punishment assessed.[33] Accordingly, the state must prove the repair or replacement costs with something more than "off the wall guesses."[34] Expert opinion from police officers, repair technicians, insurance adjusters, and the like may be needed to establish the monetary level of damage.[35]

Also similar to the law of theft, certain forms of property receive special penalties. Texas affords enhanced penalties regardless of monetary value of the damage to habitations damaged by firearms, livestock fencing, and railroad property.[36] A diversion of utilities is deemed a Class A misdemeanor. Damage to places of worship, burial sites, public monuments, and certain forms of community centers elevates to a state jail felony.[37] Often, this form of vandalism exhibits the characteristics of a hate crime.

For tampering with property that causes only a substantial inconvenience, the behavior is generally deemed to be a Class C misdemeanor.

Reckless Damage or Destruction

If the damage or destruction of property is unintended, no offense occurs. However, if the damage was produced in a reckless manner, then a reckless damage or destruction charge might be appropriate. Suppose Mary is driving her car while intoxicated. Because of her impaired condition, the vehicle runs off the edge of the roadway and strikes a highway sign. The sign post is knocked over. Mary brings the car to a stop and notices that the sign is bent and mangled as is her right front fender. Mary has committed reckless damage or destruction. Her reckless operation of her automobile resulted in the damage to the sign. The offense is classified as a Class C misdemeanor regardless of the value of the property that was damaged.

§ 28.04. Reckless Damage or Destruction

a. A person commits an offense if, without the effective consent of the owner, he recklessly damages or destroys property of the owner.

b. An offense under this section is a Class C misdemeanor.

Anti-graffiti Statutes

One modern problem concerning criminal damage has been the spread of graffiti, particularly in urban areas. Many such markings are made with aerosol spray paints, which have proven difficult to remove. Graffiti often appears on public property, such as highway overpasses and signs, and the sides of public buildings. The walls of abandoned properties and railroad boxcars are also fertile sites for the paintings. The shear volume of graffiti has taxed the ability of municipalities to remove it and identify the offenders.

The placement of the graffiti is motivated by a variety of reasons. In some instances the graffiti constitutes gang territory **tagging**. Other forms are considered "street art" and a dynamic part of American urban folklore. Some graffiti may contain political messages. Anti-war graffiti has been common during the last century. In many other incidents the markings lack any artistic value and are simply destructive acts of vandalism, often perpetrated by juveniles. Sometimes the meaning of the graffiti is unknown.[38] But in its most pernicious form, graffiti can carry messages of racial and gender bias rising to the level of a hate crime.

To avoid allegations that the author of graffiti is being punished for his or her speech contrary to the First Amendment, Texas anti-graffiti laws are **content neutral**. This means that the crime occurs because of the destructive act, not due to what the writing actually says. Thus, if "Stop the War" is sprayed on the side of the public library, the level of offense is not punished differently than if the author had painted "Go Bearkats!"

Texas has two forms of anti-graffiti statutes. The first is the criminal mischief statute discussed above. Note that Sec. 28.03(a)(3) declares it a form of criminal mischief to make markings, *et cetera* on another's property without permission. The penalty is assessed based on the same statutory factors as other forms of criminal mischief.

In 1997, the Texas Legislature, believing that the existing penalties for graffiti were too limited to act as a deterrent, enacted a comprehensive anti-graffiti law.[39] Instead of expanding the criminal mischief statute, an entirely new section was added to the Penal Code, Sec. 28.08. Additionally, the legislation established a graffiti eradication fund collected through court costs, and restricted the sale of aerosol paint to persons 18 years old and older.

The criminal conduct proscribed by this statute overlaps Sec. 28.03(a)(3) somewhat but is directed primarily at the use of spray paint and other permanent forms of markings. The minimum penalty is a Class B misdemeanor. Graffiti placed on school or college property, churches, public monuments, burial sites, and community centers raises to a state jail felony.

Suppose Mack paints "Hook'em Horn" on the side of a building at Texas A&M University using a can of aerosol spray paint. He has committed a state jail felony. If he paints the same message using a paintbrush, does the conduct not violate Sec. 28.08?

CRIMEGRAPH

Arson

Offense	Culpable mental state	Conduct	Specific intent	What?	Result?	Where or When?	Penalty
Arson 28.02(a)(1)	1. Intentionally <u>or</u> 2. Knowingly	1. Starts fire <u>or</u> 2. Causes explosion	With intent to: 1. Damage <u>or</u> 2. Destroy	1. Vegetation, <u>or</u> 2. Structure, <u>or</u> 3. Fence		On open-space land	F2 or F1
Arson 28.02(a)(2)	1. Intentionally <u>or</u> 2. Knowingly	1. Starts fire <u>or</u> 2. Causes explosion	With intent to: 1. Damage <u>or</u> 2. Destroy	1. Building, <u>or</u> 2. Habitation, <u>or</u> 3. Vehicle		1. Knowing within city limits, <u>or</u> 2. Knowing it is insured, <u>or</u> 3. Knowing subject to mortgage, <u>or</u> 4. Knowing located on property of another, <u>or</u> 5. Knowing it has property of another within, <u>or</u> 6. Is reckless about whether life or property is endangered.	F3 to F1
Arson 28.02 (a-1)	1. Recklessly	1. Starts fire <u>or</u> 2. Causes explosion			Damages: 1. Building, <u>or</u> 2. Habitation, <u>or</u> 3. Vehicle	While manufacturing a controlled substance	SJF or F3

191

CRIMEGRAPH
Criminal Damage to Property Offenses

Offense	Culpable mental state	Conduct	What?	Who?	When?	Special Circumstances?	Penalty
Criminal Mischief 28.03(a)(1)	1. Intentionally or 2. Knowingly	1. Damages or 2. Destroys	Tangible property	Of the owner	Without effective consent		CM to F1
Criminal Mischief 28.03(a)(2)	1. Intentionally or 2. Knowingly	Tampers with	Tangible property	Of the owner	Without effective consent	1. Pecuniary loss or 2. Substantial inconvenience	CM to F1 CM
Criminal Mischief 28.03(a)(3)	1. Intentionally or 2. Knowingly	Makes markings	On tangible property	Of the owner	Without effective consent		CM to F1
Reckless Damage or Destruction 28.04(a)	Recklessly	1. Damages or 2. Destroys	Property	Of the owner	Without effective consent		CM
Graffiti 28.08(a)	1. Intentionally or 2. Knowingly	Makes markings	On tangible property	Of the owner	Without effective consent	1. Uses aerosol paint, or 2. Uses indelible marker, or 3. Uses an etching/engraving device	BM to F1

192

Notes

1. Certainly some number of arsons are committed which go undetected. For many years, the FBI resisted including arson in its Part I offenses. The FBI argued that its national crime index was composed of crimes known to police and many arsons go undetected, thereby producing an inaccurate picture of crime in the United States. Data collection was expected to present problems. Nonetheless, in 1979 by congressional mandate, arson was added to the existing seven Part I crimes.

2. TEX. DEP'T OF PUB. SAFETY, THE TEXAS CRIME REPORT FOR 2006 (2007).

3. 4 WILLIAM BLACKSTONE, COMMENTARIES *220.

4. *Id.* at *222.

5. While the Great Fire of London is believed to have started accidentally in a bakery, it did have an unintended positive effect. Scholars argue that the fire hastened the end of the Great Plague by killing off disease-bearing rats.

6. State v. Spiegel, 83 N.E. 722, 723 (Iowa 1900).

7. For a review of cases considering the question of when a burning occurs, see Jay M. Zitter, Annotation, *What Constitutes "Burning" to Justify Charge of Arson*, 28 A.L.R.4TH 482 (1984).

8. See discussion of curtilage in Chapter 11 — Burglary.

9. TEX. PENAL CODE § 19.03(a)(2).

10. See TEX. PENAL CODE § 19.02(b)(3) and the discussion in Chapter 5 — Criminal Homicide.

11. Taylor v. State, 735 S.W.2d 930, 948 (Tex. App. — Dallas 1987).

12. A Molotov cocktail is an incendiary device usually made of glass containing an accelerant such as gasoline. A wick, generally a piece of rag or paper, is then placed in the top of the glass container. The wick is lit and the device is thrown at the intended target.

13. Mosher v. State, 901 S.W.2d 547 (Tex. App. — El Paso 1995).

14. Miller v. State 566 S.W.2d 614 (Tex. Crim. App. 1978).

15. Greer v. State, 882 S.W.2d 24 (Tex. App. — Tyler 1994).

16. This rule does not hold true for the 2005 amendment to the arson statute that declared it a crime to recklessly start a fire while manufacturing a controlled substance. TEX. PENAL CODE § 28.02(a-1).

17. *See* TEX. LOC. GOV. CODE § 352.011 and § 352.081.

18. *See* Federal Bureau of Investigation, *Hate Crime Statistics 2006, at* http://www.fbi.gov.

19. See State v. Council, 1 Tenn. 305 (1808), wherein the defendant used a knife to stab his neighbor's horse.

The horse frequently broke a fence to get into the defendant's field and eat corn.

20. *See* THE TEXAS CRIME REPORT FOR 2006, *supra.*

21. TEX. PENAL CODE § 28.05. See Tackett v. State, 2003 Tex. App. LEXIS 3760, upholding criminal mischief conviction of wife who "keyed" estranged husband's automobile.

22. *See National Transportation Statistics*, Bureau of Transportation Statistics, *at* http://www.bts.gov/ publications/national_transportation_statistics.

23. Cullen v. State, 832 S.W.2d 788, n. 2 (Tex. App. — Austin 1992).

24. Retana v. State, 2007 Tex. App. LEXIS 2796.

25. *Id.*

26. See discussion in Chapter 9 — Theft.

27. See State v. Bartee, 894 S.W.2d 34 (Tex. App. — San Antonio 1994), holding that wild animals in their natural state are not subject to the law of criminal mischief or theft.

28. TEX. PENAL CODE § 42.092.

29. Barnstein v. State, 2006 Tex. App. LEXIS 268.

30. See TEX. PENAL CODE § 28.06 for the method of establishing the value of the damage or destruction.

31. See Petros v. State, 2002 Tex. App. LEXIS 7098, where the defendant was convicted of criminal mischief, felony of the first degree, for damaging over $1,000,000 in hospital equipment.

32. TEX. PENAL CODE § 28.03(e).

33. Elomary v. State, 796 S.W.2d 191 (Tex. Crim. App. 1990).

34. *Id.*, at 193.

35. Barnes v. State, 2007 Tex. App. LEXIS 4261.

36. TEX. PENAL CODE § 28.03(b)(4) and § 28.07.

37. TEX. PENAL CODE § 28.03(f).

38. Not all graffiti involves paint. During 2006, San Francisco was plagued by someone plastering the city's walls, phone booths, parking meters, and newspaper racks with postcard size stickers bearing the letters "BNE." The stickers proved especially difficult to remove. No one seemed to know the identity of the person placing the stickers nor their meaning. "BNE" stickers and neatly painted graffiti subsequently began appearing in other major cities both in the United States and abroad. *See* Jesse McKinley, *In San Francisco, a Plague of Stickers Opens a New Front in the Graffiti War*, N.Y. TIMES, Sept. 17, 2006, § 1, at 14.

39. *See* Act of Jun. 9, 1997, 75th Leg., R.S., ch. 593, 1997 Tex. Gen. Laws 2072.

CHAPTER
9
Theft, Fraud, and Related Offenses

BOLO

The reader should be on the lookout (BOLO) for the meaning of the following terms. Knowledge of the meaning of these terms will greatly assist the reader in understanding the primary elements of the chapter.

- Appropriation
- Asportation
- Coercion
- Common Law larceny
- Consent
- Deception
- Dyer Act
- Effective consent
- Embezzlement
- Fair market value
- False pretenses

- False token
- Forgery
- Fraud
- Identity theft
- Intent to deprive
- Owner
- Personal property
- Receiving stolen property
- Service
- Trade secret
- Utter

INTRODUCTION TO THEFT

Kris buys a purse from a vendor at a flea market. By all outward appearances the purse is an expensive designer bag that retails for $1,000. A sign at the stall reads "Genuine Designer Handbags." Kris pays the seller $250 for the bag. She later learns that the purse is an unauthorized copy made overseas and valued at $40. Meanwhile, Jay, Kris's boyfriend, is having a beer at the local tavern. He is watching two individuals shoot pool. One of the two men, Bob, seems none too skilled at the game. Subsequently, Bob approaches Jay and asks if he would like to shoot a game. Jay agrees and wins easily. As the evening progress, the two begin betting on the games and Jay begins to lose. By the end of the evening Jay has lost $300 to Bob. Jay later learns that Bob is really a skilled pool hustler. Across town, Wanda, Jay's mother, fills her automobile with gasoline. As she finishes she is interrupted by a cellphone call. Wanda gets into her car talking on the phone and drives off without paying for the gasoline. At the same time, Kris's roommate Gail is preparing for her big date. Unhappy with her choice of clothing available, she opens Kris's closet and sees a stunning red dress. Since the two roommates are the same size, Gail decides to wear Kris's dress on the date. Gail puts on the dress and leaves to meet her date.

Do any of the previous scenarios constitute the crime of theft? How about the following situations?

Rhonda is in the market for a used car. She sees one she likes and makes inquiry about it. Honest Eddie, the car dealer, tells her it was only driven on Sundays by a little ol' lady from Pasadena. Assuming that the vehicle has not been abused, Rhonda buys it. She later learns that the automobile was actually a former rental car. Meanwhile, Cal stops to buy groceries. The groceries total $122.75. Cal writes a check for the amount. Unknown to Cal, earlier in the day Patti his wife has withdrawn $100 cash from the account at an ATM. Her withdrawal left only $68 in the account. The bank subsequently rejects payment on Cal's check. In another portion of the shopping center, Lori spies a sweater she likes. She cannot decide between a red one and a yellow one. Lori then notices that the yellow one is priced $20 lower than the red one. Upon closer examination she realizes that the yellow sweater has the wrong price tag on it. She takes the yellow sweater to the store clerk and without mentioning the erroneous price pays the lower marked amount. The clerk rings up the sale, gives her a receipt, and Lori leaves the store with the sweater.

Do any of these events constitute theft?

Theft is the most common of the nation's serious offenses, constituting about two-thirds of all crimes against property. Each year about 7,000,000 thefts are reported to police. Nearly 10 percent of those occur in Texas.[1] Add to this figure confidence games, auto thefts, thefts that occur as part of a burglary, forgeries, and robberies, of which theft is an element, and the national number easily exceeds ten million annually. The number of unreported and unknown thefts is also believed to be substantial. Within the state, over 760,000 thefts and auto thefts occur annually. But, only about 130,000 persons are arrested in Texas for theft-related conduct.[2]

"Thou shalt not steal"[3] has been a societal prohibition in Western culture for thousands of years, yet as the examples above demonstrate, application of that moral principle may prove difficult in real-life situations. Paradoxically, the law of theft is at the same time one of the easiest and one of the most difficult topics for the student of criminal law. It is easy because we all have learned from childhood that taking another's property without permission is inappropriate behavior. So if our instincts suggest that particular conduct is stealing, our instincts are probably accurate. On the other hand, the topic can be difficult to study in depth. In Texas, the various laws related to theft are expressed as a series of highly detailed statutes. These statutes often contain precise definitions of terminology. Additionally, the definitions of the terms themselves are dependent on other definitions elsewhere in the Penal Code. This hyper-technical approach is necessary to include antisocial conduct and at the same time avoid criminalizing legitimate transfers of property and appropriate business dealings.

The state's laws covering theft-like behavior, as with other criminal statutes, seek to draw the line between criminal and noncriminal conduct. These laws are essentially a statement of public policy regarding the transfer of property between individuals. The close cases, of course, are the ones that prove most difficult. For example, consider the case of Cal and the bounced check mentioned above. He has taken the groceries without paying appropriate compensation. Should we criminalize his mistake? Or how about Honest Eddie, the used-car salesman? Are his statements about the previous owner of the car sufficiently deceptive that he defrauded Rhonda and should be criminally prosecuted?

A few words are necessary about terminology. The Common Law term for stealing was "larceny." Fourteen states, largely those which retain a strong Common Law tradition, continue to use the label "larceny."[4] The clear modern trend, however, is to enact consolidated "theft" statutes. This approach, encouraged by the Model Penal Code, is followed in the vast majority of states including Texas.

COMMON LAW LARCENY

Introduction

To fully appreciate the clarification to the law that the Texas consolidated theft statute provides, a short discussion of the Common Law of larceny is necessary. The legal rules defining the crime of larceny did not become manifest the moment William the Conqueror gained control of England in the eleventh century. Rather, the law evolved over time as property ownership expanded across all classes of society. The Industrial Revolution of the eighteenth century with its corresponding urbanization of cities accelerated the expansion of the law of larceny. As individuals acquired more personal property, there was more to steal.

The crime of larceny, like most Common Law offenses, was created through case law. However, two loopholes in the unwritten law were filled by acts of Parliament when that legislative body created the offenses of **embezzlement** and **false pretenses** (see Table 9-1). Thus, the rigid definitions of larceny, embezzlement, and false pretenses influenced the structure of the American law of theft until the middle of the twentieth century.[5]

During the legal reform movement of the mid-1800s the states largely codified the existing Common Law definitions of the various larceny-like offenses. However, American statutes split the crime into two categories, grand larceny and petit (or petty) larceny, depending on the value of the property stolen, although the states were inconsistent on the monetary amount to serve as the felony–misdemeanor divide.

Elements of Larceny

Larceny may be defined as the trespassory taking and carrying away of personal property of another with intent to steal. Thus the crime had five elements.

Trespassory Taking

Larceny is a crime against the individual in possession of property, not the individual who is the titleholder of the property. Accordingly, the Common Law required a trespassory act, meaning an appropriation of the property without consent. If the offender was already in lawful possession of the property, no trespass had occurred and therefore no larceny. It is for this reason that Parliament enacted the first general embezzlement statute to sanction those who converted another's property to their own use after being entrusted with it.[6] If a bookkeeper who handled his employer's account took some of the money for his own use, he did not violate the law of larceny. After 1799, however, his conduct did violate the English embezzlement statute.

TABLE 9-1	Common Law Larceny Terminology
Larceny	The taking and carrying away of the personal property of another by trespass with the intent to permanently deprive the owner of possession of the property.
Embezzlement	The fraudulent conversion of the property of another by a person in lawful possession of the property.
False Pretenses	The false representation of a material present or past fact, known to be false, with intent to deceive and cause the transfer of title to property.
Receiving Stolen Property	The receipt of stolen property, knowing that is stolen, with intent to deprive the owner of the property.

If the offender obtained possession of the property by fraud or deceit, he committed a variant of larceny known as larceny by trick. This form of larceny was supplemented by the 1757 false pretense statute.[7] This act of Parliament covered the obtaining of the title to property by a material misrepresentation of fact. Suppose Charles approaches Harold about purchasing Harold's horse. Harold agrees to let Charles take a test ride. Charles gallops off, never to be seen again. He has committed larceny by trick. But under the same facts, if instead Charles buys the horse, giving Harold coins that are later determined to be counterfeit, Charles has committed the crime of false pretenses. Harold parted with both possession and claim of title to the horse after being deceived.

Carrying Away

For a traditional larceny to occur, the property had to be carried away. This became known by the term **asportation**. No larceny occurred until the property had been moved, even if only a short distance. Over the years the asportation requirement was given a generous definition. However, in one extreme case, a would-be thief shot a cow in a field. The cow fell to the ground. A court found that the movement of the falling cow satisfied the asportation requirement of larceny.[8]

Personal Property

Larceny was limited to theft of tangible personal property. Real estate was not subject to larceny primarily because it could not be carried away. Persons who unlawfully occupied land were dealt with through other legal procedures. Likewise, one could not steal intangible property, such as deeds, bonds, and warehouse receipts, as they were viewed as representations of valuable property, not the property itself. This rule worked reasonably well for many years until the adoption of paper currency. Statutory changes ultimately altered the rule to encompass representations of property such as currency.[9]

Suppose during his pilgrimage Friar Tuck comes upon an apple tree. Since it is lunch time and he has a hearty appetite, the friar decides to help himself to a juicy red apple. He notices a nice one lying on the ground under the tree. He picks up the apple and eats it. Relishing the sweet taste, Tuck decides to have another. This time he plucks a shiny apple from the tree and eats it. The Sheriff of Nottingham observes all of this. Has the friar committed acts of larceny? Under the old Common Law notions, the answer was that the friar committed no crime and essentially enjoyed two free apples. The legal problem here arises because the apple, while hanging on the tree, was considered real property, not personal property, and thus not subject to the law of larceny. In a similar manner, the apple on the ground, while certainly no longer real property, had yet to come into the possession of the owner and therefore, no trespassory taking had occurred.[10] This scenario illustrates the complexities that arose over trying to determine when the law of larceny did or did not apply. In particular, the hypothetical serves as an example of the legal technicalities that surrounded the early application of the criminal law generally. Fortunately modern statutes have resolved Friar Tuck-type issues by providing that crops severed from the land are the owner's personal property and are covered by the theft statute.

Of Another

Only property in the possession of someone other than the offender was subject to larceny. In cases where two or more individuals were co-owners, taking of the property by one of the owners was not larceny. If Tom and Jerry are partners in a business and one day Tom makes off with the day's receipts, no Common Law larceny had occurred.

With Intent to Steal

For a larceny, there must be a specific intent to steal. Under the Common Law this was known by the Latin phrase *animus furandi*. The idea of stealing focused on intending to permanently deprive the owner of the property and to convert it to one's own use. Suppose on a rainy day Betty takes her roommate's umbrella to avoid getting wet en route to class. As class is letting out Veronica picks up the umbrella and mistaking it for her own walks out the door with it. Despite the fact that both Betty and Veronica took the umbrella without the permission of the party in possession, no larceny has occurred because both lack the intent to permanently deprive.

Importantly, larceny concerns the intentions of the offender, not whether he is successful. Assume Marcus grabs a silver goblet in the jewelry shop and flees out the door. The shopkeeper shouts, "Stop! Thief!" Two passing citizens observe Marcus and tackle him before he has gone more than 50 feet. Marcus has committed larceny because he *intended* to steal the goblet. His lack of successful escape does nothing to alter that fact.

TEXAS LAW OF THEFT

Consolidation of Theft Statutes

For the justice system of the mid-twentieth century, the Common Law-based definitions created several significant problems. First, the case-by-case development of the law had created a patchwork of rules that both overlapped and left gaps. Constant court and legislative tinkering was necessary to respond to evolving acts of thievery. For example, as noted below, joyriding in automobiles necessitated a major change in the law. Second, American courts had also adopted the Common Law rules of pleading along with the principle that such pleadings should be construed strictly in favor of the defendant. (The term "pleading" refers to the paperwork, such as an information or indictment, filed with the court in the course of litigation.) These procedural rules required the prosecutor to "prove what he pled." Consider the case of Lance found to be in possession of a stolen bicycle. If he is charged with larceny, the state would have to prove he committed a trespass in obtaining the bicycle and intended to permanently deprive the owner of the bike. But what if the proof in court showed that he purchased the bicycle from Walter who had stolen the bicycle? Lance knew the bike was stolen when he acquired it but because he committed no trespass in its taking, he could not be convicted of larceny. He might be guilty of some other crime but the prosecutor would have to anticipate that possibility and file charges accordingly.

Suppose Phil is charged by indictment with stealing a soup bowl. At trial, the evidence establishes that the dish was a sugar bowl, not a soup bowl. Under the principle of strict construction, Phil would be found not guilty, even though he clearly had stolen a bowl.[11] The rule of strict construction developed in England when larceny was subject to the death penalty. Judges recognized the injustice of executing individuals for minor thefts and devised the rule to increase the difficulty of capital convictions.[12]

In 1973, the Texas Legislature simplified the law of theft in the state by enacting the following statute:

> § 31.02. CONSOLIDATION OF THEFT OFFENSES. Theft as defined in Section 31.03 constitutes a single offense superseding the separate offenses previously known as theft, theft by false pretext, conversion by a bailee, theft from the person, shoplifting, acquisition of property by threat, swindling, swindling by worthless check, embezzlement, extortion, receiving or concealing embezzled property, and receiving or concealing stolen property.

The statute took a dozen previously existing separate theft-type laws and combined them into one statute called simply "theft." This consolidation of the various theft offenses into a single statute relieved prosecutors of the burden of choosing the precise manner in which the theft was perpetrated (e.g., theft or shoplifting; swindling or extortion). Under contemporary Texas law, the defendant is simply charged with theft of particular property and "the state has only to allege that the accused appropriated property unlawfully with intent to deprive the owner of it."[13] For the purposes of clarity, however, justice system reports may parenthetically incorporate the manner of theft in the description of the offense. Thus, one may see a suspect described as being charged with "theft (by exercising control)" or "theft (by receiving stolen property)" or "theft (by deception)."

One negative aspect results from consolidating all forms of theft into a single statute: the statute by necessity must be quite complex. Crafting statutory language to cover virtually every means by which one person can steal property from another is a major challenge for the legislature. The Texas Legislature, relying on the development work of the Model Penal Code, has done a good job of producing such a statute without criminalizing conduct that should not be illegal nor leaving holes for the unscrupulous to exploit. While Sec. 31.03—Theft—may appear complex, it basically means "Thou shall not steal, no way, no how!"

Elements of Theft

Unlawfully

For the acquisition of another's property to constitute the crime of theft, the defendant must have acted "unlawfully." Sec. 31.03(b) states that appropriation of property is unlawful if done in any one of three ways. The Court of Criminal Appeals in interpreting Sec. 31.03 has ruled that a thief can unlawfully appropriate property in a fourth manner: with no consent whatsoever.[14] These four methods may be summarized as follows:

- Acquiring property without consent.
- Acquiring property without effective consent.
- Acquiring stolen property knowing it is stolen.
- Acquiring property represented by a law enforcement officer as being stolen property.

1. *Without Consent*   The most common method by which property is stolen is when the thief simply takes it without the consent of the owner. Shoplifting, employee thefts, theft of automobile parts, and the like are all too common examples of this form of theft. Data collected by the Texas Department of Public Safety suggests that two-thirds of all thefts are acquisitions of property without any consent from the owner.[15]

---

§ 31.03. Theft

a. A person commits an offense if he unlawfully appropriates property with intent to deprive the owner of property.
b. Appropriation of property is unlawful if:
   1. it is without the owner's effective consent;
   2. the property is stolen and the actor appropriates the property knowing it was stolen by another; or
   3. property in the custody of any law enforcement agency was explicitly represented by any law enforcement agent to the actor as being stolen and the actor appropriates the property believing it was stolen by another.

§ 31.01. Definitions

In this chapter:

* * *

(3) "Effective consent" includes consent by a person legally authorized to act for the owner. Consent is not effective if:

A. induced by deception or coercion;

B. given by a person the actor knows is not legally authorized to act for the owner;

C. given by a person who by reason of youth, mental disease or defect, or intoxication is known by the actor to be unable to make reasonable property dispositions;

D. given solely to detect the commission of an offense; or

E. given by a person who by reason of advanced age is known by the actor to have a diminished capacity to make informed and rational decisions about the reasonable disposition of property.

2. *Without Effective Consent*   Suppose Huey, Dewey, and Louie are playing high stakes poker. Huey wins every hand. By the end of the evening he has won $25,000. The reason Huey wins every hand is that the group is using his set of marked cards and Huey is cheating. Dewey and Louie certainly voluntarily played the game and knowingly bet their money. In one sense Huey had their consent to take their money. But, would they have played with Huey had they known he would cheat? Of course not. They were deceived. Their consent to play, and pay for losing hands, was not *effective* consent. Huey's appropriation of the money was wrongful because he used deceit. Similarly, suppose Lenny sends a letter to Mayor Quimby stating that unless the mayor pays him $10,000 Lenny will send to the local newspaper photos of the mayor in a sexually compromising position. The mayor responds to the blackmail letter by paying the $10,000. Lenny has committed theft because his obtaining of the money came through a coercive threat.

Absence of effective consent, and thereby a wrongful appropriation, may occur under one of several circumstances:

- **Consent is obtained by coercion**[16]—If one agrees to part with his goods or money only out of fear of physical harm to himself or harm to other property, the consent is not a valid, effective one and the taking is wrongful. Under particular factual circumstances, this form of theft might elevate to robbery (see Chapter 10). An unlawful taking occurs when the owner is coerced into parting with the property. **Coercion** need not be a physical risk but can include subjecting another to hatred, ridicule, or damage to their personal or business reputation. Blackmail and extortion are treated as theft under Texas law because they involve obtaining property through coercive conduct.

- **Consent is obtained by deception**[17]—Being fooled into parting with property is not true consent. The most frequent example is the "hot" check passer who uses deceit (tendering a presumptively valid check) to obtain the merchant's property. This aspect of lack of effective consent replaces the Common Law notion of obtaining property by false pretenses. Confidence games and other swindles are also examples of where the owner gives up his or her property willingly because of being deceived.

- **Consent from unauthorized person**—Consent obtained from one who has no authority to give it is no consent at all. A thief cannot escape prosecution through a claim that he obtained consent to take the property from someone else when that person had no legal standing to grant consent.

- **Consent given by reason of youth, mental disease, or intoxication**—Permission to take property given by a child, an individual with a mental disability, or an intoxicated person is not effective. Bill, a college student, becomes drunk at a fraternity party. He tells his pledge brother Fred, "Here. I am giving you my red sports car. I don't want it anymore." He hands Fred the keys. Bill's intoxicated condition prevents him from making a lawful transfer of the car title to Fred. Should Fred seek to take and retain the vehicle based on the alleged gift, Fred would be guilty of theft. Similarly, convincing a five-year-old child to give you the money from his piggy bank is theft because of the child's youth.[18] Note the requirement that the offender be aware that the individual is too young, mentally ill, or intoxicated to make a reasonable disposition of his property.
- **Consent given by person of advanced age**—As with young people, the law will not allow elderly persons to be deceived out of their property. This is of particular concern with confidence games and swindles, such as home repair and investment scams, which prey upon the elderly. Whether an individual is too old to make rational dispositions of property is a fact question for a jury.
- **Consent given solely to detect commission of a crime**—This section of the statute rejects a defense that thieves would occasionally raise under Common Law larceny. Suppose the police seek the cooperation of a storekeeper to help catch a thief. The storekeeper leaves the door on his warehouse open while the police hide in the shadows. An individual comes along, notes the open door, and helps himself to merchandise. He is arrested and prosecuted. Under the law of larceny, a trespassory taking was a necessary element. At trial, the accused argues that that element of the offense is missing since the storekeeper purposely left the door open so that the accused would have no trouble taking the goods. The storekeeper essentially consented for him to take the goods, thereby negating the trespass. The Texas definition of "effective consent" shuts off the possibility of this argument being made in a modern theft prosecution.

3. *Acquiring Stolen Property Knowing It Is Stolen*   Another form of unlawful appropriation of property is through possession of stolen property. Texas has merged the old offense of receiving and concealing stolen property into the general theft statute. Thus, if Charles is a fence, trafficking in stolen goods, he is in violation of Sec. 31.03 since such criminal conduct is included within the definition of theft.

One Saturday morning while walking about a flea market, Pat observes a vendor selling name-brand large screen television sets. Pat inquires at the price and is pleasantly surprised to learn the vendor only wants $600 for an item that retails around $2,000. Pat, being a suspicious criminal justice major, wonders to himself if the televisions are stolen property. Pat sets aside his concerns and purchases one of the televisions. He takes the set home and enjoys it over the weekend. On Monday afternoon the police arrive at Pat's apartment and tell him that the set he purchased was indeed stolen in a burglary of a video megastore several weeks earlier. Will the officers arrest Pat for theft by receiving stolen property?

The statute requires that "the actor appropriates the property *knowing* it was stolen by another." Sec. 6.03(b) states that a person acts with knowledge with respect to the circumstances surrounding his conduct when he is *aware* that the circumstances exist. Is Pat aware that the television is stolen property? Ought Pat have been aware of the stolen nature of the property given the low price he paid for the television? Has Pat committed theft?

Were a thief only to take property for his own use, the problems of law enforcement might be much simpler. But, much property is unlawfully taken for purposes of barter or resale to others. Certainly, society has an interest in deterring others from trafficking in stolen goods. On the other hand, the general deterrence theory will not be successful if the receiver of the stolen property is unaware of the illicit status of the item he or she acquires.

Courts in Texas have long held that in theft by receiving stolen property cases, actual awareness of the stolen nature of the property must be established.[19] The fact that the defendant suspected the property might be stolen (e.g., Pat in the example of the television set) or that the circumstances under which the item was acquired would lead the reasonable person to believe the article was stolen (e.g., the low price Pat paid for the television) is insufficient standing alone to establish the required level of culpability of knowledge.[20] Likewise, mere unexplained possession of stolen property is insufficient to establish the required culpable mental state of knowledge.[21] "It would be a dangerous doctrine to hold every citizen guilty of receiving stolen property, and send him to the penitentiary, because he was found in possession thereof."[22] However, juries are allowed to infer the existence of knowledge from the surrounding circumstances of the incident. For example, case law does hold that purchasing property from a stranger at a value far below its apparent worth is a factor to consider in determining whether the buyer had reason to believe the property was stolen.[23]

In an effort to strengthen the ability of district attorneys to prosecute commercial traffickers in stolen property, the state has imposed certain recordkeeping requirements regarding the identity of sellers of used property. Failure to maintain these records can be used as evidence that the purchaser knew the property was stolen. The state has imposed these recordkeeping requirements on dealers in second-hand property, salvaged auto parts, used cars, and restricted-use pesticides.[24] Additionally, when a person is tried for theft by **receiving stolen property**, to establish the culpable mental state of knowledge the state may introduce evidence that he previously engaged in other recent transactions involving stolen property.

4. *Property Represented as Being Stolen Property*   One law enforcement method of discovering who is trafficking in stolen property is through undercover operations, commonly called "stings." Suppose the police suspect that Wilbur, the owner of a pawnshop, is buying and selling stolen property. Randy, an undercover police officer, obtains a camera from the police property room and goes to the pawnshop in an effort to sell it. Randy tells Wilbur that he stole the camera out of an unlocked automobile. Wilbur gives Randy $25 for the camera. Under traditional rules surrounding larceny and theft, it would be difficult to prosecute Wilbur for receiving stolen property because the camera was not actually stolen property. Sec. 31.03(b)(3) resolves this problem by declaring that if a law enforcement officer asserts that an object is stolen property, it will be treated the same as actual stolen property for the purposes of a theft prosecution.[25] In a related matter, Sec. 31.03(c)(5) states that stolen property does not lose its stolen character once recovered by the police. Thus, if a police officer uses stolen property previously recovered by the department as props in a sting operation, the items do not lose their legal status of being stolen property.

§ 31.01. Definitions

In this chapter:

* * *

(4) "Appropriate" means:

A. to bring about a transfer or purported transfer of title to or other nonpossessory interest in property, whether to the actor or another; or

B. to acquire or otherwise exercise control over property other than real property.

Appropriates

The *actus reus* of theft in Texas is an **appropriation**, not a taking or an asportation as required under the Common Law. The statutory definition [Sec. 31.01(4)] covers the behaviors earlier condemned by larceny (taking from possession) and by false pretense (transfer of title). If Sam deceives Wes into giving him a deed to Wes' home, Sam has appropriated the property within the meaning of the statute because he brought about a transfer of title.

More common is the theft of personal property, such as merchandise, vehicles, and the like. The statute simply requires that the offender "acquire" or "otherwise exercise control over the property." Thus, a shoplifter acquires or exercises control of the object taken, as does an automobile thief or pickpocket. In the broader sense of the phrase, an individual who unlawfully exercises control over deposits in a bank has appropriated the funds and also thereby committed theft.[26] Likewise assume Barney is a stockbroker. He alters brokerage records to transfer ownership records of shares of stock from client accounts to his personal account. Even though no actual item, that is, a stock certificate, has moved from a client to Barney, he has exercised control over the property and thereby appropriated it for the purposes of the theft statute.

Unlike Common Law larceny, an asportation or carrying away is not an element of the offense. Thus, a car thief commits the offense when he enters the vehicle and starts the motor. Driving away is not a necessary element of theft of the vehicle.[27]

The question of when an offender has actually exercised control over the property arises occasionally. In one case, the appellate court held that the defendant exercised control over an extortion victim's money and thereby committed theft the moment the victim transferred the money to a detective and a postal inspector who subsequently mailed the funds to the defendant as part of their effort to apprehend him.[28]

Note that one cannot appropriate real estate by exercising control over it. Such conduct is excluded from the coverage of the theft statute because it is better handled as either a criminal trespass or a civil matter. An apartment tenant who has not paid the rent but refuses to vacate the apartment is certainly exercising control over the apartment but is not subject to prosecution for theft because the statute expressly excludes such conduct.

Property

Sec. 31.01(5) defines the three types of property subject to the law of theft. First is real property. The Penal Code does not explicitly define "real property," but another state statute considers the term to include land, improvements on the land, timber, and minerals in the land.[29] Under the Common Law, the law of larceny did not apply to real estate because it could not be carried away. As noted earlier, real

---

§ 31.01. Definitions

In this chapter:

$$* * *$$

(5) "Property" means:

A. real property;

B. tangible or intangible personal property including anything severed from land; or

C. a document, including money, that represents or embodies anything of value.

estate cannot be stolen simply by exercising control over it. The theft of real estate can constitute a crime but only when it occurs through transfer of title, such as execution of a deed.

Tangible and intangible **personal property** is the second type of property and the most common objects of theft. Tangible personal property is any object of value that has form and mass. It can range from a postage stamp to a multi-million dollar airplane. Note that the definition also includes anything severed from the land, thereby resolving the issues mentioned in the Friar Tuck scenario earlier.

Suppose Amos steals Debbi's secret recipe for chocolate chip cookies. The recipe is an intangible, a mere representation of something valuable. While the Common Law of larceny would not be violated by such an act, the Texas definition of "property" covers the secret recipe as well as other intellectual properties, such as patents, formulas, and copyrights. Another example of intangible property is a bank account, which represents the value of the underlying currency. Additionally, the definition covers documents that represent something of value and explicitly mentions money. Certainly theft of currency is a common problem. But, stealing wills, deeds, stock certificates, receipts, and other tokens of right or privilege is subject to the modern law of theft.

With Intent

The theft statute, like most crimes, contains a culpable mental state. Suppose at the end of class today Helen picks up her books and leaves the classroom. Thirty minutes later she discovers that she has two copies of the Penal Code, her own and one belonging to Sean who sits beside her in class. Has Helen committed theft? She certainly intended to carry Sean's book from the classroom, but that general intent is insufficient to support a charge of theft. She also needs the objective to deprive Sean of the property, an intent which she lacks in this case. In other words, Helen must intend to steal the book before a crime occurs.

Sec. 31.03 requires **intent to deprive**, arguably a slightly broader term than mere intent to steal. This is the intent requirement that converts absentmindedness or a mistake of fact into a crime. Recall this chapter's opening paragraph where Wanda drives away from the gasoline station without paying for the fuel. The facts presented show that she certainly intentionally drove away, taking the gasoline with her. But, because she was distracted by the cellphone call, it was not her conscious objective to take the fuel without paying for it.

Proof of intent is always difficult. We cannot readily determine what is transpiring in another person's brain. Rather, the judge and jury draw conclusions about a person's intentions by assessing his or her conduct. If Bud enters a grocery store, grabs a six-pack of beer, and runs out the door without paying, one can infer he intends to steal the beer. There is simply no reasonable explanation for a stranger to snatch a six-pack of beer without the owner's consent unless he intends to steal it.

Recall that Texas law does not require the offender be successful in taking and carrying away the object. Rather, it is the intent to deprive that is the element of the offense. Thus, in a real case a would-be thief picked up a roll of barbed wire in a hardware store storage room. He was startled by an employee who was hiding in the room. The actor dropped the wire and ran. His conviction was upheld on appeal; he intended to deprive the owner of the barbed wire.[30]

Proving intent to deprive for the purposes of the law of theft has proven particularly bedeviling in two areas: shoplifting and issuance of worthless checks. Suppose Brenda goes to the local discount store. Store security personnel observe her place a tube of lipstick in her pocket. Brenda then goes to the other side of the store where she collects various groceries in her basket. She exits the store after paying for the groceries but not for the lipstick. Has she committed theft of the lipstick? Or, did Brenda merely forget to pay for the lipstick? Or, more accurately, can the state prove she intended to steal the lipstick?

While the intent to deprive an owner of property can be inferred from the acts, words, and conduct of the suspect,[31] merchant policies often seek to reduce ambiguity about whether a theft has occurred. While no legal requirement exists that the merchandise being stolen leave the store premises,[32] many retailers utilize a procedure whereby a suspected shoplifter is approached only after exiting the last checkout point in the store or the actual store building. The suspect is given an opportunity to pay for the merchandise. Only after refusing to pay or after denying that goods were taken is the suspect arrested and searched. This approach, commonly used in Texas, assists in establishing an intent to steal in comparison to a simple neglect in failing to pay for the merchandise.[33]

Some states, but not Texas, have enacted concealment of merchandise statutes making it an offense to conceal unpaid items on one's person. Texas has, however, enacted a statute outlawing possession of a device intended to deactivate electronic article surveillance tags and sensors or hinder their detection (Sec. 31.15). Certainly, possession of such a device at a retail establishment would be strong circumstantial evidence that the individual was a skilled shoplifter who possesses the intent to steal. Additionally, the unlawful use of criminal instrument statute (Sec. 16.01) might have applicability in cases involving shoplifters, who use "booster boxes" or other devices exclusively constructed to commit theft.[34] Finally, an organized retail theft statute (Sec. 31.16) also seeks to punish skilled habitual shoplifters.

Recall the earlier example of Cal who wrote a $122.75 check for groceries unaware that his wife had made an ATM withdrawal from the account, leaving only $68. Assuming Cal's bank rejects the check and sends it back to the grocery store because of insufficient funds, has Cal committed theft? The answer to the question turns upon whether Cal used the check to deceive the store into giving him the groceries or whether the non-sufficient funds check was merely an oversight, the product of faulty bookkeeper. Cal would not be permitted to take the groceries until he paid for them. He could certainly deceive the store into giving him the groceries by issuing a check that he knows is worthless. To establish Cal's intentions, Texas, like many states, has enacted special legislation regarding issuance of checks. Sec. 31.06 establishes a *prima facie* case of intent to deprive if the check is drawn on a nonexistent account.[35] In the alternative, an intent to deprive is also presumed if the recipient of the check, within 30 days of its issuance, sends written notice demanding payment to the maker at the address shown on the check. If the maker of the check (Cal) fails to make good on the amount within ten days, the law presumes he intended to deceive the recipient.[36] Depending on the factual circumstances, theft by check and/or issuance of bad check (Sec. 32.41) charges may then be filed.

§ 31.01. Definitions

In this chapter:

* * *

(2) "Deprive" means:

    A. to withhold property from the owner permanently or for so extended a period of time that a major portion of the value or enjoyment of the property is lost to the owner;

    B. to restore property only upon payment of reward or other compensation; or

    C. to dispose of property in a manner that makes recovery of the property by the owner unlikely.

To Deprive

In the law of theft, the offender must possess the intent to "deprive" the owner of property. Texas statute [Sec. 31.01(2)] defines "deprive" in essentially four ways:

- Withholding property permanently
- Withholding property for extended period of time
- Restoring property only on payment of compensation
- Disposing of property in manner making recovery unlikely

Recall the earlier scenario of Gail who decided to wear her roommate Kris' red dress on a date. When she returns from the date Kris is very mad at her. Has Gail committed theft of the dress? The answer is likely "No." Under Common Law larceny, the offender had to intend to permanently deprive the owner of the property. This requirement is carried over in contemporary Texas law. But, Gail had no such intentions. Even though Gail lacked Kris' permission to wear the dress, Kris suffers no significant monetary loss in the incident as the dress was returned in a relatively short period of time. On the other hand, the teenage shoplifter who slides several video games into his trousers is committing theft since he intends to permanently deprive the store of the video games. Does it matter that he gets caught? Recall that the law requires *an intent* to permanently deprive. It does not mandate that the offender be successful in his efforts. Thus, the thief who is apprehended in the act of stealing is still guilty of theft.

But what if Gail had taken the dress and not returned it for a year? In this fact situation, she would likely have committed theft. The second definition of "deprive" covers withholding property for so extended period of time that a major portion of its value or enjoyment is lost. Being without one's favorite dress would seem to fit this definition. Thus, absolute permanent deprivation is not always required for a violation of the theft law.

The third option is directed at the unlawful possession of property. Suppose Jerry owes Frank $100. Despite Frank's insistence that the debt be repaid, Jerry has not made good on his obligation. One day Frank takes Jerry's prized bulldog from his front yard. Jerry learns of Frank's action, calls him on the telephone, and demands return of the dog. Frank says, "Give me the $100 you owe me and I will return the dog." Jerry demands the immediate return of the bulldog. If Frank refuses to return the dog unless he is paid the $100, he is committing theft. Frank has no legal right to take Jerry's bulldog, and certainly has no legal right to hold the dog for ransom.[37]

Finally, while most acts of property destruction are handled as cases of criminal mischief (Sec. 28.04), some such acts fit the definition of theft. Suppose Charlene, concerned that her employer will discover her misappropriation of funds, deletes certain files from the company computer. Could her conduct amount to theft? In a similar case, the Court of Appeals ruled that this disposal of the computer files (intangible property) established an intent to deprive the owner of his property and did indeed fit the statutory definition of theft.[38] In another case, the court ruled that the defendant's act of throwing the victim's cellphone away evidenced an intent to deprive and constituted theft when the cellphone was never recovered.[39]

The Owner

The Common Law divided its larceny-type offenses between those where the titleholder was the victim and those where the person in possession of the property was victimized. The modern Texas theft statute eliminates this distinction between title and possession

§ 1.07. Definitions

(a) In this code:

* * *

(35) "Owner" means a person who:

  A. has title to the property, possession of the property, whether lawful or not, or a greater right to possession of the property than the actor; or

  B. is a holder in due course of a negotiable instrument.

and establishes the victim as the "owner," very broadly defined. An item of personal property can have a titleholder and a person who is in actual possession of the object. The two individuals may or may not be the same person. Indeed property actually may have multiple owners.

The definition of **owner** establishes several possible victims of theft, depending on the surrounding factual circumstances. According to Sec. 1.07(a)(35) any of the following could be considered the "owner" of stolen property:

- Titleholder to property
- Party in possession of property, whether lawful or not
- Party with greater right of possession
- Holder in due course of negotiable instrument[40]

If Jeff borrows Dale's car but Darryl steals it while it is in Jeff's possession, who is the victim of the theft? Add to the facts that Dale is financing the vehicle through his credit union. Who is the owner of the car?

The credit union is the owner because the lending agency is the titleholder to the car. But Jeff is also the owner because he was the party in possession of the automobile at the time it was stolen. Dale too can be considered the owner because he has a greater right of possession to the vehicle than the thief. At Darryl's trial for auto theft, any of the three possible owners can testify that Darryl lacked consent to take the vehicle.

Assume Virginia shoplifts a tube of lipstick at the discount store. She is apprehended by store security personnel. The true titleholders to the store's wares are the thousands of stockholders. Yet, the law does not require that each testify to Virginia's lack of consent. The store manager (or his assistant) has a greater right of possession to the property than Virginia and is thereby an "owner" of the lipstick for the purposes of the prosecution for theft. Even the store security officer would fit the definition of "owner" because of her greater right of possession.[41]

Can one commit theft by taking his or her own property? Suppose Fred leaves his car to be repaired at Richard's garage. When the repairs are complete, Fred, using a spare set of keys, retrieves his vehicle and drives off without paying the repair bill. Under Texas law Richard had a legal right to retain possession of the automobile until Fred paid for the repairs. Since Richard had a superior right of possession of the vehicle, Fred's act of taking his own car would constitute theft.[42] Sec. 31.10 states that it is no defense that the actor has an interest in the property stolen if another person has the right of exclusive possession. The mechanic's lien grants Richard the right of exclusive possession even though Fred holds title to the vehicle.

The expansive definition of "owner" opens the potential for one thief being prosecuted for stealing property from another thief. Thus, assume Freddy is a dealer in stolen auto parts. One day Scott, himself a previously convicted thief, steals a stolen car radio from Freddy's store. Scott is no less a thief because the radio was stolen property or because Freddy is a thief. While Freddy had no title to the stolen radio, he did have a greater right of possession than Scott.

Of Property

Note that the language of Sec. 31.01 twice contains the term "property." The theft statute speaks in terms of unlawfully appropriating *property* with intent to deprive the owner of *property*. Recall Virginia who shoplifts lipstick at the local discount store. She has unlawfully appropriated property (the lipstick) with intent to deprive the owner of property (the lipstick). But the two properties in question need not be identical. If Dr. Evil steals the painting of the Mona Lisa from a museum and seeks a ransom of $1,000,000 for its safe return, he has, of course, committed theft. He has appropriated property (the Mona Lisa) with intent to deprive the museum of property (the $1,000,000). Thus, certain acts of extortion may involve exercising control over one form of property with the ultimate intention of obtaining some other form of property.

Penalty

Perhaps the greatest differences in the law of theft across America lie in the penalties imposed for commission of the crime. Over the years, the classifying of theft as a felony or misdemeanor and the relative grading of conduct within these two categories has become quite complex in many jurisdictions, including Texas. Often, the level of penalty is a clear statement of the economic interests and social mores of the particular jurisdiction. Under Texas law, the penalty for committing theft may depend upon the following elements:

Value of the Property Stolen

The presumptive penalty classification scheme is based on the monetary value of the property stolen. Depending on the worth of the item, the penalty for its theft can range from a Class C misdemeanor to a first degree felony. Table 9-2 depicts the monetary breakpoints for each penalty classification. Note that theft of property valued in excess of $1,500 is a felony.

One disadvantage to the monetary classification scheme is the necessity of the Legislature to revise the breakpoint upward every few years because of inflation. For example, in 1975, theft of a $250 television set in Texas was a felony! Over 30 years later, because of statutory revisions, the television would have to be worth over $1,500 for a felony theft charge to be levied.

The worth of the stolen property, and thereby the penalty level, is initially established by its fair market value at the time and place of the theft (Sec. 31.08). **Fair market value** is "the amount the property would sell for in cash, giving a reasonable time for selling it."[43] Suppose Eric steals a gold ingot valued at $1,350. Six months later he is apprehended and the ingot is recovered. Because the price of gold has risen, the ingot is now worth $1,580. Is Eric culpable for a Class A misdemeanor or a state jail felony? What if the value of the ingot had dropped from $1,350 to $450 in the intervening six months between the theft and Eric's apprehension? What level of offense has he committed? The answer is that the fluctuating price of gold has no effect on the penalty level for the theft. The fair market value of the gold is based on the time and place of the theft, not its value at time of trial. Eric is facing a Class A misdemeanor charge irrespective of the current price of gold.

If the fair market value cannot be ascertained, replacement cost is used. Suppose Jared steals a box of collectible baseball cards. The fair market value of the cards may

TABLE 9-2 Penalties for Theft and Theft of Service*

Class C Misdemeanor	Property or service valued at less than $50 Property valued at less than $20 and defendant issued a check
Class B Misdemeanor	Property or service valued at $50 or more but less than $500 Property valued at $20 or more but less than $500 and defendant issued a check
Class A Misdemeanor	Property or service valued at $500 or more but less than $1,500
State Jail Felony	Property or service valued at $1,500 or more but less than $20,000 Less than 10 head of cattle, horses, exotic livestock, exotic fowl, or any part thereof with value under $20,000 Less than 100 head of sheep, swine, goats, or any part thereof with value under $20,000 Property is stolen from person of another or from a human corpse or grave Property is a firearm Property is an official ballot or election envelope
Third Degree Felony	Property or service valued at $20,000 or more but less than $100,000 10 or more head of cattle, horses, exotic livestock, or exotic fowl stolen in single transaction with value less than $100,000 100 or more head of sheep, swine, or goats stolen during a single transaction with value less than $100,000
Second Degree Felony	Property or service valued at $100,000 or more but less than $200,000
First Degree Felony	Property or service valued at $200,000

*Chart does not list enhanced penalties for offenders with previous convictions for theft

Note: Punishment increases to next higher penalty category if the offense is committed by a public servant or government contractor or if victim is an elderly individual.

be ascertainable because an extensive secondary market exists for the items. But if instead he steals a five-year-old television set, determination of the fair market value may be more difficult. However, since television sets are available for sale, the cost of replacing the set can readily be ascertained.

Assume a thief steals a collection of photographs of the Rolling Stones band that the owner made in 1982. These photos have no readily determinable fair market value. Likewise, due to their nature, they cannot be replaced. For items where neither the fair market value nor the replacement value can be determined, a presumptive value is established by statute. Sec. 31.08(c) establishes the value of such items as being between $500 and $1,500. Thus the theft of the photographs would be treated as a Class A misdemeanor.

Suppose Marla shoplifts six items at a drug store. Has one theft occurred or six thefts? To resolve this dilemma and to improve the efficiency of the justice system, Texas, like many other states, permits the court to treat the matter as a single event, total the value of the items, and upon conviction impose punishment based on the aggregated value (Sec. 31.09). This procedure occasionally pushes a series of high value misdemeanor thefts across the line to become a single felony event.

Type of Property Stolen

Most states establish enhanced penalties for the theft of certain forms of property regardless of the value. Texas is no exception to this rule. An individual who steals an object for which the statute declares the punishment is at the felony level is facing possible prison time regardless of the fair market value of the item. A review of the various types of property afforded this special classification reveals much about the social and economic influences within the state.[44] Texas' long tradition of being a state with an extensive livestock industry is reflected in the subsection declaring it a felony to steal cattle, horse, sheep, swine, goats, and ostriches. Stealing a horse worth $100 is a state jail felony instead of a Class B misdemeanor as its value alone initially would suggest. Culture and tradition are also the likely reasons that theft of a firearm regardless of value is also a felony. Consult Sec. 31.01 and Table 9-2 to determine the types of property protected and the exact penalty level for their theft.

Manner of Obtaining Property

A relatively low value loss may also be increased to a felony depending on the manner in which the theft occurs. Texas law enhances the penalty for misdemeanor theft if the offender commits the act using a check. If George simply steals a $30 bottle of whiskey from a liquor store, he commits a Class C misdemeanor. However, if George obtains the same bottle of whiskey by writing a worthless check for it, he has committed a Class B misdemeanor.

Victim of the Offense

Texas law also declares any theft from a person, such as by a pickpocket or a purse snatcher, to be a state jail felony. This rule exists because of the potential for violence from the incident escalating to a robbery. Texas expands felony coverage to stealing from a human corpse or grave. Any theft perpetrated against an elderly person is also increased to the next higher penalty category. Thus, if a 75-year-old widow is swindled out of $50,000, the offense is punished as a felony of the second degree instead of a felony of the third degree as the value of the loss would normally dictate.

Perpetrator of the Offense

As with the elderly victim mentioned above, the penalty level for theft is enhanced one level if the offender has prior convictions for theft or is a public servant or government contractor who stole government property.

SPECIAL PROBLEMS IN THE LAW OF THEFT

Lost Property

"Finders keepers, losers weepers" may be a playground rule but is far from an accurate statement of the criminal law when considering lost property. Betty inadvertently leaves her purse in a public restroom. The purse contains $65 cash, credit cards, her driver's license, and various personal items. As Betty boards the bus she realizes she does not have her purse. A few minutes later, Wilma discovers the purse. May Wilma lawfully keep the cash and other items?

The law makes distinctions between lost, mislaid, and abandoned property. Abandoned property are items whereby the owner intentionally relinquishes any claim of title or possession. An empty aluminum soda can thrown into a public garbage container is purposely abandoned by the owner. Accordingly, if another person comes along, retrieves the can, and sells it for scrap, the original purchaser has no claim to the proceeds. Mislaid property is property that the owner purposely placed in a location but forgot to retrieve. In some instances the owner may later fail to remember where the item was placed. This is the situation with Betty and her purse. Lost property is similar except the owner did not intend to place the object at the location and generally has no idea as to what happened to the object. If the diamond in Betty's wedding ring had fallen out at some point during the day, it would be considered lost property.

"The law of larceny approaches the problems of lost (or mislaid) and found (personal property) from the standpoint of the social interests involved."[45] If an article is found and there is no reasonable likelihood of restoring it to its owner, it is socially desirable for the finder to be able to use it. On the other hand, if the found object has a clue to ownership, it is sociably desirable for the finder to take possession with an intention of returning the property to the true owner.

Chapter 31 of the Penal Code does not deal specifically with lost and mislaid property. However, in cases decided under prior penal codes, the Texas courts adopted the Common Law rule and held that failing to take reasonable efforts to locate the true owner of lost or mislaid property constituted theft.[46] When Wilma finds Betty's purse, she must either make an effort to contact Betty or turn the purse over to the lost and found department of the facility or surrender it to the police. If Wilma helps herself to anything in the purse, she is evidencing an intent to deprive Betty of her property and thereby commits theft.

But suppose Betty inadvertently drops a $5 bill on the sidewalk. Wilma finds the money. Is it theft if Wilma keeps the five dollars? Probably not as no reasonable means exists to locate the true owner (Betty). Under the theory of social utility, Wilma may make use of the money.

Mistaken Transfers of Ownership

Homer stops at the Kwik-E-Mart to purchase a cold fountain drink. He obtains the beverage and proceeds to pay the clerk. Homer hands the clerk a $10 bill but the clerk mistakenly gives him change for a $20. Is Homer under a legal obligation to advise the clerk of his error? If Homer keeps the erroneous change, has he committed theft?

In the only modern Texas case to deal with the question, a conviction of theft was affirmed where a teller at the drive-in window of a bank, through a self-induced mistake, gave the defendant funds intended for another customer. The defendant made no effort to correct the mistake and later denied that she had received the improper amount. The appellate court found that when the defendant kept the excess funds, she demonstrated an intent to deprive the true owner of the property.

In the scenario of Homer and the excessive change provided by the Kwik-E-Mart clerk, the statutory definition of "deception" includes "confirming by words or conduct a false impression of law or fact that is likely to affect the judgment of another in the transaction, and that the actor does not believe to be true."[47] If Homer fails to draw the matter to the clerk's attention and departs, has he confirmed by conduct a false impression of fact likely to affect the judgment of the clerk? Such would seem to be the case. Certainly if Homer had handed the clerk a $20 bill and received change only for a $10, he would have immediately brought the matter to the clerk's attention!

Automobile Theft

Stealing of automobiles presents technical legal difficulties under the rules defining what constitutes theft. The problems arise due to the traditional requirement that the thief intend to permanently deprive the owner of the property, in this case the car. But suppose Jim and Jessie decide to have a good time. They discover a new red sports car with the keys in the ignition. Not ones to let an opportunity pass, they climb into the vehicle and drive it around town until it runs out of gas. At that point they abandon the car. Have Jim and Jessie committed theft?

§ 31.07. Unauthorized Use of a Vehicle

a. A person commits an offense if he intentionally or knowingly operates another's boat, airplane, or motor-propelled vehicle without the effective consent of the owner.

b. An offense under this section is a state jail felony.

The existence of the unauthorized use of a vehicle (UUV) statute (Sec. 31.07) has largely resolved the problem of joyriders and their lack of intent to permanently deprive. UUV focuses not on the intentions of the offender but rather on the scope of permission the suspect had in taking the vehicle. In most instances, the vehicle operator is lacking any consent from the owner. Thus, whether the operator is merely joyriding or intending to strip the vehicle is not of concern. He commits an offense simply by operating the vehicle without appropriate permission.

If Sam, a person unknown to Janet, takes Janet's automobile but is subsequently apprehended by the police, prosecution for UUV is much simpler than trying to establish Sam's ultimate intentions. So long as Janet states that Sam did not have her consent to take the vehicle, he has committed the offense. But what if Sam thought the automobile belonged to Dick and Dick gave his permission for Sam to drive it? Has Sam committed UUV? The Court of Criminal Appeals has held that not only must lack of the owner's effective consent be shown but the state must also establish that the accused knew he lacked effective consent.[48] Thus, in the alternate scenario, Sam can be convicted of UUV only if he knew he lacked the true owner's effective consent. A reasonable mistake of fact concerning who owned the vehicle and whether he had permission to drive it could serve as a defense for Sam.[49]

It should be noted that despite the statute's label, the *actus reus* of the offense is "operate" not "use."[50] Thus, an individual who is sleeping in an automobile without the owner's consent may be *using* the car but is not *operating* it as required for a UUV charge. On the other hand, an act as preliminary as starting the engine and revving the accelerator constitutes "operating."[51] Unless the law of parties comes into play, the prosecution must put the defendant "behind the wheel" operating the vehicle to sustain a UUV charge.[52]

Certainly if the prosecution can prove intent to deprive permanently, a car thief can be successfully prosecuted under Sec. 31.03.[53] An example of such prosecutions includes "chop shop" operations where stolen automobiles are disassembled for their component parts and theft of vehicles for resale using bogus certificates of title. The conduct of the thieves in these situations is strong evidence of an intention to permanently deprive the owner of the vehicle.

The commission of UUV is a state jail felony. The penalty for theft of a vehicle under Sec. 31.03 depends on the value of the vehicle. If the vehicle's fair market value is between $1,500 and $20,000, the offense is a state jail felony. For the typical auto theft, a UUV charge would likely net the same penalty level as a theft charge.

While automobiles are the predominant form of vehicle subjected to UUV, the statute also covers other motor-propelled vehicles such as motorcycles, all terrain vehicles, and even golf cars. Additionally, boats and airplanes fall within the scope of the statute, irrespective of whether they have motors.[54] The discussion in one reported Texas case suggests that the statute would also apply to unauthorized operation of spacecraft![55]

Suppose A.J. asks Mario to loan him his car so he can go to the grocery store. Mario agrees and gives A.J. the keys. Two days later A.J. is found with the car in the next county. His story is he had additional errands to run and was going to return the car in a few days. Has A.J. committed UUV? At least two possible theories apply to this situation. If at the time A.J. asks for the loan of the vehicle he did not actually intend to go to the grocery store, he deceived Mario and thus lacked *effective* consent to take possession of the car. On the other hand, if he did indeed go to the grocery store and then decided to retain the vehicle in order to travel to another location, has he lost the right to possess the vehicle? Few Texas cases address this issue but the rule appears to be this: if a vehicle is borrowed from its owner for a specific purpose and limited time and the borrower operates it inconsistent with the terms of that consent, a UUV has occurred.[56]

Motor vehicle theft may also implicate federal law. The National Motor Vehicle Theft Act, popularly called the **Dyer Act**, creates a federal felony for knowingly transporting into interstate commerce a stolen motor vehicle.[57] Thus, if a car thief drives from one state to another in the stolen vehicle, he has violated the federal statute as well as the law of the state where the car was originally taken. While such violations fall under the jurisdiction of the FBI, as a matter of policy, Dyer Act prosecutions are normally limited to cases involving organized automobile theft rings, not single offenders.[58]

TEXAS LAW OF THEFT OF SERVICE

The current list of the Fortune 500 companies—the largest corporations in America—contains more service-oriented companies than manufacturers. The country has increasingly shifted from a manufacturing to a service economy. Yet, only in recent decades has a broad prohibition regarding theft of those services taken a place within the nation's criminal codes. This slow evolution of the law is partly the result of the Common Law limitation on the crime of larceny. Traditionally larceny has been defined in terms of theft of personal property, tangible objects of value. Indeed, the Common Law viewed disputes over the obtaining of labor or other services as a breach of contract to be handled by civil courts.

Defrauding an innkeeper was probably the first form of a statute directed at theft of service. These statutes, many enacted as local ordinances in the eighteenth century, made it an offense to obtain food and lodging from an inn and to skip out without paying. Ironically, the advent of credit cards and a prepayment requirement by hotel operators has greatly diminished this form of theft of service, although "walking the check" continues to be a significant problem for restaurants. Conversely, a large number of circumstances have arisen in society where valuable services are obtained and never paid for. The Texas theft of service statute seeks to punish some, but not all, forms of this conduct.

Just as the crime of theft applies only to property, theft of service must involve "service." Sec. 31.01(6) defines the term **service** fairly clearly.[59] In reviewing that statute, note that potential overlap exists between property and service, particularly when one considers food and beverages served in restaurants and rental property. This ambiguity will be more fully explored later.

Elements of Theft of Service

Intent to Avoid Payment for Service He Knows Is Provided only for Compensation
One of the several *mens rea* of theft of service is an intent to avoid payment. Suppose John and Martha are eating lunch together. John has an appointment and has to depart before the waiter brings the check. Martha says, "Go on. I'll pay the check and you can pay me back tomorrow." John leaves the restaurant. But one minute later so does

§ 31.01. Definitions

In this chapter:

* * *

(6) "Service" includes:

    A. labor and professional service;

    B. telecommunication, public utility, or transportation service;

    C. lodging, restaurant service, and entertainment; and

    D. the supply of a motor vehicle or other property for use.

§ 31.04. Theft of Service

a. A person commits theft of service if, with intent to avoid payment for service that he knows is provided only for compensation:
1. he intentionally or knowingly secures performance of the service by deception, threat, or false token;
2. having control over the disposition of services of another to which he is not entitled, he intentionally or knowingly diverts the other's services to his own benefit or to the benefit of another not entitled to them;
3. having control of personal property under a written rental agreement, he holds the property beyond the expiration of the rental period without the effective consent of the owner of the property, thereby depriving the owner of the property of its use in further rentals; or
4. he intentionally or knowingly secures the performance of the service by agreeing to provide compensation and, after the service is rendered, fails to make payment after receiving notice demanding payment.

b. For purposes of this section, intent to avoid payment is presumed if:
1. the actor absconded without paying for the service or expressly refused to pay for the service in circumstances where payment is ordinarily made immediately upon rendering of the service, as in hotels, campgrounds, recreational vehicle parks, restaurants, and comparable establishments;
2. the actor failed to make payment under a service agreement within 10 days after receiving notice demanding payment;
3. the actor returns property held under a rental agreement after the expiration of the rental agreement and fails to pay the applicable rental charge for the property within 10 days after the date on which the actor received notice demanding payment; or
4. the actor failed to return the property held under a rental agreement:
    A. within five days after receiving notice demanding return, if the property is valued at less than $1,500; or
    B. within three days after receiving notice demanding return, if the property is valued at $1,500 or more.

Martha without paying for their lunches. Martha has left the premises with the intent to avoid payment and commits theft of service. Has John committed theft of service? Probably not since he lacked the *mens rea* of the crime. However, even though John may not have criminal liability for his conduct, he still owes the restaurant for the value of the meal!

Although the facts surrounding a particular situation can serve as circumstantial evidence that the defendant intended to avoid payment for service, the statutes set forth several circumstances where that intent is presumed. Sec. 31.04(b) notes four possibilities:

- **Absconding or refusing to pay in hotels, restaurants, etc.** — As with the John and Martha scenario, Martha's departure without paying raises a presumption of intent to avoid payment. This rule is a carryover of the old innkeeper statutes whereby absconding from a hotel without payment was presumed to be a criminal act. The list of establishments that fall under the coverage of the presumption contains facilities that provide food and shelter on a temporary basis. The term "abscond" in the statute means to withdraw, flee, or depart secretly.[60] Likewise, simply refusing to pay for food, beverage, and the like indicates an intent to avoid payment.

- **Failing to make payment under service agreement** — If an individual contracts for the performance of a service and fails to make payment within ten days of a demand for payment, the presumption arises. Thus, an individual who chartered an airplane in Mexico and flew to various locations in Texas and then failed to pay the charter fee upon arrival at his final destination was presumed to have intended to avoid payment for the service.[61]

- **Failing to pay under rental agreement** — In a similar vein, failing to pay for property utilized under a rental agreement within ten days of demand raises the presumption of an intent to avoid the payment. It is unclear at this time whether this presumption is intended to apply to persons who fail to pay for rented real estate (e.g., vacation cabin) as well as those who fail to pay for use of rented personal property, such as automobiles and construction equipment.

- **Failure to return property held under rental agreement** — Failing to return rented property raises the presumption of intent to avoid payment. Such failure could also raise the possibility of a theft under Sec. 31.03.

One aspect of this element that has not received court attention to date is the phrase "that he knows is provided only for compensation." For a conviction to stand, the state has to establish not only that the defendant intended to avoid payment for the service but that he or she was aware that the service was provided only for compensation. One's normal day-to-day experience with commerce fairly well establishes which services are provided only for compensation. Obviously, purveyors of restaurant, bar, and hotel services expect compensation and the average individual would recognize this fact. But some other services may be more ambiguous. Assume Kate drives her car into a discount tire store and requests that the air pressure in the tires be checked. Is this a service provided only for compensation? In many establishments such a service is provided at no charge. Other locales might charge a modest fee for the service, particularly if the motorist did not purchase her tires at that location. If an individual is unaware that the service she received is provided only for compensation and she fails to pay the compensation due to her lack of awareness, the mistake of fact defense seems to be available.[62]

Secures Performance of Service by Deception, Threat, or False Token

Theft of service can be committed in any of four ways. The intentional or knowing obtaining of service by deception, threat, or false token is likely the primary means by which the offense is committed. To a large degree, the requirement of a deception, threat, or false token provides the nonconsenual element of the crime. A merchant who is deceived or threatened provides the service without effective consent. The meaning of the terms "deception" and "threat" are presumably identical to the same terms used in theft of property cases. The term **false token** is a traditional term that developed in the law of fraud. The phrase refers to any falsely made document, fraudulent coin, or other similar representation of value or privilege. In modern usage, the term would cover counterfeit currency, stolen credit cards, and counterfeit concert tickets. Even the use of metal "slugs" in pay telephones or video arcade games would be use of a false token.

Or, Diverts Services to Another

Kyle, a college student, works as a bartender at the local club near campus. When his fraternity brothers come into the club, he provides them with free drinks. The owner of the club is unaware of Kyle's benevolence to his friends. Kyle's conduct violates Sec. 31.04(a)(2). He has control over the disposition of someone else's services (in this case food and beverage) and he diverts them to someone who is not entitled to them. It would also be considered theft of service for Kyle to personally benefit from the food and beverage without the owner's permission.

Or, Holds Rental Property beyond Rental Period

Personal property (not real property) which is held beyond its contractual rental period without compensation constitutes theft of service. A common example of prosecution under this provision involves rental cars. Assume Roger rents an automobile for two days. He keeps the vehicle a week beyond the original two-day rental period. Ultimately the vehicle is found in a parking lot. It likely is easier to prosecute Roger for theft of service than for theft of the vehicle because his ultimate intentions for the vehicle may be difficult to establish.

When video rental stores entered American society in the 1980s, in some jurisdictions police reports were filed on individuals who failed to return the videotape within the contracted time frame. Late returns became so pervasive that many police agencies refused to take such reports. Ultimately the matter was resolved not with criminal prosecution but through use of deposits and late fee charges.

Or, Agrees but Fails to Pay for Service

The fourth alternative means of committing theft of service is through obtaining the service by agreeing to provide compensation but intentionally failing to pay. Jerry hires Kevin to mow his lawn. Jerry agrees to pay Kevin $20 for the job. When Kevin completes the work, Jerry pays him only $10 because Jerry is unhappy with the quality of the work Kevin performed. Has Jerry committed theft of service or is this simply a breach of contract? Theft of service laws are not intended to turn every contractual dispute into a criminal matter. Indeed, an extensive body of law exists to determine the rights of parties to a contract and the civil side of the courthouse offers amply facilities for the resolution of those disputes. Such disputes become criminal *only* when an intent to avoid payment for services exists. If Kevin wants the additional $10, he will have to sue Jerry.

But what if Jerry simply refused to pay Kevin anything after he completed the job? Suppose Jerry laughingly says to Kevin, "You've learned a valuable lesson young man. Always get your money upfront." In this version of the scenario, an argument could be made that Jerry never intended to pay Kevin for the yard work and thereby obtained his labor by deceit. Such an act could constitute theft of service.

Consider Raymond who hires undocumented immigrants to perform day labor. At the end of the day after the work is performed, Raymond refuses to pay the workers, knowing they will be reluctant to notify the police. Raymond has committed theft of service.

Penalty

The penalty for violation of the theft of service statute tracks the monetary-based schedule used for theft. See Table 9-2 above. The value of the service is solely determined by the fair market value at the time and place of the offense. The replacement value rule is not applicable to theft of service.[63]

SPECIAL PROBLEMS IN LAW OF THEFT OF SERVICE

Several common situations bear mentioning that on the surface appear to implicate theft of service. On the first of the month Mary pays her apartment rent by writing a check to her landlord Lou. Lou deposits the check. Mary's bank ultimately returns the check for lack of sufficient funds. By now it is the 15th of the month. Has Mary committed theft of service through the deceptive act of issuing a worthless check? Probably not. While the definition of "service" found in Sec. 31.01(6) lists "lodging," the presumption of intent to avoid payment in Sec. 31.04(b)(1) speaks of "hotels, campgrounds, recreational vehicle parks . . . and comparable establishments," indicating an intention on the part of the Legislature to limit the law's application to places of temporary lodging. This view is in line with the historical concern about defrauding innkeepers. Also, the law and custom provide alternatives for Lou. First, landlords commonly collect first and last month's rent when a tenant moves in, thereby protecting themselves in the event of a failure to pay the rent during the rental period. Second, a variety of civil actions ranging from a breach of lease suit to eviction are available to him. It seems unlikely that the Texas Legislature intended to criminalize the failure to pay rent in a timely fashion.[64] However, Mary may have violated the issuance of bad check law discussed below.

Mary's bad check question raises another issue under the law of theft of service. A person can steal a service through use of deception. The word "deception" [Sec. 31.01(1)(A)] is defined in terms of creating a false impression that is likely to affect the judgment of another in the transaction. Texas courts have held that if a check is used to pay for a service that has already been provided, such as tinting of car windows,[65] child care services,[66] or a hotel bill,[67] the victim's judgment was not influenced by issuance of the fraudulent check since the service had already been rendered. As a consequence, the issuance of the worthless check did not create a deception. Thus, the intent to avoid payment presumption contained in Sec. 31.06 becomes nonapplicable. For Sec. 31.06 to apply to a theft of service case, the offender must use the worthless check to induce the victim to perform a service, not as compensation for services already performed. This rule is in contrast to theft of property where the property owner will not part with the property until he receives cash or its equivalent; the worthless check acts to deceive the victim into transferring the property.[68]

Another common situation is gasoline thefts, or drive-offs as they are known. A customer, such as Wanda in the opening paragraph, fills her automobile's tank with gasoline and drives off without paying. Industry estimates of annual loss of gasoline sales range from $115 to $250 million. Is a gasoline drive-off a theft or a theft of service? Certainly tangible property has been taken but unlike the theft of a wristwatch or cash, if the thief is apprehended, the property is not easily recovered. Given the Texas statutory definition of "service," it is difficult to see where a gasoline drive-off fits in, particularly now that virtually all gasoline facilities are self-service. However, anecdotal reports suggest that in some counties the cases are filed as theft of service instead of theft, using analogous reasoning to the individual who walks a check in a restaurant after dining; the property taken is not readily recoverable.[69]

Suppose Jack and Jill go to a restaurant to celebrate their anniversary. Jack orders steak and Jill orders salmon. When the orders come, the pair taste their food and complain that the steak is too rare and the tuna is overcooked. The waiter takes the steak back to the kitchen for additional cooking time and brings Jill more salmon. This time the steak is overcooked and the salmon is raw. In disgust, Jack and Jill decide to find another restaurant. They leave the waiter a tip and depart without paying the check. Have they committed theft of service?[70]

THEFT OF TRADE SECRETS

Suppose Sara works as a secretary at Mom's Pie Factory, which produces the nation's best tasting and best selling apple pie. Mom's apple pie is based on a secret recipe kept in the office file cabinet. Sara, who has access to the file cabinet as part of her job, takes the paper containing the secret recipe and makes a photocopy. She then replaces the recipe in the cabinet. A week later, Sara quits her job. She and her husband Lee start their own bakery. She begins selling apple pies constructed and baked according to Mom's secret recipe. Has Sara committed theft of trade secrets?

An emerging area of the law of theft concerns the stealing of items that can best be described as intellectual property. Within this classification fall a wide range of information-type matters such as chemical formulas, computer programs, production techniques, photographs, maps, drawings, recordings, architectural plans, and even methods of plant propagation and genetic engineering. The advent of the information age has made many such items extremely valuable. Certainly Mom's Pie Company seeks to protect its apple pie recipe because of the economic advantage it provides over other pie makers.

Traditional elements of the law of larceny and theft do not cover Sara's conduct very well. First, she did not take anything; the recipe remains in the file cabinet. Second, she did not carry away or deprive the owner of anything; she simply made a copy. Third, Mom has suffered no permanent deprivation of the sheet of paper containing the secret recipe. Because of the shortcomings of the traditional law of theft and larceny, a special theft of trade secrets statute was enacted.[71]

A **trade secret** is essentially any commercially valuable information the owner has taken precautions to prevent becoming available to unauthorized persons.[72] Mom's apple pie recipe is a trade secret. Stealing, copying, and transmitting a trade secret without the owner's effective consent are all violations of the Texas statute. Sara violates the theft of trade secrets statute by copying the recipe without the owner's permission. In a real case, an individual was convicted of theft of trade

§ 31.05. Theft of Trade Secrets

a. For purposes of this section:
   1. "Article" means any object, material, device, or substance or any copy thereof, including a writing, recording, drawing, sample, specimen, prototype, model, photograph, microorganism, blueprint, or map.
   2. "Copy" means a facsimile, replica, photograph, or other reproduction of an article or a note, drawing, or sketch made of or from an article.
   3. "Representing" means describing, depicting, containing, constituting, reflecting, or recording.
   4. "Trade secret" means the whole or any part of any scientific or technical information, design, process, procedure, formula, or improvement that has value and that the owner has taken measures to prevent from becoming available to persons other than those selected by the owner to have access for limited purposes.

b. A person commits an offense if, without the owner's effective consent, he knowingly:
   1. steals a trade secret;
   2. makes a copy of an article representing a trade secret; or
   3. communicates or transmits a trade secret.

c. An offense under this section is a felony of the third degree.

secrets when he faxed confidential plans for machinery parts from Washington to an individual in Texas.[73]

Violation of the theft of trade secrets statute is a felony of the third degree regardless of the value or importance of the secret.

FRAUD

Introduction

Recall the opening example of Kris who buys the phony designer handbag for $250. Assuming she would not have made the purchase but for the vendor's assertion that the bag was genuine, Kris has been the victim of a fraud. She has parted with her money by relying on an assertion of fact that proved to be untrue.

In criminal law, **fraud** is the offense of deliberately deceiving another in order to obtain property or services from him or her unjustly. Fraud often is accomplished through the aid of bogus objects, such as checks or counterfeit money. Traditionally, such events were covered by the law against obtaining property under false pretenses.

Texas has not enacted a general fraud statute. Rather, the theft and theft of service statutes (Secs 31.01 and 31.04) double as fraud statutes because they prohibit obtaining property and services through deception. As is noted below, Texas has enacted several specialized statutes to cover particular forms of fraud. The statutes are somewhat a duplicate of the theft statute but establish a different penalty for the fraudulent conduct. These laws focus on such diverse topics as credit and debit card use, check forgery, and insurance fraud.

The cornerstone of fraud is a false representation of an existing or past fact that affects the decision of the victim to part with title or possession of his or her property. Did the vendor's sign induce Kris to make the purchase of the purse? Did it cause her to view the handbag as a deal too good to pass up?

But what if the vendor's sign reads "Purses For Sale. Identical to Designer Purses Costing Hundreds More." Here, there is no claim that the purses are in fact made by famous designers. But the vendor says they are "identical" to the real item but Kris discovers they are a cheaply made version. Is the "identical" claim a fraudulent representation?

The law has attempted to maintain a reasonable balance between the protection of citizens against fraud and the ability of merchants to peddle their wares successfully. Accordingly, the law has generally allowed merchants to exaggerate the quality of their goods. Terms like "Lowest Prices in Town," "Exceptional Value," "Top Quality Merchandise," and similar phrases are viewed as a matter of opinion, known as seller's puff. The fact the store does not have the lowest prices, nor provides exceptional value, nor actually sells top quality merchandise does not raise its assertions to a criminal offense. This rule appears rooted in the age old notion of *caveat emptor*—let the buyer beware! Consider Ronda's purchase of the used car from Honest Eddie discussed at the start of the chapter? Would you consider Honest Eddie's statements to be merely puff or rising to the level of criminal deception?

While modern theft statutes retain the element that words or actions creating a false impression can serve as the basis for a charge of theft by deception, most efforts to draw the line between criminal conduct and clever merchandising are handled by special consumer protection and deceptive business practices statutes. These laws specifically criminalize certain sales tactics such as offering merchandise at a discount price when no such merchandise is actually available, purporting to be going out of business when no such intention exists, mislabeling the quantity or weight of goods,

---

Hello friend,

I am Dr. Vladimir Ivanov. And I represent Mr. Mikhail Khordokovsky the former C.E.O. of Yukos Oil Company in Russia. I have a very sensitive and confidential brief from this top (oligarch) to ask for your partnership in re-profiling funds US$42.3 million.

I will give the details, but in summary, the funds are coming via Bank Menatep.

This is a legitimate transaction. You will be paid 10% for your "Management Fees."

If you are interested, please write back by mail and provide me with your confidential telephone number, fax number and email address and I will provide details and instructions.

Please keep this confidential; we can't afford more political problems.

Finally, please note that this must be concluded within two weeks.

Please write back promptly. Write me back through my personal email.

I look forward to it.

Regards,
Dr Vladimir Ivanov

FIGURE 9-1

selling reconditioned merchandise as new, and other clearly fraudulent commercial practices.[74] Federal law also weighs in on consumer protection, criminalizing conduct such as turning back odometers on previously owned automobiles.[75]

Federal law plays an important role in trying to control complex schemes of fraudulent behavior. The U.S. Code contains statutes relating to mail fraud[76] and wire fraud.[77] Since the perpetration of high dollar scams almost always involves communication by telephone, mail, or email, the federal statutes have proven particularly important in combating these crimes. The federal wire fraud statute has become increasingly useful in combating Internet-based frauds such as lottery scams, "phishing" schemes, Nigerian 419 frauds, and other efforts to obtain personal identifying information.[78] Figure 9-1 displays a typical "phishing" email. The email was obviously composed by someone whose native language is not English. Because the email originated from outside the country, federal law is implicated. Unfortunately, the international character of the swindle effort makes investigation and prosecution difficult. The name "Vladimir Ivanov" is the Russian equivalent of "John Smith."

Forgery

Introduction

LaToya finds Carrie's tax refund check lying on the sidewalk. She takes the check into the bank. LaToya endorses the check with Carrie's name. The bank gives LaToya cash in the amount of the check. LaToya has committed **forgery** because she has signed Carrie's name without her permission. Forgery would also be the offense if LaToya, without Carrie's permission, wrote a check on Carrie's account, signing Carrie's name. In both instances the check purports to be written by Carrie but in fact was written by LaToya.

Elements of Forgery

Person Forges While Sec. 32.21 does not list a general *mens rea*, it is difficult to see how anyone could commit the offense of forgery without doing so intentionally or knowingly. The statute proscribes three modes of committing forgery:[79]

§ 32.21. Forgery

a. For purposes of this section:
  1. "Forge" means:
     A. to alter, make, complete, execute, or authenticate any writing so that it purports:
        i.   to be the act of another who did not authorize that act;
        ii. to have been executed at a time or place or in a numbered sequence other than was in fact the case; or
        iii. to be a copy of an original when no such original existed;
     B. to issue, transfer, register the transfer of, pass, publish, or otherwise utter a writing that is forged within the meaning of Paragraph (A); or
     C. to possess a writing that is forged within the meaning of Paragraph (A) with intent to utter it in a manner specified in Paragraph (B).
  2. "Writing" includes:
     A. printing or any other method of recording information;
     B. money, coins, tokens, stamps, seals, credit cards, badges, and trademarks; and
     C. symbols of value, right, privilege, or identification.

b. A person commits an offense if he forges a writing with intent to defraud or harm another.

c. Except as provided in Subsections (d) and (e) an offense under this section is a Class A misdemeanor.

d. An offense under this section is a state jail felony if the writing is or purports to be a will, codicil, deed, deed of trust, mortgage, security instrument, security agreement, credit card, check, authorization to debit an account at a financial institution, or similar sight order for payment of money, contract, release, or other commercial instrument.

e. An offense under this section is a felony of the third degree if the writing is or purports to be:
  1. part of an issue of money, securities, postage or revenue stamps;
  2. a government record listed in Section 37.01(2)(C); or
  3. other instruments issued by a state or national government or by a subdivision of either, or part of an issue of stock, bonds, or other instruments representing interests in or claims against another person.

f. A person is presumed to intend to defraud or harm another if the person acts with respect to two or more writings of the same type and if each writing is a government record listed in Section 37.01(2)(C).

1. **Making a forged writing**—The act of making a false writing or altering a legitimate writing is one form of forging. The writing is false if it purports to be the act of another who did not authorize it, to have been created at a different time or place, or to be a copy of an original when no such original exists. A common example here is LaToya signing Carrie's name to her refund check without her consent. This is an unauthorized act. As a general rule, anytime an individual executes a document using other than his or her true name, a forgery has occurred. Similarly alteration of the date of a document can constitute a forgery. As can any other modifications that are false and would induce reliance by another upon that misrepresentation.

2. **Presenting a forged writing**—An individual commits an act of forgery if he presents or otherwise tries to pass the forged item, even if he did not initially produce the fraudulent item. If Jack attempts to pass off counterfeit money, he is in violation of this statute even though he was not the person who originally printed the bogus bills. Texas law continues to utilize the traditional term "utter" in regard to the presentation of a forged item. **Utter** in the context of the law of forgery simply means to put into circulation.

3. **Possession of forged writing with intent to utter**—One need not be successful in actually passing the forged items. Mere possession with an intent to place the fraudulent item in circulation constitutes forgery. If Jill is arrested carrying a suitcase full of fraudulent Super Bowl tickets, she is in violation of this provision.

Writing   While checks are the most common objects of forgery, any writing, printed document, or other symbol of value, such as credit cards, fits within the coverage of the law. Forgeries can also involve money orders, bills of sale, receipts, stock certificates, wills, and deeds. Major sporting events such as the Super Bowl and World Series are plagued by the creation of forged admission tickets. These events use extensive technology, such as holograms and special barcodes, in an attempt to thwart forgers. Passing of counterfeit money, although usually handled under federal law, violates the state forgery statutes because it is a fraudulent writing.

Falsely made driver's license, prescriptions for medicine, academic transcripts and degrees, and other bogus credentials could also fall under the scope of the forgery law. However, the Legislature has enacted special statutes to cover these items and any prosecution would normally be under these specific laws.[80]

With Intent to Defraud or Harm Another   Suppose Vic has a baseball upon which he has inscribed a signature reading "Babe Ruth." Has Vic committed forgery? He certainly has signed Babe Ruth's name without permission. But, is Vic intending to offer to sell the baseball as authentic? If so, he is intending to use the writing to defraud and such conduct constitutes forgery. If Vic only intends to set the ball on his desk as a novelty or joke, he has not committed an offense because he lacks the intent to harm. As the Court of Criminal Appeals has observed, "Intent to defraud or harm is the gist of forgery."[81]

Penalty

Unlike the theft and theft of services statutes, the penalty for forgery is not dependent upon the value of the loss but rather upon the form of item forged. A simple forgery is a Class A misdemeanor but can elevate to as high as a felony of the third degree. Check forgery, a common occurrence, constitutes a state jail felony regardless of the amount of the check. Forgery of government documents is a felony of the third degree.

Credit/Debit Card Abuse

Deceptive and fraudulent activity involving credit cards and debit cards almost always falls under Sec. 32.31. This statute covers most forms of theft and theft of service when a credit or debit card is the instrument of the deception. Under Sec. 32.31, use of a credit/debit card without the effective consent of the owner, possession of a stolen credit card with intent to defraud, buying and selling stolen credit cards, and similar fraudulent behaviors are declared to be a state jail felony regardless of the amount of loss.

Of particular note is the definition of what constitutes a "credit card" or "debit card." Not only does the plastic card itself fall within the definition, but so does the card number alone. Thus, an individual who uses a stolen credit card number to obtain goods or services has committed credit card abuse even though he is not in possession of the actual card. Even an expired credit card is still a credit card under the statutory definition.[82]

The statute establishes 11 different alternatives by which the offense may be perpetrated. Depending on the way in which the offense is committed, the prosecution must establish that the defendant either knew that the credit/debit cards were fictitious or stolen, or that he possessed the specific intent to use the card to obtain some benefit or to defraud. There is no requirement that the defendant be successful in obtaining the desired benefit. Thus, if Larry tenders a stolen credit card to pay for his dinner and the restaurant rejects the card, Larry has still committed credit card abuse under Sec. 32.31(b)(1).

Issuance of Bad Check

Remember Cal at the start of the chapter? He wrote a check to purchase groceries but the bank ultimately returned the check to the merchant because his account balance was insufficient to cover the amount of the check. Which, if any, offense has Cal committed?

Under the Texas Penal Code, at least one of three possible offenses has occurred when a bank rejects the payment of a check:

- Forgery (Sec. 32.21)
- Theft (Sec. 31.03) or Theft of Service (Sec. 31.04)
- Issuance of Bad Check (Sec. 32.41)

Which of the crimes, if any, is violated is a function of the surrounding facts of the case and the *mens rea* of the offender.

In Cal's case, he has not committed forgery because he did not purport the check to be the act of another who did not authorize it. He signed his true name. Cases involving true name checks rarely meet the definition of a forgery.[83] Did Cal commit theft by deception? Recall that theft requires an "intent to deprive" the owner of property (or avoid payment for service in the case of Sec. 31.04). Cal certainly gained property (the groceries), but does his conduct amount to an intent to deprive? Did Cal intentionally lie in order to gain the groceries when he offered the check in payment? Not according to the facts presented. The check bounced due to his lack of knowledge about his account balance. At worst he was negligent in not maintaining close scrutiny of his account balance. No theft has occurred, assuming he makes good the check in a timely manner.

But did Cal commit issuance of bad check? This offense, Sec. 32.41, is similar to theft by check but is rooted in a different social policy. The use of checks and similar bank orders to conduct business has been so prominent within the last century that when a customer presents a check for payment, there is an implied assertion that money is in the account to cover it. Merchants rarely contact the bank to determine if the check is good or hold the purchased merchandise until the check clears the bank. Unfortunately, thousands of checks annually are returned to merchants marked "account closed" or "nonsufficient funds." The Legislature has decided that offering a check in payment which the maker knows is no good should be an offense against the commercial system. But it is not much of one, being only a Class C misdemeanor regardless of the face amount of the check.[84]

These bad checks often bear the true name of the maker and their current or former address and telephone number as well as driver's license information. Yet, they are rejected by the bank because of insufficient funds. In most cases, the merchant who takes the check is interested in gaining the amount due, not in criminal prosecution of the check writer. Accordingly, issuance of bad check charges are filed primarily to collect the check and obtain restitution not to pursue a criminal conviction.

County and district attorneys statewide operate hot check units. In the typical case, merchants file issuance of bad check charges after their own efforts to collect the check have not produced satisfactory results. Prosecutor investigators attempt to locate the offender and seek restitution under threat of criminal prosecution. In the bulk of instances, the offender pays the amount owed to the merchant and the criminal charges are dropped.[85] The prosecutor's office collects a fee from the offender to offset the cost of the collection process. In the major counties, such as Harris and Dallas, these fees can total more than $5,000,000 annually. Unlike criminal fines and other revenue collected in the justice system, bad check collection fees do not go into the county's general fund but are retained by the county or district attorney's office and are not subject to the normal budgeting and appropriation process.[86] The prosecutor may spend the fees on anything related to the operation of the office except his or her own salary.[87] In most counties the bad check fees cover the cost of the operation of the hot check unit and provide supplemental funds to pay for additional prosecutors or investigators.

Other Fraudulent Acts

Chapter 34 contains a variety of statutes regarding other fraudulent behaviors. Many of these implicate white-collar criminal behavior such as Sec. 32.32 False Statements to Obtain Property or Credit, Sec. 32.42 Commercial Bribery, and Sec. 32.45 Misapplication of Fiduciary Property. Likewise, elsewhere in the Penal Code are prohibitions against other forms of fraudulent activity such as insurance fraud (Sec. 35.02) and Medicaid fraud (Sec. 35A.02).

Two forms of fraudulent behavior that have arisen in recent years are criminal simulation (Sec. 32.22) and trademark counterfeiting (Sec. 32.23). Recall the earlier scenario of Kris buying what she thought was a designer purse only to learn that it was an unauthorized reproduction. The individual who sold her that purse violated the criminal simulation statute because he defrauded Kris into believing the purse was genuine. The sale of "knock-off" purses, wristwatches, garments, perfume, and the like has become commonplace in recent years, particularly in certain areas of the state's largest cities. The criminal simulation statute declares it a Class A misdemeanor to pass such products off as genuine. This law would also apply to individuals who produce and sell bogus sports memorabilia such as game jerseys, autographed balls, autographed photos, and similar collectables.[88] Likewise, the law would apply to the offer of sale of intentionally misrepresented artwork, sculptures, and antiques. Note that simple possession of such phony material is not an offense. Thus, Kris is not violating state law if she uses her knock-off purse.

Suppose the merchant was candid with Kris when she bought the purse and told her that it was not a real designer purse but an unauthorized copy. The merchant has not defrauded or harmed Kris as is a necessary element of criminal simulation. But, he is offering for sale goods bearing a counterfeit trademark. Violation of this statute, aimed at commercial producers and distributors of counterfeit wares, can result in a sanction from a Class C misdemeanor to a felony of the first degree.

§ 32.22. Criminal Simulation

a. A person commits an offense if, with intent to defraud or harm another:
  1. he makes or alters an object, in whole or in part, so that it appears to have value because of age, antiquity, rarity, source, or authorship that it does not have;
  2. he possesses an object so made or altered, with intent to sell, pass, or otherwise utter it; or
  3. he authenticates or certifies an object so made or altered as genuine or as different from what it is.

b. An offense under this section is a Class A misdemeanor.

IDENTITY THEFT

In recent years both the federal government[89] and the state[90] have enacted laws relating to use of another's identity with intent to perpetrate a fraud, an act commonly called identify theft. An act of **identity theft** often involves utilizing another person's name and personal data, such as Social Security number, credit record, and bank account information, to commit a fraud upon a third party such as a bank or credit card company. Virtually, every deceitful act the offender commits is covered by traditional theft and fraud laws. Problems of proof as well as the personal aggravation of trying to straighten out one's financial records motivated the enactment of these specialized identity theft laws.

Unfortunately, the federal statute is limited in application. While it covers falsely made governmental documents, such as passports, birth certificates, and driver's license, like other federal statutes, a jurisdictional basis such as interstate activity or use of the mail has to be established. Also, federal prosecutors focus on ring cases not individual acts of identity theft, deferring those to state authorities.

As a general rule, the real monetary victims of acts of identity theft are financial institutions.[91] While the task of successfully correcting financial records may be daunting for the individual whose identity was fraudulently used, the economic loss is almost universally borne by the bank, credit card company, stockbroker, or other financial institution. Since by definition the offender is obtaining funds in a manner not authorized by the account holder, it is the institution, not the account holder, who is defrauded and who suffers the monetary loss.

The Texas statute (Sec. 32.51) was enacted in 1999 and creates a state jail felony for any act where the identifying information of another person is used without their consent with intent to harm or defraud another. "Identifying information" ranges from name, to Social Security number, to bank account number, to biometric data such as retina images and fingerprints. In nearly every case of identity theft, the offender will commit a violation of Sec. 32.51 while committing the underlying theft, forgery, credit card abuse, or other fraudulent act. The identity theft charge may prove to be the more serious offense.

CRIMEGRAPH
Theft

Offense	Culpable mental state*	Conduct	What?	How?	Specific intent/knowledge	Penalty
Theft 31.03(a)	1. Intentionally, or 2. Knowingly, or 3. Recklessly	Appropriates by: 1. Transfer of title or purported title	Property: 1. Real property, or 2. Personal property, or 3. Documents	Unlawfully: 1. Without consent, or 2. Without effective consent, or 3. Appropriates knowing property is stolen, or 4. Appropriates property represented by peace officer as stolen	With intent to deprive owner of property	CM to F1
Theft 31.03(a)	1. Intentionally, or 2. Knowingly, or 3. Recklessly	Appropriates by: 1. Acquiring or exercising control over	Property: 1. Personal property or 2. Documents	Unlawfully: 1. Without consent, or 2. Without effective consent, or 3. Appropriates knowing property is stolen, or 4. Appropriates property represented by peace officer as stolen	With intent to deprive owner of property	CM to F1

*Required by Texas Penal Code § 6.02

226

CRIMEGRAPH
Theft of Service

Offense	Culpable mental state	Conduct	Of what?	How?	When?	Specific intent/knowledge	Penalty
Theft of Service 31.04(a)(1)	1. Intentionally or 2. Knowingly	Secures performance	Service: 1. Labor, or 2. Telcom, utility, or transportation, or 3. Lodging, food, or entertainment, or 4. Supply of motor vehicle or other property for use	1. Deception, or 2. Threat, or 3. False token		With intent to avoid payment he knows is provided only for compensation	CM to F1
Theft of Service 31.04(a)(2)	1. Intentionally or 2. Knowingly	Diverts to: 1. Self or 2. Another not entitled to service	Service: 1. Labor, or 2. Telcom, utility, or transportation, or 3. Lodging, food, or entertainment, or 4. Supply of motor vehicle or other property for use		Having control over disposition of service to which not entitled	With intent to avoid payment he knows is provided only for compensation	CM to F1
Theft of Service 31.04(a)(3)	1. Intentionally, or 2. Knowingly, or 3. Recklessly*	Holds beyond rental period	Personal property	Without effective consent of owner	Having control under written rental agreement	With intent to avoid payment he knows is provided only for compensation	CM to F1
Theft of Service 31.04(a)(4)	1. Intentionally or 2. Knowingly	Secures performance	Service: 1. Labor, or 2. Telcom, utility, or transportation, or 3. Lodging, food, or entertainment, or 4. Supply of motor vehicle or other property for use	By agreeing to compensate and failing to pay	After receiving notice to pay	With intent to avoid payment he knows is provided only for compensation	CM to F1

*Required by Texas Penal Code § 6.02

CRIMEGRAPH
Special Theft-Related Offenses

Offense	Culpable mental state	Conduct	What?	When?	Penalty
Theft of Trade Secrets 31.05(b)(1)	Knowingly	Steals	Trade secret	Without effective consent of owner	F3
Theft of Trade Secrets 31.05(b)(2)	Knowingly	Makes a copy of	Article representing a trade secret	Without effective consent of owner	F3
Theft of Trade Secrets 31.05(b)(3)	Knowingly	1. Communicates <u>or</u> 2. Transmits	Trade secret	Without effective consent of owner	F3
Unauthorized Use of a Vehicle 31.07(a)	1. Intentionally <u>or</u> 2. Knowingly	Operates	1. Boat, <u>or</u> 2. Airplane, <u>or</u> 3. Motor-propelled vehicle	Without effective consent of owner	SJF

CRIMEGRAPH
Fraud Offenses

Offense	Culpable mental state*	Conduct	What?	When?	Specific intent/knowledge	Penalty
Forgery 32.21(a)	1. Intentionally, or 2. Knowingly, or 3. Recklessly	Forges	Writing		With intent to defraud or harm another	AM to F3
Criminal Simulation 32.22(a)(1)	1. Intentionally, or 2. Knowingly, or 3. Recklessly	1. Makes or 2. Alters	1. Whole object or 2. Partial object	It appears to have value due to: 1. Age, or 2. Antiquity, or 3. Rarity, or 4. Source, or 5. Authorship	With intent to defraud or harm another	AM
Criminal Simulation 32.22(a)(2)	1. Intentionally, or 2. Knowingly, or 3. Recklessly	Possesses	Altered object	With intent to: 1. Sell, or 2. Pass, or 3. Utter	With intent to defraud or harm another	AM
Criminal Simulation 32.22(a)(3)	1. Intentionally, or 2. Knowingly, or 3. Recklessly	1. Authenticates or 2. Certifies	Altered object	As: 1. Genuine or 2. Different from what it is	With intent to defraud or harm another	AM
Issuance of Bad Check 32.41(a)	1. Intentionally, or 2. Knowingly, or 3. Recklessly	1. Issues or 2. Passes	Check for the payment of money		Knowing issuer does not have funds to cover it and all other checks outstanding	CM

*Required by Texas Penal Code § 6.02

229

Notes

1. *See* TEX. DEP'T OF PUB. SAFETY, THE TEXAS CRIME REPORT FOR 2006 (2007).

2. *Id.*

3. Exodus 20:15.

4. Connecticut, Michigan, Mississippi, New Mexico, New York, North Carolina, Oklahoma, Rhode Island, South Carolina, Vermont, Virginia, West Virginia, Wisconsin, and Wyoming.

5. For a classic treatise providing an historical account of the development of the law of larceny, *see* JEROME HALL, THEFT, LAW AND SOCIETY (Bobbs-Merrill 2nd ed. 1952).

6. 39 Geo. III, ch. 85 (1799).

7. 30 Geo. II, ch. 24, § 1 (1757).

8. Driggers v. State, 118 So. 20 (Fla. 1928).

9. From 1863 until 1933, a U.S. one dollar bill technically represented one dollar's worth of gold or silver on deposit in the U.S. Treasury. Paper money continued to be redeemable in silver until 1968. Today, a dollar bill is backed solely by the credit of the federal government.

10. Adapted from an example in ROLLIN M. PERKINS AND RONALD N. BOYCE, CRIMINAL LAW 292–294 (3rd ed. 1982).

11. HALL, *supra,* at 122–123, relates the tale of a British case where a man was acquitted of stealing a duck when the proof established that the fowl was a drake!

12. *Id.* at 118. Today, many states have enacted statutes purporting to abolish the rule of strict construction, but some courts seem to have generally ignored these statutes and continue to impose a rigid approach to statutory interpretation. Compare Tex. Penal Code § 1.05(a) with Brown v. De La Cruz, 156 S.W.3d 560, 565 (Tex. 2004), wherein the Texas Supreme Court simply ignores the existence of the statute abolishing the strict construction rule.

13. Chavez v. State, 843 S.W.2d 586, 588 (Tex. Crim App. 1992). However, in some types of theft the manner in which the theft occurred must be alleged in more detail in an indictment.

14. Thomas v. State, 612 S.W.2d 158 (Tex. Crim. App. 1981).

15. *See* THE TEXAS CRIME REPORT FOR 2006, *supra.* In addition, the vast majority of the nearly 100,000 motor vehicle thefts annually involve the simple taking of the vehicle without permission.

16. See TEX. PENAL CODE § 1.07(9) for the definition of "coercion."

17. See TEX. PENAL CODE § 31.01(1) for the definition of "deception."

18. The age of legal majority in Texas is 18. *See* TEX. CIV. PRAC. & REM. CODE § 129.001. Can a child under 18 make reasonable dispositions of property for purposes of the law of theft?

19. See Dennis v. State, 647 S.W.2d 275 (Tex. Crim. App. 1983) and cases cited therein.

20. While Pat likely cannot be convicted of theft by receiving stolen property, he does not go unpunished. Since a thief acquires no title to property, the thief has no title to pass to Pat. Pat will be out his $600.

21. *See* Pool v. State, 528 S.W.2d 255 (Tex. Crim. App. 1975).

22. Castleberry v. State, 33 S.W. 875 (Tex. Crim. App. 1896).

23. Bradshaw v. State, 482 S.W.2d 233 (Tex. Crim. App. 1972).

24. *See* TEX. PENAL CODE §§ 31.03(c)(3); (c)(6)–(c)(8); See also TEX. FIN. CODE § 371.174 concerning recordkeeping requirements of pawnbrokers.

25. See Vargas v. State, 818 S.W.2d 875 (Tex. App.—Houston [14th Dist.] 1991), for an example of a case wherein undercover police officer conducted sting of pawnshop operator.

26. Bailey v. State, 885 S.W.2d 193 (Tex. App.—Dallas 1994).

27. Barnes v. State, 513 S.W.2d 850 (Tex. Crim. App. 1974).

28. Stewart v. State, 44 S.W.3d 582 (Tex. Crim. App. 2001).

29. *See* TEX. TAX CODE § 1.40(2).

30. Hawkins v. State, 214 S.W.3d 668 (Tex. App.—Waco 2007).

31. Castle v. State, 718 S.W.2d 86 (Tex. App.—Fort Worth 1986).

32. Hill v. State, 633 S.W.2d 520 (Tex. Crim. App. 1981).

33. But see Castle v. State; Schultze v. State, 626 S.W.2d 89 (Tex. App.—Corpus Christi 1981); and Pender v. State, 850 S.W.2d 201 (Tex. App.—Fort Worth 1993), holding that defendants' conduct in and out of store was sufficient to establish intent to deprive.

34. A booster box is typically a cardboard box that is large enough to conceal stolen items. It may be wrapped to give the impression of a securely wrapped package but one side of the box is held in place with a spring. Stolen items are inserted through this trap door. Booster coats are loose top coats with large pockets or hooks sewn in the lining to hang merchandise. Such devices are the hallmarks of skilled shoplifters.

35. *Prima facie* is a Latin expression meaning "on its first appearance" or "by first instance" used in Common Law jurisdictions to denote evidence that is sufficient, if not rebutted, to prove a particular proposition or fact.

36. Adherence to the exact language of the demand for payment outlined in the statute is not necessary to raise presumption of intent to deprive. Leon v. State, 102 S.W.3d 776 (Tex. App.—Houston [14th Dist.] 2003).

37. Under certain circumstances, property may be seized to secure payment for a debt. In most

instances such a seizure must be based on a previously issued court judgment.

38. Kelley v. State, 2002 Tex. App. LEXIS 5380.

39. Hall v. State, 2003 Tex. App. LEXIS 1428.

40. A holder in due course is one who pays in good faith a check or promissory note and has no suspicion that it might be no good. Such a holder is entitled to payment by the maker of the check or note. Assume A writes a check payable to B. B gives A cash for the check. B then deposits the check in his bank account, receiving credit for the check. Ultimately the check bounces. B and the bank are holders in due course and either could be treated as the "owner" of the check if A is prosecuted for theft.

41. Castle v. State.

42. In Texas, the mechanic maintains a lien on the vehicle for the cost of the repairs and has a legal right to retain the car until he is paid for his services. *See* TEX. PROP. CODE § 70.001.

43. Keeton v. State, 803 S.W.2d 304, 305 (Tex. Crim. App. 1991).

44. Compare the list of Texas property with California which declares it felony grand theft to steal more than $100 worth of chickens, turkeys, avocados, olives, citrus, nuts, or artichokes or any horse, mule, sheep, or pig. Florida labels as felony any theft of a will, a fire extinguisher, a stop sign, or commercially raised livestock or fish.

45. PERKINS, *supra*, at 311.

46. *See, e.g.*, Robinson v. State, 11 Tex. Ct. App. 403 (1882); Sessions v. State, 274 S.W. 580 (Tex. Crim. App. 1925); *and* Harrison v. State, 200 S.W.2d 409 (Tex. Crim. App. 1946).

47. TEX. PENAL CODE § 31.01(1)(A).

48. McQueen v. State, 781 S.W.2d 600 (Tex. Crim. App. 1989).

49. TEX. PENAL CODE § 8.02(a).

50. "The heading of a title, subtitle, chapter, subchapter, or section does not limit or expand the meaning of a statute." TEX. GOV'T CODE § 311.024.

51. Denton v. State, 911 S.W.2d 388 (Tex. Crim. App. 1995).

52. *See* Anthony v. State, 628 S.W.2d 151 (Tex. App.— Houston [14th Dist.] 1982). See also Longest v. State, 732 S.W.2d 83 (Tex. App.—Amarillo 1987), a UUV case wherein the law of parties is applied to an individual who handed over the key to a tractor that an accomplice then drove.

53. Unauthorized use of vehicle is a lesser included offense of theft. Hoffman v. State, 877 S.W.2d 501 (Tex. App.—Fort Worth 1994).

54. Under normal circumstances, operating an airplane without a motor is not a good idea. The UUV statute would apply, however, to the nonpermissioned flying of sailplanes, gliders, and the like.

55. McLemore v. State, 669 S.W.2d 856 (Tex. App.— Austin 1984).

56. *See* Villareal v. State, 809 S.W.2d 295 (Tex. App.— Corpus Christi 1991), *and* Dodson v. State, 800 S.W.2d 592 (Tex. App.—Houston [14th Dist.] 1990).

57. 18 U.S.C. §§ 2311–2313.

58. *See* UNITED STATES ATTORNEY'S MANUAL §§ 9–61. 111–9–61.113 (Oct. 1997).

59. "It is obvious that these definitions are suggested examples that are included within the term 'service.' " Prowell v. State, 541 S.W.2d 432, 433 (Tex. Crim. App. 1976). Does the language of the court mean that the statutory list of services is not all inclusive? Can other services be the basis of prosecution for theft of service?

60. Manley v. State, 633 S.W.2d 881 (Tex. Crim. App. 1982).

61. Reger v. State, 598 S.W.2d 868 (Tex. Crim. App. 1980).

62. *See* TEX. PENAL CODE § 8.02(a).

63. *See* TEX. PENAL CODE § 31.08.

64. Some jurisdictions take the position that where rent is paid in advance by a bad check, services (the right to occupy a space) have been obtained by deception and there is a clear violation of the law but, where the rent is paid by a bad check at the end of a rental period, it cannot be said that the services were obtained by means of deception, unless it can be proved that the intent of the renter at the time of the rental was to not pay the rent when due. [*See* Op. Ky. Att'y Gen. 75–273 (1975)]. No Texas appellate court cases are known to speak to this question.

65. Cortez v. State, 582 S.W.2d 119 (Tex. Crim. App. 1979).

66. Johnson v. State, 2005 Tex. App. LEXIS 10335.

67. Gibson v. State, 623 S.W.2d 324 (Tex. Crim. App. 1981).

68. See Garcia v. State, 669 S.W.2d 169 (Tex. App.— Dallas 1984), wherein presenting a stolen credit card to a merchant to purchase a ring was held to be an act of deception for the purposes of the theft statute.

69. The automatic suspension of a driver's license based on conviction of acquiring motor fuel without payment explicitly requires that the offender be found guilty of a violation of § 31.03. Sec. 31.04 is not mentioned in the statute. *See* TEX. TRANSP. CODE § 521.349.

70. *See* Manley v. State.

71. Texas courts applied the prior theft statute (Art. 1418) to theft of a computer program in 1964, certainly one of the first instances where a computer program was the object of a crime. *See* Hancock v. State, 402 S.W.2d 906 (Tex. Crim. App. 1966).

72. See McGowan v. State, 938 S.W.2d 732 (Tex. Crim. App. 1996), outlining the factors to consider in determining whether item is a secret.

73. *Id.*

74. *See* TEX. PENAL CODE § 32.42.

75. *See* 49 U.S.C. § 32703.

76. *See* 18 U.S.C. § 1341.

77. *See* 18 U.S.C. § 1343.

78. For a detailed description of many of these Internet-based scams, visit Fraud Watch International, *at* http://www.fraudwatchinternational.com.

79. Landry v. State, 583 S.W.2d 620 (Tex. Crim. App. 1979).

80. *See* TEX. TRANSP. CODE §§ 521.451; 521.453; 521.456 (fraudulent driver's license); TEX. HEALTH & SAFETY CODE § 481.129 (forged prescription); *and* TEX. PENAL CODE § 32.50 (fraudulent academic degrees).

81. Cadd v. State, 587 S.W.2d 736, 739 (Tex. Crim. App. 1979).

82. Jefferson v. State, 705 S.W.2d 717 (Tex. App.—Dallas 1986).

83. A forgery would occur if Cal signed his true name to a check he created on his computer and drawn on a fictitious bank. Such an occurrence would be rare in practice.

84. The penalty increases to a Class B misdemeanor if the worthless check was a child support payment.

85. *See* TEX. CODE CRIM. P. art. 102.007. The statute authorizes collection of a fee in cases involving forgery, theft, theft of service, and issuance of bad check. State law also permits the restitution to be made under the supervision of the court.

86. TEX. CODE CRIM. P. art. 102.007(b).

87. Op. Tex. Att'y Gen. JM-1034 (1989).

88. Presumably the sale of a bogus autograph could be prosecuted as a forgery, a somewhat more serious offense.

89. 18 U.S. Code § 1028.

90. TEX. PENAL CODE § 32.51.

91. In an unusual application of its statute, California used the identity theft law to charge the former chairwoman and the former legal counsel of a major computer manufacturer, as well as the private detectives they hired, for illegally collecting personal information about the corporation's board of directors during an internal probe. The detectives posed as the board members in order to gather personal information about them from third parties. *See* Ellen Nakashima and Yuki Noguchi, *Dunn, Four Others Charged in Hewlett Surveillance Case*, THE WASHINGTON POST, Oct. 5, 2006, at A01.

CHAPTER

10

Robbery

BOLO

The reader should be on the lookout (BOLO) for the meaning of the following terms. Knowledge of the meaning of these terms will greatly assist the reader in understanding the primary elements of the chapter.

- Common Law robbery
- Deadly weapon
- Disabled person
- Exhibits deadly weapon

- In the course of committing theft
- Places in fear
- Uses deadly weapon

> *"Now," says Ben Rogers, "what's the line of business of this Gang?"*
> *"Nothing only robbery and murder," Tom said.*
> *"But who are we going to rob?—houses, or cattle, or—"*
> *"Stuff! stealing cattle and such things ain't robbery; it's burglary," says Tom Sawyer. "We ain't burglars. That ain't no sort of style. We are highwaymen. We stop stages and carriages on the road, with masks on, and kill people and take their watches and money."*
>
> Mark Twain, *Adventures of Huckleberry Finn* (1885)

INTRODUCTION

Tom Sawyer had it mostly right even if Ben Rogers did not. Robbery is an offense misunderstood by many individuals. While the crime has a specific legal definition, many people still use the term to describe a variety of theft-related behavior. Consider the following scenarios:

Mike comes home from a weekend at the beach to find that someone has broken into his apartment and stolen his plasma screen television set. Mike calls the police and says, "I've been robbed."

Meanwhile, Carla who has been shopping at the mall returns to the parking lot to find that the window on her car has been smashed and someone has stolen the Christmas presents she had placed in the rear seat. She finds the mall security officer and tells him, "I've been robbed."

Later the same evening, Katie, who is working the late shift at her uncle's convenience store, looks up and sees a menacing individual holding a pistol. The man says, "Give me the money." Katie complies with his demand and the individual flees. Katie dials 9-1-1 and tells the police dispatcher, "I've been robbed."

Finally, Herb has a leaking roof on his home repaired by Acme Roofing Company. When Herb gets the bill, it is double what he expected. "This bill is robbery. No one else would charge this much for such a small job," he tells the roofing company owner.

In the four scenarios only one person has actually been robbed—Katie. Mike and Carla have certainly been the victims of serious crimes but their offenses are not robberies. Likewise, while Herb may well be correct that the charge for repairing his roof is excessive, his is a civil dispute unconnected to the criminal law. Only Katie had property taken from her presence through violence or intimidation, the traditional definition of robbery. For reasons unknown, when the average person suffers the loss of valuable property under suspicious or clearly criminal circumstances, they use the term "robbed" to describe their plight. The misuse of the word "robbery" is so ingrained in society that the initial role of a police officer when interviewing a crime victim is to determine if the victim's property loss was a theft, a burglary, or really a robbery.

Robbery accounts for about 30 percent of the nation's violent crime but only 3.5 percent of all serious crime.[1] In Texas, about 36,000 robberies are perpetrated annually. About one-third occur in public areas such as streets and highways. Nearly a quarter are committed in private residences. Surprisingly, only about 20 percent of robberies involve commercial establishments such as convenience stores, liquor stores, and gasoline stations.[2]

Robbery is a bit of a unique crime. Its origin lies in concerns about violent assaults of others, not the taking of their property. In fact, some scholars believe that the crime of robbery actually predates the creation of the crime of larceny. For a period of time in England, thieves were punished more severely than robbers, the logic being that thieves were less noble because they acted by stealth while robbers accomplished their deeds in the open.[3]

During the Medieval times (eleventh to fifteenth centuries for the purposes of this text) many individuals lived in walled cities. Travelers from one community to another were especially vulnerable to being attacked by thieves. Not only might they lose their money but "highwaymen" might also take the victim's horse, carriage, and clothing. Thus, the victim was left stranded with no way to continue his journey. Under the circumstances, loss of life was not beyond the realm of possibility. Indeed, one of the first ever crime prevention laws was enacted to reduce robberies of these lone travelers. In the year 1285, King Edward I commanded that

> . . . highways from one trading town to another shall be enlarged wherever there are woods, hedges, or ditches; so that there shall be neither ditches, underbrush, nor bushes for two hundred feet on the one side and two hundred feet on the other, where men can hide near the road with evil intent; yet so that this statute shall not apply to oaks or to any great trees, so long as they are cleared underneath.[4]

In practice, robbery is larceny/theft with two additional elements: the property is taken from the actual presence of the victim and it is done so through force or intimidation.

COMMON LAW ROBBERY

During the Common Law period, the crime of **robbery** consisted of the following elements. These elements still appear in some form in virtually all American robbery statutes, including Texas.

1. Forcible taking
2. From the person of another
3. Of goods or money of any value
4. By putting him in fear.[5]

Forcible Taking

Robbery is distinguished from other forms of larcenous behavior by the requirement that the property be taken by force or the threat of force. This distinguishes robbery from other Common Law offenses such as larceny, embezzlement, and extortion. None of these offenses required force although each involved the taking of property.

Assume Sam points a pistol at Andrew and demands Andrew's money. Andrew happily informs Sam that he has no money. Sam departs empty-handed. Sam has not committed robbery under the Common Law definition because he did not take any property; he did, of course, commit attempted robbery.

From the Person of Another

Taking property from the person of another requires that the items actually be located on the victim or within his immediate control. Whereas theft is traditionally viewed as a crime of stealth—the offender chooses to commit his illegal act out of the sight of others—robbery requires some level of interaction between the robber and the victim. Property is on the victim's person if it is in some way attached to the body or the clothing. Forcing an individual to turn over his wallet under threat of being stabbed with a knife certainly qualifies as a robbery because the wallet was on the victim's person. Likewise, requiring a store clerk to empty the cash drawer under threat of being shot constitutes robbery since the cash was in the clerk's presence.

Property is in the presence of the victim if the victim is sufficiently close to the property that he could prevent it from being taken but for the intimidation of the offender. The law takes a relatively broad view of this element. For example, Phillip enters a grocery store with a pistol. He forces the employees into a storeroom and latches the door. Phillip then empties the cash register. A robbery has occurred because the employees could have controlled the cash register except for Phillip's intimidating actions.

For the offense of robbery, the property sought to be stolen need not be owned by the party from whom it is taken. As an example, John's employer entrusts John with the daily receipts of the employer's business. John is to transport the monies to the bank. En route Walter assaults John and takes the money. Walter has committed robbery even though the money he obtained from John did not belong to John.

Of Goods or Money of Any Value

Robbery traditionally is limited to efforts to take personal, moveable property. (Recall the distinction between personal property and real property discussed in Chapter 9.) Forcing someone to execute a deed to real estate would not be considered robbery because no personal property is involved in the incident. Likewise, a robbery charge would not exist where an offender used force to unlawfully evict another from real estate because, once again, property, but not personal property, was seized.

Unlike theft laws, the value of the money or goods taken is irrelevant to the severity of the robbery offense. Under the Common Law and in most jurisdictions today, robbery for a $10 watch is the same level of offense as robbery for $10,000 in cash.

By Putting Him in Fear

The Common Law requirement of placing the victim in fear has been relaxed over the years to include placing the victim in reasonable apprehension of personal harm. An assault to facilitate the theft is a key factor in committing the crime of robbery. A threat to injure the victim or actual injury to the victim in accomplishing the theft elevates the behavior to robbery. If Tony threatens to strike George unless George gives Tony his money, Tony has committed robbery. If Lucy is sitting on a park bench feeding the birds and Charles from behind strikes Lucy with a stick and steals her purse, Charles has committed robbery.

On the other hand, a threat to damage the victim's property or subject him to ridicule is insufficient to establish robbery. Thus, if Mike threatens to damage Frank's new automobile unless Mike gives him $50, theft, not robbery, has occurred.

Likewise, if the victim resists an attempt to take the property, and the offender overcomes the resistance, sufficient violence has occurred to constitute a robbery. The same holds true if personal injury occurs. Assume Mitch is a diamond salesman carrying a briefcase full of precious gems. Mitch places the briefcase on the floor while tying his shoe. Phillip shoves Mitch aside, grabs the briefcase, and flees. A robbery has occurred. Under the same facts, if Mitch and Phillip had struggled over the briefcase before Phillip was successful in stealing it, a robbery likewise has occurred.

The placing in apprehension of personal harm alternative as an element of robbery raises interesting legal questions. Many robberies occur when the victim is intimidated into surrendering his or her property through a threat of harm to his or her person. Like the crime of assault, which of course is one of the bases of robbery, most jurisdictions do not require that the victim actually be afraid but merely placed in apprehension of bodily harm. Thus, one too brave to be frightened could still be in apprehension of bodily harm.

The immediacy of the violence or threat is also important. Threatening a violent act at some future time unless the victim parts with property seems better handled by the law of theft or by specialized statutes such as extortion or blackmail.

TEXAS LAW OF ROBBERY

§ 29.01. Definitions

In this chapter:

1. "In the course of committing theft" means conduct that occurs in an attempt to commit, during the commission, or in immediate flight after the attempt or commission of theft.
2. "Property" means:
    A. tangible or intangible personal property including anything severed from land; or
    B. a document, including money, that represents or embodies anything of value.

§ 29.02. Robbery

a. A person commits an offense if, in the course of committing theft as defined in Chapter 31 and with intent to obtain or maintain control of the property, he:
    1. intentionally, knowingly, or recklessly causes bodily injury to another; or
    2. intentionally or knowingly threatens or places another in fear of imminent bodily injury or death.
b. An offense under this section is a felony of the second degree.

Introduction

The Texas law of robbery is based upon an assault occurring while the offender is in the process of committing theft. Indeed, the statute is a virtual verbatim compounding of Sec. 22.01 (Assault) and Sec. 31.01 (Theft). Despite its placement within the Texas Penal Code in Title 7, Offenses against Property, Texas courts follow the Common Law principle and consider robbery to be a form of personal crime, not an aggravated form of theft. Consequently, if an offender assaults two victims during the course of the robbery, two, not one, robberies have occurred.[6] The primary interest protected by the robbery statute is the security of the person from bodily injury, or threat of bodily injury, that might occur in the course of a theft. If the assaultive conduct involves a deadly weapon or produces serious bodily injury, the conduct elevates to the offense of aggravated robbery.

Elements of Robbery

The following paragraphs highlight key elements of the robbery statute (Sec. 29.02).

In the Course of Committing Theft

The Texas robbery statute greatly expands the scope of Common Law robbery and also changes prior state law.[7] The current statute does not require an actual taking of property but rather recognizes that the process of stealing, not the actual nonconsensual seizure of property, is where the harm arises. A robbery occurs whenever the offender is **in the course of committing theft**. Sec. 29.01 contains a definition of this phrase. Under the definition, the assaultive behavior of the offender may occur anytime during the attempt to commit theft. It may occur during the actual commission of the theft. Or, it may occur during the immediate flight from the effort at theft.

Suppose John shoves down Helen and grabs her purse. Helen, however, hangs on tenaciously to the purse strap and starts to scream. John abandons his efforts and flees empty-handed. John has committed robbery because he assaulted Helen as he was attempting to commit theft. The success of his efforts matter not. He assaulted Helen while in the course of committing theft. The broadness of the definition of "in the course of committing theft" renders unnecessary an offense of attempted robbery since the definition includes attempts. A completed theft is not a necessary element of the crime of robbery. Hence, unsuccessful robbers in Texas are charged with robbery, not with attempted robbery.[8]

Had John been successful in obtaining Helen's purse, he would also have committed robbery. Sec. 29.02 would have been violated because he assaulted her in commission of the theft.

The third possibility, assault during the immediate flight, raises interesting questions of time and space. Suppose Ron grabs a six-pack of beer in the local convenience store and runs out without paying. The clerk gives chase and tackles Ron. Ron punches the clerk in the face and flees, leaving the beer behind. Has Ron committed robbery? Clearly yes. He committed a theft and in the immediate flight from the theft assaulted the store clerk. But what is meant by the term "immediate flight"? The "immediate flight" phrase has been judicially defined as "a reasonable time in view of particular facts and circumstances of case under consideration."[9] Assume that Marla, a shoplifter, is apprehended by a store security guard. She is placed in the store office pending arrival of the police. Twenty minutes later Marla becomes violent and attempts to escape. The security guard is injured trying to subdue her. In a similar case, a Texas appellate court ruled that the injury occurred "in the immediate flight" after the attempted theft and affirmed a conviction for robbery.[10] The Court of Criminal Appeals also found that a robbery had occurred when a theft suspect struggled with a police officer who was trying to arrest him 100 yards from the scene. The arrest was effected about eight minutes after the suspect had stolen money from a dry cleaner's cash register.[11] Appeals courts have shown reluctance in overturning jury determinations of what constitutes "in the immediate flight."

Likewise, robbery was held to be the offense when a van owner interrupted an individual stealing a toolbox from the vehicle. The thief dropped the box and a struggle ensued between him and the van owner. Van owner was kicked in groin and thief escaped, only to be apprehended later. At trial, the defendant argued he had abandoned the property upon discovery by the owner, therefore no robbery occurred. However, the trial court, and a subsequent appeals court, found that the defendant remained "in the course of committing theft" even if he truly abandoned the toolbox.[12]

In an unusual case, a Texas court ruled that under the prior penal code stealing a police officer's firearm during the course of resisting arrest met the definition of robbery.[13] The same finding could occur under the current penal code.[14]

With Intent to Obtain or Maintain Control of the Property

For a robbery to occur, a connection must exist between the assault element and the theft element. In particular, the assault must be geared toward obtaining the property or maintaining control of it after it is stolen. In most situations, the assault is necessary for the offender to initially gain control over the property he seeks. Recall John knocking Helen to the ground in an effort to obtain her purse. In contrast, the earlier scenario of Ron fleeing with the six-pack of beer also demonstrates the point of the connection between the assault and the theft. His subsequent assault of the pursuing clerk was in an effort to maintain control over the property he had previously stolen. Ron had already stolen the beer without using force. His use of force against the clerk was an effort to keep possession of the beer.

The Court of Criminal Appeals has recognized that while in most circumstances an assault committed during a theft will equal a robbery, there is the possibility that one of the offenses could be separate from the other and thereby not constitute robbery.[15] Assume Bob and Ray get into an argument. A fistfight erupts between the two. Ultimately, Bob beats Ray severely, knocking him prone on the ground. As Bob is departing he picks up Ray's ballcap from the ground and places it on his own head. While Bob may have committed assault and theft, he did not commit robbery because the assault did not facilitate the taking of the ballcap. In other words, Bob's assault was not committed with the purpose of obtaining the ballcap. In this scenario, Bob could be convicted of theft from the person, a state jail felony.[16]

The statutory phrase "with intent to obtain or maintain control over property" is the equivalent of the term "appropriate" found in the theft statute, Sec. 31.03.[17]

Intentionally, Knowingly, or Recklessly Causes Bodily Injury to Another

This element is identical to the offense of assault with bodily injury under Sec. 22.01(a)(1).[18] It expands the traditional law of robbery substantially by including not only purposeful injury to the victim but also circumstances wherein the victim is injured through the robber's reckless conduct. Thus, any assault with bodily injury through recklessness would qualify. Assume Frank smashes the window of a jewelry store and grabs a display of expensive wristwatches. Frank then jumps on his motorcycle in an effort to flee. Instead of driving on the street, however, Frank guides his motorcycle along the sidewalk at high speed. Several pedestrians must jump out of his way. Gwen leaps to avoid the motorcycle and injures herself when she hits the sidewalk. Frank's "smash and grab" theft has become a robbery because Gwen suffered bodily injury due to his reckless conduct in his immediate flight from the theft.[19]

It should be noted that the robbery statute only requires bodily injury to "another," not bodily injury to the "owner." Hence, a robbery is complete even if the victim of the theft and the victim of the assault are different individuals, so long as the theft and the assault are connected.[20] For example, Ed enters a store and places an article of merchandise in his pocket intending to steal it. The clerk across the room sees Ed's actions and shouts, "Hey you!" Ed panics and runs for the door. Aaron, another customer, tries to stop Ed. Ed shoves Aaron to the floor, causing Aaron to injure his hand. Ed has committed robbery because he caused bodily injury to another.[21] In a somewhat unusual real case, a conviction for robbery of a convenience store was upheld where the offender caused a three-year-old to suffer bruises when he shoved the child into a cash register.[22]

Recall the definition of "bodily injury" found in Sec. 1.07. The term encompasses harm as minor as temporary pain, bruises, strains, and sprains. Accordingly, robbery victims need not suffer great injury in order to establish the elements of the offense under Sec. 20.02(a)(1).

Or, Intentionally or Knowingly Threatens/Places in Fear of Bodily Injury or Death

The alternative means of committing robbery is by threat or placing in fear. Most robberies fall within this subform of the offense. The offender verbally threatens the victim with imminent bodily injury unless the victim complies with his demands. Bart approaches Ned on the street and in a menacing tone says, "Give me your money or I'll kill you!" Such conduct is robbery.

A verbal demand is not a necessary element of the offense.[23] Either words or acts can be threatening. Similarly a threat could be in written form. Consider the demand note that a bank robber might hand to the bank teller; that note is an intentional threat to do bodily injury unless the robber's demands are met.

While assault by threat as defined in Sec. 22.01(a)(2) is sufficient for this element of the offense of robbery, the statutory provision is slightly broader. Robbery also may be committed by placing the victim in fear of imminent bodily injury or death. While the statute requires that the offender intend or know his actions will place the victim in fear, whether or not fear results may vary with the individual victim's reaction. However, the fear must arise from the conduct of the suspect rather than the timidity of the victim.[24] The test is: would the ordinary person be in fear under the same circumstances? In one case, the defendant walked into a convenience store carrying a three-foot long machete and asked for water. Because she was fearful of the defendant, the clerk told him to get the water himself. Defendant exited the store with the water. The defendant was convicted of aggravated robbery even though he claimed he was going to his van to retrieve his wallet when police arrived and arrested him. Appellate court ruled that evidence was sufficient to establish that defendant intended to place the clerk in fear of imminent bodily injury.[25]

Assume three teenage males dressed in stereotypical urban gang-like clothing surround an elderly pedestrian who is walking down a dimly lit street late at night. One of the youths says gruffly, "Can you spare some money to help send wayward youths to summer camp?" Is this a robbery by placing in fear? Certainly the elderly individual is likely to perceive it as so and be fearful of imminent bodily injury unless he gives the trio some cash. On the other hand, are the youths intentionally placing him in fear and are they attempting a theft? Perhaps the elderly individual's reaction is based on his own biases and perspective of the event. The facts are certainly ambiguous at best at this stage.

Placing another in fear of imminent bodily injury would not necessarily require a face-to-face confrontation. A threat over the telephone might be sufficient, so long as the fear of injury was imminent. In one case, an individual robbed a shoe store by telephoning the clerk, instructing her to place cash in a bag, and place it behind a building down the street. The caller stated that he was watching the clerk from outside and would harm her if she did not follow instructions.[26] The caller's conduct would seem sufficient to constitute robbery by placing in fear.

The risk of bodily injury or death must be "imminent," however. The term "imminent" in the context of robbery means ready to take place or near at hand. If the threat is not imminent, such as Tom demanding money from Bill over the telephone and threatening to injure Bill the next time Tom sees him, the proper charge is theft by coercion.[27] Indeed, one factor that distinguishes a robbery from some forms of extortion (threat by coercion in Texas) is the lack of immediacy in carrying out the threat.[28]

Penalty

Robbery is a felony of the second degree, regardless of the factual circumstances surrounding the event. For instance, the amount of money taken is irrelevant to the level of punishment as is the degree of injury, if any, actually caused to the victim. The sentencing authority, jury or judge, would of course consider these factors in deciding the level of punishment.

Elements of Aggravated Robbery

If an offender commits robbery and one of four special conditions exist, the crime elevates to aggravated robbery. Assuming the elements of Sec. 22.02 occur, the matter rises to aggravated robbery if the robber:

- Causes serious bodily injury, or
- Uses or exhibits a deadly weapon, or
- Causes bodily injury or threatens or places in fear of imminent bodily injury, etc., a person 65 or older, or
- Causes bodily injury or threatens or places in fear of imminent bodily injury, etc., a disabled person.

§ 29.03. Aggravated Robbery

a. A person commits an offense if he commits robbery as defined in Section 29.02, and he:
1. causes serious bodily injury to another;
2. uses or exhibits a deadly weapon; or
3. causes bodily injury to another person or threatens or places another person in fear of imminent bodily injury or death, if the other person is:
   A. 65 years of age or older; or
   B. a disabled person.

b. An offense under this section is a felony of the first degree.

c. In this section, "disabled person" means an individual with a mental, physical, or developmental disability who is substantially unable to protect himself from harm.

Causes Serious Bodily Injury

The aggravated robbery statute essentially grafts the aggravated assault with serious bodily injury statute [Sec. 22.02(a)(1)] onto the theft statute. Thus, if the assaultive element of a robbery constitutes "serious bodily injury" instead of simple "bodily injury," then the matter elevates to aggravated robbery. The term "serious bodily injury" is defined in Sec. 1.07(46) as "bodily injury that creates a substantial risk of death or that causes death, serious permanent disfigurement, or protracted loss or impairment of the function of any bodily member or organ." By way of example, if Peter, in the course of stealing Paula's purse, shoves her to the ground causing her to break an arm, Peter has committed aggravated robbery due to the severity of Paula's resultant injury. For a fuller discussion of which injuries constitute "serious bodily injury" review the discussion of aggravated assault in Chapter 6.

The crime of aggravated robbery occurs even if the offender kills the victim in the course of the robbery, since death is a form of "serious bodily injury." Such an act would normally be charged as a capital murder. However, if the death occurred through recklessness, instead of intent or knowledge, the suspect would face aggravated robbery and murder charges.[29] Suppose Tony enters the bank and announces "This is a stick-up!" He then fires a pistol in the air to scare everyone. The bullet ricochets, passes through the bank's glass window, and strikes a passing motorist Jeff. Jeff dies from the wound. Since the death during the course of the aggravated robbery was unintentional, Tony would not face capital murder charges but would face aggravated robbery charges and murder charges under the Felony Murder Rule, causing a death during the course of commission of a clearly dangerous felony.[30]

While death is a form of serious bodily injury under Texas law, stealing the wallet or wristwatch from an already deceased individual would more appropriately be considered a theft, not aggravated robbery.[31]

Or, Uses or Exhibits a Deadly Weapon

Over half of the robberies committed in Texas involve use or exhibition of a firearm or knife.[32] Firearms and knives are **deadly weapons** within the statutory definition.[33] Other forms of deadly weapons also can elevate a robbery to an aggravated robbery. For example, under certain fact situations, automobiles have been ruled to have been deadly weapons for the purpose of the aggravated robbery statute.[34] Virtually anything can become a deadly weapon depending on its manner of use.[35] (A detailed discussion of which items constitute a "deadly weapon" is found in Chapter 6.)

To establish aggravated robbery under this subsection, it must be shown that the defendant used or exhibited the deadly weapon during the course of the robbery. The Texas Court of Criminal Appeals has ruled "[a] person 'uses or exhibits a deadly weapon' under the aggravated robbery statute if he employs the weapon in any manner that facilitates the associated felony."[36] The court cautioned, however, "We are not equating mere possession with 'use or exhibit' under Texas Penal Code §29.03(a)(2). Rather, the determining factor is that the deadly weapon was 'used' in facilitating the underlying crime."[37]

Discovery after a robbery that the suspect is in possession of a deadly weapon is not proof that he used or exhibited it. On the other hand, the victim need not observe the deadly weapon during the robbery. An appeals court held that the defendant's admission that he used a knife, even though the victim never saw it, was sufficient to establish use of a deadly weapon in an aggravated robbery trial.[38] In another case, the existence of the firearm was proven with the victim's testimony that she never saw the weapon but heard it being cocked and felt a hard object placed at her back.[39] Similarly, if Pat robs Mike while carrying a shotgun, Pat has committed aggravated robbery even if he never points the shotgun at Mike; he has "exhibited" the weapon.

Or, Causes Bodily Injury etc. to a Person 65 or Older

An ordinary robbery committed against a victim 65 years of age or older is elevated to an aggravated robbery. Any of the three methods of robbery (e.g., bodily injury, threat, placing in fear) qualify. An individual reaches their chronological age on the anniversary of his or her birth date.[40] No requirement exists that the perpetrator be aware of the actual age of the robbery victim.

Or, Causes Bodily Injury etc. to a Disabled Person

As with older victims, a robbery increases to an aggravated robbery if the victim is a **disabled person**. Sec. 29.03(c)(3) provides a definition of who qualifies as a disabled person. The prosecution is not required to prove that the offender knew or should have known that the victim was a person with a disability.

Penalty

All aggravated robberies are classified as felonies of the first degree.

ISSUES IN ROBBERY

The Texas robbery statute, while a relatively modern piece of legislation, leaves open to question several issues. Ultimately the Legislature or the courts will need to address them.

What about a carjacking? Carjacking, the taking of another's motor vehicle by threat of force, has increased substantially in recent years. Some experts attribute the rise to the increased difficulty in stealing unattended vehicles. Most carjackings appear to involve armed individuals who threaten a driver and steal the motor vehicle to use it for temporary transportation. Since the carjacker has no intent to permanently deprive the owner of the vehicle, the taking of the automobile alone would usually be considered a violation of Sec. 31.07, unauthorized use of a vehicle. If the theft element of robbery is viewed as covering all offenses in Chapter 31, the carjacking is an aggravated robbery. If the theft element is intended only to cover violations of Sec. 31.03, no robbery has occurred as an element of theft—intent to deprive—is absent. Texas courts have consistently ruled that the "intent to deprive" element of auto theft is not proved when the evidence indicates that the automobile was taken for temporary use.[41] To date, the Legislature has not clarified how the current robbery statute dovetails with carjacking.[42] In a 2005 unpublished decision, the Court of Appeals considered the defendant's argument that his carjacking did not violate the robbery statute because he intended to use the vehicle only temporarily. The court rejected the argument on the grounds that sufficient facts existed for the jury to find that the defendant intended to permanently deprive the owner of the car.[43]

Bucking the trend across the nation, Texas has not enacted a home invasion statute despite the fact that about one-quarter of all robberies occurs in private residences.[44] A forcible entry into a private residence for the purposes of robbing the occupants is treated under Texas law as two independent offenses: a burglary and an aggravated robbery. Since both of these crimes are felonies of the first degree, a standalone home invasion statute is unnecessary and would likely be redundant to existing law.

CRIMEGRAPH
Robbery

Offense	Underlying offense	Culpable mental state	Conduct	Who?	Specific intent/knowledge	Penalty
Robbery 29.02(a)(1)	While in the course of committing theft (Ch. 31)	1. Intentionally, or 2. Knowingly, or 3. Recklessly	Causes bodily injury	Another	With intent to obtain or maintain control of the property	F2
Robbery 29.02(a)(2)	While in the course of committing theft (Ch. 31)	1. Intentionally or 2. Knowingly	1. Threatens or 2. Places in fear of imminent bodily injury or death	Another	With intent to obtain or maintain control of the property	F2
Aggravated Robbery 29.03(a)(1)	Robbery Sec. 29.02(a)		Causes serious bodily injury	Another		F1
Aggravated Robbery 29.03(a)(2)	Robbery Sec. 29.02(a)		1. Uses deadly weapon or 2. Exhibits deadly weapon			F1
Aggravated Robbery 29.03(a)(3)	Robbery Sec. 29.02(a)		1. Causes bodily injury, or 2. Threatens, or 3. Places in fear of imminent bodily injury or death	Person: 1. 65 or older or 2. Disabled		F1

Notes

1. FEDERAL BUREAU OF INVESTIGATION, CRIME IN AMERICA-UNIFORM CRIME REPORTS 2005 (2006).

2. TEX. DEP'T OF PUB. SAFETY, THE TEXAS CRIME REPORT FOR 2006 (2007).

3. *See* 1 FREDERICK POLLOCK & FREDERIC W. MAITLAND, THE HISTORY OF ENGLISH LAW 493–494 (2nd ed. 1899).

4. Statute of Winchester, 13 Edw. I, stat. 2, ch. 4 (1285).

5. 4 WILLIAM BLACKSTONE, COMMENTARIES *241.

6. *Ex parte* Hawkins, 6 S.W.3d 554 (Tex. Crim. App. 1999).

7. Prior to 1974, the Texas robbery statute (1925 TEX. PENAL CODE art. 1408) required that threats or violence had to occur prior to the taking of the property and had to put the person from whom the property was taken in fear so that he would more readily part with his property. *See* Crawford v. State, 509 S.W.2d 582 (Tex. Crim. App. 1974).

8. Robinson v. State, 596 S.W.2d 130 (Tex. Crim. App. 1976).

9. Thomas v. State, 708 S.W.2d 580, 581 (Tex. App.—Eastland 1986).

10. *Id.*

11. Lightner v. State, 535 S.W.2d 176 (Tex. Crim. App. 1976).

12. Yarbrough v. State, 656 S.W.2d 200 (Tex. App.—Austin 1983).

13. Stout v. State, 467 S.W.2d 409 (Tex. Crim. App. 1971).

14. *See also* TEX. PENAL CODE § 38.14.

15. Ibanez v. State, 749 S.W.2d 804 (Tex. Crim. App. 1986).

16. TEX. PENAL CODE § 31.03(e)(4)(B).

17. Martinez v. State, 644 S.W.2d 486 (Tex. Crim. App. 1983).

18. See discussion of assault with bodily injury in Chapter 6.

19. Frank may also have committed burglary when he smashed the store window. *See* Chapter 11.

20. Royster v. State, 622 S.W.2d 442 (Tex. Crim. App. 1981).

21. Servance v. State, 537 S.W.2d 753 (Tex. Crim. App. 1976); Turner v. State, 2003 Tex. App. LEXIS 1809.

22. Finch v. State, 2003 Tex. App. LEXIS 10345.

23. Garza v. State, 937 S.W.2d 569 (Tex. App.—San Antonio 1996).

24. Stout v. State.

25. Robertson v. State, 2003 Tex. App. LEXIS 8650.

26. *See* Alan Sembera, *Man robs shoe store by phone*, CONROE COURIER, Mar. 15, 1990, p. 1.

27. Devine v. State, 786 S.W.2d 268 (Tex. Crim. App. 1989).

28. During the early development of the Common Law, robbery and extortion were viewed as related offenses.

29. TEX. PENAL CODE § 19.03(a)(2).

30. TEX. PENAL CODE § 19.02(b)(3).

31. See TEX. PENAL CODE § 31.03(e)(4)(B) declaring theft from a human corpse to be a state jail felony.

32. *See* THE TEXAS CRIME REPORT FOR 2006, *supra*.

33. TEX. PENAL CODE § 1.07(17).

34. McCall v. State, 113 S.W.3d 479 (Tex. App.—Houston [1st Dist.] 2003).

35. Some of the more bizarre examples include an Oregon case holding that a pair of cowboy boots with pointed toes was a deadly weapon in a robbery; an Indiana case finding a robbery with deadly weapon when the suspect used an office stapler; and a Massachusetts case where the robber's weapon of choice was a German shepherd dog. *See* State v. Bell, 771 P.2d 305 (Or. Ct. App. 1989); Cummings v. State, 384 N.E.2d 605 (Ind. 1979); and Commonwealth v. Tarrant, 326 N.E.2d 710 (Mass. 1975).

36. McCain v. State, 22 S.W.3d 497, 502 (Tex. Crim. App. 2000).

37. *Id. at* 503.

38. Herring v. State, 202 S.W.3d 764 (Tex. Crim. App. 2006).

39. Benavidez v. State, 670 S.W.2d 297 (Tex. App.—Amarillo 1983).

40. TEX. PENAL CODE § 1.06.

41. *See* Flores v. State, 888 S.W.2d 187 (Tex. App.—Houston [1st Dist.] 1994), *citing* Kiser v. State, 150 S.W.2d 257 (Tex. Crim. App. 1941).

42. Several cases involving carjackings have been reviewed by Texas courts. In one case, the defendant pled guilty to an aggravated robbery charge after unsuccessfully trying to carjack a motor vehicle. Bibaud v. State, 2001 Tex. App. LEXIS 5982. In another case, the defendant was convicted of capital murder during a carjacking. He received a life sentence. Here the appeals court simply assumed that the robbery statute was applicable to carjacking. *See* Montgomery v. State, 2002 Tex. App. LEXIS 8878. In Patton v. State, 2004 Tex. App. LEXIS 5531, the court also assumes that the temporary use of a vehicle can be the basis of a robbery. See also Nevil v. State, 157 S.W.2d 884 (Tex. Crim. App. 1941), wherein the same issue was unsuccessfully argued in the context of the now repealed robbery by assault statute (Art. 1408).

43. Williams v. State, 2005 Tex. App. LEXIS 2059.

44. *See* THE TEXAS CRIME REPORT FOR 2006, *supra*.

CHAPTER

11

Burglary and Criminal Trespass

BOLO

The reader should be on the lookout (BOLO) for the meaning of the following terms. Knowledge of the meaning of these terms will greatly assist the reader in understanding the primary elements of the chapter.

- Break into
- Building
- Coin-operated machine
- Common Law burglary
- Constructive breaking
- Curtilage
- Defiant trespasser
- Effective consent
- Enter

- Frightening trespasser
- Habitation
- Notice
- Nuisance trespasser
- Property
- Public forum
- Trespass
- Vehicle

INTRODUCTION TO BURGLARY

It is the middle of the night. You are sound asleep. Suddenly the noise of breaking glass. You awake with a start. You realize someone is trying to break into your home. Primal concerns of vulnerability and self-preservation rush through your body. You now understand all too well why the crime of burglary was created!

Under the English Common Law, **burglary** was defined as the breaking and entering the dwelling house of another in the nighttime with intent to commit a felony therein. Burglary was a felony which at one time, like all felonies, was punishable by death. The term derives from the Saxon "burg," meaning house, and "laron," meaning theft—literally theft at a house.[1]

While contemporary penal codes tend to categorize the offense as a crime against property, burglary was originally considered to be a crime against the sanctity of one's habitation. Other felonies, such as larceny and rape, already covered the conduct that might occur after the offender entered the dwelling. Thus, early Western society was concerned with more than mere theft of property. Since the law of larceny predated the rise of the offense of burglary, one can only assume that other social concerns were at work. The fact that the offense originally could occur only in the nighttime provides a clue. Unlike many members of the animal kingdom, human beings are particularly vulnerable at night. Human vision is poor in the dark. Further, humans generally sleep during the nighttime hours. Each of these factors makes the individual less able to protect himself and his property. To increase one's level of security, particularly in times of high risk, such as the night, humans retire to the safety of their homes. They close and latch the door. Protection from harm is now assumed. Thus, an intrusion into this zone of safety is particularly disturbing and raises a potential for violent confrontation between the homeowner and the intruder. The crime of burglary sought to prevent and punish this serious breach of the sanctity of one's home.

Additionally, underlying the crime of burglary is the well-known legal concept: "A man's home is his castle." When the English jurist Sir Edward Coke first wrote this maxim in 1682, he added a Latin phrase that translates "and each man's home is his safest refuge."[2] Thus, the sanctity and security of one's home is a longstanding aspect of Anglo-American culture. Intrusion into that sanctuary is particularly reviled.[3]

COMMON LAW ELEMENTS OF BURGLARY

Under the Common Law, burglary consisted of the following elements:

1. Breaking
2. Entering
3. The dwelling house
4. Of another
5. In the nighttime
6. With intent
7. To commit a felony therein

A quick review of these elements is useful in understanding the structure and rationale of the modern Texas burglary statutes.

Breaking

The old concept of "breaking" differed from the contemporary meaning of the term. Normally one thinks of forcibly prying open a locked door or window to gain entry, but the Common Law only required the creation of an opening. Entering an open doorway or window was not considered a "breaking." However, opening an unlocked door was a "breaking" because an opening was created that did not previously exist. If Fred climbed through an open window, no burglary occurred. But, if he raised the unlocked window prior to climbing through, the necessary element had occurred.

The concept of breaking appears closely tied to the idea of trespass.[4] One could not commit the offense of burglary unless a nonpermissioned trespass had occurred. The breaking had to be a trespass, that is, without the owner's consent. Consent obtained by fraud or intimidation was considered a **constructive breaking** and was sufficient to establish this element of the offense.

Entering

Entry was also a necessary element of the offense. A would-be burglar who did not manage to gain actual entry had committed only attempted burglary since the entering element was missing. Entry could take several forms: the most obvious, of course, was the offender's entire body entering the premises. But, other possibilities existed. Over the years, case law expanded "entry" to cover reaching through a window with one's arm only, using a stick or wire to reach into the premises, and even casting a fishing line through a window.[5] Entry had not occurred if the tool involved was merely used to accomplish the intrusion as opposed to committing the felony. For example, if Jose, intending to commit theft, inserts a prybar in the door jam of Maria's home and forces the door open but is apprehended before making physical entry, the traditional elements of burglary are not met. In contrast, if Jose, intending to commit theft, reaches through the window of Maria's home with the same prybar in an effort to snare Maria's purse from a nearby table, a burglary has occurred.

Dwelling House

As a crime focusing on the sanctity of a habitation, Common Law burglary applied only to "mansion houses" or "dwelling houses." Thus, breaking and entering a store or a barn would not qualify as burglary under the Common Law because those structures are not dwelling houses.

When the offense developed, however, individuals did not live as they do now. Visiting an authentically restored residence from the nineteenth century or earlier reveals the major differences. Human dwellings, particularly in rural areas, consisted of multiple buildings. Frequently, the domestic living area would consist of a main house with dining and sleeping quarters, a detached structure serving as a kitchen, and, of course, a privy or outhouse.[6] While these structures were separated from each other, they frequently were enclosed within an identifiable fenced area. The domestic buildings inside the fenced area became known as the **curtilage**. The crime of burglary covered entry into any of these domestic buildings, not just the main living quarters. On the other hand, barns, storage sheds, stables, and the like outside of the curtilage were not encompassed by the law of burglary.

The Common Law treated entry and subsequent larceny in a church as constituting a form of burglary, later labeled as the crime of sacrilege. As English jurist Sir Edward Coke quaintly observed, a church is *domus mansionalis Dei*—the dwelling house of God.[7]

Of Another

Since burglary requires a trespass to a possessory interest, one could not normally burglarize one's own home. However, assume Bob rents his home to Ralph, retaining ownership but no right of current possession to the house. An entry and subsequent theft of Ralph's property by Bob would constitute burglary because Ralph's possessory interest and sanctity of habitation were breached.

In the Nighttime

Because of concern of human safety during the nighttime, burglary was limited to that time of day. "Nighttime" became variously defined as the time during which the countenance of a person could not be discerned by natural light or the time between sunset and sunrise. In the early 1900s, the British Parliament enacted a statute establishing "nighttime" as the period of the day between 9 p.m. and 6 a.m.[8] This statute set the stage for focusing the application of the rule on the time of day, not the actual level of illumination. If a would-be burglar entered a house between the statutorily established hours, it was no defense to the charge of burglary that the residence was well lighted. Likewise, a heavy daytime fog that effectively makes visibility difficult did not constitute nighttime for the purposes of the law of burglary.

Behavior that would constitute burglary, except that it occurred in the daytime, would be punished only as the underlying offense. For example, Albert enters John's home and steals his bag of gold while John is working in the fields. Albert has committed not burglary but rather trespass and larceny.

With Intent

Common Law burglary required a general intent to engage in the prohibited conduct but, more importantly, it required that the specific intent to commit the underlying felony be in the offender's mind at the time of entry into the premises. Consequently, one could not be accountable for burglary if he entered the premises without permission but did so only as a mere trespasser, such as to take shelter from the rain. Likewise, entering with or without permission and then deciding to commit a felony could not be prosecuted as burglary. For example, Paul enters a house to avoid a sudden thunderstorm. While in the home he observes a pocket watch and decides to steal it. Paul takes the watch (larceny) and departs. Paul is liable for the larceny and trespass but not burglary.

However, the potential offender need not have been successful in his crime. A suspect who enters a house intending to steal goods but is apprehended before completing his theft is nonetheless guilty of burglary; entry *with intent* is all that the elements of the offense required.

To Commit a Felony Therein

Application of the law of burglary was limited to felonies. However, recall that under the Common Law almost all serious offenses were classified as felonies. Indeed, larceny, the most common reason for a burglary, was a felony regardless of the value of the property taken. Similarly, murder, rape, arson, and robbery were also felonies. If late one night Tommy enters the house that Jack built for the purpose of setting it afire, Tommy commits a burglary.

Unlawful entry and subsequent commission of a misdemeanor did not constitute burglary under the strict interpretation of the Common Law definition. Suppose one night, Ernie, angry with Bert, enters Bert's home without permission and threatens him—an assault. Assault, being only a misdemeanor, could not provide the necessary element of the offense of burglary.

TEXAS LAW OF BURGLARY

Introduction

The Texas law of burglary makes significant modifications to the old Common Law approach to the crime. However, the underlying purpose of the statute remains largely unchanged from those early years. As the Court of Criminal Appeals noted in 1994, "Our burglary statutes are intended to protect the sanctity of private areas, be they habitations, buildings not open to the public, or vehicles. When a burglary is committed, the harm results from the entry itself, because the intrusion violates the occupant's reasonable expectation of privacy. Indeed, once unlawful entry is made, the crime is complete, regardless of whether the intended theft or felony is actually completed."[9] The same court observed in 2006 that "A person charged with burglary . . . is guilty of the offense the moment that he crosses the threshold of a habitation without consent and with the intent to commit the underlying felony."[10]

§ 30.01. Definitions

In this chapter:

1. "Habitation" means a structure or vehicle that is adapted for the overnight accommodation of persons, and includes:
   A. each separately secured or occupied portion of the structure or vehicle; and
   B. each structure appurtenant to or connected with the structure or vehicle.

2. "Building" means any enclosed structure intended for use or occupation as a habitation or for some purpose of trade, manufacture, ornament, or use.

3. "Vehicle" includes any device in, on, or by which any person or property is or may be propelled, moved, or drawn in the normal course of commerce or transportation, except such devices as are classified as "habitation."

§ 30.02. Burglary

a. A person commits an offense if, without the effective consent of the owner, the person:
   1. enters a habitation, or a building (or any portion of a building) not then open to the public with intent to commit a felony, theft, or an assault; or
   2. remains concealed, with intent to commit a felony, theft, or an assault, in a building or habitation; or
   3. enters a building or habitation and commits or attempts to commit a felony, theft, or an assault.

b. For purposes of this section, "enter" means to intrude:
   1. any part of the body; or
   2. any physical object connected with the body.

c. Except as provided in Subsection (d), an offense under this section is a:
   1. state jail felony if committed in a building other than a habitation; or
   2. felony of the second degree if committed in a habitation.

d. An offense under this section is a felony of the first degree if:
   1. the premises are a habitation; and
   2. any party to the offense entered the habitation with intent to commit a felony other than felony theft or committed or attempted to commit a felony other than felony theft.

The prohibition against burglary is found in three distinct statutes:

- Burglary (Sec. 30.02)
- Burglary of coin-operated or coin collection machines (Sec. 30.03)
- Burglary of vehicles (Sec. 30.04)

Elements of Burglary in Texas

Effective Consent

For each of the three broad types of burglary, the absence of **effective consent** is a common and key element. This element replaces the Common Law requirement of a trespass and is much broader in its application. Consent means "assent in fact, whether express or apparent."[11] Thus, when no consent whatsoever is obtained from the property owner, there likewise can be no "effective consent." This is the situation with the overwhelming majority of burglaries. The offender enters the property secretly when the structure or automobile is unoccupied and does so without any permission from the property owner. The Texas Court of Criminal Appeals has ruled that the requirement of lack of effective consent includes the total absence of any consent.[12]

The effective consent element expands Texas burglary law far beyond burglary's Common Law application. The Texas statute requires not only consent but consent that is "effective." For consent to be "effective," it must not be the product of force, threat, or fraud, or given by someone not authorized to give consent, or by an individual who is too young, mentally ill, or intoxicated.[13] Suppose Roger, posing as an employee of the gas company, appears at Hazel's home and announces he is searching for a gas leak. He asks permission to check her kitchen stove. Hazel allows Roger to enter. While in the house Roger steals money from Hazel's purse. Roger has committed theft certainly but also has committed burglary. Thus, if a burglar obtains entry to a structure through fraud, consent was certainly obtained, but not *effective* consent.[14]

Note that Texas law does not require the act of burglary to occur in the nighttime, as was the Common Law rule. The abolition of the nighttime rule is fortunate given that of the nearly 143,000 reported residential burglaries in Texas in 2006, 57 percent occurred in the daytime. Average value of property loss was also greater in daytime burglaries.[15]

The burglary of structures statute (Sec. 30.02) lists three distinct ways a burglary may be committed. Each of the three forms is based on lack of the owner's effective consent:

1. Entering a habitation or building with intent to commit a felony, theft, or assault;
2. Remaining concealed in a building or habitation with intent to commit a felony, theft, or assault; or
3. Entering a habitation or building and attempting to commit or actually committing a felony, theft, or assault.

Enters/Remains Concealed

Two of the three subforms of burglary [Sec. 30.02(a)(1) and Sec. 30.02(a)(2)] require the offender to "enter." Note that in Sec. 30.02 the term "breaking" nowhere appears; the statute focuses on entry only. A subsection of Sec. 30.02 defines the term "enter." Under this definition, complete entry into the structure is not required, only some part of the body or an object connected with the body. Sticking a foot through door is sufficient as is sticking a head through a window.[16] If Bill smashes the display window of a jewelry store and snatches wristwatches, he has committed burglary for he has made an entry. Similarly, entry may be accomplished with a physical object connected to the offender, such as a fishnet, a stick, a pole with a hook, or similar device.[17] Force is not required for an entry and no breaking, either in the Common Law sense or within the ordinary meaning of the term, is necessary. One case holds that mere breaking of a padlock and hasp from a garage door was sufficient to constitute entry under the burglary statute.[18] Another case found that theft of an air conditioning window unit was burglary because the unit was an integral part of the house's wall. Removal of the unit left a gaping hole that destroyed the integrity of the wall. The unit itself qualified as an extension of the body of the offender when he grabbed it.[19] As the Texas Court of Criminal Appeals has noted, " 'To intrude' is the 'act' within the meaning of [the statute]; whether the accused intruded 'any part of' his body or 'any physical object connected with the body' is essentially evidentiary. In either manner employed, the defendant must use his body directly or indirectly to commit the offense."[20]

An unanswered question on the issue of the definition of "enter" concerns remote-controlled devices. No reported Texas court decision has considered whether the use of a radio-controlled robot to effect a theft inside a building would fit the definition of "enter" to establish a burglary. Logic would suggest that robots are covered by the definition as they are physical objects "connected" (albeit via radio waves) with the body. The statute does not mandate physical connection *to* the body. As the earlier cited case notes, the offender would be using his body indirectly to cause the entry and that would appear to be sufficient.[21]

The entry aspect under Sec. 30.02(a)(1) also requires that the premises not be open to the public. Presumably when a building is open to the public, the harm caused by nonconsensual entry (the traditional idea of trespass) does not exist. Note, however, that buildings and habitations are not considered either completely open or completely closed; a closed portion of an otherwise open building could be subject to burglary. If a theft occurred from the storage room of a commercial building, behind a door marked "Employees Only,"[22] or in a closed portion of a store,[23] burglary would be a proper charge because a clear nonconsensual entry had occurred.

Suppose Ron is discovered in the manager's office of a retail clothing store with a bank bag in his hand. Ron has committed a burglary because the manager's office was not then open to the public.[24] A similar ruling has found burglary when the offender was in a hospital chaplain's office after visiting hours.[25] The latter case is instructive on the issue of the changing status of a locale. Sec. 30.02(a)(1) speaks of the property being "not *then* open to the public." In the case of the chaplain's office, the premises were closed at the time of the incident being after hospital visiting hours. Had the accused perpetrated his theft during visiting hours when the chaplain's office was open to receive visitors, a burglary charge might be harder to establish.

While no reported appellate case covers the issue, the same sometimes open/sometimes closed issue would appear to be equally applicable to residences. Under normal circumstances, residential property is not considered to be open to the public. The Court of Criminal Appeals has ruled that the statutory phrase "not then open to the public" is applicable only to the word "building" in the statute, not also to "habitation."[26] However, assume Wendell offers his home for sale. One Sunday afternoon he holds a public "open house" for prospective buyers. If a theft occurs in the home during the time of the open house, presumably the law of burglary would not apply because the thief has entered with effective consent. But suppose Wendell excludes his basement workshop from the open house. If a visitor entered the workshop and stole an item, logic would suggest that the law of burglary should apply.

The second subform of the offense requires that the offender remain concealed. The provision exists primarily to cover those situations, such as in a retail store, where the offender enters with consent but stays beyond his welcome by hiding until the store is closed. No statutory or case opinion defines the phrase "remains concealed." One potential issue is whether an offender must actually hide or merely avoid detection. Suppose Peter enters a department store during normal business hours but remains on the premises after closing time by hiding in a box. He then steals property and breaks out of the store instead of breaking into it. Clearly, Peter remained concealed for the purposes of Sec. 30.02(a)(2) of the burglary statute. However, in the same scenario, if Peter overtly poses as a store employee at closing time, for example, straightening merchandise, and turning off lights, and departs with the same merchandise 30 minutes after closing time, should that conduct be considered burglary? Was he "concealed" within the meaning of the statute? Texas appellate courts have not been faced with directly answering this question. However, one case has suggested that "[w]hen a person fails to leave a business establishment after it closes for business, his original entry becomes constructively nonconsensual. If the original entry by the person was impliedly conditioned by time, place, and purpose and the consent to enter by the one in possession of the building, if he be a merchant (and it was impliedly conditioned for the purpose of doing business with the merchant only in the area set aside for that purpose), then the consent given to enter was not for all things and all purposes."[27] This language suggests that consent to enter property is subject to the limitations in place at the time of entry, whether actual or implied. Acting contrary to those limits creates a nonconsensual situation.

Habitations and Buildings

Consistent with traditional notions of burglary, application of Sec. 30.02 is limited to "habitations" and "buildings." Special forms of burglary involving vehicles and vending machines are covered by unique statutes that will be discussed below. Whether the locale of the burglary is a habitation or a building primarily affects the severity of the offense. Sec. 30.01 defines the terms "habitation" and "building."

A **habitation** must be a structure or vehicle. Neither the Penal Code nor criminal case decisions have formally defined the word "structure." However, the Texas Supreme Court, in a tax case, defined "structure" as "any construction, production, or piece of work artificially built up or composed of parts purposefully joined together."[28] While a structure need not necessarily be affixed to the earth, some durability should be expected. For example, whether a canvass tent would be considered a structure is an open question. It lacks rigidity and permanency. Indeed, a court decision a century ago found that a tent was not a "house" within the meaning of the burglary statute in force at that time.[29] Likewise, a cardboard refrigerator carton in which one could certainly spend the night is neither very durable nor permanent. It also is not likely a structure. A cave, on the other hand, is durable but also would not be considered a habitation since it does not fit the everyday definition of a "structure."

The Texas definition of "habitation" also includes vehicles. For the purposes of this definition, "vehicle" would include mobile homes, travel trailers, motor homes, and even a semi-tractor with a sleeper cab, because each is adapted for overnight accommodation of persons. The term is also likely broad enough to cover yachts, houseboats, and railroad sleeping cars. Is a commercial aircraft a habitation? Certainly it is a vehicle and many first class cabins are fitted for overnight accommodations.

The most common form of habitation is the residential dwelling, which is clearly protected under the statute. According to Texas Department of Public Safety crime records, two-thirds of all burglaries involve private residences.[30] But a "habitation" can also include hotels, motels, apartment houses, dormitories, and other similar multi-family dwellings. Even the Harris County jail has been deemed to be a habitation for the purposes of this chapter of the Penal Code.[31]

Suppose you reside in the Lone Star Apartments, apartment number 714. While at work, your apartment is burglarized. Upon your return home you discover that three of your neighbors' apartments were also burglarized. How many burglaries have occurred? One or four? The answer is four because Sec. 30.01(a)(1) states that the term "habitation" includes "each separately secured or occupied portion of the structure." In a similar vein, while the local Motel 6 may consist of a single structure, it contains 125 separate, rented rooms. Unlawful entry and thefts from rooms 101, 205, and 317 would constitute three burglaries, not one.

Similarly, the definition speaks to "each structure appurtenant to or connected with the structure." This provision is a modern update of the Common Law curtilage concept discussed earlier and a recognition that a residential facility may consist of multiple structures. Thus, burglary of an automobile garage located next to a residence is the equivalent of burglarizing the main home itself. Whether or not the garage is attached to the home is irrelevant.[32] The same would hold true of residential outbuildings, such as a pool-house or a storage building for lawn care equipment.[33] Also, entry onto a residential balcony falls within the statute as the balcony is "connected to the structure."[34]

One particularly bedeviling question has been at what point in time does a structure become a habitation? For example, is a vacant apartment a habitation?[35] What about a house under construction? What about a derelict abandoned house? What about a cabin in the woods used with a deer lease? The current view holds that a structure is a habitation based on how the reasonable person perceives it. Factors to consider include whether the structure is currently being used as a residence, whether the structure contains bedding, furniture, food, and other items commonly found in a residence, whether utilities are connected, and whether the structure is of such a character that it was intended to accommodate persons overnight (e.g., apartment, condominium, mobile home).[36] The determination is a fact question for the jury.

By way of example, suppose Rod steals a dishwasher from a house that is under construction. Has Rod committed burglary of a habitation or the lesser offense of misdemeanor theft? The answer would appear to depend solely upon how far along is the house construction. If the house is merely framed with no exterior walls, it does not yet rise to the definition of a "habitation." However, assume the house is a few days from being turned over to its new owners. It has siding, doors, and windows. The electricity and water service have been turned on. The air conditioning is running. Under these circumstances, a reasonable jury could conclude that the structure is a habitation and a burglary has occurred. The house is adapted for overnight accommodations; someone could reside there in reasonable comfort.

Edward is a previously convicted sex offender. He lures a six-year-old child into a vacant house for the purposes of molesting her. Once in the empty house, the child becomes frightened and successfully flees. As odd as it may seem, Edward has committed a burglary. He has entered a structure with intent to commit a felony. Whether the conduct rises to the level of burglary of a habitation, a felony of the first degree, would depend on whether the house in its current condition was adapted for overnight accommodations.

The definition of a **building** is also subject to occasional argument. The statute requires an enclosed structure. Interestingly, the structure need not be actually enclosed at the time of the crime but rather only enclosable. For example, a storage building with a moveable overhead door is an enclosed structure even if the door is in the up position. The leading court decision on the question held that a fully roofed masonry structure surrounded by a fenced parking lot was not enclosed for the purpose of the burglary statute because the entry portals had no doors.[37] The fence was not considered part of the structure for the purpose of the legal definition. The offender had not "broken the close" when he entered the structure and took building materials. Had the portals been equipped with doors, even if the doors were open at the time of the crime, the structure would have been a "building" because it was capable of being enclosed.

In another decision, the court ruled that a floating boathouse was a building since it was an enclosed structure.[38] Likewise, a fireworks stand sitting on concrete blocks has been ruled to be a building even though it also had an axle with wheels attached.[39] However, a covered outdoor bandstand, picnic pavilion, or basketball court would not be considered to be a building for the purposes of the burglary statute because they cannot be closed up. The same rule would hold true of a covered parking spot at an apartment complex and a self-serve carwash. The key factor in determining whether a structure is a building is whether it is capable of being closed up.

Intent to Commit a Felony, Theft, or Assault

Two of the three forms of burglary mandate that the offender possess the intent to commit a felony, theft, or an assault. Consistent with the Common Law rule, the offender need only possess the specific intent to commit an offense; he need not be successful at his criminal enterprise.[40] Thus, suppose one night Caleb, a previously convicted burglar, takes a prybar and forces open the window to Abe's bedroom. Abe is awakened by the noise and grabs his pistol. As Caleb enters the house, Abe declares that Caleb should stop or be shot. Abe calls the police. Caleb has committed burglary, even though he was stopped before the matter proceeded very far.

Under the burglary statute, the offender must enter the premise or remain concealed on the premises and possess the conscious objective to commit a felony, theft, or an assault. As with Caleb above, the crime is complete upon the entry, irrespective of whether he is successful in carrying out his intentions.

Proof of a burglar's intent might at first glance seem difficult to accomplish. However, Texas courts have consistently held that the intent element can be proven solely through use of circumstantial evidence.[41] Additionally, Texas courts hold to the rather logical view that entry without consent at nighttime is presumed to be with intent to commit theft.[42] Other circumstantial factors establishing intent can include the offender's efforts to flee the scene upon discovery,[43] the offender's words and conduct at the scene,[44] the presence of the defendant's fingerprints at the burglary scene,[45] and the offender's recent unexplained possession of property taken from the scene.[46]

Texas statute expands the Common Law view of burglary in several ways. First, while burglary under the Common Law concerned itself only with felonious conduct, modern Texas law covers not only felonies but also misdemeanor theft and misdemeanor assault. Thus, entry for the purposes of committing a sexual assault, arson, murder, and robbery—all felonies—would constitute burglary. In addition, since theft can be a misdemeanor or felony depending on the circumstances, unlawful entry for any theft is covered under the burglary law. The same is true of assault since assault by threat and assault with bodily injury are normally misdemeanors. If Fred is angry with his neighbor Jed and enters Jed's house without permission for the purposes of beating up Jed, Fred has committed burglary even though the underlying assault he intends is only a misdemeanor. In an actual case, the burglary conviction of an individual was upheld after he entered a neighbor's garage and poured paint on the owner's truck and cut his waterbed. Since the act of criminal mischief exceeded the felony–misdemeanor monetary threshold, a burglary had been committed.[47] Once again the traditional public policy of protecting the sanctity of one's habitation comes into play in both cases.

Sec. 30.02(a)(3) covers nonconsensual entries where the requisite intent is formed after, not before, the entry is made. For instance, a trespasser in a building who assaults a security guard who is trying to eject him could face burglary charges. Likewise, an individual who steps into a residential garage to get out of the rain and subsequently decides to steal a bicycle he observes there has committed burglary. In this scenario, the intent to commit theft arose after the nonpermissioned entry but constitutes burglary under Sec. 30.02(a)(3) nonetheless.

One reading of Sec. 30.02(a)(3) could consider as burglary a felony that occurs when the offender enters a building open to the public but does so for a purpose for which the owner would certainly not grant permission. In other words, the suspect obtains entry by fraud. For example, consider an offender who buys a ticket to a movie but his real intent is to expose himself to a child in the theatre, indecency with a child being a felony.[48] The theatre manager certainly would have not given consent for the offender to enter and commit the offense had he known the offender's true purpose.

In some states, a burglary conviction could be had under these facts. The availability of such a conviction under Texas law is unclear.[49]

While most burglaries involve an entry and subsequent theft from the premises, the statute is broad enough to cover circumstances wherein the offender unlawfully enters one premises with intent to commit a theft at another location. Accordingly, a burglary conviction was upheld when the suspect entered a bank president's residence with intent to force the bank officer to take him to the bank to gain money. Police were alerted and thwarted the plot. An appeals court ruled that burglary of a habitation had occurred since the offender entered the habitation with intent to commit theft. It mattered not that the act of theft would occur at a different location.[50]

Texas courts also appear to accept the notion that intent to commit any of the various forms of theft is sufficient to sustain a burglary conviction. While most acts of burglary involve efforts to steal property, theft can be committed in a variety of other ways. Thus, entering a premises with intent to commit theft of services (Sec. 31.04) or theft of trade secrets (Sec. 30.05) appears to violate the burglary statute as well.[51] In one case, the appeals court refused to uphold a burglary of a vehicle conviction against an illegal alien who hitched a ride aboard a freight train. The defendant had been convicted of burglary based on an alleged act of theft of service, that is, obtaining transportation without pay for it. The court reversed the conviction on the basis that since the relevant portion of the theft of service statute [Sec. 31.04(a)(1)] required an intent to avoid payment for service that is provided only for compensation, no theft occurred because this was a freight train, not a passenger train. The railroad did not provide passenger service for compensation; therefore, the defendant could not have stolen such a service. The opinion gives no indication that the justices were concerned about theft of service being the foundation offense for a burglary-related charge.[52] Whether other offenses in Chapter 31 of the Penal Code, such as theft of trade secrets, can serve as the foundation felony for a burglary charge has not been decided.

Where the intent of the offender is to commit a misdemeanor, other than theft or assault, the offense of burglary does not apply. For example, Charles, a 17-year-old high school student, angry about his grades, breaks into the high school and spray-paints obscenities on the wall of the cafeteria. Charles has committed criminal trespass and criminal mischief, not burglary, assuming the damage done by his vandalism is at the misdemeanor level. But if Charles destroys computer equipment or other high value items and the aggregate total exceeds $1,500, a felony has been committed and a burglary charge would stand.

Since any felony can be the underlying offense to establish burglary, persons who enter buildings and habitations for the purpose of committing murder, sexual assault, kidnapping, robbery, or arson, all felonies, may also be culpable for burglary. In a most unusual application of this rule, the defendant's burglary conviction was upheld where he hid in a woodshed next to a house after fleeing the police. Evading arrest through use of a vehicle is a state jail felony.[53] The defendant had fled the police in his car. He later abandoned the vehicle and ran on foot. He was located in the shed about ten hours after the initial chase began. The Court of Appeals ruled that evading an arrest is a continuing offense. Since the defendant began the chase in a car, the offense became a felony. When he trespassed into the woodshed, he was committing a felony and that equals burglary.[54]

Under the appropriate set of facts, criminal trespass can be a lesser-included offense of each of the three forms of burglary contained in Sec. 30.02.[55]

Penalty

Burglary of a building is punished as a state jail felony. Burglary of a habitation is sanctioned as a felony of the second degree. If the burglary of a habitation involves a felony other than theft, such as sexual assault, robbery, arson, or murder, the punishment level is raised to a felony of the first degree.

Whether a suspect can be prosecuted for burglary, as well as any underlying felony or theft he commits, is more of a question of judicial economy than of law. Assume Dick unlawfully enters Jane's home and sexually assaults her. Dick has committed both burglary and sexual assault. While Texas law permits both offenses to be charged and handled at the same trial, the statute also provides that under most circumstances upon conviction the sentences shall run concurrently.[56] On the other hand, the defendant enjoys the absolute right to separate trials for each of the two offenses.[57] In the latter case, the sentences could be assessed concurrently or consecutively.[58]

Burglary of Coin-operated or Coin Collection Machines

The burglary of a **coin-operated machine** statute (Sec. 30.03) applies to most mechanical and electronic vending machines, pay telephones, electronic video games and similar devices, as well as nonmechanical collection devices such as open newspaper ranks and candy boxes that rely on an honor system for payment. The formal complaint filed against a defendant, however, must state which type of coin device was burglarized: Was it a coin-operated machine? A coin collection machine? Or, a coin collection receptacle? Thus, where an offender was convicted of burglary of a coin-operated machine for stealing money from a parking lot metal collection box, the appeals court ruled that such a box was not a machine. Deposit of the coin did not cause any mechanical, hydraulic, or electrical activity to occur. The coin simply sat passively in the box. Thus the device was not "operated" by the coin. The conviction was overturned because the charge should have been filed as burglary of a coin collection receptacle.[59]

While no appellate case law on the point exists, the statute's focus on coin has not kept up with the times. The wording of the current statute would appear to preclude the law's application to devices that lack the capacity to accept or dispense coins. For example, suppose a vending machine takes only credit cards or paper currency. A breaking into such a device and subsequent theft of its contents likely falls outside the plain language of the statute. The offender could be charged with theft and criminal mischief but not burglary of a coin-operated machine. The same would seem to hold true for a standalone automatic teller machine (ATM). An ATM is not operated by coins.[60]

§ 30.03. Burglary of Coin-operated or Coin Collection Machines

a. A person commits an offense if, without the effective consent of the owner, he breaks or enters into any coin-operated machine, coin collection machine, or other coin-operated or coin collection receptacle, contrivance, apparatus, or equipment used for the purpose of providing lawful amusement, sales of goods, services, or other valuable things, or telecommunications with intent to obtain property, or services.

b. For purposes of this section, "entry" includes every kind of entry except one made with the effective consent of the owner.

c. An offense under this section is a Class A misdemeanor.

Since numerous ways exist to defeat these coin-operated devices, the Legislature did not attempt to specify the forms of illegal entry. Rather, the statute outlaws every kind of entry without the owner's consent. Thus, use of a wire to trip the machine, use of a metallic slug, insertion of a screwdriver, or simply reaching in with one's hands are all unlawful if done without the owner's effective consent.

Following the traditional law of burglary, the breaking or entering must be with intent to obtain the goods or services. Hence, the crime is complete when the breaking or entering is accomplished, regardless of whether the offender is successful in obtaining the goods or services from the machine. Nearly 5,000 burglaries of coin-operated machines are known to occur in this state annually.[61]

Burglary of a coin-operated machine is a Class A misdemeanor.

Burglary of Vehicles

Vehicle burglaries are a commonly occurring crime with about 190,000 taking place annually within the state.[62] The behavior normally involves entry into a commercial vehicle, such as a railcar or commercial trailer, to steal its contents or entry into the interior of a private passenger vehicle to steal items inside, such as a purse, or a portion of the vehicle itself, such as the radio, battery, or airbags.

The Texas statute, however, covers entry not only for the purposes of theft of the vehicle's contents or accessories but also for any effort to commit a felony in the vehicle. For example, Ginger stops her automobile at a traffic signal. Rodney opens the car door and climbs in intending to kidnap and sexually assault Ginger. Ginger jumps from the vehicle and flees on foot. Rodney has committed burglary of vehicle as he entered the car with intent to commit a felony. In addition, anytime an offender enters a vehicle in an attempt to steal it, he would appear to violate the burglary of vehicles law, although the motor vehicle theft itself is generally the more serious crime.

To commit the offense the suspect must either **break into** or **enter** the vehicle. "Breaking into" has been defined as opening of the vehicle's latch, locking device, or opening an unlocked door.[63] The "enter" element is defined in the statute and is identical to the definition used for burglary of habitations and buildings [Sec. 30.02(b)].

§ 30.04. Burglary of Vehicles

a. A person commits an offense if, without the effective consent of the owner, he breaks into or enters a vehicle or any part of a vehicle with intent to commit any felony or theft.

b. For purposes of this section, "enter" means to intrude:
   1. any part of the body; or
   2. any physical object connected with the body.

c. For purposes of this section, a container or trailer carried on a rail car is a part of the rail car.

d. An offense under this section is a Class A misdemeanor unless the vehicle or part of the vehicle broken into or entered is a rail car, in which event the offense is a state jail felony.

e. It is a defense to prosecution under this section that the actor entered a rail car or any part of a rail car and was at that time an employee or a representative of employees exercising a right under the Railway Labor Act (45 U.S.C. Section 151 et seq.).

It includes entry through use of physical objects, such as poles, nets, and the like. As with the traditional offense of burglary of structures, the offense is complete when entry is made, regardless of whether property is taken or some other underlying offense is committed.[64]

The object of the burglary has to be a **vehicle**. The statute [Sec. 30.01(1)(3)] uses a broad definition of the term "vehicle." The definition does not require that the vehicle be motorized or that it have wheels. An airplane or a boat is covered by the definition.[65] Even a truck with no motor or rear wheels is still a vehicle under the statute.[66] If the target vehicle falls within the definition of a "habitation," such as a travel trailer or motor home, the more serious charge of burglary of a habitation under Sec. 30.02 would appear to be more appropriate.

Perhaps the most troublesome application of the burglary of vehicles statute regards the theft of automobile parts and accessories. Texas case law holds that theft of tires, wheel covers, hood ornaments, and radio antenna does not violate the burglary of a vehicle statute because there has not been a breaking or an entry as required by the statute. But theft of a vehicle's battery will normally be considered a burglary of a vehicle because entry under the hood is necessary to accomplish the theft.[67] Likewise, removal of tools from the locked toolbox of a pickup truck is a violation as there is an entry into the closed box.[68]

But suppose Jack spies a case of beer in the bed of Billy's pickup truck. Jack reaches into the truck bed and helps himself to the beer. Is Jack's conduct a burglary of a vehicle or merely a Class C theft? Prior case law holds that removal of personal property from the open bed of a truck violates Sec. 30.04.[69] Initially, this ruling would appear inconsistent with the general burglary requirement discussed earlier that the area entered be capable of being closed.[70] The Court of Criminal Appeals indicated that the purpose of the laws against any form of burglary is to protect an individual's reasonable expectation of privacy. Intrusion into the bed of a pickup truck violates that privacy expectation. The court held that the bed is "clearly a portion of the interior of the truck" for the purposes of the statute. To hold otherwise would leave pickups, flatbed trucks, and jeep-type vehicles unprotected under the statute. Such likely was not the intent of the Legislature in crafting the burglary of vehicles statute.[71]

Burglary of a vehicle is a Class A misdemeanor. The offense elevates to a state jail felony if the vehicle entered is a rail car or trailer carried on a rail car.

INTRODUCTION TO CRIMINAL TRESPASS

Another offense that concerns intrusion onto another's property is criminal trespass. Under the Common Law, a **trespass** was a broad term originally defined as any unlawful damage to or intrusion on another's personal or real property. Additionally, such conduct was normally a civil matter and resulted in the award of monetary damages to the owner of the damaged property. Even today in many states, the historical law of trespass is used as a basis for lawsuits over ownership, use, and injury to real estate.

During early development of English law, the distinction between criminal and civil matters was blurred. The only forms of trespass that were considered criminal under the Common Law were those committed with "great violence, and with a multitude of persons," for these constituted a breach of the peace.[72] The Common Law did afford all landowners the legal privilege to exclude others. This right to control who comes and goes on one's real estate gave rise to the modern crime of criminal trespass.

MODERN CRIMINAL TRESPASS STATUTES

It should be emphasized that not all trespasses to property constitute the crime of criminal trespass. The free movement of persons, occasionally even onto the private land of another, is important to the operation of society. Individuals frequently go upon another's real property without expressed or even implied permission. For instance, Chris, a high school student, cuts across a vacant lot on his way to school each day. Chris is a trespasser, but not a criminal trespasser unless the lot is fenced or posted. Mike, selling magazines door-to-door, must necessarily come upon private property without express permission. Even though the homeowner may not be interested in purchasing the magazines and may even find door-to-door salesmen annoying, Mike has not committed criminal trespass by entering upon the property.

Criminal trespass statutes are attempting to sanction three decidedly different types of offenders:

- Frightening trespassers
- Nuisance trespassers
- Defiant trespassers

Frightening trespassers are those individuals who are discovered prior to the commission of some more serious offense. For example, late one night Tom is found walking on the roof of a retail store. A quick check of police records reveals Tom has two previous convictions for burglary. Tom, who has no credible explanation for being on the roof, is arrested for criminal trespass, the police believing they have likely interrupted a possible burglary. In another example, late one evening a homeowner calls police to report a prowler. Responding officers discover Bob, intoxicated in the fenced backyard of the residence. Bob is arrested for criminal trespass.

Nuisance trespassers are those who go upon property without permission but are not there to commit a more serious offense. In these cases, the landowner does not wish others to be on his property because of concerns of civil liability, littering, or damage to the premises. For instance, without asking permission Tom, Dick, and Harry go swimming in a pond on their neighbor's property. The owner of the property has previously posted "no trespassing" signs. Tom, Dick, and Harry have committed criminal trespass. In another example, Larry and Moe ride their motorcycles on Curly's wooded acreage. Curly has "posted" the land. Larry and Moe are committing criminal trespass.

Defiant trespassers are those who enter property with consent but the consent is revoked because of their later behavior. David enters a restaurant for dinner. After 30 minutes he becomes disruptive because of slow service. The manager asks David to leave the restaurant. David refuses, saying he is going to stay until his meal is finished. The manager summons police who arrest David for criminal trespass. Another example of the defiant trespasser is the individual who purposely trespasses in protest of some political, economic, or social issue. The legal aspects of this behavior are discussed below.

TEXAS LAW OF CRIMINAL TRESPASS

Introduction

Many forms of trespass are not violations of the Texas Penal Code.[73] Only those limited behaviors that meet the elements of the offense constitute a crime. Sec. 30.05 sets forth the elements of the offense. However, even if an individual's conduct does not violate Sec. 30.05, a property owner may still use reasonable force to terminate the ordinary trespass.[74]

§ 30.05. Criminal Trespass

a. A person commits an offense if he enters or remains on or in property, including an aircraft or other vehicle, of another without effective consent or he enters or remains in a building of another without effective consent and he:
 1. had notice that the entry was forbidden; or
 2. received notice to depart but failed to do so.

b. For purposes of this section:
 1. "Entry" means the intrusion of the entire body.
 2. "Notice" means:
    A. oral or written communication by the owner or someone with apparent authority to act for the owner;
    B. fencing or other enclosure obviously designed to exclude intruders or to contain livestock;
    C. a sign or signs posted on the property or at the entrance to the building, reasonably likely to come to the attention of intruders, indicating that entry is forbidden;
    D. the placement of identifying purple paint marks on trees or posts on the property,

       * * * *

    E. the visible presence on the property of a crop grown for human consumption that is under cultivation, in the process of being harvested, or marketable if harvested at the time of entry.

       * * * *

c. It is a defense to prosecution under this section that the actor at the time of the offense was a fire fighter or emergency medical services personnel, as that term is defined by Section 773.003, Health and Safety Code, acting in the lawful discharge of an official duty under exigent circumstances.

d. An offense under Subsection (e) is a Class C misdemeanor unless it is committed in a habitation or unless the actor carries a deadly weapon on or about the actor's person during the commission of the offense, in which event it is a Class A misdemeanor. An offense under Subsection (a) is a Class B misdemeanor, except that the offense is a Class A misdemeanor if:
 1. the offense is committed:
    A. in a habitation or a shelter center; or
    B. on a Superfund site; or
    C. on or in a critical infrastructure facility; or
 2. the actor carries a deadly weapon on or about his person during the commission of the offense.

e. A person commits an offense if without express consent or if without authorization provided by any law, whether in writing or other form, the person:
 1. enters or remains on agricultural land of another;
 2. is on the agricultural land and within 100 feet of the boundary of the land when apprehended; and
 3. had notice that the entry was forbidden or received notice to depart but failed to do so.

   * * * *

Elements of Criminal Trespass in Texas

Mens rea *Requirement*

Note that the express language of Sec. 30.05 makes no mention of a culpable mental state. However, the language of the statute does not expressly dispense with the *mens rea* requirement. Since the language of the law does not plainly dispense with this requirement, one is implied by law and the prosecution must show that the behavior was at least reckless.[75] In most instances, trespassers are acting intentionally.

Enters or Remains

Unlike burglary, which also may require an entering, the legal element of entering under the Texas criminal trespass statute requires that the entire body come onto the property. Thus, merely setting one foot on your neighbor's lawn is insufficient to constitute a criminal trespass. This is the rule in most other states as well. It is no crime for an individual to reach through a fence to retrieve his hat.

No definition of the term "remains" is contained in the Penal Code but would likely be given its ordinary meaning of refusing to depart.

On Property

Texas case law interpreting the criminal trespass statute traditionally held that the word **property** meant real estate.[76] In recent years, however, the Legislature has expanded the scope of the statute, first to cover airplanes and then to cover all vehicles. Thus, not only does the offense occur if an individual intrudes upon posted land but presumably also covers the individual who enters a vehicle without express permission. If Joe finds Oscar, a homeless person, asleep in the backseat of Joe's automobile, Oscar has committed criminal trespass. Likewise, if Mona becomes unruly on a public bus and refuses the driver's order to exit the bus, Mona has committed criminal trespass. As noted previously, reasonable force could be used to eject the bus passenger as she has lost permission to remain on the bus.

The statute uses the preposition "in" as well as "on," indicating that a plain reading of the statute would cover individuals who are physically present within the interior of a vehicle, such as a bus or airplane, as well as those who might be standing on a piece of real estate or seated in a movie theatre.

Of Another

Criminal trespass violates one's superior possessory interest. Consequently, the statute is violated if anyone with a greater right of possession than the trespasser complains; it need not be the titleholder of the premises.[77] Thus, if a high school principal orders Alberto, a nonstudent, to leave the school campus, Alberto's failure to depart is a violation of the criminal trespass statute even though the principal is not the titleholder to the school property.[78] Or, consider John, an apartment house owner, who enters Marsha's apartment without permission. John violates the criminal trespass statute even though John is the titleholder of the property. Marsha, as the tenant, has a superior possessory interest. To prevent this circumstance from arising, the law, as well as most apartment leases, grants the owner consent to enter the apartment at reasonable hours to inspect the premises and make repairs. Similarly, a restaurant manager may act in the owner's stead in filing a complaint against a trespasser, the restaurant manager having a greater right of possession to the premises than the unruly patron.

Texas courts have further ruled that even governmental property, such as parks and schools, is subject to the coverage of the criminal trespass statute. The fact that a location is generally considered public property does not preclude the barring of certain individuals.[79] Additionally, access to certain publicly owned facilities may be limited and intruders subjected to prosecution. For example, in Bader v. State,[80] a Texas Court of Appeals upheld the criminal trespass conviction of a nonstudent who came upon the campus of The University of Texas after having received a written no trespassing warning from a campus police officer nearly one year earlier. Bader was found in the university's computer lab, an area not open to the general public. What if Bader had been found in the library or the football stadium during a game? Can the university lawfully ban particular individuals from locations where the general public is otherwise welcome and even encouraged? The appeals court panel in its opinion noted, "The public, including appellant [Bader], has a limited right of access to the University of Texas campus." The justices did not, however, define the scope of that limited right.

Without Effective Consent

Like burglary, lack of effective consent is a key element of the offense. Consent obtained by fraud, threat, or deception is not effective. Thus, if Mark poses as a university maintenance worker in order to gain access to the women's dormitory and deceives the counselor into granting him admittance, Mark is committing criminal trespass, assuming other elements of the offense are present.

Had Notice that the Entry was Forbidden

Notice that entry is forbidden is the cornerstone of criminal trespass. Indeed, to a large degree it is the element that distinguishes criminal trespasses from other forms of trespass. The rule is simple: No notice, no violation of the statute. Under Texas law, notice that entry is forbidden may be in the form of:

- Written notice.
- Verbal notice.
- Fencing or other enclosure to exclude intruders or contain livestock.
- Signs.
- Purple paint marks on trees.
- Crops under cultivation.

Placement of "No Trespassing" signs is probably the most common form of written notice. Displaying signs that read "Posted," "Private Property," or "No Hunting" is insufficient notice that entry is forbidden because such language does not explicitly ban trespassers. However, "Keep Out," "Do Not Enter," "Authorized Personnel Only," or "Entry Forbidden" is likely sufficient notice. Regarding signage, the statute requires that it be reasonably likely to come to the attention of intruders. This means that the signs must be legible and visible. Their placement must be such that the average person would likely see them. This might mean placing multiple signs along a property line at eye level. As to signage, Texas law does not specify the exact wording of the signs, their color, the type font, or even the height and frequency of their placement. Rather, the Legislature has left it to the trier of fact, jury or judge, to decide whether signage in a particular case was likely to come to the attention of intruders and whether it indicated that entry is forbidden.[81]

Written trespass warnings are commonly issued by Texas campus police officers to nonstudents who are creating a problem on campus. The written warning alerts the recipient that he or she will be arrested and charged with criminal trespass if they return to campus within a specified period of time. Some municipal police agencies provide similar forms to trespassers when so requested by a property owner.

In rare instances, a property owner may send notice by mail or email. Such notice often involves landlord–tenant disputes or other quarrels over access to property.

As to verbal notice, a vocal "get off my property" or "keep out" is sufficient. That certainly takes care of the immediate notice requirement but what is the life span of such notice? No Texas appellate court has passed specifically on the question of the time limitation for verbal or written notice. Is a person who has been told to stay off property forever barred from the premises? Should written notice have a longer term than verbal notice? Neither of these questions has been answered by Texas courts.

Fencing designed to exclude intruders, such as a ten-foot chain-link, is obvious to the average person that entry is forbidden. A two-foot white picket fence around a residential lot, however, is not likely intended to exclude others but rather to be purely decorative. Given the long ranching heritage of Texas and the historical problem of livestock theft, the Legislature considers barbed wire and other forms of livestock fencing to be the equivalent of signage. No other notice is necessary. Apparently, the fencing need not even be in good repair or capable of containing livestock, only be designed to contain livestock. Crossing a rusty string of barbed wire will constitute criminal trespass.

Assume a security guard discovers Jason inside a closed theatre. Jason is not an employee and has no valid reason to be in the closed theatre. The "other enclosure" portion of Sec. 30.05(b)(2)(B) would appear to make Jason a criminal trespasser. In this case, the "other enclosure" is the walls, room, and doors of the building.[82] Jason, and any other reasonable human being, knows he has no legal right to be inside the closed theater. As to a trespasser in a residence, one appeals court has adopted the position that "a habitation gives notice inherently," meaning the fact the property is a habitation by definition constitutes notice that entry is forbidden.[83]

The purple markings on trees alternative recognizes the inability to economically fence or place signs around large expanses of timberland or other acreage. One might argue that such marks do not give fair notice since purple paint is not universally accepted to mean "no trespassing."[84] Is the average urban resident out for a day in the woods likely to know that a purple mark on a pine tree means "no trespassing"? No appellate court has ruled on this aspect of the statute.

The same may be said of the existence of crops for human consumption. The Legislature recognizes the impracticality and expense of fencing or posting signs around large groves of citrus or watermelons in agricultural regions such as South Texas. On the other hand, passersby have been known to help themselves when no one is around. In such cases it is difficult to prove theft unless the thief is apprehended actually picking the fruit and leaving the premises with the items. In a bit of redundancy, subsection(e) of the statute declares it unlawful to enter more than 100 feet beyond the boundary of agriculture land if one has notice that entry is forbidden.

Receives Notice to Depart and Fails to Do So

Since a property owner has a right to admit or exclude whomever he or she chooses, the owner also has the right to change his or her mind. An individual who has entered onto property, with either expressed or assumed permission, can have that consent revoked. Failing to depart after receiving notice converts the individual's status into that of a criminal trespasser. Thus, Craig, a spectator at a professional sporting event, is being crude and unruly. Despite several requests from the usher to change his behavior Craig continues to act inappropriately. Finally, the usher asks Craig to leave the stadium. Craig refuses. Craig has committed criminal trespass by failing to depart after receiving notice to do so.[85]

The statute is silent as to who is empowered to give the notice to depart. Normally, the complainant in the case would provide the verbal notice but often it may be a security officer or police officer who is called to the scene.[86]

Penalty

Criminal trespass is a Class B misdemeanor unless the site of the trespass is a habitation, shelter center, Superfund site, or the actor carries a deadly weapon during the offense, in which case the violation is a Class A misdemeanor.

CRIMINAL TRESPASS AND THE CONSTITUTION

The law of criminal trespass is often invoked by authorities to terminate unruly labor pickets, protests, sit-ins, and other forms of demonstrations on social, political, moral, and economic issues. Three possible locations exist for such demonstrations: private property, privately owned public space, and public property.

In the case of purely private property, the law of criminal trespass clearly applies and unwanted demonstrators can be ordered to leave the premises or face arrest. Thus, a labor picket on the premises of a manufacturing plant need not be tolerated by management and the demonstrators may be ordered off of the premises under threat of arrest for criminal trespass. For this reason, it is common to see strikers demonstrating across the street from the target company or otherwise not on their employer's land.

Privately owned public space may create a different problem. A location such as a shopping mall, theatre, hospital, or grocery store parking lot may well be owned by private investors but is generally open to anyone without any special grant of permission. Indeed, the establishment by its very nature may encourage the general public to enter onto the premises. Assume a group of animal rights protestors are picketing in front of a department store that sells fur coats. Can the protestors lawfully be ordered to leave the premises or be arrested for criminal trespass? The answer would appear to be that the protestors have no First Amendment right to demonstrate on privately owned property and would be subject to criminal trespass laws. While in 1968 the Supreme Court upheld the right of citizens to engage in expressive conduct in the parking lot of a shopping center,[87] the court significantly narrowed the ruling in 1972, finding a mall owner could enforce a no hand-billing rule against anti-war protestors.[88] In 1976, the justices reaffirmed the principle that private property need not always be considered a **public forum** for protestors to convey their message.[89]

Use of publicly owned property for protests is the least restrictive for protestors. The government, like any landowner, can certainly limit access to property to those with legitimate business on the premises, for example, the grounds of the Governor's Mansion in Austin or the upper floors of the local police station. In 2003, the U.S. Supreme Court ruled that use of the Virginia criminal trespass law and a public housing development board's policy to bar nonresidents from the premises in an effort to control drug-dealing did not violate the First Amendment.[90] The court noted that no First Amendment right was being trampled as it was the individual's presence, not his speech, which was the object of the enforcement effort.

However, government land that is a "public forum" must normally be opened to all. Because of the First Amendment rights of free speech, peaceful assembly, and petition, the government may not choose which ideas to endorse and which to suppress. Consequently, if the protestors are in a public forum open to all (e.g., county park, plaza in front of city hall), the government cannot regulate their activity except in extremely limited circumstances.[91] The government may place reasonable time, place, and manner restrictions on such protests. For example, a city need not permit two political parades to occur on the same street at the same time. But so long as the protestors are peaceful and comply with regulations applicable to all (e.g., closing time of a park, traffic laws, and anti-noise ordinances), the protestors may not be considered criminal trespassers. This principle is so revered in our society that the U.S. Supreme Court has even struck down a federal law that sought to limit protests outside the Supreme Court Building![92]

ISSUES IN THE LAW OF CRIMINAL TRESPASS

Like any criminal law that attempts to sanction a broad spectrum of conduct, the language of the criminal trespass statute raises some questions as to its intended application. Historically, the law exempted from charges of criminal trespass individuals who were privileged to go onto property. Such individuals included meter readers, mail carriers, tax appraisers, and other persons whose occupation routinely required them to access private property. The Texas statute is unclear as to who now falls within this privileged class. In particular, the question arises as to whether public safety personnel are exempt from the law?

Sec. 30.05(c) exempts firefighters and emergency medical services personnel from the statute's coverage. Thus, firefighters and paramedics may perform their duties, including entering upon property without express permission, without fear of violating the criminal trespass statute. But what about police officers? To date, Texas appeal courts are split as to whether the same legal privilege exists for police officers or other government employees. While police officers are not likely to be prosecuted for criminal trespass, the discovery of evidence during a trespass could be subject to suppression in court under the state exclusionary rule.[93] The statutory rule mandates suppression of evidence obtained in violation of the "laws of the State of Texas." The appeal courts disagree on whether police officers are exempt from application of the statute when performing their duties.[94]

Another issue that has not been resolved by Texas courts is whether the criminal trespass statute is violated when an individual fails to comply with restrictions the landowner has placed on entry. For example, signs such as "No skateboarding," "No dogs," and "No alcoholic beverages" are commonplace at various venues. Is the statute violated when one skateboards with his dog while drinking a beer? No Texas court has ruled on this issue to date. However, logic would suggest that one who violates the terms of entry onto premises is a trespasser subject to removal but not a criminal trespasser. To hold such an individual as a criminal trespasser would essentially cede to a private landowner the power to create criminal law through personal decree. It is unlikely the Legislature intends to grant such unbridled power to private citizens.

Perhaps the most common restriction placed on the entry of premises is an admission fee, such as at movies, sporting events, and theatrical performances. Here, one who enters without paying the fee is certainly a trespasser subject to ejection. In the rare cases where criminal charges follow the nonpermissioned entry, the theft of service statute,[95] not the criminal trespass statute, would seem the more appropriate law.

Trespass by Holder of Concealed Handgun License

The Legislature has granted landowners the authority to bar individuals who possess state-issued concealed handgun licenses (CHL) from bringing their weapons onto private property (Sec. 30.06). Invocation of this power is most commonly found in commercial business establishments. Interestingly, unlike the criminal trespass statute, this statute is very explicit in terms of the style of the signage that must be displayed, including the notice being written in both English and Spanish.

A CHL holder commits the trespass offense if he or she carries a handgun on to the posted property without effective consent. The offense is a Class A misdemeanor.[96]

CRIMEGRAPH
Burglary

Offense	When?	Culpable mental state	Conduct	Where?	Specific intent/knowledge	Penalty
Burglary 30.02(a)(1)	Without effective consent of owner	1. Intentionally, or 2. Knowingly, or 3. Recklessly*	Enters	1. Habitation or 2. Building or portion not open to public	With intent to commit: 1. Any felony, or 2. Theft, or 3. Assault	SJF to F1
Burglary 30.02(a)(2)	Without effective consent of owner	1. Intentionally, or 2. Knowingly, or 3. Recklessly*	Remains concealed	1. Habitation or 2. Building	With intent to commit: 1. Any felony, or 2. Theft, or 3. Assault	SJF to F1
Burglary 30.02(a)(3)	Without effective consent of owner	1. Intentionally, or 2. Knowingly, or 3. Recklessly*	Enters	1. Habitation or 2. Building	Commits or attempts to commit: 1. Any felony, or 2. Theft, or 3. Assault	SJF to F1
Burglary of Coin-operated Machines 30.03	Without effective consent of owner	1. Intentionally, or 2. Knowingly, or 3. Recklessly*	1. Breaks or 2. Enters	Coin-operated machine/device providing amusement, goods, services, or telecommunication services	With intent to obtain: 1. Property or 2. Services	AM
Burglary of Vehicles 30.04	Without effective consent of owner	1. Intentionally, or 2. Knowingly, or 3. Recklessly*	1. Breaks into or 2. Enters	Vehicle or any part	With intent to commit: 1. Any felony or 2. Theft	AM to SJF

*Required by Texas Penal Code § 6.02

267

CRIMEGRAPH
Criminal Trespass

Offense	Culpable mental state	Conduct	Where?	When?	Specific intent/knowledge	Penalty
Criminal Trespass 30.05(a)\(1)	1. Intentionally, or 2. Knowingly, or 3. Recklessly*	1. Enters or 2. Remains on	Property	Without effective consent of owner	Had notice entry was forbidden	BM to AM
Criminal Trespass 30.05(a)\(1)	1. Intentionally, or 2. Knowingly, or 3. Recklessly*	1. Enters or 2. Remains in	Building	Without effective consent of owner	Had notice entry was forbidden	BM to AM
Criminal Trespass 30.05(a)\(2)	1. Intentionally, or 2. Knowingly, or 3. Recklessly*	1. Enters or 2. Remains on	Property	Without effective consent of owner	Received notice to depart and failed to do so	BM to AM
Criminal Trespass 30.05(a)\(2)	1. Intentionally, or 2. Knowingly, or 3. Recklessly*	1. Enters or 2. Remains in	Building	Without effective consent of owner	Received notice to depart and failed to do so	BM to AM
Criminal Trespass 30.05(e)\(\)	1. Intentionally, or 2. Knowingly, or 3. Recklessly	1. Enters or 2. Remains on	Agricultural land within 100 feet of boundary	Without express consent of owner	Had notice entry was forbidden	CM to AM
Criminal Trespass 30.05(e)\(\)	1. Intentionally, or 2. Knowingly, or 3. Recklessly	1. Enters or 2. Remains on	Agricultural land within 100 feet of boundary	Without express consent of owner	Received notice to depart and failed to do so	CM to AM

*Required by Texas Penal Code § 6.02

268

Notes

1. Anderson v. State, 48 Ala. 665 (1872).
2. *et domus sua culque est tutissimum refugium.*
3. This principle also extends broad protection to individuals in using force to protect their home. See Chapter 15—General Defenses and Justification.
4. Criminal trespass is discussed elsewhere in the chapter. However, one form of criminal trespass is the uncompleted burglary.
5. An unusual example of "entering" is a 1909 Texas case involving an individual who attempts to kill another by shooting at the victim through a window. The Texas court ruled that the behavior violated the state's then existing burglary laws. Rainey v. State, 121 S.W. 1120 (Tex. Crim. App. 1909).
6. Separation of the kitchen served to keep the heat of the fire out of the main home. Additionally, if the fire flared out of control—apparently a fairly common occurrence—the main house was not threatened.
7. 4 WILLIAM BLACKSTONE, COMMENTARIES *224–228.
8. 6 & 7 Geo. V, c. 50, § 46 (1916).
9. Richardson v. State, 888 S.W.2d 822 (Tex. Crim. App. 1994).
10. Langs v. State, 183 S.W.3d 680, 686 (Tex. Crim. App. 2006).
11. TEX. PENAL CODE § 1.07 (a)(11).
12. Thomas v. State, 621 S.W.2d 158, 161 (Tex. Crim. App. 1981).
13. TEX. PENAL CODE § 1.07 (a)(19).
14. See also Gordon v. State, 633 S.W.2d 872 (Tex. Crim. App. 1982), wherein offender gained entry by asking to use the telephone.
15. TEX. DEP'T OF PUB. SAFETY, THE TEXAS CRIME REPORT FOR 2006 (2007).
16. *See* Moore v. State, 54 S.W.3d 529 (Tex. App.—Fort Worth 2001).
17. The statutory definition of "enter" appears to eliminate the prior Texas law that discharging a firearm into a house with intent to injure constitutes burglary. See note 5 above.
18. Williams v. State, 997 S.W.2d 415 (Tex. App.—Beaumont 1999).
19. Alexander v. State, 873 S.W.2d 793 (Tex. App.—Beaumont 1994).
20. Marrs v. State, 647 S.W.2d 286, 290 (Tex. Crim. App. 1983).
21. *Id.*
22. Hughes v. State, 625 S.W.2d 827 (Tex. App.—Houston [14th Dist.] 1981)
23. See Johnson v. State, 664 S.W.2d 420 (Tex. App.—Amarillo 1983), upholding burglary conviction of individual found behind counter of pharmacy department of supermarket. Pharmacy was closed at the time.
24. *See* Evans v. State, 677 S.W.2d 814 (Tex. App.—Fort Worth 1984).
25. *See* Williams v. State, 537 S.W.2d 936 (Tex. Crim. App. 1976).
26. *See* Garza v. State, 522 S.W.2d 693 (Tex. Crim. App. 1975).
27. Grinage v. State, 634 S.W.2d 863, 866 (Tex. Civ. App. 1982), *quoting* Levesque v. State, 217 N.W.2d 317 (Wis. 1974).
28. Matagorda County Appraisal District v. Coastal Liquids Partners, 165 S.W.3d 329 (Tex. 2005).
29. Callahan v. State, 41 Tex. 43 (1874).
30. *See* THE TEXAS CRIME REPORT FOR 2006, *supra.*
31. Olaniyi-Oke v. State, 827 S.W.2d 537 (Tex. App.—Houston [1st Dist.] 1992).
32. Johnson v. State, 844 S.W.2d 872 (Tex. App.—Amarillo 1992).
33. Jones v. State, 690 S.W.2d 318 (Tex. App.—Dallas 1985).
34. Torres v. State, 117 S.W.3d 891 (Tex. Crim. App. 2003).
35. *In re* E.P., 963 S.W.2d 191 (Tex. App.—Austin 1998), holding that a vacant apartment is a habitation.
36. Blankenship v. State, 780 S.W.2d 198 (Tex. Crim. App. 1989)
37. Day v. State, 534 S.W.2d 681 (Tex. Crim. App. 1976).
38. Gilliam v. State, 746 S.W.2d 323 (Tex. App.—Eastland 1988).
39. Allen v. State, 719 S.W.2d 258 (Tex. App.—Waco 1986).
40. Ford v. State, 632 S.W.2d 151 (Tex. Crim. App. 1982).
41. Tabor v. State, 88 S.W.3d 783 (Tex. App.—Tyler 2002).
42. Simmons v. State, 590 S.W.2d 137 (Tex. Crim. App. 1979).
43. Davis v. State, 783 S.W.2d 313 (Tex. App.—Corpus Christi 1990).
44. *See* Denison v. State, 651 S.W.2d 754 (Tex. Crim. App. 1983).
45. Villarreal v. State, 79 S.W.3d 806 (Tex. App.—Corpus Christi 2006).
46. Poncio v. State, 185 S.W.3d 904 ((Tex. Crim. App. 2006).
47. Bolyard v. State, 198 S.W.3d 806 (Tex. App.—Eastland 2006).
48. TEX. PENAL CODE § 21.11.
49. See Ashby v. State, 604 S.W.2d 897, 898 (Tex. Crim. App. 1979), where in a retail theft case the court noted, "No authority is cited by the State for the novel proposition that one who enters the store with the fraudulent intent to unlawfully appropriate property has rendered the commercially provided consent of the store ineffective for purposes of our theft statute."
50. Robles v. State, 651 S.W.2d 868 (Tex. App.—Houston [1st Dist.] 1983).
51. *See* Mohammed v. State, 2001 Tex. App. LEXIS 4198, n. 4.

52. Ramirez v. State, 711 S.W.2d 408 (Tex. App.— El Paso 1986).

53. Tex. Penal Code § 38.04(b)(1).

54. Hobbs v. State, 175 S.W.3d 777 (Tex. Crim. App. 2005).

55. Aguilar v. State, 682 S.W.2d 556 (Tex. Crim. App. 1985).

56. Tex. Penal Code § 3.02.

57. Tex. Penal Code § 3.04(a).

58. Tex. Penal Code § 3.04(b).

59. Morris v. State, 928 S.W.2d 282 (Tex. App.—Fort Worth 1996).

60. Breaking into an ATM that is mounted in the wall of a bank would violate the general burglary statute, Sec. 30.02.

61. *See* The Texas Crime Report for 2006, *supra*.

62. State crime data tracks the format used in the FBI Uniform Crime Reports. As such, most vehicular burglaries are recorded as thefts from motor vehicles. *See* The Texas Crime Report for 2006, *supra*.

63. *See* Garcia v. State, 732 S.W.2d 673 (Tex. App.— Corpus Christi 1987), *and* Reed v. State, 767 S.W.2d 293 (Tex. App.—Fort Worth 1989).

64. Chavez v. State, 479 S.W.2d 687 (Tex. Crim. App. 1972).

65. See Wade v. State, 833 S.W.2d 324 (Tex. App.— Houston [1st Dist.] 1992), upholding conviction for theft of chairs from a boat.

66. Van Dalen v. State, 789 S.W.2d 334 (Tex. App.— Houston [14th Dist.] 1990). See also Trevino v. State, 697 S.W.2d 476 (Tex. App.—San Antonio 1985), holding that an automobile without a motor was still a "vehicle" for purposes of the burglary of vehicle statute.

67. Griffin v. State, 815 S.W.2d 576 (Tex. Crim. App. 1991).

68. Soto v. State, 782 S.W.2d 17 (Tex. App.—San Antonio 1989).

69. Richardson v. State.

70. *See* Day v. State.

71. Richardson v. State.

72. State v. Wheeler, 3 Vt. 344 (1830).

73. Municipal ordinances often expand the definition of criminal trespass.

74. Tex. Penal Code § 9.41(a). See also Chapter 15 for discussion on justification and use of force.

75. Tex. Penal Code § 6.02(b) and (c). See discussion of culpable mental state in Chapter 3. *See also* West v. State, 567 S.W.2d 515 (Tex. Crim. App. 1978).

76. Williams v. State, 605 S.W.2d 596 (Tex. Crim. App. 1980).

77. Arnold v. State, 867 S.W.2d 378 (Tex. Crim. App. 1993).

78. Alberto has also violated Tex. Educ. Code § 37.107—Trespass on School Grounds.

79. See Otwell v. State, 850 S.W.2d 815 (Tex. App.—Fort Worth 1993), upholding conviction of criminal trespasser involving city-owned park and building; Reed v. State, 762 S.W.2d 640 (Tex. App.—Texarkana 1988), applying the statute to high school premises; and Arnold v. State, 867 S.W.2d 378 (Tex. Crim.

App. 1993), upholding conviction of an individual for trespassing at a federal courthouse. However, see State of Texas v. Carley, 885 F. Supp. 940 (W.D. Tex. 1994), wherein a federal judge ruled that one could not be charged with criminal trespass for being on a public road or a road the defendant had good reason to believe is public.

80. 15 S.W.3d 599 (Tex. App.—Austin 2000).

81. In contrast, the Legislature has specified the exact wording that must be contained in the registered letter to an individual who has written a "hot" check in order to raise the presumption of intent to deceive. *See* Tex. Penal Code § 32.41(c)(3). Additionally, the posting requirements on a private parking lot necessary to legally tow vehicles are precise as to size, content, and placement. *See* Tex. Transp. Code §§ 684.031–684.035.

82. The statute could certainly be improved by adopting the view of Model Penal Code § 221.2, which criminalizes entering or remaining in any building without permission.

83. Moreno v. State, 702 S.W.2d 636 (Tex. App.— El Paso 1986).

84. Arkansas, Missouri, and Kansas also reportedly use purple paint. At least ten other states use paint colors ranging from orange to lime green.

85. Whether or not Craig gets the price of admission returned is a civil matter grounded in the law of contracts.

86. In contrast, see Tex. Penal Code § 42.04, which specifically authorizes a "peace officer, a fireman, a person with authority to control the use of the premises, or any person directly affected by the violation" to give an order to disperse in cases of obstructing a passageway.

87. Amalgamated Food Employees Union v. Logan Valley Plaza, 391 U.S. 308 (1968).

88. Lloyd Corp., Ltd. v. Tanner, 407 U.S. 551 (1972).

89. Hudgens v. National Labor Relations Board, 424 U.S. 507 (1976). *See also* International Society for Krishna Consciousness, Inc. v. Lee, 505 U.S. 672 (1992).

90. Virginia v. Hicks, 539 U.S. 113 (2003).

91. Edwards v. South Carolina, 372 U.S. 229 (1963).

92. United States v. Grace, 461 U.S. 171 (1983).

93. Tex. Code of Crim. P. art. 38.23.

94. Compare State v. Hobbs, 824 S.W.2d 317 (Tex. App.—San Antonio 1992), holding peace officers not exempt from coverage of criminal trespass statute and Rosalez v. State, 875 S.W.2d 705 (Tex. App.— Dallas 1993), and Rue v. State, 958 S.W.2d 915 (Tex. App.—Houston [14th Dist.] 1997), holding statute does not apply to law enforcement officers because of availability of defense of necessity under Tex. Penal Code § 9.21.

95. Tex. Penal Code § 31.04.

96. *Id.*

CHAPTER
12
Offenses Against Government Operations

BOLO

The reader should be on the lookout (BOLO) for the meaning of the following terms. Knowledge of the meaning of these terms will greatly assist the reader in understanding the primary elements of the chapter.

- Benefit
- Bribery
- Community supervision
- Consideration
- Custody
- Escape
- Frankpledge

- Materiality
- Misprision
- Parole
- Perjury
- Probation
- *Terry* stop
- Writ of *habeas corpus*

INTRODUCTION

Given that the government holds the power to decide which forms of conduct constitute offenses among its citizens, it is not surprising that over the years the government has also wielded that authority to decide when a crime is perpetrated against it. Recall that in Common Law-based countries like the United States all offenses are viewed as affronts to the government in the broad sense. Yet some offenses are indeed affronts to the government in the narrow sense. In these offenses, the king (or in modern times, the institutions of government at the federal, state, or local levels) is the actual as well as theoretical victim.

This authority of the sovereign to define when conduct constituted a crime was widely abused by various English rulers. British history is full of incidents of the incarceration or execution of individuals who wronged the monarch through a variety of real or perceived acts. The demise of the various wives of King Henry VIII (1491–1547) has been the stuff of literature, motion pictures, and television shows for decades. Sometimes the unwritten law turned against the lawmakers. King Charles I (1600–1649) and his successor Oliver Cromwell (1599–1658) were both beheaded for their alleged treasons against England.[1] In each instance, the sovereign declared that some conduct of the individual constituted treason, which was punishable by death. Such an approach was possible, of course, in a system where the "law" was often the product of monarchial decree.

When America's founding fathers considered the nature of government for the new nation, they understood the need for the sovereign to be able to specify when conduct was a crime against the operation of government. But, they also recognized the need to control such power to prevent the abuses their British forbearers had experienced. Accordingly, contained in the U.S. Constitution and in most state constitutions is the prohibition against the enactment of *ex post facto* laws. As discussed in Chapter 1, the *ex post facto* prohibition bars the creation of retroactive criminal statutes. Additionally, the U.S. Constitution requires that any conviction for treason be based upon the testimony of two witnesses.[2] The two witness rule is unique in all of American criminal law. While the *ex post facto* protection applies to any criminal offense, the historical basis for this restriction as well as the two witness rule lies in curtailing the ability of governmental officials to punish individuals purely for political reasons.

Some of the government-as-victim crimes exist to facilitate the orderly operation of the justice system. The justice system, both the criminal and civil forms of it, cannot function reasonably effectively and efficiently unless certain principles are adhered to. Over the years, society has decided that certain of the justice system principles are so important that their violation should result in prosecution. A few offenses, such as those mandating accurate reporting of the occurrence of a crime, place an affirmative duty on all citizens to assist the justice system in functioning. Some other offenses, such as bribery, perjury, and tampering with evidence, are critical to ensuring the fairness of the operation of the justice system, while other crimes, like evading arrest, resisting arrest, and escape, exist to encourage persons affected by the decisions of public officials to comply with those decisions. Additionally, at least one offense, obstruction or retaliation, is in place to protect law-abiding individuals who perform their duty in serving as witnesses or jurors and public officials from being the object of personal harm based upon their service.

OFFENSES CONCERNING REPORTING OF CRIME

Introduction

You are driving down the freeway and observe an apparently intoxicated motorist driving on the wrong side of the road. Oncoming traffic is dodging his vehicle. Obviously a dangerous situation exists. What do you do? Many of us will grab our cellular telephones, dial 9-1-1, and apprise the police dispatcher of the situation. Similarly, in the unlikely event that we were to observe an armed robbery in progress, we would likewise alert the nearest law enforcement agency. The overwhelming bulk of serious criminal offenses come to the attention of authorities by a citizen report. A citizen reports a criminal act and the police respond. Despite utilizing their best strategies, police agencies uncover relatively few serious criminal instances through their own efforts.

But the question is, Why? Why do citizens alert authorities to criminal incidents when the citizen is not the victim of the crime or even at risk of becoming a victim? Most of us view the calling of the police as our civic duty. That is, as members of society we believe we have a responsibility for the collective security of each other. We call the police when we see our neighbor being victimized because we assume that the neighbor would alert authorities if we were the victim. This system of collective protection and responsibility arose formally in early England with the creation of the system of **frankpledge**, the custom whereby the inhabitants of a district were responsible for any crime or injury committed by one of their number. Indeed the first king of modern England, William the Conqueror (1027–1087), ordered that "everyone who wishes to be regarded as free must be in a pledge, and that the pledge must hold and bring him to justice if he commits any offence." Thus arose the Anglo-American notion that each member of society had mutual rights and obligations regarding the suppression of crime and the reporting of offenders.[3]

Over the course of American history, citizens have continued to notify authorities when serious crime occurs, even though the formal system of frankpledge has long since vanished from the legal and social landscape. The failure to report serious crime has not proven to be a major problem in this country. Certainly some crimes may go unreported due to the victim's fear of retaliation, the protection of the perpetrator, or other reasons, but these unknown crimes appear not to constitute a significant percentage of serious offenses.[4]

But is the failure to report a crime itself a crime? Many jurisdictions have general failure to report laws, often labeled either misprision of a felony or compounding a crime. The term **misprision** is used in law to refer to the failure to act.

Failure to Report a Felony

Only since 2003 has the Texas criminal law imposed a general duty on citizens to report felonious conduct. Sec. 38.171 requires any person who observes the commission of a felony potentially involving serious bodily injury or death to immediately report the same to a peace officer or law enforcement agency. However, the reporting requirement exists only if the individual can act without placing himself or herself in serious danger. The statute, which is punished as a Class A misdemeanor, applies only to felonies. Failure to report a misdemeanor is not an offense.

Since the statute is relatively new, its scope of coverage and its practical uses have not been fully fleshed out by courts, prosecutors, and police. The law would appear to exist more to encourage the reporting of crimes by reluctant witnesses than to actually punish the average citizen who observes a serious crime and does nothing. Indeed, anecdotal evidence suggests that the charge is being filed primarily against individuals who are actually parties to another crime or are protecting relatives and friends! In one instance, a Central Texas mother whose three-year-old son ate her LSD-laced candy pled guilty to failure to report a felony.[5] In another case, the husband of a schoolteacher who was engaging in sex acts with male students in her home was charged with failure to report a felony in addition to a charge of sexual assault of a child after participating in sexual contact of one of the boys.[6] Similarly, a man suspected of participating in a gang-related slaying in Laredo was initially charged with failure to report a felony while the police investigated the extent of his involvement.[7]

Specialized forms of failure to report criminal offense statutes also exist in the state. The best known are failure to report child abuse[8] and the requirement of drivers

---

§ 38.171. Failure to Report Felony

a. A person commits an offense if the person:
　1. observes the commission of a felony under circumstances in which a reasonable person would believe that an offense had been committed in which serious bodily injury or death may have resulted; and
　2. fails to immediately report the commission of the offense to a peace officer or law enforcement agency under circumstances in which:
　　A. a reasonable person would believe that the commission of the offense had not been reported; and
　　B. the person could immediately report the commission of the offense without placing himself or herself in danger of suffering serious bodily injury or death.

b. An offense under this section is a Class A misdemeanor.

to report being involved in a vehicular accident.[9] But Texas law also criminalizes the failure to report the existence of a dead body,[10] the failure to report incidents of school hazing,[11] and the failure of medical professionals to report gunshot wounds,[12] drug overdoses,[13] and incidents of physical or sexual abuse of a minor.[14] Photo processors are required to report suspected child pornography.[15] Justice personnel also have a duty, under threat of criminal prosecution, to report the death of a prisoner in custody.[16] Once again, the goal of all such statutes is less to punish individuals who fail to report the incidents and more to encourage the act of reporting. Many of these specialized criminal statutes are coupled with a civil immunity absolving from liability an individual who makes a good faith report of a suspected crime. Thus, if Ed, a schoolteacher, suspects that one of his students is being physically or sexually abused, Ed can report his suspicions to appropriate authorities without fear of a civil suit should his suspicions prove unfounded.[17]

False Report to Peace Officer

Just as the government seeks to encourage the reporting of serious crimes, albeit through the threat of criminal sanction, it also desires to discourage false reporting of criminal incidents. Suppose Monika is angry at her boyfriend Tyrone. She has discovered that Tyrone has been seeing another woman. Monika, in an effort to make Tyrone's life miserable, calls the police and reports that Tyrone raped her. The police launch an investigation and arrest Tyrone. Monika has a change of heart and tells the police that she made up the entire story. Tyrone is released but Monika is subject to being charged with making a false report to the police.

False reporting, while not a major problem for law enforcement, does result in the expenditure of time and resources to pursue a situation for which there is no basis in fact. False reporting statutes are designed to discourage the improper diversion of the limited resources of police agencies.

Individuals may make false reports for a variety of reasons. Revenge, such as in the case of Monika, might be one motivation. In another case, a psychological need to draw attention to oneself, such as the individual who falsely claims to have been kidnapped, may be the reason for the report. Some individuals may attempt to cover-up an embarrassing incident or lack of good judgment, such as the teenager who wrecks the family car while intoxicated but reports it stolen to avoid the wrath of his parents. Or perhaps an individual is seeking to defraud an insurance company. She reports her diamond ring mysteriously missing even though she actually had

§ 37.08. False Report to Peace Officer or Law Enforcement Employee

a. A person commits an offense if, with intent to deceive, he knowingly makes a false statement that is material to a criminal investigation and makes the statement to:
   1. a peace officer conducting the investigation; or
   2. any employee of a law enforcement agency that is authorized by the agency to conduct the investigation and that the actor knows is conducting the investigation.

b. In this section, "law enforcement agency" has the meaning assigned by Article 59.01, Code of Criminal Procedure.

c. An offense under this section is a Class B misdemeanor.

sold it to raise cash to pay her credit card bill. Insurance companies often require that a police report be filed in any case involving a suspected theft or unexplained disappearance of expensive property.

It is important to bear in mind that false reporting is a circumstance surrounding conduct crime.[18] The offender must be aware that his or her report is not true. A mere error in reporting is not sufficient. Thus, assume Carl is driving down the street. He observes a man exit an automobile and seize a young girl who is walking on the sidewalk. The child struggles with the man and is screaming. The man succeeds in forcing the girl into his vehicle. Carl calls the police to report the incident. A subsequent investigation reveals that the child had run away from home and the man who seized her was her father. Carl has not committed any offense since his report was merely mistaken, not knowingly in error.

Sec. 37.08 requires that the false report be made with "the intent to deceive." The statute also mandates that the false statement be "material." To be "material," the information has to matter. The requirement of **materiality** prevents an individual from being prosecuted based on a false statement that has no effect on the investigation.[19] Materiality is explained further in the section covering perjury.

Suppose Tony is stopped for speeding. The highway patrol trooper asks Tony if he has been drinking. Tony says he had one beer an hour earlier. Suspecting Tony is intoxicated, the trooper takes him to the police station where a breath test is administered. Tony's blood alcohol level is determined to be over the legal limit. In addition to his driving while intoxicated charge, did Tony commit another offense when he made the clearly false statement about having drunk only one beer?

Certainly suspects in criminal cases often give false statements to the police with the clear purpose of confusing or misleading the police in their investigations.[20] Few such individuals like the intoxicated driver Tony are ever charged with making false statements. Police officers come to expect that some people will be less than forthcoming when interviewed, while others will simply lie to further their own or someone else's interest. Police officers also possess wide discretion in deciding against whom to file charges. In cases involving lying to police officers, whether to file charges often turns upon whether the additional charges will accomplish a larger purpose. Rarely is the suspect in a major investigation, such as a burglary or sexual assault, the object of false statement charges. Logically, the suspect is facing more serious charges and the fact the suspect uses every means at hand, including lying to the police, is seen by many as a common, if undesirable, aspect of the justice system.

On the other hand, one occasionally will see the filing of false statement charges against those who directly obstruct police investigative efforts. For example, suppose the police are seeking to execute an arrest warrant for Cain. The police go to his last known address. The door is answered by his roommate Abel. Abel tells the police that he has not seen Cain in the last two weeks. The police search the apartment and find Cain hiding in a bedroom closet. Should Abel be charged with making false statements to the police?[21] How is this situation different from that of Tony the drunk driver?

Individuals who are queried by the police can avoid charges of making a false statement by a very simple means. They can invoke their Fifth Amendment privilege against compulsory self-incrimination. With limited exceptions, this privilege not to respond to the questions of government officials is near absolute. The citizen can simply choose to speak to the police or not. While the right to remain silent has been long revered, the Constitution does not grant the right to lie.

OFFENSES INTERFERING WITH INVESTIGATION AND PROSECUTION

Tampering with or Fabricating Physical Evidence

A suspect or third party who tampers with or destroys evidence of a crime can be prosecuted for the additional misconduct. If Jeff robs a liquor store and then throws his mask and pistol in the river, he will certainly be charged with aggravated robbery but is highly unlikely to be charged with destruction of evidence. On the other hand, if after the robbery Jeff gives the mask and pistol to his brother Mutt who carries out the task of throwing the objects in the river, Mutt may well be prosecuted for destruction of evidence. Mutt's act is supplemental to Jeff's, and the interests of justice are such that the law seeks to discourage conduct that obstructs the prosecution of a criminal offense.

Under Texas law (Sec. 37.09), a person who "alters, destroys, or conceals" any item with intent to affect its accuracy or availability as evidence in an investigation or court proceeding commits an offense. The conduct is a felony of the second degree. The statute requires as an element of the offense that the individual know an investigation is being conducted at the time of the destruction of the evidence and that the item is evidence.[22] This element can create arguably curious results. Suppose Jeff in the robbery scenario above disposes of the mask and pistol before the police focus on him as a suspect. In this case he apparently does not violate the destruction of evidence law. But if he disposes of the evidence while the police are chasing him down the street following the robbery, he does commit the offense because he knows an investigation is underway.

Texas courts have treated the phrase "alters, destroys, or conceals" as three different forms of illegal behavior. Thus, when an arrested subject tore a marijuana cigarette in two parts and tossed it out the window of her car, she did not destroy the evidence because the police immediately recovered the pieces and used them to convict her of possession of marijuana. The court ruled that something is destroyed within the meaning of the statute when its evidentiary value is destroyed. Changes in the form of the evidence without a loss of evidentiary value should be charged as either attempts to destroy or alterations.[23]

Similar logic is followed when a suspect attempts to swallow evidence, such as illegal narcotics. In one case, cocaine was obtained from a suspect through a hospital procedure of pumping his stomach. The court held that swallowing the cocaine was an effort to conceal the evidence and violated Sec. 37.09.[24] In contrast, a suspect who was found with crack cocaine in his mouth was ruled not guilty of violating Sec. 37.09 because users commonly carry the drug in their mouths and there was no evidence that the defendant was intending to impair the availability of the evidence.[25]

For a violation, only the intent to alter, destroy, or conceal the item need be proven. Successful alteration or destruction is not an element of the offense.[26]

But consider the following relatively common occurrence. A police officer is signaling a motorist to stop following commission of a traffic violation. Prior to stopping, the motorist tosses several unknown objects out of the vehicle. Subsequent investigation reveals the objects to be cans of beer and the motorist and his passengers to be juveniles. Have the vehicle's occupants committed tampering with evidence? Probably not. Texas case law suggests that since the officer was not initially stopping the youths for the crime of minor in possession[27] or violating the open container law,[28] the abandonment of the beer was not an effort to conceal evidence while an investigation was "pending" or "in progress" as required by the statute's language. The court decisions appear to require a connection between the investigation the officer is conducting and the evidence alleged to have been damaged or concealed.[29] In contrast, a suspect who crushes his crack pipe after an officer discovered it in a stop-and-frisk encounter was guilty of damaging evidence.[30]

However, at least one Court of Appeals takes the position that the term "pending" means about to happen. Thus, according to this appellate court, efforts to destroy evidence immediately prior to its discovery during an unrelated investigation violate Sec. 37.09.[31] The Court of Criminal Appeals has yet to resolve this interpretation conflict across the various lower courts.

Many states that have considered the matter view the dropping of contraband within the view of a police officer as an act of abandonment, not an attempt to conceal or destroy evidence. The primary rationale for this view is that a destruction of evidence charge is often more serious than the underlying possession charge; it would be illogical to assume that the Legislature intended to punish an offender more severely for destroying evidence of a crime than for the crime itself.[32]

The tampering statute has also been applied to peace officers who are overly zealous in the performance of their duties. In an unusual application of the statute, a Dallas narcotics officer was convicted of tampering after he filed an affidavit for a search warrant which contained sworn statements he knew to be false.[33] Sec. 37.09(a)(2) declares it an offense to present a false document with intent to affect the outcome of an investigation.[34] The narcotics officers lied in the affidavit about the previous track record of his informant.

Failure to Identify

Late at night in a part of town that has been plagued with residential burglaries, a police officer observes a car driving very slowly through the neighborhood. Is the driver a would-be burglar? Or maybe drunk? Or merely lost? Everyday police officers face such ambiguous situations and must decide whether the observed conduct is potentially criminal or simply innocent or stupid behavior. But, for many years the scope of the officer's authority to act in such situations was ambiguous at best. Police officers would fall back on pretext offenses (e.g., driving too slowly), suspicious persons laws, and vagrancy statutes to justify the stopping or arresting of individuals who were engaging in unusual or suspicious behavior. The officer's goal was often to deter the commission of a crime or buy time until the officer could gather additional information to make a decision about more serious charges.

In 1968, in the landmark case of Terry v. Ohio,[35] the Supreme Court ruled that whenever a peace officer had a reasonable suspicion to believe criminal activity was afoot, the officer, after identifying himself, could stop the individual and make reasonable inquiries. If the officer believed the individual was armed, a frisk for weapons could be conducted. *Terry* and subsequent court rulings established guidelines for officers handling suspicious persons in a constitutional manner.[36]

The Supreme Court granted officers the authority during **Terry stops** to make reasonable inquires. Among the forms of inquiry approved by the court is the asking of the suspect's name.[37] But what if the suspect refuses to respond or responds with a fictitious name? Can such deceptive or noncooperation itself be made a crime? What if the suspect refuses to produce identification? Can the state constitutionally criminalize that failure to cooperate with the officer?

In 2004, the Supreme Court answered at least a portion of these questions. The high court upheld the conviction of a Nevada man who refused to give his name to a police officer who was investigating a suspected assault.[38] The man was convicted under the state's resisting a public officer statute. The law criminalized resisting or obstructing a police officer in the performance of a legal duty. A five to four majority of justices noted that about two dozen states have enacted statutes authorizing peace officers to stop

§ 38.02. Failure to Identify

a. A person commits an offense if he intentionally refuses to give his name, residence address, or date of birth to a peace officer who has lawfully arrested the person and requested the information.

b. A person commits an offense if he intentionally gives a false or fictitious name, residence address, or date of birth to a peace officer who has:
   1. lawfully arrested the person;
   2. lawfully detained the person; or
   3. requested the information from a person that the peace officer has good cause to believe is a witness to a criminal offense.

c. Except as provided by Subsections (d) and (e), an offense under this section is:
   1. a Class C misdemeanor if the offense is committed under Subsection (a); or
   2. a Class B misdemeanor if the offense is committed under Subsection (b).

d. If it is shown on the trial of an offense under this section that the defendant was a fugitive from justice at the time of the offense, the offense is:
   1. a Class B misdemeanor if the offense is committed under Subsection (a); or
   2. a Class A misdemeanor if the offense is committed under Subsection (b).

e. If conduct that constitutes an offense under this section also constitutes an offense under Section 106.07, Alcoholic Beverage Code, the actor may be prosecuted only under Section 106.07.

and detain suspicious individuals. These statutes are generally in accord with the *Terry* rule governing the stopping of suspects. The justices concluded that under the circumstances presented neither the Fourth Amendment right to be free of unreasonable searches and seizures nor the right to remain silent afforded by the Fifth Amendment were violated. Reasonable grounds existed to detain the suspect and ask him questions about the incident. His refusal to give his name obstructed the investigation. The high court ruled that giving one's name during the course of an investigation normally did not tend to incriminate the person.

The Supreme Court's ruling would appear to allow all states to treat a failure to identify during a *Terry* stop as a form of obstructing a peace officer, providing the statutory language is sufficient.[39] However, the Texas Legislature has chosen not to enact a statute that criminalizes failure to identify oneself to a police officer during a temporary detention. Rather, despite its name, a close reading of Sec. 38.02 reveals that it only criminalizes a refusal to identify oneself if the suspect has already been arrested for some other offense. For individuals who are the object of a *Terry* stop, refusal to provide identification is not itself a crime.[40] However, it is an offense for a lawfully detained party to provide a false or fictitious name, residence address, or date of birth. Assume Aaron is lawfully detained by Officer Harold, a uniformed city police officer.[41] Officer Harold asks Aaron his name and address. If Aaron simply refuses to provide this information, he commits no violation of Sec. 38.02. But if Aaron provides a name or address other than his true name, an offense has been committed. During its 2007 session, the Legislature considered a bill to expand the coverage of this statute to criminalize the refusal of anyone who has been lawfully stopped to identify themselves on request. The state House of Representatives rejected the proposal. The matter was never considered by the state Senate.[42]

The Supreme Court decisions on the topic of failure to identify have left open the constitutional question of whether documentary evidence of identity must be provided on request of a police officer.[43] While Texas and most other states require the driver of a motor vehicle to produce his or her operator's license upon demand of a peace officer, this statutory requirement is limited to the vehicle's driver.[44] Whether Texas or any other state can criminalize failure to produce an identifying document in other situations is an open question. The American tradition, unlike most other countries of the world, has been not to require citizens to possess proof of identity or citizenship. Following the attacks of September 11, 2001, some suggested that America adopt a national identification card system to help thwart terrorists. Those suggestions failed to gain broad political support.[45] It would appear illogical to criminalize failing to produce identifying documents unless some preexisting statute required those same documents to be carried on one's person. To date, no federal or state statute requires citizens to carry proof of identity.

Interference with Public Duties

State law bars individuals from interfering with peace officers, firefighters, EMS personnel, and certain other government employees in the performance of their duties. Sec. 38.15 lays out the various elements of the crime but generally prohibits interrupting, disrupting, impeding, or otherwise interfering with these public safety personnel in the course of their jobs. The *actus reus* of the offense is quite broad but such expansive language is necessary to cover the range of situations where a citizen might obstruct the work of a peace officer or firefighter. In enacting the statute, the Legislature is empowering public safety personnel, judges, and juries to use their respective judgments in determining when citizen conduct at a crime scene or fire crosses the line and becomes an interference to the safety personnel at the scene.

If Sam blocks entry of a fire truck responding to a fire, Sam commits a violation. If Mary, an intoxicated driver, resists efforts of the police to impound her vehicle, she violates this statute. When Arthur seeks to prevent a deputy constable from evicting a tenant who is behind in their rent, Arthur commits interference with public duties.

While the offense is a Class B misdemeanor, the statute does provide two interesting defenses. First, the statute is not violated when an individual warns another of the presence of a police officer who is enforcing traffic laws. Thus the flashing of headlamps to warn oncoming motorists of the presence of a police officer over the next hill has been specifically exempted from the scope of the law. Apparently, the Legislature feared overzealous enforcement of the statute in this situation.

The other defense has its origin in a decision of the U.S. Supreme Court. Sec. 38.15(d) provides that no offense occurs if the alleged interference consists of speech only. In 1987, the high court reviewed a Houston city ordinance which was similar in scope to the state statute.[46] A police officer had arrested a community activist who had verbally criticized the officer's interactions with a pedestrian who was attempting to stop traffic to permit a friend's automobile to back onto a busy street. The activist was found not guilty of interfering with the officer's official duties and then sued the city seeking to have the ordinance declared unconstitutional. After a federal appeals court found the ordinance conflicted with the First Amendment, the city appealed to the Supreme Court. The justices affirmed the determination of unconstitutionality on the grounds that the ordinance improperly provided the police with unfettered discretion to arrest individuals for words or conduct that were simply annoying or offensive. Such broad discretion conflicted with the free speech rights protected by the First Amendment.

The Legislature has essentially incorporated this decision into the state interference statute. However, the conviction of a belligerent individual who argued with police officers during a disturbance call was affirmed not because of the argument but because he refused to comply with an officer's command to stay on the sidewalk.[47] For safety reasons, the officer was attempting to keep the defendant separated from another individual. In another case, a detained suspect who told her child to run from the police was found to have committed interference with public duties. The Court of Criminal Appeals in affirming the conviction ruled that her speech fell outside the statutory defense because it was designed to prompt action.[48] But in another case, arguing with an officer was ruled not to be a violation of the statute.[49]

Special statutes also exist that prohibit taking a weapon from a peace officer or correctional officer and interfering with police service animals.[50]

Evading Arrest

Suppose a police officer observes Juan Pablo engaging in reckless driving. The officer turns on his patrol vehicle's lights and siren to signal Juan Pablo to stop. But instead of stopping, Juan Pablo speeds up. The officer gives a chase. In addition to possible reckless driving charges, Juan Pablo is now facing charges of evading the officer. This offense is variously known as evading, fleeing, or eluding an officer and most commonly comes into play in traffic encounters. Every jurisdiction penalizes flight from a police officer who is attempting a traffic stop. The public policy basis for such an offense is to encourage compliance with official action and to deter placing the officer and the general public at risk when a chase ensues. A significant number of police chases terminate after the suspect has crashed his automobile into some innocent third party. Civil lawsuits arising out of such chases have cost police agencies substantial amounts of money in recent years.

While the Common Law apparently lacked an evading arrest law, the Texas statute on the topic contains the following elements:

1. An individual intentionally
2. Flees
3. A person he knows
4. Is a peace officer
5. Who is attempting lawfully to arrest or detain him.

A core component of the offense is the *mens rea*. The offender must intentionally flee the officer and know the officer is attempting to arrest or detain him.[51] Suppose Ethel, an elderly woman who is hearing impaired, is observed by a police officer committing a traffic violation. The officer activates his vehicle lights and siren and pulls behind Ethel in an effort to signal her to stop. Ethel is oblivious to the officer's signal and continues driving for several miles. Is Ethel guilty of evading arrest? Probably not as she is neither purposefully fleeing nor consciously aware of the officer's efforts to stop her. Likewise, suppose late one night a police car pulls in behind Maria and begins flashing its lights in an effort to get Maria to stop. Maria refuses to stop her car because she has heard of individuals posing as police officers who stop young women and rape them. Has Maria violated Sec. 38.04?

---

§ 38.04. Evading Arrest or Detention

(a) A person commits an offense if he intentionally flees from a person he knows is a peace officer attempting lawfully to arrest or detain him.

Like many misdemeanor offenses, appellate courts have had few opportunities to explain the precise meaning of the elements of the offense. Note that despite the statute's label, it does not criminalize evading an officer but rather fleeing the officer. For example, the verb "flee" is used in its ordinary sense and is an attempt to cover all possible circumstances where the offender fails to submit to the officer's efforts to detain or arrest him or her. Is a suspect committing an offense if he merely hides from the officer? Secreting oneself is certainly evading detection but is the act of hiding a part of "fleeing"?

While one usually thinks of flight as involving moving as fast as possible, the statute does not require that the flight involve any particular speed or mode of transport. As one Texas judge observed, "Neither the accused nor the peace officer is required to be in a motor vehicle, airplane, bicycle or ox-cart."[52] Indeed many offenders simply flee the police on foot.

While an offender's involvement in a high speed chase may elevate the charge because of the danger he creates, one can commit evading an officer by driving at low speed. Given that police are reluctant to use force to halt a fleeing misdemeanor offender, an intoxicated driver who refuses to stop while driving at 15 mph creates an odd police pursuit situation.[53]

Much like resisting arrest laws, evading arrest statutes are applicable only to efforts by governmental officials, not private citizens. Thus if the shopkeeper attempts a citizen's arrest, the flight of the offender does not constitute evading arrest or fleeing an officer.

A lawful action by the police officer is a required element of the evading charge. Even in Texas where the illegality of the arrest is no defense to a resisting arrest charge, the illegality of the arrest or detention is a defense to an evading charge. Put another way, to convict an individual of evading arrest or detention, the prosecution must establish that the arrest or detention was lawful. If, for example, the officer lacked probable cause to make an arrest, no crime is committed by the offender evading the arrest effort.

While evading is normally a Class B misdemeanor, the crime elevates to a state jail felony if the actor is fleeing in a motor vehicle.[54]

Resisting Arrest

The most common entry point to the criminal justice system is the act of arrest. A peace officer arrests an offender and takes him to jail. At some point, usually within 48 hours of the arrest, the offender is taken before a magistrate where formal charges are initiated. The subsequent steps in the justice system follow in due course.

But suppose the offender doesn't desire to be arrested. Or the offender believes that the arrest is illegal or unjustified under the circumstances. What immediate recourse does the offender have? Not much. An arrest is not intended to be the point at which an individual is determined to be guilty or innocent of a criminal charge. Indeed the standard of proof for a lawful arrest, probable cause, is a relatively low one. Society and the institution of law expect the suspect to submit peacefully to the arrest; the legality of the act can be litigated at some point later in the justice system. The purpose of resisting arrest statutes is to prevent injury to the officer and the citizen during the arrest encounter. Accordingly, the courts tend to interpret them consistent with this goal.

Curiously, no state is known to have enacted a statute explicitly requiring a citizen to make himself or herself available to be arrested. Rather, the law of arrest focuses on the grant of authority to peace officers to arrest under particular circumstances or the establishment of the requirements of an arrest warrant. An arrest warrant is a court

§ 38.03. Resisting Arrest, Search, or Transportation

a. A person commits an offense if he intentionally prevents or obstructs a person he knows is a peace officer or a person acting in a peace officer's presence and at his direction from effecting an arrest, search, or transportation of the actor or another by using force against the peace officer or another.

b. It is no defense to prosecution under this section that the arrest or search was unlawful.

c. Except as provided in Subsection (d), an offense under this section is a Class A misdemeanor.

d. An offense under this section is a felony of the third degree if the actor uses a deadly weapon to resist the arrest or search.

order to the sheriff or other peace officer to seize the body of the named suspect. An arrest warrant does not require the suspect himself or herself to do anything. For example, if Herby learns that an outstanding arrest warrant for him exists, Herby is under no legal obligation to turn himself in or otherwise make the job of the police easier in finding him.[55] The one thing Herby is prohibited from doing is physically resisting the effort to arrest him.

The Texas statute unifies resisting arrest, search, and transportation into a single law. Since an arrest is usually considered complete when effected, resistance at some later point in the justice process is not resisting arrest.[56] Thus the law criminalizes resisting transportation to cover the movement of a prisoner in a post-arrest situation. Likewise, the resisting a search aspect of the crime applies to the physical search incident to arrest of a suspect as well as any other lawful search of a person, such as during a temporary detention or jail processing.[57] Obstructing the search of property, such as during execution of a search warrant, is an offense under Sec. 38.15, interference with public duties.

Suppose a constable comes to John and Marsha's home. The constable holds an arrest warrant for Marsha for writing a bad check. Marsha is willing to submit to arrest but John, believing the arrest to be unnecessary to resolve the matter, steps between Marsha and the officer. John pushes the officer in an effort to prevent him from taking Marsha into custody. Has John committed resisting arrest? The answer is affirmative. While normally the object of a resisting an arrest charge is the party being arrested, statutory language is broad enough to permit the offense to be filed against anyone who forcibly interferes with the officer's effort to take another person into custody.

But suppose the reason John is trying to prevent Marsha's arrest is that Marsha is the victim of identity theft and someone else used her name on the check. This matters not. The officer has a presumably valid warrant and Marsha's guilt or innocence will be determined later in court. While the Common Law and early Texas law allowed an individual to resist an unlawful arrest, currently it is no defense to prosecution that the arrest or search was unlawful.

While some states criminalize any effort to prevent an arrest, Texas limits the application of the law to forcible resistance against the officer. Suppose Jack and Jill are staging a protest against pollution of the town water supply. They are lying in the middle of the street in front of the water department. Traffic has come to a stop. The police arrive and order the protestors to disperse. Instead of leaving as ordered, Jack and Jill continue to lie passively in the street. Police officers place them under arrest and carry them to police cars for transportation to jail. In addition to other possible charges, have Jack and Jill committed resisting arrest?

The answer to the question in Texas appears to be no. Jack and Jill are simply not using any force. State courts have held that passive refusal to cooperate with the police does not rise to the offense of resisting arrest because the conduct does not endanger the officer.[58]

Texas appellate courts are divided on what constitutes the use of force in the context of resisting arrest.[59] However, one court has defined force as "power dynamically considered, that is, in motion or in action; constraining power, compulsion; strength directed to an end."[60] On the other hand, a person can forcefully resist an arrest without successfully making physical contact with the one making the arrest.[61] Thus it was resisting arrest for the suspect to kick at a police officer who was trying to arrest him.[62] Likewise, resisting arrest occurred when the suspect unleashed a pit bull on a police officer, although the officer was not bitten by the dog.[63] But, it was not considered forcible resistance for a suspect to twice pull his arm *away* from the arresting officer.[64]

Physical resistance to arrest is likely more common than going limp or other passive acts. The strong law enforcement interest in less than lethal devices such as batons, pepper spray, stun guns, Tasers, and the like exists because the police are concerned with means to temporarily subdue uncooperative offenders. If physical resistance by a suspect occurs, the suspect can often be charged with three offenses: the initial charge for which the arrest was being made, resisting arrest, and assault. The assault charge arises because the use of force against the arresting officer will likely constitute assault by contact or assault with bodily injury.

Since resisting arrest is an offense against the orderly operation of government, the statutes in most states, including Texas, are applicable only to arrests attempted by public servants such as deputy sheriffs or police officers. Private citizens and private security officers do not fall within the coverage of the statutes in most states unless operating under the direct supervision of a peace officer. Thus, if Bob shoplifts merchandise in a store, the store owner or the store security guard can lawfully attempt to arrest him but any resistance Bob puts up will not constitute the separate offense of resisting arrest.

Escape

Once in custody a criminal suspect is expected to adhere to the established processes of the justice system. If the suspect seeks to be freed from jail, he must do so by making bail, by being adjudicated as not guilty of the offense charged, or by successfully obtaining a **writ of *habeas corpus*,**[65] whichever the circumstances might require. What the suspect may not do is decide to leave on his own accord. The offense of **escape** criminalizes unauthorized departures from lawful custody.

The statute applies to those who are in custody in prison or jail and extends also to those who are under arrest by a peace officer. Further, the scope of the law covers anyone in custody pursuant to a court order. The latter would likely include persons jailed as material witnesses and individuals housed in mental health facilities under an involuntary commitment order. Juvenile detainees are also covered under the statute.

While the Common Law distinguished between escapes involving force (breach of prison) and those where no force was used, Texas law makes no such distinction.[66] In any case, the offender must be in **custody**. The requirement of custody distinguishes escape from evading arrest or resisting arrest, two offenses where the offender is not in custody. Sec. 38.01 defines "custody" in the context of being under arrest by a peace officer, being under restraint by a public servant, such as in a Department of Criminal

§ 38.06. Escape

(a) A person commits an offense if he escapes from custody when he is:

1. under arrest for, charged with, or convicted of an offense;
2. in custody pursuant to a lawful order of a court;
3. detained in a secure detention facility, as that term is defined by Section 51.02, Family Code, or
4. in the custody of a juvenile probation officer for violating an order imposed by the juvenile court under Section 52.01, Family Code.

Justice prison unit, and being under restraint in a privately operated jail. The state's escape law covers both any form of restraint by a police officer and incarceration in jail or prison. In addition, "[c]ustody is not limited to actual, physical 'hands-on' restraint, but in the context of escape, is more than the right to control; it implies a degree of physical limitation, restraint, or control the nature and scope of which depends on the facts of each case."[67] An inmate who dressed in doctor scrubs and was permitted by guards to exit the prison infirmary still fits within the definition of escaping.[68]

Clint, a convicted felon housed in a high security prison, concocts a plan to escape. He crawls under a prison dump truck and hoists himself up, clinging to the vehicle's undercarriage. When the evening count of inmates is taken, Clint is discovered not to be in his cell. Correctional officers search the prison grounds and ultimately discover Clint holding on to the underside of the truck. Has Clint committed any criminal offense or has he only violated prison rules? Has Clint "escaped" within the meaning of Sec. 38.01 defining the term?

In one sense, the law of escape when applied to post-conviction offenders is rather simple: the offender is either in the correctional institution where he belongs or not. But this rule becomes complicated when convicted offenders are placed on community supervision, parole, or in work release programs. **Community supervision**, also called **probation**, normally consists of suspension of a convicted offender's sentence, while he or she is allowed to remain in the community often under direction of a probation officer. The probationer must adhere to certain behavioral rules or face revocation and incarceration. **Parole** is the supervised release of an offender from prison before completion of sentence. Here too, the offender must abide by certain rules while reintegrating into the community. Work release programs involve incarcerated prisoners who are permitted to go into the community on a daily basis in order to work. They are expected to return to the correctional facility at the end of their workday.

Texas is in accord with the overwhelming majority of jurisdictions and views probationers as not being in custody. Thus, any violation of the rules of probation or actual flight from the jurisdiction is not considered an escape for the purposes of the Penal Code. The misconduct simply subjects the offender to the potential of having his or her probation revoked and possibly being remanded to jail or prison to serve the original sentence. Similarly, persons on parole are being allowed to complete a portion of their sentence in the community and are often regarded as still being within the custody of the state. However, errant parolees are also not viewed as escapees. Texas law specifically excludes parole violators from the coverage of the escape statute.[69] Parole violations simply place the parolee in jeopardy of revocation and being returned to prison.

Work release rule violations may manifest into a criminal offense, but do not always do so. Since by definition an individual must be in the custody of the government in order to participate in a work release program, failure to return to the designated time and place is treated as an escape.[70] Escape charges are nearly universally filed against individuals who escape from a penitentiary or jail. But, authorities tend to exercise more discretion in the filing of escape charges against errant work release participants. Suppose Rodney, a convicted forger, is a participant in a work release program. Each day he takes the bus to the city to work as a butcher in a meatpacking plant. He is supposed to return to the correctional facility by 6:00 p.m. everyday. But one day, because he is late cleaning up after his work shift, he misses the bus. The next bus does not get him back to the correctional facility until 7:30 p.m. Should he be charged with escape? Is Rodney's situation different than his fellow inmate Peter who works at the same meatpacking plant? One Friday Peter fails to return to the correctional facility. Subsequent investigation reveals Peter has hitchhiked across the state to visit his girlfriend. He is located at the girlfriend's apartment in a drunken condition. Should escape charges be filed against Peter?

Under Sec. 38.08, it is no defense to the crime of escape that the custody was unlawful. If an individual asserts that his confinement is contrary to law, he or she must use the judicial system to contest the lawfulness of the detention. Seeking a writ of *habeas corpus* is the traditional means by which to contest the lawfulness of one's confinement.[71] However, in rare cases, the courts have recognized the defense of necessity as justification for a prisoner's escape from custody.[72]

OFFENSES AFFECTING THE INTEGRITY OF THE JUSTICE SYSTEM

Bribery

The criminal justice system, as with our entire system of government, is dependent upon honest people performing their jobs in an appropriate, consistent manner. Every individual who becomes involved with the justice system deserves equal and fair treatment. Similarly, the public as a whole holds a strong interest in a fair justice system. Any act that casts doubt upon the fairness of the system is viewed by society with particular distain.

One part of this concern is that each employee will perform his or her job in a fair manner. Suppose, for example, that a judge was paid only if the defendant were found guilty. One can certainly expect that even the most honest judge would have difficulty being fair if his or her livelihood was dependent on guilty verdicts. Fortunately, the U.S. Supreme Court ruled many years ago that such a system was unconstitutional.[73]

Now suppose you are a college student charged with DWI. A conviction for that offense would greatly diminish your chance of obtaining employment with a federal investigative agency, your life goal. Consider the possibility that the judge in your case sends word that he will find you not guilty if you place $500 cash in an envelope and deliver it to his spouse by the close of the day. Further, suppose you don't have a spare $500. Putting aside the ethical question, would it be a fair system to acquit those who could pay $500 and convict those who could not? Obviously not. That is why acts of bribery are unlawful. Bribing public officials to perform their jobs, not to perform their jobs, or to perform their jobs in a favorable manner corrupts our system of government. This is particularly true in the criminal justice system. Over the entrance to the U.S. Supreme Court Building in Washington, D.C., are the words "Equal Justice under Law." That phrase embodies the American ideal of justice. If decisions by the police, the prosecutor, and the courts were controlled by personal profit, an equal and just system would not exist.

Successful bribery of justice officials, as well as other governmental personnel, is a crime in every state. It is also a crime for a public official to solicit a bribe or for a citizen to offer a bribe. Depending on the jurisdiction, these separate behaviors may constitute three distinct offenses—soliciting a bribe, offering a bribe, and accepting a bribe. Texas places all three behaviors into a single bribery statute, Sec. 36.02.

The elements of **bribery** consist of:

1. A person intentionally or knowingly
2. Offers, confers, or agrees to confer on another, or solicits, accepts, or agrees to accept from another
3. Any benefit as consideration
4. For vote, exercise of discretion by public servant, or other official act.

Bribery is an offense that can only be committed in a purposeful manner. In other words, the actor must offer or solicit the bribe intentionally or knowingly. This means that either or both parties to the incident intend for the conduct to be a bribe. Suppose John gives a $100 bottle of wine to Wallace, a state legislator. Is that a bribe? It depends on John's purpose. The bottle of wine might be a Christmas gift. Or if John gives Wallace a $100 bill instead of a bottle of wine, the $100 bill might be intended as a campaign contribution. The facts may initially be ambiguous concerning John's intentions.

Consider each of the following variations to the same factual scenario.

1. Doug is stopped for speeding by a deputy sheriff, Rick. Doug says to Rick, "My insurance can't stand another speeding ticket. What if I give you my two tickets to this Sunday's football game? Can we call it even?" Rick replies, "Sounds like a good deal to me. Thanks for the tickets. Go on and be careful."

2. Doug is stopped for speeding by a deputy sheriff, Rick. Doug says to Rick, "My insurance can't stand another speeding ticket. What if I give you my two tickets to this Sunday's football game? Can we call it even?" Rick replies, "No thank you. I'm writing you a citation for doing 70 in a 55 zone."

3. Doug is stopped for speeding by a deputy sheriff, Rick. Rick says to Doug, "You look like a nice guy and otherwise safe driver. Tell you what. Let's cut out the middleman. Just give me $20 and you can go on about your business." Doug responds, "I don't think so. You best just give me the citation."

4. Doug is stopped for speeding by a deputy sheriff, Rick. Rick says to Doug, "You look like a nice guy and otherwise safe driver. Tell you what. Let's cut out the middleman. Just give me $20 and you can go on about your business." Doug responds, "That's the best deal I've heard all week. Here is a nice new crisp $20 bill."

Which of the four hypothetical scenarios constitute bribery? They all do, in one form or another. In scenario 1, Doug commits bribery by offering the tickets to Rick, a public servant, in an effort to influence Rick's exercise of his official discretion in whether or not to issue a traffic citation. Likewise, Rick commits bribery because under the Texas consolidated bribery statute it is an offense for a public servant to accept a bribe. In scenario 2, Doug commits the offense by his mere offer. Note that apparently there is no such crime as attempted bribery because the attempt is criminalized in the underlying statute. Rick, however, commits no offense because he does not accept the bribe. However, in scenario 3, Rick commits the crime but not Doug. The statute criminalizes a public official's efforts at soliciting a bribe. Scenario 4 presents a case where once again both parties violate the law, Rick by soliciting the bribe and Doug by paying the bribe.

The elements of offering or soliciting and accepting a bribe are sometimes difficult to prove directly. Frequently, the conduct occurs without any third-party witness. However, on occasion, one of the participants to the event may be cooperating with the investigation. As such, he or she may tape record the offer of the bribe and use previously marked currency. In cases where neither party is cooperating, the payment of the bribe must be established by other evidence, such as the unexplained existence of cash in the public official's bank account.

If you give your little brother 25 cents not to tell your mother about some misconduct in which you engaged, your conduct does not violate the state bribery statute. While you may have bribed your brother in the ordinary sense, bribery as a crime is concerned with corruption of public officials and employees, ranging from elected officeholders to police officers to schoolteachers. Note that in virtually every bribery situation one of the parties must be a public servant. The only private individuals who can be bribed for the purposes of the statute are political party officials and voters. This latter application covers the public's interest in fair elections.

Bribery occurs only if the conduct involves a **benefit**. The term is defined in Sec. 36.01 in the context of "anything reasonably regarded as pecuniary gain or pecuniary advantage." While cash certainly falls within the definition, other economic gain would also fit, for example, the tickets to the professional football game in the scenarios above. However, goods and services of nominal value, such as unsolicited food treats, a key chain or coffee cup, and the like, are normally not viewed as providing pecuniary advantage.[74] But, a county sheriff's offer of the chief deputy position to an opposition candidate contingent on his withdrawal from a run-off election was a benefit within the meaning of the statute.[75]

Sexual favors do not appear to fit the definition of "benefit." A public servant offering or accepting sex acts in exchange for making an official decision likely does not constitute bribery. But under certain factual circumstances, such conduct might violate the official oppression statute (Sec. 39.03).

A connection must exist between the benefit and the decision of the official. The benefit must be **consideration** for the decision. As one court noted, bribery is an inducement to engage in an illegal contract.[76] It is worthy to note that efforts to influence conduct and decisions of public officials occur with great regularity. Indeed, the First Amendment explicitly grants the right to petition the government. As a consequence, bribery occurs only when the public officer is offered or receives a benefit which he or she is not legally permitted to receive. In an earlier example, the $100 bottle of wine given as a Christmas gift to the legislator would not fit the bribery statute as it would be difficult to prove that the gift was in consideration of a decision. To limit allegations of bribery of elected officials, state law establishes rules whereby public servants must report acceptance of gifts and campaign contributions. Similarly, if a city council member is given $1,000 by a vendor who does business with the city, the payment would seem to be intended as a bribe. But, if the city council member reports the cash in his periodically required disclosure of campaign contributions, the matter is normally not viewed as a bribe. Did the vendor expect the council member to vote in a favorable manner? Most likely. But, the vendor's motives do not make his conduct bribery so long as the transaction is above board and disclosed as required by law.

Because bribery goes to the core of corrupting governmental operations, it is a very serious offense. Bribery is categorized as a second degree felony.

An individual who attempts to influence a voter or public servant through coercive conduct as opposed to a bribe commits the crime of coercion of a public servant or voter, Sec. 36.03.

Obstruction or Retaliation

While the integrity of the government can be corrupted through bribery or coercive influences on public servants, the system can also be stymied if public servants fear doing their duty or citizens are fearful of reporting crime or testifying as witnesses. To assist in preventing this from occurring, Sec. 36.06 was enacted. This statute declares it to be a felony to harm or threaten to harm another through an unlawful act in retaliation for the person's status as a public servant, witness, prospective witness, informant, or individual who reported a crime.[77]

While a threat to do harm to another might constitute assault or terroristic threat, the elements of this offense do not require that the threat of harm be imminent. A threatening letter from a prison inmate to a prospective witness at his trial was sufficient to constitute the offense.[78] Similarly, a threat by a prison inmate to do harm to another inmate "snitch" constitutes retaliation because the victim was a prospective witness.[79] Likewise, repeated threats by an arrestee that he would kill his arresting officer constituted unlawful retaliation.[80]

Retaliation was also the appropriate charge against a juvenile who threatened to obtain a gun and shoot a high school administrator unless the administrator returned certain property to the juvenile.[81] A threat to harm a Child Protective Services worker was the crime of retaliation where the CPS worker advised the actor she was going to report his act of threatening his son with a knife.[82]

Obstruction or retaliation is a felony of the third degree but advances to a felony of the second degree if the victim is a juror. Recall that if a person is murdered during the commission of this offense, the crime becomes capital murder.[83]

Perjury

"I solemnly swear to tell the truth, the whole truth, and nothing but the truth, so help me God." The swearing-in of witnesses prior to giving courtroom testimony is a mainstay of both the civil and criminal justice systems. Although the notion of requiring an oath prior to testifying goes back to Roman law, the current language of the oath dates from thirteenth-century England. During the early Common Law period, however, no criminal penalty for false swearing existed. Rather it was assumed that God's vengeance would take care of those who lied after giving an oath. False swearing, or **perjury**, as a criminal offense did not arise until the mid-sixteenth century. The giving of knowingly false testimony is a crime today in every American jurisdiction.

In Texas, the offense of perjury takes two forms: perjury and aggravated perjury. The distinction between the two offenses is not the degree to which a statement is false

---

§ 37.02. Perjury

a. A person commits an offense if, with intent to deceive and with knowledge of the statement's meaning:

1. he makes a false statement under oath or swears to the truth of a false statement previously made and the statement is required or authorized by law to be made under oath; or

2. he makes a false unsworn declaration under Chapter 132, Civil Practice and Remedies Code.

b. An offense under this section is a Class A misdemeanor.

§ 37.03. Aggravated Perjury

a. A person commits an offense if he commits perjury as defined in Section 37.02, and the false statement:
1. is made during or in connection with an official proceeding; and
2. is material.

b. An offense under this section is a felony of the third degree.

§ 37.04. Materiality

a. A statement is material, regardless of the admissibility of the statement under the rules of evidence, if it could have affected the course or outcome of the official proceeding.

b. It is no defense to prosecution under Section 37.03 (Aggravated Perjury) that the declarant mistakenly believed the statement to be immaterial.

c. Whether a statement is material in a given factual situation is a question of law.

but rather the circumstances of the making of the statement. Perjury (Sec. 37.02) is committed when the false assertion is made or required to be made under oath. Aggravated perjury (Sec. 37.03) occurs when the false utterance is made in an official proceeding, such as court, and is material.

The elements of perjury are essentially

1. With intent to deceive
2. And with knowledge of the statement's meaning
3. A person makes a false statement
4. Under oath, and
5. The statement is required by law to be made under oath.

The offense becomes aggravated perjury when the following elements are added;

6. The statement is made in an official proceeding, and
7. The statement is material.

Perjury applies only to statements that are false and made with an intent to deceive.[84] Suppose Matt testifies that he saw Chester at the saloon Saturday afternoon. Chester testifies that he was not at the saloon that date but rather was at the church picnic. Which of the two is committing perjury? Quite possibly neither is making a false statement. One of the two's statements may be untrue, but not considered false by the witness. For the purpose of the law of perjury, an honest belief, though erroneous, is not a false statement. If Matt is simply confused regarding the day on which he saw Chester in the saloon, his testimony fails to constitute perjury. Matt is not making the statement with an intent to deceive, even though the statement is not factually accurate.

Additionally, a statement that is literally true but not responsive to the lawyer's question and is calculated to mislead normally will not be considered to be perjury.[85] For example, Peter is called as a witness at his brother Paul's trial for burglarizing the Acme Pie Factory. The prosecutor asks Peter, "Did Paul tell you that he had broken into the Ajax Pie Factory?" Peter answers, "No. He told me no such thing." Assuming Peter had in fact told Paul of his exploits at the Acme Pie Factory, Paul is not committing perjury because he answered truthfully, even though Paul knows that the prosecutor meant to say Acme instead of Ajax. As the U.S. Supreme Court once noted with a unanimous decision in a similar case,

> [T]he perjury statute is not to be loosely construed, nor the statute invoked simply because a wily witness succeeds in derailing the questioner—so long as the witness speaks the literal truth. The burden is on the questioner to pin the witness down to the specific object of the questioner's inquiry.[86]

Suppose Ibraham is registering to vote and lies on the application by saying that he is a citizen when he is not. He has committed perjury. State law requires that the accuracy of the information on a voter registration application be sworn to.[87] In a similar vein, a police officer who knowingly lies on the application for an arrest warrant commits the offense of perjury because the law requires the affidavit to be sworn to. Often the declarant is alerted to this legal requirement of truthfulness by a statement on the document, such as "I swear under penalty of perjury that the foregoing is true to the best of my knowledge and belief."

While a violation of the perjury statute is a Class A misdemeanor, aggravated perjury is a felony of the third degree. The falsity fits within the more serious statute when the sworn statement is offered in an official proceeding, such as a courtroom, an administrative hearing, or legislative hearing.[88]

Although a few states have modified the traditional rule by statute, Texas and the vast majority of American jurisdictions hold that for a false statement to be considered aggravated perjury, the statement must be "material."[89] A statement is material if it could affect the outcome of the proceedings. Assume Randy testifies that he saw the defendant Dick attempting to break into an automobile. On cross-examination, Dick's attorney asks Randy his occupation. He later asks if Randy wears glasses. In response to the lawyer's questions Randy says he is a college student and he does not wear glasses. The attorney subsequently produces evidence that Randy flunked out of college a year ago and that he indeed must wear glasses to correct rather poor eyesight. Did Randy commit perjury with his false answers? Which of the two answers could have affected the outcome of the trial? In Texas and the majority of jurisdictions, the question of whether a false statement is material is one for the judge to determine.[90]

A traditional companion offense to perjury is subornation of perjury. This offense criminalizes the conduct of an individual who induces another to make a false statement under oath.[91] Suppose Chip is on trial for murder. He convinces Dale to testify falsely that he and Chip were together at the movies when the murder occurred. Dale has committed perjury and Chip has committed subornation of perjury. Under Texas law, an act of subornation of perjury is included within the tampering with witness statute.[92]

CRIMEGRAPH
Offenses Against Government Operations—Part One

Offense	Specific intent	Culpable mental state	Conduct	Who or What?	When?	Penalty
Failure to Report a Felony 38.171		1. Intentionally, or 2. Knowingly, or 3. Recklessly*	1. Observes a felony involving serious bodily injury/death and 2. Fails to immediately report it	1. To peace officer or 2. To law enforcement agency	Under circumstances in which: a. reasonable person would believe it not yet reported and b. report can be made without placing actor in danger	AM
False Report to Peace Officer or Law Enforcement Employee 37.08	With intent to deceive	Knowingly	Makes a statement that is: 1. False and 2. Material	1. To peace officer or 2. To employee of a law enforcement agency	Who is conducting an investigation	BM
Tampering/Fabricating Evidence 37.09(a)(1)	With intent to impair: 1. verity, or 2. legibility, or 3. availability as evidence	1. Intentionally, or 2. Knowingly, or 3. Recklessly*	1. Alters, or 2. Destroys, or 3. Conceals		1. Knowing that: a. investigation is pending or b. official proceeding is pending, or 2. Knowing that: a. investigation in progress or b. official proceeding is in progress	F3 to F2
Tampering/Fabricating Evidence 37.09(a)(2)	1. With intent to affect the course of: a. investigation or b. official proceeding, or 2. With intent to affect the outcome of: a. investigation or b. official proceeding	1. Intentionally, or 2. Knowingly, or 3. Recklessly*	1. Makes, or 2. Presents, or 3. Uses	1. Record, or 2. Document, or 3. Thing	With knowledge of its falsity	F3 to F2

(continued)

291

Offense	Specific intent	Culpable mental state	Conduct	Who or What?	When?	Penalty

Tampering/Fabric-ating Evidence 37.09(d)(1)	1. With intent to impair:
	  a. verity, <u>or</u>
	  b. legibility, <u>or</u>
	  c. availability as evidence in subsequent related investigation, <u>or</u>
	2. With intent to impair:
	  a. verity, <u>or</u>
	  b. legibility, <u>or</u>
	  c. availability as evidence in subsequent related official proceeding
		1. Intentionally, <u>or</u>
		2. Knowingly, <u>or</u>
		3. Recklessly*
			1. Alters, <u>or</u>
			2. Destroys, <u>or</u>
			3. Conceals
				1. Record, <u>or</u>
				2. Document, <u>or</u>
				3. Thing
					Knowing that offense has been committed	F3 to F2

*Required by Texas Penal Code § 6.02

CRIMEGRAPH
Offenses Against Government Operations—Part Two

Offense	Culpable mental state	Conduct	Who or What?	When?	Penalty

Tampering/Fabricating Evidence 37.09(d)(2)	1. Intentionally, or
	2. Knowingly, or
	3. Recklessly*
		1. Observes human corpse and
		2. Fails to report to law enforcement agency:
		  a. existence of corpse and
		  b. location of corpse.
				1. When reasonable person would believe offense has been committed and
				2. Knows or should know law enforcement agency is unaware of existence and location
					AM

Failure to Identify 38.02(a)	Intentionally	Refuses to give	1. Name, or 2. Residence, or 3. Date of birth	To peace officer who has lawfully arrested the person	CM to BM
Failure to Identify 38.02(b)	Intentionally	1. Gives a false or 2. Gives a fictitious	1. Name, or 2. Residence, or 3. Date of birth	Upon request by a peace officer who has: 1. lawfully arrested the person, or 2. lawfully detained the person, or 3. good cause to believe is a witness	BM to AM
Interference with Public Duties 38.15(a)(1)	Criminal negligence	1. Interrupts, or 2. Disrupts, or 3. Impedes, or 4. Interferes with	Peace officer	1. While officer performing a legal duty or 2. While officer is exercising legal authority	BM
Interference with Public Duties 38.15(a)(2)	Criminal negligence	1. Interrupts, or 2. Disrupts, or 3. Impedes, or 4. Interferes with	Emergency medical personnel	1. Providing medical services to ill or injured persons or 2. Transporting ill or injured persons	BM
Interference with Public Duties 38.15(a)(3)	Criminal negligence	1. Interrupts, or 2. Disrupts, or 3. Impedes, or 4. Interferes with	Fire fighter	1. Fighting a fire or 2. Investigating the cause of a fire	BM

*Required by Texas Penal Code § 6.02

293

CRIMEGRAPH
Offenses Against Government Operations—Part Three

Offense	Culpable mental state	Conduct	Who or What?	When?	Penalty
Interference with Public Duties 38.15(a)(4)	Criminal negligence	1. Interrupts, or 2. Disrupts, or 3. Impedes, or 4. Interferes with	Animal under the supervision of: 1. peace officer, or 2. corrections officer, or 3. jailer	Knowing animal is being used for: 1. law enforcement purpose, or 2. corrections purpose, or 3. prison security purpose, or 4. jail security purpose, or 5. investigative purpose	BM
Interference with Public Duties 38.15(a)(5)	Criminal negligence	1. Interrupts, or 2. Disrupts, or 3. Impedes, or 4. Interferes with	Transmission over citizen's band radio	1. For purpose of informing about emergency or 2. For purpose of inquiring about emergency	BM
Interference with Public Duties 38.15(a)(6)	Criminal negligence	1. Interrupts, or 2. Disrupts, or 3. Impedes, or 4. Interferes with	1. County animal control officer or 2. Municipal animal control officer	1. Performing legal duty or 2. Exercising legal authority	BM
Interference with Public Duties 38.15(a)(7)	Criminal negligence	1. Interrupts, or 2. Disrupts, or 3. Impedes, or 4. Interferes with	State, county, or municipal: a. health officer, or b. environmental officer, or c. radiation officer, or d. safety officer	1. Performing legal duty while investigating a site or 2. Exercising legal authority while investigating a site	BM

CRIMEGRAPH

Offenses Against Government Operations—Part Four

Offense	Culpable mental state	Conduct	Who or What?	When?	Penalty
Evading Arrest or Detention 38.04	Intentionally	Flees	Peace officer	He knows is attempting to: 1. lawfully arrest him <u>or</u> 2. lawfully detain him	BM to F2
Resisting Arrest, Search, or Transportation 38.03	Intentionally	By using force: 1. Prevents <u>or</u> 2. Obstructs	Person actor knows is: 1. peace officer <u>or</u> 2. person acting in presence and at direction of peace officer	From effecting: 1. arrest of actor, <u>or</u> 2. arrest of another, <u>or</u> 3. search of actor, <u>or</u> 4. search of another, <u>or</u> 5. transportation of actor, <u>or</u> 6. transportation of another	AM to F3
Escape 38.06	1. Intentionally, <u>or</u> 2. Knowingly, <u>or</u> 3. Recklessly*	Escapes	From custody	1. Under arrest for offense, <u>or</u> 2. Charged with offense, <u>or</u> 3. Convicted of offense, <u>or</u> 4. In custody pursuant to lawful court order, <u>or</u> 5. Detained in secure juvenile detention facility, <u>or</u> 6. In custody of juvenile probation officer pursuant to court order	AM to F1

*Required by Texas Penal Code § 6.02

Offenses Against Government Operations—Part Five

Offense	Culpable Mental State	Conduct	Who or What?	Why?	Penalty
Bribery 36.02(a)(1)	1. Intentionally <u>or</u> 2. Knowingly	1. Offers, <u>or</u> 2. Confers, <u>or</u> 3. Agrees to confer on another, <u>or</u> 4. Solicits, <u>or</u> 5. Accepts, <u>or</u> 6. Agrees to accept from another	Any benefit on: 1. public servant, <u>or</u> 2. party official, <u>or</u> 3. voter	As consideration for recipient's: 1. decision, <u>or</u> 2. opinion, <u>or</u> 3. recommendation, <u>or</u> 4. vote, <u>or</u> 5. exercise of discretion	F2
Bribery 36.02(a)(2)	1. Intentionally <u>or</u> 2. Knowingly	1. Offers, <u>or</u> 2. Confers, <u>or</u> 3. Agrees to confer on another, <u>or</u> 4. Solicits, <u>or</u> 5. Accepts, <u>or</u> 6. Agrees to accept from another	Any benefit	1. In judicial proceeding as consideration for recipient's: a. decision, <u>or</u> b. opinion, <u>or</u> c. recommendation, <u>or</u> d. vote, <u>or</u> e. exercise of discretion, <u>or</u> 2. In administrative proceeding as consideration for recipient's: a. decision, <u>or</u> b. opinion, <u>or</u> c. recommendation, <u>or</u> d. vote, <u>or</u> e. exercise of discretion	F2

Offense	Culpable Mental State	Conduct	Who or What?	Why?	Penalty
Bribery 36.02(a)(3)	1. Intentionally or 2. Knowingly	1. Offers, or 2. Confers, or 3. Agrees to confer on another, or 4. Solicits, or 5. Accepts, or 6. Agrees to accept from another	Any benefit on: 1. public servant or 2. party official	As consideration for violation of a duty imposed by law	F2
Bribery 36.02(a)(4)	1. Intentionally or 2. Knowingly	1. Offers, or 2. Confers, or 3. Agrees to confer on another, or 4. Solicits, or 5. Accepts, or 6. Agrees to accept from another	Any benefit that is a: 1. political contribution or 2. political expenditure	As consideration pursuant to an express agreement to take or withhold exercise of official discretion	F2

CRIMEGRAPH
Offenses Against Government Operations—Part Six

Offense	Culpable mental state	Conduct	Why?	Penalty
Obstruction or Retaliation 36.06(a)(1)	1. Intentionally <u>or</u> 2. Knowingly	1. Harms <u>or</u> 2. Threatens to harm by unlawful act	1. In retaliation for service or status as: a. public servant, <u>or</u> b. witness, <u>or</u> c. prospective witness, <u>or</u> d. informant, <u>or</u> e. person who reports or intends to report a crime, <u>or</u> 2. On account of service or status as: a. public servant, <u>or</u> b. witness, <u>or</u> c. prospective witness, <u>or</u> d. informant, <u>or</u> e. person who reports or intends to report a crime	F3 to F2
Obstruction or Retaliation 36.06(a)\(2)	1. Intentionally <u>or</u> 2. Knowingly	1. Harms <u>or</u> 2. Threatens to harm by unlawful act	To prevent or delay the service of another as: 1. public servant, <u>or</u> 2. witness, <u>or</u> 3. prospective witness, <u>or</u> 4. informant, <u>or</u> 5. person who reports or intends to report a crime	F3 to F2

CRIMEGRAPH
Offenses Against Government Operations—Part Seven

Offense	Underlying offense	Specific intent/knowledge	Culpable mental state	Conduct	Who or What?	Why or When?	Penalty
Perjury 37.02(a)(1)		1. With intent to deceive and 2. With knowledge of statement's meaning	1. Intentionally, or 2. Knowingly, or 3. Recklessly*	1. Makes false statement under oath or 2. Swears to the truth of previously made false statement		Statement is required or authorized to be made under oath	AM
Perjury 37.02(a)(2)		1. With intent to deceive and 2. With knowledge of statement's meaning	1. Intentionally, or 2. Knowingly, or 3. Recklessly*	Makes a false unsworn declaration	Written declaration is made by prison inmate		AM
Aggravated Perjury 37.03	Perjury Sec. 37.02			Makes material false statement		During official proceeding	F3

*Required by Texas Penal Code § 6.02

299

Notes

1. Lord Protector Cromwell's beheading came three years after his death when his body was exhumed following the restoration of the monarchy.

2. The two witness rule was apparently inspired by the British Treason Act of 1695 (7 & 8 Will. III c. 3), which sought to prevent future abusive prosecutions. England dropped the two witness rule in 1800.

3. *See generally* BRACTON, ON THE LAWS AND CUSTOMS OF ENGLAND (Samuel E. Thorne trans., 1968–1977).

4. Legal scholars have long suggested a substantial underreporting of sexual assaults. However, the reasons for this underreporting lie more with issues of fear and embarrassment on the part of the victim than with any conscious rejection of the traditional cultural norm of calling the police when a crime occurs.

5. *See Charge dropped in drug case,* AUSTIN AMERICAN-STATESMAN, Jan. 11, 2007, at B03.

6. *See* Robert Crowe, *Teacher accused of luring 5 boys: Woman allegedly had sexual contact with 5th-graders in theaters, class,* HOUSTON CHRONICLE, Dec. 15, 2006, at B1.

7. *See News Roundup,* SAN ANTONIO EXPRESS-NEWS, Aug. 24, 2004, at 2B.

8. TEX. FAM. CODE § 261.101.

9. TEX. TRANSP. CODE § 550.061.

10. TEX. PENAL CODE § 37.09(d)(2).

11. TEX. EDUC. CODE § 37.152(a)(4).

12. TEX. HEALTH & SAFETY CODE § 161.041.

13. TEX. HEALTH & SAFETY CODE § 161.042.

14. TEX. FAM. CODE § 33.008.

15. TEX. PENAL CODE § 43.27. It is unclear whether this duty to report is actually a criminal offense since no penalty is mentioned in the statute.

16. TEX. PENAL CODE § 39.05.

17. TEX. FAM. CODE § 261.106.

18. See Chapter 2 for discussion of *mens rea* in circumstances surrounding conduct offenses.

19. Because of constitutional concerns, Texas courts have imposed a heightened level of proof in cases concerning allegations of official misconduct. *See* Wood v. State, 577 S.W.2d 477 (Tex. Crim. App. 1979).

20. Texas law also separately criminalizes false reports of child abuse (TEX. FAM. CODE § 261.107); missing children or missing persons (TEX. PENAL CODE § 37.081); and, of course, false alarms (TEX. PENAL CODE § 42.06).

21. See Washington v. State, 127 S.W.3d 111 (Tex. App.—Houston [1st Dist.] 2003), upholding conviction for false report where defendant lied about whereabouts of juvenile fugitive who was in defendant's house.

22. *See* Pannell v. State, 7 S.W.3d 222 (Tex. App.—Dallas 1999).

23. Spector v. State, 746 S.W.2d 945 (Tex. App.—Austin 1988).

24. *See* Lewis v. State, 56 S.W.3d 617 (Tex. App.—Texarkana 2001). See also Whitlock v. State, 2006 Tex. App. LEXIS 5301, and Nichols v. State, 2004 Tex. App. LEXIS 5718, upholding convictions of suspects who swallowed illegal drugs during traffic stops.

25. Hollingsworth v. State, 15 S.W.3d 586 (Tex. App.—Austin 2000).

26. Lewis v. State.

27. TEX. ALCO. BEV. CODE § 106.05.

28. TEX. PENAL CODE § 49.031.

29. Pannell v. State.

30. Williams v. State, 2007 Tex. App. LEXIS 892.

31. Lumpkin v. State, 129 S.W.3d 659 (Tex. App.—Houston [1st Dist.] 2004).

32. For a discussion of these issues, see the decision in Vigue v. State, 987 P.2d 204 (Alaska 1999).

33. Delapaz v. State, 228 S.W.3d 183 (Tex. App.—Dallas 2007).

34. Perjury (§ 37.02) would appear to have been a more appropriate charge in this case. Both offenses are Class A misdemeanors.

35. 392 U.S. 1 (1968).

36. *See* Davis v. State, 829 S.W.2d 218 (Tex. Crim. App. 1992), *and* Woods v. State, 956 S.W.2d 33 (Tex. Crim. App. 1997).

37. Adams v. Williams, 407 U.S. 143 (1972).

38. Hiibel v. Sixth Judicial Dist. Court, 542 U.S. 177 (2004).

39. Only six states in addition to Nevada have enacted broad failure to identify statutes. *See* ARK. CODE § 5–71–213(a)(1); CAL. PEN. CODE § 647(e); DEL. CODE, TIT. 11, § 1321(6); FLA. STAT. § 856.021(2); GA. CODE § 16–11–36(b); N. M. STAT. § 30–22–3; *and* VT. STAT., TIT. 24, § 1983.

40. *See* Matt Schwartz, *City to pay $55,000 settlement for mistaken arrest of judge,* HOUSTON CHRONICLE, Nov. 30, 2000, at A39.

41. Case law holds that a violation occurs only if the defendant knows that the requesting party is a peace officer. *See* Green v. State, 951 S.W.2d 3 (Tex. Crim. App. 1997).

42. Tex. H.B. 855, 80th Leg., R.S. (2007). *See also* Jane Elliott, *ID bill killed by personal appeals,* HOUSTON CHRONICLE, Apr. 13, 2007, at B1.

43. *See also* Brown v. Texas, 443 U.S. 47 (1979), *and* Kolender v. Lawson, 461 U.S. 352 (1983).

44. *See* TEX. TRANSP. CODE § 521.025.

45. *See National ID Cards and REAL ID Act,* Electronic Privacy Information Center, *at* http://www.epic.org/privacy/id_cards.

46. City of Houston v. Hill, 482 U.S. 451 (1987).

47. Key v. State, 88 S.W.3d 672 (Tex. App.—Tyler 2002).

48. Barnes v. State, 206 S.W.3d 601 (Tex. Crim. App. 2006).

49. Carney v. State, 31 S.W.3d 392 (Tex. App.— Austin 2000).

50. Tex. Penal Code § 38.14 and § 38.151.

51. Hobyl v. State, 152 S.W.3d 624 (Tex. App.—Houston [1st Dist.] 2004).

52. Alejos v. State, 555 S.W.2d 444, 449 (Tex. Crim. App. 1977).

53. Perhaps the best known low speed pursuit was the 1994 flight of murder suspect O.J. Simpson in his white Ford Bronco after Simpson failed to voluntarily surrender to police. Millions nationwide watched part of the televised chase which occurred on Los Angeles freeways often at speeds well below the posted limit.

54. The Texas Transportation Code contains the similar offense of fleeing or attempting to elude police officer (§ 545.421). This offense declares refusing to stop a motor vehicle at request of a police vehicle is a Class B misdemeanor. It can elevate to a Class A if the evasion creates a danger of serious bodily injury.

55. If Herby flees from one state to another to avoid arrest, however, he may be in violation of the federal Fugitive Felon Act (18 U.S.C. § 1073).

56. "A person is arrested when he has been actually placed under restraint or taken into custody by an officer or person executing a warrant of arrest, or by an officer or person arresting without a warrant." Tex. Code Crim. P. art. 15.22.

57. Vactor v. State, 181 S.W.3d 461 (Tex. App.— Texarkana 2005).

58. See, e.g., Sheehan v. State, 201 S.W.3d 820 (Tex. App.—Waco 2006).

59. Thompson v. State, 987 S.W.2d 64 (Tex. Crim. App. 1999).

60. Haliburton v. State, 80 S.W.3d 309, 313 (Tex. App.— Fort Worth 2002).

61. *Id.*

62. *Id.*

63. Gary v. State, 195 S.W.3d 339 (Tex. App.—Waco 2006).

64. Raymond v. State, 640 S.W.2d 678 (Tex. App.— El Paso 1982).

65. A writ of *habeas corpus* is a judicial order affording a hearing to an incarcerated individual for the purposes of challenging the legality of his confinement.

66. 4 William Blackstone, Commentaries *129–130.

67. Russell v. State, 90 S.W.3d 865, 870 (Tex. App. 2002).

68. *Id.*

69. See definition of "escape" contained in Tex. Penal Code § 38.01(2).

70. *See* Annotation, *Failure of Prisoner to Return at Expiration of Work Furlough or Other Permissive Release Period as Crime of Escape,* 76 A.L.R.3d 658 (1977).

71. *See* Tex. Code Crim. P. art. 11.01 *et seq.*

72. See discussion in Chapter 15.

73. Tumey v. Ohio, 273 U.S. 510 (1927).

74. *See, e.g.,* Tex. Ethics Comm. Op. No. 61 & 62 (1992).

75. Kaisner v. State, 772 S.W.2d 528 (Tex. App.— Beaumont 1989).

76. McCallum v. State, 686 S.W.2d 132 (Tex. Crim. App. 1985).

77. See Morrow v. State, 862 S.W.2d 612 (Tex. Crim. App. 1993), for a discussion of the difference between a witness, a prospective witness, an informant, and an individual who reported a crime.

78. Cochran v. State, 783 S.W.2d 807 (Tex. App.— Houston [1st Dist.] 1990).

79. Morrow v. State.

80. Stafford v. State, 948 S.W.2d 921 (Tex. App.— Texarkana 1997).

81. *In re* B.M., 1 S.W.3d 204 (Tex. App.—Tyler 1999).

82. Webb v. State, 991 S.W.2d 408 (Tex. App.—Houston [14th Dist.] 1999).

83. Tex. Penal Code § 19.03(a)(2).

84. Presumably a true statement made with intent to deceive does not constitute perjury as well.

85. *See* John D. Perovich, Annotation, *Incomplete, Misleading, or Unresponsive but Literally True Statement as Perjury,* 69 A.L.R.3d 993 (1976).

86. Bronston v. United States, 409 U.S. 352, 361 (1973).

87. See Tex. Elec. Code § 13.007 explicitly declaring that a false statement on a voter registration application constitutes perjury.

88. See Tex. Penal Code § 1.07(33) defining "official proceeding."

89. See State v. Nelson, 546 P.2d 592 (Alaska 1976), holding that materiality is not an element of the crime of perjury in Alaska.

90. *See* John E. Theuman, Annotation, *Materiality of Testimony Forming Basis of Perjury Charge as Question for Court or Jury in State Trial,* 37 A.L.R.4th 948 (1985).

91. "Subornation of perjury is the offence of procuring another to take such a false oath as constitutes perjury in the principal." 4 William Blackstone, Commentaries *137–138.

92. Tex. Penal Code § 36.05.

CHAPTER

Public Disorder and Safety Offenses

13

BOLO

The reader should be on the lookout (BOLO) for the meaning of the following terms. Knowledge of the meaning of these terms will greatly assist the reader in understanding the primary elements of the chapter.

- Abusive language
- Carrying of weapons
- Disorderly conduct
- "Fighting" words
- Intoxicated
- Lewd purpose
- Mutual combatants

- Prohibited weapon
- Public place
- Public view
- Reasonable man standard
- Riot
- Unreasonable noise

INTRODUCTION

Each year over 10,000 persons in Texas are arrested for the commission of violent felonies such as murder, robbery, aggravated assault, and sexual assault. Yet, 16 times that many persons are annually taken into custody for disorderly conduct and public drunkenness violations![1] In addition, an unknown number are issued a citation for their unruly behavior. Indeed the average citizen is far more likely to face criminal charges for one of these petty offenses than for commission of a violent crime or serious property offense. Public disorder offenses, although admittedly minor in nature, also consume a substantial portion of the resources of the justice system ranging from police call for services to jail space to court time. This chapter will explore two of the most common public disorder offenses: disorderly conduct and public intoxication. Additionally, the Texas law regarding carrying of weapons will be examined. No offenses in the Penal Code are more the subject of legend and folklore than the state's weapons laws.

DISORDERLY CONDUCT

Introduction

It is Saturday night in a college town. Nu Upsilon Tau is hosting an end of semester party at the fraternity house. About 100 partygoers are enjoying the music of a live band as well as various alcoholic beverages. Things are a bit rowdy. Unfortunately for the fraternity, its house sits on the edge of campus in an otherwise quiet middle-class neighborhood.

Needless to say, the group's neighbors are less than tolerant of the noise, the crowds, the traffic, and the general disorder surrounding the party. Ultimately a neighbor calls the police to complain. Officer Elaine is dispatched to the scene. Which, if any, criminal offenses are Officer Elaine likely to discover? Who is legally responsible for the offenses? What action may the officer take regarding each offense?

Or consider Ricardo who decides to celebrate New Years by standing in his front yard and discharging his shotgun into the air at the stroke of midnight. How about Albert who is attending a professional football game? He verbalizes his displeasure with the home team's performance by shouting obscenity-laced phrases at the coach and players. The fans sitting near Albert are becoming increasingly agitated by his conduct. Or maybe Roger, the neighborhood "Peeping Tom," who late one evening walks into his neighbor's backyard and peers through her bedroom window. Each of these actions and a host of others disturb the tranquility of the community and implicate the law of disorderly conduct.

In other jurisdictions, the catchall phrase for such unruly or offensive behavior may be known as breaching the peace or disturbing the peace. In Texas, the offense is labeled **disorderly conduct**. The illegal conduct commonly includes noise-related incidents but also frequently encompasses many activities that are simply disruptive,

§ 42.01. Disorderly Conduct

a. A person commits an offense if he intentionally or knowingly:
   1. uses abusive, indecent, profane, or vulgar language in a public place, and the language by its very utterance tends to incite an immediate breach of the peace;
   2. makes an offensive gesture or display in a public place, and the gesture or display tends to incite an immediate breach of the peace;
   3. creates, by chemical means, a noxious and unreasonable odor in a public place;
   4. abuses or threatens a person in a public place in an obviously offensive manner;
   5. makes unreasonable noise in a public place other than a sport shooting range, as defined by Section 250.001, Local Government Code, or in or near a private residence that he has no right to occupy;
   6. fights with another in a public place;
   7. discharges a firearm in a public place other than a public road or a sport shooting range, as defined by Section 250.001, Local Government Code;
   8. displays a firearm or other deadly weapon in a public place in a manner calculated to alarm;
   9. discharges a firearm on or across a public road;
   10. exposes his anus or genitals in a public place and is reckless about whether another may be present who will be offended or alarmed by his act; or
   11. for a lewd or unlawful purpose:
      A. enters on the property of another and looks into a dwelling on the property through any window or other opening in the dwelling;
      B. while on the premises of a hotel or comparable establishment, looks into a guest room not the person's own through a window or other opening in the room; or
      C. while on the premises of a public place, looks into an area such as a restroom or shower stall or changing or dressing room that is designed to provide privacy to a person using the area.

* * * *

b. An offense under this section is a Class C misdemeanor unless committed under Subsection (a)(7) or (a)(8), in which event it is a Class B misdemeanor.

shocking, or offensive to the general population. While the state statute lists nearly a dozen forms of disorderly behavior, most Texas cities have by ordinance supplemented the Penal Code and outlawed additional behaviors that bother or offend the public. For example, in several of the state's municipalities urinating in public, other than in a public restroom, is a form of disorderly conduct. State law is silent on the topic.[2]

Defining "Public Place"

With the exception of the "Peeping Tom" provision in subsection 11, all other forms of disorderly conduct have as an element the requirement that the incident occur in a "public place." The Penal Code in the general definitions (Sec. 1.07) states **public place**

> means any place to which the public or a substantial group of the public has access and includes, but is not limited to, streets, highways, and the common areas of schools, hospitals, apartment houses, office buildings, transport facilities, and shops.[3]

This definition is divided into two parts. First, an identified set of locations are deemed always to be public places. These include

1. Streets
2. Highways
3. Common areas of schools
4. Common areas of hospitals
5. Common areas of apartment houses
6. Common areas of office buildings
7. Common areas of transport facilities
8. Common areas of shops.

Thus, any street or highway is a public place as would the hallways of schools and hospitals. The lobby of an apartment house or office building as well as the waiting room of a bus station fit the definition. Similarly, the open shopping areas of retail businesses are by definition public places.

However, the myriad of locales in society in which the public is invited or has access is too broad to list. Accordingly, the statutory definition of "public place" includes *any place* to which the public or a substantial group of the public has access. "The definition of public place is cast in broad language."[4] This method utilizes a fact-dependent approach to determining which locales are or are not public places. The relevant inquiry is whether the public has access to the place. For example, a street on Bergstrom Air Force Base in Austin was ruled to be a public place even though the base is fenced, gates are guarded, and a pass is required to enter. The evidence revealed that under appropriate circumstances virtually anyone could gain access to the base.[5] Similarly, the roads in a gated residential community were found to be a public place because the general public could gain access to the community with little effort.[6]

Whether the property in question is privately owned property or public property is not determinative of whether it is a public place; rather the question is whether the public has access. For example, the sheriff's office housed at the county jail is located in publicly owned property but would not normally be viewed as a public place, at least when the sheriff had closed the door or the sheriff's aide controlled access to the office. In a like manner, movie theaters are private property but are viewed as public places when open for business. Note that in the latter example, the fact that a fee is charged for admission does not remove the facility from the definition of a "public place" since a substantial group of the public (those willing to buy a ticket) have access. Case law holds that a college classroom is a public place.[7] In one case, the appeals court concluded the obvious and ruled that a fenced backyard containing two pit bulls whose purpose was to keep strangers out was not a public place.[8] Could a private residence ever be a public place? How about during an open house when the residence is up for sale? Or when a large number of persons are gathered for a party in the backyard?[9]

Many states' criminal codes distinguish among offenses that occur in a public place and those that occur in **public view**. For example, what if an individual is standing nude in the front window of his residence? He is located in a private place but appears in public view. For many years, Texas statutes did not make this distinction thereby creating a level of uncertainty as to whether the hypothetical nude individual was in violation of Sec. 42.01(a)(10).[10] Case law was similarly less than clear in explaining when a person physically in a private place but viewable from a public place met this element of the offense.[11] The Legislature appears to have resolved this conundrum by enacting Sec. 42.01(c)(1), which holds that "an act is deemed to occur in a public place or near a private residence if it produces its offensive or proscribed consequences in the public place or near a private residence." Thus, the rule is that if the offensive conduct is viewable, or hearable, or can be smelled from a public place, the particular offense has occurred in a public place for purposes of the disorderly conduct statute.[12] The nude individual above would be in violation of Sec. 42.01(a)(10), disorderly conduct by exposure.

Elements of Disorderly Conduct

Intentionally or Knowingly

Disorderly conduct can only be committed by the purposeful conduct of the actor. An individual whose conduct is merely reckless or criminally negligent does not commit the crime. For example, if a chemical tank truck springs a leak and noxious chlorine gas expels into the atmosphere, no disorderly conduct under Sec. 42.01(a)(3) has occurred because at most the truck owner is negligent in not maintaining his equipment in proper condition. Similarly, an accidental discharge of a firearm in a public place does not equate to disorderly conduct under Sec. 42.01(a)(7).

Uses Abusive, Indecent, Profane, or Vulgar Language in Public Place [Sec. 42.01(a)(1)]

A common form of disorderly conduct relates to certain speech uttered in a public place. The statute outlaws indecent, profane, and vulgar language terms that are nearly synonymous. Also, prohibited is **abusive language**. While the statute does not define these four terms, the courts apply their ordinary, everyday meanings. Indeed, individuals are presumed to know the type of words or gestures likely to provoke violence.[13] However, any effort to criminalize speech collides with the protections of the First Amendment. How can one's constitutional right of free speech be reconciled with the criminalization of speech-based disorderly behavior?

Some years ago, the U.S. Supreme Court resolved the conflict, at least in theory, by declaring that the First Amendment right of free speech is not absolute at all times under all circumstances.[14]

> There are certain well-defined and narrowly limited classes of speech, the prevention and punishment of which have never been thought to raise any Constitutional problem. These include the lewd and obscene, the profane, the libelous, and the insulting or "fighting" words—those which by their very utterance inflict injury or tend to incite an immediate breach of the peace. It has been well observed that such utterances are no essential part of any

exposition of ideas, and are of such slight social value as a step to truth that any benefit that may be derived from them is clearly outweighed by the social interest in order and morality. Resort to epithets or personal abuse is not in any proper sense communication of information or opinion safeguarded by the Constitution, and its punishment as a criminal act would raise no question under that instrument.[15]

Texas case law limits the application of Sec. 42.01(a)(1) to "fighting" words only.[16] The test is what a person of common intelligence would understand to be words likely to cause an average addressee to fight. Not only must the actor utter the words but the words must tend to incite an immediate breach of the peace.

Words alone, however, are insufficient to complete the elements of the offense. It is the context in which the words are used that is crucial. If Tom is laughing at his brother Ray's struggling efforts at changing a flat tire and the frustrated Ray tells Tom to "go to hell," the phrase is unlikely to cause Tom to react in a violent way. Thus, Ray has not committed disorderly conduct. On the other hand, suppose Ray gets into a dispute with another motorist over who is at fault in a minor traffic collision. If Ray tells the motorist to "go to hell," is the utterance of the phrase in this context likely to cause a violent response? Were the latter case to go to trial, a jury must first determine if Ray's utterance was indecent, profane, vulgar, or abusive and, if so, did actual violence result or was the utterance highly likely to cause violence? Only if the second question is also answered in the affirmative is Ray guilty of disorderly conduct. Texas courts have cautioned that language that is merely harsh and insulting does not rise to the level of "fighting" words. For example, calling someone "an idiot" is not the use of a "fighting" word.[17] However, consider the case of a college teacher who stopped his class lecture due to loud cursing in the hallway. Efforts to remedy the situation were met by the female defendant belligerently hurling various well-known curse words back at the teacher. Defendant was ultimately arrested by a campus security officer. An appeals court upheld the defendant's disorderly conduct conviction on the grounds that her words were profane and abusive and tended to incite a violent response.[18]

As a rule of thumb, statements will be considered **"fighting" words** and thereby subject to a disorderly conduct charge if they meet the following five conditions:

1. The words constitute a direct personal insult;
2. The words are directed to the addressee personally and individually and not a generalized insult to a large group;
3. The words must be addressed to the person face to face;
4. The words must be of such a nature as to be likely to provoke the average addressee to an immediate violent response; and
5. The words must be likely to provoke the actual addressee to violence in light of all the surrounding circumstances.[19]

Makes an Offensive Gesture or Display in a Public Place [Sec. 42.01(a)(2)]
This subsection recognizes that all communication is not verbal. Communication can occur in a variety of expressive means ranging from physical gestures and printed signage to bumper stickers and T-shirts.[20] However, such symbolic communication may also be protected by the First Amendment. Thus, any expressive conduct must tend to incite a breach of the peace and meet the test of being equivalent to "fighting" words.

In one case, a graduating senior who "gave the finger" to the high school principal upon being awarded his diploma was held to have violated this subsection of the Penal Code. The principal testified that he had to resist his "animal instinct to retaliate" against the youth. The appeals court found the gesture offensive and the equivalent of "fighting" words.[21] However, in another case where a motorist exhibited a mild case of road rage by "flipping the bird" at another driver, the motorist was found not to have violated the statute. The reaction of the victim, an off duty county jailer, was to call the police. In reversing the defendant's conviction, the appeals court found that the gesture, while offensive, did not tend to incite a breach of the peace. The victim, although angry, was not moved to violence. Instead he called the police. Thus, no offense had occurred.[22]

The statute also declares certain conduct to be disorderly when it has no communicative value or expressive conduct whatsoever. If the conduct is not "speech," it is not subject to First Amendment protection. Here the law may well be more expansive. While communication must constitute "fighting" words to be criminalized, an offensive display not intended to communicate a message only needs to tend to incite a breach of the peace. A breach of the peace has long been defined in Texas as follows:

> The term "breach of the peace" is generic, and includes all violations of the public peace or order, or decorum; in other words, it signifies the offense of disturbing the public peace or tranquility enjoyed by the citizens of a community; a disturbance of the public tranquility by any act or conduct inciting to violence or tending to provoke or excite others to break the peace; a disturbance of public order by an act of violence, or by any act likely to produce violence, or which, by causing consternation and alarm disturbs the peace and quiet of the community. By "peace," as used in this connection, is meant the tranquility enjoyed by the citizens of a municipality or a community where good order reigns among its members.[23]

For example, in one case a female who appeared topless at a Texas beach festival was convicted of making an offensive display when her mere appearance upset many in the crowd. The U.S. Supreme Court refused to consider her argument that punishing topless females but not topless males violated the Equal Protection Clause of the Fourteenth Amendment.[24] In a similar manner, females "flashing" their breasts during Mardi Gras parades constitutes disorderly conduct.[25] Since neither incident implicates activity protected by the First Amendment, no incitement to violence need be shown.

Creates a Noxious or Unreasonable Odor in a Public Place [Sec. 42.01(a)(3)]
This subsection of the disorderly conduct statute covers stink bombs and other noxious odors. As noted above, the emission of such odors must be intentionally or knowingly done. The rare application of the statute is primarily to pranksters as air quality laws are normally used in cases involving industrial air pollution.

Abuses or Threatens Another in a Public Place in Offensive Manner [Sec. 42.01(a)(4)]
Suppose Rob and Carl get into an argument in a restaurant. Rob threatens to punch Carl in the nose. While this conduct may constitute assault by threat, the fact that the incident occurs in a public place implicates the interests of the public as a whole. Other diners at the restaurant are going to be disturbed by Rob and Carl's personal dispute. Regardless of whether Carl would cooperate in pursuing charges against Rob, Rob has committed disorderly conduct.

While case law has defined "threat," the term "abuses" has not been explicitly defined by Texas courts.[26] Although the issue has never been directly considered on appeal, the courts hold to the view that by implication the Legislature intended for the terms "threatens" and "abuses" to apply only in situations meeting the "fighting" words test.[27] This view seems to be a logically questionable application of the "fighting" words doctrine. This interpretation makes Sec. 42.01(a)(4) virtually redundant to subsection (a)(1) and the law of assault, Sec. 22.01. As a general rule, acts of the Legislature are to be construed to avoid redundancy. Nonetheless, until the Court of Criminal Appeals addresses the matter head-on, the "fighting" words requirement will remain an unwritten element of this subsection.

In the confrontation between Rob and Carl, if Rob's threat to punch Carl was a result of provocation by Carl, it is a defense since Rob had significant provocation for his threatening conduct [Sec. 42.01(b)].

Makes Unreasonable Noise in Public Place/Near Private Residence [Sec. 42.01(a)(5)]
Noise is all around us, from the beeping sound of a delivery truck backing into a loading dock to a youthful motorist playing the latest rap song on his car radio with his windows down. The disorderly conduct statute does not criminalize noise but only that sound that is unreasonable and which occurs in a public place or near a private residence. "Noise commonly means a loud, confused, or senseless outcry, or a sound noticeably loud, harsh, or discordant."[28] Whether noise is unreasonable and thereby potentially a criminal act depends on the time, place, and circumstances under which it is made. Whether or not sound is "noise" is judged by the **reasonable man standard**.[29] Recall the previously mentioned Nu Upsilon Tau fraternity party. If nearby neighbors complain to the police about the sound, Officer Elaine may go to the fraternity house and advise the members of the complaints. Indeed, it is common practice for police officers to make multiple efforts to quiet such parties, recognizing that resolution of the disturbance is more important than criminal prosecution.[30]

In most situations, the individuals making the noise and those hearing it are likely to disagree about whether the noise is unreasonable for the time and place. In an effort to define when a noise is "unreasonable," the Legislature has created a presumption that sound violates the statute if it exceeds 85 decibels and the individual has previously received notice from a peace officer or magistrate that the sound is a public nuisance [Sec. 42.01(c)(2)].[31] Prior to approaching the fraternity house, Officer Elaine might stand in the street, a public place, and use a decibel meter to measure the intensity of the noise. The brothers of Nu Upsilon Tau will be notified by Officer Elaine as to the complaint. If the party noise continues to exceed the 85 decibel threshold and does not diminish after several contacts by the police, a citation, or occasionally a custody arrest, may result. While many police agencies use decibel meters to measure sound intensity, the statute does not require such a measurement. Rather the presumption simply makes it easier to prove a violation. Assume Officer Elaine does not have a decibel meter, what other evidence exists that the fraternity party was producing an unreasonable noise?

Noises that disturb the public or nearby residents can take a variety of forms other than loud parties. Although the statute is rarely enforced in these circumstances, many consider loud car stereos, motorcycles with little or no muffling of engine sound, and construction noise occurring early in the morning to constitute unreasonable noise. In one case, however, the court held that an individual who was loudly complaining about the size of the food portions and the quality of service in a restaurant was lawfully arrested for disorderly conduct.[32] Likewise, an individual who was shouting and disturbing other customers in a convenience store was appropriately arrested.[33] Each was making an unreasonable noise in a public place.

Application of the statute is limited to public places and near private residences which the actor has no right to occupy. For example, disorderly conduct does not occur when an individual complains to the police that his roommate is making an unreasonable noise. Since the noisemaker has a legal right to be at the residence, his disorderly behavior is not "near a private residence he has no right to occupy" as the statute requires.[34]

On occasion, noise may be the result of constitutionally protected speech. Assume that a group of individuals are protesting the performing of abortions at a community health center. Their protest includes shouting anti-abortion slogans in a loud manner. Is this disorderly conduct? Or assume the Reverend Jones stands on a downtown street corner, Bible in hand, and loudly proclaims his religious message to passersby. Is this disorderly conduct? Both the protestors and the street corner preacher possess a First Amendment right to freely express their respective views. But, they do not have a right to do so in a manner that disrupts the public peace. To resolve this conflict of interests the Texas Legislature, following the lead of Supreme Court decisions, enacted Sec. 42.04. This provision of the Penal Code declares that if the unreasonable noise is made by persons who are expressing in a nonviolent manner a position on a social, economic, political, or religious question, authorities must follow certain specified procedures before a disorderly conduct arrest may be made. A peace officer, firefighter, or person in charge of the premises where the speech is occurring must first order the speaker to move, disperse, or otherwise remedy the violation. If the unreasonable noise ends, no arrest is to be made. If the speaker refuses to terminate the disruptive speech after the order, then a disorderly conduct arrest and subsequent charge is lawful. This is one of the few criminal offenses where an opportunity must be afforded to the actor to cease the unlawful conduct.[35]

Fights with another in a Public Place [Sec. 42.01(a)(6)]

When two individuals engage in a fight, one would assume that an assault is occurring. But recall that an individual can consent to being assaulted.[36] Thus, **mutual combatants** commit no offense as to each other if each party is consenting. However, fighting in public can be disturbing to the broader community. Accordingly, the Legislature has decreed fighting with another in a public place to be a form of disorderly conduct. Under the Common Law and prior Texas statutes, this behavior was called "affray."[37] It should be noted that justification defenses, such as self-defense, can be raised if relevant.[38]

Suppose you are attending a professional baseball game. The pitcher hits the batter with a fastball. The batter charges the mound and a fight ensues on the field. Several players take swings at each other. Meanwhile, you and another fan get into an argument about whether the batter was justified in going after the pitcher. You and the fan begin to exchange punches. A police officer arrives. Of the fight on the field and the fight in the stands, who is likely to be arrested? Is this fair?

Discharges a Firearm in a Public Place [Sec. 42.01(a)(7)]

Several provisions of the Penal Code ranging from aggravated assault and attempted murder to deadly conduct relate to the discharge of firearms. The disorderly conduct statute adds to that list. It is concerned with the potential harm that occurs when a weapon is fired, even if the actor does not intend to scare or harm anyone. The mere discharge of the weapon in public places others at risk. In the opening example, Ricardo commits an offense when he fires his shotgun into the air to celebrate New Years. The pellets must come down somewhere and someone else could be injured. Bear in mind that such an act must be done intentionally or knowingly. Therefore, an accidental firing is not a violation. The statute also specifically excludes discharging a firearm at a shooting range. Nor is it a violation to discharge the weapon in self-defense or when in fear of injury by a dangerous animal.[39]

Displays a Firearm or Deadly Weapon in a Public Place [Sec. 42.01(a)(8)]

Just as discharging a firearm in public can lead to personal injury, the mere display of the gun or other deadly weapon can also upset the community. The statute criminalizes any public display of a firearm or other deadly weapon (e.g., Bowie knife, baseball bat, hammer) "in a manner calculated to alarm." The weapon need not be used in a threatening manner (this would constitute aggravated assault) nor actually pointed at a particular individual (this might constitute deadly conduct). Rather its display must be such that any member of the public would be alarmed.

While appellate court interpretation of this form of disorderly conduct is nearly nonexistent,[40] the crime likely includes actions such as an individual appearing at a PTA meeting carrying a shotgun or a group of tax protestors parading with loaded rifles. In both circumstances, others gathered at the meeting or parade are likely to become very uneasy about what might happen. Presumably the reasonable man test would be used by the court to determine whether display of the weapon was "in a manner calculated to alarm."

Discharges a Firearm on or across a Public Road [Sec. 42.01(a)(9)]
This subsection is a companion to the prohibition barring discharging a firearm in a public place. The subsection also covers firing across a public road. Shooting from one side of a roadway to another places the passing public in danger.[41]

Recklessly Exposes Anus or Genitals in Public Place [Sec. 42.01(a)(10)]
Several sections of the Penal Code criminalize the display of private parts under certain circumstances. An individual who exposes his genitals for sexual gratification commits indecent exposure (Sec. 21.08), while one who with sexual motives exposes himself to a minor commits a form of indecency with a child (Sec. 21.11). The disorderly conduct statute criminalizes display of the anus or genitals in public and being reckless about whether someone is present who might be offended or alarmed.

Note that the statute is limited to exposure of anus or genitals,[42] two specific portions of the anatomy. In one case, an individual who was bungee jumping at a beach festival would pull down his swim trunks and expose his buttocks. Does that conduct violate this subsection? Probably not as the buttocks and the anus are separate parts of the body.[43] However, the crude bungee jumper likely violates Sec. 42.01(a)(2) in making an offensive display. Under similar logic, display of female breasts does not fit this subsection because they are not genitals, but such a display might be offensive under a particular set of circumstances. (Recall earlier discussion of topless female at beach festival.) Texas law, however, grants mothers the right to breastfeed infants.[44]

Consider Ronald who enters the men's restroom at a movie theater to urinate. He will stand at the urinal exposing his penis but is not being reckless about whether others present will be alarmed; such conduct is expected in that setting. But if instead Ronald stops his automobile by the side of the roadway, turns his back to traffic, and proceeds to urinate, is he being reckless about whether someone might be present who would be offended? Is Ronald aware of that risk?

The statute only requires the possibility of someone being present who will be offended or alarmed. It does not require that a member of the public actually be present or that a third party actually view the actor's genitals or anus.[45]

In one unusual case, disorderly conduct by exposure occurred when one individual complained about 100 nudists who were frolicking on a secluded public beach near Austin. Although the beach was remote and difficult to access, the Court of Criminal Appeals upheld the conviction of one of the nudist on the basis that the disorderly conduct statute does not exclude isolated or secluded public places.[46]

Enters on Property for Lewd or Unlawful Purpose [Sec. 42.01(a)(11)]
The final subsection of the statute is predominantly a "Peeping Tom" law. The first portion criminalizes entering on property of another for a lewd or unlawful purpose and looking through a window or other opening into the dwelling. Since entry on to

another's property is an element of the offense, some, but not all, situations also will constitute a criminal trespass (Sec. 30.05). For the criminal trespass violation to occur, however, the property must be fenced or posted.

Second, a lewd or unlawful purpose must be established. Most such intrusions and surreptitious viewings are for sexual gratification, a **lewd purpose**. But, a prospective residential burglar also violates the statute because his entry is for an unlawful purpose.

Similarly, one who peeps into a restroom stall, shower stall, or dressing room in a public place violates the statute. Individuals expect privacy in those stalls and someone who peeps into the stall for lewd purposes commits disorderly conduct.[47]

For many years, hotels were constructed in a square with an open center or in an H-shape. Such architecture allowed both exterior and interior rooms to have natural light and ventilation. It also created the opportunity for an occupant in an interior room to view other guests residing in interior rooms. The statute declares it an offense for an individual who is occupying a hotel guestroom to look into another guestroom window for a lewd or unlawful purpose. This subsection is a bit arcane and rarely enforced today as few modern hotels and motels are constructed in a style that facilitates the commission of the offense.

Suppose each evening Jim sits in the bedroom of his home and watches his neighbor Sherry undress. Jim finds this activity sexually gratifying. Is he committing an offense? Apparently not. While Jim's conduct may be viewed as lewd, he has not entered Sherry's property nor is he conducting the viewing from one hotel room to another. The solution to this invasion of Sherry's privacy is for her to be sure to draw the drapes each evening.

Penalty for Disorderly Conduct

With two exceptions, the penalty for disorderly conduct is a Class C misdemeanor fine. The prohibitions against discharging and displaying firearms in public places are Class B misdemeanors.

OTHER DISORDERLY BEHAVIOR

Chapter 42 contains a variety of other specialized disorderly behavior laws. Individuals are prohibited from obstructing public passageways (Sec. 42.03). This offense is often related to protest activity. In one case, a disabled individual in a wheelchair was convicted after she blocked vehicular traffic while protesting the manner in which she had been treated by a local bank.[48] Similarly, an anti-abortion protestor was found to have violated the statute when he blocked the sidewalk in front of a place of business.[49] But in a case not involving a protest, an individual's conviction was upheld after she refused to pay a road toll. The toll booth employee refused to accept her $50 bill and the motorist refused to provide any smaller bill or sign an IOU. Her stubbornness blocked the toll booth lane and required the opening of another lane for other vehicles.[50]

Other specialized offenses include disrupting meetings and processions (Sec. 42.05), disrupting funerals (Sec. 42.055), and discharging firearms within city limits in cities over 100,000 population (Sec. 42.12).[51]

Perhaps the ultimate form of disorderly behavior is rioting—essentially disorderly behavior by a group of individuals. In the long tradition of Anglo-American law, the Penal Code (Sec. 42.02) outlaws knowingly participating in a riot.[52] A **riot** requires seven or more persons to be creating an immediate danger to persons or property, substantially obstructing governmental operations, or using force or the threat of force to deprive any person of a legal right. The origin of the minimum participation of at least seven persons is unknown. The Common Law required a minimum of three for a riot.[53]

While the riot statute is not often used, riot by arson convictions were upheld against several workers who burned an office trailer during a labor strike.[54] The statute is also applicable to prison riots.[55] The Texas riot statute has been criticized both for its redundancy to other offenses in the Penal Code and its possible unconstitutionality.[56]

PUBLIC INTOXICATION

Introduction

"Public drunkenness has been a crime throughout our history, and even before our history it was explicitly proscribed by a 1606 English statute . . ."[57] So noted Justice Hugo Black in a 1968 Supreme Court opinion. While this case, Powell v. Texas,[58] upheld the state's application of its drunk in public place law[59] to an individual afflicted with alcoholism, the matter caused many jurisdictions to reassess the scope of their public intoxication statutes. As a consequence, today no criminal offense exhibits more variation across the 50 states' criminal codes than public intoxication. In some jurisdictions, the penal code contains no mention of public drunkenness, while in others the behavior is listed as a petty misdemeanor on the order of disturbing the peace. Meanwhile, some states criminalize the conduct only if the offender is disorderly in addition to being intoxicated. Other jurisdictions have decriminalized public drunkenness but empower the police to take intoxicated individuals into custody for their own safety. Even others, such as Texas, maintain the behavior as a criminal violation but grant broad discretion to the police and courts in regard to how to process offenders.

The differences in the nation's laws have developed over time influenced by:

- The argument that the drunk person is hurting only himself, not society;
- The traditional Puritanical view that drinking intoxicating liquors is a sin;
- The lessons learned from the nation's experiment with the prohibition of liquor in the 1920s;
- The public's desire for alcohol to be available in retail stores, restaurants, bars, and clubs;
- Anti-alcohol public interest groups (e.g., Mothers Against Drunk Driving);
- The recognition that chronic use of alcohol may lead to permanent physiological and psychological damage; and
- The acknowledgement that the judgment of intoxicated individuals may be so impaired that he or she creates a danger to themselves or others.

For each state legislature certain of these factors are more influential than others. Modern statutes, or lack thereof, reflect the importance a particular legislature has given each factor.

Public intoxication has been a state-level offense since 1879.[60] In recent years, however, while the conduct officially remains a Class C misdemeanor, the Legislature has empowered the police and the courts to divert the intoxicated individual out of the normal justice system.

Elements of Public Intoxication

Person Appears

Sec. 49.11 explicitly eliminates the necessity of proving a culpable mental state in cases involving public intoxication. Thus, whether the intoxicated actor intentionally appears

§ 49.01. Definitions

In this chapter:

* * * *

(2) "Intoxicated" means:

  A. not having the normal use of mental or physical faculties by reason of the introduction of alcohol, a controlled substance, a drug, a dangerous drug, a combination of two or more of those substances, or any other substance into the body; or

  B. having an alcohol concentration of 0.08 or more.

* * * *

§ 49.02. Public Intoxication

  a. A person commits an offense if the person appears in a public place while intoxicated to the degree that the person may endanger the person or another.

a-1. For the purposes of this section, a premises licensed or permitted under the Alcoholic Beverage Code is a public place.

  b. It is a defense to prosecution under this section that the alcohol or other substance was administered for therapeutic purposes and as a part of the person's professional medical treatment by a licensed physician.

  c. Except as provided by Subsection (e), an offense under this section is a Class C misdemeanor.

  d. An offense under this section is not a lesser included offense under Section 49.04.

  e. An offense under this section committed by a person younger than 21 years of age is punishable in the same manner as if the minor committed an offense to which Section 106.071, Alcoholic Beverage Code, applies.

in a public place or was dumped there by friends after he passed out would appear to be irrelevant to the charge.

Courts have not been afforded the opportunity to define the term "appears." One court did note that the term relates to the location of public place rather than the individual's degree of intoxication. In other words, the offense is not that the actor "appears to be intoxicated" but rather "appears in a public place."[61]

In Public Place

The offense is captioned *public* intoxication. Thus, the individual who is intoxicated in the privacy of his home is not in a public place and is not committing an offense. The general definition of what constitutes a "public place" discussed earlier in this chapter is fully applicable to the crime of public intoxication. But, two particular problematic circumstances tend to arise in public intoxication cases: the individual who is intoxicated on his own property and the individual who is intoxicated in a vehicle.

Suppose Roger is drinking beer and sitting in a lawn chair in his front yard. After about a dozen cans he is highly intoxicated. Maybe he has even passed out. Is he violating the public intoxication statute? Certainly all elements of the offense seem in place except for the question of whether his front yard is a public place. While a 1906 Court of Criminal Appeals case, which has never been expressly overturned, holds that "a private residence is not a public place, nor has the yard or driveway of a private residence ever been construed as such,"[62] the modern trend is to take the opposite view. Several court decisions in recent years have applied the definition of public place to individuals who are standing in their front yards or driveways.[63] The test of whether these private property locales constitute public places is based on the access the general public has to the property. If the postman, a door-to-door salesman, or a neighbor has unimpeded access, then the exterior area of the residence is a public place.[64]

Suppose police respond to a loud party call at an apartment. The resident opens the door in response to the officer's knock. Through the open door the officer observes several individuals who are clearly intoxicated, including one who seems unconscious on the living room couch. Is the offense of public intoxication being committed? To date, the appellate courts have not been afforded the opportunity to determine whether one who is intoxicated in his private residence but within public view is in violation of Sec. 49.02. Given the statute's focus on potential danger to the individual or others, so long as the actor remains within his home it makes little sense to arrest him. To adopt the opposite view would effectively expand the paternalism of the state to anyone who was intoxicated and potentially dangerous, regardless of his or her location.[65]

Assume Officer Jennifer stops a suspected intoxicated motorist. Field sobriety tests strongly indicate that Bobby, the driver, is intoxicated. Officer Jennifer places him under arrest. But, Bobby's wife Phyllis, a passenger in the vehicle, is also intoxicated. What is to be done with Phyllis? She was not operating the vehicle so she has not committed DWI. Can she be taken into custody for public intoxication? More explicitly, is the interior of Bobby's automobile a public place?

For many years, the answer to the question of whether the passenger compartment of a private motor vehicle was a public place had been muddled at best, dependent upon the state showing the public nature of the vehicle.[66] Thus, a convertible with its top down was a public place because the public had visual access, but not a vehicle with tinted glass parked in an unlighted lot at night.[67] In one case, a vehicle passenger intoxicated by drugs was arrested after police approached the car which was blocking an intersection. The Court of Criminal Appeals appears to assume that under the circumstances the passenger was located in a public place.[68]

In practice, the issue of whether the intoxicated Phyllis is in a public place is often resolved by the officer asking her to step out of the car. Once Phyllis is standing on the roadway, she is by definition in a public place. No appellate court has considered whether Phyllis is placed in an untenable legal dilemma in this situation. If she complies with the officer's request and exits the vehicle, she completes the elements of public intoxication.[69] If she refuses to exit the vehicle, she might be subject to charges of interference with public duties.[70] The Legislature could remedy this ambiguity by simply declaring that the interior passenger compartment of a private vehicle on a public roadway is a public place for the purposes of the public intoxication statute. This would be consistent with the public policy underlying the prohibition on the possession of alcoholic beverages in a motor vehicle (Sec. 49.031). Note that the statute [Sec. 42.02(a-1)] already expressly declares that a licensed premises is a public place. Thus, an intoxicated individual in a bar is subject to potential arrest and prosecution.

While Intoxicated

The definition of **intoxicated** found in Sec. 49.01 is used for all offenses contained in the chapter including driving while intoxicated. The term covers both the intoxication *per se* standard of a blood alcohol concentration of 0.08 and not having normal use of mental or physical faculties due to ingestion into the body of alcohol, drugs, or any substance. The 0.08 standard is virtually never used in public intoxication cases. The reason is that the necessary machinery or blood and urine tests to measure the alcohol concentration are simply too time consuming and expensive to use to prove such a minor offense. Such tests are reserved for DWI and intoxication manslaughter cases.

In nearly every case, the standard is whether the individual has consumed alcohol, drugs, or other substances sufficient to impair normal use of mental or physical faculties. Note that any substance that impairs psychomotor functions can serve as the basis of the intoxication. While alcohol and drugs (e.g., marijuana, cocaine, and heroin) are the most common intoxicants, other substances such as glue, paint thinner, and aerosol propellants can also produce intoxication.

Intoxication is established by the effect the substances manifest. A suspect might be unconscious or his ability to walk or stand impaired. Slurred speech, swaying, and bloodshot and glassy eyes have all been held to be evidence of intoxication. Such factors are particularly relevant if the suspect also has the odor of alcohol on his breath or is found to be in possession of drugs. Appellate courts grant fairly broad discretion to peace officers in determining whether or not an individual is intoxicated. The key seems to be whether the officer can articulate specific observable factors to support his or her claim.

If a person is intoxicated as a result of medical treatment, such a treatment program is a defense to a public intoxication charge.[71] In contrast, intoxication as a result of medical treatment is not a defense to DWI or intoxication manslaughter.[72]

To a Degree He May Endanger Person or Another

Unlike prior statutes which basically viewed being intoxicated in public as a violation of community moral standards, the current law is concerned with the harm the intoxicated individual potentially poses to himself or other persons. If the individual is intoxicated but not found under circumstances where he is a danger, presumably no offense occurs. Drunken revelers at Mardi Gras in Galveston or Washington's Birthday in Laredo or at Texas-OU weekend in Dallas are less likely to be taken into custody than a drunk individual who is passed out on a cold winter night in an alley in Amarillo. In the latter situation, the actor's well-being is in danger. Commonly, intoxicated individuals who are about to get behind the wheel of an automobile may be arrested for public intoxication; allowing them to operate a motor vehicle places others in danger.

The danger need not be immediate. Indeed a specific identifiable danger need not even be apparent to the arresting officer.[73] Only the possibility that the actor may endanger himself or another is sufficient to meet this element of the crime.[74] Thus the public intoxication conviction of an individual was upheld where the arresting officer testified he feared the defendant, who was found in the alley of a high crime neighborhood, might become a crime victim. Likewise, the officer was concerned that the defendant might seek to drive away in his automobile.[75] In another case, the defendant was found asleep behind the wheel of a car. He posed a potential danger to others.[76] Likewise, an intoxicated individual who was walking down the middle of a street was found to be a danger to himself.[77]

Penalty for Public Intoxication

Public intoxication is graded as a Class C misdemeanor. However, the offense differs procedurally from other Class C offenses in at least two respects. First, an arresting officer is authorized by state law to release a Class C misdemeanant with a citation instead of making a full custody arrest.[78] However, public intoxication is the sole exception to this law. It would be of questionable logic to take a person into custody because he poses a danger to himself or others and then immediately release him on his written promise to appear in court.

On the other hand, officers are granted specific authority to release intoxicated individuals without filing formal charges or without taking them before a magistrate as is normally required after an arrest. Art. 14.031 of the Texas Code of Criminal Procedure grants peace officers the discretion to release the intoxicated individual into the care of a responsible adult or to place the individual, with his or her consent, into a substance abuse treatment facility. In such cases, no formal criminal charges would be filed.

The power to divert intoxicated individuals away from the justice system is consistent with the protective philosophy of the statute. However, the law still permits the arrest and prosecution of an intoxicated person under the same terms as any other Class C offender. Which approach is taken lies within the sole discretion of the arresting officer as dictated by his or her department policies. Thus, if a peace officer observes Freddy, an intoxicated individual, the officer is empowered to take any of the following four actions:

1. The officer can simply ignore Freddy, reasoning that he is not a danger to himself or others.
2. The officer may arrest Freddy, take him to jail, and file a public intoxication charge. When he sobers up, Freddy will be allowed to be released on bail. He will later come to court on the charge and, if convicted, be subject to a fine up to $500.
3. The officer may detain Freddy and release him to a responsible adult, such as by taking him home to his wife.
4. The officer may detain Freddy and with Freddy's consent check him into an alcohol treatment facility.

The unfortunate aspect of these choices is that the option selected is often solely dependent on the policy of the arresting agency. In some counties, anecdotal evidence suggests that municipal officers may largely ignore intoxicated individuals unless they cause a disturbance while sheriff's deputies treat them like other Class C offenders and book them into jail. At the same time, the local constable may simply take the individual into protective custody and take him to his residence. Thus, what happens to the intoxicated Freddy is based solely on which agency first encounters him. Such a random result seems contrary to one of the stated objectives of the Penal Code: "to systematize the exercise of state criminal jurisdiction."[79]

WEAPONS OFFENSES

Introduction

No set of statutes in the Texas Penal Code are the subject of more legend, lore, and misinterpretation than the weapons laws found in Chapter 46. This circumstance is the product of two factors: the Old West heritage and cowboy image of the Lone Star State and the fact that the principal statute, the unlawful **carrying of weapons** (UCW) law, is little different in wording than its predecessor 150 years ago! Until recently, a law enacted when Comanche rode the Llano Estacado remained the basis for the contemporary statutes that attempted to regulate weapons. Modern urban society certainly presents its share of dangers to life and property ranging from drive-by shootings to carjackings but Comanche attacks are no longer one of them!

Any discussion of weapons laws must also include mention of the Texas Constitution. Article I, Sec. 23 states

> Every citizen shall have the right to keep and bear arms in the lawful defense of himself or the State; but the Legislature shall have power, by law, to regulate the wearing of arms, with a view to prevent crime.

Unlike the Second Amendment to the U.S. Constitution which is less than clear on the issue of private possession of firearms, the Texas Constitution does grant such a right to citizens. Importantly, the state constitution gives the Legislature the authority "to regulate the wearing of arms, with a view to prevent crime."[80] The current statutes reflect this power and corresponding limitation. As will be explored subsequently, the UCW statute criminalizes unlawful *carrying*, not unlawful possession. Similarly, the only persons who are prohibited from possessing a firearm are convicted felons (Sec. 46.04). However, even that legal disability is lifted five years after completion of sentence. Further, with an eye toward crime prevention, the items contained in the prohibited weapons law (Sec. 46.05) are useful primarily for killing people or for other criminal purposes, not for self-defense or hunting.

Three statutes serve as the primary laws regulating weapons in Texas: the prohibited weapons statute, the places weapons prohibited statute (Sec. 46.03), and the UCW statute. Each will be discussed in order. It should be noted that various federal laws also regulate ownership and sale of firearms.[81] One must be in full compliance of each jurisdiction's statutes and rules to be in lawful possession of certain weapons.

Prohibited Weapons

Sec. 46.05 outlaws the intentional or knowing possession, manufacturing, transporting, repairing, or selling certain forms of weaponry. These devices include machine guns, sawed-off firearms, silencers, and other gangster-type weaponry. Additionally, gang-related devices such as switchblade knives, knuckles, and zip guns[82] are also unlawful for the private citizen to have. Explosive weapons, such as bombs, are similarly banned under this statute. Possession of a switchblade knife or knuckles is a Class A misdemeanor while custody of any of the other prohibited weapons is a Third Degree felony.

The statute does exempt from its coverage the military, correctional officers, and law enforcement personnel who possess the weaponry in the performance of their duties. For example, SWAT members often use fully automatic rifles. Such possession is limited to on duty use only.

Places Weapons Prohibited

Prohibited weapons, illegal knives, clubs, and firearms generally, whether lawfully possessed or not, are banned from certain locations. The Legislature envisions that even though many weapons may have lawful and appropriate uses, no need exists for those same weapons to be at certain specified locales. Thus, Sec. 46.03 stipulates that a felony of the third degree occurs if these weapons are intentionally, knowingly, or recklessly brought:

- On premises of school or educational institution
- To a polling place on election day
- Into a courtroom
- To a racetrack[83]
- Within the secured area of airport
- Within 1,000 feet of Department of Criminal Justice execution site on day of execution.

Areas not specifically addressed by the law include non-court government offices, banks, churches, athletic contests, community centers, amusement parks, and jails. Curiously, for holders of a concealed handgun license, carrying a pistol at many of these locations does constitute an offense.[84]

Unlawful Carrying of Weapons

Arthur is a diamond salesman who travels around the state. He is always concerned about being robbed of his samples. To protect his property, Arthur carries a pistol in his pocket. Jaime works as a long-haul truck driver. He logs many miles traveling across

Texas delivering watermelons. Because he often drives late at night, he keeps a revolver in the cab of his truck. Joan works the night shift at a convenience store. The store owner has placed a pistol under the cash register for employees to use to protect themselves against the possibility of being robbed. Joan keeps the pistol nearby during her shift. Mike is a member of the school board. Because of suspected financial improprieties, the board recently terminated the contract of the local high school football coach. The coach had been very successful and was popular with the players' parents. In recent days Mike has received several anonymous phone calls threatening his life. Mike has begun wearing a pistol. Are these individuals violating Texas law regarding the carrying of a firearm?

For many years, Texas statute prohibited an individual from carrying on or about his person a firearm, illegal knife, or club. This law changed little from its first enactment in 1856. On its face, the statute was one of the most severe gun control laws in the nation. However, a companion statute, now Sec. 46.15, set forth a wide range of exceptions to the law's application. Many of these exceptions, such as the infamous "traveling" exemption, were the source of much courtroom—and barroom—debate.[85] Over time, court decisions similarly resulted in the creation of other exclusions to the law's application.[86] Compounding the matter was the absence of any recognized means for a private citizen to obtain a permit to carry a pistol. Various strategies, most of dubious legality such as obtaining a permission letter from a sheriff or judge, were tried by individuals who had an arguable need to carry a handgun but no method by which to do so legally.

Finally, beginning in 1995, the Legislature created a system by which a private citizen may obtain a concealed handgun license.[87] As of 2007, about 250,000 Texans held this license. Accordingly, many individuals with legitimate need to carry a weapon now have a mechanism by which that need can be lawfully met.

In a second step, the Legislature in 2007 clarified the right of individuals to possess weapons on their own premises or while in their motor vehicles. Previously existing law excused peace officers, correctional officers, soldiers, private security personnel, and such from application of the UCW statute. Table 13-1 displays a summary of the current exceptions and exemptions to the principal weapons laws in Chapter 46.

Several specific aspects of Sec. 46.02 bear particular mention. First, the law's application is limited to handguns, illegal knives, and clubs. It does not criminalize possession of all firearms or all potential forms of weaponry (e.g., bow and arrows). Thus, it has no application to rifles and shotguns. Such weapons may be carried lawfully providing the circumstances do not place the actor in violation of some other law. For example, transporting a loaded rifle in a rack in the cab of a pickup truck generally violates no Texas law. But if the operator drives the vehicle onto the grounds of a public school he runs afoul of the places prohibited by law (Sec. 46.03).

Sec. 46.01 defines the terms "handgun," "illegal knife," and "club." Case law holds that the UCW statute is applicable even if the handgun is not loaded.[88] Second, the UCW statute, unlike similar laws in other states, makes little distinction between concealed weapons and those in open view. With one exception [Sec. 46.02(a-1)] discussed below, whether the individual has the weapon concealed or in open view is not an element of the offense of UCW. Suppose Dean, a South Texas rancher, wears a pistol on his belt because he has had prior unfortunate encounters with rattlesnakes. In determining whether he is violating the UCW statute, it matters not whether the pistol is visible on his hip or covered with his jacket.

As noted earlier, Sec. 46.02 applies to unlawful carrying on or about the person, not unlawful possession.[89] Thus, an individual who has a pistol in the trunk of his car is not carrying it about his person. However, if the pistol is in the passenger compartment of

TABLE 13-1   Availability of Defenses and Exemptions To Selected Texas Weapons Statutes

Person Holding Defense or Exemption	Unlawful Carrying of Weapons Sec. 46.02	Places Weapons Prohibited Sec. 46.03	Prohibited Weapons Sec. 46.05
Person on own premises	X		
Person on premises under person's control	X		
Inside person's motor vehicle	X		
En route to person's motor vehicle	X		
Person who is a traveler	X		
Person engaged in lawful hunting, fishing, or other sport	X		
Peace officer	X	X	X
Qualified retired peace officer	X	X	
On duty parole officer	X	X	
On duty probation officer	X	X	
State or federal judge holding CHL*	X	X	
Prosecutor/assistant. prosecutor holding CHL*	X	X	
Court bailiff holding CHL* while escorting judge	X	X	
On duty member of armed forces	X	X	
On duty member of State or National Guard	X	X	X
On duty guard of penal institution	X	X	X
On duty officer of the court			
On duty licensed uniformed private security officer	X	*partial*	*chemical dispensing device only*
On duty licensed bodyguard	X	*partial*	
Person holding CHL*	X	X	
Holder of alcoholic beverage permit	X		
Police cadet	X		
Security officer employed by state adjutant general	X		
Persons engaged in historical reenactments	X		
University security guard	*club only*		
Person driving on public road		*partial*	
Person at residence		*partial*	
Person at place of employment		*partial*	
Person in compliance with National Firearms Act			X
Antique or curio dealer			*partial*

Note: *CHL = concealed handgun license

the vehicle, the courts do view this as falling within the statutory prohibition, assuming the owner is physically in the vehicle.[90] Having a weapon in one's pocket or purse or secured on a belt would also constitute carrying on or about the person. "In order to have the gun on or about his person [an individual] need not have had actual, physical possession of it. It is sufficient that the weapon was nearby, close at hand, convenient of access and within such a distance that he could reach it without materially changing his position."[91] If John has a collection of pistols in his study at home, he is certainly in possession of those weapons but is not carrying them. The spirit of the Texas UCW law seems to be directed at those individuals who go armed, not individuals who simply own weapons. As a rule of thumb, if the individual has reasonably quick access to the pistol or other unlawful weapon, he will be viewed as falling within the purview of the UCW statute.

Texas law has long exempted application of the UCW statute to possession of weapons on one's own premises. While an appellate court has yet to rule on this question, the current version of the UCW statute appears to require the prosecution to establish that the violation did not occur on the defendant's own premises rather than placing this burden of proof on the defendant as was previously the rule. In like manner, property which the individual does not own but is under his control is similarly exempt. In the earlier example regarding Joan the convenience store clerk, she is likely not violating the UCW statute because the pistol is on premises under her control.

As a practical matter, few UCW violations are detected without some other offense occurring. An individual who is creating a disturbance may attract the attention of the police and be found in possession of a handgun. A suspect may be arrested for shoplifting and found to have a pistol in her purse. Anecdotal evidence suggests that the bulk of UCW charges flow from discovery of a weapon during routine traffic stops. For instance, a police officer discovers a handgun while detaining a motorist for speeding. The UCW charge follows. In years past the obligation fell on the motorist to convince the judge or jury that he or she fit within the "traveling" exemption.[92] While Texas courts have never explicitly defined "traveling," they generally considered the distance, time, and mode of travel.[93] This exemption essentially became a question of fact for the court. Some judges held a more generous view of this exemption than others. In an effort to clarify this defense to the UCW law and create a presumption in favor of the motorist, the Legislature amended Sec. 46.02. Sec. 46.02(a) now requires the prosecution to establish that the defendant was not "inside of or directly en route to a motor vehicle" under his control.[94] In other words, the actor does not appear to be in violation of Sec. 46.02(a) if he and his weapon (i.e., handgun, illegal knife, or club) are inside his motor vehicle. In like manner, Sec. 46.02(a-1) creates a specific offense of carrying a handgun in a motor vehicle. But, the crime occurs only if the actor has the handgun in plain view, or is engaged in criminal activity other than a Class C misdemeanor traffic violation, or is prohibited by law from possessing the weapon, or is a member of a criminal street gang. This presumption in favor of the vehicle operator will likely diminish the need for defendant's to assert the traveling defense. Thus, Jaime, the watermelon truck driver mentioned earlier, does not violate either section of Sec. 46.02 so long as he keeps his pistol in the glove box, under the seat, or otherwise out of sight.

But what about Arthur the diamond salesman and Mike the fearful school board member? While either man is in his personal automobile they would appear to fall under the same rule as Jaime. Outside of their vehicles they would have to find some other exemption to fit their situations. Prior case law holds that there is no recognized exception permitting one to carry a handgun solely on the basis of self-protection.[95] Additionally, today's courts may be less understanding of these situations now that a relatively simple procedure exists for obtaining a concealed handgun license.

UCW is a Class A misdemeanor, which elevates to a felony of the third degree if the offense occurs at a location licensed to sell alcoholic beverages. It should be noted that the felony level punishment does not come into play until a violation exists. For example, a convenience store clerk who carries a pistol does not commit a felony even though beer is sold at the store; the clerk is on premises under his control and therefore no violation of Sec. 46.02 is occurring. Without a violation, the issue of the level of penalty is irrelevant.

CRIMEGRAPH
Disorderly Conduct—Part One

Offense	Culpable mental state	Conduct	Who/What?	Where?	Special circumstances	Penalty
Disorderly Conduct 42.01(a)(1)	1. Intentionally or 2. Knowingly	Uses: 1. Abusive language, or 2. Indecent language, or 3. Profane language, or 4. Vulgar language		In a public place	Utterance tends to incite immediate breach of peace	CM
Disorderly Conduct 42.01(a)(2)	1. Intentionally or 2. Knowingly	Makes: 1. Offensive gesture or 2. Offensive display		In a public place	Gesture or display tends to incite immediate breach of peace	CM
Disorderly Conduct 42.01(a)(3)	1. Intentionally or 2. Knowingly	Creates by chemical means	1. Noxious and 2. Unreasonable odor	In a public place		CM
Disorderly Conduct 42.01(a)(4)	1. Intentionally or 2. Knowingly	1. Abuses or 2. Threatens	A person	In a public place	In an obviously offense manner	CM
Disorderly Conduct 42.01(a)(5)	1. Intentionally or 2. Knowingly	Makes	Unreasonable noise	1. In a public place or 2. Near a private residence he has no right to occupy		CM
Disorderly Conduct 42.01(a)(6)	1. Intentionally or 2. Knowingly	Fights	With another	In a public place		CM
Disorderly Conduct 42.01(a)(7)	1. Intentionally or 2. Knowingly	Discharges	A firearm	In a public place	Other than a public road	BM

CRIMEGRAPH
Disorderly Conduct—Part Two

Offense	Culpable mental state	Conduct	Who/What?	Where?	Special circumstances	Penalty
Disorderly Conduct 42.01(a)(8)	1. Intentionally or 2. Knowingly	Displays	1. A firearm or 2. Deadly weapon	In a public place	In manner calculated to alarm	BM
Disorderly Conduct 42.01(a)(9)	1. Intentionally or 2. Knowingly	Discharges	A firearm	1. On a public road or 2. Across a public road		CM
Disorderly Conduct 42.01(a)(10)	1. Intentionally or 2. Knowingly	Exposes	1. Anus or 2. Genitals	In a public place	1. Reckless whether another may be present who will be offended or 2. Reckless whether another may be present who will be alarmed	CM
Disorderly Conduct 42.01(a)(11)(A)	1. Intentionally or 2. Knowingly	1. Enters on property of another and 2. Looks into dwelling through: a. window or b. other opening in dwelling			1. For lewd purpose or 2. For unlawful purpose	CM
Disorderly Conduct 42.01(a)(11)(B)	1. Intentionally or 2. Knowingly	Looks into another's guest room through: 1. Window or 2. Other opening in room		While on premises of: 1. Hotel or 2. Comparable establishment	1. For lewd purpose or 2. For unlawful purpose	CM
Disorderly Conduct 42.01(a)(11)(C)	1. Intentionally or 2. Knowingly	Looks into: 1. Restroom, or 2. Shower stall, or 3. Changing room, or 4. Dressing room, or 5. Area designed to provide privacy		While on premises of public place	1. For lewd purpose or 2. For unlawful purpose	CM

CRIMEGRAPH
Weapons—Part One

Offense	Culpable mental state	Conduct	What?	Where?	Penalty
Unlawful Carrying Weapon 46.02(a)	1. Intentionally, or 2. Knowingly, or 3. Recklessly	1. Carries on person or 2. About person	1. Handgun, or 2. Illegal knife, or 3. Club	1. Other than on own premises, and 2. Other than on premises under control, and 3. Other than inside personal vehicle, and 4. Other than en route to personal vehicle	AM to SJF
Unlawful Carrying Weapon 46.02(a-1)	1. Intentionally, or 2. Knowingly, or 3. Recklessly	1. Carries on person or 2. About person	Handgun	In motor vehicle: 1. In plain view and 2. Person is: a. engaged in criminal activity, or b. prohibited by law from possessing firearm, or c. member of criminal street gang	AM to SJF
Places Weapons Prohibited 46.03(a)	1. Intentionally, or 2. Knowingly, or 3. Recklessly	1. Possesses or 2. Goes with	1. Firearm, or 2. Illegal knife, or 3. Club, or 4. Prohibited weapon	1. School premises, or 2. Premises where school sponsored activity, or 3. School transportation vehicle, or 4. Polling place, or 5. Courtroom, or 6. Court offices, or 7. Racetrack, or 8. Secured area of airport, or 9. Within 1000 feet of TDCJ execution site	F3

323

CRIMEGRAPH
Weapons—Part Two

Offense	Culpable mental state	Conduct	What?	Where?	Penalty
Prohibited Weapons 46.05(a)	1. Intentionally or 2. Knowingly	1. Possesses, or 2. Manufactures, or 3. Transports, or 4. Repairs, or 5. Sells	1. Explosive weapon, or 2. Machine gun, or 3. Short-barrel firearm, or 4. Firearm silencer, or 5. Switchblade knife, or 6. Knuckles, or 7. Armor-piercing ammunition, or 8. Chemical dispensing device, or 9. Zip gun		AM to F3

CRIMEGRAPH
Public Intoxication

Offense	Conduct	Where?	Special circumstances	Penalty
Public Intoxication 49.02	Appears	In a public place	While intoxicated to degree: 1. May endanger self or 2. May endanger another	CM

Note: No culpable mental state required per § 49.11.

Notes

1. Tex. Dep't of Pub. Safety, The Texas Crime Report for 2006 (2007).
2. *See, e.g.*, Abilene, Tex., City Code § 20-5; Amarillo, Tex., Municipal Code § 10-3-42; Carrollton, Tex., Code § 130.14; Galveston, Tex., Code § 24-18; Houston, Tex., Code of Ordinances § 28-19; *and* Victoria, Tex., Code § 15-14.
3. Tex. Penal Code § 1.07(40).
4. Shaub v. State, 99 S.W.3d 253, 256 (Tex. App.—Fort Worth 2003).
5. Woodruff v. State, 899 S.W.2d 443 (Tex. App.—Austin 1995).
6. State v. Gerstenkorn, 239 S.W.3d 357 (Tex. App.—San Antonio 2007).
7. Ross v. State, 802 S.W.2d 308 (Tex. App.—Dallas 1990).
8. *In re* A.G.O., 1999 Tex. App. LEXIS 8775.
9. Nixon v. State, 928 S.W.2d 208 (Tex. App.—Beaumont 1996).
10. Contrast the approach taken in the public lewdness law, Tex. Penal Code § 21.07.
11. *See, e.g.*, Honeycutt v. State, 690 S.W.2d 64 (Tex. Crim. App. 1985).
12. The statute does not mean that "near a private residence" is the legal equivalent of a "public place." The two locales are not synonyms but rather relate to specific subsections of § 42.01. *See In re* A.G.O., *supra*.
13. Seth S. Searcy & James R. Patterson, *Practice Commentary*, V.T.C.A., Penal Code § 42.01 (1974).
14. See Michael J. Mannheimer, *The Fighting Words Doctrine*, 93 Colum. L. Rev. 1527 (1993), for an extensive discussion of the "fighting" words doctrine and its application.
15. Chaplinsky v. New Hampshire, 315 U.S. 568, 571–572 (1942).
16. Jimmerson v. State, 561 S.W.2d 5 (Tex. Crim. App. 1978).
17. Duran v. Furr's Supermarkets, Inc, 921 S.W.2d 778 (Tex. App.—El Paso 1996).
18. Ross v. State.
19. Adapted from Mannheimer, *supra*, at 1551.
20. *See* Roger Croteau, *T-shirt lands teen obscenity charge*, San Antonio Express-News, Jan. 17, 1998, at B2.
21. Estes v. State, 660 S.W.2d 873 (Tex. App.—Fort Worth 1983).
22. Coggin v. State, 123 S.W.3d 82 (Tex. App.—Austin 2003). The court's decision contains an extensive discussion of the history of using the middle finger to express an opinion.
23. Woods v. State, 213 S.W.2d 685, 687 (Tex. Crim. App. 1948).
24. Carreras v. State, 936 S.W.2d 727 (Tex. App.—Houston [14th Dist.] 1996), *cert. denied*, 522 U.S. 933 (1997).
25. *See* Claire Osborn, *Austin police trying to topple topless Mardi Gras tradition*, Austin American-Statesman, Feb. 2, 2002, at A1.
26. See discussion of the word "threat" in Chapter 6—Assault and Sexual Assault.
27. Jimmerson v. State.
28. Blanco v. State, 761 S.W.2d 38, 42 (Tex. App.—Houston [14th Dist.] 1988).
29. *Id.*
30. See Del Luensmann v. Zimmer-Zampese & Associates, Inc., 103 S.W.3d 594, 599 (Tex. App.—San Antonio 2003), suggesting that notification by a peace officer or magistrate is an element of the offense that must be proven. This position seems unsupportable given the clear language of the statute.
31. By way of example, normal conversation is about 60 db while a telephone's dial tone is 80 db. The noise of city traffic, heard from inside a car, is approximately 85 db as is the backup alarm on commercial vehicles. A gasoline lawnmower engine is over 100 db while a rock concert measures 115 db. 85 db is also the sound level of an IPOD set at 80 percent of its volume.
32. Brown v. State, 594 S.W.2d 86 (Tex. Crim. App. 1980).
33. Edwards v. Scott, 1999 U.S. Dist. LEXIS 17960.
34. Searcy & Patterson, *supra*.
35. *See also* Tex. Penal Code § 42.03 and § 42.055.
36. Tex. Penal Code § 22.06.
37. *See* 1925 Tex. Penal Code art. 473.
38. Tex. Penal Code § 9.02.
39. Tex. Penal Code § 9.31 and § 42.01(e).
40. Only one appellate case, a matter involving a juvenile's possession of a pellet gun at school, makes mention of the statute. The opinion notes that the defendant was not proven to be in violation of the statute. *See In re* K.H., 169 S.W.3d 459 (Tex. App.—Texarkana 2005).
41. The hunting laws also prohibit discharging a firearm across a property line. *See* Tex. Parks & Wild. Code § 62.0121.
42. Or any portion of the genitals. *See* Claycomb v. State, 988 S.W.2d 922 (Tex. App.—Texarkana 1999).
43. See Wright v. State, 693 S.W.2d 734 (Tex. App.—Dallas 1985), discussing difference between anus and buttocks.
44. *See* Tex. Health & Safety Code § 165.002.
45. Tarr v. State, 2004 Tex. App. LEXIS 8986.
46. Lacour v. State, 8 S.W.3d 670 (Tex. Crim. App. 2000).
47. In 2007, a U.S. Senator was charged under a similar Minnesota statute for looking several times into an occupied restroom stall at the Minneapolis airport. *See* David Chanen, *Craig's arrest one of many in restroom*, Minneapolis Star Tribune, Aug. 29, 2007, at 1B.

48. Lauderback v. State, 789 S.W.2d 343 (Tex. App.—Fort Worth 1990).

49. Smith v. State, 772 S.W.2d 946 (Tex. App.—Dallas 1989).

50. Mobley v. State, 2003 Tex. App. LEXIS 8425.

51. Many smaller cities have enacted ordinances banning the discharge of firearms within their corporate limits. *See, e.g.*, CASTROVILLE, TEX., CODE OF ORDINANCES § 78–2; EAGLE PASS, TEX., CODE OF ORDINANCES § 19–15; HUNTSVILLE, TEX., CODE OF ORDINANCES § 21.01.07; *and* WYLIE, TEX., CODE OF ORDINANCES § 74–81.

52. Hirschi v. State, 683 S.W.2d 415 (Tex. Crim. App. 1984).

53. In 1714 the British Parliament passed the Riot Act (1 Geo. 1, c. 5), raising to 12 the number of individuals necessary for an unlawful assembly. Local authorities were empowered to "read the Riot Act" to any such unruly group. If the group did not disperse within 20 minutes, the members were guilty of a felony. The law was ultimately repealed in 1973 but the phrase "read the Riot Act" remains in popular language to mean giving an individual a severe verbal scolding.

54. Faulk v. State, 608 S.W.2d 625 (Tex. Crim. App. 1980).

55. *See ex parte* Lozano, 982 S.W.2d 511 (Tex. App.—San Antonio 1998).

56. Searcy & Patterson § 42.02, *supra*. But see Ferguson v. State, 610 S.W.2d 468 (Tex. Crim. App. 1979), upholding the constitutionality of the statute.

57. Powell v. Texas, 392 U.S. 514, 538 (1968).

58. *Id.*

59. 1925 TEX. PENAL CODE art. 477.

60. Act of Feb. 21, 1879, 16th Leg., R.S.

61. *See In re* R.R., 714 S.W.2d 25 (Tex. App.—Amarillo 1986).

62. Pugh v. State, 117 S.W. 817 (Tex. Crim. App. 1909).

63. *See, e.g.*, Aguilera v. State, 2004 Tex. App. LEXIS 11399.

64. Loera v. State, 14 S.W.3d 464 (Tex. App.—Dallas 2000). See also, Banda v. State, 890 S.W.2d 42 (Tex. Crim. App. 1994), upholding warrantless arrest for public intoxication where actor jumped fence into backyard. Court found suspect had previously been in public place (i.e., neighbor's yard) prior to officer's arrival.

65. Art. 477 of the 1925 PENAL CODE specially excluded the public intoxication law's reach into an individual's own residence. Even earlier case law held that a private residence was not a public place. Pugh v. State, 117 S.W. 817 (Tex. Crim. App. 1909).

66. *See* Kirtley v. State, 585 S.W.2d 724 (Tex. Crim. App. 1979). The interior of a city bus, a passenger train, airplane, or other commercial passenger vehicle would constitute a public place under the statutory definition.

67. *Compare* Henderson v. State, 2000 Tex. App. LEXIS 2763, *to* Honeycutt v. State, 690 S.W.2d 64 (Tex. App.—Houston [14th Dist.] 1985).

68. Britton v. State, 578 S.W.2d 685 (Tex. Crim. App. 1978). *See also* Kelly v. State, 529 S.W.2d 554 (Tex. Crim. App. 1995).

69. See Maryland v. Wilson, 519 U.S. 408 (1997), holding that a police officer making a traffic stop is permitted, consistent with the Fourth Amendment, to order passengers to get out of car pending completion of stop. *See also* Brendlin v. California, 127 S. Ct. 2400 (2007).

70. TEX. PENAL CODE § 38.15.

71. TEX. PENAL CODE § 49.02(b).

72. TEX. PENAL CODE § 49.10.

73. Padilla v. State, 697 S.W.2d 522 (Tex. App.—El Paso 1985).

74. Segura v. State, 826 S.W.2d 178 (Tex. App.—Dallas 1992).

75. Padilla v. State.

76. Dickey v. State, 552 S.W.2d 467 (Tex. Crim. App. 1977).

77. Balli v. State, 530 S.W.2d 123 (Tex. Crim. App. 1975).

78. *See* TEX. CODE CRIM. P. art. 14.06(b).

79. TEX. PENAL CODE § 1.02(6).

80. See Miller v. Texas, 153 U.S. 535 (1894), holding that Art. 1 § 23 of the Texas Constitution does not violate U.S. Constitution.

81. *See generally* 18 U.S.C. §§ 921–929. *See also* BUREAU OF ALCOHOL, TOBACCO, FIREARMS AND EXPLOSIVES, FEDERAL FIREARMS REGULATIONS REFERENCE GUIDE (2005), *at* www.atf.treas.gov.

82. A zip gun is essentially a homemade or improvised firearm. *See* TEX. PENAL CODE § 46.01(16).

83. "Racetrack" refers to dog and horse racing tracks regulated by the state. *See* TEX. PENAL CODE § 46.01(15). Automotive racetracks are not within the scope of the prohibition.

84. *See* TEX. PENAL CODE § 46.035.

85. *See* Jack Staggs, Note and Comment, *Have Gun, Will Travel? The Hopelessly Confusing Journey of the Traveling Exception to the Unlawful Carrying Weapons Statute*, 57 BAYLOR. L. REV. 507 (2005).

86. See, e.g., Pettit v. State, 627 S.W.2d 453 (Tex. App.—Houston [1st Dist.] 1981), holding that individual may carry weapon between home and work if transporting large sums of money, and Britton v. State, 124 S.W. 684 (Tex. Crim. App. 1910), authorizing carrying pistol to gunsmith to be repaired. The defense of necessity (§ 9.22) is also available to an individual charged with UCW. *See* Johnson v. State, 650 S.W.2d 414 (Tex. Crim. App. 1983).

87. *See* TEX. GOV'T. CODE § 411.171 *et seq. See also* TEXAS DEP'T OF PUBLIC SAFETY, TEXAS CONCEALED HANDGUN LAWS AND SELECTED STATUTES (Oct. 2007), *at* www.txdps.state.tx.us.

88. Christopher v. State, 819 S.W.2d 173 (Tex. App.— Tyler 1991).

89. "Carrying" within meaning of statute does not require actual movement from one location to another. ontreras v. State, 853 S.W.2d 694 (Tex. App.—Houston [1st Dist.] 1993). An individual who was found asleep with a pistol in pocket was properly convicted of carrying a weapon on or about his person. Tijerina v. State, 578 S.W.2d 415 (Tex. Crim. App. 1979).

90. Harkness v. State, 139 S.W.3d 4 (Tex. App.—Fort Worth 2004).

91. Linvel v. State, 629 S.W.2d 94, 96 (Tex. Crim. App. 1981).

92. In jury trials, the jury determines the meaning of the term.

93. Birch v. State, 948 S.W.2d 880 (Tex. App.—San Antonio 1997).

94. Apparently in an oversight, the Legislature failed to exempt carrying the weapon en route *from* the motor vehicle.

95. Evers v. State, 576 S.W.2d 46 (Tex. Crim. App. 1978). *See also* Slack v. State, 296 S.W. 309 (Tex. Crim. App. 1927).

CHAPTER
Preparatory Offenses
14

BOLO

The reader should be on the lookout (BOLO) for the meaning of the following terms. Knowledge of the meaning of these terms will greatly assist the reader in understanding the primary elements of the chapter.

- Court of Star Chamber
- Criminal attempt
- Criminal instrument
- Criminal conspiracy
- Criminal solicitation
- Factual impossibility
- Inchoate crimes
- Inherent impossibility

- Legal impossibility
- Mere preparation
- Overt act
- Pinkerton Rule
- Plurality requirement
- Renunciation defense
- Wharton's Rule

INTRODUCTION

In recent weeks, John has had numerous conflicts with his business partner Ron. Ron claims that John is not working as hard as he is and is contributing little to the business enterprise. The arguments have become heated and near violent. John decides that he cannot tolerate Ron anymore. John believes that the way to resolve the problem is to kill Ron. However, John does not have the stomach for such a violent act. Instead, John approaches his old high school classmate Don about doing the deed. John offers Don $10,000—half now and half when the job is completed—to kill Ron. Don agrees. John gives Don $5,000 cash. The next day, Don purchases a pistol. A few nights later, Don, armed with the pistol, climbs through the window of Ron's home and goes into his bedroom. Don fires five shots into the figure in the bed and then flees. The next day, John and Don learn that Ron has been out of town on a fishing trip and that Don actually shot and killed Ron's Saint Bernard dog which had a habit of sleeping in his master's bed. Relative to their effort to kill Ron, have John and Don committed any criminal offenses? What if Don had originally turned down the deal, would John be blameworthy for any offense? Or, suppose Don is caught in the house prior to discharging his pistol, could he be convicted of attempted murder?

The foregoing scenario raises a variety of questions regarding the criminal liability of individuals who are unsuccessful at committing their intended criminal acts and at what point in time do their failed efforts themselves constitute a crime. It would certainly be foolish public policy for the government to stand idly by while persons with evil intent plot to violate the criminal law. Or to fail to sanction the would-be murderer simply because he was a bad shot or ignore the actions of a burglar who flees the scene because he trips an audible alarm prior to entering a building. Likewise, is it good social policy to permit individuals to attempt to employ others to perform criminal acts on their behalf?

Certainly society should not have to wait for an individual to fire a shot at his intended victim or start prying on the door of a closed business before some enforcement action may be taken. If there is harm in conduct society labels as "crime," there is also potential harm in the preparation to commit those same criminal acts. On the other hand, a traditional goal of the American criminal law is to restrict individual freedom as little as possible. Merely thinking about committing a criminal act is itself not a crime in our modern society. Even engaging in one or more of the elements of a crime does not implicate society's interest in maintaining order. The question is, Where should society draw the line between harmless behavior and conduct that sufficiently threatens society as to be worthy of sanction? The answer to this question lies in examining the law of preparatory offenses, also known as **inchoate crimes** or preliminary crimes. Texas establishes three forms of preparatory offenses:

- Criminal attempt
- Criminal conspiracy
- Criminal solicitation

In each instance, the legislation seeks to use the criminal sanction as a means to deter and punish conduct that moves beyond innocent behavior but falls short of the commission of a traditional substantive crime. Each of these three types of preparatory offense is discussed in the following sections as is another form of preliminary crime, possession of a criminal instrument.

CRIMINAL ATTEMPT

History of the Law of Criminal Attempt

Like many topics of criminal law, an appreciation of the history of the legal rule is desirable in order to understand the contemporary implementation of that rule. So it is with the law of criminal attempt. Authorities generally agree that, with the possible exception of the crimes of treason and robbery (and in rare instances attempted murder), the Common Law courts did not sanction attempted offenses; for criminal liability to attach, the full measure of the actual elements of murder, rape, larceny, arson, and other felonies had to be committed before the criminal sanction was imposed. Since the historical record is hazy, one can only surmise that our Common Law forbearers adhered to the view that the "broad aim of the criminal law is . . . to prevent harm to society."[1] Since attempted offenses produced no actual harm, they were not deemed criminal. The focus of early criminal law was an objective one. The law concerned itself with the nature of harm done, not the *potential* evilness of the offender.

While some authorities suggest that the notion of criminal attempts as crimes originated with the notorious **Court of Star Chamber**[2] in the early 1600s,[3] one scholar asserts that careful examination of decisions shows little embrace of criminal attempts by the Common Law courts post-Star Chamber.[4] While a few court rulings in the mid-seventeenth century did involve punishing incomplete criminal offenses, no general law of criminal attempt had yet developed. Indeed, Sir William Blackstone, in the fourth book of his frequently referenced COMMENTARIES ON THE COMMON LAW OF ENGLAND (1769), makes no mention whatever of a general doctrine of criminal attempt. Thus, the idea of sanctioning incomplete offenses was virtually nonexistent until the latter part of the eighteenth century.

The modern view of criminal attempt dates from the 1784 British opinion in *Rex v. Scofield*.[5] Scofield was indicted for arson after placing a lighted candle and kindling in a house in which he was residing but did not own. No proof was presented that the house actually burned, as was required by the Common Law definition of arson. The English Chief Justice, Lord Mansfield, rejected the argument that no crime had occurred and noted, "It makes a great difference, whether an act was done; as in this case putting fire to a candle in the midst of combustible matter (which was the only act necessary to commit a misdemeanor) and where no act at all is done. The intent may make the act, innocent in itself, criminal; nor is the completion of an act, criminal in itself, necessary to constitute criminality."[6] Seventeen years later, Lord Mansfield's observation gained concrete form: "All offences of a public nature, that is, all such acts or attempts as tend to the prejudice of the community, are indictable," the King's Bench ruled in *Rex v. Higgins*.[7] By the early 1800s, the criminalization of attempts was commonplace under English law.[8] However, the English law treated all attempts as misdemeanor offenses.

The first instance in the United States of the application of the law of criminal attempt is unclear. The U.S. Supreme Court in 1809 reviewed a matter involving an alleged attempt to evade customs duties by misstating the value of some goods imported from England.[9] In an opinion consisting of less than 100 words, Chief Justice John Marshall affirmed the restoration of the goods to the owner. Marshall noted that "The law did not intend to punish the intention, but [rather] the attempt to defraud the revenue [department]."[10] Marshall's observation was consistent with the Common Law rule of the time that intent alone was insufficient to constitute the crime of attempt.[11]

Because American criminal law of the early nineteenth century remained largely rooted in English law, U.S. courts freely cited British cases for authority. American decisions adopting the law of criminal attempt began appearing in state court decisions as early as 1805.[12] However, like the British, the rules regarding the law of attempt at this time were often intertwined with other preparatory offenses, such as solicitation and conspiracy. Courts seemed to consolidate these preparatory offenses into a single generic category of attempted crimes. The few reported early American cases involving criminal attempt were generated primarily by specific statutes declaring to be criminal the committing of a particular offense with intent to perform some other act.[13]

Following the codification movement of the mid-nineteenth century, the states slowly disaggregated preparatory offenses. This movement ultimately resulted in statutes defining when an attempt to commit an offense became a crime itself. Interestingly, despite the broad existence of state criminal attempt statutes,[14] the federal criminal code contains no general attempt law. Efforts to sanction criminal attempts are included within the elements of the various substantive offenses. Thus, robbery of a federally insured bank and an attempted robbery of the same bank are defined under the very same statute.[15]

Elements of Criminal Attempt

In modern American criminal codes, such as the Texas Penal Code, criminal attempts normally involve two elements: (1) an intent to commit some substantive offense and (2) an act that falls short of the completion of the intended offense. Possessing an intent to commit a crime without acting upon that desire is no offense. Similarly, nearly causing some societal harm, but doing so unintentionally does not constitute an attempted offense.

§ 15.01. Criminal Attempt

(a) A person commits an offense if, with specific intent to commit an offense, he does an act amounting to more than mere preparation that tends but fails to effect the commission of the offense intended.

Mens rea *of Attempt*

As to the *mens rea* element, Texas limits criminal attempts to specific intent crimes. The Legislature and courts have shown reluctance to expand general attempt laws to offenses other than those requiring a culpable mental state of intent. Suppose Suzy secretly follows her husband Jack to a motel where he is meeting his girlfriend Brenda. As Jack is crossing the parking lot, an angry Suzy accelerates her automobile and hits Jack. She then backs up over Jack's prone body. Luckily for Jack he survives Suzy's homicidal efforts. Clearly Suzy is attempting to kill Jack. The facts show her behavior to be purposeful and directed toward a goal of causing Jack's death, although her efforts are unsuccessful.

But suppose Mary is speeding in her sports car. She runs a red light and strikes Will, a pedestrian who is crossing the street. Will is seriously injured but survives the incident. Has Mary committed attempted manslaughter? No. Although Will could have been killed in the incident, Mary's conduct was at the most reckless. She may have violated various statutes, such as deadly conduct or aggravated assault, but she would not be culpable for an attempted criminal homicide. The same principle would apply if she had barely avoided hitting Will as he crossed the street. Her dangerous conduct might constitute a criminal violation but one would not expect to see a charge of attempted manslaughter or attempted deadly conduct because the underlying offenses involve a *mens rea* lower than intent.

Actus reus *of Attempt*

While the *mens rea* requirement of criminal attempt is fairly straight forward, the same cannot be said of the conduct element. In a formal sense, the *actus reus* of criminal attempt is conduct that goes beyond mere preparation that tends but fails to effect the commission of the desired offense. Three forms of behavior are implicated in this definition. First, the act must be beyond **mere preparation**. Texas, like every other jurisdiction, recognizes the principle that a criminal attempt must involve more than the initial groundwork for committing the crime. However, it need not reach the level of an almost complete offense. Secondly, Texas requires only an "active effort" to carry out the offender's purpose.[16] Sufficiency of that effort to constitute an attempt is determined on a case-by-case basis.[17] Finally, the act must be unsuccessful. In one case, the appeals court upheld an attempted indecency with a child conviction wherein the defendant had verbally offered a 16-year-old male $10 to engage in sexual contact.[18]

Recall the opening scenario of John and Don and their effort to murder Ron. When does Don commit attempted murder? Are any of his acts simply "mere preparation?" Certainly a strong argument can be made that the discussions Don had with John about killing Ron did not go beyond mere preparation. (These discussions would be an important element of a criminal conspiracy charge against John and Don, however.) Likewise, Don's purchase of the pistol could be viewed as a mere preparatory act. On the other hand, all would agree that the discharge of the pistol is an act well beyond mere preparation. The issue, of course, is when did Don cross the line between mere preparation and the required *actus reus*? Was it when he left his home en route to Ron's house? Was it when he exited his car at Ron's house? Was it when he crawled through the window? Or, was it at some other point in time?

Identifying from the facts of a case when a suspect moves from mere preparation to a criminal attempt has proven difficult for courts. Texas, whose criminal laws are influenced by the Model Penal Code, requires that the suspect complete a substantial step toward commission of the offense. Each case requires a determination by the judge or jury that the accused's actions amount to a "substantial step." Reasonable persons could certainly disagree regarding whether various forms of conduct are a substantial step or not.

The point at which the conduct threshold is crossed seems to be occurring earlier and earlier in contemporary applications of the criminal law. Anecdotal evidence suggests that prosecutors are increasingly willing to accept criminal attempt charges in cases where the suspect is nowhere near consummation of the underlying crime or where the circumstances even create a factual impossibility that preclude the commission of the offense. For example, the use by adults of Internet chat rooms and other social networking websites to solicit sexual contact with underage boys and girls has led many jurisdictions to file attempted sexual assault of a child charges against these sexual predators. Before accepting criminal attempt charges, some district attorneys require that the cyber-suspect actually make some affirmative effort toward engaging in the sexual behavior, such as appearing at the youthful victim's home. However, many prosecutors hold to the view that the online chat between the suspect and the child is sufficient conduct beyond the mere preparation stage to justify prosecution for an attempted sexual assault offense. To avoid claims of overcriminalization, the problem of online sexual predators is probably better handled through the criminal solicitation of a minor statute (Sec. 15.031) instead of the law of criminal attempt.

LIMITATIONS ON LAW OF CRIMINAL ATTEMPT

The application of the criminal attempt statute has its limitations. Despite the generic nature of such laws, courts have been reluctant to apply them in situations that produce illogical results, even when the suspect is acting in a purposeful manner. Thus, efforts at criminalizing attempts to drive while intoxicated have been struck down.[19] One would also expect that attempted disorderly conduct, attempted public intoxication, and any attempted traffic violation would fail to pass judicial scrutiny. Logically, most *malum prohibitum* offenses do not lend themselves to application of the law of criminal attempt.

Likewise, Texas, like most jurisdictions, holds that an attempt to attempt a crime is no crime (Sec. 15.05). The conduct and the potential harm are simply too remote to warrant the invocation of the criminal code.

ISSUES IN LAW OF CRIMINAL ATTEMPT

One of the more controversial issues in recent years regarding application of the law of criminal attempt focused upon whether an individual who was infected with HIV could be prosecuted for attempted murder when he or she bit, spat at, or otherwise tried to transfer tainted bodily fluids to another person. The controversy arose in the 1980s as society was deciding how to compassionately deal with HIV-positive individuals while at the same time recognizing the potential for innocent persons to be exposed to the deadly virus. In the intervening decades, several hundred HIV-infected individuals are believed to have been prosecuted for attempted murder because of their malicious efforts to transmit the virus to others.[20] These type of attempt cases present several challenges for prosecutors. First, since criminal attempt is a specific intent offense, most courts hold that mere knowledge of the HIV-positive condition is insufficient to support a charge of attempted murder. For example, if Bruce, aware that he has HIV, engages in unprotected sex with Monica and Monica is unaware of his condition, Bruce is legally reckless at best. Exposing Monica to the risk of HIV might be deadly conduct but no evidence exists that Bruce is trying to cause her death. On the other hand, where the defendant has manifested by words or deeds an intent to try to cause death, attempted murder charges have been sustained. In one Texas case, an HIV-infected prisoner who spat at a correctional officer was convicted of attempted murder, his words and actions manifesting an intent to cause harm.[21]

DEFENSES TO CHARGE OF CRIMINAL ATTEMPT

Because society would rather prevent crime than punish its commission, Texas, like the majority of jurisdictions, provides a **renunciation defense** to charges of criminal attempt (Sec. 15.04). A prospective offender who voluntarily renounces his criminal goal may be found not guilty of criminal attempt. Thus in the earlier example, if Don, after entering Ron's house changes his mind about killing John and abandons the plot, he has a defense to any charge of attempted murder. Not surprisingly, this defense is not available when the police intercede and prevent the commission of the underlying crime. The decision to abandon must be the affirmative choice of the prospective offender. Renunciation as a defense is not commonly raised.

Suppose via an Internet chat room Rudy solicits Hannah for sex. Hannah agrees to meet Rudy for sexual intercourse. In her messages to Rudy, Hannah has told him that she is a 14-year-old female. In fact, Hannah is a 30-year-old male police officer. Can Rudy be convicted of attempting to have sex with a child?

Even though there is no way Rudy can accomplish his desired goal (sex with a child), Rudy can still be convicted of *attempting* to engage in the illegal conduct. This situation is known in the law as a **factual impossibility**. A fact or circumstance unknown to the offender is the only thing that prevents him from committing the substantive crime. The law has long held that such factual impossibility is not a defense to a charge of criminal attempt. The suspect's conduct meets the requirements for a criminal attempt: intent to commit the offense and an unsuccessful act in furtherance of the commission of the crime. The notion that the suspect could never complete the offense is of little concern. In the opening example, Don's mistaken shooting of the dog, believing it to be Ron, would not save Don from a charge of attempted murder.

On the other hand, **inherent impossibility** is a defense. If Maria tries to kill Jack by sticking pins in a voodoo doll representing Jack, Maria has not committed attempted murder. While she has the requisite *mens rea*, she is missing an important part of the *actus reus*, an act in furtherance of the commission of the underlying crime. Her conduct of sticking pins in a doll does not further the potential for harm to Jack.

Similarly, recall that intent alone is insufficient to constitute a criminal attempt. This rule comes into play with the defense of **legal impossibility**. Suppose Mike decides to steal apples from the nearby apple orchard. Late one night, he goes to the orchard and helps himself to a dozen apples. Because it is dark, Mike does not see a big sign that reads, "Free apples. Take all you want." Mike possesses the culpable mental state to steal the apples, but no matter how hard he tries he cannot commit theft of the apples because the owner has consented for anyone to help themselves. Likewise, suppose Judy has gone to Mexico on spring break. She buys several items of gold jewelry while there. Because Judy had previously heard that it is illegal to bring gold into the United States, she conceals the jewelry in the lining of her luggage in the hopes that the U.S. Customs inspector will not find it. If the inspector finds the jewelry, has Judy committed attempted smuggling? She certainly has the intent to smuggle but no law exists barring the importation of gold jewelry. Since American law does not punish individuals for their criminal intentions only, Judy cannot be convicted of attempting to violate a statute that does not exist; it is a legal impossibility.

Suppose that one night Harry is apprehended inside the local bank using an acetylene torch on the bank vault. The prosecutor charges Harry with attempted burglary. At trial, Harry raises a somewhat novel defense to the charge: he is not guilty of attempted burglary because he has actually committed all of the elements required of burglary! Will Harry's unusual defense be successful? Probably not. State statute explicitly provides that it is no defense to a criminal attempt charge that the offense attempted was actually committed.[22] There appears to be at least two reasons for this view. First, since an attempt contains some but not all of the elements of the primary offense, commission of the primary crime includes all of the elements of the attempt. By definition, an attempted burglary is a lesser included offense of burglary. Thus, if the elements of burglary have been committed, the offender has also committed the elements of attempted burglary. The second reason for rejecting Harry's defense is rooted in the discretionary authority of the public prosecutor. Under the American system of law, district attorneys are granted wide discretion in choosing which offenses to prosecute and, importantly, the type and level of charges to be levied against a particular offender. Strategic and policy reasons may exist as to why a prosecutor would choose to pursue attempt charges even though the facts suggest the actual completion of the substantive offense. Maybe a rule of courtroom evidence would make prosecution difficult or perhaps establishing the constitutionally required level of proof would be demanding. The prosecutor may simply believe it would be easier to prove an attempted crime instead of the more serious substantive crime. Whatever the reason, the prosecutor generally gets to choose the level of offense he or she will seek to prove in court.

Penalty

American criminal law generally sets punishment based on the amount of harm produced. A criminal attempt produces less harm than the actual offense attempted. An attempted murder, while socially undesirable, is less harmful than a consummated murder. Accordingly, the Texas Penal Code sets the penalty for a criminal attempt at one level less than the underlying offense. For example, since murder is a felony of the first degree, attempted murder is a graded as a felony of the second degree. What is the penalty, if any, for attempted theft under $20, a Class C misdemeanor?

CRIMINAL CONSPIRACY

Introduction

The Common Law declared it a crime to conspire with others to commit a criminal offense. This prohibition has carried over to contemporary criminal law so that the offense of criminal conspiracy now exists by statute in every state. Conspiracy may be defined as an agreement by two or more people to commit an unlawful act or to commit a lawful act by unlawful means. Conspiracy statutes exist primarily for two public policy reasons. First, the government should not have to stand idly by and wait

> ## § 15.02. Criminal Conspiracy
>
> a. A person commits criminal conspiracy if, with intent that a felony be committed:
>   1. he agrees with one or more persons that they or one or more of them engage in conduct that would constitute the offense; and
>   2. he or one or more of them performs an overt act in pursuance of the agreement.
> b. An agreement constituting a conspiracy may be inferred from acts of the parties.

for potential offenders to actually cause harm before intervening in their undesirable social conduct. Second, the potential harm that individuals can cause in concert with others is greater than the harm a single person can cause. For example, organized crime creates a greater potential for harm than a series of individual offenders.

Criminal conspiracies are basically criminal partnerships where two or more individuals agree to engage in criminal behavior. And, much like the law of business partnerships, each partner becomes legally responsible for the behavior of his or her associates and employees. In a conspiracy, however, the parties may not even know each other so long as they are part of a common criminal group.

Elements of Criminal Conspiracy

Mens rea of Criminal Conspiracy

Criminal conspiracy is a crime grounded in purposeful or intentional behavior. Individuals must agree to be part of the conspiracy and intend that one or more criminal acts flow from the agreement. Merely having knowledge of the existence of the conspiracy is insufficient to establish the required culpable mental state. As with other offenses, the mental state of the participants can be inferred from their conduct.

Actus reus of Criminal Conspiracy

The *actus reus* of the offense consists of two parts: the agreement and the overt act. The agreement to commit the criminal offense need not be a written one and indeed rarely would be reduced to writing. Further, a co-conspirator need not explicitly verbalize that he wishes to be part of the conspiracy. A conspirator's assent to the conspiracy is often established by his subsequent conduct.

Assume Jake says to George, "I've got a great idea on how to make money. Let's print our own using your scanner and computer." Consider George's potential responses:

1. "That's not only a bad idea, that's illegal."
2. "I'm in. I could use some extra cash."
3. "The scanner is in my office. Let's see what kind of image it will generate."
4. "My scanner is broken but I know where I can get another one."

Which of George's responses suggests his willingness to participate with Jake in a scheme to counterfeit money? All but the first. The first response does not reject participation in the plot but clearly is not itself a sufficiently explicit agreement to participate. Note that only the second potential response is an unambiguous statement of support for the plan. Statements three and four require a reasonable inference that George will willingly participate in the scheme.

Jake's idea and George's agreement alone are not sufficient to constitute a conspiracy. Texas law requires that some **overt act** be taken in furtherance of the conspiracy. This overt act requirement serves several purposes. It confirms that under

American law harm is established not by state of mind alone but by conduct. Accordingly, some conduct in support of the conspiracy, no matter how minor, is needed. Second, the legal requirement also recognizes the old adage that talk is cheap. Persons sometimes talk about what they are going to do, both legal and illegal, but do not always carry out their stated intentions. Consider three individuals sitting in a bar drinking beer. They are discussing the recent tax hike. One individual says, "We ought to go and burn down city hall." "Yea!" exclaims his drinking buddies. So long as they make no move to actually set fire to city hall, no offense has been committed.

Recall Jake and George's counterfeiting plot. Suppose Jake goes in search of appropriate paper upon which to print the money. His act is likely sufficient to seal the conspiracy charge.[23]

ISSUES IN LAW OF CRIMINAL CONSPIRACY

While conspiracy charges can be filed in almost every case where two or more offenders participate, the law of conspiracy is particularly useful in establishing criminal responsibility for individuals who do not directly participate in the underlying substantive offense. For example, suppose "Mad Dog," the leader of the "Demon Hogs" motorcycle gang, decides to raise money by making and selling "crystal meth." Three members of the gang manufacture the drug while six other members actually sell the illegal substance to customers. Suppose "Mad Dog" is involved in neither the actual production nor direct sale of the drug. The law will still consider him a co-conspirator because he agreed to the conspiracy and a fellow conspirator has committed one or more overt acts (manufacture and sale of the drug) on behalf of the conspiracy. "Mad Dog" can be successfully prosecuted for conspiracy to manufacture and sell a controlled substance even though he did neither act directly. Additionally, he bears criminal responsibility for the other acts of his crime partners. Under a legal principle known as the **Pinkerton Rule**, "Mad Dog," or any other member of a conspiracy, is criminally responsible for the reasonably foreseeable acts of his crime associates.[24] Because of the ability to reach these "hidden hands" behind criminal enterprises, the law of criminal conspiracy is a popular tool in the prosecution of organized crime-type cases. Indeed the potential reach of the law of conspiracy is so broad that one judge called conspiracy "the darling of the modern prosecutor's nursery."[25]

Recall Jake and George and their counterfeiting plot. Assume they successfully print bogus currency and pass a few of the bills to merchants before being apprehended. Can they be successfully prosecuted for both forgery and conspiracy to commit forgery?[26] Unlike criminal attempt, conspiracy is not a lesser included offense of the primary crime but rather a standalone offense. If conspirators are successful in carrying out their illicit plans, the conspiracy does not merge into their criminal objective and they can be prosecuted for both the conspiracy and the actual offense committed. No double jeopardy problem arises. Likewise, the offenders can be prosecuted for the conspiracy whether or not the objective crime is successfully perpetrated.

While one normally thinks of conspiracy as involving a minimum of two persons, in a few instances more than two persons are necessary to sustain a charge. Consider the offense of bribery. Rex offers a bribe to Oliver, a juror in Rex's personal injury lawsuit, if Oliver will vote in Rex's favor. Oliver accepts the bribe. In addition to violating the bribery statute, have Rex and Oliver engaged in a conspiracy to commit bribery? No. Although two individuals are involved and an overt act has occurred, American courts decline to apply the law of conspiracy to offenses that inherently require two persons to commit, such as bribery, prostitution, adultery, incest, and gambling, under a principle of law called Wharton's Rule.[27] **Wharton's Rule** states that an agreement by two persons to commit a particular crime cannot be prosecuted as a conspiracy when the crime is of such a nature as to necessarily require the participation of two persons for its commission.[28] But suppose that Perry, Rex's attorney, offered Oliver the bribe on Rex's authorization. Under this scenario, Perry and Rex would be guilty of conspiracy to commit bribery regardless of whether Oliver chooses to accept the bribe. Oliver is not a part of the conspiracy.

Note that the Texas law of conspiracy is limited to felony offenses. It is no offense in this state to conspire to commit a misdemeanor. Thus, if John and Paul agree to enter the music store and John will steal a CD while Paul distracts the salesclerk, the two will be liable for a theft charge but not also a conspiracy charge.

As with the law of criminal attempt, factual impossibility is no defense to a conspiracy charge. That is, the fact that for reasons beyond the perpetrators' control they would be unable to commit the desired crime does not serve to negate a conspiracy charge. If Larry, Moe, and Curly plot to steal money from a bank in downtown San Antonio by tunneling under the River Walk and into a bank vault, the fact that the scheme has no realistic chance of being successful will not protect them from prosecution for conspiracy, providing the agreement and overt act elements can be established.

Penalty

As with criminal attempt, the Texas Penal Code establishes the penalty for conspiracy at one penalty category below "the most serious felony that is the object of the conspiracy."[29]

DEFENSES TO CHARGE OF CRIMINAL CONSPIRACY

Suppose Frank, Peter, and Dean agree to rob a bank tomorrow. Dean goes to the bank to examine its layout and reports back to Frank and Peter, describing the number of guards present and the floor plan of the bank. The next day as the trio is driving to the bank, Peter has a change of heart and declares he will not participate. While Frank and Dean are entering the bank without him, Peter calls the police and reports the imminent robbery. While Peter is not culpable for the actual robbery, can he still be prosecuted for conspiracy to commit robbery? The traditional rule is that Peter's withdrawal will not relieve him of liability for a conspiracy charge; he made an agreement with Frank and Dean to commit the crime and an overt act occurred in furtherance of that agreement has occurred. All elements of the offense of conspiracy are complete. However, the Texas Penal Code (Sec. 15.04) recognizes voluntary renunciation, or withdrawal, as a defense even after the overt act has occurred. But, the defendant must have taken action to thwart the commission of the object offense. Merely withdrawing from participation in the plot is insufficient to raise the defense. As one court noted, renunciation is voluntary only if there is repentance or a change of heart.[30] Does Peter's telephone call to the police department fit this requirement?

Fred, Ed, Ned, and Ted are charged with conspiracy to commit theft through use of a bogus Internet website. Fred is tried first and found not guilty. Ed, because he is only 16 years old, is referred to the juvenile justice system. Ned dies in a car wreck prior to trial. Can Ted be prosecuted for conspiracy now that no one is left who is legally considered a co-conspirator? Ted's situation falls under the so-called **plurality requirement**. This traditional rule of law holds that since a conspiracy requires a combination of two or more persons, a single conspirator cannot be convicted if none of his partners are found to be criminally responsible. However, the Texas Penal Code [Sec. 15.02(c)] departs from

§ 15.02. Criminal Conspiracy

* * *

(c) It is no defense to prosecution for criminal conspiracy that:

1. one or more of the coconspirators is not criminally responsible for the object offense;

2. one or more of the coconspirators has been acquitted, so long as two or more coconspirators have not been acquitted;

3. one or more of the coconspirators has not been prosecuted or convicted, has been convicted of a different offense, or is immune from prosecution;

4. the actor belongs to a class of persons that by definition of the object offense is legally incapable of committing the object offense in an individual capacity; or

5. the object offense was actually committed.

this view slightly and treats the trial of each conspirator as a separate event. Under this approach, each case stands on its own merits and the outcome of one offender's case should not influence the potential culpability of his partner in crime. However, the Texas statutory rule continues to adhere to the traditional view that a conspiracy conviction cannot occur if all other conspirators have been acquitted except the conspirator on trial. Ted could probably be convicted of conspiracy because Ed, the juvenile, has not been acquitted. Examine the precise language of Sec. 15.02(c) to see how the sequencing of the trials of multiple co-conspirators could affect the ability to convict the last person placed on trial.

Under the Common Law, spouses were considered to be one legal person and thereby legally incapable of being co-conspirators.[31] However, the Texas law of marriage is rooted in the Spanish civil law. This law rejected the Common Law notion that a wife lost her individual identity upon marriage. Accordingly, the law in Texas has long been that a wife could be convicted of being a co-conspirator with her husband.[32]

The Texas Penal Code contains a second statute that is based in a large part on the theory of conspiracy. Sec. 71.02, engaging in organized criminal activity, creates a separate felony for individuals who work together (e.g., criminal combinations and criminal street gangs) to profit from a variety of serious felonious acts ranging from murder to gambling to promotion of prostitution. Unlike Sec. 15.02 which applies to two or more persons, Sec. 71.02 requires at least three participants in the criminal activity. As with conspiracy, the connection between the defendants in a Sec. 71.02 case need not be substantial. In fact, the state need not prove the defendants are acquainted with each other, only that they "collaborate in carrying on criminal activities."

CRIMINAL SOLICITATION

Introduction

At the beginning of the chapter, John approaches Don about killing his business partner. As the scenario plays out, Don agrees to commit the murder and attempts to do so. Under the facts posed by the hypothetical, Don could properly be convicted of conspiracy to commit murder and attempted murder. Likewise, John would be guilty of conspiracy and also culpable for attempted murder under the law of parties. But what if Don had rebuffed John's effort to hire him? Don simply turns down John's offer. Has any crime occurred? Don certainly has committed no offense as he declined to become involved in the homicidal plot. But what about John? Is it an offense to ask another individual to commit a crime, regardless of whether the other person accepts the enticement?

Soliciting another to commit a criminal offense was considered a misdemeanor under the Common Law.[33] Certainly the government has an interest in preventing individuals from seeking to induce others into committing criminal offenses. This interest is manifested in modern criminal codes through establishment of the crime of criminal solicitation. Criminal solicitation in this context is not to be confused with solicitation of prostitution. The latter is a different offense with different elements.[34]

Elements of Criminal Solicitation

The elements of criminal solicitation consist of:

- an individual who possesses a specific intent that a capital felony or felony of the first degree be committed
- requests, commands, or attempts to induce another to commit the offense.

The *mens rea* of the offense is twofold. First the offender must knowingly make the solicitation, but more importantly, he or she must possess the specific intent that a capital felony or first degree felony be committed.[35] It must be the offender's conscious desire (intent) that the crime be carried out. Note that the statute limits criminal solicitation to efforts to persuade another to commit a capital felony or felony of the first degree. Not surprisingly, the overwhelming bulk of criminal solicitation cases involve solicitation of capital murder, that is, murder for hire.

Sec. 15.03 is not violated if the solicitation is to commit a lesser felony or a misdemeanor. Assume Roderick tells Ray, "I'll give you $50 to beat up Bubba real badly." Regardless of whether Ray accepts the offer or not, criminal solicitation is not committed because even an aggravated assault with serious bodily injury is only a felony of the second degree. Should Ray agree to the deal and actually cause serious bodily injury to Bubba, Roderick would likely have liability under the law of parties. Criminal solicitation would occur if Bubba is a peace officer and Roderick seeks to have him beaten because of his official position. Such an aggravated assault would be a felony of the first degree and serve as the basis for the criminal solicitation charge.

The offense is complete when the solicitation is made, even if the other party rejects the overture. Thus, when John tries to hire Don to kill Ron, John commits solicitation of capital murder even though Don declines the job offer. In short, the crime is complete with the asking.[36]

The Texas statute, like most state's criminal solicitation laws, uses fairly generic terms to describe the *actus reus*: "commands, requests, entices, encourages, or requests." The Legislature could have just as easily used terms such as asks, entreats,

---

§ 15.03. Criminal Solicitation

(a) A person commits an offense if, with intent that a capital felony or felony of the first degree be committed, he requests, commands, or attempts to induce another to engage in specific conduct that, under the circumstances surrounding his conduct as the actor believes them to be, would constitute the felony or make the other a party to its commission.

orders, persuades, influences, convinces, and the like. The statutory terms seem chosen less for their specific definitions and more to convey the notion that the actor is the originator of an effort to cause another to commit a crime. Texas courts have not been presented with many opportunities to explore the boundaries of the *actus reus* of this offense. Most criminal solicitation cases are straightforward: the actor makes a clear request to another person to commit a crime. But a conviction must be based on evidence that the actor engaged in conduct that fits the definition of one of the verbs in the statute.

Many criminal solicitation cases involve one party offering money or other remuneration to another party if the second party will commit a crime, usually murder. Note, however, that the statute is silent on the issue of compensation. If Mary solicits her boyfriend Al to murder George, her ex-husband, Al's motive, love or money, is not an element of the offense that must be proven.

Issues in Law of Criminal Solicitation

Suppose Jill is seeking someone to kill her husband Jack. She approaches Ned and offers him $5,000 to kill Jack. Ned accepts the deal. Unbeknownst to Jill, Ned is an undercover police officer who has no intention of killing Jack.[37] Can Jill be convicted of solicitation of murder? Most certainly. The Texas rule is that acquiescence by the party solicited is not an element of the offense. The crime is complete when the offender makes the solicitation regardless of whether the proposal is accepted or whether the solicited person actually carries out the crime. Further, even though the undercover police officer has no intention of committing the murder, the law looks at the plot from the perspective of what Jill perceives the circumstances to be, not what the circumstances are in reality. Jill believes the officer will do the deed. She has committed solicitation of murder.

Criminal solicitation prosecutions occasionally raise issues regarding the accomplice testimony rule discussed in Chapter 4. Recall that the Texas Code of Criminal Procedure, Art. 38.14, states that "A conviction cannot be had upon the testimony of an accomplice unless corroborated by other evidence tending to connect the defendant with the offense committed; and the corroboration is not sufficient if it merely shows the commission of the offense." The criminal solicitation statute contains a more restrictive variant of the accomplice testimony rule in Sec. 15.03(b):

> A person may not be convicted under this section on the uncorroborated testimony of the person allegedly solicited and unless the solicitation is made under circumstances strongly corroborative of both the solicitation itself and the actor's intent that the other person act on the solicitation.

This section requires "strongly corroborative" evidence of both the solicitation and the defendant's intent to solicit the other party. Thus, if Ralph calls the police and reports that Kevin offered him $100 to kill Kevin's wife, Ralph's testimony is, by itself, not sufficient to convict Kevin. In actual practice, and to comply with the corroboration requirement, the police would likely request that Ralph contact Kevin and engage him in further discussion about the plan while Ralph is wearing a concealed recording device. The recording would serve as the "strongly corroborative" evidence required of the statute.

Texas case law holds that an undercover police officer is not an accomplice witness and the accomplice testimony rule is inapplicable to the officer. However, the corroboration required in the criminal solicitation statute is more specific and applies to all persons who are solicited, including peace officers.[38]

Penalty

The Texas Penal Code treats criminal solicitation as an offense generally punishable under the same penalty scheme as the other inchoate offenses; that is, if the crime solicited is a capital felony, criminal solicitation is a felony of the first degree. If the offense is a felony of the first degree, criminal solicitation is punished as a felony of the second degree.[39]

SUMMARY OF PREPARATORY OFFENSES

Assume Jill contacts Jack and offers him $5,000 to kill Hazel, her employer at the water company. Jack agrees. One evening Jack hides in the bushes outside of Hazel's home. As Hazel is walking up the driveway, Jack appears and fires one shot at her. Jack flees. The shot hits Hazel in the arm but the wound is only minor. An investigation reveals Jack and Jill's plot. For which preparatory offenses are Jill and Jack responsible?

Jill committed solicitation of capital murder when she offered the money to Jack to kill Hazel. Once Jack agreed and went to Hazel's home (an overt act), Jill and Jack are guilty of conspiracy to commit capital murder. When Jack fires the shot, he has committed attempted capital murder and Jill, under the law of parties discussed elsewhere in the text, is also culpable for attempted capital murder.

UNLAWFUL USE OF CRIMINAL INSTRUMENT

Introduction

Statutes prohibiting possession of criminal instruments, such as burglar tools, are common throughout the country.[40] Here, the problem of when a would-be offender crosses the threshold between mere preparation and an attempted offense has been avoided by declaring the possession of tools of the trade—certainly a very preliminary step toward committing a burglary—to be a crime in itself. The burglar needs to be neither near the potential burglary site nor actually prying on the door for his preparatory behavior to be criminalized. On the other hand, the prosecutor must establish the specific intent to use the tools or the knowledge that the tools are usable only for criminal purposes. Thus, what might be considered an innocent act becomes a criminal one when a *mens rea* exists along with some *actus reus*, although the latter may be relatively insignificant.

§ 16.01. Unlawful Use of Criminal Instrument

a. A person commits an offense if:
  1. he possesses a criminal instrument with intent to use it in the commission of an offense; or
  2. with knowledge of its character and with intent to use or aid or permit another to use in the commission of an offense, he manufactures, adapts, sells, installs, or sets up a criminal instrument.

b. For the purpose of this section, "criminal instrument" means anything, the possession, manufacture, or sale of which is not otherwise an offense, that is specially designed, made, or adapted for use in the commission of an offense.

c. An offense under Subsection (a)(1) is one category lower than the offense intended. An offense under Subsection (a)(2) is a state jail felony.

Texas, however, has rejected this common approach. While on its face the language of Sec. 16.01 suggests that the statute is much broader than a possession of burglar tools-type law, Texas courts has given it a much more narrow and restricted reading. The statute presumably applies to any offense where the offender possesses a **criminal instrument** with intent to use to commit a crime. On the surface, this would mean that a would-be burglar's prybar, a prospective murderer's pistol, and a pornographer's movie camera could all be criminal instruments. The problem arises in how Texas courts have interpreted the definition of "criminal instrument."

The general rule is that an object that has a legitimate use can be considered to be a criminal instrument only in the most unusual of circumstances. This conclusion draws from the language of the definition requiring the object to be "specially designed, made, or adapted" to commit an offense. "The statute [Sec. 16.01] was obviously designed to deal with a very small class of property which can be used only for the commission of crime and to deal with persons in possession of such property or engaged in the manufacture or adaptation of the property exclusively for use in criminal activities, before the criminal activities are undertaken or completed."[41] Thus, a "slim jim"[42] used to unlock automobile doors was found not to be a criminal instrument.[43] Likewise, a flashlight, prybar, and circuit tester were ruled not to fit the statutory definition.[44] Even the possession of an electric service lockband key by a private citizen was not deemed a criminal instrument.[45] These rulings are based on the principle that each item has a legitimate use and thereby is not *specifically* made for use in commission of a criminal offense.

The few reported instances where the appeals courts have upheld convictions for possession of a criminal instrument involve cases where the circumstances indicated that the device had virtually no lawful purpose. Thus, a homemade device consisting of a wire with a loop on the end to facilitate opening locked cars was ruled to be a criminal instrument[46] as was a homemade key to coin-operated washing machines in a Laundromat.[47] These cases suggest that homemade items used in criminal acts are more likely to be found to be criminal instruments than commercially produced objects.

Given the stringent Texas definition, are lock picks criminal instruments? How about an automotive radar detector?

The definition of "criminal instrument" excludes items otherwise declared to be an offense. For example, short-barrel firearms,[48] switchblade knives,[49] audio surveillance equipment,[50] drug paraphernalia,[51] and equipment to manufacture illicit distilled spirits ("moonshine")[52] are covered under specialized statutes.

CRIMEGRAPH
Preparatory Offenses

Offense	Specific Intent or Knowledge	Culpable mental state	Conduct	What?	Penalty
Criminal Attempt 15.01(a)	With specific intent to commit an offense	1. Intentionally, or 2. Knowingly, or 3. Recklessly*	Does an act more than mere preparation	That tends but fails to commit offense	CM to F1
Criminal Conspiracy 15.02(a)	With intent that a felony be committed	1. Intentionally, or 2. Knowingly, or 3. Recklessly*	1. Agrees with one or more persons that one or more engage in criminal conduct and 2. Commits an overt act in pursuance of agreement		AM to F1
Criminal Solicitation 15.03(a)	With intent that: 1. Capital felony be committed or 2. Felony of the first degree be committed	1. Intentionally, or 2. Knowingly, or 3. Recklessly*	1. Requests, or 2. Commands, or 3. Attempts to induce another	To engage in specific conduct that would constitute a felony	F2 to F1
Unlawful Use of Criminal Instrument 16.01(a)(1)	With intent to use in commission of offense	1. Intentionally, or 2. Knowingly, or 3. Recklessly*	Possesses	Criminal instrument	CM to F1
Unlawful Use of Criminal Instrument 16.01(a)(2)	1. With knowledge of its character and 2. With intent to: a. Use, or b. Aid, or c. Permit another to use 3. In the commission of an offense	1. Intentionally, or 2. Knowingly, or 3. Recklessly*	1. Manufactures, or 2. Adapts, or 3. Sells, or 4. Installs, or 5. Sets up	Criminal instrument	SJF

*Required by Texas Penal Code § 6.02

343

Notes

1. WAYNE R. LaFAVE, CRIMINAL LAW 13 (4th ed. 2003).
2. The Court of Star Chamber was an English court that sat between 1487 and 1641. Its primary purpose was to hear political libel and treason cases. During the reign of King Charles I (1600–1649), the court became synonymous with the abuse of and misuse of power by the king.
3. *See* 2 STEPHEN, HISTORY OF CRIMINAL LAW 223–224.
4. *See* Francis B. Sayre, *Criminal Attempts*, 41 HARV. L. REV. 821, 829 (1928).
5. Cald. 397 (KBD 1784).
6. *Id.* at 400.
7. 2 East 5 (1801).
8. Sayre, *supra*, at 836.
9. U.S. v. Riddle, 9 U.S. 311 (1809).
10. *Id.* at 312.
11. Sayre, *supra*, at 826–827.
12. State v. Beeler, 3 S.C.L. 482 (S.C. 1801), upholding a conviction for attempting to pass a counterfeit coin.
13. *See* Commonwealth v. Barlow, 4 Mass. 439 (Mass. 1808).
14. See MODEL PENAL CODE § 5.01 (1962) and state statutes cited in commentary.
15. 18 U.S.C. § 2113.
16. Flores v. State, 902 S.W.2d 618 (Tex. App.—Austin 1995).
17. *Id.*
18. Henson v. State, 173 S.W.3d 92 (Tex. App.—Tyler 2005).
19. See Strong v. State, 87 S.W.3d 206 (Tex. App.—Dallas 2002), holding no such offense as attempted driving while intoxicated.
20. *See* Rorie Sherman, *Criminal Prosecutions on AIDS Growing*, NAT'L LAW JOURNAL, Oct. 14, 1991, at 3.
21. *See, e.g.*, Weeks v. State, 834 S.W.2d 559 (Tex. App.—Eastland 1992).
22. TEX. PENAL CODE § 15.01(c).
23. Walker v. State, 828 S.W.2d 485 (Tex. App.—Dallas 1992).
24. Pinkerton v. U.S., 328 U.S. 640 (1946).
25. Harrison v. U.S., 7 F.2d 259, 263 (2nd Cir. 1925).
26. While counterfeiting of currency violates federal law (18 U.S.C. § 471), the conduct also violates the Texas forgery statute (§ 32.21).
27. The rule owes its name to Francis Wharton (1820–1889) author of A TREATISE ON THE CRIMINAL LAW OF THE UNITED STATES (1846). Wharton originally identified the doctrine and stated its rationale.
28. *See* CHARLES E. TORCIA, 4 WHARTON'S CRIMINAL LAW 684–685 (15th ed. 1996).
29. TEX. PENAL CODE § 15.02(d).
30. Chennault v. State, 667 S.W.2d 299 (Tex. App.—Dallas 1984).
31. 1 Hawkins, PLEAS OF THE CROWN 192 (4th ed. 1762).
32. Marks v. State, 164 S.W.2d 690 (Tex. Crim. App. 1942). All American jurisdictions which have faced the issue in modern times have rejected the Common Law rule and permitted a spouse to be charged as a co-conspirator.
33. Oddly the offense of criminal solicitation was not confirmed as part of the Common Law until 1801. *See* King v. Higgins, 102 Eng. Rep. 269 (1801).
34. *See* TEX. PENAL CODE § 43.02(a)(2).
35. Sheffield v. State, 847 S.W.2d 251 (Tex. App.—Tyler 1992).
36. Underwood v. State, 853 S.W.2d 858 (Tex. App.—Fort Worth 1993).
37. Many murder-for-hire plots are uncovered because the offender solicits an undercover police officer or police informant.
38. See Varvaro v. State, 772 S.W.2d 140 (Tex. App.—Tyler 1988), for a discussion of this distinction.
39. TEX. PENAL CODE § 15.03(d).
40. *See, e.g.*, CAL. PENAL CODE § 466 *and* 720 ILL. COMP. STAT. 5/19–2.
41. Universal Amusement Co. v. Vance, 404 F. Supp. 33, 51 (S.D. Tex. 1975), cited with approval in Fronatt v. State, 543 S.W.2d 140 (Tex. Crim. App. 1976). But see Janjua v. State, 991 S.W.2d 419 (Tex. App.—Houston [14th Dist.] 1999), reviewing the history of the prior possession of burglar tools statute and comparing it with the current law. The Court of Appeals argues that the Legislature intended for § 16.01 to be interpreted more broadly, not more restrictively, than the prior statute.
42. A "slim jim" is a thin strip of metal that can be slid between the window weather striping of a car door and used to trip the locking mechanism.
43. Van Danzi v. State, 101 S.W.3d 786 (Tex. App.—El Paso 2003).
44. Eodice v. State, 742 S.W.2d 844 (Tex. App.—Austin 1987).
45. Harris v. State, 790 S.W.2d 778 (Tex. App.—Houston [14th Dist.] 1990).
46. Carrasco v. State, 712 S.W.2d 623 (Tex. App.—Corpus Christi 1986).
47. Simmons v. State, 690 S.W.2d 26 (Tex. App.—Beaumont 1985).
48. TEX. PENAL CODE § 46.05.
49. *Id.*
50. TEX. PENAL CODE § 16.02(d)(1).
51. TEX. HEALTH & SAFETY CODE § 481.125.
52. TEX. ALCO. BEV. CODE § 103.02.

CHAPTER

15

General Defenses and Justification

BOLO

The reader should be on the lookout (BOLO) for the meaning of the following terms. Knowledge of the meaning of these terms will greatly assist the reader in understanding the primary elements of the chapter.

- Affirmative defense
- Battered spouse syndrome
- Deadly force
- Defense
- Diminished mental capacity
- *doli incapax* rule
- Duress
- Entrapment
- Exception
- Force
- General defense

- Identity defense
- Infancy
- Insanity
- Legal excuse
- Legal process
- M'Naghten Test
- Mistake of fact
- Mistake of law
- Mitigation
- Post-traumatic stress disorder
- Spiritual treatment defense

THE PROCESS OF CRIMINAL DEFENSES

Introduction

Mark finds a car with the keys in the ignition. He takes the car for a drive. Mark does not have the owner's permission. John is arrested by postal inspectors and charged with possession of child pornography, which he had received through the mail. Will Mark and John be found guilty by a court? Maybe not. What if Mark, the car thief, is only 12 years old? Or suppose John was entrapped into receiving the child pornography through the mail? In both of these incidents, what would otherwise appear to be a straightforward criminal offense becomes no crime at all because the defendant possesses a legally established defense, otherwise known as a **legal excuse**. Similarly, suppose Sara shoots Eric with a pistol. Ordinarily, one would immediately think that Sara has committed aggravated assault or attempted murder. But if the shooting occurs when Eric is attempting to burglarize Sara's home, her conduct is legally justified.

Courts have long accepted various defenses that relieve a defendant of criminal responsibility, even though the facts of the case initially indicated that a crime had occurred. Traditionally, these defenses were categorized as either excuses or justifications. An excuse is a defense based on public policy considerations—that is, conduct that would otherwise be illegal is excused because society has deemed it inappropriate to hold the offender morally responsible for his behavior. Insanity, age, duress, and entrapment are examples of legal excuses. Societal assumptions about who should be held accountable and other public policy concerns underlie excusing an otherwise guilty party from a penalty for his harmful conduct. On the other hand, what would otherwise be deemed illegal conduct is considered legally justified due to the factual circumstances under which the behavior occurs. An extraordinary set of facts, such as defending oneself or damaging property to rescue another from a raging fire, establishes a justification for the actor's otherwise wrongful behavior. Society will forgive the individual for his criminal behavior because the individual's harmful conduct prevents or terminates a potentially greater harm. As one scholar observed, justified conduct is "a good thing, or the right or sensible thing, or a permissible thing to do."[1]

Under the early Common Law, conduct that was justified resulted in an acquittal while excusable conduct simply allowed a guilty person to petition the monarch to exempt him or her from the death penalty.[2] Today, conduct that is legally excused or justified normally results in a complete defense to the charge.

Unlike criminal offenses, which are nearly exclusively the product of statutory enactments, defenses can be created by legislative action, established by court decisions, or arise from the Common Law tradition. Some defenses are **general defenses**, meaning they may be used in any criminal prosecution, while others are unique to a particular type of crime. For example, insanity is available as a defense to any crime.[3] On the other hand, consent is a defense to sexual assault but not to murder. This chapter first discusses the common defenses raised by criminal defendants. Many, but not all, of these are contained in Chapter 8 of the Texas Penal Code. The defenses unique to particular offenses, such as consent in an assault, are covered in the chapters related to the specific offense. Defenses relative to justifiable conduct, such as use of force and deadly force, are discussed in the second portion of this chapter.

Procedural Issues in Establishing a Defense

With a singular exception, raising a legal defense (as opposed to a factual defense) normally requires that the accused bring forth evidence that meets the requirements of the defense. For example, if the defendant wishes to assert that he is not guilty because he was entrapped, the prosecution is under no obligation to negate that defense until the defendant has raised the matter in court. Depending on the nature of the defense, the burden of persuasion that a defendant must carry varies. States, such as Texas, that have enacted modern criminal codes often establish three possible levels of persuasion when bringing forth a defense:

Exceptions—A statutory exception is not so much a defense as an element of the offense that the prosecution must disprove.[4] For example, Texas criminalizes the communicating of wagering information with intent to further gambling.[5] The statute, however, states that it is an exception that the information communicated is intended for placing a lawful wager consistent with state law regulating horse and dog racing. Thus, if Billy the Bookie is charged with communicating betting lines on professional football games, the prosecution, as part of its proof, must establish beyond a reasonable doubt that Billy's conduct does not fall within the scope of the laws concerning horse and dog racing. Very few statutory defenses in Texas are characterized as exceptions.

Defenses—Most defenses are labeled just that defenses. Procedurally, this means that once the defendant places some proof into evidence that he qualifies for the defense, the prosecution must disprove the defense beyond a reasonable doubt.[6] Assume Bob is approached by Ray, an old high school acquaintance, about joining in a plan to sell marijuana Ray has grown. Bob rebuffs Ray's offer but several days later, Ray approaches him again and tells Bob that he needs quick cash to pay for medical treatment for his child and selling the marijuana is the only way he has to raise money. Bob reluctantly agrees to help sell the marijuana. A few days later Bob is arrested for conspiracy to deliver marijuana. He subsequently learns that Ray is working as a confidential informant for the police narcotics unit and the story about his sick child was totally false. At trial, Bob raises the defense of entrapment. To convict Bob of the drug charge, the state must prove beyond a reasonable doubt that Bob's conduct fits the elements of the offense and does not fall within the state's law regarding entrapment. If Bob's testimony about Ray's methods of persuasion places a reasonable doubt in the minds of the jurors on the issue of entrapment, the prosecution has failed to carry the constitutional burden of proof and Bob is entitled to be found not guilty. The raising of a legal defense certainly complicates the job of the prosecution in obtaining a conviction.[7]

Affirmative defenses—Suppose Mary is charged with being the getaway driver for her bank robber boyfriend Lou. At trial, Mary testifies that Lou threatened to kill her if she did not aid him. Mary has raised the defense of duress. In Texas, duress is categorized as an affirmative defense. This level of defense places the burden on the accused not only to raise the matter at trial but to establish the defense by the "preponderance of the evidence." If Mary fails to bring forth sufficient evidence to overturn the presumption that she acted voluntarily, she will be found guilty. Similarly, a defendant who pleads not guilty by reason of insanity must establish the defense with sufficiently persuasive proof to negate the presumption of sanity. Failing to convince the jury of the existence of insanity will result in a conviction.

This greater burden of persuasion for certain defenses exists because the prosecution has limited access to the information it needs to negate the defendant's claim. Only the defendant Mary knows whether she was really in fear of her life at the time of the robbery and only she knows for sure her mental state at the time. Courts view claims of involuntary behavior and mental disease as being too easy to feign and too difficult to disprove. Thus, if a defendant wishes to use these defenses, he or she must put forth a more substantial level of evidence. Such a requirement does not violate the defendant's constitutional right to due process. As the Supreme Court has noted, "So long as a State's method of allocating the burdens of proof does not lessen the State's burden to prove every element of the offense charged . . . a defendant's constitutional rights are not violated by placing on him the burden of proving mitigating circumstances sufficiently substantial to call for leniency."[8]

What happens if Rita, Mark, John, Ray, Mary, or any other defendant successfully raises a legal defense at trial? Recall the discussion of double jeopardy found in Chapter 3. The Fifth Amendment to the U.S. Constitution prohibits a person from being tried twice for the same criminal offense. Accordingly, when a not guilty verdict is rendered, the defendant is no longer subject to prosecution for that crime or any other offense containing the same elements.[9] The state no longer has grounds to hold the individual. With the sole exception of a successful insanity defense discussed below, the defendant will be discharged and free to go about his or her life.

Mitigation

In some instances, the defendant in a criminal case may not deny that he or she caused the harm but argues that the charge is too severe for the facts. The defendant may produce evidence in an effort to reduce or mitigate the level of offense for which the jury might convict.[10]

Suppose Ginger learns that her husband Fred is having an affair. This is the third time Fred has been unfaithful to Ginger. When Fred comes home, Ginger confronts Fred with a loaded pistol. An argument ensues and the pistol discharges. Fred dies as a result of the injury. Ginger is charged with murder. At her trial, Ginger seeks to establish that the firearm discharged inadvertently and that her behavior constitutes the crime of manslaughter, not murder.

Such a trial tactic keeps the jury from facing an all or nothing decision. In cases such as the previous scenario, it is clear that Ginger caused the death of Fred and has no legal justification for her behavior. The state asserts that she did so purposefully. A jury is placed in the position of convicting her for murder, an arguably harsh result under the circumstances, or acquitting her, an unlikely outcome since she clearly killed Fred. By injecting a third choice, the jury is afforded the chance to convict Ginger without creating an overly harsh result.

An alternative method of mitigating Ginger's culpability would be to convict her of murder but during the punishment phase of the trial, treat the matter as a felony of the second degree as is permitted under Sec. 19.01(d). In this manner the punishment is mitigated.

INFANCY/AGE

Recall Mark the auto thief. Because of his young age he will not be processed within the adult justice system but rather routed to the juvenile justice system. Modern criminal codes establish an age threshold that must be attained before the offender will be considered to be an adult for prosecution purposes. This legal excuse is known variously as the defense of **infancy**, age, or immaturity. While the Common Law basis for drawing an age line for criminal responsibility was rooted in the notion that children were incapable of forming malicious intent, modern policies seem based largely on the broader societal goal of rehabilitating youthful offenders instead of punishing them. With the rare exception of incarceration of particularly violent children, the modern juvenile system operates at the community level with a goal of rehabilitation and prevention of more serious crimes in future. This philosophy is further manifested in juvenile court proceedings being considered to be civil in nature, not criminal, even though the youth's conduct fits within the penal code definitions.

The Common Law followed the *doli incapax* **rule**,[11] conclusively presuming that children under the age of seven were incapable of forming the required malicious intent necessary to commit a criminal act. Young children were thereby excused from any criminal accountability. Individuals at least 14 years of age were treated as adults for the purpose of the application of the criminal law. Children between the ages of 7 and 14 were presumed to be without criminal capacity, but that presumption could be rebutted in individual cases through proof of awareness of wrongful behavior (e.g., concealing evidence).[12]

Modern American statutes track a structure similar to the Common Law although different chronological ages are used.[13] The age of responsibility varies from state to state with age 18 being the most common. The federal government, 38 states, and the District of Columbia adhere to the 18-year-old dividing line for criminal responsibility. Ten states, including Texas, use age 17 while two set age 16 as the demarcation between adult and juvenile offenders. However, in recent years, many states, including Texas, have dropped the qualifying age for certain particularly violent offenses.

Penal Code Sec. 8.07 sets forth the somewhat complicated rules for determining when a person under 17 in Texas is subject to the adult criminal sanction. Table 15-1 displays the current Texas rules on sorting which offenders initially go to juvenile court and which are processed through the adult justice system.

In every jurisdiction, a juvenile who has attained a statutorily established minimum age and commits any serious crime can be transferred to stand trial as an adult. This procedure involves the district attorney seeking a discretionary waiver of

TABLE 15-1	Processing of Offenders in Texas by Age (Texas Penal Code § 8.07 and Texas Family Code § 54.02)

Offender Processed in Adult Justice System

A. 17 years of age or older at time of offense

B. Any age for following offenses:
   a. Perjury if understands nature of oath;
   b. Operation of motor vehicle by minor (fine only);
   c. Municipal motor vehicle ordinance;
   d. State misdemeanors punishable by fine only, other than public intoxication; or
   e. Municipal or county ordinance

C. 14–16 years of age at time of offense
   a. Offense charged is:
      1. Capital felony;
      2. Aggravated controlled substance felony; or
      3. Felony of first degree; and
   b. Juvenile court waives jurisdiction

D. 15–16 years of age at time of offense
   a. Offense charged is:
      1. Felony of second degree;
      2. Felony of third degree; or
      3. State jail felony; and
   b. Juvenile court waives jurisdiction

E. 10–16 years of age at time of offense
   a. Offender is over 18 at time of court proceeding;
   b. Offense charged is:
      1. Capital felony; or
      2. Murder; and
   c. Juvenile court waives jurisdiction;

F. 14–16 years of age at time of offense
   a. Offender is over 18 at time of court proceeding;
   b. Offense charged is:
      1. Aggravated controlled substance felony; or
      2. Felony of first degree other than murder; and
   c. Juvenile court waives jurisdiction;

G. 15–16 years of age at time of offense
   a. Offender is over 18 at time of court proceeding;
   b. Offense charged is:
      1. Felony of second degree;
      2. Felony of third degree; or
      3. State jail felony; and
   c. Juvenile court waives jurisdiction;

Offender Processed in Juvenile Justice System

10–16 years of age

All other misdemeanors and felonies

jurisdiction from the juvenile court. The process normally involves the juvenile court conducting a hearing upon request of the prosecutor.[14] The juvenile judge reviews such factors as the seriousness of the offense, the age of the minor, whether the act was aggressive, the minor's court history, the interests of the public, and the adequacy of the juvenile justice system to deal with the minor. After consideration of the statutory factors, the judge decides whether or not to waive jurisdiction and transfer the youth's case to the adult justice system. Upon conviction in the adult system, the youthful offender can receive any sentence an adult could receive except death. The death penalty cannot be imposed on an individual who was under 18 at the time of the commission of the capital crime.[15]

While the discretionary transfer system is in place for youthful offenders who commit serious offenses, Texas, like every other state, has established a lower age of responsibility for minor misdemeanors. If Jimmy, age 16, violates the traffic laws or engages in petty criminal behavior, such as disorderly conduct, vandalism, shoplifting, or violation of city ordinances, he will be processed through the adult criminal justice system rather than referring him to the juvenile court. The underlying logic is that the adult system is equipped to handle these youthful indiscretions; Jimmy and other youth who commit minor offenses will likely outgrow their misdirected behavior without any need for formal intervention from the juvenile court. Additionally, the petty nature of the offenses does not warrant use of the specialized juvenile justice system. Jimmy's sanction will often be a monetary fine or some form of community service such as picking up litter.

As a general rule, the defense of infancy is available only if the offender was below the majority age at the time of the commission of the act. The offender's age at time of trial is not a concern. However, an underlying assumption of the processing of juveniles is that their offenses will be detected in a timely manner. Thus, in the bulk of cases the young offender will still be legally a child when his or her case comes before the juvenile court. But consider the case of Ralph, a 14-year-old who commits a murder. The murder remains unsolved for years. Twenty years later, Ralph is identified as the killer. Ralph is now 34. Should the juvenile court exercise jurisdiction over Ralph? Should he be certified as an adult for trial? Would he have been so certified if he had been caught shortly after the killing? What should be done with Ralph, a juvenile when the crime was committed but a mature law-abiding adult when apprehended?

ENTRAPMENT

One of the prime objectives of the criminal law is to deter the commission of crime. Once a crime has been committed, however, modern society expects law enforcement officials to use all reasonable means, including setting traps, to identify and apprehend those who chose to violate the criminal law. On occasion, these two goals can come into conflict. Consider Chris, a veteran cocaine dealer. John approaches Chris and seeks to buy cocaine. John gives Chris $50 and Chris hands John a small envelope containing cocaine. John then identifies himself as a police officer and arrests Chris. Or consider

§ 8.06. Entrapment

a. It is a defense to prosecution that the actor engaged in the conduct charged because he was induced to do so by a law enforcement agent using persuasion or other means likely to cause persons to commit the offense. Conduct merely affording a person an opportunity to commit an offense does not constitute entrapment.

b. In this section "law enforcement agent" includes personnel of the state and local law enforcement agencies as well as of the United States and any person acting in accordance with instructions from such agents.

Jennifer, a police officer assigned to the vice squad. Jennifer, in provocative clothing, is assigned to stand on a street corner late in the evening. When Tom, a college student, approaches her and offers her money for sex, she directs him to meet her at a nearby hotel room. When Tom arrives at the hotel room, other members of the vice squad arrest him. Do Chris or Tom possess any defense to their criminal charges? Specifically, were they entrapped?

Entrapment may be defined as the government's unlawful inducement of a citizen to commit a crime. Arguably, the government has no interest in creating crime or in prosecuting otherwise innocent citizens. However, law enforcement officers often need to operate in undercover capacities in order to detect and apprehend criminal offenders. Use of such covert tactics is lawful. But the law will excuse from conviction those who are *unlawfully* induced into committing a crime.[16]

Drawing the line between lawful and unlawful inducement begins with the principle that government agents must be responsible for the inducement. No entrapment defense is available for the individual who is persuaded to commit a crime by a friend, family member, or even private security personnel.[17] However, the unlawful inducement need not be made by a police officer. Texas, as with all other states, permits the entrapment defense to be raised when the inducement comes from private citizens who are working with the police, such as confidential informants [Sec. 8.06(b)]. Thus, if an informant lures another into committing a crime, the defense of entrapment may be available. States differ on the question of whether the defense of entrapment can arise when the inducement is made by a government official who is not a police officer. For example, a Texas court rejected a claim by a motorist who argued that he was entrapped into committing a traffic violation through the placement of confusing traffic control signs.[18] The court ruled that the entrapment statute limited the defense to the action of law enforcement personnel. Highway department workers did not fall within the scope of the law.

Because the entrapment defense does not derive from the Constitution, legislative bodies and courts have had a relatively free hand in determining the circumstances under which a criminal defendant will be considered to have been entrapped. While all jurisdictions permit a defendant to raise entrapment as a defense, they disagree on the elements to establish a successful defense. Generally, one of two approaches is used. The majority of jurisdictions take the view that their legislatures in creating substantive criminal statutes did not intend them to apply to someone who is led into crime by a government agent. A minority of states shape their entrapment defense on the principle that as a matter of public policy, police officials should not manufacture crime because the danger exists that innocent persons will be caught in the snare. Spinning off the first reason, the majority of states and the federal government use the "subjective test," also known as the "origin of intent test" of entrapment.[19] The minority view is known as the "objective test," also called the "police conduct test."[20]

The majority origin of intent test focuses on the question of where the *mens rea* to commit the crime originated. If the defendant had the predisposition to commit the offense, regardless of the later behavior of the police, no entrapment has occurred. If the idea to commit the crime originated with the police or a police informant and the defendant was thereby induced into committing it, then the defendant was entrapped and is entitled to be found not guilty. Reconsider the case of Chris. Where did the intention to sell cocaine start? With Chris or John? How about Tom? Did the idea of paying for sex originate with him or the undercover officer?

In both instances, the offenders were predisposed to commit the crime. Chris was a veteran drug dealer.[21] He apparently was willing to sell cocaine to anyone with money. He treated the covert police officer like any other customer. Other than inquiring about the availability of the cocaine, the officer took no action to prompt Chris to commit a crime that he was not otherwise ready and willing to commit given the opportunity. Similarly, Tom took the affirmative step of soliciting Jennifer and offering her money. Jennifer was standing on the street corner, and while dressed in a manner that many might consider socially inappropriate or sexually tempting, Tom voluntarily initiated the contact and engaged in the elements of the offense.

The plight of Chris and Tom illustrates the extreme difficulty a defendant has in successfully mounting an entrapment defense. Merely affording an opportunity to commit a crime does not constitute entrapment. In both scenarios, the undercover police officers simply afforded an opportunity for Chris and Tom to commit their crimes. Chris could have refused to sell drugs to the undercover officer and Tom could have simply driven past Jennifer without stopping and seeking sex for money, as did a large number of other males.

The "police conduct test" might arguably hold more hope for Chris and Tom. This rule seeks to deter the police from using methods likely to lure otherwise innocent persons into committing crime. Whether the particular defendant who is on trial was induced or even predisposed to commit the offense is rarely the central issue. The manner in which the police behaved becomes the core question for court consideration.

In a uniquely Texas fashion, the Court of Criminal Appeals has interpreted Sec. 8.06 to encompass a combined "subjective/objective" test of entrapment, merging elements of both tests.[22,23] To prevail on the defense of entrapment, the accused must show that he or she was actually induced by the police to commit the offense and that the police used methods likely to induce the average citizen. As to the subjective element, if the defendant were predisposed to engage in the illicit conduct, he was not induced by the police behavior and was not thereby entrapped. In the scenario above, Chris was not induced to commit the crime. On the other hand, if the actor were indeed lured into committing an offense he would not have otherwise committed, was the police conduct likely to so induce the ordinary law-abiding person of average resistance? With respect to this objective element, prohibited police conduct can include pleas based on extreme need, sympathy, pity, or close personal friendship, offers of inordinate sums of money, and other methods of persuasion that are likely to cause the otherwise unwilling person, rather than the ready, willing, and anxious person, to commit an offense.[24]

However, Texas courts are reluctant to second-guess police investigative methods unless the tactics are outrageous. Thus, while reasonable persons might differ regarding the appropriateness of attractive, scantily dressed female police officers posing as prostitutes, the tactic is not so outrageous that a danger exists that innocent persons will be entrapped into soliciting sex for money. Similarly, assigning covert officers to ask citizens to sell drugs to them is not likely to motivate an innocent person to suddenly become a drug dealer. Indeed, it is difficult to contrive factual situations that would lure truly innocent persons into committing crime.[25] Couple this reality with the legal principle that merely affording an opportunity to commit a crime is not entrapment, and it is not surprising that few defendants are successful in asserting an entrapment defense under any legal standard.

Although entrapment is a general defense, it is raised primarily in cases where there is a direct contact between the defendant and a covert police officer or informer. Delivery of a controlled substance, solicitation of prostitution, and bribery of a public official are the most common instances where the entrapment defense is raised. These events often involve use of undercover police officers who make their cases through direct contact with the offender. The evidence of the offense is often the officer's word against that of the defendant. Officers frequently use recorders or other means of corroboration in an attempt to negate entrapment allegations. It is rare to see entrapment raised as a defense to robbery, burglary, theft, or other similar offense.

In raising the defense of entrapment, a defendant has two options. He or she can admit committing the act but assert that they should be found not guilty because of the entrapment. Failure to establish entrapment will result in a guilty verdict. As to the second option, a defendant who pleads not guilty and does not take the witness stand nor offer any testimony inconsistent with commission of the offense also can raise the defense of entrapment. In this circumstance, he or she is not required to admit actual commission of the crime to raise the defense.[26] Because the question of entrapment is highly fact-dependent, Texas treats the defense as a determination for the jury to make, although in extreme circumstances where the facts of the case are not in dispute, a trial judge can rule that a defendant was entrapped as a matter of law.[27]

MISTAKE OF LAW

Doug is driving down the highway. He observes a police cruiser with flashing lights pull in behind him. Doug checks the car's speedometer. He is going 60 miles per hour. After Doug stops the vehicle, the police officer approaches and tells Doug that the speed limit in the area is 45 miles per hour. Doug responds, "I did not realize that. I thought it was 65." Has Doug committed the offense of speeding?

Doug's mistaken knowledge of the speed limit will not provide him a defense. One of the best known legal maxims is *ignorantia juris quod quisque tenetur scire, neminem excusat* (ignorance of the law, which every one is bound to know, excuses no one).[28] As a matter of public policy, all persons are presumed to know the law and actual lack of knowledge is not a legal excuse. Accordingly, failure to realize that one's conduct is illegal will not serve as a defense. Texas has codified this principle in Sec. 8.03.

But do citizens know the law in actuality? Of course not. The existence of a written penal code and the frequent posting of highway speed limit signs are evidence that no one actually is aware of all of the law under all circumstances. The legal fiction presuming that all persons know the law is necessary for an effective justice system. If no such presumption existed, a criminal defendant would need only to assert that he did not realize that his conduct was illegal. It would be exceedingly difficult for the prosecution to establish what the defendant did or did not know at the time of the commission of the crime.

Since serious offenses such as murder, robbery, and theft are *malum in se* in our society, it is not necessary to remind the citizenry of the existence of these crimes. Most

§ 8.03. Mistake of Law

a. It is no defense to prosecution that the actor was ignorant of the provisions of any law after the law has taken effect.

b. It is an affirmative defense to prosecution that the actor reasonably believed the conduct charged did not constitute a crime and that he acted in reasonable reliance upon:
   1. an official statement of the law contained in a written order or grant of permission by an administrative agency charged by law with responsibility for interpreting the law in question; or
   2. a written interpretation of the law contained in an opinion of a court of record or made by a public official charged by law with responsibility for interpreting the law in question.

major *malum prohibitum* offenses are well known within society as well. Through one's upbringing, social interaction, and educational experiences everyone knows that driving while intoxicated is unlawful as is disorderly conduct, to name only two examples. No one is likely to stumble into committing a serious criminal offense because of ignorance of its illegality.

But reconsider Doug's circumstance. As a licensed driver, Doug actually studied the traffic laws in order to pass the licensing exam. Additionally, he knows he has a legal responsibility to operate his vehicle within the posted speed limit. He is also aware that he has the obligation to pay attention for changes in the speed limit and adjust his vehicle's speed accordingly. But, while the government presumes that Doug knows the maximum allowable speed limit within the state, it does not presume Doug is aware of a variation from that speed limit at a particular location. In fact, the government alerts Doug to the change in the speed limit by posting signs. When the limit goes up or down, new signs alert the motorist to the change. Thus, the motorist is not likely to be unfairly cited for speeding due to lack of actual knowledge of the speed limit.

Similar steps are taken in any case where the presumption of knowing the law may conflict with the reality of the situation. Consider "30 minute parking" signage. Or, "no smoking" placards. Or, "do not enter" notices. Each of these signs puts the citizen on actual notice that what would normally be perfectly lawful conduct is restricted or prohibited at this specific location or time, and is thus subject to criminal sanction.[29]

Can a mistake about the law ever be a defense? Suppose Colin is a shrewd businessman. In conjunction with his accountants and attorneys, Colin creates a complicated method of trading stock options whereby he believes he can avoid paying sales tax on his monetary gains. Several experienced tax attorneys tell him the technique is lawful and not contrary to state tax laws. Subsequently, prosecutors file tax fraud charges against Colin. Colin's defense is that his attorneys told him the scheme was lawful. Will the defense be successful? Probably not. Tradition and case law hold that bad private legal advice does not negate one's responsibility to comply with the criminal law.[30] To hold otherwise would encourage collusion between criminals and attorneys whereby for a fee an attorney could effectively immunize an offender from criminal responsibility. Indeed, such a rule might actually encourage, instead of discourage, bad legal advice.[31]

But suppose Colin received the same advice in an official advisory letter from the Comptroller of Public Accounts, the official responsible for the collection of sales tax? Should he be subject to prosecution for violating the tax laws if the agency responsible for interpreting the laws told him his conduct was permissible?

Texas statute [Sec. 8.03(b)] creates the defense of mistake of law when the defendant made a good faith reliance on a court opinion or an official opinion issued by the public officer charged with interpreting the law. Use of the mistake of law defense appears to be quite rare.[32]

MISTAKE OF FACT

Another type of mistake upon which a criminal defendant might rely to dodge culpability is **mistake of fact**. In rare occasions, a good faith mistake of a factual nature may absolve the offender of responsibility. Suppose one rainy day as Brandi is leaving the student union she takes an umbrella from the umbrella rack. Upon reaching her dorm room, Brandi realizes that the umbrella is not hers but is similar in color and style to the one she owns. Does her act of taking the wrong umbrella constitute theft? No.

§ 8.02. Mistake of Fact

(a) It is a defense to prosecution that the actor through mistake formed a reasonable belief about a matter of fact if his mistaken belief negated the kind of culpability required for commission of the offense.

Brandi has not committed theft because her mistake negated an element of the offense. Recall that theft requires an intent to deprive another of property. Brandi lacks the requisite *mens rea* to complete the elements of the crime.

The mistaken umbrella scenario affirms the oft-stated principle that a mistake of fact is a defense if it negates an element of the offense. Texas has codified this principle in Sec. 8.02. However, anytime one element of an offense fails to be established, no crime has occurred. One way to view Brandi's conduct is to realize that she commits no offense because all of the elements of theft are not present. So the matter is not really so much of a question of a defense, as simply the failure to establish all of the elements of the offense.

What if the factual mistake made by the offender does not affect an element of the offense? Suppose Jay shoots and kills May in the dark, mistaking May for her twin sister Kay. Jay is still culpable for murder because he intentionally killed another human being. No state limits the law of murder only to purposeful deaths of intended victims. Recall the doctrine of transferred intent whereby an offender is responsible for the death of an unintended victim. Likewise, if Romeo has consensual sexual intercourse with Juliet, a minor, he is guilty of sexual assault of a child even though he reasonably believed Juliet was of age. All state statutes criminalize having sex with a child, in contrast to criminalizing having sex with a child and knowing that the victim is a child. Romeo's belief as to Juliet's age, even if reasonable, is not a defense in Texas because the belief does not negate an element of the offense.

Despite the general rule, as a practical matter, mistake of fact might result in no criminal charges being filed. Suppose Tom, a traveling salesman, has gone on a multi-day sales trip. His wife, Katie, expects him home on Friday. Because of bad weather, Tom cuts his trip short. He returns home late Thursday night. Not wanting to awaken his wife, Tom quietly slips into the house. Katie, hearing Tom walking toward the bedroom, awakes. She sees Tom's shadowy figure in the hallway. Mistaking Tom for a burglar, Katie draws a pistol from under the mattress and fires at Tom. The bullet strikes him but fortunately he is not seriously injured. Has Katie committed attempted murder? As a practical matter, most prosecutors would be reluctant to take charges under this scenario. While Katie purposely shot at the figure, her mistake of fact about the individual's identity was a reasonable one which the average person could understand, given the surrounding circumstances. Tom certainly is unlikely to press charges. Arguably, none of the traditional purposes of the criminal law would be served by prosecuting Katie.[33]

DURESS

The American criminal law system is based on an assumption of free will—individuals make conscious, voluntary choices to engage in criminal conduct. But what if the individual is coerced into participating in a criminal act? Should he or she still be held criminally responsible? The answer clearly is no. Such an act is not the result of free will.

§ 8.05. Duress

a. It is an affirmative defense to prosecution that the actor engaged in the proscribed conduct because he was compelled to do so by threat of imminent death or serious bodily injury to himself or another.

b. In a prosecution for an offense that does not constitute a felony, it is an affirmative defense to prosecution that the actor engaged in the proscribed conduct because he was compelled to do so by force or threat of force.

c. Compulsion within the meaning of this section exists only if the force or threat of force would render a person of reasonable firmness incapable of resisting the pressure.

d. The defense provided by this section is unavailable if the actor intentionally, knowingly, or recklessly placed himself in a situation in which it was probable that he would be subjected to compulsion.

e. It is no defense that a person acted at the command or persuasion of his spouse, unless he acted under compulsion that would establish a defense under this section.

Consider the bank robber who points his pistol at the teller and tells her to fill the bag with money. The money does not belong to the teller and the robber could not be successful unless the teller follows his instructions. Yet, few would suggest that the teller should be prosecuted for assisting in the robbery. The teller complies with the robber's order only because she is in fear of her life. She is under duress.

In Texas and most other states, for the defense of **duress** to arise, there must be a threat by one person that places a person of reasonable firmness in fear that he or she will suffer imminent serious bodily injury or death. The bank teller's situation fits this rule. In examining the elements of the defense, it should be noted that the "reasonable person" standard is used in determining the availability of the defense. If the defendant was a particularly timid person who was coerced into committing a crime, his timidity is irrelevant. Rather, the question is how a person of reasonable firmness would have responded to the same circumstance.

Likewise, duress is limited to the threat of serious physical harm to the defendant or another. Suppose Martha works in an art gallery. John kidnaps Martha's baby Sunshine. John threatens to kill Sunshine unless Martha steals an expensive work of art from the gallery and brings it to John. The duress defense would be available for Martha even though the threat was made against Sunshine's life. But assume instead that John is Martha's live-in boyfriend. He threatens to harm Sunshine unless Martha periodically steals artwork from her employer and provides it to John to sell in order to support his cocaine habit. Here, the defense of duress would not likely be available for Martha because the threat is arguably not imminent or immediate but rather one of a future nature.[34] Martha has the opportunity to notify the police or take other reasonable, noncriminal means to protect her child.

Karl is Sheila's former boyfriend. The relationship ended after Sheila learned that Karl supported himself by committing burglaries. During their relationship Karl made a video of the two engaged in sexual intercourse. Six months after the breakup, Karl contacts Sheila and says that unless she obtains the combination to the safe at the office where she works, he will post the video on the Internet. Embarrassed by the existence of the tape and fearful that its release will cause her to lose her job, Sheila obtains the safe combination and later provides it to Karl. Will the defense of duress be available to Sheila if she is prosecuted for aiding Karl in the burglary? Probably not. By statute in this state the law of duress is limited to imminent risks of serious bodily injury or death. Fear of embarrassment or job loss would appear to be insufficient to excuse one's commission of a felony.

Is the defense of duress available to a spouse who is forced into committing a crime through the coercion of their husband or wife? Texas law [Sec. 8.05(e)] allows anyone who is charged with a criminal act to attempt to establish the duress defense, regardless of whether the third party who made the threat was a stranger or their spouse. Early American courts did recognize the Common Law defense of coverture. Under the concept of coverture, married women were viewed as having no legal existence independent of their husbands. Accordingly, a married woman who was coerced by her husband to commit any crime, other than murder or treason, was excused from criminal sanction because she was expected to follow her husband's commands.[35] The coverture defense is now abolished by the Texas statute and is believed to no longer be available in any American jurisdiction.

Criminal defendants rarely raise the defense of duress. The circumstances are usually quite clear on whether a potential defendant was in fact under duress at the time of the event. Prosecutors tend not to file charges against individuals who assisted the commission of a crime while under threat of physical harm. Only when the actual role of the defendant is unknown or ambiguous will the case go to trial and the defendant be required to establish that he or she acted under duress.

INSANITY

The 1981 video of John Hinckley's attempted assassination of President Ronald Reagan has been seen by millions. Viewers observe Hinckley purposefully discharge multiple gunshots, striking the President, a top presidential aide, a Secret Service agent, and a District of Columbia police officer. Yet despite the clearly calculated nature of the act, Hinckley is subsequently found not guilty by reason of **insanity**.[36] Earlier, in 1970, Charles Manson was convicted of seven counts of murder in California after directing his "family" to perpetuate several killings in an effort to ignite an apocalyptic race war. For many, the wild-eyed Manson exemplifies the height of lunacy.[37] Yet, he did not even raise the defense of insanity. In more recent times, Andrea Yates drowned her five children in the family's Houston bathtub in 2001. In 2003, Deanna Laney beat her two young sons to death with rocks and injured a third in East Texas. Lisa Ann Diaz drowned her two daughters in a Plano bathtub, and Dena Schlosser severed her ten-month-old daughter's arms with a kitchen knife in 2004. Each was ultimately found not guilty by reason of insanity. These and other similarly shocking incidents illustrate the difficulty the public has in understanding how some persons who engage in deliberate acts can be ruled not to be criminally responsible for their conduct while others are held blameworthy. This seeming inconsistency has bedeviled the criminal law for several hundred years as society has sought to strike a balance between holding citizens responsible for their conduct while recognizing that the primary purposes of

§ 8.01. Insanity

a. It is an affirmative defense to prosecution that, at the time of the conduct charged, the actor, as a result of severe mental disease or defect, did not know that his conduct was wrong.

b. The term "mental disease or defect" does not include an abnormality manifested only by repeated criminal or otherwise antisocial conduct.

the criminal law, particularly deterrence, will not be served by punishing individuals who cannot make rational decisions or otherwise control their conduct. "No problem in the drafting of a penal code presents greater intrinsic difficulty than that of determining when individuals whose conduct would otherwise be criminal ought to be exculpated on the grounds that they were suffering from mental disease or defect when they acted as they did."[38] Under the Anglo-American legal tradition, punishment may be meted out only to those who engage in freewill behavior. An insane person is incapable of making rational freewill decisions and thus is not subject to punishment under our system.

Despite the public interest generated by a plea of not guilty by reason of insanity, the defense is raised in a very small percentage of cases. First, individuals who are so obviously mentally ill that they are incapable of rational thought are also frequently incompetent to stand trial. Thus, they never reach the criminal court system and are never required to establish their insanity. Second, while insanity is a general defense that theoretically can be raised in any criminal case, as a practical matter the defense is used largely in murder cases, although a defendant will occasionally raise the sanity question in selected arson, sexual assault, and, in some instances, theft cases.[39] The costs and complexity of the defense tend to relegate it to cases where the potential sanction is high. Consider as an example Bert, a homeless individual who suffers from mental illness. Bert is arrested for shoplifting, a misdemeanor. While the insanity defense might be available to him, it is unlikely to be used for a wide variety of practical reasons. Experts estimate that the insanity defense is raised in less than one percent of all criminal cases.[40] The number seems higher because the cases where the defense is pled tend to be high profile ones.[41] The American Psychiatric Association once went so far as to say, "While philosophically important for the criminal law, the insanity defense is empirically unimportant."[42]

While all but four states recognize the defense of insanity, the states do not agree on the definition of the term.[43] Similarly, the procedural manner in which the plea is raised varies across jurisdictions. Currently, the test of insanity in Texas and most other states is derived from the so-called M'Naghten Rule.[44] The rule originated in 1843 by way of the English House of Lord's decision in M'Naghten's Case.[45] Thus, in a somewhat odd way modern courts use a criterion for criminal culpability that was created before the advent of modern theories of psychology and psychiatry. This fact leads to the important point that insanity is a legal concept, not a psychological or psychiatric diagnosis. While the opinions of mental health professionals are used to assist the jury in its determination, ultimately a person is insane when he or she meets the legal standard. This explains why socially deviant individuals such as Charles Manson, who may be viewed by the general public as "crazy," are not considered legally insane. Manson and others of his ilk simply fail to meet the high required legal standard necessary for the defense.

To be found not guilty by reason of insanity under the Texas version of the M'Naghten Rule, a criminal defendant must establish that:

1. At the time of the conduct charged
2. As a result of a severe mental disease or defect
3. He did not know his conduct was wrong.

Note that the test of insanity focuses on the mental state of the defendant at the time of the criminal act, not his or her current state.[46] Obvious difficulties arise in making an after-the-fact determination of a person's mental condition weeks or months following the commission of the crime. On the other hand, mental disease does not turn on and off like a light bulb. So an assessment of the accused days after the crime usually proves sufficient. Because mental disease is not a fleeting matter, individuals who seek to raise a defense of temporary insanity, saying in effect "I was insane then but I am okay now," are faced with a difficult challenge. (Texas does recognize a form of temporary insanity based on intoxication. This is discussed subsequently.)

For a successful insanity defense, the accused must establish that he or she suffers from a recognized mental disease or defect. Interestingly, the law does not attempt to specifically define the term "severe mental disease or defect." Rather, medical and psychological experts are used to make that determination. The mental disease could be a condition such as paranoid schizophrenia or other recognized mental illness.[47] In rarer instances the defendant may suffer from organic conditions such as brain trauma or tumors. Because psychological assessments are not an exact science, experts testifying for the prosecution and the defense may come to different conclusions regarding the defendant's mental health. Thus, the very existence of the accused's mental disease becomes a fact question for the jury to resolve.

Suppose Ted is a serial murderer. At his trial he raises the insanity defense. Ted says, "I must be insane or else I would not have murdered all of those people." Is Ted's logic a good explanation of insanity? No. Note that Sec. 8.01(b) specifically prohibits the use of the insanity defense in cases where the only evidence of mental disease is repeated antisocial behavior. Ted's horrendous conduct by itself is insufficient to establish that he has the required "severe mental disease" needed to establish an insanity defense.

Although John Hinckley, the would-be assassin of President Reagan, was found not guilty by reason of insanity largely due to a procedural quirk, many jurisdictions, including Texas, tightened their definitions of insanity. As a result of the Hinckley case, Texas, the federal system, and a few other states now limit the application of the insanity defense to "serious" or "severe" mental illnesses.[48] This change is intended to restrict the use of post-traumatic stress disorder and other less debilitating mental illnesses from serving as a basis for an insanity claim.

The third element of the test requires the accused to demonstrate by the preponderance of the evidence that he or she did not know the wrongfulness of their criminal conduct. This places a heavy burden on the defendant because court rulings establish that the term "know" means absolute lack of cognitive awareness. Thus, if the accused believed he was splitting a coconut when actually he was striking the deceased in the head with an ax, the standard is met. Clearly a significant degree of mental illness is necessary to possess this level of disassociation from reality.

What if the accused knew what he was doing but believed God told him to do it? This insane delusion presents another approach to the lack of knowledge of the wrongfulness of one's conduct. For example, Andre Yates apparently believed that the slaying of her children was morally appropriate because God told her to do it. On the other hand, the state argued she knew the wrongfulness of her conduct because she telephoned the police shortly after committing the killings.

While some states have modified M'Naghten to include behavior based on an "irresistible impulse," current Texas law rejects the concept. Thus, if Greta is a kleptomaniac (a compulsive thief) she would have no defense in Texas to a charge of theft based on the psychological abnormality that causes her to be unable to control her behavior.[49]

A cousin to the insanity defense is the defense of **diminished mental capacity**, sometimes called diminished responsibility. The defendant, realizing that he or she cannot meet the insanity standard, nonetheless claims lack of legal accountable because his or her normal mental capacity was diminished or impaired at the time of the criminal act.

The accused may claim that he was under severe emotional distress at the time of the crime, or is mentally retarded, or suffers some other abnormal mental condition insufficient to meet the test of insanity. He argues, however, that his level of culpability should be lessened because of the mental condition beyond his control. Texas follows the majority of jurisdictions and holds to the position that insanity is the only defense available by which an accused can place his or her mental state in question.[50] Thus, evidence of a mental disability short of insanity is not admissible.

Under state statute, a defendant seeking to raise insanity as a defense must provide the state notice of this intention at least 20 days prior to the trial date.[51] The defendant will then be examined by qualified psychiatrists or psychologists who will later testify to their findings.[52] If the jury, or judge in case of a bench trial, finds the defendant not guilty by reason of insanity, the defendant is considered to have been acquitted of the charge.[53] Acquitted defendants who are potentially dangerous to themselves or others may be subject to civil commitment proceedings that could confine them in a mental hospital.

INTOXICATION AS A DEFENSE

Suppose Brad is depressed because he has broken up with his girlfriend Jennifer. Brad becomes intoxicated from drinking large quantities of whiskey. In his drunken state, he smashes the furniture in the hotel room where he resides. The hotel manager summons the police who arrest Brad and charge him with criminal mischief. At trial, Brad points out that he has no prior criminal record and would not have destroyed the property had he been sober. He asks the court to excuse his behavior because he was intoxicated. Will such a defense be successful? Probably not.

Anglo-American law has long viewed voluntary intoxication as no excuse for criminal behavior. Indeed one early view of intoxication saw it as an aggravating, not an excusing, factor in a criminal act.[54] An early American jurist noted, "This is the first time, that I ever remember it to have been contended, that the commission of one crime was an excuse for another."[55] The underlying logic appears to be that since the defendant voluntarily consumed the intoxicating substance, he or she will be held responsible for the results of that decision. The U.S. Supreme Court has ruled that no constitutional violation occurs if a state refuses to allow the intoxication defense in any form.[56]

Texas law (Sec. 8.04) follows the general rule that voluntary intoxication is no defense to a criminal charge. Intoxication is considered to be voluntary if the defendant exercised independent judgment in consuming the intoxicant.[57] Since intoxication is no defense, Texas courts refuse to permit a defendant to argue that his or her intoxicated condition negated the required culpable mental state for the crime. So the fact that an individual was intoxicated does not prevent him from forming the specific intent to commit burglary or from being aware of a risk when recklessly causing bodily injury.[58]

In addition, recall that Sec. 49.10 clearly states that lawful use of intoxicating substances is no defense to the charge of intoxication manslaughter, intoxication assault, driving while intoxicated, and similar offenses. Only the public intoxication statute (Sec. 49.02) provides a defense to the charge if the intoxicating substance was administered for therapeutic purposes by a medical professional.

Texas does provide a small caveat for intoxicated offenders. A convicted defendant can introduce evidence of temporary insanity caused by voluntary intoxication for purposes of mitigation of punishment.[59] To benefit from this rule, the defendant must establish that his drunken condition reached the point that he did not know that his conduct was wrong. Even if a defendant is successful in establishing temporary insanity due to intoxication, the jury need not adjust its punishment decision based on this fact; the defendant simply enjoys the right to argue the fact before the jury in the penalty phase of the trial.

Insanity caused by involuntary intoxication is a recognized defense.[60] Once again, the level of intoxication must be such that the accused did not know his conduct was wrong. Because the defense requires that one "know" the wrongfulness of his or her conduct, Texas courts have refused to allow the defense to be used by persons who are unconscious due to intoxication.[61]

NONSTATUTORY DEFENSES

Identity

One essential part of the prosecutorial role is to establish that the defendant is in fact the individual who committed the crime. This burden goes largely to the facts of the case, not the legal elements of the offense. A criminal defendant often seeks to refute this factual assertion. Thus, a common defense raised in crimes against persons, such as criminal homicides, sexual assaults, and robberies, is that of identity. A stranger accosts the victim and perpetrates some criminal offense. The victim has the opportunity to view the offender. In some instances, such as a robbery, eyewitnesses to the event may also exist. At trial, the defendant simply denies that he or she is the individual who committed the crime. The defendant may choose not to contest the actual occurrence of the criminal act. Rather, by pleading not guilty he or she is saying, "*I* did not do it." The defendant is contesting the factual accuracy of being the one accused of the offense.

Identity will be raised as an issue mostly in cases where the defendant was not arrested at the crime scene. If Willie is arrested following a police chase after robbing a bank, denying at trial that he is the robber would normally prove futile. But what if Willie is arrested weeks after the robbery following an extensive police investigation? Maybe Willie's fingerprint was found on the counter in front of the victim teller. Maybe the victim teller identified a photograph of Willie. Could there be a legitimate reason for Willie's fingerprint to be on the counter? Could the teller be mistaken in picking out Willie's photo?

Contesting identity is mustered in several ways. First, the defense attorney may attempt to discredit or otherwise cast doubt on the accuracy of any eyewitness identification of the defendant. Rigid cross-examination will focus on matters such as the time period the witness had to view the offender, the lighting conditions, the distance between the witness and the offender, the quality of the witness' eyesight, and issues in cross-racial identification, as applicable to the particular case. Allegations of faulty police procedures may also arise if the witness viewed photos of the defendant prior to trial or if a pre-trial lineup were conducted.

If appropriate under the facts, the defense attorney may seek to discredit any circumstantial evidence establishing identity, such as fingerprints and DNA. The methods by which the physical evidence was collected may be critiqued. The integrity of the chain of custody of evidence will be scrutinized. The credentials of the laboratory examiner may be called into question as well. Each of these attacks seeks to weaken the quality of the prosecution's case in establishing the identity of the offender.

Another strategy is use of alibi.[62] By calling to testify so-called alibi witnesses, as well as the defendant's own testimony, efforts are made to convince the jury that the defendant was not at the location of the crime at the time the offense occurred. In

Willie's case he may admit to having cashed a check in the bank the day before, thereby hoping to explain the presence of his fingerprint and the recognition of his face by the teller. If eyewitness testimony alone is used in an effort to establish guilt, the defendant will suggest the witness is mistaken by seeking to prove that the defendant was physically at another location at the time of the crime. Since the prosecution must establish identity beyond a reasonable doubt, any question as to identity induces doubt in the minds of the jury and can result in an acquittal.

Religious Beliefs

John and Mary are parents of baby Charles. Charles contracts an infection. He manifests a fever and other signs of being ill. John and Mary, however, are faithful members of a religious sect that believes in prayer to cure all ills. Their faith prohibits them from using medical treatment for their child's illness. Baby Charles subsequently dies from his condition. John and Mary are charged with involuntary manslaughter. Can their sincere religious beliefs save them from a manslaughter conviction?

The First Amendment to the U.S. Constitution grants the right of free exercise of religion. Although the clause absolutely protects religious belief, religiously motivated conduct "remains subject to regulation for the protection of society."[63] The state's interest in intruding into religious practices is particularly heightened when minors are concerned. While over 40 states, including Texas, provide a statutory **spiritual treatment defense** to charges of injury to a child, all but a few states hold that the exemption is limited to minor illnesses and will not serve as a defense to criminal homicide charges.[64] Over the years dozens of individuals who held sincere religious beliefs have been convicted of manslaughter or criminally negligent homicide for failing to seek medical care for ill or injured minor children who subsequently died.[65]

Religious beliefs are a defense to charges of possession of peyote, a controlled substance. Texas and federal statutes exempt Native Americans from prosecution for using the peyote cactus during religious services.[66] Use of the hallucinogen has been traditional among certain Native American groups for hundreds of years. The exemption is limited to members of these federally recognized tribes.

Psycho-social Syndromes

In recent decades, defense attorneys have sought to raise a series of psycho-medical syndrome defenses, usually in murder cases. These defenses argue that due to an organic medical or psychological circumstance beyond the control of the accused, he or she should be excused from criminal responsibility. Critics counter that the proliferation of such defenses could undermine a fundamental purpose of the legal system: to ascribe blame for unlawful conduct.[67] Because of their unusual nature, raising of these excuses often receives substantial media attention. To date, most courts have refused to recognize many of these defenses. However, a few have been permitted and are worthy of mention.

Perhaps the best known psycho-medical defense is **post-traumatic stress disorder** (PTSD). PTSD is an anxiety disorder that develops after a severe traumatic event or experience. It first gained official recognition by the American Psychiatric Association in 1980 in the aftermath of the Vietnam War. Mental health professionals had noted a disproportionately high number of psychological problems experienced by individuals who had served in combat. An individual who has been exposed to an extreme traumatic event may exhibit persistent re-experiencing of the traumatic event as well as extreme psychological stress when faced with reminders of the incident.[68] One source suggests that as many as half of combat veterans and crime victims suffer some level of PTSD. The disorder is usually raised as the basis of the insanity defense, particularly on the issue of diminished capacity. Another study found that PTSD was no more successful than other insanity defenses.[69]

A somewhat more controversial anxiety disorder is the **battered spouse syndrome** (BSS).[70] BSS was first proposed following research by an activist in the women's rights field.[71] Critics argue that the syndrome has never been validated through empirical research and does not enjoy wide support from forensic psychologists. They suggest that victims who are chronically battered may more reliably be diagnosed as suffering from PTSD.

In a limited number of cases defendants have sought to escape criminal responsibility due to so-called social syndromes. The accused has offered as an excuse for his behavior the inability to control his conduct based on the influence of his social environment. Among the defenses that have been raised are urban psychosis, black rage, and media intoxication.[72]

The urban psychosis defense suggests a form of PTSD spawned by repetitive exposure to violence while growing up in an inner-city environment. A few courts have allowed expert testimony on this topic when the defendant seeks to establish an insanity defense.

Defendants raising the black rage defense assert that endemic societal racism or the use of a racial epithet produced an uncontrollable reaction due to mental disease leading to their criminal acts. While this defense was raised as early as 1846, the best known case involved an individual convicted of killing six and wounding 19 passengers on a New York commuter train in 1993. In this latter case, the black defendant, who selected his victims based on their race, was not permitted to assert the defense.[73] Evidence of black rage was permitted to support an insanity defense in a 1989 case wherein a black stockbroker murdered his white supervisor after being terminated from his job.[74]

At least a half-dozen offenders have claimed that violence in the media affected their mental functioning and caused them to engage in criminal behavior. These defendants asserted that their mental state was involuntarily altered by watching a particular movie, viewing violent pornography, listening to rock lyrics, or simply by being subliminally intoxicated by a constant stream of violent television shows. Court acceptance of media intoxication as a basis for an insanity defense has been mixed.

In the past the effort of Texas defendants to use these psycho-social syndromes as a basis of a defense has been restricted on relevancy grounds. However, Art. 38.36 of the Texas Code of Criminal Procedure establishes a rule that both the state and the defendant in a murder case shall be permitted "to offer testimony as to all relevant facts and circumstances surrounding the killing and the previous relationship existing between the accused and the deceased, together with all relevant facts and circumstances going to show the condition of the mind of the accused at the time of the offense." But the Court of Criminal Appeals has been reluctant to expand the traditional rules of evidence and permit trial courts to consider *all* surrounding circumstances in a murder case, once again on the basis of relevancy.[75] Art. 38.36 expressly provides that in cases where self-defense is raised by the defendant, evidence that the defendant had been a previous victim of family violence is admissible. Additionally, expert testimony regarding a family violence victim's state of mind may be introduced. This statute essentially permits courts to hear evidence regarding battered spouse syndrome, providing the testimony can be shown to be relevant to the case at hand.

INTRODUCTION TO JUSTIFICATION

On occasion, factual circumstances arise whereby conduct that would be considered to be a crime under normal circumstances is treated as noncriminal by the law because the actor was legally justified in engaging in the behavior. Suppose Ronald and Jack engage in an argument during a game of billiards. Jack draws a large knife from his boot and attempts to slash Ronald. As Jack swings the blade Ronald strikes him with a pool cue and Jack slumps to the floor with a bad gash in his scalp. Ronald's conduct, which might otherwise be viewed as an assault, becomes defensible because he was repelling Jack's unlawful use of deadly force. In more common terms, Ronald acted in self-defense.

Most, but not all, forms of justification recognized in the Texas Penal Code involve the threat of or actual use of force or deadly force. Depending on the circumstances, legally justified action might also involve damaging or destroying property or confining another against their will.

It should be noted initially that the statutory forms of justification found in Chapter 9 of the Texas Penal Code are treated procedurally as defenses.[76] Recall from the discussion earlier that this means the burden is upon the defendant to raise the defense at trial. A jury will consider the defense only if some evidence has been admitted at trial supporting the defense.[77] For example, in the opening scenario of Ronald and Jack, at Ronald's trial for aggravated assault, he would bear the responsibility of advising the court that he acted in self-defense.

Sec. 9.06 states that if conduct is justified under the Penal Code, such justification does not affect any remedy available in a civil suit. The language of this statute suggests that an individual may be justified in his conduct and thereby not criminally responsible, but such justification does not necessarily absolve him from civil liability. For example, police officers are rarely charged with assault or murder in the shooting of suspects but are often sued as a result of such encounters. Another recently enacted statute may have effectively neutered the effect of Sec. 9.06, however. In 2007, the Texas Legislature amended the Civil Practices and Remedies Code, which establishes the various grounds for civil suits, to provide that an individual is immune from liability for personal injuries or death through the use of force or deadly force if the individual's conduct is justified under Chapter 9.[78] This new law would seem to establish the same use of force standard for both criminal prosecutions and civil suits.

Finally, even though an individual might be justified under the law, he or she will still be responsible if his or her conduct recklessly causes harm to an innocent third party (Sec. 9.05). Assume Officer Jan is chasing a robber down a crowded city street. The robber turns and fires a shot at Officer Jan. Under state law Officer Jan would certainly be justified in returning fire.[79] However, suppose Officer Jan shoots at the robber and misses, striking and killing a patron in a nearby barbershop. While the shooting at the robber is justified, the circumstances under which Officer Jan fired arguably evidenced a reckless disregard for the safety of others. Would the average police officer have fired under the same circumstances? Was Officer Jan aware of the risk of harm to innocent bystanders if her shot misses its mark? Officer Jan could face manslaughter charges for the death of the barbershop patron.

PUBLIC DUTY

Suppose Jack is a suspect in a series of sexual assaults wherein the offender wears black clothing and threatens his victims with a Bowie knife. Detectives Bob and Ray seek a warrant to search Jack's house. The appropriate sworn statement of probable cause is filed and a magistrate issues the search warrant.[80] In executing the warrant the officers break open the front door to gain entry. Once inside they examine the contents of the house and seize certain articles of clothing belonging to Jack as well as a Bowie knife. The detectives take the items to the police station. Normally if someone breaks into a house and takes property from within, they would be considered a burglar, or at the very least a thief and criminal trespasser. But because the detectives conduct their seizure under the authority of a search warrant, their behavior is justified. The public duty statute (Sec. 9.21) exempts from criminal liability individuals who engage in conduct that they reasonably believe is required or authorized by law. Indeed, the language of a search warrant not only grants permission for a search to be conducted but actually commands the peace officer to carry out the court's order. Federal and state case law authorizes the breaking of doors to enter the premises to be searched.[81]

Because of the court order (the warrant) and other relevant state statutes, Bob and Ray will not be subject to criminal prosecution for their intrusion into Jack's home. This is true even if the warrant is later ruled to be invalid because probable cause is absent or the magistrate failed to sign it or for any of a variety of other technical violations of search and seizure law that may affect the courtroom admissibility of the evidence. Sec. 9.21 only requires that the actor, that is, Bob or Ray, "reasonably believes the conduct is required or authorized . . . in the execution of legal process." In this context the term **legal process** is synonymous with written orders from a court, such as arrest and search warrants.

Texas courts have found that an officer's general responsibility to prevent crime and enforce the criminal statutes fits within the meaning of this section. Thus, Sec. 9.21 prevented a peace officer from being in violation of the criminal trespass statute when he chased a fleeing offender into an abandoned apartment house bearing "no trespassing" signage.[82]

Sec. 9.21(c) justifies the use of deadly force only in the lawful conduct of war and when "specifically required by statute." It is this subsection that releases from any criminal liability the individual who serves as the executioner at the Texas Department of Criminal Justice. A judicially issued death warrant orders the execution of the prisoner. Employees of the prison system carry out that judicial order and are thereby exempt from criminal responsibility in the death of the condemned inmate.

NECESSITY

Donnie is injured on a construction site when he accidentally slices off his finger with a power saw. Fearing he may bleed to death, his co-workers place Donnie in the bed of a pickup truck and drive toward the hospital emergency room. Should the truck driver stay within the speed limit? Should he remain stopped at red traffic signals until the signal changes? What if the driver could reach the hospital faster if he drove the wrong way down a one-way street?

While the law exists to help maintain social order, in some instances the greater good of society may be served by violating the law. Such is the case with Donnie's finger injury. Which is more important: to save Donnie's life or to adhere to the requirement of staying within the speed limit? Clearly the former.

Sec. 9.22 recognizes that on occasion the more socially useful thing to do is to violate the law. This is known in Texas as the defense of necessity. The statute authorizes deviation from the law to avoid imminent harm when "the desirability and urgency of avoiding the harm clearly outweigh, according to ordinary standards of reasonableness, the harm sought to be prevented by the law proscribing the conduct." For the harm to be imminent there must exist an emergency situation requiring immediate action or a split second decision to avoid the harm.[83] Does Donnie's medical emergency raise the possibility of imminent harm? Does the desirability of saving Donnie's life clearly outweigh the harm that the traffic laws seek to prevent? The answer to both questions is certainly yes. While it is unlikely the driver of the pickup would be cited for his Transportation Code violations, he would have available to him the defense of necessity.

Texas courts have also applied the necessity defense in cases where a defendant claimed he forcibly resisted a deputy sheriff who was using excessive force against him during an arrest.[84] The defense was also available in a case where an escaped prison inmate was charged with unlawfully carrying a firearm. He claimed he needed the pistol to protect himself from former prison gang members who earlier had tried to kidnap him.[85] Similarly, the Court of Criminal Appeals has held that necessity was a possible defense to the crime of escape from prison for an inmate who held a real fear that he would be killed or sexually assaulted by other inmates.[86] On the other hand, a court refused to recognize necessity as a defense to a possession of marijuana charge wherein the defendant alleged he needed the marijuana to stay off the effects of PTSD.[87] The defense was also rejected for a prison escapee who burglarized an apartment in order to obtain food and clothing.[88] Texas courts have also rejected the necessity defense for charges of criminal trespass and obstructing a public passageway committed by anti-abortion protestors. The courts held that the action the demonstrators sought to prevent (legal abortions) did not meet the legal definition of "harm" and thereby did not qualify under Sec. 9.22.[89]

SELF-DEFENSE

"The right of self-defense is a God-given right which the laws of man cannot take away."[90] So noted a Texas judge in 1909. Despite that ruling being a century old, the view is still widely held today. The Common Law and every state's statutes recognize the power of the individual to defend himself or herself from another person's use of unlawful force. However, jurisdictional variations exist regarding the circumstances under which a citizen will be excused from criminal liability for using force or deadly force in self-defense.

Texas law, as codified in Secs 9.31–9.34, provides individuals fairly broad rights in using force and deadly force to protect themselves from aggressors. Before examining the specific statutory provisions, however, several background matters must be considered. The first is the definition of "force." Most of the provisions of Chapter 9, including the sections on self-defense, are stated in terms of the use of force and deadly force. While Chapter 9 contains the word "force" nearly 50 times, this important term is nowhere defined within the Penal Code! Likewise, state appellate courts have not formally defined the word "force" within the meaning of the justification statutes. In fairness to the appellate courts, they have had few opportunities to consider the definition of "force." As a general rule, only serious criminal convictions are appealed. Accordingly, many appellate decisions discuss the definition and scope of *deadly* force because its unlawful use will likely result in a felony conviction. Most uses of ordinary force concern misdemeanors or other petty activity and convictions are rarely appealed. As a result, the fact finder, be it jury or judge, must rely on the ordinary dictionary definition of the term "force." Thus, the concept of **force** can be viewed as "the use of physical power or violence to compel or restrain."[91]

However, **deadly force** is statutorily defined in Sec. 9.01:

> "Deadly force" means force that is intended or known by the actor to cause, or in the manner of its use or intended use is capable of causing, death or serious bodily injury.

The definition is similar, though not identical, to the definition of "deadly weapon" contained in Sec. 1.07(17). Note that deadly force need not actually cause serious bodily injury or death but must only be capable of doing so. Thus, thrusting a knife at another constitutes use of deadly force even when the knife does not actually cut the victim. Also, no degrees of deadly force exist. For example, if Jeff is justified in using deadly force to protect himself, it does not matter whether he uses a brick, a knife, a pistol, a machinegun, or a hand grenade! So long as his use of deadly force is legally justifiable, Jeff can use any device capable of causing death or serious bodily injury. Suppose Jeff opts for a pistol. Does it matter under the law whether he shoots his assailant once or eight times? While Texas courts have not directly considered this question, the rule would appear to be that one bullet and eight bullets are legal equivalents. The defense of justification does not recognize the concept of excessive deadly force.

One's forcible conduct is justified only if he or she is repelling another's use of *unlawful* force or deadly force. One has no right to resist by force the *lawful* use of force. Thus, use of force to avoid being arrested constitutes the offense of resisting arrest, the officer's efforts to arrest the individual being authorized by law.[92] Consistent with this principle, however, the statute does permit use of force to resist the officer's use of unlawful or excessive force.[93]

Finally, the use of force and deadly force is judged from the standpoint of the actor. Note that the various statutes consistently use the phrase "to the degree the actor reasonably believes." This means that so long as the individual's perspective of what occurred is not unreasonable, he must be given the benefit of the defense; what some other person might do under the same circumstances is not relevant. Consider this scenario. Cedric enters a liquor store. He places his hand in his coat pocket and uses his finger to simulate a pistol barrel. Cedric then demands the store clerk give him the money out of the cash register. The clerk responds by shooting Cedric with his own pistol. While Cedric did not actually have a pistol, the clerk believed that he did and responded consistent with that belief. He was thus justified under state law in using deadly force against Cedric. The fact that some other clerk might simply give Cedric the money, duck under the table, ignore Cedric's demands, or respond in some other manner has no bearing on the availability of the defense. The clerk's response was not unreasonable under the circumstances.

While the self-defense law, Sec. 9.31, is complex, its focus is on the immediate need to use force to protect against the other's use of unlawful force. If the need is not immediate, the defense is not available. For example, assume Jack and Walt get into a verbal argument in a bar. As tempers escalate Walt strikes Jack with his fist. Jack falls to the floor. While Jack is lying on the floor, Walt exits the bar. Jack arises and follows Walt out the door. As Walt reaches the parking lot, Jack strikes him from behind with a chair. While Jack may have been justified in using the chair to defend himself in the bar, his use of the chair in the parking lot is no longer "immediately necessary" to protect himself.

Because an individual may not always view a set of circumstances accurately, the law of self-defense is based on perceived danger, not actual danger. The reasonable apprehension of danger is a subjective matter determined from the viewpoint of the actor.[94]

The factual circumstances that may arise under which an individual is justified in using force in self-defense are wide indeed. The Legislature cannot anticipate every possible situation where it is reasonable for an individual to engage in an act of self-defense. However, lawmakers have confirmed the right of self-defense in certain specific situations. Sec. 9.31(a)(1) presumes that the actor's belief in the need to use force is reasonable if three criteria are meet:

1. The party against whom the force was used:
   a. unlawfully entered the actor's habitation, vehicle, place of business, or place of employment; or
   b. was attempting to unlawfully remove the actor from his or her habitation, vehicle, place of business, or place of employment; or
   c. was committing aggravated kidnapping, murder, sexual assault, aggravated sexual assault, robbery, or aggravated robbery; and
2. The actor did not provoke the other party; and
3. The actor was himself or herself not engaged in criminal activity, other than a minor traffic law violation.

If the actor's use of force fits within these three criteria, the actor's conduct is considered to be done in self-defense and is legally justified. Thus if Gail kicks Waldo in the groin to protect herself from being sexually assaulted, she has engaged in an act of self-defense. If Rosa threatens to use force to thwart a potential intruder into her residence, she has engaged in self-defense. If Jacob punches Billy in the nose because Billy is attempting to take Jacob's lunch money from him, Jacob has committed an act of self-defense.

Under limited circumstances individuals may defend themselves through the use of deadly force. Note that the actor must first be legally authorized to use force before the use of deadly force can be justified. Sec. 9.32 authorizing the use of deadly force reads similarly to the self-defense statute except it speaks to the question of the aggressor's unlawful use of *deadly force*. In other words, if the aggressor is unlawfully using force, the actor can respond with like force. But if the actor is using unlawful deadly force, the actor likewise is lawfully authorized to protect himself or herself by reacting with deadly force. However, the actor may not lawfully repel ordinary force with deadly force. In the previous example, Gail, instead of kicking Waldo, could lawfully shoot him because he is attempting to commit a violent felony, sexual assault. Likewise, suppose Gordon is attempting to carjack Oscar's automobile. He threatens to harm Oscar with a knife unless Oscar exits the running vehicle. Oscar responds with blast of pepper spray. Oscar has lawfully used force. But what if Oscar's response was to draw a pistol on Gordon? That too would be lawful. Gordon is committing a robbery and the statute authorizes the use of deadly force to protect oneself against another's immediate commission of a robbery. But if Mike punches Steve in the nose with his fist, Steve normally would not be justified in stabbing Mike with a knife in the name of defending himself. Can you think of a factual situation where Steve might be legally justified in using deadly force to respond to Mike's assault upon him?

Sec. 9.33 grants an individual the same justification for using force and deadly force to protect others. The only additional requirement is that the actor reasonably believes that his intervention is immediately necessary to protect the third party. So if Gail is being sexually assaulted as in the example above, she can lawfully use both force and deadly force to protect herself. Likewise, if Gail comes home to find her roommate Lisa being sexually assaulted, Gail can use force or deadly force to protect Lisa.

A recent addition to the Texas law of self-defense is the "no retreat rule," sometimes called the Castle Doctrine. In 2007, the Texas Legislature clarified the law of self-defense by adding Sec. 9.31(e) & (f).[95] The statute says that an individual who is otherwise lawfully using force or deadly force in self-defense is not required to retreat prior to using the force. Recall the carjacking scenario above. Oscar could certainly mash the accelerator and drive away from Gordon. Instead Oscar sprays (or shoots)

Gordon. Oscar's conduct is legally justified in self-defense even though one could argue that simply fleeing (retreating) would be the more rational act. The Texas statute does not require Oscar to retreat. It only requires him to act under a reasonable belief that his forceful conduct was necessary. Additionally, jurors are not permitted to consider the issue of retreat when determining whether the defendant (Oscar) held a reasonable belief that the use of the pepper spray or the pistol was necessary under the circumstances.

According to the statute, the use of force (and thereby deadly force) against another is not justified:

1. In response to verbal provocation alone
2. If the actor consented to the exact force used against him
3. If the actor provoked the other party
4. If the actor sought an explanation from the other party while carrying a weapon

Thus punching someone in the nose for what they say is an assault, not self-defense. However, using force to reject an impending assault prompted by the assailant's words may be justified. For example, if Fred says to Pete, "You are a lying rat," Pete is not justified in striking Fred. But if Fred draws back his arm and says to Pete, "You are a lying rat and I'm going to kick your butt," Pete need not wait until Fred strikes him before defending himself. In this situation Pete could reasonably believe that he must use force to protect himself from Fred's attempted use of unlawful force.

Sec. 9.34 provides a broad justification for the use of force to protect others. First, force, but not deadly force, can be used to prevent another from committing suicide or causing serious bodily injury to himself. Likewise, force and deadly force can be used to preserve life in an emergency. For example, stories of heroism exist wherein an individual who was partially crushed in a building collapse was saved when someone cut off their trapped leg in order to free the ensnared individual from the rubble. The amputation of the leg is use of deadly force. The law is not going to punish someone who acts in a reasonable manner in an effort to save another's life, even if extreme measures are necessary. In a less dramatic example, bystanders are known to attempt to restrain individuals who experience a grand mal seizure. The forceful efforts at restraint are intended to prevent the individual from hurting himself and would be justified under Sec. 9.34(a), even if medically unnecessary.

On rare occasion, the law of self-defense can be applied as justification for committing offenses involving property. In one case, the Court of Criminal Appeals held that a defendant had a right to invoke the law of self-defense as justification for smashing the windshield of a truck. The defendant, who was subsequently tried for criminal mischief, claimed the driver of the truck was trying to run over him and he used a flashlight to smash the window in order to protect himself. The court said the defendant's conduct implicated self-defense even though no assault on a person occurred. The defendant was entitled for the jury to consider his self-defense claim.[96]

DEFENSE OF PROPERTY

While the desirability of allowing individuals to use force and deadly force to protect themselves or other humans is generally recognized across all jurisdictions, the same cannot be said for use of force to protect property. Some states have concluded that lost or damaged property is not of sufficient social importance as to permit property owners to injure or kill thieves and trespassers. Texas, however, has a long tradition of protecting property rights and the law regarding use of force reflects this culture.

For example, Sec. 9.41 permits the use of force to prevent or terminate trespasses to land or other unlawful interference with property. Both real estate and tangible, moveable property are covered by the statute. The party using the force must be in lawful possession of the property; thus, a thief is not justified in using force to prevent someone else from taking his stolen property.

The justification afforded under Sec. 9.41(a) is most commonly used as the basis of ejecting trespassers from property. Assume Jeremy is in a local dance hall. After consuming several beers he becomes obnoxious. Several patrons complain to the dance hall owner. The owner asks Jeremy to leave the premises. Jeremy refuses. Jeremy has become a trespasser once the dance hall owner revokes his permission to be on the premises. The dance hall owner (or more likely a bouncer or security officer acting on his behalf) is justified in using force to eject Jeremy from the premises. Note that the use of force relative to ejecting trespassers is not limited to individuals in violation of the criminal trespass statute (Sec. 30.04). The Legislature appears to desire the law to apply to any trespasser whether or not they are committing the offense of criminal trespass. Similarly, force may lawfully be used to end someone's effort at tampering with property.

In a like vein, Sec. 9.41(b) authorizes the use of force by the lawful owner of property to regain what is rightfully his. In the case of real estate, force may be used to reenter the land if the true owner has been unlawfully dispossessed of the land. But, the owner would not be justified in forcibly entering his property if he was dispossessed by a court order. In that case, the owner would not have been in *lawful* possession. As for personal property, the owner can use force to regain custody of it. But, the forcible regaining of possession of the property must be done in fresh pursuit. The fresh pursuit requirement seeks to encourage resort to court processes in property disputes except in cases where self-help would likely occur anyway. John observes Harry stealing wheel covers from his sports car. John chases Harry and wrestles the wheel covers from him. John is legally justified in using force to recover the wheel covers.

One of the more controversial portions of the Penal Code concerns the use of deadly force to protect property. Here the law provides Texans with far greater legal immunity than most other states. Sec. 9.42 justifies the use of deadly force to protect land and personal property if the actor is justified in using force and he reasonably believes use of deadly force is immediately necessary to

1. prevent the imminent commission of:
   a. arson
   b. burglary
   c. robbery
   d. aggravated robbery
   e. theft during the nighttime, or
   f. criminal mischief during the nighttime[97]

2. or, to prevent an offender from fleeing after committing:
   a. burglary
   b. robbery
   c. aggravated robbery, or
   d. theft during the nighttime

3. and the actor reasonably believes the land or property:
   a. cannot be protected or recovered by other means, or
   b. the use of other than deadly force would expose the actor to substantial risk of injury or death.

To use deadly force to protect real estate or personal property, the actor must meet the justification for using ordinary force. If that standard is met, deadly force can be utilized to prevent the commission of certain property-based crimes or to prevent the perpetrator from escaping after committing some, but not all, of the same property-based crimes. For example, a homeowner is justified in using deadly force to prevent a burglary and to stop a burglar who is fleeting with the owner's property. However, if a burglar or robber flees without actually taking any property, use of deadly force is not permitted. Note that while deadly force can be used to prevent an arson, it cannot be used to stop the fleeing arsonist. The arsonist has done his deed and stopping his flight in no way protects the individual's property or assists in stopping the fire.

The authorization to use deadly force to prevent criminal trespass in the nighttime likely exists to cover the nonconsummated burglary. A homeowner should not be required to wait until a would-be burglar actually enters the residence before using deadly force.

Suppose as a prank late one night several teenagers decide to throw rolls of toilet paper in the trees at a friend's house. Unfortunately, the teens go to the wrong address and paper the neighbor's trees. The neighbor awakes, observes the teens, and does not realize what is happening. The neighbor fires his shotgun over the heads of the teens. Are the teens committing criminal mischief in the nighttime? Is the neighbor's use of deadly force justified under the Penal Code?

The statute is silent regarding any duty to retreat prior to using force to protect one's property. If it is reasonable under the circumstances to flee a home during a burglary instead of apprehending or shooting the burglar, must the homeowner retreat from his residence? As noted above, while the 2007 session of the Legislature clarified that issue in the context of self-defense, the lawmakers did not modify Sec. 9.42. However, the long-time American tradition has been that an individual has no duty to retreat instead of using deadly force to protect his home or business.[98] No Texas appellate court case has explicitly adopted this position, however.[99]

Just as individuals can use force and deadly force to protect third parties, so can coercive power be applied to protect property belonging to someone else. Sec. 9.43 permits an individual to use force or deadly force to protect a third person's property if he could lawfully use the force or deadly force himself and he believes that a theft or criminal mischief is occurring to the other's property. Various other Texas laws grant wide authority to all citizens to prevent theft and to use force to recover stolen property, regardless of whether they or someone else owns the tangible property.[100]

Similarly both forms of force can be used if the property owner has requested the actor's protection of the property, the actor has a legal duty to protect the property, or the property belongs to a spouse, parent, or child who resides with the actor. Recall the earlier scenario of the robbery of the liquor store. The clerk in the liquor store is authorized to use deadly force to protect the store owner's property. Similarly, this portion of the statute authorizes contract private security personnel to use force to protect property.

Use of force through deployment of mechanical devices is permitted under limited circumstances. For example, it is lawful to use chain-link fencing to protect property. However, Texas law does not permit the use of potentially deadly devices to protect property. Under Sec. 9.44 the justification afforded to use force would not be available if the individual protected his property with spring guns, man-traps, or similar means. For example, suppose Ralph's bakery has been burglarized several times in recent weeks. In an effort to stop the burglaries, Ralph electrifies the doors and windows with 220 volts of current. The burglar is killed when he touches the back doorknob. Ralph cannot rely on the use of deadly force to protect property statute to defend himself in a prosecution for the death of the burglar. The prohibition on use of lethal devices is premised on at least two notions. First, a danger exists that an innocent party might be injured or killed by the device, such as a child who touches the doorknob in passing. Second, any use of deadly force must be reasonable under the existing circumstances at the time. In the case of a burglar, in some factual situations the use of deadly force might be reasonable but not reasonable in other situations. Accordingly, the law will not allow the citizen to set into motion a set of automatic circumstances where deadly force would always be used, such as with the electrified door or a firearm activated by a tripwire.

LAW ENFORCEMENT USE OF FORCE

States commonly enact special use of force laws for their criminal justice personnel apart from the laws applicable to the citizenry as a whole. Sometimes these laws grant extraordinary authority to public safety personnel and sometimes the laws also place special restrictions on an officer's use of force. In Texas, these laws speak to the special authority that peace officers have to use force to make arrests and conduct searches.[101] Additionally, the authority to use force, and sometimes deadly force, to maintain security in correctional facilities and prevent prisoners from escaping is also spoken to in the statutes.

Sec. 9.51 empowers a peace officer to use force to make an arrest, conduct a search, or prevent escape after an arrest so long as the officer reasonably believes his conduct is lawful and he identifies himself as an officer prior to using the force. For example, police officers respond to a barroom brawl. The officers can use reasonable force to subdue the brawlers and effect necessary arrests. Upon making the arrest the officers can also use reasonable force to conduct a search of the arrestees. Likewise, the statutory language is broad enough to justify an officer's use of handcuffs to restrain an arrested suspect. Interestingly, the statute does not distinguish between felony and misdemeanor offenders. The officer is authorized to use just as much force to arrest a shoplifter as an armed robber. The amount of necessary force is determined by the level of resistance by the suspect, not the severity of the offense.

According to the statute, the amount of force the officer uses in any given circumstance must be reasonable. Peace officers receive extensive training in the practical application of using force. Additionally, most law enforcement agencies have written policies concerning which form of force (e.g., baton, pepper spray, Taser) may be used in a given situation. These policies are frequently more restrictive in nature than the authority provided under Sec. 9.51. Most agencies follow a use of force continuum whereby the amount of force administered is progressive depending on the amount of resistance manifested by the suspect.

Peace officers are justified in using deadly force to make arrests or prevent an escape when the officer "reasonably believes the conduct for which arrest is authorized included the use or attempted use of deadly force" or the officer reasonably believes the arrestee will cause serious bodily injury to the officer or another if arrest is delayed.[102] The officer has no duty to retreat prior to using deadly force. Thus, if Officer Ollie is chasing an armed robber who shot a convenience store clerk, Officer Ollie is justified in using deadly force to stop the robber. But if he is chasing an individual who has stolen a gold watch, use of deadly force is not justified because the offender did not commit a violent crime nor does reason exist to believe he poses a threat to Officer Ollie or any other person.

But suppose Officer Ollie is chasing an armed robber who merely threatened the store clerk but did not actually harm her. May Officer Ollie lawfully use deadly force to prevent the robber from escaping? A close reading of Sec. 9.51(c)(1) reveals that the offender must have used or attempted to use "deadly force." Mere display of a deadly weapon during the commission of the offense may not be sufficient to meet the definition of *using* "deadly force."

On the other hand, assume Officer Ollie receives a radio broadcast telling him that shots were fired by the robber. Upon discovery of the robber, Officer Ollie shoots him when he fails to stop on command. Officer Ollie later learns that the broadcast was erroneous as no shots were ever fired by the robber. Officer Ollie's use of deadly force was still justified because all the statute requires is a reasonable belief, which he obviously had, that the offender used deadly force.

Unlike most parts of substantive criminal law, use of force and deadly force has a constitutional aspect. In 1985, the U.S. Supreme Court held that shooting a fleeing suspect was a seizure within the meaning of the Fourth Amendment's prohibition on unreasonable searches and seizures. In *Tennessee v. Garner*[103] the high court ruled that the old Common Law rule that permitted officers to use deadly force to stop any fleeing felon was unreasonable and thereby unconstitutional. "It is not better that all felony suspects die than that they escape. Where the suspect poses no immediate threat to the officer and no threat to others, the harm resulting from failing to apprehend him does not justify the use of deadly force to do so," Justice White wrote in the majority opinion.[104] Garner was an unarmed juvenile who was shot in the back of the head as he fled the scene of a residential burglary. The Supreme Court ruled that such use of deadly force to stop unarmed fleeing property offenders was unconstitutional. The *Garner* decision has had little effect on Texas law since Sec. 9.51 limits police use of deadly force to violent or potentially violent offenders.[105]

While Sec. 9.51 grants peace officers unique authority to use force and deadly force in performing their duties, there is no indication that the Legislature intended to exclude officers from the coverage of the other sections of Chapter 9. Accordingly, a peace officer retains the authority to use force or deadly force in self-defense or the defense of third parties. Presumably a working peace officer also has the benefit of the necessity defense (Sec. 9.31) and the defense of protection of life or health (Sec. 9.34).

Sec. 9.52 and Sec. 9.53 excuse from criminal responsibility the use of force by peace officers and correctional personnel to prevent escape from jail or prison and to maintain order and security within correctional facilities. Sec. 9.52 authorizes the use of deadly force to prevent escape from a correctional facility. Is this provision constitutional under the reasoning of the *Garner* case? Is the Fourth Amendment reasonableness standard different for suspects than for offenders who have been convicted of a crime?

USE OF FORCE IN SPECIAL RELATIONSHIPS

State law exempts from criminal responsibility the use of force by one person upon another when certain special relationships exist. Specifically, statutes authorize parents to use reasonable force to safeguard and discipline minor children, teachers to use force to maintain class order, and guardians to use force to control mentally incompetent individuals.

Under Sec. 9.61, a parent or other person acting in the stead of the parent, can use reasonable force, but not deadly force, "to discipline the child or to safeguard or promote his welfare." For the purposes of the statute, the child must be under 18 years of age. This authority to use force prevents a parent from being accused of unlawful restraint for restricting the movements of the child or from facing an injury to a child charge for using corporal punishment.[106] As to the latter conduct, such as spanking a child, the parent's conduct must be reasonable under the circumstances then existing. While the law grants parents some latitude in the manner in which they discipline their children, disciplinary acts that are abusive, excessive, or place the child at risk of serious bodily injury or death are not permitted. The parent may face aggravated assault, injury to a child, or endangering a child charges in these cases.[107]

In a similar manner, individuals entrusted with the care of others are permitted to use reasonable force to maintain discipline and to further the special purpose in which they are engaging. This statute, Sec. 9.62, is somewhat curious. While it is labeled as "Educator-Student," neither of those terms actually appears in the language of the statute. Rather the law speaks of individuals entrusted with the care and supervision of others "for a special purpose," a phrase not otherwise defined. Likewise, unlike Sec. 9.61, the law is not limited solely to children. Unfortunately, appellate case law interpreting Sec. 9.62 is scant. Thus, it is difficult to speculate regarding how courts might interpret the scope of the law's coverage. In the case of a schoolteacher, "special purpose" means controlling, training, and educating the child.[108] It is long established in Texas that a teacher has a right to "inflict moderate corporal punishment for the purpose of restraining or correcting the refractory" student.[109] The statute thereby exempts from criminal prosecution teachers or coaches who paddle a student. However, Texas education law requires that any use of corporal punishment in schools must be consistent with school board policy.[110]

Arguably, the authority to use force to further a special purpose might logically extend to medical personnel in controlling patients, such as paramedics subduing a belligerent individual who is in need of medical attention. Does the law provide immunity from prosecution to a college professor who uses force to maintain class decorum? Would the concept apply to lifeguards at swimming pools? Camp counselors? Dormitory managers? Baby sitters?[111]

In like manner, Sec. 9.63 establishes the authority of a guardian of a mentally incompetent person to use force, but not deadly force, to safeguard the incompetent's welfare. The statute also authorizes the employees of a mental institution to use force to maintain discipline within the institution. This section may overlap Sec. 9.34 (protection of life or health) in situations where the incompetent must be placed in a straitjacket or confined in a padded room.[112]

Notes

1. J.L. Austin, *A Plea for Excuses, in* FREEDOM AND RESPONSIBILITY 6 (Herbert Morris ed., 1961).
2. JOSHUA DRESSLER, UNDERSTANDING CRIMINAL LAW 221 (4th ed. 2006).
3. While in Texas no bar exists to raising insanity as a defense to even minor misdemeanors, such a tactic is generally impractical. The cost in both time and money of mounting the defense pretty much restricts its use to serious felonies such as murder and arson. Additionally, the social stigma of being adjudicated as insane is generally perceived as far more severe that the stigma of being convicted of a minor crime.
4. *See* TEX. PENAL CODE § 2.02.
5. TEX. PENAL CODE § 47.05.
6. *See* TEX. PENAL CODE § 2.03.
7. Acts that are justified, such as self-defense or use of force to protect property, are normally treated procedurally as defenses with regard to the allocation of burden of proof.
8. Walton v. Arizona, 497 U.S. 639, 650 (1990). See also Leland v. Oregon, 343 U.S. 790 (1952), wherein the

Court upheld a state law requiring the defendant to establish insanity beyond a reasonable doubt.
9. Blockburger v. U.S., 284 U.S. 299 (1932).
10. The degree to which this strategy is the result of failed plea bargaining is unknown.
11. A Latin phrase translating as "incapable of wrong."
12. *See* WAYNE R. LAFAVE, CRIMINAL LAW 485–486 (4th ed. 2003).
13. The age of criminal responsibility in England is now set at 10 for all cases.
14. *See* Kent v. U.S., 383 U.S. 541 (1966).
15. Roper v. Simmons, 543 U.S. 551 (2005).
16. At least one court has suggested that the entrapment defense is mislabeled. "It is not the entrapment of a criminal upon which the law frowns, but the seduction of innocent people into a criminal career by its officers is what is condemned and will not be tolerated." People v. Braddock, 264 P.2d 521, 525 (Cal. 1953).
17. *See* United States v. Martinez, 979 F.2d 1424 (10th Cir. 1992); United States v. Leroux, 738 F.2d 943 (8th Cir. 1984); *and* U.S. v. Mattox, 492 F.2d 104 (5th Cir. 1974).

18. Drago v. State, 553 S.W.2d 375 (Tex. Crim. App. 1977).

19. *See* Munoz v. State, 629 So.2d 90 (Fla. 1993); People v. Tipton, 401 N.E.2d 528 (Ill. 1980); People v. McGee, 399 N.E.2d 1177 (N.Y. 1979); *and* Sorrells v. United States, 287 U.S. 435 (1932).

20. *See* People v. Barraza, 591 P.2d 947 (Cal. 1979).

21. While during a trial courts generally restrict the introduction into evidence of a defendant's previous criminal convictions, such prior convictions can be offered by the prosecution to rebut an entrapment claim. If Chris has prior convictions for drug dealing, the state can introduce that fact to negate his claim that he was not predisposed to sell drugs.

22. England v. State, 887 S.W.2d 902 (Tex. Crim. App. 1994).

23. Curiously, § 31.03(d) appears to codify the subjective test alone for cases where entrapment is raised in theft prosecutions. Would a theft defendant who alleges entrapment be entitled to consideration of this test *and* the combined subjective/objective test?

24. Hernandez v. State, 161 S.W.3d 491 (Tex. Crim. App. 2005).

25. But see Oliver v. State, 703 P.2d 869 (Nev. 1985), wherein the Nevada Supreme Court found defendant was entrapped into committing larceny when a police officer posed as a vulnerable intoxicated vagrant with a ten dollar bill sticking out of his coat pocket. Court found the conduct was "calculated to tempt any needy person in the area, whether immediately predisposed to crime or not."

26. Norman v. State, 588 S.W.2d 340 (Tex. Crim. App. 1979).

27. *See* Hernandez v. State.

28. 4 WILLIAM BLACKSTONE, COMMENTARIES *27.

29. The author's son once avoided payment of a fine for parking in a handicap restricted space because the designating sign was completely hidden by the leaves of a nearby tree.

30. *See* Barrera v. State, 978 S.W.2d 577 (Tex. App. 1992).

31. For a contrary argument asserting that competent legal advice should be considered as a defense to criminal charges, see ROLLIN M. PERKINS & RONALD N. BOYCE, CRIMINAL LAW 1042–1043 (1982).

32. See Tovar v. State, 949 S.W.2d 370 (Tex. App. 1997), rejecting a public official's mistake of law claim that he did not know that his conduct was in violation of the state's open meeting law.

33. Additionally, Katie's conduct would be a justifiable use of deadly force in the prevention of a crime against her or her property. As more fully discussed later in the chapter, justification in the use of force is based on the user's perception of the circumstances, not on the actual facts of the situation.

34. See Kessler v. State, 850 S.W.2d 217 (Tex. App. 1993), rejecting duress defense to charge of burglary wherein burglary companion's threats of harm were found not to be imminent.

35. 4 WILLIAM BLACKSTONE, COMMENTARIES *28. The husband was criminally responsible for acts of his wife that were committed under his direction.

36. As of 2008, despite efforts to gain his freedom, Hinckley remains an involuntary patient in a Washington, D.C., area mental facility.

37. Manson initially received the death penalty but he was spared when the California Supreme Court nullified the state's capital punishment law. As of 2008, he remained in custody in California's Corcoran State Prison. His parole eligibility will be reviewed in 2012.

38. MODEL PENAL CODE § 4.01 cmt. at 164 (1985).

39. But see Beasley v. State, 810 S.W.2d 838 (Tex. App. 1991), holding the insanity defense to be inapplicable in DWI prosecutions because the offense lacks a culpable mental state.

40. *See* RITA J. SIMON & DAVID E. AARONSON, THE INSANITY DEFENSE 7–8 (1988).

41. The low frequency of use of the defense is in sharp contrast to the fact that a substantial number of criminal defendants suffer from some level of mental disorder. See *Louisa Van Wezel Schwartz Symposium on Mental Health Issues in Correctional Institutions: Symposium Introduction*, 7 UDC L. REV. 111, 115 (2003), citing Bureau of Justice Statistics "showing that 16 percent of all persons in the criminal justice system have serious mental disorders."

42. Board of Trustees of the American Psychiatric Association, *American Psychiatric Association Statement on the Insanity Defense 5* (Dec. 1982).

43. Idaho, Kansas, Montana, and Utah do not utilize the traditional insanity defense. These states do permit introduction of evidence regarding the relationship of the defendant's mental condition and his or her ability to form the required *mens rea*.

44. M'Naghten's name appears in legal literature variously as McNaughten, M'Naughten, or M'Naughton.

45. 10 C & F 200 (1843).

46. Mental state at trial is known as competency to stand trial. The test of trial competency involves whether the defendant has an understanding of the proceedings and is capable of aiding in his own defense. *See* TEX. CODE CRIM. P. art. 46B.003.

47. The various definitions found in the DIAGNOSTIC AND STATISTICAL MANUAL OF MENTAL DISORDERS—FOURTH EDITION (DSM-IV) serve to standardize any diagnosis of a mental disease or condition.

48. *See* Insanity Defense Reform Act of 1984, *codified as* 18 U.S.C. § 17.

49. Irresistible impulse was a recognized defense in Texas until 1993 when the Legislature modified the statute.

50. For a list of states that recognize the defense of diminished mental capacity, see C.T. Drechsler, Annotation, *Mental or Emotional Condition as Diminishing Responsibility for Crime*, 22 A.L.R.3D 1228 (1968).

51. TEX. CODE CRIM. P. art. 46C.051.

52. TEX. CODE CRIM. P. art. 46C.102.

53. TEX. CODE CRIM. P. art. 46C.155.

54. 4 WILLIAM BLACKSTONE, COMMENTARIES * 25–26.

55. U.S. v. Cornell, 25 Fed. Cas. 650, 657–658 (C.C.R.I. 1820).

56. Montana v. Egelhoff, 518 U.S. 37 (1996).

57. Watson v. State, 654 S.W.2d 730 (Tex. App.—Houston [14th Dist.] 1983).

58. Witherspoon v. State, 671 S.W.2d 143 (Tex. App.—Houston [1st Dist.] 1984).

59. *Ex parte* Martinez, 195 S.W.3d 713 (Tex. Crim. App. 2006).

60. Mendenhall v. State, 77 S.W.3d 815 (Tex. Crim. App. 2002).

61. *Id.*

62. "Alibi" is a Latin word meaning "elsewhere."

63. Cantwell v. Connecticut, 310 U.S. 296, 303–304 (1940). *See also* Church of the Lukumi Babalu Aye, Inc. v. City of Hialeah, Florida, 508 U.S. 520 (1993).

64. *See* TEX. PENAL CODE § 22.04 (l). See also www.childrenshealthcare.org/legal.htm for list of states that provide religious exemption defense to various charges.

65. *See, e.g.*, Walker v. Superior Court, 763 P.2d 852 (Cal. 1988); State v. Chenoweth, 71 N.E. 197 (Ind. 1904); Craig v. State, 155 A.2d 684 (Md. App. 1959); Commonwealth v. Twitchell, 617 N.E.2d 609 (Mass. 1993); State v. McKown, 475 N.W.2d 63 (Minn. 1991); People v. Pierson, 68 N.E. 243 (N.Y. 1903); Funkhouser v. State, 763 P.2d 695 (Okla. Crim. App. 1988); State v. Hays, 964 P.2d 1042 (Ore. Ct. App. 1998); Commonwealth v. Barnhart, 497 A.2d 616 (Pa. Super. Ct. 1985); *and* State v. Norman, 808 P.2d 1159 (Wash. Ct. App. 1991).

66. *See* TEX. HEALTH & SAFETY CODE § 481.111(a) *and* 42 U.S.C. § 1966a.

67. *See* Karla K. Leeper & Jon Bruschke, *The Prevalence of the Abuse Excuse: Media Hype or Cause for Concern?* 17 COMM. & THE LAW 47 (1995).

68. *Sec. 309.81 Post Traumatic Stress Disorder*, AMERICAN PSYCHIATRIC ASSOCIATION, DIAGNOSTIC AND STATISTICAL MANUAL OF MENTAL DISORDERS (DSM-IV) (1994).

69. *See* P.S. Appelbaum et al., *Use of Posttraumatic Stress Disorder to Support an Insanity Defense*, 150 J. AM. PSYCH. ASSN.229 (1993), *and* Constantina Aprilakis, *The Warrior Returns: Struggling to Address Criminal Behavior by Veterans with PTSD*, 3 GEO. J. L. & PUB. POL'Y 541 (2005).

70. A variant of the defense is battered child syndrome. *See, e.g.*, State v. Nemeth, 694 N.E.2d 1332 (Ohio 1998).

71. *See* LENORE WALKER, THE BATTERED WOMAN (1979).

72. See Patricia J. Falk, *Novel Theories of Criminal Defense Based upon the Toxicity of the Social Environment: Urban Psychosis, Television Intoxication, and Black Rage*, 74 N.C. L. REV. 731 (1996), and Henry F. Fradella, *From Insanity to Beyond Diminished Capacity: Mental Illness and Criminal Excuse in the Post-Clark Era*, 18 J.L. & PUB. POL'Y 7 (2007), for a more complete discussion of these social syndrome defenses.

73. *See* Peter Marks, *L.I.R.R. Case Again Raises Sanity Issue*, N.Y. TIMES, Aug. 12, 1994, at B1.

74. *See* Doris S. Wong, *Gilchrist Convicted of First-Degree Murder*, BOSTON GLOBE, Apr. 18, 1989, at 1.

75. *See* Smith v. State, 5 S.W.3d 673 (Tex. Crim. App. 1999). See also Werner v. State, 711 S.W.2d 639 (Tex. Crim. App. 1986), Teague, J. dissenting, for a list of psycho-social syndromes ranging from Holocaust syndrome to policeman's syndrome.

76. TEX. PENAL CODE § 9.02.

77. *See* TEX. PENAL CODE § 2.03.

78. Act of Mar. 20, 2007, 80th Leg., R.S., ch. 1, § 4, 2007 Tex. Sess. Law Serv. 1 (Vernon) (amending TEX. CIV. PRAC. & REM. CODE § 83.001).

79. *See* TEX. PENAL CODE §§ 9.32; 9.42; and 9.51.

80. For the procedures in obtaining a search warrant, see Chapter 18 of the TEXAS CODE OF CRIMINAL PROCEDURE.

81. *See* Wilson v. Arkansas, 514 U.S. 927 (1995).

82. Rue v. State, 958 S.W.2d 915 (Tex. App.—Houston [14th Dist.] 1997).

83. McGarity v. State, 5 S.W.3d 223 (Tex. App.—San Antonio 1999).

84. Bowen v. State, 187 S.W.3d 744 (Tex. App.—Fort Worth 2006).

85. Vasquez v. State, 830 S.W.2d 948 (Tex. Crim. App. 1992).

86. Spakes v. State, 913 S.W.2d 597 (Tex. Crim. App. 1996).

87. Stefanoff v. State, 78 S.W.3d 496 (Tex. App.—Austin 2002).

88. McFarland v. State, 784 S.W.2d 52 (Tex. App.—Houston [1st Dist.] 1990).

89. *See generally* Erlandson v. State, 763 S.W.2d 845 (Tex. App.—Houston [14th Dist.] 1988); Brumley v. State, 804 S.W.2d 659 (Tex. App.—Amarillo 1991); *and* Cyr v. State, 887 S.W.2d 203 (Tex. App.—Dallas 1994).

90. Railey v. State, 121 S.W. 1120 (Tex. Crim. App. 1909).

91. THE AMERICAN HERITAGE DICTIONARY OF THE ENGLISH LANGUAGE 686 (4th ed. 2000).

92. TEX. PENAL CODE § 38.03. The statute does provide that it is no defense to the charge that the arrest was unlawful.

93. TEX. PENAL CODE § 9.31(c).

94. Semaire v. State, 612 S.W.2d 528 (Tex. Crim. App. 1980); Juarez v. State, 886 S.W.2d 511 (Tex. App. 1994).

95. Act of Mar. 20, 2007, 80th Leg., R.S., ch. 1, § 2, 2007 Tex. Sess. Law Serv. 1 (Vernon).

96. Boget v. State, 74 S.W.3d 23 (Tex. Crim. App. 2002).

97. While "nighttime" is not defined in the Penal Code, prior case law holds that it is any time between 30 minutes after sunset and 30 minutes before sunrise. Laws v. State, 10 S.W. 220 (Tex. Crim. App. 1889).

98. LaFave, *supra*, pp. 547–548.

99. In 1979, the Court of Criminal Appeals noted that the language of § 9.42 was different than the language of § 9.31 and thereby raised a question as to whether an individual has a duty to retreat prior to using deadly force to protect property. Valentine v. State, 587 S.W.2d 399 (Tex. Crim. App. 1979).

100. *See, e.g.*, Tex. Code Crim. P. art. 18.16 *and* Tex. Civ. Prac. & Rem. Code § 124.001.

101. These statutes apply both to peace officers and individuals acting in an officer's presence and at his direction. See Tex. Code Crim. P. art. 2.12 for list of who are peace officers.

102. Note that deadly force is never authorized solely to conduct a search.

103. 471 U.S. 1 (1985).

104. *Id.* at 11.

105. The *Garner* case was a civil case in which the deceased burglar's next of kin sued the responding police officer and the City of Memphis. While the decision establishes the circumstances under which peace officers and their employing governmental entities may be liable for money damages when an unarmed property offender is injured or killed through the use of force, the Supreme Court's opinion does not answer the question of whether a state can still excuse the officer from criminal liability.

106. See Tex. Fam. Code § 151.002 setting forth rights and duties of parents, including the right to use corporal punishment for the reasonable discipline of a child.

107. *See* Assister v. State, 58 S.W.3d 743 (Tex. App.—Amarillo 2000).

108. Hogenson v. Williams, 542 S.W.2d 546 (Tex. Civ. App. 1976).

109. Dowlen v. State, 14 Tex. Ct. App. 61 (1883).

110. *See* Tex. Educ. Code § 22.0511 *and* § 22.0512. *See also* Op. Tex. Att'y Gen. No. GA-0374 (2005).

111. See Seth S. Searcy & James R. Patterson, *Practice Commentary*, V.T.C.A., Penal Code (1974) § 9.62, suggesting that statute's coverage extends beyond educator-student relationships.

112. *Id.* at § 9.63.

Using the Texas Penal Code
and Court Decisions

To fully study Texas criminal law, the reader must examine both the current provisions in the Texas Penal Code and the relevant case decisions interpreting and applying the statutes. Current versions of the Texas Penal Code are available for sale from a variety of law book publishers. Additionally, the code is available online through the Legislature's website http://tlo2.tlc.state.tx.us/statutes/statutes.html and private websites such as www.texaspolicecentral.com/penal_code.html. The reader should ensure that any copy reviewed is up to date through the most recent session of the Legislature. The process of how to take greatest advantage of the Penal Code and interpretive case law is overviewed in this appendix.

A penal code, called a criminal code in some jurisdictions, is a compilation of the primary criminal offenses of a state. Often, the penal code does not contain all criminal statutes. For instance, in Texas, while the offenses of murder, burglary, robbery, and similar serious matters are found in the Texas Penal Code, traffic laws, game and fish laws, and drug laws are located in one of the other 26 codes. Likewise, rules of court procedure are located in the Code of Criminal Procedure while rules of courtroom evidence are found in the Texas Rules of Evidence. This textbook makes occasional reference to these two sources.

The word "code" derives from the concept of codification of the law. Until the mid-1800s many laws were not formally recorded, or if recorded and printed in bound volumes, they were not well-organized. With the advent of inexpensive printing and expanded literacy within society, states began arranging their criminal and noncriminal statutes into formal, organized volumes. The word "code" suggests a structured, organized compilation of legislative enactments. How well-structured and organized the statutes may be varies widely from jurisdiction to jurisdiction, however. The California Penal Code, which has not been comprehensively revised since 1873, only roughly places like offenses

together in the same chapters. On the other hand, the Texas Penal Code, enacted in its current form in 1973, is organized in an outline style with like offenses generally clustered together.

An examination of the Table of Contents of the Texas Penal Code reveals that it is divided into 11 Titles. These 11 categories place the criminal law into major topical groups such as "Offenses against the Person" and "Organized Crime." The general material applicable to all subsequent statutes is found in the early Titles. For the typical student of the criminal law, in which "Title" an offense appears is virtually of no importance.

Within each Title, however, are one or more Chapters. And within each Chapter are Sections. These designations are important as many statutes cross-reference to other Chapters and Sections, and offenses are most commonly referred to by Section number. Thus, the crime of burglary is located in Title 7, Chapter 30, Sec. 30.02. In normal discussion of the crime of burglary, a criminal justice practitioner would simply refer to the offense by its section number, 30.02. Note that the first digit or two of the Section number is identical to the Chapter number in which the statute appears. The next two (or three digits) are the numerical sequence in which the statute appears within the chapter. So in the example, Burglary, Sec. 30.02, is the second entry in Chapter 30. (In a few instances, the Legislature has added a statute between two existing statutes by adding a third digit. For example, Sexual Assault is Sec. 22.011, placed between Sec. 22.01 and Sec. 22.02. The penchant for inserting statutes also exists at the Chapter level with Chapter 33A Telecommunications Crimes being wedged between Chapters 33 and 34.)

Within each section may be found multiple subsections and sub-subsections. Attempting to decipher all of this can be a challenge. But, if the reader views the Texas Penal Code not as a textbook but as a detailed outline, its structure and content become far easier to understand. Although each section is written in an outline format, printers of the Texas Penal Code do not always indent each subsection appropriately. This failure to indent prevents the text from becoming shifted too far to the right margin and wasting paper but also makes it difficult for the reader to keep the various subsections parallel and correctly related to each other. The following guidelines should assist the Texas Penal Code reader in understanding the outline sequencing.

Most of the time—but not always—the hierarchical relationship within each Penal Code section follows this sequence:

(a)

    (1)

        (A)

            (i)

Lines beginning with (a), (b), (c), and so forth are of equal status to each other as are (1), (2), (3), and so forth. Sentences starting with (1), (2), (3), and so forth are subordinate to the category above just as (A), (B), and (C) are subordinate to (1), (2), and (3). By way of example, examine in a copy of the Texas Penal Code this excerpt from Sec. 22.021 Aggravated Sexual Assault. If the printer indented the text as would normally be done when outlining, Sec. 22.021 would appear as:

(a) A person commits an offense:

    (1) if the person:

        (A) intentionally or knowingly:

            (i) causes the penetration of the anus or sexual organ of another person by any means, without that person's consent;

            (ii) causes the penetration of the mouth of another person by the sexual organ of the actor, without that person's consent; or

            (iii) causes the sexual organ of another person, without that person's consent, to contact or penetrate the mouth, anus, or sexual organ of another person, including the actor; or

        (B) intentionally or knowingly:

            (i) causes the penetration of the anus or sexual organ of a child by any means;

            (ii) causes the penetration of the mouth of a child by the sexual organ of the actor;

            (iii) causes the sexual organ of a child to contact or penetrate the mouth, anus, or sexual organ of another person, including the actor;

            (iv) causes the anus of a child to contact the mouth, anus, or sexual organ of another person, including the actor; or

            (v) causes the mouth of a child to contact the anus or sexual organ of another person, including the actor; and

    (2) if:

        (A) the person:

            (i) causes serious bodily injury or attempts to cause the death of the victim or another person in the course of the same criminal episode;

            (ii) by acts or words places the victim in fear that death, serious bodily injury, or kidnapping will be imminently inflicted on any person;

            (iii) by acts or words occurring in the presence of the victim threatens to cause the death, serious bodily injury, or kidnapping of any person;

            (iv) uses or exhibits a deadly weapon in the course of the same criminal episode;

            (v) acts in concert with another who engages in conduct described by Subdivision (1) directed toward the same victim and occurring during the course of the same criminal episode; or

            (vi) administers or provides flunitrazepam, otherwise known as rohypnol, gamma hydroxybutyrate, or ketamine to the victim of the offense with the intent of facilitating the commission of the offense;

        (B) the victim is younger than 14 years of age; or

        (C) the victim is an elderly individual or a disabled individual.

If the reader follows the outlining format, the reader will note that the statute establishes two general requirements for committing the offense: (1) *and* (2). Within subsection (1) are two possibilities, (A) or (B), which are then coupled with any of the three possibilities: (A), (B), or (C) in subsection (2). Potentially confusing are the sub-subsections in each main section. However, note the placement of the words "and" and "or" within the statute. The word "and" requires all of the possibilities—in this example both parts (1) *and* (2)—while the word "or" mandates any one of the sequence of choices. Hence, any of eight possibilities in subsection (1) when coupled with any of the eight behaviors in subsection (2) constitute the crime of Aggravated Sexual Assault.

Finally, to a large degree, the law is about the meaning of words. Murder has an explicit definition within the Texas Penal Code just as burglary, robbery, or any other offense. Unless an individual engages in the explicit behavior prohibited by the words of the statute, the individual has not committed that offense. Within each statute, however, certain individual words may also need to be defined. These definitions may be found in one of four places:

- within the particular statute itself;
- by reference to another statute;
- in the first section of the Chapter in which the statute is placed; or
- in the General Definitions located at Sec. 1.07.

Thus, Sec. 28.02 Arson contains a definition of the term "explosive weapon" in a subsection of the statute. But, for the definition of "firearm," the section cross-references to Sec. 46.01. Further, the definitions of "building," "habitation," and "property" for the purposes of the offense of arson are found in the Chapter definitions in Sec. 28.01. Finally, the word "another," which is an element of several forms of arson, is defined in the General Definitions in Sec. 1.07.

Whenever the reader seeks the definition of a term within a statute, he or she should determine whether it is defined at one of the four previously mentioned possibilities. When no written definition has been provided by the Legislature, the courts must decide what the Legislature meant. In such circumstances, courts interpret words according to their common usage.

Many of the comments in the text are referenced to court decisions. With a single exception not relevant to this text, only appellate courts normally issue written opinions. Thus, the opinions reported in the text originate primarily from the state's highest court with criminal jurisdiction, the Texas Court of Criminal Appeals, or from one of the 14 intermediate Courts of Appeals. In a few instances, citations to decisions of the U.S. Supreme Court, the U.S. Courts of Appeal, or the appellate courts of other states are provided.

Each case citation is listed by name of the parties and an alphanumeric citation describing the book title (known as the "reporter"), the volume number, and the beginning page number of the decision. An abbreviation of the court name and the year of the decision follows. This standardized citation system has been used by lawyers for over 150 years. Decisions of the Court of Criminal Appeals and the various Texas Courts of Appeals are published in a set of volumes entitled South Western Reporter. South Western Reporter is one of seven geographically designated reporters that contains case opinions from the various states. South Western Reporter, which also contains decisions from Arkansas, Kentucky, Missouri, and Tennessee, is currently in its third series (S.W.3d). The prior second series is abbreviated S.W.2d while the original series is simply S.W. For example, the citation of *Rodriguez v. State*, 146 S.W.3d 674 (Tex. Crim. App. 2004), means that the opinion can be found in volume 146 of the third series of South Western Reporter beginning on page 674. The opinion was rendered by the Court of Criminal Appeals in 2004. Similarly, the case of *Williams v. State*, 629 S.W.2d 791 (Tex. App.—Dallas 1981), is to be found in volume 629 of the second series of South Western Reporter starting on page 791. This opinion was handed down in 1981 by the Court of Appeals situated in Dallas.

In some instances in this textbook, the opinions cited have not been published in South Western Reporter either because they are too new or because the appellate court has decided they lack sufficient value as precedent to be worthy of official publication. In these cases, the citation is to one of the electronic legal databases. LexisNexis® citations are primarily used in this text. This service uses its own citation coding system. For example, a LexisNexis citation will appear as *Trejos v. State*, 2007 Tex. App. LEXIS 4045. Entering the citation into the electronic database will retrieve the case. For the few cases which are not available in LexisNexis, a citation to Westlaw® (e.g., *Trejos v. State*, 2007 WL 1500276) is provided.

Readers interested in viewing the case opinion references have four options. First, the clerk of the issuing court can be contacted and a copy of the opinion requested. Since court opinions are public records, citizens can obtain copies just like any other public record. This process can be slow and cumbersome, particularly if the decision is some years old.

Second, researchers can subscribe to fee-based legal databases such as LexisNexis, Westlaw, or VersusLaw®. In addition to rapid access to court decisions, these services offer a wide range of legal research materials. However, many may view them as expensive, particularly for the casual user. However, many university libraries offer their students free access to legal materials in LexisNexis and Westlaw. LexisNexis Academic™ service is available without charge through many university libraries as is the Westlaw Campus Research™ database.

Third, a reader can use the traditional method of case location by looking in the printed volumes. This is relatively easy providing one has access to the reporters in question. Because of cost and storage requirements, most practicing lawyers do not maintain extensive collections of case reporters. However, any Texas lawyer is likely to have copies of South Western Reporter and access to U.S. Supreme Court opinions. Law schools hold the most extensive collections of case reporters and other legal research materials, but many public and private universities that do not host a law school nonetheless subscribe to a portion of the case reporters. If a law school library is not readily accessible, a reader should seek help at a major university library or at a Texas college that operates a paralegal or criminal justice degree program. They are likely to maintain copies of Texas case reporters.

The fourth means of accessing case reports is via the Internet. Most federal and state appellate courts maintain a searchable database for case opinions. Accessing these cases is normally cost free. Many of these databases contain only the court's opinions from the last few years, however. All opinions of the U.S. Supreme Court may be found by entering the case name in a search engine such as Google. Recent opinions of the Supreme Court may be accessed at the court's website www.supremecourtus.gov. Current opinions from the Texas Court of Criminal Appeals may be found at www.cca.courts.state.tx.us. Opinions from the 14 Courts of Appeals may be located by using the portal www.courts.state.tx.us. Some files may require the use of Adobe Acrobat Reader® software that is available free from www.adobe.com.

Glossary of Terms

Abduction—The carrying away of another person unlawfully with intent to secret them, as in a kidnapping.

Accessory after the fact—Traditionally, an individual who knowingly assists a criminal offender after the commission of the criminal act, as in providing him assistance in escaping or destroying evidence.

Accessory before the fact—Traditionally, an individual who knowingly assists a criminal offender before the commission of the criminal act, as in providing him transportation to the crime scene or tools to commit the offense.

Accomplice—An individual present at a crime who knowingly assists the primary offender.

Accomplice testimony rule—Rule of courtroom evidence that requires that the testimony of an accomplice when offered in evidence against the principal to be corroborated by independent proof.

Actor—Person whose criminal responsibility is at issue in the case.

Actus reus—Latin term for "guilty act." Used to refer to the forbidden conduct element of a criminal offense.

Affirmative defense—An excuse or justification for otherwise criminal conduct whereby the defendant bears the evidentiary burden of establishing the excuse or justification beyond a reasonable doubt, e.g., insanity, duress.

American bystander rule—Principle of law holding that an individual has no legal obligation to assist a fellow citizen who is in peril unless a law mandates such assistance. Thus, bystander is not obligated to attempt rescue of drowning man but law requires parents to care for welfare of minor children. Failure to perform latter legal duty is a criminal offense.

Appropriation of property—Under Texas law, the act of stealing property. Property may be appropriated in a variety of ways, the most common being without consent.

Arson—Traditionally, the willful and malicious burning of another's dwelling. Texas statutes have altered and expanded the scope of this offense.

Asportation—A Common Law term meaning the taking and carrying away of property during a larceny. Also used in law of kidnapping to refer to the abduction of the victim.

Assault—Traditionally, a threat to commit a battery. Under Texas law, assault includes both threats to do bodily injury and the actual causing of bodily injury.

Attempt—Intentional conduct that exceeds mere preparation to commit a crime but falls short of all elements of the desired offense.

Attendant circumstances—Factual conditions related to the *mens rea, actus rea*, or resultant harm of an event that convert otherwise lawful behavior into a criminal act.

Battered spouse syndrome—Variant of post-traumatic stress disorder (PTSD) whereby victim asserts their behavior is the result of long-term physical and psychological abuse from husband or wife. Occasionally raised as a legal defense in murders resulting from incidents of domestic violence.

Battery—Traditionally, the unwanted touching of another or bodily harm to another; incorporated into the law of assault under Texas law.

Bias crime—See hate crime.

Bifurcated trial—Rule of Texas court procedure whereby criminal trial is divided into two parts. In the first part, the jury hears evidence related to guilt and returns verdict of guilty or not guilty. If guilty verdict is returned, jury or judge hears evidence related to sentencing and then determines sentence.

Breach of peace—Any disruption of the tranquility of the community whether by noise or offensive conduct.

Bribery—Traditionally, the offering, soliciting, or accepting by a public servant of a monetary benefit in exchange for taking or withholding some official action.

Burden of proof—Rule of courtroom procedure in which the prosecutor or the defendant bears the obligation of bringing forth evidence and persuading the factfinder. The state bears the overarching burden of proof in obtaining a criminal conviction but the defendant may bear the burden when certain excuses or justifications are raised.

Burglary—Traditionally, the breaking and entering of the dwelling house of another in the nighttime with intent to commit a felony therein. Texas statutes have altered and expanded the scope of this offense.

"But for" test—Statutory test of causation under Texas criminal law. Assuming other elements of offense are present, actor is criminally liable if the result would not have occurred "but for" his conduct.

Capital murder—Under Texas law, those forms of intentional or knowing murder that may be punished with the death penalty.

Carjacking—The violent theft of an automobile from the presence of the owner. Considered as a form of robbery in Texas.

Causation—The connection between an actor's conduct and the resultant harm.

Civil law—The body of American law that does not involve criminal sanctions. Includes tort law, the law of contracts, probate law, and the like.

Code—A group of laws related to the same topic which are placed into one or more volumes in a logically organized format. For example, the Penal Code, the Code of Criminal Procedure, and the Parks and Wildlife Code.

Common Law—The law of England that has evolved over the years through custom, tradition, and judicial rulings. The Common Law dates from 1066, the year of the Norman Conquest. The Common Law is the basis of much American and Texas law and legal procedure. Because of the enactment of extensive statutory law in America, the Common Law no longer wields much influence over the definition of criminal offenses.

Complaint—In Texas, the affidavit made before a prosecutor or magistrate charging commission of a criminal offense. A complaint may also serve as the basis for issuance of an arrest warrant.

Concurrence—The requirement that for criminal liability to attach, the *mens rea* and the *actus rea* must exist at the same point in time.

Conspiracy—An agreement of two or more persons to commit a crime coupled with an overt act in furtherance of the commission.

Constructive possession—Exercising care, custody, or control over an object without having the object in one's immediate presence.

Corpus delicti—Latin term meaning "body of the crime." Requirement that the prosecutor establish the existence of a crime independent of the accused's confession.

County Court—Texas general trial court responsible for hearing all misdemeanors that have a possible penalty of jail time, i.e., Class A and B misdemeanors. Term may refer to any of the 254 constitutional County Courts, County Courts-at-Law, or County Criminal Courts-at-Law.

Court of Appeals—Primary criminal appellate court of Texas. With exception of death cases, the court is the first level of appeal for all other felonies and Class A and B misdemeanor cases. Court is actually 14 separate courts dispersed throughout the state on a geographical basis.

Court of Criminal Appeals—Highest Texas criminal appellate court. Conducts mandatory review of death penalty cases. Has discretion to hear criminal appeals from the Courts of Appeal.

Crime involving moral turpitude—Criminal offense that offends the core moral values of society. Generally includes offenses involving deceit, dishonesty, and immoral conduct.

Criminal homicide—A death of a human being caused by the action of another human being who possesses the required *mens rea*. Capital murder, murder, manslaughter, intoxication manslaughter, and criminally negligent homicide are the criminal homicides in Texas.

Criminal instrument—A device specially designed, made, or adapted for use in the commission of a criminal offense.

Criminal negligence—The lowest level of *mens rea* in Texas criminal law. Focus is on what the actor ought to have done under the circumstances.

Criminal solicitation—Effort to induce another person to commit a criminal offense. Texas law punishes such conduct only if the offense solicited is a capital felony or felony of the first degree.

Criminally negligent homicide—Least serious form of criminal homicide in Texas. Requires *mens rea* of criminal negligence.

Culpable mental state—See *mens rea*.

Curtilage—Traditionally, the domestic outbuildings which surround a person's home. Important concept in the law of arson and burglary.

Deadly force—Force intended or known to be capable of causing death or serious bodily injury.

Deadly weapon—A firearm or any device that in its design or manner of use is capable of causing death or serious bodily injury.

Defense—An excuse or justification which absolves a defendant from liability for commission of a criminal offense.

Direct filing—The formal filing of criminal charges by a peace officer without first obtaining approval from the local prosecutor. Used most often in misdemeanor cases.

District Court—Texas general trial court responsible for hearing all felonies and those misdemeanors involving official misconduct.

Doctrine of transferred intent—Legal fiction whereby for the purposes of criminal prosecution, an actor's intent to harm one individual is transferred to any other victim who is inadvertently harmed.

Doli incapax rule—Legal presumption that a child under a certain age is incapable of committing a crime. Age at Common Law was ten.

Double jeopardy—Constitutional prohibition against being tried more than once for the same criminal conduct or being punished more than once for the same criminal act. The right is found in the Fifth Amendment to the U.S. Constitution.

Dual sovereign doctrine—Principle that under our federal system of government both the U.S. government and a state may have an interest in prosecuting an individual for the same criminal act. Such dual prosecution does not violate the constitutional prohibition against double jeopardy.

Duress—A defense to criminal charges wherein the defendant asserts he or she committed the offense only because another person coerced them by threatening imminent death or serious bodily injury.

Effective consent—Consent given by property owner that is not the result of deception, threat, or fraud. Important concept in the law of theft.

Elements of an offense—The components that constitute a particular criminal offense. In Texas, the components consist of the forbidden conduct, required culpable mental state, and any required result.

Embezzlement—Traditional term used to describe theft of property by an individual who was initially entrusted with the property.

Entrapment—An unlawful inducement of an innocent party to commit a crime. Entrapment is a legal defense to a criminal charge.

Ex post facto law—A retroactive criminal law; a criminal law that provides for punishment for behavior that occurred prior to the date of the law's enactment.

Excuse—A defense to a criminal charge rooted in public policy considerations, e.g., infancy, insanity.

False Pretense—The false representation of a material present or past fact, known to be false, with intent to deceive and cause the transfer of title to property.

Felony—Under Texas law, a criminal offense in which the punishment is to be served in the custody of the state.

Felony murder rule—Legal rule treating as the crime of murder any unintended death that occurs during the commission of a dangerous felony.

Fighting words—Words that would cause the person of average temperament to want to respond with violence. Because of the First Amendment protection of free speech, normally an actor's speech can be criminalized only if it consists of "fighting words."

First degree murder—Traditional American label for an intentional killing with malice.

Force—An assertion of power against another person or object.

Forgery—Traditionally, the creation of a fraudulent document or other writing. Forgery often involves falsely representing a document as the work of another person who did not authorize it. Texas statutes have altered and expanded the scope of this offense.

Frankpledge—The custom whereby the inhabitants of a district were responsible for any crime or injury committed by one of their number.

Fraud—Traditional term used to describe an intentional act of deception of another person. In Texas, most frauds are covered by the theft statute.

General defense—A legal defense that is available for use against any criminal charge, e.g., insanity.

General deterrence—Criminological theory that holds that if behavior is made a crime subject to punishment,

individuals will not engage in the behavior. The focus is on general prevention of crime by making examples of specific offenders.

Habitation—A building or vehicle adapted for the overnight accommodation of persons.

Handgun—A firearm designed, made, or adapted to be operated with one hand.

Hate crime—A criminal offense motivated by the offender's bias or prejudice against a group based on their race, color, disability, religion, national origin, ancestry, age, or sexual preference.

Homicide—The killing of one human being by another human being. Not all homicides are crimes.

Identity theft—Any of a series of criminal offenses wherein the actor uses another's name and financial information without that person's permission to perpetrate a fraud on a third party.

Incapacitation—Criminological theory that supports the incarceration of convicted criminal offenders as a means of ensuring public safety.

Inchoate crime—A preparatory or preliminary offense, such as criminal attempt, criminal conspiracy, and criminal solicitation.

Indictment—The formal charging document issued by a grand jury. In normal practice, the document charges an individual with the commission of a felony.

Individual—Under Texas law, a human being who is alive, including an unborn child from fertilization to birth.

Infancy defense—The legal excuse of being under the required chronological age for criminal responsibility in the adult justice system.

Information—The formal charging instrument filed by the district or county attorney in a misdemeanor prosecution. May also be used in felony cases where the defendant waives the right to be indicted by a grand jury.

Insanity—The defense that the defendant's mental condition at the time of the commission of the crime should excuse him or her from criminal responsibility. The Texas statutory test for insanity is a variant of the M'Naghten Rule.

Intentionally—The *mens rea* of possessing a conscious objective or desire to engage in particular conduct or cause a result.

Intoxication manslaughter—In Texas, a death by accident or mistake brought about by an intoxicated individual who was operating a motor vehicle.

Involuntary manslaughter—Traditionally, an unintended death brought about by the offender's reckless behavior.

Justice Court—Lowest level of the Texas criminal court system. Justice Court has jurisdiction to try misdemeanors which result in a penalty of a monetary fine only.

Kidnapping—Traditionally, the abduction of an individual and the removal of him or her from his own country. Texas statutes have altered and expanded the scope of this offense.

Knowingly—The *mens rea* of being aware of the nature of one's conduct or aware that the conduct is reasonably likely to cause a particular result.

Larceny—Traditionally, the term used to describe the stealing of personal property.

Legal process—The various documents issued by a court to assert its power and authority, e.g., summons, subpoenas, warrants.

Lesser included offense—A crime that is a component element of a larger crime but has a lesser *mens rea* or produced a lesser harm. For example, manslaughter is a lesser included offense of murder and theft is a lesser included offense of robbery.

M'Naghten Rule—The test of legal insanity which holds that as a result of a mental disease or defect the actor did not know that his conduct was wrong. If an individual meets the test, he is entitled to a not guilty verdict.

Magistrate—Under Texas law, the term used to designate persons who perform judicial functions. For the most part the terms "judge" and "magistrate" are synonyms.

Malice—Traditionally, the notion that an offender had evilness in his or her heart. Today, malice is generally assumed if the actor intentionally causes harm.

Malum in se—Latin phrase meaning "evil in itself." Refers to crimes that are viewed as inherently bad within society, e.g., murder, theft, rape.

Malum prohibitum—Latin phrase meaning "wrong because prohibited." Refers to crimes that exist only because the legislature has chosen to criminalize the conduct, e.g., speeding, unlawful carrying a weapon, public intoxication. Offenses may not be considered morally evil.

Manslaughter—Traditionally, an intentional killing without malice. Under Texas law, a death that results from reckless behavior.

Mens rea—Latin for "guilty mind." Used to refer to the blameworthy mental state of the offender. Under Texas law, the *mens rea* of a crime is either intent, knowledge, recklessness, or criminal negligence.

Misdemeanor—A criminal offense punishable by either a fine only or incarceration in a county jail.

Misprision of a felony—Traditional phrase referring to concealing the existence of a felony.

Mistake of fact—A legal excuse rooted in a mistaken belief of factual circumstances. The defense is available only if the mistake negates the required *mens rea* of the crime.

Mitigation—to reduce; as in reducing the level of criminal responsibility.

Motive—The reason the actor committed the crime. Often used in court to establish that the defendant's conduct was intentional.

Municipal Court—Lowest level of the Texas criminal court system. A municipal court has jurisdiction to try misdemeanors which occur within the limits of an incorporated city and have a penalty of a monetary fine only. Court also has jurisdiction over violations of the city's ordinances.

Murder—Traditionally, the intentional killing of another human being with malice. Under Texas statute, murder can be committed in three different ways, none of which involve malice.

Necessity—A legal defense justifying the commission of a criminal offense when the desirability and urgency of avoiding harm clearly outweighs the harm sought to be prevented by the statute that is violated, e.g., speeding in an automobile while transporting a seriously injured person to the hospital.

Parole—Supervised release of a felon from prison before completion of his or her sentence.

Perjury—Knowingly making a false statement under circumstances where the law requires truthful statements.

Personal property—Property that can be moved from one location to another, in contrast to real estate (real property).

Pinkerton Rule—Rule of law that holds any member of a criminal conspiracy responsible for all criminal acts of his fellow co-conspirators.

Possession—Actual care, custody, or control of property.

Post-traumatic stress disorder (PTSD)—A psychological anxiety disorder that can develop after exposure to a terrifying event or ordeal in which grave physical harm occurred or was threatened. PTSD has been asserted as a legal defense in some cases.

Preemption doctrine—Rule permitting a governmental entity to exert total responsibility over a particular area of law and thereby deny lesser governmental entities the power to legislate in that field. For example, in Texas the state exercises virtually complete control over legislation relative to the manufacture and sale of alcoholic beverages. Local governments are powerless to legislate in that field.

Premeditation—The act of consciously planning out a criminal act before committing it. Traditionally premeditation was an element of murder.

Principal in first degree—Traditionally, the party to an offense who personally perpetrated the crime.

Principal in second degree—Traditionally, a party to an offense who assisted the commission of a crime and was present at the scene but did not commit the elements of the offense, e.g., a getaway car driver.

Principle of legality—Before an accused can be convicted and punished for engaging in some conduct, that conduct must be prohibited by statute; *nullum crimen sine lege* (no crime without law).

Probation—A correctional measure characterized by suspension of sentence and community-based supervision of a criminal offender.

Proof beyond reasonable doubt—The level of proof needed to support a criminal conviction. Texas courts have been reluctant to provide a precise definition of the term, leaving the matter of interpretation to the jury.

Public place—A location to which the public or a substantial group of the public has access.

Rape—Traditionally, the sexual penetration of a female by a male, not her husband, by force and without her consent. Texas law, now called sexual assault, greatly expands the concept.

Rape shield law—A law that limits criminal defendants' ability to cross-examine sexual assault victims about their past sexual behavior.

Recklessly—The *mens rea* of being aware of a substantial risk and consciously disregarding it. Intending to engage in risky conduct but not intending the harm the conduct produces.

Rehabilitation—A criminology theory that holds that through education, counseling, and treatment convicted offenders' behavior can be altered sufficiently to return them to society and they will commit no additional offenses.

Respondeat superior—Latin phrase meaning "the master is responsible for the servant." Concept used in ascribing criminal responsibility to a corporation for the acts of its employees.

Restitution—Court-imposed requirement that a convicted offender pay the medical costs or property loss and damage costs suffered by the victim. Often used as a term of probation.

Retribution—A criminology theory that maintains that proportionate punishment is a morally acceptable response to crime, regardless of whether the punishment produces any tangible benefits. Also called "just deserts."

Robbery—Traditionally, the taking of personal goods from the presence of another by force or placing in fear. Texas statutes have altered and expanded the scope of this offense.

Second degree murder—Traditionally, an intentional killing other than one that was premeditated.

Serious bodily injury—Bodily injury that creates a substantial risk of death or serious permanent disfigurement or loss of use of a body member or organ.

Specific deterrence—A criminology theory that seeks to prevent specific individuals from re-offending by instilling in them the consequences of any future misbehavior.

Stare decisis—A Latin phrase meaning "let the decision stand." The concept underlies the rule of precedent whereby courts create stability in the law by leaving undisturbed previously decided points of law.

Status crime—An offense which sanctions individuals for what they are, not what they do. Such crimes are unconstitutional and thereby legally unenforceable, e.g., vagrancy.

Statute of limitations—Rule requiring the government to bring formal charges against a criminal offender within a designated time period following commission of an offense. Various crimes have different statutes of limitations.

Strict liability—A criminal offense that does not require a *mens rea* as an element. Most such crimes are regulatory in nature and result in a fine.

Substantive criminal law—The portion of criminal law concerned with the definition of criminal offenses and their punishments, in contrast to procedural criminal law which is concerned with how the criminal law is implemented.

Territorial jurisdiction—The geographical area where a governmental entity or agency may lawfully assert its authority and control.

Terry **stop**—A temporary detention and search of a criminal suspect by a police officer. Also known as a stop-and-frisk. The name derives from the U.S. Supreme Court decision authorizing such detentions, Terry v. Ohio.

Tort—A civil wrong for which the law provides a remedy. Most torts result from one person negligently breaching a duty of care owed to another. The remedy is often an award of money damages.

Treason—The crime of disloyalty to one's sovereign or nation. According to the Constitution, "Treason against the United States, shall consist only in levying War against them, or in adhering to their Enemies, giving them Aid and Comfort."

Trespass—Traditionally, the unlawful interference with property of another. In modern times, trespass is the entry onto the land of another without consent. Under Texas law, only certain trespasses are crimes.

Utter—To attempt to pass a forged writing.

Vicarious responsibility—Responsibility imposed on an individual by law based on the conduct of some other person.

Victimless crimes—Criminal conduct in which no identified individual has been personally harmed by the behavior, e.g., prostitution, use of a controlled substance.

Voluntary manslaughter—Traditionally, an intentional killing committed in an act of sudden passion from adequate provocation.

Wharton's Rule—Legal principle that a conspiracy charge cannot be maintained where the agreement of two persons is necessary for the completion of the object crime, e.g. bribery, gambling.

Writ of *habeas corpus*—A Latin term for "you have the body." The writ is a court order directing a prison official to bring a particular inmate before the court to review the legality of his or her confinement.

Year-and-a-day rule—Traditional rule holding that a criminal homicide victim must die within one year and one day from the infliction of the fatal wound in order for charges to be brought. Texas and most other states no longer adhere to this rule.

Index